CW00552424

THOUSAND MILE TRIAL

THE
1,000
MILE
TRIAL
1900
-
2000

THOUSAND MILE TRIAL

Elizabeth Bennett

Published by Elizabeth Bennett
2000

First published 2000

ISBN: 0-9537930-0-1

Published by Elizabeth Bennett, Heathfield, E. Sussex, Tel: 01435 863499

Typeset and designed by The Wadsley Workshop
Printed by Ian Allan Printing Ltd
River Dene Estate, Molesey Road, Hersham, Surrey, KT12 4RG

Half-title photograph: Rose bowl presented to Ernest Pitman Esq.

Acknowledgements

The author wishes to thank everyone who has kindly assisted in many ways to make production of this book possible.

Tim Scott
Daniel Ward
Peter Heilbron
Jonathan Bingham
Geoffrey Wadsley
Marion H. Wadsley
Derek Copson
Tom Clarke
National Motor Museum Beaulieu Library
Veteran Car Club of Great Britain Library
Malcolm Jeal
Margaret Goding
Royal Automobile Club Library, London.
Joan Williamson
The Autocar
David N. Card
Justin Otto-Jones
Martin Ashby
James Riddell
Gowan Coulthard
Margaret Duff Collection
John Olorenshaw
Air Marshall Sir Freddie Sowrey
John Mellors
Peter Bazalgette
Barrie Hinson
Jack Pitman
Ron Clark
And many others
Thank you

Authors' Dedication

To Tim Scott for making the production of this book possible, and my husband Graham Bennett for his support throughout.

CONTENTS

AUTHOR'S NOTE

THIS BOOK HAS been a wonderful opportunity to evoke the feeling of the year 1900 in Britain. This has been done as far as possible by using contemporary accounts to tell the story. The use of the English language has changed over the last 100 years, and this adds to the 'period' feel. Some stories are told more than once by different narrators; giving amusing insights into reaction of the time to the introduction of the motorcar. Factual differences in narrative will be noticed by the reader, adding amusement to the experience of reliving the excitement of 1900 in your imagination.

The people you will meet within these pages were mostly young, all were vigorous, and undeniably tough. They were, in their later years, mostly pillars of the motor industry in Britain; but this narrative catches them at a stage of life before they had made their mark. For instance, we get a glimpse of S. F. Edge (accompanied by 'bully' his bull-terrier) as 'unbeatable' amateur boxing champion for his cycle club, taking on all-comers and a force to be reckoned with. John Stocks, who thought nothing of riding his trike home to Birmingham (120 miles) on a winters' night after a visit to the theatre in London – so that he could be at work the next morning! Two of his friends accompanied him for the first 20 miles, just for a lark. Women were also appearing driving motorcars; and one even made her own private entry in this Thousand Mile Trial of 1900. Many stories just waiting to be told ...

Elizabeth Bennett
February, 2000

PREFACE

ONE HUNDRED YEARS is a mere entry in the historian's book – in reality it is a great deal more. When asked to become involved with the Re-enactment of *The 1900 One Thousand Mile Trial* I was both delighted and honoured as, in my view, the original Trial was the first milestone in the collective promotion and design appraisal of the motor car. A view encapsulated previously by S. F. Edge in his book 'My Motoring Reminiscences' in which he stated *'the public saw that motor vehicles were a thoroughly practicable form of road locomotion'* and *'the car designer saw that weaknesses existed in unexpected quarters'*.

The One Thousand Mile Trial was an awesome undertaking in 1900 and rightly achieved a notable place in motoring history. Its success was due in no small part to the pioneering spirit of the participants. Many would ultimately become synonymous with the industry, like Claude Johnson (whose remarkable organisational and marketing skills would lead him to promote possibly the world's most renowned marque, the Rolls-Royce,) the Hon. C. S. Rolls, Alfred Harmsworth (later Lord Northcliffe), Frederick Simms, Count Zborowski, Worby Beaumont, J. Scott Montagu (later Lord Montagu), E. M. Iliffe (later Lord Iliffe), J. D. Siddeley (later Lord Kenilworth), Herbert Austin (later Lord Austin), Napier, Egerton (later of Mann Egerton) S. F. Edge, J. W. Stocks, and the only lady driver, Mrs Bazalgette, along with many more.

Thousand Mile Trial, although written one hundred years after the original event, is the first book that brings together contemporary photographs and articles from newspaper reports as well as participants' own accounts. It is, by any measure, a remarkable accomplishment and I am sure those involved in the original Trial would have been proud that their achievements had been so impressively recorded. Thanks go to Elizabeth Bennett, the author, for not only undertaking such a mammoth task but for compiling an outstanding record that will forever serve all who have an interest in early motoring.

There may be many reasons for being interested in the original Trial and the Centennial Re-enactment. These range from admiration for those early pioneers and an interest in early motoring, to the evolution of the motor car that over the last 100 years, has eclipsed most other 20th Century engineering achievements. What will the next 100 years hold? Presently we talk of electric cars, fuel cells, zero emissions – currently tomorrow's technology; but all of these may be just as dated to those attending the bicentenary as the cars of the original Trial are to us. In truth, if the past rate of progress is maintained, what will have been achieved by the bicentenary is impossible to imagine even by the most prophetic of us.

I am confident those people at the bicentenary of the year 2100 will have the same pioneering spirit, passion and interest as epitomised by both the original entrants, and the current participants. There can be no doubt that these qualities are nowhere better illustrated than by Daniel Ward, the organiser of the Centennial Re-enactment Run, for the year 2000 'Thousand Mile Trial'. This very special publication will continue to serve all such people for many years to come.

Tim Scott

FOREWORD

THE THOUSAND MILE TRIAL RE-ENACTMENT 2000

SOMETIMES YOU WONDER what might first have sparked your interest; someone, somewhere or something, but in the case of the Thousand Mile Trial I vividly remember what originally drew my attention to it. I was viewing a Sotheby's sale held at the Honourable Artillery Company in London on 22nd May 1993 and browsing through the books in the automobilia offerings I came across the Argent Archer photograph album of the Thousand Mile Trial. I was completely transfixed by the message that this book of photographs was giving me. Here was an indelible record of a tremendously significant watershed in the development of the thing that interests me most – Early Motorcars.

I was unable to afford the album at that time but nevertheless had been inbued with a powerful recognition of the significance of the Thousand Mile Trial and the phenomenal achievement it represented in 1900 of the efforts of Claude Johnson, in what must have been extremely difficult conditions, staging this spectacular and daring event. The more I found out about the event, the reasons for the need for a public demonstration of the motor car in a hostile political environment, the financial risk of the enterprise, and the evident team spirit and camaraderie of the entrants, the more convinced I was that we should at some point try to re-create it as a Veteran Car Club main event.

The Millennium, being the hundredth anniversary, and the wishes of the VCC to stage an important rally to mark this moment in time, was the ideal opportunity to re-enact the centennial of the Trial. This proposal was suggested to the Committee of the Veteran Car Club and endorsed as being suitable for the Headquarters main event for the year 2000.

The task of planning the trial has not been particularly onerous given that the route was already known, and I could draw on the fabulous original program still extant and held in the library of The Veteran Car Club. This document again is the enduring evidence of the original event and underpins the value of printed media as the historical record. Producing a rally at this end of the 20th Century with the benefit of telephones, commonly accepted bank cheques, the fax machine, e-mail, well mapped and signposted roads with a reliable consistent service, means that such a task is considerably easier than that faced by Claude Johnson in December 1899.

In formulating the re-enactment the major difficulties encountered have principally been finding a route which is safe for Veteran Cars and not too busy, and trying to encourage those with very early motor cars to actually attempt such a great distance today in a historic vehicle, given the advantage of easy availability of petrol, comfortable hotels, modern breakdown facilities and trailers in support, and the mobile telephone offering a degree of independence and safety unknown to the Pioneer Motorist.

No-one will fail to appreciate the irony that the very object of the original pioneers of motoring – to gain acceptability for their machines, despite the widespread contempt of the governing elite; should have been so phenomenally successful that now the motorcar is accessible to virtually all of our society, and that it again attracts contempt and the greatest body of governing law for any activity practised by a free society.

The wheel has almost turned full circle and those privileged few who now own the remaining automobiles of the pioneering age, consider themselves lucky indeed to still be able to exercise their freedom on the public highway, and as long as we can continue to travel in the tyre tracks of those intrepid early motorists we can still call ourselves free men.

It is such a fitting tribute to the entrants in the 1900 Trial that Elizabeth Bennett has freely given her time to compile this comprehensive work which is founded on the generosity of Tim Scott. He not only was the purchaser of the Argent Archer Album that I first saw at Sotheby's in 1993 and has generously lent this as the foundation for this book, but also has given his financial support to enable the publication in its entirety in order that we might all benefit from seeing them. Claude Johnston had a similar benefactor in Alfred Harmsworth, like Tim, a fellow owner of a 'sixty horse' Mercedes. Every great man should have one!

Daniel Ward

Busy London Streets at the time of Queen Victoria's Diamond Jubilee 1897

SET THE SCENE 1

THIS IS A STORY of Daring, Desperation and Design. The how, what, and why, of the Thousand Mile Trial of the year 1900. Contemporary reports tell us what and how, and now one hundred years later we are able to judge the results and the answer to – why?

Horse-drawn traffic around 1900. (Photo courtesy of J. Otto-Jones)

Daring, describes the concept, the development of the idea.

Desperation, applies to the stagnant state of the automobile industry, engendered by public ignorance and draconian laws relating amongst other things to speed limits (8 mph in town, 12 mph outside towns in England:10 mph outside towns in Scotland).

Design, this event was surely the birth of the British motor industry, highlighting ways that the foreign imports could be improved for the British market. The immediate result of the Trial in 1900 was in the field of motorcar design. Ideas that were state of the art on April 23rd 1900 were outdated by May 12th 1900. This was a novel situation. Never before had motorcars been tested in this country on a thousand mile trial in close proximity to their rival products. It was truly the first show piece of the infant British motorcar industry. It became a matter of patriotic pride to see how the first products of British workshops measured up to the more experienced foreign manufacturers. Men who were selling foreign made cars in England realised that they could make their own, and better! This was the contribution of Claude Johnson's organising genius to the history and development of motoring in Great Britain. His attention to detail provided the building blocks. He compressed years of development into 3 short weeks, by bringing together the best minds in this country to test their ideas against each other, enabling them to learn together and from one another. This event highlighted many shortcomings in current design. It signalled the beginning of the end for hot tube ignition, tiller steering, solid tyres, single cylinder engines, belt transmission, and illustrated that there was a better alternative to steam motive power for passenger carrying road vehicles. These design developments will be discussed in a later chapter. Subsequent developments came fast and furious, compressing history as never before.

How the streets of London were c. 1900.
(*right:*) The junction of St. James's and Picadilly.
(Photos courtesy of J. Otto-Jones)

Daily Mail

LONDON, MONDAY, MAY 4, 1896.

MOTOR CAR TRAVEL.

Lovers of the horse, after all, need not be jealous of the homely little petroleum engine that disputes the road with their favourite. The motor carriage will never displace the smart trotting pony or the high-stepping team, but it will end the cruel labours of the poor equine drudges that strain before omnibus and dray, and save the broken-down favourite of the Turf from the bondage of the nocturnal cab.

The first motorbus service in London 1899, passing Charing Cross.
(Photo: Argent Archer)

THE MOTOR 'BUS.

Fussy Old Gent. "Hi! Stop! stop! I want to get down." *Driver.* "I can't stop the bloomin' thing!!"

The first petrol motorbus service in London 1899, crossing Westminster Bridge.
(Photo: Argent Archer)

Every Participant in the 1900 Trial had a fund of stories to tell. This book creates an umbrella to collectively shelter them. To retain the original flavour the story has been told as far as possible using contemporary reports drawn from many sources. Never before have all these accounts been gathered together within the covers of one book. As you read through these wonderfully atmospheric accounts from *The Autocar* and *The Motor-Car Journal* of the year 1900 and many other sources, please bear in mind that although the Event was spendidly organised one source says that 'one cannot say the same for the reporting of the event. Nor is this surprising, as the lay reporters' ignorance of automobile matters was matched by the hostility of the majority of their readers, and the specialist craft of motor journalism was in its infancy and naturally prone to error.' Indeed the Automobile Club of Great Britain and Ireland was at pains to point out that even their published facts and figures, while as accurate as possible at time of publication 'were subject to revision'. So, while the material used to tell the story will give us the broad view, minute examination will show discrepancies which may have depended upon the writers point of view. That is why sometimes it will be found within this text that the same story is recounted more than once, with amusing differences.

It has been said that the famous Run from London to Brighton in November 1896 was the birth of the motorcar industry in Great Britain. I would like to offer the reader the following thoughts. During the period 1896 to early 1900 the automobile industry in Britain did not noticeably develop. In point of fact the motorcar was a subject of ridicule and much ignorance. It was not until the Thousand Mile Trial demonstrated to people of all persuasions the length and breadth of Britain that it was a preferable means of road transport to the horse-drawn variety, that the motorcar industry in Britain really got launched. Soon the 12 mph speed limit was raised, royal patronage was gained, and the industry began to organise itself. So, it is a strange fact to relate, that this momentous event in 1900 has not been very widely celebrated until now, while the London to Brighton Run annual celebration is a world class event!

'The Present Times' at Brighton 1896. Herr Daimler is seen in the back seat. (Photo: Argent Archer)

First run from London to Brighton in 1896 at Hotel Metropole Brighton. (Photo: Argent Archer)

In this the year Two Thousand AD, the motor cars of 1900 AD look strange and remarkable. As the participants of the 2000 Commemorative Run follow in the tyre tracks of those motoring pioneers recalled in these pages, people stop and stare and marvel to see these strange machines on the road. Think how strange and remarkable the same sight was in 1900, seen through the eyes of a population most of whom had never before in their lives seen a motorcar!

Racing driver Phil Hill 1996 – Emancipation Centenary – on 1896 Panhard et Levassor 4 cylinder 8 h.p. (Photo: Elizabeth Bennett)

1900 2 cylinder Georges Richard. (Photo: Elizabeth Bennett)

1899 4 cylinder 12 h.p. Daimler driven by Hon. John Scott-Montagu in Thousand Mile Trial 1900. (Photo: Elizabeth Bennett)

1898 2 cylinder 4 h.p. Daimler wagonette. (Photo: Elizabeth Bennett)

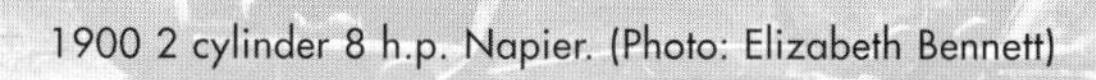

1900 2 cylinder 8 h.p. Napier. (Photo: Elizabeth Bennett)

38
36

1899 1 cylinder 3½ h.p. Wolseley that Herbert Austin drove on the Thousand Mile Trial 1900 now in the hands of the British Motor Industry Heritage Trust, precedes Lord Montagu driving the 12 h.p. Daimler that his father Hon, John Scott Montagu drove on the Thousand Mile Trial 1900, at the start of the London to Brighton Veteran Car Run, 7th November 1999. (Photo: Elizabeth Bennett)

Two 1900 New Orleans 3½ h.p. voiturettes, at the start of the London to Brighton Veteran Car Run, 7th November 1999. (Photo: Elizabeth Bennett)

1898 Benz 4½ h.p. vis à vis at the start of the London to Brighton Veteran Car Run, 7th November 1999. (Photo: Elizabeth Bennett)

1899 Decauville 3½ h.p. at the start of the London to Brighton Veteran Car Run, 7th November 1999. (Photo: Elizabeth Bennett)

1900 Georges Richard at the start of the London to Brighton Veteran Car Run, 7th November 1999. (Photo: Elizabeth Bennett)

The State of Automobilism in 1899

RACING IN BRITAIN was out of the question, so a long distance rally would be the next best thing, although the ability to average the legal maximum speed of 12 mph (outside of towns) would appear no great achievement compared with the daring races in France.

At the end of July 1897 the formation of the 'Automobile Club of Great Britain' was announced by Frederick Simms to champion the cause of all motorists. Like the computer 100 years later, the early supporters were regarded with suspicion. Indeed Lord Kelvin, a distinguished Victorian Scientist had commented to the effect that it was not in reason that vehicles propelled by a series of explosions, and using an engine not on a solid base, could reach a practical and permanently useful stage.

> "In France and Belgium impetus has been given to the automobile industry by racing at fearful speeds along the high roads to the accompaniment of official bands and with the assistance of the police authorities. The result has been the apparent popularisation of the automobile as a means of sport, and the development of high speed cars specially designed for record breaking. Fortunately in England no such venturesomeness has manifested itself."

The Motor-Car Journal,
Friday, April 27th 1900

An initial meeting of the new Club was held in August 1897, but even amongst the enthusiasts there was little accord. The Rules were based upon the Automobile Club de France. It was only when Simms sent out a rallying call in the national interest that the Club came into being.

A series of demonstrations and Exhibitions still failed to win any general support. In fact they had lost money for The Automobile Club of Great Britain, so they were very cautious about what the next step should be. If automobilism was to prosper in Great Britain something would have to be done soon. Something dramatic and courageous was called for. The first full-time Secretary, Claude Johnson, was appointed.

Against this discouraging backdrop Claude Johnson at the age of 36, conceived an idea. He decided to organise a tour along the lines that would be most likely to appeal to the practical character of the British people. It was to test the temper, patience and skill of the drivers, no less than the construction and design of the cars taking part. Instead of great speed over specially selected roads of a uniformly level surface, it was intended to show that the cars could successfully make daily runs aggregating 1,000 miles in a certain number of days. A car that could go through such a trial should be more suited for ordinary pleasure or commercial purposes than one designed merely for speed. He turned to a friend for help.

One of the first motorcars in London mingling with the horse-drawn traffic. (Photos courtesy of J. Otto-Jones)

Harmsworth Steam lorries.
(Photo: Argent Archer)

ALFRED HARMSWORTH was the eldest son of a family of fourteen. When he was eighteen he was writing articles and earning £3 per week; he was absolutely determined that he was going to make a lot of money and so solve one of the family's major problems. Alfred had a natural flair for writing and for a while worked as a freelance. He wrote for the magazine '*Tit-Bits*', but it was really '*Answers*' that started him on his meteoric career. The first newspaper he bought was the *Evening News*, which was making extremely heavy losses; no one had been able to make it pay and he bought it for £25,000. It was losing money at the rate of £100 per week; in its' first week of ownership by Alfred Harmsworth it made £7 profit; its' third week it made £50, This was in 1894. Two years later he started the *Daily Mail*, which gave an entirely new approach to newspapers and heralded modern journalism.

Alfred Harmsworth 1899.
(Courtesy P.H.H.)

At an early age Alfred Harmsworth was a very keen automobilist and motored all over Europe in his Gardner-Serpollet steam car or 'Travelling Carriage' as he called it, and was an enthusiastic member of the Automobile Club of Great Britain. In the summer of 1899 Claude Johnson Secretary of the ACGBI suggested a 1,000 mile trial run as a further demonstration to the general public that the motor car was a practical means of conveyance. The idea was for the members to visit practically every major town and city in Great Britain. The ACGBI Committee felt that this project was far too ambitious and the scheme was foundering for lack of support, but Harmsworth heard of it and was very enthusiastic. He said that not only would he give it wide publicity in all his newspapers, but he would also finance the undertaking indemnifying the Club against any losses, and placing money in the prize fund; so Claude Johnson delightedly set about the tremendously difficult task of organising this epic trial.

What were cars like in the early days of the year 1900?

S. F. Edge gives us some idea in his book *My Motoring Reminiscences*

'A large number of cars were fitted with tube ignition, and ignition burners gave far more trouble than batteries and coils. In a wind, particularly in exposed spots, it was very difficult to keep them alight.'

The hot tubes of the 1898 Peugeot are in the ventilated compartment at the rear (see also below).

The Operation of Hot Tube Ignition

'The starting of the motor is only a matter of a few minutes. It is first necessary to heat the tubes. This is accomplished by lighting a small quantity of methylated spirit below the burners. In the space of half a minute, the burners are sufficiently heated to vapourise the petrol. The latter is now fed to the burners from the supply tank. If the tank is placed at a low level, the petrol is forced out of the tank by means of air pressure created by a hand pump, which causes the oil to flow both to the burners and to the float chamber, this pressure being kept up afterwards automatically by the motor when in motion. With gravity fed engines, it is only necessary to open the supply cock. As soon as the ignition tubes are at a red heat, the motor is started by means of the detachable starting-handle which fits on the end of the crank-shaft. A few revolutions of the starting handle draws in the first explosive charge, after which the motor will continue to work as long as the supply tank feeds it. This supply tank will usually take a carriage a distance of 80 miles.'

Extract from Daimler Company Catalogue

Burners heating hot tubes on 1898 Peugeot. (Photos: Elizabeth Bennett)

'Cars that were not hot tube ignition had electric ignition. The car ran on one battery and a second one was carried as spare, which meant disconnecting the terminals from the exhausted battery and fitting them to the spare one. It was also common to find that by some mysterious means the spare one had exhausted itself when it was most needed.

Tyres were a constant source of delays. The life of the average pneumatic tyre did not exceed one thousand miles, and luck was needed to cover that distance on a set of tyres. There were no such things as spare or detachable wheels. When a puncture occurred, which happened very often, due, both to the quality of the tyres and the numbers of horse-shoes and nails found on the roads, it was almost impossible for one man, unassisted, to remove a cover, and still as difficult to refit it again. Each cover was held on by numbers of so-termed security bolts which easily nipped the tube and punctured it again during the process of re-fitting. Valves varied, and it was not uncommon, unless one was very careful, to be stranded with a pump connection which would not fit the particular valve.

The driving chains ran in a constant bath of grit, mud and water, as they were unprotected. For driving after dark, candle lamps, as fitted to carriages were common, bicycle lamps were often used, special paraffin lamps were more or less a luxury, while large acetylene head-lamps were considered to be almost futuristic. Many cars had no rear mudguards at all – the Napier had none; front mudguards consisted of about one yard of bent wood, four inches across, with no side protection for the bonnet.

An engine that ran at 750 revolutions per minute was normal, while 1,000 rpm was considered to be fast-running. There was no throttle for engine-control; engine-speed was controlled by a centrifugal governor which could be cut out of action by the driver.

On many cars, notably the Peugeot, De Dion, Decauville, etc., the steering column was quite vertical, and on others such as the Panhard, Daimler, M.M.C. and the Napier, it was only slightly inclined. Wheel steering was by no means universal; the radiator, as we know it to-day, was unknown; cooling of the engine was effected by a huge water tank at the rear of the car, beneath which could be found a series of coiled tubes with small discs attached with which to catch the air. The water was conveyed to the engine by means of a friction pump in contact with the fly-wheel, and in wet weather this friction pump often slipped owing to wet getting on the fly-wheel, thus causing the engine to overheat.

Inlet manifolds, as they are termed to-day, were often a yard or more in length, which made starting in cold weather very uncertain. Cars weighing 1½ tons often had two-cylinder engines which were supposed to develop 6 h.p. but usually did nothing of the kind.

Lawson Motor wheel
(Photo: Argent Archer)

Control of car-speed was effected by changing gear; if one wished to go slower, which was very seldom, one merely changed down to a lower gear and allowed the engine to cut out, and it was quite common to have to change gear half-a-dozen times within a mile. The slightest incline, unless it could be 'rushed,' meant a change of gear, and to miss one's gear on a steep hill nearly always resulted in the car running backward as brakes would only operate in a forward position. They consisted of nothing more substantial than a brass brake-drum attached to the rear sprocket, round which was wound some wire rope, with numbers of wooden blocks attached to it, which rubbed against the drum when the brake-lever was applied. There was also a brake on the countershaft, and sometimes a third brake which acted against the back tyres; if these punctured the third brake became ineffective.

Such, briefly, was the condition of motordom when we all assembled to take part in the Thousand Miles Trial.'

S. F. Edge *My Motoring Reminiscences*

Motor vehicles prior to 1900 frequently resembled a carriage without the horse.
(***Right:***) 1898 Brougham
(***Below:***) 1899 convertible Phaeton.
(Photos: Argent Archer)

THE 1,000 MILE MOTOR TEST.

COUNT DE DION, VICE PRESIDENT OF THE AUTOMOBILE CLUB, ON HIS DION-BOUTON LIGHT MOTOR CARRIAGE.

WHY ARE WE BEHIND THE WORLD?

THE great motor test which is to start from London on April 23 will, it is hoped, do something to awaken us to our strange position in what is destined to be one of the world's greatest industries.

This test, by the way, is not a race, for racing is, perhaps wisely, perhaps unwisely, forbidden, even on lonely roads, to those who wish to submit British inventions to practical tests.

The trial involves the journey from London to Edinburgh and back, and is, at the moment of going to press, arranged to last from April 23 to May 12.

Its object is to prove how far the various forms of motor vehicles are reliable or not, and their makers will try to prove that their vehicles are capable not only of going over all roads that are used for horse-drawn traffic, but that at a time when roads are in far from their best condition the motor-car can during a day cover a distance far greater than could be covered by a horse.

The list of towns through which the motor-cars will pass is given at the end of this article. Our illustrations represent some of the cars which will make this unique tour.

That England is behind any other country in the manufacture of motor-cars or anything else is still grudgingly and unwillingly admitted by the majority of Englishmen.

MR. T. B. BROWNE'S 6-HORSE POWER PANHARD MOTOR-CAR.

2

INTRODUCTION

TO THE FIRST GREAT BRITISH MOTORING ADVENTURE

THE YOUNG ARE always in search of adventure. This is a story of a new technology breaking onto the scene in Great Britain at the end of the 19th century. About every hundred years technology lobs a spinning ball. The technological revolution in process at the end of the 20th century concerns the microchip. This fragment of silicon with its awesome power to affect our lives, occupied the position at the end of the 20th century held by the internal combustion engine in 1899, and the computer with all its life changing possibilities in the year 2000 is where the motor-car was in 1900.

Late Victorians travelled by train. They also went to Europe and America by boat. They saw the automobile industry growing in other countries and yearned to throw off the yoke of protectionism of the railway companies in Britain. The fun of being in control with more immediacy than the reins of a horse – master of their own destiny – blended with the thrill of speed and the stimulus of travel, was a heady mixture to hand to a vigorous young generation!

The attraction of a new and exciting unknown to conquer was a magnet to the young. The cream of any generation will associate themselves with a new and growing industry. A brief analysis of the ages of the Participants in the Thousand Mile Trial of the year 1900 shows the average age to be below 30 years. Some were as young as 22-23, whilst St. John Nixon who was aged just 14 rode as mechanician for S. F. Edge.

The first twin-cylinder 8 h.p. Napier car – as driven by S. F. Edge. (Photo: *The Autocar*)

The problem in 1900 was that most of the population of Great Britain had never seen a motorcar, let alone think it could play a part in their lives. In order for the industry to grow the population at large must be educated.

S. F. Edge *My Motoring Reminiscences* with reference to The Thousand Miles Trial of 1900 has this to say:

> 'At the end of 1899, there were still numbers of people who had never seen a motor car, and a greater number who laughed at the idea of their ever becoming a commercial or practical success. This scepticism existed chiefly in the Midlands and in the west of England, and it was for the object of enlightening the public that the Automobile Club decided that an extensive trial should be held in the Spring of 1900, in which a large number of motor vehicles of all kinds should take part.'

ORGANISATION OF THE 1,000 MILE TRIAL

3

23rd APRIL–12th MAY 1900

FEW MOTORISTS HAD at that time driven 100 miles in a single day. When the plans were conceived no-one knew how to plan a schedule that could be maintained. Some drivers wanted a 2 hour lunch break to allow for coffee and liqueurs, while others grudged any stop at all! It was clear though that if the public were to be given a chance to examine the motorcars at close quarters, then set breaks must be adhered to. Then having introduced the motorcar, the intent was to test not just human endurance, but also the machinery for reliability and safety. C. S. Rolls was only too aware of this, and he is recorded as saying:

'People now take no notice whatever of a bicycle going along at 20 miles an hour; they have got used to it, and it no longer shocks them; but when they see a heavy motor vehicle driven by a man in a mask, with a weird-looking shining black jacket, and overall appearance of being in armour plate, travelling at 30 miles an hour, raising a cloud of dust, and propelled by a force which they do not understand, and leaving behind it a smell, which, sweeter than eau de Cologne to the motorists, is to them abominable, they naturally say we are 'madmen in motors', and that such practices must end in the death of thousands of people.'

The Hyphen in Rolls Royce, biography of Claude Johnson by Wilton J. Oldham. (ch 5) *Source:* Royal Automobile Club Pall Mall library

Above:
F. R. Simms founder and first President of A.C.G.B.I.

Left:
A Postcard of the day.

'The Hare and the Tortoise' retold: the hare leads. (From the *London Illustrated News* June 9, 1900)

'The Hare and the Tortoise' retold: the tortoise wins. (From the *London Illustrated News* June 9, 1900)

A Pennington with a full load at Coventry 1897 (Photo: Argent Archer)

Cannstatt Daimler convertible cab 1899 (Photo: Argent Archer)

Reconnaissance of route for 1,000 Mile Trial, Claude Johnson and Montague Grahame-White

Claude Johnson

CLAUDE JOHNSON, Secretary to the Automobile Club, threw himself into the arrangements for the 1,000-mile trial. It was to consist of driving from one town to another, with hill-climbs, brake tests, etc., en route. At each overnight stopping place the cars would be on view to the general public. It was to take place during the months of April and May 1900. Local authorities would have to be consulted and their co-operation won. No doubt a good many people, never having seen or even heard a car but having spent their lives amongst horses (in some cases making them part of their means of livelihood), would not be very pleased at this new mode of transportation.

THE ONLY principal car makes of British origin were Daimler, Napier, Lanchester and Wolseley; there were beginning to be others but many of these were really French or German marques imported and sold after being thinly disguised as British. The number of enthusiastic people in the trade was so small that everybody knew everybody else and CJ knew J. S. Critchley of the Daimler Company quite well. He had learned to drive on a Daimler and always liked them, so he asked Critchley to lend him a car and driver to go over the route he had mapped out; Critchley was only too pleased and agreed immediately, suggesting Montague Grahame-White, one of their keenest young men.

Montague Grahame-White was born 27 July 1877 at Bursledon Towers, Bursledon, Hampshire, his parents' home on the Southampton side of the Hamble River, overlooking the Solent. His grandfather was at one time High Sheriff of the County and for several years Mayor of Southampton. He was a large landowner in the district, young Montague was, therefore, the son of wealthy parents. At an early age he showed a natural aptitude for anything mechanical and in 1897, when aged twenty, he obtained a position with the Daimler Company in Coventry, partly through the influence of his friend the Hon. Evelyn Ellis. He was delighted at the thought of accompanying Claude Johnson on the trial, and below are extracts from his own book *At the Wheel Ashore and Afloat:*

Montague Grahame-White aged 23. (Photo: Argent Archer)

'On November 16th Mr. Critchley had received a request from Mr. Johnson, who was responsible for the route to be traversed, to provide the Club with a car and driver for this purpose.

I was sent for by Mr. Critchley and he informed me of the purport of Claude Johnson's letter and suggested I should undertake the job.

Needless to say, I felt flattered at being selected for this undertaking, although fully realising the probable difficulties to be faced

Montague Grahame-Whites' personal photograph album. (Courtesy N.M.M. Beaulieu)

under winter conditions in the north of England.

After considerable discussion and, I might add, persuasion on my part, it was decided to prepare for the tour one of the 'Critchley' belt-driven cars fitted with a 5½ h.p. motor in place of the original one of 3½ h.p., thus giving a reserve of power on the stiff gradients included on the route. (*This car is later described as 6 h.p. in Montague Grahame-Whites' personal photograph album.*)

Some days later Johnson arrived at the works when it was decided he and I should make a start from London on December 16th

... This little car, when fitted with a 4½ h.p. engine had seen considerable service on demonstration runs since the Richmond Trials, and the only troubles experienced were caused by the belt transmission, especially on gradients.

It was chiefly due to my faith in the possibility of removing these failings that I tried my persuasion on Mr. Critchley to use the car bearing his name in preference to the gear-driven type, both of which were built by the Daimler Company.

The excessively short wheel base allowed in the design, with a consequent limited belt drive, was responsible for much of the trouble experienced later on.

The first part of the tour from London to Bristol, a distance of 118 miles, was commenced, however, on an 8 h.p. Panhard, kindly lent by Mr. Alfred Harmsworth, the run being accomplished at an average of just over 14 miles per hour in a heavy snowstorm during part of the journey.

Here certain arrangements for the exhibition proposed to be held were discussed with the Club's local representatives overnight, and at

6am the following morning a start was made for Birmingham, passing through Cheltenham, a run of 93 miles in very rainy weather.

The next day was devoted by Johnson to various organising arrangements, and he then returned to London. On December 19th Johnson arrived at Coventry in readiness to leave with me the following day on the Critchley car for Birmingham.

Leaving at 5.30 a.m. on the 20th (Johnson was an early riser as later accounts will show), Manchester was reached much to our delight after a highly successful run. There we remained until the following morning when a start was made for Kendal.

The run to Kendal, a distance of seventy-four miles, took us through uninteresting country, passing through Bolton, Preston and Lancaster. At first rain, then sleet, and finally snow accompanied by high winds, were encountered the whole way and were accountable for repeated stops to relight the burners, and for rejointing or adjustment of the driving belts until our arrival at 5pm.

The ascent of Shap the following day, a distance of ten miles, during which the road rises from 300 to 1,400 feet above sea level, was begun with three inches of snow on the road.

is composed of a colourless transparent material of no weight. It is invisible under an ordinary veil, and protects the face from cold winds as effectually as if the wearer were sheltered behind a glass screen, while it does not interfere with free respiration. When protected by the Mask Veil, a lady can drive on a motor car at the highest speed, facing the keen east wind, with perfect comfort, and after a day's journey will find herself as clean and smart as when she started, instead of showing dishevelled hair, a red nose adorned with smuts, discoloured cheeks, and watery eyes. The open carriage constitutional in the park would be far more enjoyable if the refreshing breezes were not followed by flushed faces on entering warmed rooms.

Black or White Lace Veil, 5/- Postage 1d.

MEN'S MASK. 2/6

Mask Veil for Ladies for inclement weather, covers ears and chin, **7/6** Postage 2d.

(*Prov. Patent* 21347/99.)

O. CLAXTON, 62, STRAND, W.C.

The driving snow and sleet made it extremely difficult to see, the car having neither hood nor windscreen, and the higher we climbed the more wind we encountered. I suggested to Johnson that we should stop at a local haberdashery and provide ourselves with some black veiling to place under our caps and over our faces to obtain protection and better visibility.

In the higher stretches of the pass, however, we found it necessary to remove these, the snow clogging the net and rendering sight impossible.

6HP CAR formerly a 2cyl 4½ HP, Belt driven Critchley Daimler driven by M.G-W from Coventry - B'ham - Derby, Manchester - Preston, over Shap to Kendal (Xmas eve 1899) Carlisle - Moffat - Edinburgh - Berwick - N'castle Durham - York. Here the back axle gave out & the remaining distance was completed on a 6HP heavy Daimler to London. Claud Johnson accompanied the driver throughout the run, which mapped out the 1000 mile trial the following year. This car did 37.35 mph on the Coventry - B'ham road. with a 6hp motor. GW

Under the loose snow that had been falling for seven hours there was a layer of frozen snow over loose stones which caused considerable side slip on the gradient, calling for extreme caution in handling the car.

Between the start of the ascent and reaching the summit of Shap, Johnson and I must have got out on more than a score of occasions, either to fit new belt fasteners, new sections of belting or to relight the extinguished burners.

To endeavour to reduce the belt slip, powdered resin was dropped on the inside of the belts whilst the car was running, by means of a small funnel penetrating a hole drilled in the flooring of the car.

It took us 6¼ hours to cover the ten miles to reach the summit, where we encountered half a gale which drove the loose snow into snow-drifts in the most exposed places. The run down to Shap, a somewhat tricky venture, completed the day's 'amusement'.

On completion of ninety miles in this kind of weather in an open car, no two men were

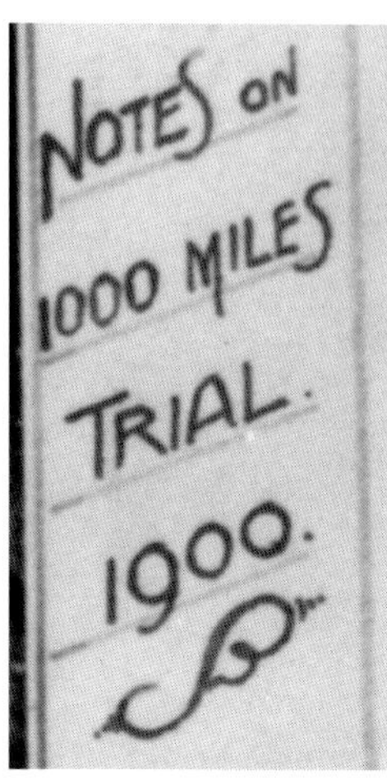

Extract from Montague Grahame-White's Album. (Courtesy of N.M.M. Beaulieu)

more eager for a hot supper and warm bed at the local inn than my companion and myself.

Johnson fell asleep in an armchair in front of the parlour fire on rising from the table, and it was with difficulty I roused him to 'turn in' an hour or so later. Contemplating a late start the following morning I soon followed suit and counted on a well-earned rest. My hopes were, however, dashed to the ground, Johnson being in favour of an early start, the day in store promising to be full of adventure and unforeseen possibilities owing to the probable state of the weather and roads.

Banging on my room door at 5.15 am when it was absolutely dark he urged me to 'get a move on'.

He was unaware that after supper I had returned to the stable and by the light of two carriage lamps had put in a couple of hours on my back fitting new belts, roughing the driving pulleys, and making an additional wind shield round the burners, ready for the mornings departure.

Breakfast over, I went to the stable where I found a farmhand awaiting my arrival. With his assistance I pushed the car out of the yard and then proceeded to replenish the petrol tank from a five gallon reserve drum, before lighting the car lamps and burners.

Although it was dark I was able to feel sufficiently well for the purpose. The farm hand, however, thought otherwise and, striking a match close to the tank, leant towards the spot where I was standing, oblivious to the danger he was courting.

By a stroke of luck it blew out and thus saved the position. My subsequent remarks to the poor fellow were more expressive than polite.

Our journey from Shap to Carlisle, thirty miles, was covered without incident, the work carried out on the previous night proving beneficial to the car's running.

The remainder of the day was devoted by Johnson to local arrangements at Carlisle and by myself in adjusting brakes, and oiling the car.

Christmas Eve was to be a memorable day for us, as Johnson surprised me by saying he had decided to make a return trip over Shap back to Kendal in order to try the alternative Lake route from Kendal to Carlisle.

The night of December 23rd witnessed a severe frost and on this account the radiator and cylinder jackets of the motor were emptied before leaving the car in the garage overnight.

To describe my fears in regard to the behaviour of the car on the morrow's run might appear unreasonable, so I will here give a verbatim report of our experiences as sent by Claude Johnson to Mr. Frederick R. Simms, Chairman of the Automobile Club Committee:

Windermere by moonlight
(J. Riddell collection)

'We – Mr. Montague Grahame-White driving and myself – set out from Carlisle for Kendal at 5.30 this morning, taking the route over Shap which we traversed on the 22nd inst.

The little car took us up Shap the whole way with the exception of about ten yards where the road was extremely bad. The snow on the summit had thawed and refrozen; the road surface was, in fact, ice.

The descent was, therefore, not without incident and it required the nerve and skill of a driver like Grahame-White to keep the car on the road at all.

The road from Kendal to Thirlmere via Banerigg Hill, with a gradient of one in ten, was then attempted and was only negotiated by resorting to pushing, the engine having developed carburation trouble.

The road passes along Windermere Lake through Ambleside to Grasmere, after which Dunmail Raise (which includes about one mile of I in 10 and 1 in 12) was ascended in good style, after having cleared water from the carburetter, the cause of the misfiring of the motor.

Trouble, however, soon presented itself again and the car began to run badly – inexplicably so, much to the concern of Grahame-White – just before reaching the summit, in a heavy hail storm and strong wind.

Then followed a weird drive in the dark along the Thirlmere Road, the car gradually losing speed and the belts either slipping or breaking continuously.

Stopping the car, we discovered that although the engine when running free, was quite in order, it required considerable effort to even move the car on the level by hand.

Getting underneath it and feeling the back axle and brake drum, Grahame-White discovered considerable over-heating of the former which he cooled down with snow from the road and subsequently oiled by the aid of two carriage-lamps.

For the next mile or two the car ran up to its former pace, but gradually slowed up until it would scarcely travel with the aid of the engine down the steep hill into Keswick which was finally reached at 1.30 a.m. on Christmas morning.'

This concluded Johnson's report, and Montague Grahame-White remembered a little episode connected with their arrival at Keswick.

The small town was in darkness as we groped our way down what appeared to be the main Street, until we arrived at an inn that seemed the most inviting of those we had seen.

Not a soul was about, so blowing the horn and shining one of our lamps on an upstairs window to awaken the landlord and get a 'shake-down' for the night, we awaited results.

Several minutes elapsed when finally there appeared at a window an old woman in a nightcap who told us to 'Go home' and then closed the window.

Renewed horn-blowing, however, brought her once more to the window and as I steered the car closer to the house, Johnson enquired if we could put up for the night.

' "George and the Dragon" have gone to bed,' was the reply.

'I know that,' said Johnson, 'but get George to come down and let us in.'

After waiting what seemed like a quarter of an hour, we heard footsteps descending the stairs ... a light appeared on the ground floor and the door was opened by the landlord.

Johnson explained matters and, much to my delight, beckoned me into the house.

The host of 'The George' at Keswick is a man to be remembered with gratitude by us both. Instead of grumbling at being turned out in the early hours of a Christmas morning, he and his wife and daughter gave us a hearty welcome and a good supper before a rekindled log fire within half an hour of our arrival.

Eleven o'clock the following morning found Johnson and I still snug in bed when the landlord's daughter knocked at our door to bring in breakfast and our boots, which she had dried overnight over the kitchen stove.

Johnson was the first to move, and as he caught sight of the boots uttered just one word ... 'Hell'.

His thick-soled Scotch brogues were shrivelled like Bombay ducks, whilst my high-topped shooters were dried as stiff as cold glue, each boot resembling a half-extended accordion placed on end.

Owing to the courtly reception we had received, we said nothing and put on spare shoes in our kits to go and inspect the car after breakfast.

Having jacked up the back axle, I found it was almost impossible to revolve either rear wheel. The strain to which it had been

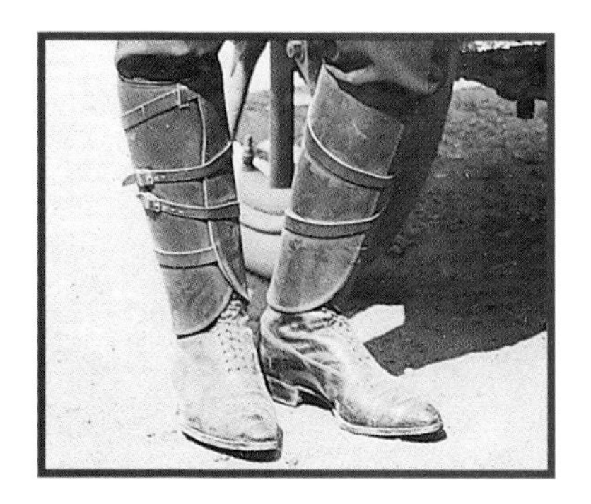

subjected in crossing and re-crossing Shap, with an almost continuous jerk in bringing up side-slips on the borders of the ice-covered roads, had twisted the interior shaft causing its mis-alignment.

Despite my entreaties to Johnson to allow me time to dismantle the axle and get it straightened at the local blacksmith's, he decided it would be more expedient to put the car on rail to Coventry and telegraph to the Edinburgh Autocar Co. for another to be sent to Keswick.

On the 27th a 5½ h.p. gear-driven Daimler was despatched to Johnson, and the tour was continued to Newcastle with Mr. Rowland Outhwaite the owner, as its driver, I, myself, returning to Coventry by rail with the other car.

In answer to Johnson's request, however, on December 30th another gear-driven Daimler car was substituted at Newcastle-on-Tyne and I continued the route with him, driving to York, Leeds, via Harrogate, Bradford, Wakefield to Sheffield, which was reached without encountering any trouble whatever on January 4th, 1900.

The following day the run was made to Nottingham via Lincoln. We reached London, a further distance of 124 miles, in the afternoon, so completing the task we had set ourselves.'

Claude Johnson had laid the foundation of his plans for Great Britain's First Great Motoring Adventure. Returning to Montague Grahame-White's commentary:

'It is worthy of mention here that the following month, after receiving a full report of this tour of inspection and its successful conclusion, His Royal Highness the Prince of Wales ordered his first motor carriage, a 6 h.p. mail phaeton from the Daimler Company, so giving considerable encouragement to manufacturers in England.'

Source: *At the Wheel Ashore and Afloat*
Montague Grahame-White

The following is taken from Claude Johnsons' book *An Early History of Motoring*, which demonstrates his natural modesty:

I CRAVE THE indulgence of my readers if I attach too much importance to the 1,000 miles trial of the Automobile Club of Great Britain and Ireland of 1900. Very probably the writer overrates its value. But it must be borne in mind that no public demonstration of motor vehicles had previously been held in England in which a long distance was covered by a number of vehicles.

The ever-memorable run to Brighton in 1896 was a comparatively short affair witnessed by Londoners and Brightonians and those living on the route between these two places. The Club tours had excited interest and the 50 miles and 100 miles trials of the Club had at least proved something.

Every endeavour was made prior to the Trial to interest the authorities on the route. The police were consulted as to controls, the surveyors were written to as to roads, and the editors of every newspaper published in the districts through which the Trial passed, were kept informed from day to day of the progress of the organisation of the Trial.

During the Trial, long telegrams were sent every night to the principal newspapers throughout the kingdom, giving the results of the day's run.

The itinerary was as follows:

April 23rd	London to Bristol, 118½ miles.
24th	Exhibition at Bristol.
25th	Bristol via Cheltenham to Birmingham, 92½ miles.
26th	Exhibition at Birmingham.
27th	Birmingham to Manchester, 110 miles.
28th	Exhibition at Manchester.
30th	Manchester to Kendal, 73¾ miles.
May 1st	Kendal to Carlisle, 61½ miles.
2nd	Carlisle via Berkhill to Edinburgh, 100 miles.
3rd	Exhibition at Edinburgh.
4th	Edinburgh to Newcastle-on-Tyne, 121½ miles.
5th	Exhibition at Newcastle.
7th	Newcastle to Leeds, 103 miles.
8th	Exhibition at Leeds.
9th	Leeds to Sheffield, 74 miles.
10th	Exhibition at Sheffield.
11th	Sheffield to Nottingham, with speed trials at Welbeck, 82¼ miles.
12th	Nottingham to London, 123½ miles.
	Total: 1,060 miles.

An Early History of Motoring, Claude Johnson
(You will notice – no activity on Sundays)

Below:
Entry forms (Courtesy John Mellors)

AUTOMOBILE CLUB—1,000-MILE TRIAL, 1900.

FORM OF ENTRY.

*To THE COMMITTEE,
Automobile Club of Great Britain,
4, Whitehall Court,
London, S.W.

SIRS,

We hereby beg to enter for the 1,000-Mile Trial of the Automobile Club, to be held, probably, from Monday, 23rd April, to Friday, 11th May, 1900, the vehicle or part specified on the back hereof.

Cheque Enclosed. We are enclosing cheque for †£______ being entrance fees for the same.

And we hereby agree to abide by, and to be bound by, the Rules of the Club Committee affecting the same, a copy of which we have received and read.

We are, SIRS,

Yours obediently,

*This Form should be sent, with Cheque, to the Accountants' Department, Messrs. Andw. W. Barr & Co., 30, Moorgate Street, London, E.C.

†Cheques should be made payable to the "Automobile Club Trials Account," and should be crossed, "Union Bank of London."

AUTOMOBILE CLUB—1,000-MILE TRIAL, 1900.

FORM OF ENTRY.

Section (*see* Rule 2)______

Class (*see* Rule 3)______

SECTIONS I & II:—

Type of Motor (Petrol, heavy—oil, steam, etc.)______

Number of Cylinders______

Brake Horse-Power______

Weight of Vehicle unladen______

Designed to carry______persons, including driver.

Transmission (gear or belt)______

Speeds at normal revolutions of engine______ miles per hour.

______ " "

______ " "

______ " "

Engine feed (gravity or pressure)______

Ignition—lamp or electric______

If lamp, is lamp feed gravity or pressure?______

Price (*see* Rule 17) £ ______

Signature ______

Date______

**If the vehicle be driven by power other than oil or spirit, please fill in similar particulars.
If more than one vehicle be entered, fill in, please, a fresh form for every vehicle.**

SECTION III:—

Class (*see* Rule 3.)______

Description______

We have noted what is required of us in Rule 5.

Signature______

Date______

Address______

Over Shap in the Snow

The following extract from the diary of the Secretary of the Automobile Club of his inspection run over the route selected for the one thousand miles trial next April is not without interest. Only those who have been over Shap by road can fully appreciate the following:

Wednesday, 20th December – The route at first selected between Birmingham and Manchester, viz, by Stafford and Newcastle-under-Lyme, was abandoned in favour of that by Burton, Derby, Matlock, and Buxton to Manchester. This journey was made on the original Critchley five and a half horse-power car, kindly placed at the disposal of the club by the Daimler Company, and driven for the greater part of the journey by Mr. Montague Grahame-White. Day's run, 102 miles.

Friday, 22nd December – On the same car, from Manchester to Preston, where snow commenced and continued for seven hours, making the roads very heavy, with the result that Kendal (seventy-three miles) was not reached until 5 p.m. The ascent of Shap (ten miles, during which the road rises from 130 to 1,400 feet above the sea) was begun with three inches of snow on the road. In the higher parts it was found that underneath the new snow there was much old snow, this being on the top of loose stones. With the aid of considerable muscular assistance, the motor vehicle at last reached the top, and the run down to Shap completed the day's work – ninety miles, mostly through heavy snow.

Saturday, 23rd December – On the same car. Shap to Carlisle, twenty-nine and a half miles, the remainder of the day being devoted to inquiries as to local arrangements at Carlisle.

Sunday, 24th December – Carlisle back over Shap to Kendal in order to try the alternative lake-route from Kendal to Carlisle. The little car took Mr. M. Grahame-White and the Secretary all the way up except about ten yards, where the road was very bad. The snow on Shap summit had thawed and refrozen. The road surface was, in fact, ice. The descent was, therefore, not without interest. The road from Kendal via Thirlmere was then attempted. Banerrigg is a stiff hill – one in ten. The car needed help here. It was not travelling well. The road passes along Windermere Lake, through Ambleside to Grasmere, after which Dunmail Raise (which includes about one mile of one in ten and one in twelve) was ascended. The car was going very badly, inexplicably so. But with patience and pushing the top was reached in a rattling hailstorm and strong wind. Then followed a weird drive in the dark along the new road by Thirlmere. The car was going worse and worse. The belts either slipped or broke continually; the engine, however, was working splendidly. More pushing up hill, and, at last, with a car which would scarcely run with the aid of the engine down the steep hill, Keswick was entered at 1.30 on Christmas morning. The host of the George Inn, Keswick, is a man to be remembered with gratitude, since, instead of grumbling at being required to get up at this hour, he and his wife and daughter gave us a hearty welcome and a good supper.

A postcard of the day
Lance Thackeray (Raphael Tuck)

Christmas Day, 25th December – Examination of the car on Christmas Day morning showed that the axle of the back wheels, which had some time previously been bent and re-straightened, had, owing probably to the severe strain imposed on it by frequent side-slips on icy roads, become bent again. When jacked up, the engine could scarcely start the one wheel, which had unfortunately also suffered too severely from unequal strain to make it safe to use the car without considerable repair. It was, therefore, put on the train for Coventry: a great disappointment, since the motor had worked admirably.

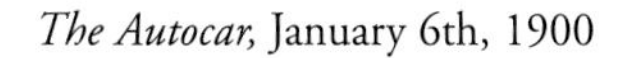

The Autocar, January 6th, 1900

Preparations in Hand!

There now appears every probability that the one thousand mile run of the Automobile Club will include Lincoln. Mr. Johnson, the secretary of the club, was to be in Lincoln yesterday (Thursday) on his way from Sheffield to Nottingham and London. The A.C. would undoubtedly be giving the movement a great lift in Lincolnshire by taking the run through Lincoln. The roads are good.

The Autocar, January 6th, 1900

“ The Automobile Club

Meeting in Newcastle – Arrangements for the 1,000 Miles Trial

A meeting of members and others interested in automobilism was held in the County Hotel, Newcastle, last Friday. As our readers are aware, the object of the gathering was to forward arrangements for the one thousand miles trial, which will probably commence on April 23rd. It is also proposed to hold day exhibitions at seven of the principal cities on the line of route, namely, Bristol, Birmingham, Manchester, Edinburgh, Newcastle, Leeds, and Sheffield. The object of the trial is to popularise the automobile, and to do something to dispel the opinion entertained by many people that the motor vehicle is a most unreliable machine. Mr. J.W. Ellis presided, and there was a good attendance.

From Edinburgh approaching Newcastle, Bridge Street Morpeth as it appeared at the time of the Trial. (Courtesy J. Riddell)

Mr. C. Johnson (secretary), who had travelled overnight from Edinburgh by autocar, explained the objects of the 1,000 miles trial. He said the Automobile Club was an entirely independent body, and had nothing to do with any firm, company, or financial undertaking. In 1894 certain of the French newspapers, recognising that the then very imperfect machines were the forerunners of machines which would eventually revolutionise to a great extent road locomotion, offered prizes for a race on the road. The race was a great success, although the speed at that time was not very great. The result was a number of sporting gentlemen in France formed themselves into a committee, with the view of organising further races. The Automobile Club of France was thus formed. It had now a membership of two thousand, an income of £16,000 a year, and the finest clubhouse in the world. Similar clubs followed in Berlin, Brussels, London, Turin, Geneva, and New York. The committee of the club of Great Britain had felt for some time that the industry enjoyed in France advantages which it did not possess in this country. It had been found that the road racing had done great good to the industry, having shown where the construction was faulty, where weight might be reduced, and had thus, so to speak, improved the breed. Races had taken place in all parts of France, with the result that the people in rural France knew that the motor vehicles were extraordinarily speedy, and also reliable machines. The people of this country, on the contrary, had come to the conclusion that automobiles were most unreliable machines, whereas with experienced drivers, as in France, autocars could be driven without any serious breakdown. The trial had been designed to remove as far as possible the impression as to the unreliability of the machines. The projected tour would be in no sense a race. Road racing was illegal in this country, and the tour was simply a test of reliability. At the seven big centres on the line of route exhibitions were proposed to be held. On the proposition of the Chairman, seconded by Mr. W. Philipson, it was agreed that the gentlemen present form themselves into a local committee, with power to add to their number, in order to make the necessary local arrangements. On the proposition of Mr. F. G. Lundi, seconded by Mr. W. Dunn, it was resolved to invite contributions to a local guarantee fund in the event of the expenses exceeding the receipts.

It was further resolved that the committee should make enquiry as to the hiring of a hall for the proposed exhibition, to approach the mayor and leading men of the city with a view to securing their patronage, to confer with the police as to suitable control of the traffic, and to make other arrangements. Messrs. W. Philipson and R. Barnett were appointed hon. local secs. The itinerary provides that Newcastle shall be reached from Edinburgh on Friday, May 4th, and that the suggested exhibition of cars shall be held on May 5th.

Besides the meeting at Newcastle, equally successful gatherings have been held during the course of the inspection run over the one thousand miles trial course at Bristol, Birmingham, Leeds (where a branch of the Automobile Club has been formed), and Edinburgh. In another column we give some particulars of Mr. Johnson's experiences on the road. It will be seen his adventures in the snow drifts on the barren slopes of Shap deterred him not, as he borrowed another car and drove down from Edinburgh to Newcastle in the night. ”

The Autocar, January 6th, 1900

"The 1,000 Miles Trial Run

This great autocar trial of the Automobile Club, suggested more or less by the Tour de France, made by our chauffeur brethren on the other side of the Channel, is now taking definite shape. Mr. Claude Johnson, by the courtesy of autocar manufacturers and private owners, has been enabled to cover all but a small portion of the proposed trip on autocars, and pronounces every yard of the selected route to be entirely practical. Finding Mr. Johnson with a few spare moments at his command at the Club in Whitehall Court the other day, we sought to get his views of the whole project.

Recalling what had appeared in the club circular, we suggested that he and Mr. Grahame White, who accompanied him as far as Keswick, had had rather a bad time so far as the weather and roads were concerned.

'Yes,' was the reply, 'even when on the first stage, travelling between London and Bristol, on Mr. Harmsworth's eight horse-power Panhard, we ran into very heavy snow between Newbury and Marlborough. It was freezing hard, too.'

'Not quite an ideal trip?' we suggested.

'Not quite, but very pleasant all the same.'

'Did you find the Bristol folk well disposed towards the idea?' was our next question.

'Oh, extremely well disposed; indeed, quite enthusiastic. They are anxious to have us. The Bristol press throughout were profuse in their promises of support, and more than one representative of the principal papers are acting upon the local committee. Mr. W. M. Appleton, who is an enthusiastic autocarist, and who, I think, was at one time a prominent cyclist and keen military cyclist, acts as secretary.'

'You will give Cheltenham a visit, Mr. Johnson?'

'Well, we shall only be able to give a two-hours' show in the middle of the day there, as we have to get on to Birmingham, where a vast amount of interest is being taken in the tour. The *Birmingham Post* and other papers have already accorded our suggestions the warmest welcome in print, and promise to do all they can for us. There will be a day show in Birmingham, and the next day we shall push on to Manchester, via Burton, Derby, Matlock, and Buxton.'

'That's rather a hilly route?'

'Oh, no, nothing that a good autocar should not easily tackle. The hill into Buxton is a trifle stiff, certainly, but it will be coped with.'

'You were on the original Critchley five and a half horse-power over this part of the route, were you not?'

'Yes,' said Mr. Johnson, 'Mr. Grahame White was with me from Birmingham, and the car ran splendidly.'

'According to *Notes and Notices* you seem to have had a bit of a bad time between Manchester and Kendal,' we remarked, recalling the way at which the suggested climb over Shap Fell was objected to at the meeting called by the Club.

'Well, to tell the truth, we did,' smilingly returned the Secretary, 'but then, you see, the snow began to fall at Preston, and it fell steadily for seven hours, so that the ascent of Shap was begun with three inches of snow on the ground. The ten miles climb raises one 1,330 feet, and on the upper grades a depth of old snow and newly-laid stones were found under the snow of the day. However, by dint of some pushing we got over the worst parts, but we had such a freezing that we stopped at Shap instead of going on to Carlisle. Still ninety miles in such weather and over such roads was not bad.'

'Carlisle, then, is to be honoured with a show?' we queried.

'Oh, yes, but on the tour itself it is probable that the Lake route from Kendal will be followed. You see we may have several members of the Automobile Club of France with us, and we may as well give them an opportunity of seeing one of England's beauty spots, particularly as the road, with the exception of Banerigg and Dunmail Raise, is an easier one.'

'But you had rather a bad time on this stage,' we slyly remarked.

'Ah,' returned Mr. Johnson, 'but that was due to a bent axle, which had been previously bent in an accident, and which the awful twisting it received from the deep frozen ruts had again put out of the straight. So holding were the roads, and so strong the winds, accompanied by stinging hailstorms, that we did not get into Keswick until 1.30 on Christmas morning.'

'Nice time to arrive; how did you get put up at that unearthly hour?

The Autocar, January 13th, 1900

'Oh, we found the landlord of the George at Keswick a good fellow. He got up himself, roused his wife and daughter, cooked us a hot meal, and then blew merry calls on a post-horn outside the hotel to announce our arrival to the neighbourhood.'

'Then you did not go on to Edinburgh, across the Border?'

'No, that section yet remains to be explored, but later the Edinburgh Autocar Co. placed a five and a half horse-power Daimler car, which Mr. Outhwaite drove, at the disposal of the Club, and conveyed me from hard frost and snow at Edinburgh to rain in torrents at Newcastle.'

'The Club, then, will be welcomed at Edinburgh?'

'Oh, yes, as warmly as at Newcastle, Leeds, Bradford, Harrogate, Sheffield and Nottingham. At Edinburgh, in addition to a large number of influential gentlemen who attended the meeting, the Rt. Hon. the Lord Justice Clerk is keenly interested in the success of the arrangements. At Newcastle, too, Mr. W. C. B. Cowan, the late M.P. and well-known newspaper proprietor, warmly supports us. Then, again, at Leeds the ex-mayor of Halifax attended the meeting.'

'You completed the run to London from Newcastle, of course?' we asked.

'Yes, on a five and a half horse-power Daimler waggonette, lent by the Daimler Co. I went through Thirsk and Northallerton to York, and then on three subsequent days back to London, *via* Harrogate, Bradford, Wakefield, Barnsley, Sheffield, Worksop, Lincoln, and Nottingham to London *via* Leicester and Northampton.'

'Then with the exception of the Carlisle-Edinburgh section, you have satisfied yourself that the route is practical throughout?'

'Undoubtedly it is,' replied Mr. Johnson with assurance, 'and the cars that take part and go through will obtain very valuable publicity.'

'Now with regard to the entries, how are you off for these?'

In reply Mr. Johnson handed us the following list of manufacturers, agents, amateurs and parts makers who have intimated their intention of entering vehicles:

SECTION I. MANUFACTURERS AND AGENTS – Daimler Motor Co., Ltd., Motor Manufacturing Co., Ltd., Hewetson Ltd., Motor Carriage Supply Co., Ltd., Motor Vehicle Co., Automobile Association, Ltd., De Dion Bouton Syndicate, Ltd., Souvestre and Co., Ltd., Delahaye Motor Co., Mr. F.W. Lanchester, Marshall and Co., London Motor Van and Waggon Co., Ltd., Stirling's Motor Carriages, Ltd., the Edinburgh Autocar Co., and the Locomobile Co. of America, a steam carriage.

SECTION II. AMATEURS – No. 1: Mr. Ernest J. Hutton, J.P., 12 h.p. Panhard. No. 2: Mr. Frank H. Butler, 6 h.p. Panhard; Mr. T. B. Browne, 6 h.p. Panhard; the Hon. John Scott Monatgu, M.P., 12 h.p. Daimler, Mr. Alfred Harmsworth, 20 h.p. Daimler, 12 h.p. Panhard, 6 h.p. Daimler; Count Zborowski, 24 h.p. Cannstatt Daimler; Mr. Oscar Gregoire, President of the Sports Committee of the Belgian Automobile Club, Belgian Daimler; Mr. J. Hargreaves, J.P., 12 h.p. Daimler; and Mr. Charles Parker, 3¼ De Dion tricycle.

SECTION III. PARTS – The Dunlop Pneumatic Tyre Co., the Clipper Pneumatic Tyre Co., and the New Grappler Pneumatic Tyre Co.

'We hear something of a prize fund, how is that shaping?'

'Well, that list will show you,' replied the Secretary, handing another list.

	£	s.	d.
The *Daily Mail*, London	150	0	0
The *Daily Mail*, London, for every motor vehicle entered by a manufacturer or agent, which may be successful in covering the 1,000 miles *per vehicle*	10	0	0
Sir David Salomons, Bart.	50	0	0
Mr. Stanley Spooner	10	10	0
Mr. Walter C. Bersey	10	0	0
Mr. Jno. Love	1	1	0
Mr. John Simpson	1	1	0

Mr. Ernest Owers has announced his intention of giving a silver cup value £21 to the owner of the motor carriage which shall be most successful in the amateur class.

The Automobile Club de France has promised three medals: A silver gilt medal, a silver medal, and a bronze medal. These will probably be allotted to the three vehicles irrespective of class which may make the three best records in the trial.

'Then you think success promises?'

'Undoubtedly I do,' replied the Secretary, 'with luck I think the tour will be a triumphal progress. ”

The Autocar, January 13th, 1900

INTRODUCTION.

The Purpose of the 1,000-Mile Trial.

The 1,000-Mile Trial of Motor Vehicles is organized by the Automobile Club of Great Britain and Ireland, with the object of advancing the Automobile movement in the United Kingdom.

This important branch of the Engineering industry has already attained very considerable proportions on the Continent, where many thousands of men are engaged, at high wages, in the manufacture of Motor Vehicles, the demand for which is far greater than the supply, with the result that the best vehicles are selling at premiums of from 33 to 100 per cent.

The Committee of the Club are of opinion that this Kingdom should not remain, as it does at present, in the rear of foreign countries as regards this new industry; and it is hoped that the passage of some eighty Motor Vehicles over 1,000 miles of the roads of Great Britain, and their exhibition at big centres of population, may have the effect not only of proving that the best of these vehicles are capable of covering long distances and of mounting steep hills, but also of demonstrating what are the respective capabilities of the various vehicles.

The Committee of the Club desire to point out that, in framing the rules, they have taken every precaution to prevent the passage of the Trial vehicles being a source of annoyance or danger to other users of the road; and they earnestly beg the drivers of vehicles not to exceed the legal limit of speed and to show the greatest consideration to the drivers of restless horses and other users of the road.

The Trial is in no sense a race, as on the open road no speed in excess of the legal limit of twelve miles an hour (ten in Scotland) will be recognised, and in towns any speed in excess of a maximum of eight miles an hour is prohibited.

AUTOMOBILE CLUB,
4, WHITEHALL COURT,
LONDON, S.W.

April, 1900.

AUTOMOBILE CLUB OF GREAT BRITAIN AND IRELAND
WITH WHICH IS INCORPORATED
THE SELF-PROPELLED TRAFFIC ASSOCIATION.
4, WHITEHALL COURT, LONDON, S.W.

1,000-MILE TRIAL,
23rd April to 12th May, 1900.
PRIZE FUND.

Particulars of Subscriptions, which form the nucleus of the Prize Fund, are given in the current number of "NOTES AND NOTICES." The 1,000-Mile Trial will be the most important Automobile event, both from a Commercial and a Sporting aspect, which has taken place in this country. The Committee of the Club is anxious that the Prize Fund should be worthy of the occasion, and it therefore invites every Member of the Club to aid the movement by subscribing from £1 1s. upwards to this Fund. As it is desired to publish particulars of the Prize Fund prior to the date fixed for the formal entry of vehicles, viz., the 1st February, Members are requested to kindly **fill in and post** this stamped and addressed form **immediately.**

FORM OF SUBSCRIPTION.

To the Committee of the Automobile Club,

I have pleasure in promising to contribute a sum of ____________ Guineas to the Prize Fund of the 1,000-Mile Trial, 1900.

Signature ____________

Address ____________

Date ____________

[illegible]:—It is intended that this form should be folded in two, and then crosswise into three equal parts, so that one end may be inserted in the other.

PRIZE FUND.

Automobile Club de France ... — A Silver-Gilt Medal.
Mr. Ernest Owers ... — A Silver Medal.
The *Daily Mail*, London ... — A Bronze Medal.
A Silver Cup to the value of £21.
£10 to every Vehicle satisfactorily completing the Trial.

	£	s.	d.
The *Daily Mail*, London (additional)	150	0	0
Sir David Salomons, Bart.	50	0	0
Lord Llangattock and The Hon. C. S. Rolls	10	10	0
Mr. Stanley Spooner	10	10	0
Mr. Charles Cordingley	10	10	0
Mr. Walter C. Bersey	10	0	0
Mr. Hugh Weguelin	10	0	0
Count Zborowski	5	5	0
Dr. J. J. Acworth	5	5	0
Mr. W. G. D. Goff	5	5	0
Mr. Worby Beaumont	2	2	0
Mr. W. H. Cox	2	2	0
Capt. the Hon. Cecil Duncombe, J.P.	2	2	0
Mr. Edward Jones	2	2	0
Mr Bayntun Hippisley, J.P.	2	2	0
Mr. Fred. P. Pullar	2	2	0
Mr. Roger H. Fuller	2	2	0
Mr. Ernest Pitman	2	2	0
Mr. J. Broughton Dugdale, J.P.	2	2	0
Mr. W. H. Taylor	2	2	0
Mr. E. J. Halsey, J.P.	2	2	0
Mr. A. C. Poole	2	2	0
Mr. C. Vernon Pugh	2	2	0
Mr. J. S. Taylor	2	2	0
Mr. Nevill Copland	2	2	0
Lieut.-General John Sprot	1	1	0
Captain H. R. Langrishe, J.P.	1	1	0
Mr. Ernest Brown	1	1	0
Mr. T. B. Browne	1	1	0
Mr. Albert Brown	1	1	0
Mr. Edmund Howl	1	1	0
Mr. John Taylor	1	1	0
Colonel Clark-Kennedy	1	1	0
Mr. Jas. A. Cooke	1	1	0
Mr. H. Hewetson	1	1	0
Mr. John Love	1	1	0
Mr. John Simpson	1	1	0
Colonel S. R. Bevington	1	1	0
Mr. Wm. Bracewell	1	1	0
Mr. A. H. Barkworth	1	1	0
Mr. Jules de Castro	1	1	0
Mr. H. W. Egerton	1	1	0
Mr. Julius Harvey	1	1	0
Mr. Louis Knoblanch	1	1	0
Professor William Unwin	1	1	0
Mr. F. Howard Mercer	1	1	0
Major-General Montgomery	1	1	0
Mr. V. de Michele	1	1	0
Mr. A. F. Mulliner	1	1	0
Mr. Edgar Soames	1	1	0
Mr. W. Beckett Hill	1	1	0
Dr. Dawson Turner	1	1	0
Mr. H. E. Zacharias	1	1	0
Colonel J. Magrath	1	1	0
Mr. James W. Butler	1	1	0
Mr. Frank H. Butler	1	1	0
Mr. William Exe	1	1	0

S. F. Edge comments on the story so far ...

It was arranged that this trial, which was the first one of its kind to be held in this country should be of one thousand miles, and the route chosen was from London to Bristol, Birmingham, Manchester, Kendal, Carlisle, Edinburgh, Newcastle, Leeds, Sheffield, Nottingham and back to London. Accommodation in these towns for so many motor vehicles required a good deal of organisation, while the necessary supply of petrol and oil was also an essential feature. It was arranged that the motor vehicles should be on exhibition for at least one day in each of these towns, and two days in several. The local authorities promised to give considerable assistance to the club in arranging accommodation in the various drill halls or otherwise, and an admission charge was to be made, the proceeds of which were to go to one of the many charities in existence in connection with the South African War, which was then at its height. It was arranged that hill-climbing tests should be carried out en route, some of which should be compulsory and others optional, while the Duke of Portland was kind enough to place a straight piece of road on his estate at Welbeck at the disposal of the club for a speed test. This, too, was optional.

This Thousand Miles Trial attracted a large number of people interested in the motor movement. Entries literally poured into the club in respect of cars, motor-tricycles, quadricycles and in fact every form of motor vehicle then being made in Europe, both petrol and steam. The start of the trial was to be on April 23, and it was to terminate on May 12.

S. F. Edge *My Motoring Reminiscences*

Consider the logistics of supplying fuel. To supply all the cars on the Trial Claude Johnson estimated that about 250 gallons of petrol would be needed each day. With the help of local Members a list of suppliers and price per gallon was published in the programme. Entrants needed to reserve their supplies and pay for them in advance. (Could be tricky if your car broke down and you did not need it!) Garages were virtually non-existent in 1900. Petrol was hard to find, and one had to rely on Chemist's shops and the generosity of ACGBI Members who may maintain supplies at their country houses. (Importance of a Members list!) The list of petrol suppliers in the programme was not exhaustive, but indicated suppliers who were willing to take (pre-paid) advance petrol orders. A list of Repairing Shops located on the route was also compiled.

"Where to Obtain Motor Spirit."

The above booklet (pocket size) has just been issued by the Proprietors of "The Autocar" for the convenience of Touring Automobilists. It contains, in addition to a very exhaustive list of Agents and others in every town of any size in Great Britain who supply petrol, a list of charges made by the Proprietors of the leading hotels in the country for storing the car or motor cycle.

The price is 1/- net, post free 1/1; and the book can be obtained from the Publishers, "The Autocar," 3, St. Bride Street, Ludgate Circus, London, E.C.

The Autocar, February 10th, 1900

“ The carriage of Petroleum Spirit

So far no suggestion of a workable character has been made in regard to a solution of the petrol transport deadlock, which appears likely to be brought about by the action of the railway companies, who wish to make the sender or receiver of any spirit they carry responsible for any damage which may occur through careless handling on the part of their (the railway companies') servants. The obnoxious Clause 2 has already been published in our columns, so we need not repeat it here, but the Automobile Club, in their letter to the general managers of railway companies, conclude it by the following very reasonable and sensible suggestion:

'The committee of this club, having for its purpose the general advancement of automobilism in this kingdom, naturally desire that every possible precaution should be taken to prevent accident in connection with the transport of petroleum spirit, which is largely used in connection with a certain class of automobile vehicles. They would be prepared, if desired, to appoint a committee composed of gentlemen who are not commercially connected with the petroleum trade, and scientific men who have a knowledge of the properties of petroleum spirit to examine into the methods employed by the sellers in packing petroleum spirit for transmission by railway, and to report to the railway companies what, in the opinion of the committee, would be the safest method of packing, and the club would uphold the policy of the railway companies in insisting on a thoroughly safe and recognised form of packing being adopted, and on the sender of the spirit being, in the event of damage, subject to a fixed penalty for improper packing, such as that which obtains under the explosive substances clauses. The committee trust that your company may see its way not to insist on the provisions of Clause 2 referred to, pending a thorough enquiry into the matter.'

The suggestion made by the Motor Manufacturing Co.'s secretary, that petrol should be transported by road by means of automobile vehicles, whilst a very good one indeed, is, in our mind 'too previous,' as we fear the pastime is not yet big enough for such a service to be organised on a paying basis. Even if it would pay, it would take a long time to develop, and in the meantime, if the railway companies were not brought to reason, there would be a petrol famine in most outlying districts. So we can only hope that the companies will accept the club's offer. ”

The Autocar, March 3rd, 1900

THE WHOLE BUSINESS of obtaining petrol was at an embryonic stage. There was no infrastructure for distribution, and private users bought from the importers using the railway for despatch. One Company involved in the supply of petrol was Messrs. Carless, Capel, and Leonard, the well-known distillers of petrol. At the time of the Trial a Notice was published in *The Autocar* announcing that they had issued a supplement to their book '*Petrol, What it is and Where it may be Obtained*, in which they gave 'a list of agents' and others at whose stores their spirit may be had. Further than that at the suggestion of Mr. A. J. Wilson, they have added a table of densimeter readings for petrol at various temperatures from 30 degrees to 90 degrees Fahr., provided that it is of the standard specific gravity of 0.680 at 60 degrees Fahr'. This will undoubtedly be a convenience to many autocarists, as they will be able to tell at once whether they have the right density of petrol without troubling about the rule of adding one to, or subtracting one from, the densimeter readings for every two degrees in the change of temperature. Messrs. Carless, Capel, and Leonard inform us they will be pleased to send a copy of the book to any of our readers who let them know that they want one. They are also issuing a special List of their agents on the route of the 1,000 miles trial.

The Autocar Advertisement
April 7th, 1900

Pratt's petrol
(Photo: Elizabeth Bennett)

192 1,000-Mile Trial.

PETROLEUM SPIRIT STORES.

(*a*) *Authorised Agents of Messrs. Carless, Capel & Leonard.*

(*b*) *Agents of the Anglo-American Oil Company.*

(*c*) *Agents of the Bristol, West of England & South Wales Petroleum Association (Pratt's Spirit).*

SPECIAL NOTICE.

As some 250 Gallons of Petroleum Spirit will be required for each day's run during the Trial, gentlemen and firms who have entered are advised to give their orders to the Agents on the Route not later than the 1st of April. The Agents will not, in many cases, accept orders unless accompanied by a proper remittance, owing to the expense to which they are often put to by having spirit ordered from them but subsequently not called for.

		Price, Per Gallon. s.	d.
Slough	Fullbrook & Co. (*a*), Cycle Works	1	4
	Parker, F. (*a*), Cycle & Motor Works, High Street	1	2
Maidenhead ...	Thompson & Walton (*a*), Chemists	1	6
		1/4 for 2 gals. or more.	
	Smith, E. C. (*b*), 13, Cordwallis Road (*b*)	1	4
Reading	Fuller, J. H., & Co. (*a*), 51, Minster Street	1	6
	Speedwell Electrical Motor Car Co. (*b*), 83, Oxford Street	1	3
Newbury	Stradling & Plenty (*a*), 78, Northbrook Street	1	6
	Bendy, H. T. (*a* & *b*), Bartholomew Street ... { *a*	1	6
	{ *b*	1	4
Marlborough ...	Milburn, J. (*a*), 139, High Street	1	8
Bath	Whiting, W. (*a*), 7a, Northgate Street	1	4
Bristol	Bristol Motor Co. (*c*), Redcross Street	1	6
	Hawkes, W. H. (*c*), The Quay	1	6
	Howe, F. J. (*c*), Bedminster Parade	1	6

194

PETROLE

(*a*
(*b*
(*c*

Bristol—*cont.*

Gloucester

Cheltenham
Worcester
*Birmingham

Lichfield ..

Burton-on-Tre

Derby ...
Belper ...

Manchester

Bolton ...
Chorley ...
Preston ...

202

REPAIR

Slough.—Mr. F. Parker.
Messrs. J. Fulbrook & Co.
Reading.—Messrs. Speedwell Elect. M. C. Co.
Newbury.—Messrs. Stradling & Plenty.
Bristol.—The Bristol Motor Co.
Gloucester.—Messrs. The Gloucester Cycle Co.
Messrs. Clarke & Morgan.
Cheltenham.—Messrs. Clarke & Morgan.
Messrs. The Cheltenham Engineering W
Messrs. Meats & Co.
Tewkesbury.—Mr. S. J. Osborne.
Messrs. McNaught & Co.
Worcester.—Mr. W. J. Bladder.
Messrs. Jno. Cam & Sons.
Messrs. Sanders & Co.
Messrs. The Worcester Cycle Co.
Messrs. Larkworthy & Co.
Messrs. Whiteman & Co.
Droitwich.—Messrs. Harrison & Son.
Messrs. Smith & Co.
Bromsgrove.—Messrs. C. Cound
Manchester.—Messrs. J. Bennett & Co.
Bolton.—Mr. J. V. Madgwick.
Lancaster.—Messrs. Atkinson's Electric Cycle Works.
Carnforth.—The Cycle Co.
Kendal.—Messrs. Croft.
Messrs. Wright, Heaps & Westwood.
Messrs. Jilkes.
Messrs. Jas. Parker.
Windermere.—Messrs. Braithwaite.
Keswick.—Mr. J. Hodges, Cycle Agent.
Carlisle.—Messrs. Bulmore & Co.
Messrs Deas & Co.
Mr. Fendley.
Mr. John Robinson, Warwick Road.
Portobello.—Mr. J. S. Ewan, High Street.
Musselburgh.—Mr. J. Hurry.
Haddington.—Mr. Rose.
Dunbar.—Mr. H. Duncanson.
Durham.—Mr. Wilkinson.
Berwick.—Mr. Robson.
Mr. G. Smith, Tweedmouth.

PIRIT STORES (*continued*).

d Agents of Messrs. Carless, Capel & Leonard.
f the Anglo-American Oil Company.
f the Bristol, West of England and South Wales
n Association (Pratt's Spirit).

	Price Per Gall s. d
s, Thos., & Son (*c*), Wine Street & Thomas treet ...	1 6
r & Co. (*c*), Stokes Croft ...	1 6
& Morgan (*a*), 1, Worcester Street ...	1 3
n, W. J., Lady Bellgate Street (*a* & *b*) ... { *a* / *b*	1 6 / 1 6
& Morgan (*a*), 22, Clarence Street ...	1 3
man & Co. (*a*), 40, Silver Street ...	
s-Turrell (*a*), Holford Works, Perry Barr ...	1 4
nd Motor Agency, Acock's Green ...	1 6
ley's, Ltd. (*b*), Snow Hill ...	1 6
ms, A., & Son (*b*), 72, Broad Street ...	1 2
Francis Williams Oil Co. (*a* & *b*), 281-3, Broad treet, and 100-102, Bristol Street	1 5
& Co. (*b*) ...	1 6
ns, J. J. (*b*), Tamworth Street ...	
n Bros. Cycle Co. (*a*), 23, Bridge Street ...	2 0
s, C. M. (*b*), High Street ...	1 9
e, E. C., Ltd. (*a*), 5, Irongate ...	1 6
rt & Son (*b*), Chemists ...	1 6
on & Co. (*a* & *b*), 50, Blackfriars Street {	(*a*) 1 9 / (*b*) 1 9
ll, F. D. (*b*), 219, Stretford Road ...	1 6
h Brooks & Co., Ltd. (*a*), 42, Shudehill ...	1 6
rop, Thos., & Co. (*b*), 1-3, Fold's Road ...	1 6
, Sons & Co., Ltd. (*b*), Corporation Street ...	1 6
sley, Paul, & Son (*b*), Drysalters, Bamber's Yard	1 3
Parkinson (*b*), 265, North Road	1 8
...	2 0
reet ...	1 6
...	1 9

al.

istol Street, to supply

HOPS.

-Messrs. J. Ryan & Sons.
—Messrs. The Alnwick Cycle Co.
Messrs. Arvis & Atkinson.
—Mr. A. Hogg.
-on Tyne.—Messrs. Rowland Burnett & Co.
Mr. J. Duncan Hodgson.
Mr. John Teasdale.
Messrs. W. Kirsop & Co.
Messrs. Atkinson & Philipson.
Messrs. Toward and Co.
n.—Mr. W. Hall.
rton.—Messrs. Weignell & Co.
Mr. H. Meek.
Messrs. Dent & Co.
Messrs. The Cyclists' Supply Co.
.—Mr. Slee.
Mr. J. Dyson.
—Mr. J. Dyson.
Mr. W. Jowett.
Mr. W. Howath.
Messrs. The Yorkshire Motor Vehicle Co.
Mr. Albert Farnell.
—Messrs. Whitehead & Co.
Mr. Chas. Knowles.
-Mr. E. Frost.
Messrs. Thompson & Sons.
—Mr. G. Vardy.
Mr. H. P. Forest.
-Messrs. Gilbert & Son.
—Messrs. Ford & Co.
m.—Messrs. Ford & Sons.
Messrs. The George Hunt Cycle Corporation.
Messrs. Pearson & Sons, Market Place.
ugh.—Mr. Geo. Minor.
Mr. J. J. Porter.
-Messrs. H. A. Clarke & Co.
The Clyde Cycle & Motor Co.
Messrs. J. Parr & Co.
Mr. S. H. Shakespear.
ton.—Messrs. A. E. Mulliner.
Pagnell.—Messrs. Salmon & Low.

PETROLEUM SPIRIT STORES (*continued*).

(*a*) *Authorised Agents of Messrs. Carless, Capel & Leonard.*
(*b*) *Agents of the Anglo-American Oil Company.*

		Price, Per Gallon. s. d.
Carlisle ...	Ritson, F. (*b*), Chemist ...	1 4
Edinburgh ...	Finlayson & Stuart (*b*), Regent Arch ...	
	Edinburgh Autocar Co., Ltd. (*b*), Gilmore Place ...	1 6
	Reid, A. & M. (*b*), 25, Commercial Street, Leith ...	1 6
Newcastle-on-Tyne	Rowland Barnett & Co. (*b*), 74, Northumberland Street	Motor Spirit 1 2 / C. C. Petrol, 1 6
	City Motor Car Co., Ltd. (*b*) ...	1 3
	Arnott, Jas. (*b*), Dean Street ...	
Sunderland ...	Duncan, S., 36, Queen's Crescent ...	1 6
	Milburn & Surtees (*b*) ...	
	Sunderland Motor Car Co. (*b*) ...	
	Farrow, Robt., William Street (*b*) ...	
Thirsk ...	Ayre, G., & Son (*b*) ...	2 0
* Northallerton ...	J. Ernest Hutton (*a*) "Solberge" (*a*) ...	1 5
York ...	Wasling, F. E., 22, Blake Street ...	1 4
	Dresser Folkard & Co. (*b*), Pavement ...	1 4
Leeds ...	Exley & Co. (*b*), Hunslet Lane ...	1 2
	Leuchters & Co. (*b*), 41, Aire Street ...	1 2
Bradford ...	Dyson, T. (*a*), Cycle Works, College Road ...	1 6
	Calvert, M. (*b*), 112, Westgate ...	1 3
	Matthews, W. A. (*b*), 81, Godwin Street ...	1 6
	Yorkshire Motor Vehicle Co., Vaughn Motor Works (*b*)	1 8
Wakefield... ...	Pollard, W. (*b*), Westgate ...	1 3
Sheffield	Dobb, J. T., & Son (*b*), West Bar ...	1 5
Mansfield	Benjamin Adams, Market Place (*a*) ...	1 8
	(*b*) ...	1 9
Lincoln ...	Wright, R. M. & Co. (*a*), Mint Street ...	1 6
	Battle, Son & Maltby (*b*), 294, High Street ...	1 6
	Gilbert & Son, Ltd., Lindum Works (*a* & *b*) ...	
Newark ...	Cherrington, G. W. (*b*), Chemist ...	2 0
Nottingham ...	Imperial Cycle Agency, 19, Wheeler Gate ...	1 6
	Springfield Cycle Co. (*a*), Sandiacre ...	1 6
	Haynes, W. (*b*), Lincoln Street ...	1 6
Loughborough ...	Oram & Lewin (*b*), Derby Square ...	1 6
Leicester	Leicester Motor Car Co., Ltd., 31, Rutland Street (*a*)	1 6
	Jacques, R., & Son (*b*), Cank Street ...	
	Clarke, H. A., 31, Rutland Street ...	1 6

* At Northallerton, Mr. Hutton, a member, has kindly arranged to have a supply of Petrol ready with a man in attendance at the "Golden Lion" Hotel, during Luncheon. Orders (without remittances) must be sent before April 6th.

A time-table was produced for the Trial. Meticulous recording of hotels, with as far as possible, prices for various services, together with aforesaid suppliers of petrol and repairers of vehicles, was done by Claude Johnson on his recconnaisances, and supported by help from local ACGBI Members and local Automobilist's Clubs in larger towns.

1,000-Mile Trial. 25

APPROXIMATE TIME-TABLE.

From the "Automotor Journal" for April, 1900.

Date.	Depart.	Arrive about	Intermediate distances.
April 23rd (Monday)	London, 7 a.m.	Maidenhead, 9.45 a.m.	26¼
		Reading, 10.35 a.m.	12¾
		b. Calcot Park, 10.55 a.m.	3¼
	Calcot Park, 11.25 a.m.	Newbury, 12.35 p.m.	13¾
		l. Marlborough, 2.5 p.m.	18½
	Marlborough, 2.50 p.m.	Chippenham, 4.20 p.m.	18¾
		t. Bath, 5.25 p.m.	12¾
	Bath, 5.40 p.m.	Bristol, 6.40 p.m.	12½
			118½
April 24th (Tuesday)	Exhibition	at Bristol.	
April 25th (Wednesday)	Bristol, 7 a.m.	b. Gloucester, 10 a.m.	33¾
	Gloucester, 10.55 a.m.	l. Cheltenham, 11.40 a.m. (Exhibition here till 3 p.m.)	9
	Cheltenham, 3 p.m.	Tewkesbury, 3.52 p.m.	8¾
		t. Worcester, 5.9 p.m.	15¼
	Worcester, 5.30 p.m.	Droitwich, 6.5 p.m.	6¾
		Bromsgrove, 6.35 p.m	5¾
		Birmingham, 7.45 p.m.	13
			92¼
April 26th (Thursday)	Exhibition	at Birmingham.	
April 27th (Friday)	Birmingham, 7 a.m.	b. Lichfield, 8.30 a.m.	15¾
	Lichfield, 9 a.m.	Burton-on-Trent, 10.5 a.m.	12¾
		Derby, 11.5 a.m.	11
		l. Matlock Bath, 12.30 p.m.	16
	Matlock Bath, 1.15 p.m.	t. Buxton, 3.15 p.m.	21½
	(Hill-Climbing	Trial—Taddington.)	
	Buxton, 3.30 p.m.	Manchester, 5.40 p.m.	24¾
			101¾
April 28th (Saturday)	Exhibition	at Manchester.	
April 30th (Monday)	Manchester, 7 a.m.	Bolton, 8.5 a.m.	11
		Chorley, 9.10 a.m.	11
		b. Preston, 10 a.m.	9¼
	Preston, 10.30 a.m.	l. Lancaster, 12.20 p.m.	21½
	Lancaster, 1.5 p.m.	Kendal, 2.50 p.m.	21
	(Hill-Climbing Trial—	Optional. 10 miles.)	
	Kendal, 4.30 p.m.	Shap Summit, 6.30 p.m.	
	Shap Summit, 7.30 p.m.	Kendal, 8.50 p.m.	
			73¾
	Evening Exhibi	tion at Kendal.	
May 1st (Tuesday)	b. Kendal, 9.30 a.m.	Windermere, 10.30 a.m.	8½
		Ambleside, 11 a.m.	5
		Foot of Dunmail Raise, 11.35 a.m.	6½
	(Hill-Climbing	Competition.)	
		Keswick, 2.10 p.m.	10
	Keswick, 2.55 p.m.	Bothel, 4.25 p.m.	12¾
		Carlisle, 6 p.m.	18¾
			61½
	Evening Exhibi	tion at Carlisle.	
May 2nd (Wednesday)	b. Carlisle, 9.30 a.m.	Gretna Green, 10.15 a.m.	9½
		Ecclefechan, 11.5 a.m.	9¼
		Lockerbie, 11.35 a.m.	6
		Beattock, 1.10 a.m.	14
		Moffatt, 1.20 a.m.	1½
	(Hill-Climbing	Competition.)	
		Birkhill Summit, 3 p.m.	3¾
		l. St. Mary's Loch, 3.25 p.m.	5
	St. Mary's Loch, 4.10 p.m.	t. Peeb'es, 6.10 p.m.	20
	Peebles, 6.25 p.m.	Edinburgh, 8.25 p.m.	23¾
			100
May 3rd (Thursday)	Exhibition	at Edinburgh.	
May 4th (Friday)	Edinburgh, 7 a.m.	b. Haddington, 8.25 a.m.	16¼
	Haddington, 9 a.m.	Dunbar, 10 a.m.	11
		l. Berwick, 1 p.m.	30½
	Berwick, 1.45 p.m.	Belford, 3.5 p.m.	15½
		Alnwick, 4.20 p.m.	14½
		t. Morpeth, 6 p.m.	19¼
	Morpeth, 6.15 p.m.	Newcastle, 7.35 p.m.	14½
			121½
May 5th (Saturday)	Exhibition	at Newcastle.	
May 7th (Monday)	Newcastle, 7 a.m.	b. Durham, 8.20 a.m.	14¼
	Durham, 9 a.m.	Darlington, 10.30 a.m.	18
		l. Northallerton, 11.50 a.m.	15¾
	Northallerton, 12.35 p.m.	Thirsk, 1.20 p.m.	9
		York, 3.20 p.m.	23
	Exhibition	at York.	
	York, 5.20 p.m.	Leeds, 7.45 p.m.	23
			103
May 8th (Tuesday)	Exhibition	at Leeds.	
May 9th (Wednesday)	Leeds, 7 a.m.	b. Harrogate, 8.30 a.m.	15
	Exhibition	at Harrogate.	
	Harrogate, 9.30 a.m.	Shipley, 11 a.m.	18
		l. Bradford, 11.30 a.m.	3½
	Exhibition	at Bradford.	
	Bradford, 2.30 p.m.	Wakefield, 3.50 p.m.	13¼
		t. Barnsley, 4.50 p.m.	10½
	Barnsley, 5.5 p.m.	Sheffield, 6.35 p.m.	14
			74
May 10th (Thursday)	Exhibition	at Sheffield.	
May 11th (Friday)	Sheffield, 7 a.m.	b. Worksop, 8.45 a.m.	18¼
	Worksop, 9.15 a.m. (Optional run, Worksop	to Welbeck and back, through	
	the Duke of Portland's	Estate. If this route be fol-	
	lowed, add one hour.)		
	l. Linco	ln, 11.45 a.m.	28½
	Exhibition	at Lincoln.	
	Lincoln, 3.45 p.m.	t. Newark, 5.5 p.m.	15¾
	Newark, 5.20 p.m.	Nottingham, 7 p.m.	19¾
			82¼
	Evening Exhibi	tion at Nottingham.	
May 12th (Saturday)	Nottingham, 7 a.m.	Loughboro', 8.30 a.m.	14¾
		b. Leicester, 9.30 a.m.	11
	Exhibition (Tempo	rary) at Leicester.	
	Leicester, 11 a.m.	l. Northampton, 2 p.m.	31½
	Northampton, 2.45 p.m.	Newport Pagnell, 4.5 p.m.	14¾
		Hockliffe, 5.10 p.m.	13
		Dunstable, 5.35 p.m.	4
		t. St. Albans, 6.45 p.m.	12¾
	St. Albans, 7 p.m.	London (probably Prince's Skating Club, Knightsbridge), 9.30 p.m.	21
			122¾

b. Stop for Breakfast. l. Stop for Lunch. t. Stop for Tea.

The times given above can only be said to be approximate, since some vehicles will arrive earlier and others later than the hours stated, and in view of the large number of entries it is possible that some of the vehicles may be started at 5 a.m. or even earlier, and therefore the times of some vehicles may be two or more hours earlier, while others may be two or more hours later than the times stated.

This Map appeared in the "AUTOMOTOR JOURNAL" for March, and is here reproduced by the kind permission of the Proprietors, Messrs. F. KING & Co., Ltd., 62, St. Martin's Lane, London, W.C.

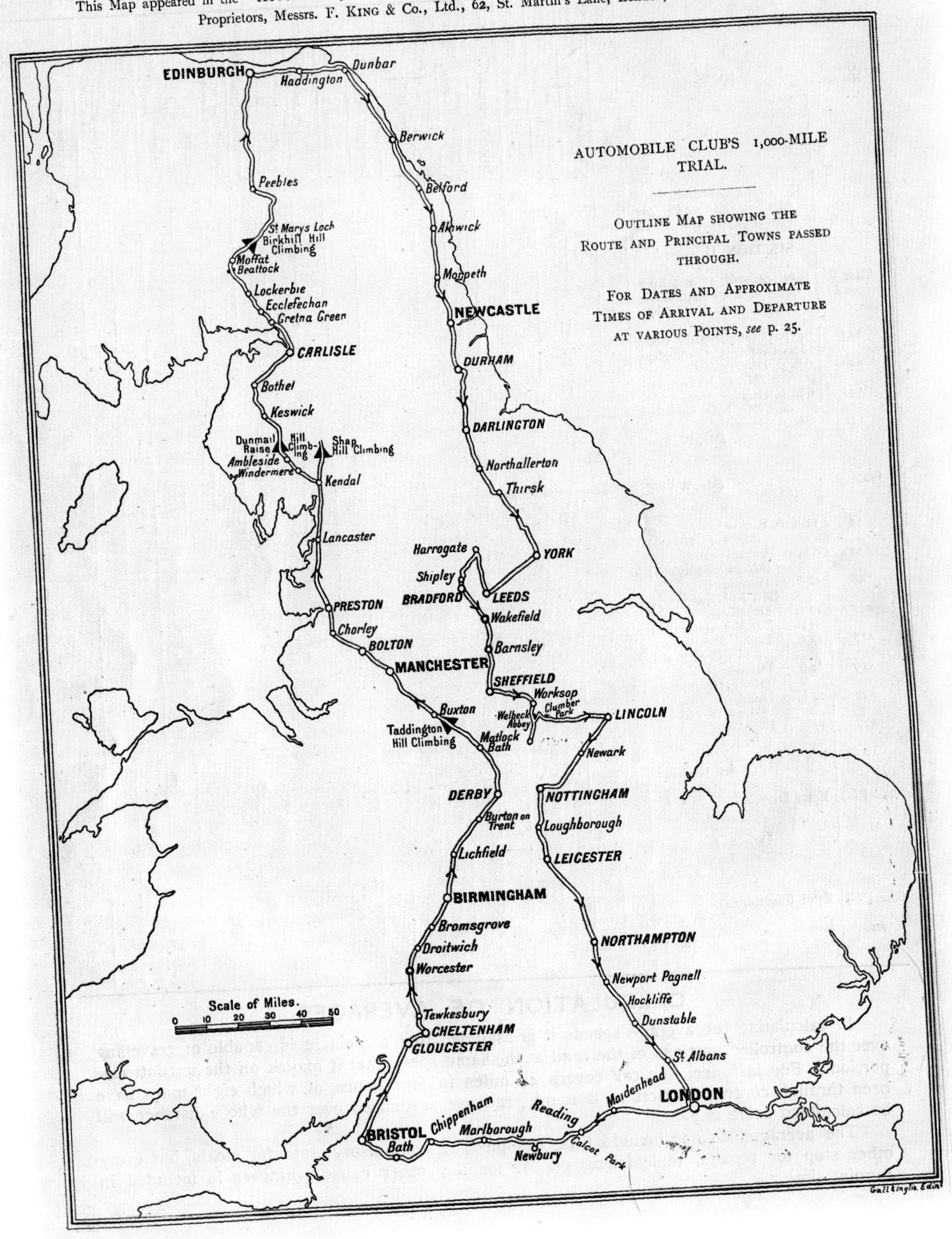

Hotels

The following is a List of Hotels with the prices charged. Automobilists taking part in the Trial are advised to secure as early as possible the necessary Hotel accommodation, and in giving orders, to state that they form a part of the 1,000-Mile Trial Party, and that the charges must be in accordance with the Tariff supplied to the Club. The number of the vehicle should be given in ordering Meals, so as to facilitate identification in telegraphing as to time at which Meals are required, etc.—

A. Breakfast of tea (or coffee, if specially ordered), two eggs with bread and butter, with attendance, will be ______ per person.

B. Breakfast of tea (or coffee, if specially ordered), eggs and bacon, or a chop, marmalade and bread and butter, with attendance, will be ______ per person.

C. Luncheon of six sandwiches and bread and cheese, with attendance, will be ______ per person.

D. Luncheon of cold beef, or chicken and ham, hot potatoes, sweets, cheese, bread and butter, with attendance, will be ______ per person.

E. Tea, bread and butter, will be ______ per person.

F. Tea, bread and butter, cake, jam, and eggs, will be ______ per person.

G. Dinner of chop, steak, or joint, two vegetables, bread and cheese, with attendance, will be ______ per person.

H. Dinner of soup, fish, joint, or grill, sweets, cheese, bread and butter, and coffee, including attendance, will be ______ per person.

J. Small bedroom in valets' wing, with lights and attendance, per night.

K. Single bedroom in guests' portion of Hotel, including lights, attendance, boot-cleaning, and bath (hot or cold, as desired), per night.

L.

M. Storage under lock-and-key, with supply of water and attendance, but not of labour for washing of vehicle, per night.

N. Number of people who can be accommodated in guests' portion of Hotel.

O. Number of people who can be accommodated in valets' portion of Hotel.

	A	B	C	D	E	F	G	H	J	K	L	M	N	O
MARLBOROUGH.														
Aylesbury Arms			1/6	2/6									100	
Castle and Ball			2/0	3/0									50	
BATH.														
Grand Pump Room	3/0				1/6	2/6							120	
Angel					1/0	2/0							10	10
Castle					1/3	1/9							20	
Christopher					1/0	2/0							12	
Reynolds					1/6	2/6							4	4
Royal					1/6	2/0								
Seven Stars					0/9	1/3							12	
Fortt & Sons					0/9	1/6								

As well as having the comprehensive route card that was incorporated in the Programme, the route was to be marked by flags. A Lemon coloured flag to indicate 'Turn to the Left': a Royal blue coloured flag to indicate 'Turn to the Right'. Red flag for Stop. Green flag for slow down to 8 mph. White flag for resume normal speed.

A note in *The Autocar* on Jan 20th 1900 says:

> 'The Committee of the Automobile Club ask the co-operation of cycling clubs, individual cyclists, and autocarists in properly marking out and flagging the course for their forthcoming one thousand miles tour.'

FLAGS.

A **LEMON**-coloured flag being displayed, indicates, " Turn to the **LEFT**.'

A **ROYAL BLUE** flag indicates, " Turn to the **RIGHT**."

At points where a road splits into more than two roads, the road to be taken will be indicated by a Lemon Flag on its Right-hand side, and a Blue Flag on its Left-hand side.

(*Note.*—These flags may be readily remembered by : Lemon=Left, and Royal blue=Right.)

SIGNS AND ABBREVIATIONS IN DESCRIPTION OF ROUTE.

■ = Red flag. STOP.

▨ = Green flag. Slow down to 8 m. p. h.

□ = Right away. Resume normal speed.

✕ = Record sheets must be filled in here.

|||| = Level railway crossing.

m. p. h. = Miles per hour.

R = Turn to Right.

L = Turn to Left.

Drivers must stop at White flags at end of Red flag controls. Drivers should carefully follow the notes as to route as provided in the Official Programme, as the Committee cannot guarantee that flags will be shown at all the points indicated therein, or that flags of direction, when displayed, may not be tampered with and misplaced by unauthorised persons.

Above inset:
Original flag from 1000 Mile Trial, 1900.

Left:
Boys mingle with the participants cars selling *The Autocar*.
(Courtesy P.H.H.)

Fire Regulations for Exhibitions.

THE Committee of the Automobile Club, after having had the advantage of a consultation with Professor BOVERTON REDWOOD, F.R.S.E., specially urge upon the Provincial Committees that every precaution should be taken to PREVENT THE POSSIBILITY OF FIRE within any Exhibition Building. The Attendants and Firemen employed should be especially instructed :—

(I.) To prevent the spirit tanks of any motor vehicles being opened under any pretext whatever, whilst the vehicles are within the Exhibition Building.

(II.) To prevent drums, tins, or other vessels containing spirit, other than the permanent tanks affixed to the vehicles, being introduced into the Exhibition Building.

(III.) To prevent any unauthorised person from having access to the buildings containing the vehicles during the time that such buildings are not open to the public.

(IV.) To prohibit SMOKING and the use of matches, and the lighting up of motor burners within the Exhibition Building, and to insist that vehicles which have not electric ignition should be pushed, not driven, in and out of the Exhibition Building.

It is also urged that there should be provided in the Exhibition Buildings an ample supply of buckets, filled with fine sand, which may be ready at hand for use in the event of a le[illegible] motor spirit becoming ignited.

Minutes of a meeting of the Club Committee held at the Club, 4 Whitehall Court London, SW, on Monday 19th March 1900 at 5 pm.

Present: Mr Roger W. Wallace, QC, (in the chair).
Mr Frederick R. Simms.
Sir Edward Jenkinson.
Mr W. Worby Beaumont
Mr Frank Butler
Mr C. Cordingley
Mr J. W. Staplee Firth
Mr John Henry Knight
Colonel John Lee
Mr Richard Muirhead
Mr C. Harrington Moore
Mr Arthur Paget
The Hon. C. S. Rolls
Mr Stanley Spooner

In attendance C. Johnson Secretary

Extract from A.C.G.B.I. Minutes in Claude Johnson's hand

300 Thousand Miles Trial Speed

A resolution of the Judges Committee to the effect that in making awards, concerning 1000-mile trial vehicles, they will not take into consideration the records of any speeds over 12 miles an hour was refused.

(The meeting then terminated.)

R W Wallace
Chairman

Extract from minutes

The arrangements had to be put in place for the Exhibitions of the vehicles at all the important stopping places. Suitable locations for display and secure overnight garaging had to be found, mostly Drill Halls etc., and given the suspicion with which the vehicles were regarded a strict form of 'Fire Regulations for Exhibitions' was drawn up. Apart from the domestic arrangements, (the logistics were formidable for so large a group of people); Claude Johnson also drew up Rules, which were discussed at great length by the Committee of the ACGBI, being a regular item in their Minutes of Meetings in early 1900. On Tuesday 9th of March 1900, they discussed the following points:

1 There should be an Exhibition of a few hours at Lincoln
2 They should advertise the Thousand Mile Trial event in a magazine called 'Le Velo' at a cost of £10.
3 That the question asked about the introduction of Belgian made Daimlers into England for the Trial should be repeated in a letter to the British Motor Company
4 That Mr. Leonard of the MMC should be informed that if he could obtain 3 entries of motor bicycles, a special class shall be established.
5 A letter was read asking whether gentlemen other than Members of the Club may enter for the competition for which Mr. Edmunds offers £10. It was decided that the competition should be open to gentlemen who are not Members
6 It was also agreed that certificates should be given to professional drivers who satisfactorily drive motor vehicles throughout the 1,000 Mile trial. Rule 19 was extended to apply also to an owner or unpaid driver who may drive a vehicle shall successfully accomplish the Trial, and that the owner or unpaid driver who may drive a vehicle in Sec II, provided that the vehicle shall successfully accomplish the Trial, and that the owner or unpaid driver concerned shall accompany the vehicle throughout, and shall himself drive and steer it at least half the distance.
7 The alterations of the Rules of the 1000-Mile trial were adopted as recommended by the Standing Committee

The ACGBI Minutes dated 10 March 1900 records Proposed additions to the 1000 Mile Trial Rules:

Roger Wallace President ACGBI 1899. (Courtesy P.H.H.)

Sprocket Wheels shall not be changed during the course of a running day.

Any alteration, temporary or otherwise on the load or the number of passengers during the hill-climbing Trial shall be declared by the driver to the next time-keeper.

The Minutes also hint at much wrangling and nit-picking as to how entries should be defined where trade and private ownership appeared to overlap!

Claude Johnson had to work within these parameters, but undeterred he pressed on. He arranged for the manning of the frequent 'control' points, in collaboration with local enthusiasts (see reports of Meetings etc on his reconnaissances), and collation of results therefrom. These were intended to be on show, together with the car concerned, at the various Exhibitions in major towns. This was to demonstrate to the public the prowess of the vehicle upon which they were gazing; so they had a measure of performance before their very eyes. The Exhibitions had Rules of course (*see insert*), and the Official Openings etc organised. Publicity was a high priority, and seats were provided for Journalists, both national and local, which were drawn by ballot. Arrangements were made to telegraph reports to London Newspapers every day.

ACGBI 'Notes and Notices

'Committee will endeavour to secure seats for members. The charge will probably be about 10s 6d seat per day.'

A Trip from Kendal to Edinburgh

Latest Arrangements for the 1,000-Mile Trial

By C. Johnson, the Secretary of the Automobile Club

NO DESCRIPTION HAS, so far as I am aware, appeared in your columns of what is probably the most interesting portion of the 1,000-mile Trial route both from a trial and a picturesque point of view. Owing to circumstances which have already been recorded in your columns, it was impossible to include the route from Kendal to Edinburgh in the inspection of the roads which was made at Christmas time. On hearing of this Dr. Dawson Turner, a member of the Automobile Club and one of the most prominent motorists in Scotland, kindly offered to drive me from Edinburgh to Kendal. The Club and those who are about to take part in the Trial owe a debt of gratitude to Dr. Dawson Turner for thus enabling the Club to indicate in its official programme carefully prepared instructions as to the turnings to be taken and other points of difficulty, seeing that on the road from Kendal to Edinburgh, especially in the wild moorland and hill districts which are to be traversed, it will be impossible to provide flags of direction. Dr. Turner was good enough to drive me from Edinburgh to Windermere and back, but for the purpose of this article it will suffice if a description of the arrangements at and road from Kendal to Edinburgh are given.

Postcard of Ambleside and Windermere c. 1900. (Courtesy J. Riddell)

On Wednesday, the 21st inst., a meeting took place of the committee which has been formed at Kendal to undertake the arrangements there in connection with the Trial. Mr. Edward Boundy is acting as honorary secretary, and has been most energetic in forming the committee. The town council have granted the free use of their splendid market hall for the purpose of the exhibition of the trial vehicles at Kendal. It was pointed out at the meeting that if the vehicles are to ascend Shap Fell on the evening of their arrival at Kendal, and if on their return to Kendal they are allowed to be removed from the exhibition building for three hours for the purpose of cleaning, lubrication, etc., the exhibition, which is being looked forward to with considerable interest, would be more or less a fiasco. The committee were of opinion that the exhibition would be more attractive if the vehicles were seen in their uncleaned condition after they descend from Shap. It has, therefore, been decided that the vehicles shall remain uncleaned until the Tuesday morning, and that on the Tuesday morning breakfast shall be taken at Kendal before the start, that the vehicles shall be cleaned and lubricated from 6 a.m. till 9 a.m., and that the start shall take place at 9.30 a.m. The proposed stop at Ambleside for breakfast will thus be abandoned, and the day's run from Kendal to Carlisle will include only one stop, namely, at Keswick for luncheon, except the timekeepers' stop at Dunmail Raise.

On leaving Kendal, the road comprises a number of small hills, the first really steep one being Bannerigg, at the summit of which Windermere Lake is seen for the first time. There follows a magnificent run down for about 2½ miles, but seeing that the road is at points precipitous, that it passes through Windermere town, contains many turnings, and is used by a fair amount of traffic, the rules provide that the speed should be limited to a maximum of 10 miles an hour, and that no vehicle shall pass another during the descent. If the morning be fine no one will regret that a moderate speed should enable them to enjoy a view of Windermere and the hills which surround it. The road passes through Ambleside and Grasmere, and shortly the long ascent of Dunmail Raise commences, but it will not be until Mill Bridge is reached that the hill-climbing contest will commence. From here to the summit is a distance of 3,013 yards, the average gradient being about 1 in 15. The road is, however, at points considerably steeper, and is reputed by the county surveyor to include 83 yards of 1 in 6¾. On the summit, which is about 780ft. above the sea, the county of Cumberland is entered, and, in descending, a sharp turn is made to the left in order that the vehicles may pass over the western road constructed by the Manchester Corporation, from which is obtained a fine view of Thirlmere. On the other side of the lake is Helvellyn (3,118ft.) This road by the side of Thirlmere is beautifully engineered. It twists and turns through cuttings made in the solid rock, and will require all the attention and skill of drivers; but in proof of the fact that it presents no serious difficulties I may state that Mr. Grahame Montague-White, who had never seen the road before, drove me over it in the pitchy darkness of the night of Christmas Eve by the aid of the light of two candles only. There is some stiff hill-climbing between Thirlmere and Keswick, but, on the whole, the surface of the road is so excellent that the hills should present no difficulties to vehicles in which horse-power and weight are properly apportioned. The descent into Keswick is really very steep, but no one in their senses would be inclined to 'rush it,' seeing that there is presented before one a magnificent view of Derwentwater, Skiddaw, and the surrounding valleys and hills. From Keswick the road by Bassenthwaite is excellent as far as Castle Inn. From there to Bothel a moorland road is taken from which is seen in the distance the sea. After getting clear of Bothel the surface of the road into Carlisle, about 19 miles, is magnificent.

At Carlisle, Mr. Hayton, a solicitor, and others are kindly undertaking the local arrangements. Application has been made to the markets' committee for permission to use the butter market for the exhibition of the vehicles. If this be granted on the evening of Tuesday, 1st May, the arrangement which has been made at Kendall will also obtain here, namely, that the vehicles shall not be removed from the exhibition building until 6 a.m. on the Wednesday morning; that breakfast shall be taken at Carlisle instead of at Lockerbie, and that the start from Carlisle shall take place at 9.30 a.m., thus enabling the time-keepers, by starting early, to arrive at Birkhill in ample time to take the records of the vehicles in the hill climbing competition there.

The road from Carlisle to Moffat, a distance of 40 miles, is truly magnificent. There is very little traffic on it, it is wide and straight. It has a fine surface, and the only hill worthy of notice is that at Ecclefechan. Scotland is entered on crossing the river Sark. From Moffat the character of the road changes, and very shortly becomes a winding mountain road, which leads to Birkhill. The road lies in a valley bordered on each side by many hills of over 2,000ft. altitude. If the morning of Wednesday, 2nd May, be fine, the road selected by Dr. Dawson Turner will here delight everyone. The scenery is indeed magnificent. The hill-climbing trial will commence at nine miles from Moffat, that is, two miles from the summit. In the first mile the road ascends 150ft., in the second mile it ascends 300ft., that is to say, an ascent of 100 yards in 1,760 yards. The gradient just before the summit is very steep, and in the opinion of those who have been over both hills Birkhill is considered worse than Dunmail Raise. The summit of Birkhill is 1,100ft. above the sea. From the summit there ensues a splendid run down to St. Mary's Loch, which stands 730ft. above the sea. Luncheon will be taken at the Rodono Hotel, which overlooks this loch. After luncheon a run along the loch and the River Yarrow will bring one to the Gordon Arms Inn and the County Police Station, from whence an ascent of 300ft. follows with a run down to the valley of the Tweed, which is crossed at Innerleither, and the course of which is followed as far as Peebles, where tea is to be taken. It should be stated that the run down from the top of the hills to the valley of the Tweed is made on a road which cannot be treated light-heartedly, inasmuch as it is divided from a drop into the valley beneath only by an earth barricade about one foot in height. From Peebles, the road, which has a good surface, passes through pretty scenery to Penicuik, after which place the surface deteriorates, but the scenery still continues interesting, as Arthur's Seat and the sea on the right come nearer, and a splendid view of Edinburgh is obtained.

Postcard of Princes Street, Edinburgh by moonlight c. 1900.
(Courtesy J. Riddell)

At Edinburgh the committee of the Scottish Automobile Club are making arrangements for the exhibition of the vehicles at the Waverley Market, and they are also undertaking the time-keeping and flagging arrangements between Peebles on the one hand and Berwick-on-Tweed on the other. The secretary, Mr. Newton, has promised to go over the route next week with a view to securing that every detail is properly attended to. ”

The Motor-Car Journal, Friday, March 30th, 1900

Review of the Rules & Regulations for 1000 Miles Trial 1900

The rules were a weighty production, and the major points are summarised thus:

Every competitor shall be supposed to be acquainted with these Rules, and by entering undertakes to abide by them

Sections

I Trade

II Privately owned

III Parts which must be fitted to a vehicle with a Club Observer

I & II were divided thus:

A Car price £200 or less

B Priced £200-£300

C Priced £300-£500

D more than £500

E MotorCycles

(a) Tricycles (1 person)

(b) Tricycles or quadricycles for 2 or more people

F Public Service vehicles (must carry at least 6 people or equivalent weight at rate of 10½ stone per person in ballast – tools and parts not allowed)

Passengers can only be changed at control points. Seats can be placed at the disposal of the Club for Press representatives.

Disqualification will be implemented. Protests within 24 hours in writing.

Entry fees non-refundable: early entry £20, late entry £40 for cars etc.

No advertising. Official rally plate only. Trade – white figures on black ground.

Private entries – black letters on white ground.

Road stewards will govern speeds

No 'cutting in' on other entrants.

Controls either side of towns. Only 8mph allowed between these controls.

Record sheets must be filled in where marked with red flag (or lantern after dark) controls close at 10 pm.

Starts at 7am, first day in Sections, subsequent days in order of arrival, with 30 secs between departures; if start time missed go to back of queue, but start time will be counted as though it had been at the correct time.

2½ hours allowed for cleaning, greasing and lubrication either evening or morning, and refuelling all by written pass-out system. None of this allowed in Exhibitions.

Excess time will be added to running time.

Record sheets must be completed daily.

Prizes Daily Mail gives £10 to each successful vehicle.

Private entries Gold, Silver, Bronze medals in each class; certificates to successful paid drivers.

The Judges

a

b

c

d

e

f

The Judges for the 1000 mile trial. (Courtesy P.H.H.)

Of course with so many Rules and Regulations, and so much potential benefit to future trading from the results of the Trial for the motor industry at stake, an impressive array of Judges needed to be appointed. They were from the senior echelon of the Club or having particular qualifications, as can be seen from the impressive list:

Judges.

a) Prof. Archibald Barr, D. Sc., M. Inst. C.E.
b) Prof. Hudson Beare, B. Sc., M. Inst C.E., M.E.
c) W. Worby Beaumont, Esq., M. Inst C.E., M. Inst. M.E.
d) Prof. C. Vernon Boys, F.R.S.
e) Prof. D. S. Capper, M. Inst. C.E., M. Inst. M.E.
f) Dugald Clerk, Esq., M. Inst C.E.
g) Bryan Donkin, Esq., M. Inst C.E., M. Inst. M. E.
h) Prof. Hele-Shaw, LL.D., F.R.S., M. Inst. M.E.
i) Major H. C. L. Holden, R.A., F.R.S.
j) Sir William Preece, K.C.P., F.R.S., P.P. Inst. C.E.
k) Prof. Boverton Redwood, F.R.S.E., assoc. M. Inst. C.E.
l) Sir David Salomons, Bart., M.A., Assoc. M. Inst. C.E., M. Inst F.F.
m) James Swinburne, Esq,. M. Inst. C.E., M. Inst. M.E.
n) Prof. William C. Unwin, F.R.S., M. Inst. C.E.
o) A. F. Yarrow, Esq., M. Inst. C. E., M. Inst. M.E.

During the period up to close of entries, attempts were made to 'drum up' support. The Automobile Club had to try and live down the failures of the previous exhibitions that were having a depressing effect upon trade interest. An announcement on Feb 3rd 1900 tried to allay these fears.

Drumming up Commercial Support

" If any of our trade readers are holding out from the 1,000 miles tour of the Automobile Club in the belief that their display at the previous exhibition will be all that will be necessary for trade, they are making a great mistake. The firms who take part in and figure well in the tour will get infinitely better advertisement than by taking part in any stationary exhibition. Some appear to think the trial entrance fees are high, but we know they will fall considerably short of paying the club's expenses in the matter, and the fact must not be overlooked that the fee paid by participants in the tour covers free exhibition in most of the principal towns in the kingdom, to say nothing of the exhibition at Prince's Skating Club at the completion of the tour, where all the carriages taking part in the trials will find a place. Indeed, this exhibition appears to us likely to prove the draw of the season, and certainly it will be for all practically interested in automobilism, for although the machines may not look quite so spick and span as when run into a covered exhibition directly they leave the painter's hands, each car will bear absolute and positive testimony as to its practical value as a road machine, and, after all, that is what the buying public are after. There will doubtless be many new and untried contrivances rushed into the show for the first time at the preparatory exhibition, but, unless these take part in the tour – which many of them will not do – the public will still be sceptical as to their capabilities, and orders will undoubtedly go more fully to those firms whose cars have successfully gone through the club run. "

The Autocar February 3rd, 1900

The Autocar ran a series of articles called 'Thousand Miles Trial Machines that will be used.' Some of these, come the day, did not in fact run on the Trial.

I

The first such featured was described (Feb 17th 1900) as 'Mr. Alf. Chas. Harmsworth's new 12 h.p. Panhard purchased from Paris.' This column was a good 'shop window' for the marque, describing the novel features of the car: 'the hydraulic brake, hydraulic in the sense that the brake drum is formed by a rectangular section ring, which is water cooled, and has the strap so actuated that a pull is obtained at each end, and the brake acts whether the car is running forwards or backwards. All lubricators and grease boxes are mounted on the dashboard directly under the eye, and ready to hand of the driver. The radiator is fixed high up on the motor bonnet, and well exposed to the draught.' It is not clear why this car did not in fact participate in the Trial; perhaps Mr. Harmsworth had other plans for it come April 23rd. It was in fact seen at Calcot Park on that day.

Other marques that benefited from this fine form of free advertising were:

II

Gladiator voiturette from the Motor Power Co. Described as a little carriage with a 3½ h.p. water cooled De Dion engine.

The motorshaft runs crossways of the car, and the drive is conveyed to the countershaft, carried under the centre of the car, by a cycle chain and chain-wheels, and thence by another cycle chain and chain-wheels to the live driving axle, upon which the differential gear is carried. On the countershaft is mounted a Crypto gear, which by application a band brake to its containing drum can he put into use for climbing very steep grades. Otherwise the driving mechanism has but one relation of speed to motor revolutions, the speed of the latter being controllable through the sparking in the usual way.

A circulating pump driven by a light cycle chain off the motorshaft, and an efficient flanged radiator are fitted. The body of the car is well hung on laminated steel springs. Wheel steering with a wheel of ample diameter is fitted. This car entered in Section I number 16

III

Featured the privately owned 6 h.p. Panhards belonging to Mr. Frank H. Butler, and Mr. T. B. Browne

IV

Déchamps 9 h.p. which entered as number 25 but did not run. Described as 4 cylinder front engined with cylinders in pairs at 45 degrees to vertical. The idea was to double up on the 2 cylinder 4½ h.p. version already made. The cylinders were 3" diameter by 3½" stroke. Fan assisted air cooling. The large fan was driven from the motor-shaft at 4,500 revolutions per minute with air screens so arranged that the fierce current of cool air impinges chiefly upon the regions of the valve chambers. This had withstood a 100 mile non-stop high speed test and was said to be probably the highest-powered pleasure car made with a live axle. Electric ignition with 4 trembling coils. 'The car has the appearance of a self-contained self-propelled vehicle, and does not present any lost horse appearance.'

Despite all this it failed to report at the start of the Trial.

Déschamps

V

Featured the Marshall car belonging to Mr. J. J. Mann entry no. 24 in Section I. Manufactured in Manchester this was a horizontal 5 h.p. rear engined vehicle with automatic lubrication. It had electric ignition and belt drive, giving 2 positive speeds together with intermediate speed from ignition variation. The smart looking semicircular front gave it a different appearance from any horse-drawn vehicle. A light folding hood and detachable front windows were an option 'to allow use in the worst of weather without risk of undue exposure to the fierceness of the elements.

Marshall No. 24

The Century Tandem Motor Tricycle

VI

The Century Tandem Motor Tricycle with 3½ h.p. De Dion engine is lavishly described. The steering gear was arranged so that not only do the front wheels run in the proper concentric curves when turning, but also incline inwards at the correct angle at the same time. The seat for the passenger was described as luxuriously hung on big C springs, and the exhaust can be turned at will into the footplate which is cellular, and thus serves as a foot warmer in cold weather. This ingenious design had already made a trip of 500 miles without mishap.

VII

The M.C.C. Triumph was a 3½ h.p. De Dion engined voiturette with Panhard gear and Renault transmission. Two of these were entered Section I, numbers 31 & 32 by the Motor Car Company Ltd. 168 Shaftesbury Avenue, London.

M.C.C. Triumph

VIII & IX

Featured again the Panhards of Mr. T. B. Browne and Mr. Frank Butler. Mr. Browne fits hill-climbing sprockets on the car when in regions like Wales, and gets a top speed of about 20 mph despite having no accelerator.

IX

This featured the Brown Whitney Steam Car. The vertical steel tubular boiler was fired with petrol; the gas supply to the furnace controlled by automatic governor operated by steam pressure. The boiler was fed by a pump worked off the engine. An injector and hand feed pump were supplied, so that water could be put in under any conditions. The water tank was at the rear, and the petrol reservoir inside it. A water lifter was fitted so that the tank could be filled from the roadside. Section I entry No. 23.

Browne-Whitney Steam car entry No. 23

So ended *The Autocar* Series called 'Thousand Miles Trial Machines that will be Used.'

Above: Argent Archer, photographer, was well known for his work by the year 1900. One of his specialities was transport pictures. His photograph of A.C.G.B.I. Committee Member Mr. Staplee Firth, with Mr. Armstrong is shown above.

Right: Argent Archer's label that he used c. 1900. (Courtesy David N. Card)

The Automobile Club appointed an official photographer *Argent Archer Photographer 195a, Kensington High St., London W. (Telegrams: 'Likenesses, London')* and we are fortunate to be able to reproduce this fine record of the 1900 Thousand Mile Trial in this book.

Argent Archer rode with the Trial but it appears that between the dates 27th April to May 1st inclusive he had no success. One contemplates the variety of things that could have gone wrong when carrying delicate equipment and glass plates on such a hazardous dusty journey!

Hubert Egerton, one of the Participants has left a hand written note as follows:

'The Official Photographer to the Automobile Club at the time of the 1000 Miles Trial (April and May 1900) was ARGENT ARCHER – I remember him vividly – He came with us – taking photos at each town in which we parked our cars for the night and for the public to inspect – His Photographer Shop was in Kensington not far from Harrods and on the opposite side of the road, and took countless photos of the 1000 mile trial, both for photos and lantern slides.'

GIVEN THE ATMOSPHERE of fear and caution associated with automobilism, it was something of an achievement to insure the event. It was reported in *Automotor Journal* – Mar. 1900: 'Ocean Accident & Guarantee Corp. have arranged to grant a special policy of insurance to cover the third-party risks of persons and property of those taking part in the Thousand Miles Trial at a premium of two guineas, the policy to cover a total sum of £500 (on the understanding that no claim shall exceed £250) and to cover damage to the car itself, up to £35.'

A full page advertisement extolling the virtues of The Ocean Accident & Guarantee Corporation Ltd appeared in the Trial Programme. A £35 contribution towards damage to a car for example like Hon C S Rolls Panhard (value £900) was perhaps a little derisory, but the thought was there. A million pounds sterling of backing funds must have seemed like untold riches in the year 1900.

Advertisements. I

The OCEAN

Accident and Guarantee Corporation,

(FOUNDED 1871.) LIMITED.

(Empowered by Special Act of Parliament.)

36 to 44, MOORGATE STREET, E.C.,

Has from the inception of the Industry offered special facilities to Motor Car Owners and Makers for Insurance against all risks.

The Automobile Club and many of its Members have availed themselves of the protection afforded by an "Ocean" Policy, which being backed by Funds (exclusive of uncalled Capital) amounting to

£1,016,696

and being free from all the vexatious conditions usually imposed in such contracts, is absolutely

THE MOST DESIRABLE POLICY OFFERED.

THE CORPORATION also issues Policies for:

Fidelity Guarantees.	Workmen's Compensation and Employers' Liability Insurance.
Burglary Insurance.	
Sickness Insurance.	
Accident Insurance.	Mortgage Insurance.
Combined (Accident and Disease) Insurance.	Lift and Boiler Insurance.

For Prospectuses and further particulars, apply to the

LAW COURTS BRANCH,

27, CHANCERY LANE, W.C.

Subject to Amendment.

AUTOMOBILE CLU
WITH WHICH IS INCO
1,000 MILE
LONDON
23rd Apr.
ONE-D
AT SEVEN PRC
AUTOMOBILE
Under the Patronage
Business Directors:
AT THE AGRI
Saturday, 14th
AN
The Automobile
Which h
THE PRINCE'S SK
OR AT

Automobile Club of Great Britain & Ireland

with which is Incorporated the Self-Propelled Traffic Association.

Official Programme

OF THE

1,000-MILE MOTOR VEHICLE TRIAL,

Starting from London on Monday, April 23rd, 1900, at 7 a.m. and returning to London on Saturday, May 12th, 1900,

Passing through Bath, Bristol, Gloucester, Cheltenham, Worcester, Birmingham, Lichfield, Matlock, Buxton, Manchester, Preston, Lancaster, Kendal, Keswick, Carlisle, Moffat, Peebles, Edinburgh, Berwick, Newcastle-on-Tyne, Durham, Northallerton, Thirsk, York, Leeds, Harrogate, Bradford, Wakefield, Barnsley, Sheffield, Worksop, Lincoln, Newark, Nottingham, Loughborough, Leicester, and Northampton.

AND INCLUDING

ONE-DAY EXHIBITIONS

OF THE MOTOR VEHICLES, OF WHICH THERE WILL BE AT LEAST EIGHTY.

At Bristol, Birmingham, Manchester, Edinburgh, Newcastle-on-Tyne, Leeds, and Sheffield.

This Trial and the Exhibitions have been organized by the Club in the interests of the Automobile Movement.

Certificates will be granted to the vehicles, in Section I, which successfully accomplish the Trial.

The vehicles entered for the Trial will also be on view, previous to the Trial, at the Agricultural Hall, Islington, on Saturday, April 21st, and also on their return, from Saturday, May 12th, to Saturday, May 19th, 1900, at THE CRYSTAL PALACE, SYDENHAM, LONDON.

A 2

At first the plan was to run the Trial from 19th March to 6th April 1900. (*Automobile Club Notes and Notices Wed. 15th November 1899*), but by 5th December the date, 23rd April to 11th May 1900 was settled upon.

...obile Club Notes and Notices" of Wednesday, 15th November, 1899.

OF GREAT BRITAIN AND IRELAND,

...ORATED THE SELF-PROPELLED TRAFFIC ASSOCIATION.

MILES MOTOR VEHICLE TRIAL

TO EDINBURGH AND BACK,

... to 6th April, 1900,

INCLUDING

...Y EXHIBITIONS,

...INCIAL CITIES AND TOWNS.

...es entered by Manufacturers and Agents.
...ned Motor Vehicles driven by Members of the Club
...anches, or of any of the recognised Continental
...ibs.

...OBILE CLUB OF GREAT BRITAIN with the co-operation of

, London.
, London.
, London.
, London.
, London.
, London.
, London.
, London.

, Bristol.
, Birmingham.
, Liverpool
and
The Liverpool Branch of the Automobile Club (The Liverpool Self-Propelled Traffic Association).
, Leeds.
, Carlisle.
, Glasgow.
, Edinburgh.
, Newcastle-on-Tyne.
, Sheffield.

SPECIAL NOTE.

The Date, some details in the Itinerary, and the Classification of Prizes are subject to variation, as they are to be further discussed by Representatives of the Firms which will participate in the Trials at a Meeting to be held at the Automobile Club, on MONDAY, 20th NOVEMBER, 1899, AT 5.30 P.M.

If it be decided to hold the Trials after the Agricultural Hall Exhibition, the Cars taking part in the Trial may, first, be exhibited there, and, after the Trial, at a Special Exhibition at the Prince's Skating Club or elsewhere.

...TOR VEHICLE TRIAL

...BURGH AND BACK,

11th May, 1900,

...UDING

...XHIBITIONS,

...L CITIES AND TOWNS,

...EDED BY THE

...MOTOR EXHIBITION

the Automobile Club of Great Britain.

...EY & CO., 39, SHOE LANE, LONDON, E.C.

...RAL HALL, LONDON,

...Saturday, 21st April, 1900,

...O BE FOLLOWED BY

...hibition of Motor Vehicles

...n the 1,000-mile Trial, at

...B, KNIGHTSBRIDGE, LONDON,

...SUITABLE BUILDING,

Above:
(Courtesy John Mellors)

The Official Programme price sixpence (10d post free) was boldly printed with a red cover, promising 84 competing vehicles at the various Exhibitions. The inside cover position insert (also red) was taken by Daimler Motor Company Ltd., who were immediately into aggressive advertising by listing the number of entries of other makes of motorcar in the Private Section claiming that out of 31 entries 14 were Daimler; and clearly stating themselves to be British from Coventry despite what must have appeared to the population of Great Britain to be an unpronounceable and foreign sounding name.

Several other advertisers took full page advertisements, and on page 6 we have a statement from The Automobile Club Preface to explain how the public could use it to compile a record of the cars' performance.

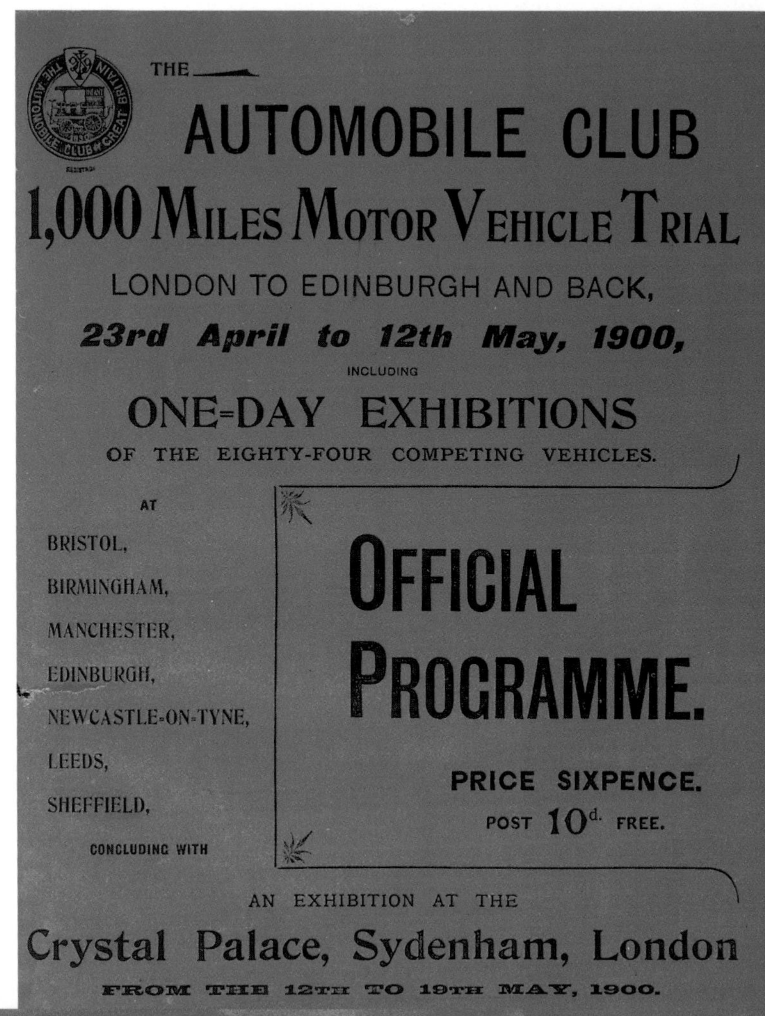

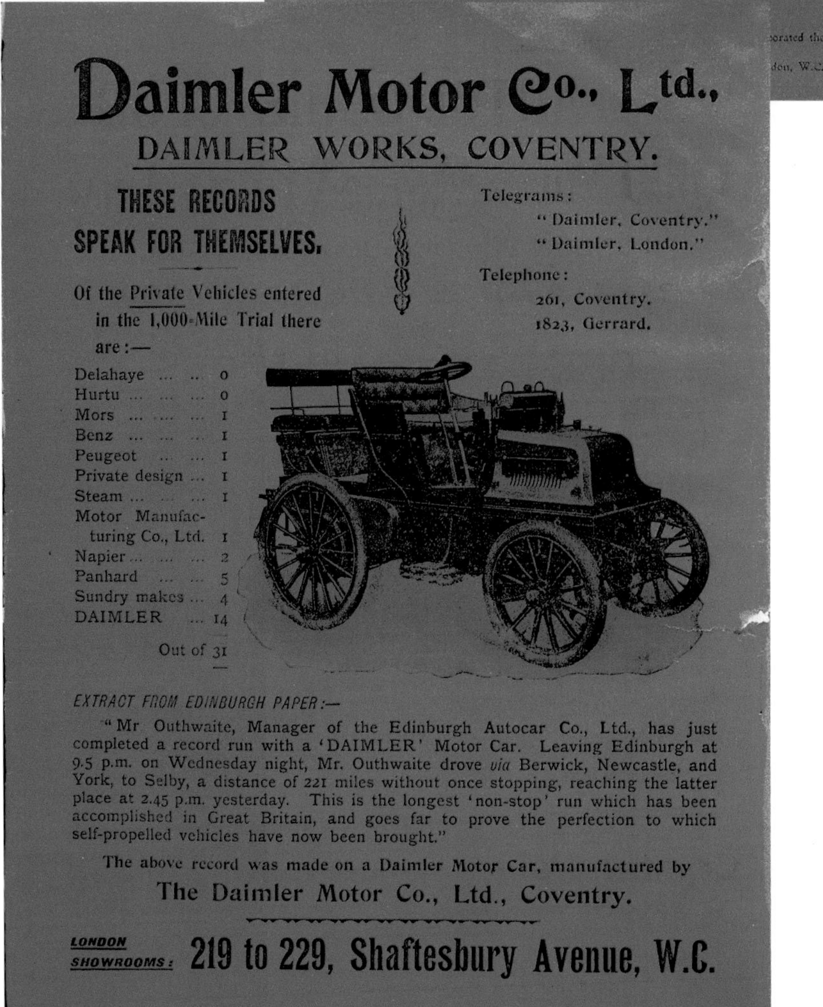

The Autocar commented upon Claude Johnsons' efforts:

> "The Official Programme provided for the Entrants is a volume of more than 200 quarto pages, compiled by Mr. C. Johnson. The organising genius of Mr. Johnson is well known, but on this occasion he has eclipsed his former records. Every detail has been considered, and the only way in which the arrangements can be upset will be owing to the zeal of members in arriving early at the various stopping places.
>
> On opening the programme of the Trial the official list of controls appeared very formidable, but in active operation they have proved simplicity itself, causing practically no inconvenience."

1,000-Mile Trial.

The Official Programme.

PREFACE.

THIS Official Programme has been prepared by the Automobile Club at considerable cost, and is to be sold at a nominal charge, in order that the public, and especially those who contemplate the purchase of a motor vehicle, may be possessed of the fullest possible information concerning the Route of and the Vehicles taking part in the Trial. It is hoped that the Press may publish the Official Reports of the average speed of the various vehicles, in order that owners of this Programme may be able to fill in therefrom the figures for which space is left in the tables specially provided for that purpose on page 32 *et seq.*

An Official Table of the averages will be issued, and will be on sale, price 1*d.*, or post free, 2*d.*, or with Official Programme, post free, 11*d.*, after the Trial, at the Printers, Messrs. F. King & Co., Ltd., 62, St. Martin's Lane, London, W.C.

It is believed that this Programme will form, for a buyer of a motor vehicle, the most valuable collection of information which has ever been brought together in one volume in this country.

The Committee of the Club beg to thank the Local Committees, the Local Honorary Secretaries, the Officers and men of the County, City, and Borough Police, the County, City, and Borough Surveyors, members of Cycling Clubs and others who have rendered most valuable assistance in the organization of this Trial.

THE AUTOMOBILE CLUB,
4, WHITEHALL COURT,
LONDON S.W.

Advertising in the 'Official Programme'

Another way of joining the publicity trail was to take an advertisement in the Official Programme.

In fact there are more than a dozen **non-starting** vehicles in the programme. But how was anyone to know? In automobilism 1900 anything can happen.

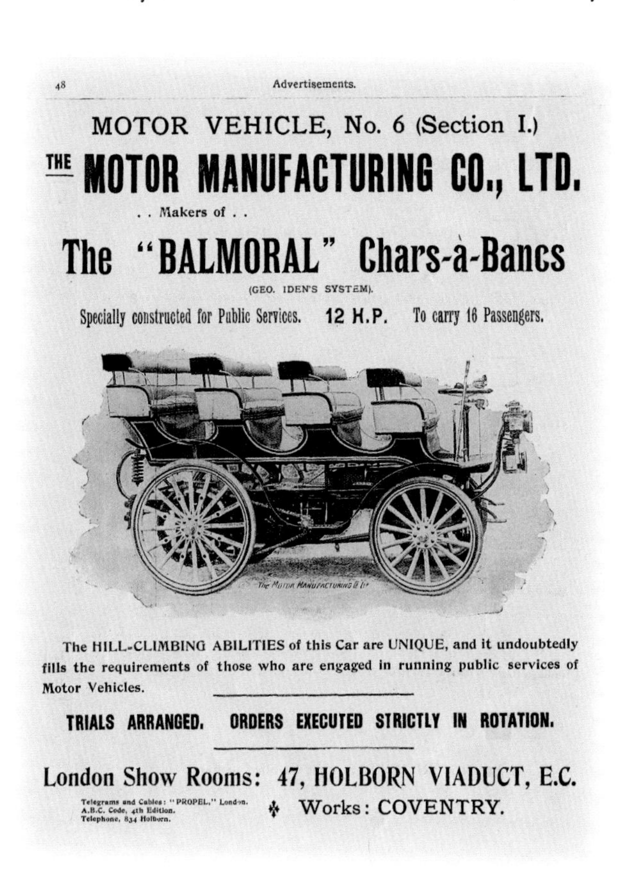

Section I No. 6

Page 48 had a full page advertisement describing the virtues of the MMC entry the 'Balmoral' Char-a-Bancs. (George Iden's System) Specially constructed for Public Services this 12 h.p. to carry 16 passengers resembled a horse drawn bus without shafts, and claimed unique hill-climbing abilities.

Section I No. 7

Page 50 full page advertisement
12 h.p. MMC Phaeton (again George Iden's System). Specially built for speed and comfort, made entirely at MMC's own works Coventry.

Section I No. 10

Full page advertisement on page 56, again from MMC; offering The 'Princess' 4½ h.p. or 6 h.p. 'The most Luxurious and Easy-riding Carriage Constructed. Undoubtedly the most popular English-made Two-seated Car or the Market'. Sadly did not appear at the start of the Trial.

Section I No. 11

Full page advertisement on page 58, again from MMC; offering The Princess Car 'recently remodelled and improved. It is now thoroughly well built, and is eminently satisfactory.' But was absent from the Start.

Other manufacturers were also too optimistic with their capabilities to meet the start line:

Section I No. 13
(page 62) was planned to be an Ariel Panhard Voiturette. Offered by The Ariel Motor Company Birmingham, this light vehicle had a water cooled 3½ h.p. engine, two brakes (one band brake operated by foot pedal: one tyre brake operated by hand lever) and 3 speeds. The spur wheels were always in mesh, each side being keyed separately to shaft connected to motor by friction clutch. Motive power transmitted to wheels by chains.

Section I No. 17
This was a highly optimistic advertisement for the Napier Autocar, offered by The Motor Power Company Ltd., of 14, Regent Street London. The Proprietors were Harvey du Cros, and S. F. Edge. It offered the 8 h.p. carriage that was still being built (see S. F. Edge's version of the full story a littlc latcr) for £500; and a 16 h.p. carriage offered at £1,300 that was not really ready on April 23rd 1900. Montague Napier had made a very successful engine, and S. F. Edge tried it out in a Panhard car. This was followed by the first Napier ever built, and entered in the Private Entries Section II as the Motor Power Co had sold it to Mr. E. Kennard. A range of claims were made for the 16 h.p. 'carriage to seat from two to sixteen persons' including 'Ample Guarantee', and 'All business dealt with by the Proprietors personally.'

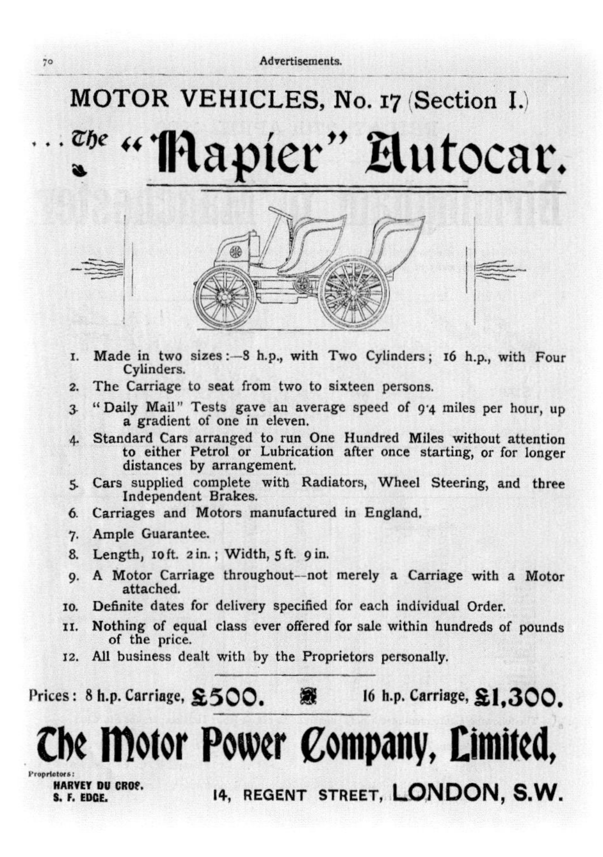

Section I No. 25
The aforementioned Déchamps that had been featured in 'The Autocar Machines that will be used' series, with further descriptions of the 'wheel and worm steering gear which was pillar hinged to permit easy ingress; four band brakes, and aluminium crank case and gearbox. No water. No pump. No condenser.' (Also no-show!) Sole selling agent J. Burns 44, Berners Street, Oxford Street, London.

Section I No. 48

Humber Motors of Beeston, Wolverhampton and Coventry (London Office 32, Holborn Viaduct) had entered a 3 h.p. voiturette called the Humber Phaeton. Three speed and reverse, air cooled, electric ignition, wheel steering; the body supported on springs bearing onto axles, while to reduce vibration the engine and gearing were mounted on a separate frame. Failed to be at the start.

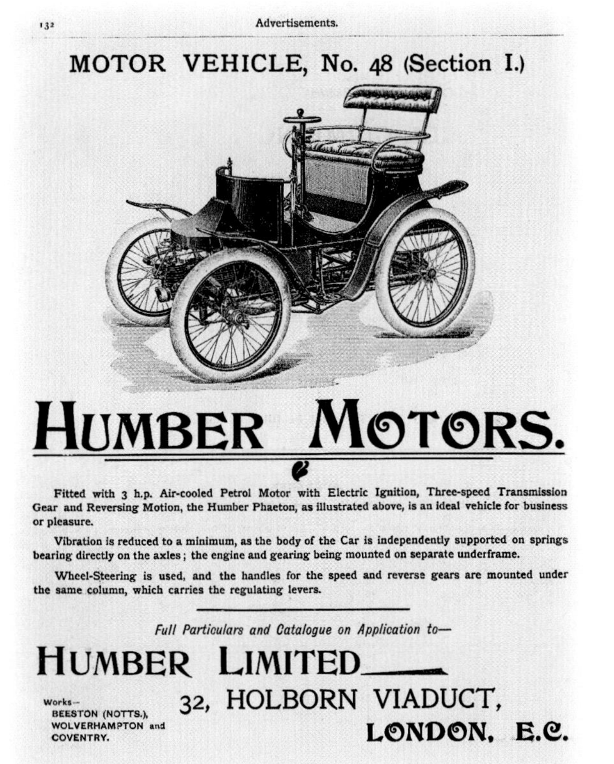

Section I No. 50

Marshall & Co Belsize Works, Manchester entered the Renaux 3⅓ h.p. Motor Tricycle. This had won the Paris to St. Malo 226 mile race in 7 hours 11 minutes non-stop averaging 31¼ mph; and held 'The Hill-Climbing Record of the World'. A special feature was the engine placed horizontally with the valve box directly facing into the wind facilitating cooling. Did not appear at start of Trial.

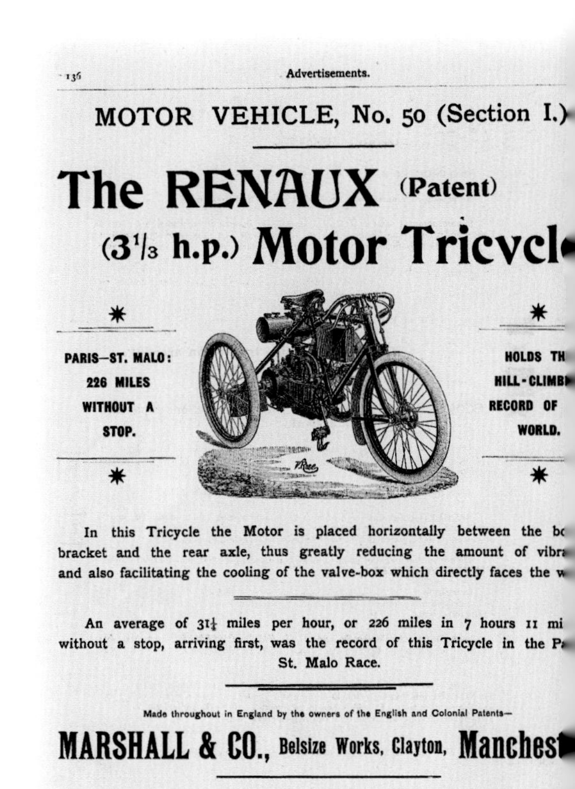

Entered but did not start:

Section II Private Entries

Entered but did not start:			*Entered by*
A1	Panhard	12 h.p.	J. Ernest Hutton Esq J.P.
A5	Steam Car	12 h.p.	Cyril Gooch
From Times Engineering, Brighton			
A9	Napier	8 h.p.	Harvey du Cros jun.
A13	Daimler	6 h.p.	Ernest Estcourt, Esq.
A14	Napier	8 h.p.	W. D. G. Goff, Esq.
A15	petrol Phaeton	5 h.p.	Robert McCay Wilson
A18	Light Daimler	6 h.p.	Neville Copland

"

Arrangements

The Automobile Club's 1,000-Mile Trial

Interest in this event continues to increase, and by Saturday, the 14th inst., the entries will be complete, that being the last day for both private owners and manufacturers to send in their applications to the secretary of the Automobile Club. On the same day the Exhibition at the Agricultural Hall will open, and on Wednesday, the 18th inst., the arrangements for the Trial will be detailed by the Hon. C. S. Rolls at a dinner at the Agricultural Hall. Then, on the following Saturday, there will be a meeting of all the 1,000-mile Trial vehicles for examination and sealing by the judges.

The start will take place at 7 a.m., on Monday, April 23rd, from the club house, Whitehall Court. Meanwhile the local arrangements are proceeding briskly and everything points to a very successful time. Below we record some of the arrangements which have already been made:

BRISTOL – The local committee has decided to abandon the proposed parade round the Downs, and to obtain estimates for a band to perform in the Drill Hall during the exhibition. The committee will also undertake the flagging of the route between Marlborough and Bath. On entering the city the cars will go via Victoria Street, St. Augustines, and Park Street to the Drill Hall, and leave via Whiteladies Road and Redland Road to the Barracks, where the outward control ceases. There will be a fully adequate supply of petroleum spirit obtainable, and the public are showing considerable interest in the forthcoming event.

CHELTENHAM – The cars are expected to arrive in Cheltenham about 11.30 a.m., and a short exhibition (under the patronage of the mayor) will be held in the Winter Gardens; the admission will be 1s. and the profits will be given to some patriotic fund. The cars will leave Cheltenham at three o'clock. The Cheltenham committee have undertaken to be responsible for that portion of the route which lies between the Cheltenham 'inward control' and the Tewkesbury 'outer control,' and for the time-keeping duties at the latter town they have secured the assistance of Mr. Osborne, Mr. F. Paxman, and Mr. Palmer. The following are the gentlemen secured by Dr. Abbott to act as time-keepers at the Cheltenham Controls, viz.: Messrs. W. Turner, F.S.S., W. W. Whittard, B.A., E. E. Bick, T. George, W. Hughes, G. Rudge. Although no great effort has yet been made to dispose of the tickets, they are already going well, and there will no doubt be a considerable sale for them.

BIRMINGHAM – Three members of the local committee at Birmingham went over the course between Worcester and Lichfield last Saturday and Sunday, and completed the organisation for the timekeeping. By order of the Chief Constable, competitors upon entering the Birmingham control, at Selly Oak, will proceed at 8 miles per hour until they reach the Horse Fair, a distance of 3 miles, whereupon they will have to further reduce speed to 6 miles per hour, until Bingley Hall is arrived at, a distance of ¾ mile. The same rate of speed (6 miles per hour) will be insisted on at the commencement of the outward journey, until Gosta Green, a distance of 1¼ miles, is reached, but from Gosta Green to Four Oaks Station, a distance of 8½ miles, the limit will be 8 miles per hour. The exhibition will be held in Bingley Hall annexe. In Bingley Hall an Industrial Exhibition is proceeding, and the manager, Mr. Stanley, has invited through the local committee, all members of the Automobile Club to pass from the annexe to the main hall at their pleasure. As several military bands have been engaged no doubt this invitation will be cordially appreciated. The cleaning of the vehicles on the morning of the 26th will be done at Messrs. Mulliner's Gas Street Works, quite close to the exhibition buildings.

MANCHESTER – The Chief Constable of Macclesfield has expressed his intention of assisting as far as possible, and Messrs. Coulthard and Co., will help in making the arrangements at Preston. Between Bakewell and the outward control for Buxton, Mr. J. Walton, the secretary of the Buxton Cycle Club, will do all that is necessary.

NEWCASTLE-ON-TYNE – The Mayor of Newcastle will open the exhibition at the Drill Hall on May 5th, and there will be a reception of the Automobile Club in the evening. Mr. J. Duncan Hodgson has agreed to act as guide from Berwick to Newcastle.

LEEDS – The size of the exhibition building at Leeds is 138ft. by 172ft., and the charges for entrance will be 1s. on the evening of May 7th, 1s. up to 5 o'clock on the following day, and 6d. after 5 p.m. "

The Motor-Car Journal, Friday, April 6th, 1990

The Exhibition of the Entrants Cars at the Agricultural Hall, Islington from Saturday 14th April to Saturday 21st April was given a full page advertisement in the programme.

IN ORDER that the public might have an opportunity of seeing the vehicles which were going to take part in the Thousand Miles Trial, it was arranged that an exhibition should be held at the Agricultural Hall, Islington, from Saturday, April 14th, to the following Saturday, and during the week the public had free access to make thorough inspection of all the exhibits. Sunday, April 22nd was reserved for an official inspection by the judges of the Automobile Club, in order that the competing vehicles could be passed by them, as each vehicle had to be stamped in various places.

At that time, a mild sensation had been caused at the Alhambra Music Hall by E. J. Coles, who was driving one of the Benz cars in the trial in question, giving an exhibition of trick driving. This consisted of driving up a flight of wooden steps with a reputed grade of 1 in 4, and down the other side, which was varied by Coles doing the same thing while he steered the car with his foot and kept his arms folded. It was arranged that he should give a demonstration in the hall during this exhibition. He had an assistant who stood in front of the car, and his duty was not to move in any circumstances. Coles would rush up towards him, but stop just short. On one occasion, the assistant appeared to think Coles was becoming a little too daring, for as he approached at speed, the man gave a leap for life, to the huge amusement of the crowd.

A catalogue for the show was published, but this proved to be a complete farce as, with the exception of one or two accessory agents, not a single exhibitor made the slightest attempt to show what was in the catalogue. It was a long business for the judges to pass all the vehicles which were to line up at the starting point on the Monday, but at length the task was completed, and all was ready for the start of this great trial.

My Motoring Reminiscences S. F. Edge

1,000-Mile Trial. 15

AN EXHIBITION

WILL BE HELD AT THE

AGRICULTURAL HALL, LONDON,

ON

Saturday, 14th April, to Saturday, 21st April, 1900,

OF THE

MOTOR VEHICLES

Entered for the 1,000-Mile Trial, and others,

UNDER THE PATRONAGE AND CONTROL OF THE AUTOMOBILE CLUB OF GREAT BRITAIN

From 10 a.m. to 10 p.m., each Day.

PRICE OF ADMISSION, ONE SHILLING.

For Prices for Space and other Particulars apply to the Business Directors, Messrs. CORDINGLEY & CO., 39, Shoe Lane, London, E.C.

Cole's 'Fancy Driving'. (Courtesy P.H.H.)

THE FOLLOWING, AMONG OTHER FIRMS, HAVE ALREADY BOOKED SPACES

AT THE

AUTOMOBILE CLUB'S EXHIBITION

OF

MOTOR CARS, MOTOR CYCLES, MOTORS, PARTS, ACCESSORIES, MACHINE TOOLS, ETC.,

To be held from SATURDAY, APRIL 14th, to SATURDAY, APRIL 21st, 1900,

At the ROYAL AGRICULTURAL HALL, ISLINGTON.

Ailsa Craig Company
Allard & Company
Andrews
Anglo-America Oil Company
Automobile Association
Automobile Supply Company
Bayley's Limited
Bersey & Company
Blake, F. C.
Brampton Brothers
Brown Brothers
Bundy & Company
Burford, Van Toll & Company
Burgess, W. H. M.
Burns, J.
Carless, Capel & Leonard
Champion Friction Clutch Company
Churchill, C.
Collier Tyre Company
Clarkson & Capel
Clipper Tyre Company
Connolly, J. W. & T.
Crowden, C. T.
Curzon, Robey & Company
Daimler Motor Company, Limited
De Dion Motor Company
Dennis Brothers
Dunhill, Alfred
Dunlop Tyre Company, Limited
Eadie Manufacturing Company
Eclipse Engineering Company
Electrical Undertakings, Limited
Farman & Company
Fleet Wheel Works
Friswell, Limited
Gibbon Brothers
Hall & Company
Hart Accumulator Company
Headland Battery Company
Hewetson's Limited
Iliffe, Sons & Sturmey Ltd.
International Motor Car Company
Joel Engineering Company
Lanchester Engine Company
Lane & Fitte
Le Carbone
Locomobile Company
London Autocar Company, Limited
London Motor Van & Waggon Company
Lucas & Co.
Marshall & Company
Maxim, Hiram S., Company, Limited
McLachlan Engine Company
Mo-Car Company, Limited
Mossberg Roller Bearings, Limited
Motor Carriage Supply Company, Limited
Motor Car Company
Motor Manufacturing Company, Limited
Motor Vehicle Company
Napier Motor Vehicle Company
National Gas Engine
North British Rubber Company
Oppermann, Carl
Palmer & Company
Pennington Motor Company
Peto & Radford, Ltd.
Price's Candle Company
Progress Motor Company
Protector Company
Remington Sholes Syndicate, Limited
Roots & Venables
Rubery & Company
Salsbury Lamp Company
Selig, Sonnenthal & Company
Sellers & Company
Shippey Bros., Ltd.
Simpson & Bodman
Sirdar Rubber Company
Slingsby, H. C.
Stern Brothers
Stirling Motor Car Company
The Star Motor Company
United Industries
Wellington, F. F.
Wellington Motor Company
White & Poppe
Etc., etc., etc.

Business Directors: CORDINGLEY & CO.

Offices: 39 and 40, SHOE LANE, LONDON, E.C.

The Autocar advertisement, March 10th 1900.

The cars awaiting the Judge's Examination and Official Sealing in the Arena of the Agricultural Hall, Islington, Saturday, April 21st 1900.

“The Autocar show at the Agricultural Hall

The show at the Agricultural Hall opened on Saturday last under the auspices of the Automobile Club of Great Britain, whilst Messrs. Cordingly and Co. were responsible for the business management of the exhibition. On the opening day, it must be confessed that the general unreadiness of the stands and backwardness of things in general somewhat disappointed early visitors, but by Monday morning matters had improved considerably, and only a few stands were still unoccupied. It is a pity these empty stands could not be filled up by exhibits which are now in comparatively out-of-the-way places, as it so happens that most of the vacant stands are in rather prominent positions. The centre of the hall is devoted to driving demonstrations, and almost all day there are at least three or four machines being manoeuvred about the arena. As we said last year, we think it is a mistake that exhibitors should be allowed to take machines from their stands to drive in the arena, as this results in some exhibits presenting an incomplete appearance during a large portion of the day, and so creating a bad effect on the casual visitor. It would be much better if duplicate machines were used for the driving demonstrations. This is done by a few exhibitors and there is plenty of room for a full stud of machines to be kept in the Barford Street yard and Minor Hall. We hope before another show is held it will be made a stringent rule that no car shall be removed from a stand, as the general effect of the show would be greatly enhanced by systematically separating the stationary from the moving exhibits. It would also be a good plan if all machines in the driving arena had their names fixed on them in legible style, so that the uninitiated could at once identify them. Driving under cover at the slow speeds necessary in a restricted space is not altogether a good feature of the show, as noise of most of the machines is greatly intensified, and tends to mislead the general public, especially in the case of motor cycles, which show at their very worst under the conditions named. Scarcely a stand in the hall was numbered on Monday, so that the catalogue was of little service to the man who wished to quickly find any given exhibit, especially as many of the stand attendants did not even know of their own exhibit. However, despite these defects in organisation, the show is undoubtedly a very fine one, and every automobilist and all the individuals interested in the movement who possibly can should make a point of carefully examining the many interesting and beautiful specimens of the self-propelled carriage which are to be found at Islington, and we feel sure that all who attended last year's shows will agree with us that a real advance has been made, especially in regard to workmanship as there are very few poorly-built cars on view today. Designs are in many cases admirable, and the outlines of some cars are perfect in the view of those gifted with any sense of mechanical proportion. We are afraid the public attendance will have been discouraging, so far as the opening days are concerned, on account of the inappropriate date fixed for the show, but we think most exhibitors were agreeably surprised at the interest evinced by the 'holiday gate.' ”

The Autocar, Saturday, April 21st, 1900

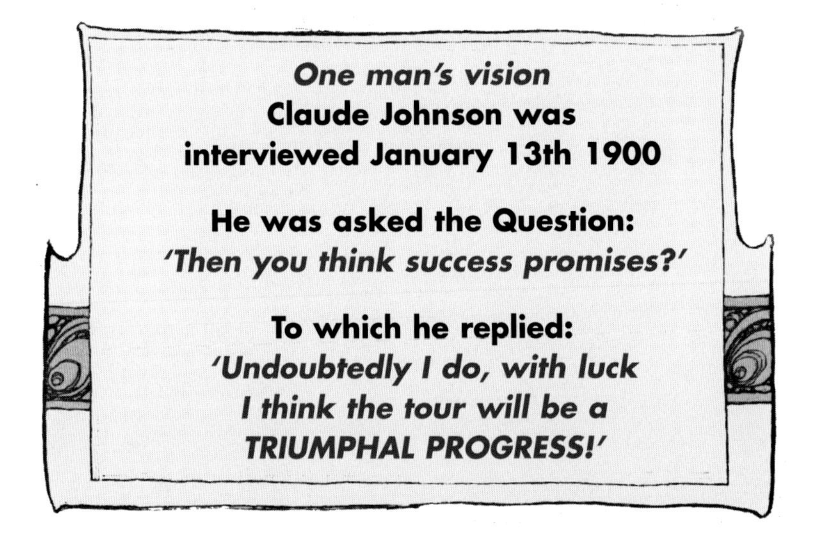

THE ENTRANTS

23rd APRIL 1900

Sections printed in GREEN INK are Manufacturers claims

Section I TRADE ENTRIES

No. 1 Benz

3 h.p. 1cyl
Entered by Hewetson's
Class A (for cars up to £200)
price £173-5s-0d weight 7½ cwts

Henry Hewetson drove a 1 cylinder 3 h.p. **Benz Ideal;** and his Company entered 2 other cars of this type, one driven by a certain E. J. Coles, who would give exhibitions of trick driving as a "Music Hall" entertainment. Hewetson's friend Mrs Louise Bazalgette, the only woman driver, entered another Benz Ideal (supplied by Hewetsons of course), in the Private Entries – Section II.

There is a story that has passed in to folk-lore concerning Henry Hewetson, who was a commodity broker, and variously described as a tea importer, and car importer. He travelled widely. "He was stopping with friends in Mannheim during August 1894 when he saw a belt driven Benz car. He ordered one at a cost of 1,642 marks, and it was delivered to him before the end of the year at Catford where he lived." He claimed to have imported the first car in to Britain: but Malcolm Jeal's researches have revealed that the car to which Hewetson attached his claim, number 260, was not despatched from the factory until November 29th 1895.

Right:
Benz Velo sold by Hewetson as a Benz Ideal. (Photo Elizabeth Bennett)

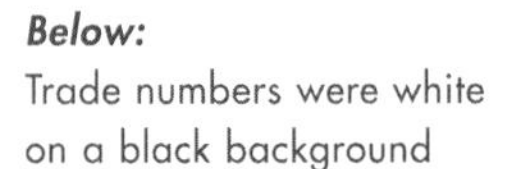

Below:
Trade numbers were white on a black background

Left:
Henry Hewetson accompanied by Mrs Louise Bazalgette on early Benz. (P.H.H.)

Henry Hewetson and Louise Bazalgette were photographed together at the London to Brighton Emancipation Run on 14th November.1896; and there is also a picture of them in his "early type" Benz car "about 1897".

Hewetson claimed to be the sole direct importer of the Benz Cars from Mannheim; and generally had 40-50 cars in stock at his Oxford St, London premises in 1900. To economise on space the cars were stored around the walls standing up on end. As required they were taken down and fitted with Connolly tyres and Hewetson-Brampton chains. The cars are described thus:

Hewetsons Limited, BENZ'S SYSTEM

These magnificently built and finished carriages are a result of 20 years experiment and trials: they are upholstered and fitted in the most comfortable and improved style, and are propelled by Patent Spirit Gas Motors, which give of no heat or smell, and no

Above:
Hewetson's showrooms
(Photo: *The Autocar*)

vibration is felt when the car is in motion. On a good smooth road they are adapted to run from 10 to 18 miles an hour according to the h.p. and with the third speed will climb very steep gradients. Both carriages and wheels are strongly constructed, and can therefore travel over bad roads, and even over frozen roads and snow.

The cost of running the small cars is under a half penny a mile, the larger cars slightly more. Sufficient benzolene (or petrol) is carried in the tank for a drive of 60 to 70 miles, and a supplementary supply can be taken in a spare metal container, which will enable a journey of double this distance to be undertaken; moreover benzolene can be cheaply bought in nearly every town in the kingdom.

Left:
Henry Hewetson

All the carriages are fitted with two powerful brakes which are capable of stopping them on the deepest down grade or hill; moreover, the engine itself forms a most efficient third brake if the supply of gas and air to the cylinder be turned off, this alone being sufficient to descend most hills. There is not the slightest danger of the carriages catching fire from the engine, even in the very remote and unlikely event of an upset, as the mixture of gas and air is fired at the proper moment by an electric spark in the cylinder.

The carriages are complete, with all requisite fittings and tools, duplicate parts and accessories, and two lamps; each car has also a double set of (2 volt) accumulators, each of which will work continuously for 500 miles, and when one set requires re-charging, the second or spare set, can be switched on; the accumulator can be re-charged at any place fitted with a direct current electricity at a small cost, or by a primary carbon battery, three cells of which in series at £1- 1s, would charge two sets of accumulators at the cost of about 5d.

No. 2 Benz

3 h.p.
Entered by Hewetsons
Class A (for cars up to £200)
price £173-5s-0d weight 7½ cwts
See No. 1 above.

Ernest James Coles was famous for his Music hall Act of "Fancy Driving" with his 3 h.p. **Benz Ideal** (*see picture on previous page*)

Right:
Ernest James Coles on No. 2 Benz Ideal.
(Photo: Argent Archer)

Left:
John William Stocks

No. 3 Ariel quad

3½ h.p.
Entered by Ariel Motor Co Birmingham
Class E (b)
price £115-10s-0d weight 3 cwts

John William Stocks drove an **Ariel Quadricycle** 3½ h.p. entered by Ariel Motor Co Birmingham, fitted with a petrol driven De Dion engine,.

From 1897 to 1901 he was Department Manager, Components Ltd Birmingham **Makers of motor-bicycles, tricycles & motor-cars.**

He was born in Hull in Oct. 1871, and was riding an ordinary by the time he was 12. John Stocks became an outstanding bicycle rider. He rode at Herne Hill in 1893 and became the first man to drive just over 25 miles in the hour. He was Yorkshire champion both on cycles and tandems. He eventually achieved 29 miles in the hour and broke many records including fastest in the world for one mile and one hour in 1897. He even beat a New Beeston motor-bicycle over one hour by 300 yards the same year. Stocks loved driving long distances and was the first man to succeed in getting from Lands End to John O'Groats on an auto-cycle after various attempts.

Stocks became involved with the Ariel Cycle Co. Birmingham in 1898.

Left:
No. 3 John William Stocks on Ariel Quadricycle.
(Photo: Argent Archer)

No. 4 Ariel Tricycle

2¼ h.p.
Entered by Ariel Motor Tricycle 15A, Baker Street London
Class E (b)
price £100 weight 2½ cwts

It is possible that **Lance Newton** drove the **Ariel Tricycle** 2¼ h.p. (petrol driven), with **Edwin S. Cheel** on the **Whippet Trailer** Manufactured by Ariel Motor Co Birmingham, Price of the Tricycle alone eighty guineas, with trailer £100. **Every part is made in England, and the workmanship of the whole machine is exquisite.**

The trailer was detachable.

Right:
No. 4 Lance Newton on the Ariel Tricycle with Edwin S. Cheel (in 'Pork Pie' hat) on the Whippet Trailer.
(Photo: Argent Archer)

No. 5 Locomobile Steam Carriage

2 h.p.
Entered by The Locomobile Co of America. South Kensington London.
Class A (for cars up to £200)
price £160 weight 5¼ cwts
Steam powered. Ideal vehicle for business or pleasure. Free from noise, odour or jar. Can run at any speed, or climb any hill. The power, steam, is always reliable, and easily controlled.

Left:
No. 5 Locomobile Steam Carriage

• No. 6 MMC Balmoral Charbanc

12 h.p.
Entered by Motor Manuf Co London & Coventry
price £650 weight 35cwts (petrol driven)

• No. 7 MMC Phaeton

12 h.p.
Entered by Motor Manuf Co London & Coventry
price £650 weight 29cwts (petrol driven)

No. 8 MMC Panhard

6 h.p.
Entered by Motor Manuf Co London & Coventry
Class C (for cars £300-£500)
price £412-10s-0d weight 20¼ cwts (petrol driven)
The latest improvements are embodied in this car and it fills the great demand for a 6 h.p. carriage at a reasonable figure.
Mr. Alfred Burgess is credited with driving it.

Right:
No. 8 M.M.C. Panhard

No. 9
MMC Iveagh Phaeton (Daimler)

6 h.p.
Entered by Motor Manuf Co London & Coventry
Class C (for cars £300-£500)
price £380 weight 20¼ cwts (petrol driven)
The best English car constructed. Although Mr. Schofield was named as driver, William White is credited with driving this entry.

Right:
No. 9 MMC Iveagh Phaeton (Daimler)

• No. 10 MMC 'Princess'

4½ h.p.
Entered by Motor Manuf Co London & Coventry
Geo. Iden's System
Class B (price £200-300)
price £235 weight 11½ cwts (petrol driven)

• non-starter on April 23rd 1900

No. 11 MMC 'Princess'

4½ h.p.
Entered by Motor Manuf Co London & Coventry
Class B (price £200-300)
price £235 weight 11½ cwts (petrol driven)
Cheapest and most luxurious British-made two seated carriage on the market. Now thoroughly well-built, and is eminently satisfactory. Joined for last stage only.

Left:
No. 11 MMC 'Princess'
(Photo: Argent Archer)

No. 12 Motor Manufacturing Co's Tricycle

2¼ h.p.
Entered by Motor Manuf Co London & Coventry
Class E (a)
price £75 weight 1¾ cwts (petrol driven)
The engine fitted to this machine is made by the Motor Manufacturing Co. It has been considerably improved, is much more powerful, and less noisy than any French made 'De Dion' motor of the same type.
E. Buck is credited with driving it throughout the Trial

Left and right:
No. 12 Motor Manufacturing Co's Tricycle

● No. 13 Ariel Panhard Voiturette

3½ h.p.
Entered by Ariel Motor Co Birmingham
Class B (price £200-£300)
price £250 weight 5 cwts (petrol driven)
Two brakes, one band brake, operated by foot pedal, one tyre brake operated by hand-lever.

No. 14 De Dion Voiturette

3 h.p.
Entered by De Dion Syndicate, Ltd
Driven by Mr Grierson
Class B (price £200-£300)
price £204-15s-0d weight 4½ cwts (petrol driven)
Mr. Grierson was a friend of Hubert Egerton (*see 15 below*).
Direct transmission. No belts or chains. Speeds up to 20 mph in top speed, low speed 7 miles per hour up a hill 1 in 10. Engine cooled with forced circulation. Almost noiseless, no vibration. Hung on perfectly balanced springs. Price 195 gns.

Right:
No. 14 De Dion Voiturette
(Photo: Argent Archer)

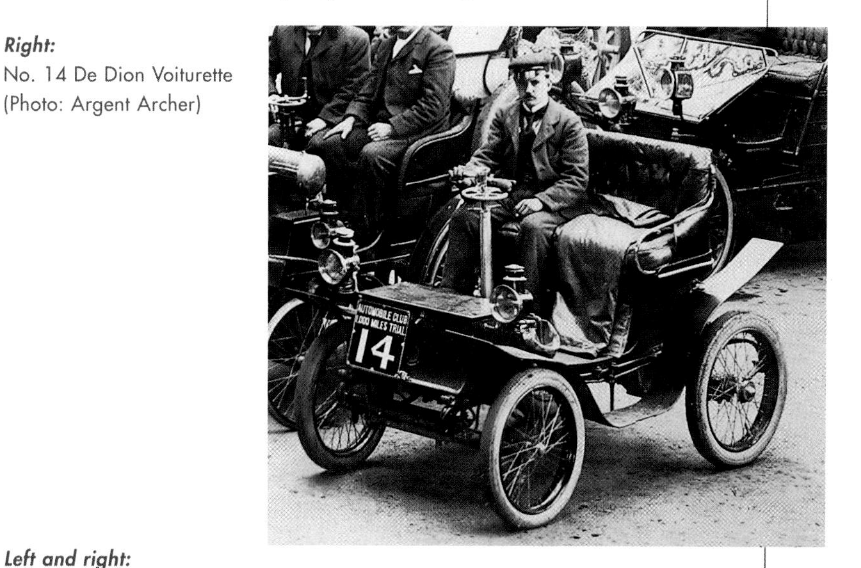

● non-starter on April 23rd 1900

No. 15 De Dion Voiturette

3 h.p.
Entered by De Dion Syndicate
Driven by Mr Hubert Egerton
Class B (price £200-£300)
price £204-15s-0d weight 4½ cwts (petrol driven)

Hubert Egerton was Sales Manager for the English De Dion Syndicate. This car was one of the first 6 to reach England from the De Dion works at Puteaux, Paris. A 3 h.p. voiturette price 195 gns delivered in London. It was Hubert Egerton's personal car, but he entered using his Company's name.

Left:
Hubert Egerton driving No. 15 De Dion Voiturette. (His passenger is Grierson)
(Photo: Argent Archer)

Right:
No. 16 Gladiator
(Photo: Argent Archer)

Left:
An original Rally Number Plate from Trade entry No. 15 (H. Egerton) now displayed at Royal Automobile Club, Pall Mall
(Photo Elizabeth Bennett)

No. 16 Gladiator

3¼ h.p.
Entered by the Motor Power Co London
Class A (price up to £200)
price £185-15s-0d weight 3½ cwts (petrol driven)

Seat 2 people. Two speeds. No belts. Speeds from zero up to 23 mph. Water cooled. Wheel steering. Graceful design. Simple and practical on the road.

Roland le Bars drove No. 16 throughout the Trial.

• No. 17 Napier

16 h.p.
Entered by Motor Power Co London
Class D (price over £500)
price £1,300 weight 18½ cwts (petrol driven)

This entry was projected to be the 16 h.p. **Napier Autocar** price £1,300. The fact that this price appeared in the Official Programme excited the Press of the day to quote it to shock the readers! In fact the car did not compete, as it was not finished in time. It was projected to have 4 cylinders and seat up to 16 persons. Standard Cars arranged to run 100 miles without attention to either petrol or lubrication after once starting, or for longer distances by arrangement. Supplied complete with radiators, wheel steering, and 3 independent brakes. Carriages and motors manufactured in England.

● non-starter on April 23rd 1900

No. 18 Endurance Car

5 h.p.
Entered by Endurance Motor Co Ltd.
Class A (price up to £200)
price £190 weight 10 cwts (petrol driven)

British material and workmanship throughout. Crank running in oil bath. Variable electric ignition controlled from seat; circulation maintained by rotary pump, efficient cooler fitted in front of car, 3 speeds, reverse gear (A. Hallett's patent), band brake on countershaft and on each rear wheel, double silencer fitted. Dunlop tyres, Brampton chains, and tangent spoke wire wheels.

Left:
No. 18 Endurance Car

No. 20 Simms Motor Wheel

2¾ h.p.
Entered by Motor Carriage Supply Ltd
Class E (a)
price £115 weight 3 cwts (petrol driven)

Fitted with 2 speed gear for hill-climbing. Extremely silent, simple, safe, strong, comfortable and fast. Absolutely reliable and entirely automatic. Rear wheel steered.

The driver was said to be **Samuel Rowbottom**

Right:
No. 20 Simms Motor Wheel
(Photo: Argent Archer)

Right:
Simms Motor Wheel entry No. 20
(Photo: *The Autocar*)

No. 19 Orient Express

6 h.p.
Entered by the English supplier Automobile Association Ltd. Holland Park London
Class A (price up to £200)
price £200 weight 12 cwts (petrol driven)

Water cooled motor; magneto-electric ignition, therefore none of the trouble of accumulators, self-mixing automatic carburettor; belt transmission with jockey pulleys, therefore impossible for belts to slip, 3 speeds and reverse; artillery wood wheels. The finest coachbuilding. Speed from 1 to 22 mph.

Retired after collision with cow Carlisle to Edinburgh section.

Left:
No. 19 Orient Express

No. 21 Lanchester Carriage

8 h.p.
Entered by Lanchester Engine Co.
retired Manchester with split body
Class D (price over £500)
price £525 weight 14½ cwts (petrol driven)

George H. Lanchester Born Dec.1874 was the youngest of the Lanchester brothers. He was indentured to his eldest brother 'Dr Fred' six years his senior, at the age of 15 in 1889. Thus George was 26 when the 1000 miles trial took place. The Lanchester Engine Co. entered two cars for the 1000 miles trial and Archie Millership who drove the second car (No. 22) for the Company was aged about 22. Their exploits on the trials are well recorded – it is now perceived that perhaps the Lanchesters might have come out better than they did as fortune was not on their side.

They had won awards with their Gold Medal Phaeton (entered as No. 22), and they built a replica. The backers insisted that this replica (entered as No. 21) should have a coachwork body. A well known Birmingham coachbuilder constructed a 4 seater Hooded Mail Phaeton body for it. It was very high and unwieldy and looked like a horse vehicle without the horse.

Right:
No. 22 Lanchester Motor Carriage
(Photo: Argent Archer)

No. 22 Lanchester Carriage

8 h.p.
Entered by Lanchester Engine Co.
Armourer Mills, Birmingham
Class D (price over £500)
price £525 weight 14½ cwts (petrol driven)

Driven by **J.W. Archibald Millership**. Born around 1878, Archie Millership was apparently quite well heeled at a young age. It seems he became interested in motoring before he reached the age of twenty. Although he at first trained as an accountant he was more interested in things mechanical and was a very early owner of a Léon Bollée. The Lanchester brothers took him on as a demonstrator at the Ladywood Road factory, Birmingham, about 1898. Archie was about 22 at the time of the trial and lived at Mosley where he was a member of the Midlands Automobile and Birmingham Cycle Clubs. He drove the 1897 Gold medal Phaeton (No. 22) for Lanchesters on the Trial. This Gold Medal Phaeton had won awards for "Perfection in Design". It claimed **Vibrationless, balanced motor, safety tiller steering, electric magneto ignition, no batteries, range of speed at command, any speed up to 20 miles per hour.**

No. 23
Brown-Whitney Steam Car

Entered by Brown Bros., Ltd
Class C (price £300-£500)
price £350 weight 8¾ cwts (steam driven)

Being steam-driven, it is free from vibration when running, also when at rest, as the motor ceases to work on bringing the car to a stop. No transmission gear (which according to ACGBI Trials absorbs 30% of entire engine power) as the engine drives direct on the back

Left:
George Lanchester and Archie Millership
(Photo: Argent Archer)

Right:
Brown-Whitney Steam Car No. 23

axle by a simple chain. Boiler is fired by petrol, which is automatically regulated so the steam pressure is always regularly maintained. This allows the car to be left standing any length of time without attention and yet ready for immediate use. The petrol supply cistern is carried inside the water-tank, at the back of the car thus protecting it from all chance of damage. Speed can be obtained from zero to 30mph.

E. R. Banks is credited with driving it throughout the Trial

Right:
Charles Hain Friswell (P.H.H.)

No. 24 Marshall Carriage

5 h.p.
Entered by Marshall & Co. Belsize Works, Manchester
Class B (price £200-300)
price £260 weight 12 cwts (petrol driven)

This car was badly damaged in a collision with a railway van a few days before the start. The true damage – cracking the stay holding the engine – was only discovered on the last day of the Trial, and is the explanation for heated bearings etc.

This car is thoroughly reliable and well made.

Left:
Entry No. 24 5 h.p. Marshall Carriage

• No. 25 Déchamps

9 h.p.
Entered by J. Burns Oxford St., London
Class C
price £350 weight 12 cwts (petrol driven)

No. 26 Peugeot

8 h.p.
Entered by Friswell Ltd 18 Holborn Viaduct
Driver C. H. Friswell
Class C (price £300-500)
price £500 weight 14 cwts (petrol driven)

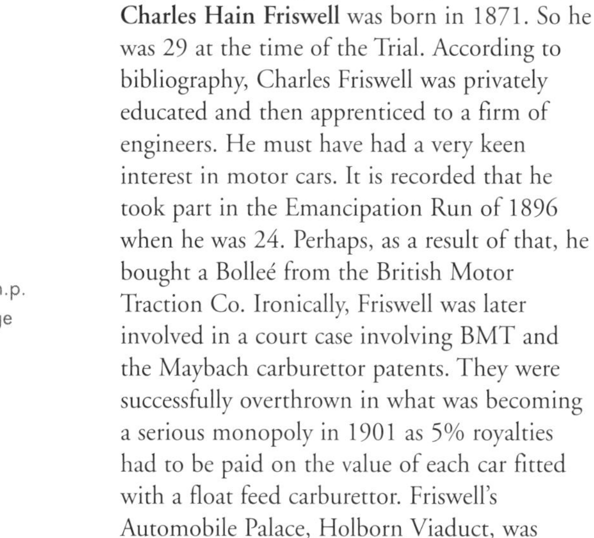

Charles Hain Friswell was born in 1871. So he was 29 at the time of the Trial. According to bibliography, Charles Friswell was privately educated and then apprenticed to a firm of engineers. He must have had a very keen interest in motor cars. It is recorded that he took part in the Emancipation Run of 1896 when he was 24. Perhaps, as a result of that, he bought a Bolleé from the British Motor Traction Co. Ironically, Friswell was later involved in a court case involving BMT and the Maybach carburettor patents. They were successfully overthrown in what was becoming a serious monopoly in 1901 as 5% royalties had to be paid on the value of each car fitted with a float feed carburettor. Friswell's Automobile Palace, Holborn Viaduct, was

Right:
Mr. & Mrs C. H. Friswell on 8 h.p. Peugeot. (Photo: Argent Archer)

● non-starter on April 23rd 1900

registered in 1900 with a capital of £40,000. Interestingly, Mark Mayhew was one of the first directors. Friswell entered the 1000 miles Trial as an agent with an 8 h.p. Peugeot.

No. 27 New Orleans

3 h.p.
Entered by Burford, van Toll & Co Twickenham
Class A (price up to £200)
price £130 weight 4 cwts (petrol driven)
The simplest and Best two-seated Car made.
This New Orleans was driven by **Mr. Astell.**

Right:
No. 28 I. C. Forrow on New Orleans.
(Photo: Argent Archer)

Left:
No. 27 3 h.p. New Orleans
(Photo: Argent Archer)

No. 28 New Orleans

3 h.p.
Entered by Burford, van Toll & Co Twickenham
Class A (price up to £200)
price £130 weight 4 cwts (petrol driven)
No Time Starting Engine.

I. C. Forrow is said to have driven this entry.

No. 29 Eureka car

2¼ h.p.
Entered by Motor Car Co., Ltd London
Class A (price up to £200)
price £145 weight 3¼ cwts (petrol driven)
With the little friction clutch. 2 speeds, no belts, no chains. Simple as a tricycle.

Right:
Nos 29/30 Eureka 2¼ h.p.

6 THE AUTOCAR. ADVERTISEMENTS. MARCH 10TH, 1900.

Our New Orleans Voiturette

Eclipses all previous and present makes yet offered to the public. For size is the cheapest, lightest, strongest, most durable, reliable, and trustworthy car on the market.

NEW ORLEANS — OTHER MAKES OF VOITURETTES. — VOITURETTES.

No time wasted starting motor.

No breaking of chains.

SOLE MAKERS:
BURFORD, VAN TOLL & CO., Orleans Works, TWICKENHAM.

No. 30 Eureka car

2¼ h.p.
Entered by Motor Car Co., Ltd
Class A (price up to £200)
price £145 weight 3¼ cwts (petrol driven)

No. 31 M.C.C. Triumph

3½ h.p.
Entered by Motor Car Co., Ltd. London
Driven by Maurice and Henry Farman
Class B (price £200-300)
price £230 weight 6 cwts (petrol driven)

Thomas Farman was a Parisian Englishman who was correspondent for the *'Standard'* newspaper. He had three sons, Henry, Maurice and Dick. Henry and Maurice raced successfully on tandem bicycles before becoming interested in automobiles like many of their racing friends.

Above:
Maurice Farman
(P.H.H.)

Henry worked with Voisin to produce one of the earliest successful aeroplanes and was the first man to fly one kilometre. Both he and Maurice were excellent racing motorists and took part in a number of events in Europe. The Farman brothers represented various motor manufacturers as sales agents. (They eventually reached into air transport and manufactured a high quality car under their own name following WW1.) Maurice was born in 1877 (aged 23 on Trial), and Henry was three years older (hence 26 at the time of the 1000 Miles Trial). **Henry (Harry) Farman** is in fact credited with driving throughout the whole Trial.

The MCC Triumph had a 3½ h.p. water-cooled De Dion engine; Panhard gear; Renault transmission; and Dunlop tyres.
The Best of Everything. To seat two people with Dickey for Attendant.

Left:
Nos 31/32 M.C.C. Triumph

No. 32 M.C.C. Triumph

3½ h.p.
Entered by Motor Car Co., Ltd, London
Class B (price £200-300)
price £230 weight 6 cwts (petrol driven)
This car was similar to entry No. 31.

R. Moffat Ford is credited with driving entry No. 32 throughout the whole Trial

No. 33 Decauville

3½ h.p.
Entered by Motor Car Co, 168 Shaftesbury Ave., London
Class A (price up to £200)
price £200 weight 5 cwts (petrol driven)
The Decauville Sociable was To seat two people with seat for occasional party. 3 speeds; no belts; no chains; travels up to 22 mph; started from the seat. Watch it climb the hills!

Frank Strange is credited with driving No. 33 throughout the entire Trial.

Right:
Frank Strange on Decauville No. 33 and Jules Debois on Decauville No. 34.
(Photo: Argent Archer)

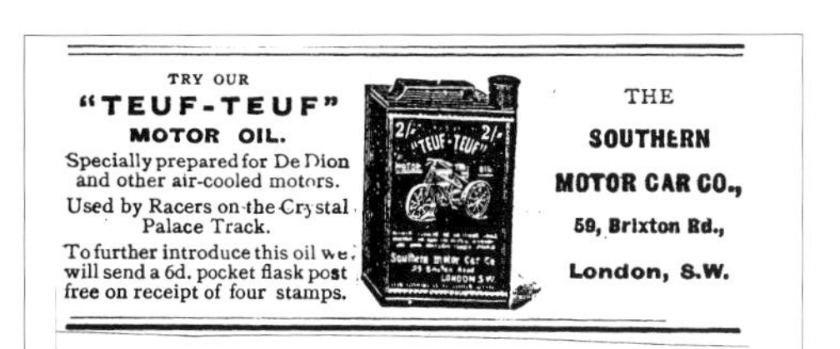

No. 34 Decauville

3½ h.p.
Entered by Motor Car Co, 168 Shaftesbury Ave., London
Class A (price up to £200)
price £200 weight 5 cwts (petrol driven)

As Entry No. 33. "Magnificent Hill-Climber." This Decauville was driven by **Jules Dubois.** H. K. Hales was also involved with this entry.

Right:
Mr. J. S. Critchley
(P.H.H.)

Left:
Entry No. 34 Jules Dubois on 3½ h.p. Decauville

No. 35 Daimler

6 h.p.
Entered by Daimler Motor Co Ltd
Driven by Mr. J. S. Critchley
Class C (price £300-500)
price £432 weight 18 cwts (petrol driven)

Daimler Motor Vehicles are constructed of the best material only, and the finest workmanship alone is employed.

Frame for 2 or 4 seated Phaeton from £400, pneumatic tyres and special fittings extra.

J. S. Critchley was Manager of the Daimler Works from 1896. He drove the 6 h.p. Daimler No. 35, but his responsibilities on the Trial were far reaching. 13 of the Daimlers on the Trial were under his supervision.

No. 36 Daimler

6 h.p.
Entered by Daimler Motor Co Ltd
Driven by Mr Richardson
Class C (price £300-500)
price £460 weight 19 cwts (petrol driven)

Mr. Richardson had as his passengers Lord Kingsburgh (Lord Justice Clerk of Scotland) and Colonel McGrath, who accompanied him for the whole of the Trial in this new 6 h.p. Daimler.

Above:
Mr. J. S. Critchley on a Daimler 6 h.p.
(Photo: Argent Archer)

Section I TRADE ENTRIES

No. 37 Daimler Parisian

6 h.p.
Entered by Daimler Motor Co Ltd
Driven by Mr Montague Grahame-White
Class C (price £300-500)
price £472 weight 187 cwts (petrol driven)

Left:
Montague Grahame-White

The programme advertisement is a little ambiguous, offering motor vehicles from 6 to 24 B.H.P. (Perhaps a strange coincidence that M G-W started with a 12 h.p. and changed to a 6?)

It would appear that Montague Grahame-White drove a 12 h.p. 1898 Daimler previously owned by Sir David Salomons as far as Cheltenham, and probably a little further. The Trial paused in Birmingham, which would have been the closest point to the Daimler Coventry Works, and we can speculate that he swapped onto a new Daimler Parisian 6 h.p., which may have not been ready for the Start (this is discussed in a later chapter). Certainly the Daimler Company was exceedingly keen to demonstrate the new light Daimler with all its improvements.

Left:
Daimler No. 37
(Photo: Argent Archer)

No. 38
Daimler Public Service Vehicle

9½ h.p.
Daimler Motor Co Ltd
Class F Public Service Vehicle
price £500 weight 28 cwts (petrol driven)
Wheel and screw steering gear. Water cooler and geared pump. 3" vulcanised tyres. Compensating sprocket brake and double acting pulley brake. Speeds from 3 to 12 mph Side lever controlling gear, forced lubrication, aluminium gear box and engine base. Geared direct from motor to road wheels; no chains.

Right:
No. 38 Daimler Public Service Vehicle

No. 39 Century Tandem Tricycle

2¼ h.p.
Entered by Century Engineering Manchester
Class E (a)
price £120 weight 3 cwts (petrol driven)
The design of the frame was new and immensely rigid. It is not possible by any ordinary or fair means to upset the machine. Steering was by a special device whereby the 2 front or steering wheels are coupled together and so arranged that they incline at varying and correct angles according to the circumference of the radius of the turn. Steering is rendered so safe and sure that it is possible to negotiate right-angle turns at top speed with perfect ease and safety. Vibration is entirely overcome, and a powerful brake enables the driver to bring the machine to a standstill in a very short distance. Direct chain-driving is

Left:
No. 39 Century Tandem
(Photo: Argent Archer)

Right:
Mr. Herbert C. Austin
(P.H.H.)

adopted, the result being a pliable drive, and elimination of shock and noise. Other features included a footwarmer (warmed from the exhaust).

Ralph Jackson drove.

No. 40 Wolseley

3½ h.p.
Entered by Wolseley Sheep Shearing Machine Co B'ham
Driven by Mr. Herbert C. Austin
Chief designer and Engineer Wolseley
Class B (price £200-300)
price £225 weight 12 cwts (petrol driven)

Herbert Austin was the son of a farmer, born Aug.1866 at Little Missenden, Bucks. He trained as an engineer and was apprenticed to the Great Northern Railway Co. An uncle, also an engineer, who worked in Australia and was in England in 1883 persuaded the young Austin, aged 18, to accompany him back to Australia in 1884. He married Helen Dron in 1887 and joined the Wolseley Sheep-Shearing Machine Co where he proved to be capable and inventive, In 1889 the Company's activities were transferred to England and Austin was appointed its manager in 1893.

A new department was opened in 1895 which included the manufacture of bicycle parts. Austin's Directors had no faith in motor cars so he secretly developed his first Bollée-type vehicle that same year.

The Twentieth Century dawned, and during the first week of it came an announcement regarding the Wolseley autocar, the result of three years' work on the part of the Wolseley Sheep Shearing Machine Company and its works manager, Mr. Herbert Austin. The machine was normally a 2-seater, but could carry four "at a slightly reduced speed."

It had a 3½ h.p. engine, located at the front, water-cooled by forced circulation, with good radiation and the "breech" of the cylinders well exposed to the air. The patented speed change and reverse were accomplished by two cone, stepped pulleys and a belt; any intermediate speed, it was declared, could be obtained by tightening or slackening the belt. This model won a silver medal at the Birmingham Show in February, 1900.

Herbert Austin drove this first Wolseley on the Trial.

Centre of gravity low. Very silent, little vibration. Most comfortable to ride in. Every detail carefully thought out. Nothing flimsy.

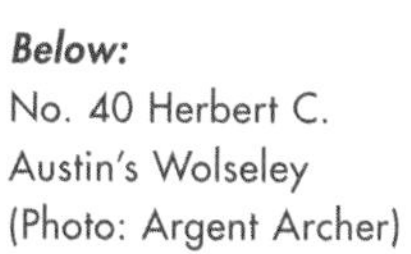

Below:
No. 40 Herbert C. Austin's Wolseley
(Photo: Argent Archer)

Section I TRADE ENTRIES

No. 41 International Victoria

3 h.p.
Entered by International Motor Car Co London
Driven by Mr O. Seyd
Class A (price up to £200)
price £160 weight 8½ cwts (petrol driven)

Left:
No. 40 International Victoria
(Photo: Argent Archer)

Right:
No. 43 Phaeton

No. 43 Parisian Daimler Phaeton

5½ h.p.
Entered by London Motor Van & Wagon Co Ltd., London
Class C (price £300-500)
Price £365; radiator £10 extra
Retired after first day

No. 44 International Victoria

3 h.p.
Entered by International Motor Car Co L'don
Driver Mr. H. Cappellan
Class A (price up to £200)
price £160 weight 8 cwts (petrol driven)
Another driver was Mr. Billing

Right:
Entry No. 44 International Victoria
(Photo: Argent Archer)

• No. 42 Hurlingham Voiturette

3½ h.p.
Entered by London Motor Van & Wagon Co Ltd., London
Class A (price up to £200)
price 160 gns; hamper 1gn extra

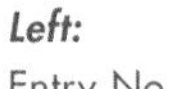

Left:
Entry No. 42 Hurlingham Voiturette

● non-starter on April 23rd 1900

No. 45 S.S. Carriage

5½ h.p.
Entered by S.S. Motor Co., London
Class B (price £200-300)
price £262 weight 8½ cwts (petrol driven)

The car has been designed to permit the utmost accessibilty to all working parts, and there is no part of the engine or gearing that cannot be exposed in an instant. The body of the carriage can also be wholly removed to facilitate cleaning, etc., by unscrewing 6 bolts.

Retired at Birmingham.

Right:
No. 46 Richard 7 h.p. with the Mayor of Reading.
(Photo: Argent Archer)

No. 46 Richard

7 h.p.
Entered by the English supplier Automobile Manufacturing Co London
French driver
Class C (price £300-500)
price £450 weight 16 cwts (petrol driven)

Speeds 7, 14, 21, and 28 mph, and reverse.

Believed to have French drivers from the Club De l'Auto.

Below:
No. 46 Richard 7 h.p.
(V.C.C. Archives)

No. 47 Richard

7 h.p.
Entered by Automobile Manufacturing Co London
W. C. Bersey + passenger M. Berduil
Class C (price £300-500)
price £450 weight 16 cwts (petrol driven)

Below:
Two Richard cars No. 46 and No. 47
(Photo: Argent Archer)

• No. 48 Humber Voiturette

6 h.p.
Entered by Humber & Co Holborn Viaduct London
Class A (price up to £200)
price £175 weight 6 cwts (petrol driven)
To reduce vibration the body of the car is independently supported on springs bearing directly on the axles; the engine and gearing being mounted on separate underframe.

No. 49 Marshall

5 h.p.
Entered by Marshall & Co. Belsize Works, Manchester
Driver Mr. J. J. Mann
Class B (price £200-300)
price £260 weight 12 cwts (petrol driven)
Born 1872 **Mr. Mann** was 28 at the time of the Trial, and Works Manager at Marshalls. He was a Trade Representative on the Competitors Committee.

The car was advertised with a **Gold medal for efficiency. Made throughout in England. For use on English Roads.**

• No. 50 Renaux Tricycle

Marshall & Co Belsize Works Manchester
Class E (a)
price £80
"Paris-St.Malo 226 miles without a stop (ave 31½ mph). Holds the hill-climbing record of the world."

No. 51 Star Voiturette

3½ h.p.
Star Motor Co., Wolverhampton.
Class A (price up to £200)
price £173-5s-0d weight 9 cwts (petrol driven)
This **Star voiturette** was driven by **Mr. Lisle** or **Mr. Prew** – records are unclear

Entirely of British manufacture. Most economical in consumption of petrol and water. Splendid hill climbers. Price complete with cushion tyres 164 gns

Right:
Entry No. 51 Star Voiturette
(Photo: Argent Archer)

Right:
Mr. J. J. Mann with 5 h.p. Marshall
(Photo: Argent Archer)

● non-starter on April 23rd 1900

Section I TRADE ENTRIES

No. 52
Roots & Venables Oil Carriage

2⅞ h.p.
Entered by Roots & Venables
Class A (price up to £200)
price £175 weight 7 cwts
Fuel was petroleum oil (paraffin)
Retired Manchester

Right:
No. 52 Roots & Venables Oil Carriage

No. 53 Wolseley Carriage

15 h.p.
Wolseley Sheep Shearing Machine Co
Birmingham
Class B (price £200-300)
Price £300 weight 15 cwts (petrol driven)
An untried vehicle, not ready in time for the start, this entry joined at Birmingham, and retired Manchester

The Motor Carriage - - Supply Company, Ltd.

MOTOR CARRIAGES, MOTOR CYCLES AND MOTOR LAUNCHES.

Speciality CANNSTATT DAIMLER MOTOR VEHICLES from 4 to 20 h.p.

Manufactured in accordance with designs and instructions by Mr. FRED. R. SIMMS, C.E., and fitted with bodies of best English construction.

Daimler Motor Carriages. Daimler Motor Char-a-Bancs.
Daimler Motor Omnibuses.
Daimler Motor Delivery Vans. Daimler Motor Lorries.
Daimler Motor Tramcars.
Daimler Motor Railway Cars. Daimler Motors for Launches.
Daimler Motors for Stationary purposes.

Sole Licensees of the SIMMS-BOSCH MAGNETO-ELECTRIC IGNITION for explosion engines of every description. No Battery, Accumulators, or Re-Charging necessary. Simple, Reliable, and Economical.

Makers of the SIMMS LIGHT MOTOR VEHICLES, the only Motors which work entirely automatically.

SIMMS' PATENT PETROL MOTORS (2½ and 3 h.p.).

THE MOTOR CARRIAGE SUPPLY COMPANY, LTD.,
Donington House, Norfolk Street, Strand,
LONDON, W.C.

Left:
Advertisement 1900

Below
Private entries were denoted by letter A for Amateur and were black on white background.
(Photo: Argent Archer)

● No. A1 Panhard

12 h.p.
J Ernest Hutton Esq JP
Class D (price over £500)
Weight 20 cwts (petrol driven)

Classed as **Non Starter** by Official records, but J. Ernest Hutton J.P., was not pleased. He wrote to *The Autocar:*

I was much annoyed to see in your last week's issue a statement that my twelve horse-power Panhard broke down on the first day of the thousand miles trial owing to the gearing giving way through having been converted from six to twelve horse-power.

This statement is wholly inaccurate. The fact was that one of the engines developed a knock two days before the trial, and my car did not start, as we were not ready. I went down to Bristol the following day without a hitch, and the car showed very good speed. Unfortunately, just as we were entering the exhibition building at Bristol (it being dark at the time) I drove the car into a steep gutter at the side of the road, which broke the radiator and sprung several water joints.

I accordingly gave up the idea of completing the tour, but have since been running the car, which is showing a very high speed, and there is nothing whatever wrong with the gearing.

As you are no doubt aware, in Panhard cars alteration of horse-power (from four to twelve) does not affect the gearing.

It may be of interest to you to know that the car on Monday, 21st ult., ran twenty-five miles in fifty minutes on a very trying road, and that it has run 230 miles in the last three days with not a single involuntary stop.

Above:
J. E. Hutton J.P. (P.H.H.)

Below:
Frank Hedges Butler with his daughter Vera in his 6 h.p. Panhard. (Passenger – Hon. C. S. Rolls) (Photo: Montague Grahame-White's personal album, courtesy N.M.M. Beaulieu)

No. A2 Panhard

6 h.p.
Entrant Frank Butler
Driver Frank Butler
Class C (price £300-500)
price £500 (petrol driven)

continued overleaf

● non-starter on April 23rd 1900

A 6 h.p. Panhard manufactured by Messrs Panhard & Levassor. Avenue D'Ivry, Paris

Frank Hedges Butler [FRGS] b. 1855. This remarkable man was the fifth son of James Butler, wine merchant and Frances Hedges of London. He was educated at private schools then joined the family business of Hedges & Butler founded in 1667. He became a partner in 1882 aged 27.

He acquired a Benz car in 1897 and in the same year became the first Hon. Treasurer of the ACGBI. His daughter Vera accompanied him on the 1000 miles Trial and on many balloon journeys. He abandoned motoring soon after the turn of the Century to become an avid balloonist like Rolls, and suggested the formation of an Aero Club as a branch of the Automobile Club.

Frank Hedges Butler in his Benz. (Photo Argent Archer)

Right: Frank Hedges Butler was a man of many interests s shown by his book plate. (P.H.H.)

No. A3 Panhard

6 h.p.

Entrant & Driver T. B. Browne Esq.

Class C (price £300-500)

price £500 (petrol driven)

A 6 h.p. Panhard manufactured by Messrs Panhard & Levassor. Avenue D'Ivry, Paris Business James & Browne. Private owners representative on Competitors committee.

Below: No. A3 Mr. and Mrs T. B. Browne in his 6 h.p. Panhard (Photo Argent Archer)

Left:
Lt. Mark Mayhew L.C.C. in his regimental levee dress.
(P.H.H.)

No. A4 Panhard

8 h.p.
Entrant Mark Mayhew L.C.C.
Class D (price over £500)
price £500 weight 19 cwts. (petrol driven)

An 8 h.p. Panhard manufactured by Messrs Panhard & Levassor. Avenue D'Ivry, Paris

Mr. Mark Mayhew at the age of 29 is said to have driven this entry 651 miles. He also owned and entered No. A29.

His first car was a small Benz in November 1898. Within 3 months he had graduated to a 6h.p. Benz. He then had 3 four cylinder Mors dog-carts, followed by a De Dion quadricycle. He joined the ACGBI, and shortly afterwards purchased the 8 h.p. Panhard that he ran on the Trial. Educated at Harrow, he unsuccessfully contested for the representation of Wandsworth in the House of Commons in 1895. He was a lieutenant in the Middlesex Yeomanry, and the portrait shows him in his regimental levee dress.

• No. A5 Steam Car

12 h.p.
Entered by Cyril Gooch
Class C (price £300-500)
price £350 weight 25 cwts (steam driven)

From Times Engineering, Brighton

No. A6 Panhard

12 h.p.
Entered by Alfred Harmsworth, Esq
Class D (price over £500)
price £900 weight 20 cwts (petrol driven)

A 12 h.p. Panhard manufactured by Messrs Panhard & Levassor. Avenue D'Ivry, Paris This car ran parts of the Trial non-competitively; bringing Alfred Harmsworth to join various sections.

No. A7 Daimler

6 h.p.
Owner/entrant Alfred Harmsworth, Esq
Driver Capt Hercules Langrishe
Class C (price £300-500)
price £472-10s-0d weight 16 cwts (petrol driven)

A 6 h.p. Parisian Daimler manufactured by The Daimler Motor Co., Ltd., Coventry & London.

Alfred Charles William Harmsworth [Viscount Northcliffe] b. 1865

Eldest son of Alfred Harmsworth – barrister, Dublin. Alfred was brought to London on his father exchanging from the Irish Bar for the Inner Temple. He attended Stamford Grammar school for two years and in1876 attended as a day boy at Henley

Below:
No. A7 Alfred Harmsworth's 6 h.p. Daimler driven by Capt. Hercules Langrishe.
(Photo: Argent Archer)

● non-starter on April 23rd 1900

Left:
Alfred Charles Harmsworth. (P.H.H.)

Right:
Captain Hercules Robert Langrishe who drove 6 h.p. Daimler entry No. A7 for Alfred Harmsworth. (P.H.H.)

House, Hampstead, run by John Vine Milne, father of A. A Milne.

At the age of 13 he founded for his school fellows the Henley House magazine. By 1880 he was occasional reporter for the *Hampstead & Highgate Gazette* and composed articles for *Bicycling News.* He was an ardent cyclist and was interested in the latest scientific discoveries. An attack of pneumonia brought on by riding from Bristol to London in pouring rain and without food resulted in his living away from London to slowly recover. He thus joined Iliffe & Sons, Coventry.

By the time he was 21 he had saved £1,000 and in 1887 formed his own publishing business.

1896 saw the foundation of the *Daily Mail* with his brother Harold who later became Viscount Rothermere. The paper sold for a halfpenny. Inventions of the day – motoring, flying, wireless, as examples, came in turn. They were all advertised, stimulated and prizes were offered. Alfred was a keen motorist and was elected a life member of the ACGBI in 1899. He was a great friend of Claude Johnson.

Alfred did not drive the trial, but joined it occasionally in his 12 h.p. Panhard, (A6).

Meanwhile his other entry (A7) a 6 h.p. Daimler was driven by Captain Hercules Langrishe.

Hercules Robert Langrishe. Although of English stock, the Langrishe family was settled in Ireland, County Kilkenny in the 18th Century. His forbear Hercules Langrishe owned over 1000 acres of land. He was a politician and a friend of Burke, and was created a Baronet in 1777.

Hercules Robert was born in 1859. He married Helen Hume in 1887, was a High Sheriff in 1891, also a J.P. and D.L. He was a Captain in the Army Motor Reserve, and Hon. Major 3rd battalion the Oxford Light Infantry. He served in the Med. and Russia in WW1.

He had various escapades in the 1000 Miles Trial driving for Alfred Harmsworth, he was then 41.

No. A8 (not allocated)

No. A9 Napier

8 h.p.
Owned by Harvey du Cros Junior Esq.
Class C (price £300-500)
price £500 weight 21 cwts (petrol driven)

There was a connection with the Motor Power Co., Ltd., Regent Street London. This Napier was a converted 6 h.p. Panhard which only ran to Bristol.

No. A10 Napier

8 h.p.
Owner E Kennard Esq D.L., J.P.
Driver S. F. Edge with St. John Nixon as riding mechanic
Class C (price £300-500)
price £500 weight 21 cwts (petrol driven)
Manufactured by Motor Power Co., Ltd., Regent Street London.

This entry bought together several famous names on the Trial. The owner was the

● non-starter on April 23rd 1900

Left:
No. A10 Napier owner Edward Kennard in driving seat. St. John Nixon in his mechanician seat.
(Photo Argent Archer)

sportsman **Edward Kennard**, who did not drive himself. His wife Mary Kennard was a novelist and a keen automobilist. She was seen on various stages of the Trial in her De Dion, but was not an Entrant as such.

The car No. A10 was built by Montague Napier, and was driven by Selwyn Francis Edge at the age of 32. St. John Nixon at the age of 14 was his riding mechanic.

Montague Stanley Napier A man of striking appearance, standing nearly 6 feet high with a face not unlike an apostle is how S. F. Edge describes him. He was not a keen motorist, always preferring to be driven in a car to driving himself, and he never drove a racing car. He was an engineer of outstanding ability, and in the early days it was his goal to have a workshop with perfect organisation.

Left:
Montague Stanley Napier (P.H.H.)

This was his obsession. He was also resourceful in an emergency, as demonstrated by the repair he made to the carburettor of the Napier car A10 which had broken in half, using solely copper wire and plaster of paris.

His father's company D. Napier & Son, Lambeth, built precision testing and coin weighing machines for mints and banks. Napier built a 7 h.p. engine that so impressed S. F. Edge that he had the French motor taken out of his Panhard car, and the Napier motor built in its place. It is described in *The Autocar* Sept 16th 1899 as follows: "The engine was of double-cylinder vertical type, having the valve gear enclosed in the crank chamber, which is thus protected from damage, dust etc., and ensured perfect lubrication. The exterior of the engine also thereby offers a neat and clean appearance which must recommend it to those whose sense of order is always offended by gear of sorts projecting and surrounding the motor case." So, appreciation of exterior design of an engine rears its head! Discerning people, with an eye to a good horse also wished to appreciate the lines of an engine, even if they knew no more about what went on inside it any more than they were familiar with the inside of their horse. Napier's first engine had many attractive design features, providing amongst other things ease of starting and flexibility of engine revs from 10 to 1,200. High speeds were controlled by a centrifugal governor. This modified Panhard was so successful that Napier went on to build his first motorcar that was in turn purchased by Mr. Kennard before completion. Mr. Kennard's car was used by S F Edge on the Thousand Mile Trial prior to H. Mulliners fitting the body.

Messrs Napier and Son had another speciality; altering cars fitted with tiller steering to the wheel form of steering, which was proving so much safer.

Hubert Edgerton handwritten notes describe the situation:

The first complete Napier Car ever made (*was on the Trial*). Napier had made a very successful ENGINE and SFE had tried it out in a Panhard car The (*Trial*) car belonged to Mr. Kennard.

Left:
Selwyn Francis Edge, driver of entry No. A10. (Photo Argent Archer)

Selwyn Francis Edge was born in Sydney, New South Wales, Australia in 1868; and came to England quite young to continue his studies. By 1887 he was winning tricycle awards, and was known as an amateur boxer. No one tangled with SF or his bull terrier dog called Bully.

He became involved with Harvey du Cros (Sr) in the Dunlop Tyre Company, which SF was managing at 14 Regent Street in 1896; the same year in which he purchased his first De Dion motor-tricycle. This was the first of a long series of motors, with SF winning races and taking up challenges at every turn.

By 1899 a group of friends had set up "The De Dion-Bouton British and Colonial Syndicate Ltd. 14, Regent Street", to be the sole representatives of that marque, the Directors being Hon. John Scott Montagu, Chairman; S. F. Edge, Roger H. Fuller, and Thomas H. Wegulin. S. F. Edge and Harvey Du Cros were also Directors of Motor Power Co Ltd. 14, Regent Street, London S.W. Everyone in automobilism in 1900 knew everyone else. This did not stop S. F. Edge becoming involved with Napier and he drove the first Napier car on the 1900 Thousand Mile Trial event. It so happened that when the Trial was announced this car had already been purchased by Mr. E. Kennard, a well known sporting figure of the day. The new owner agreed that his car could be used on this trial, prior to the body being fitted at Mulliner's coachworks.

Above:
No. A10 Napier – Driver: S. F. Edge Mechanic: St. John Nixon – standing right owner Edward Kennard.
(Photo: Argent Archer)

(extract: *My Motoring Reminiscences* S. F. Edge)
"It was obvious that if the improvements in the Napier car were to be ventilated and the public were to hear of them in the only practical manner, a Napier would have to be entered for this event. The great difficulty was that the first one was very far from completion; it existed at the end of 1899 on paper only with the exception of the chassis frame, a few castings and such like. Napier, however, saw what a golden opportunity would be lost if we were unable to enter the first car, so every possible effort was made to get it running in time. Looking back on past events, it was a bold move to enter an entirely unknown and untried car for the most severe trial ever held in England. The outlook would have been better if we had been able to run the car for a couple of months beforehand and overcome its teething troubles, but far from this being a possibility, we should be fortunate if the car were ready to run straight from the factory to the starting point.

Never had Napier's small factory (*in a Lambeth slum*) witnessed such hectic work as it did for three months prior to April 23, 1900. The car was by no means an exact copy of the Panhard. What we considered would prove themselves to be decided improvements had been introduced into its design as, for example, a type of roller bearing on the countershaft to overcome a common fault with early Panhards; but there was a distinct element of risk putting this and other features to the test with public limelight on the car.

In actual fact, the first Napier car which we had ear-marked for the Thousand Miles Trial, had been sold before it was manufactured. It had been purchased in chassis form by Arthur Mulliner, the well-known coachbuilder of Northampton, who was designing a body for it to the order of Mr. Edward Kennard, J.P. This gentleman was famous in the hunting world: he had an estate at Market Harborough. and although his whole life had been devoted to horses, he did not let his love for them obscure his vision of the future. His wife was famous as a novelist, and she was a woman of unusual mechanical instincts. They had owned a small Benz car and a De Dion motor tricycle prior to ordering the Napier, and Mrs Kennard had become a skilled mechanic. She had a suit of mechanic's overalls, and it was quite common for her to carry out her own repairs and overhauls in company with Brooks, her chauffeur.

I well remember stopping a week-end with the Kennards at Market Harborough shortly before the Thousand Miles Trial. I had driven Mr. Kennard down on Number "8" (*the Panhard with a Napier engine*), and we had had almost incessant tyre trouble en route, due largely to my experimenting with a new set of wired-on tyres instead of the usual beaded-edge type. The following morning. Mr. Kennard showed us round his beautiful estate. We did not miss Mrs Kennard during this journey, but on entering the stable-yard we saw her dressed in mechanic's blue overalls, perched on the side of a petrol can, busy mending the tyres of the car with a tin of solution, patching rubber and tyre levers all around her. I had not met Mr. Kennard until I was introduced to him by Mulliner, and I had to ask him whether he had any objection to my driving his car through the Thousand Miles Trial. I was assured by Mulliner that it was very unlikely he would mind, as he had such a sporting nature, and so it turned out; he even enquired whether he could occupy the passengers seat. The body which would be used was only a rough one, with two seats, but I told him that if he would put up with a certain amount of discomfort, I should be delighted to have him with me.

Only five days before the trial began, the first Napier car left the factory. It was entirely untried, and as a certain amount of tuning-up, if nothing more serious, would be necessary. Napier and I spent every minute we had in running the car about. We covered, in those ten days, long distances, and as the mileage increased and no unforeseen difficulties occurred, my confidence in the car increased. Napier refused to have anything to do with tube ignition, and so the car had electric ignition only, which, in those days, was considered a somewhat bold move.

By the time April 23 arrived, I appreciated that there was very little cause for worry; the car had been put though some severe tests and had given practically no trouble."

St. John Nixon
(Photo: Argent Archer)

St. John Nixon. was known as young Mr. Cousins (*Cusens*) on the Thousand Mile Trial, St. John Cousins Nixon life spanned from the dawn of motoring.

How did a 14 year old boy come to take part in the 1900 Thousand Mile Trial? S. F. Edge tells the story ...

"The recognised place for the mechanic to sit in those days was on the footboards, with his feet on the step, and I had to consider whom I should take as mechanic. There was a youngster named St. John Nixon with me at 14, Regent Street, who had had a good deal of experience in driving my various motor tricycles. Nixon used to work on cars and motor cycles with the Motor Vehicle Company, and I lent him one of my tricycles to ride backwards and forwards to his home at Putney.

He rode several of my racing tricycles at race meetings at the Crystal Palace and owing to his extremely light weight he did exceedingly well. So St. John Nixon was invited to ride with S. F. Edge on No. A10 Napier on the Thousand Mile Trial."

Napier car No. A8 driven by S. F. Edge

Left:
Hon. John Scott-Montagu M.P. Hampshire volunteer. (P.H.H.)

No. A11 Daimler

12 h.p.
Entrant and Driver Hon J. S. Montagu M.P.
Class D (price over £500)
price £800 weight 20 cwts (petrol driven)
A 12 h.p. Parisian Daimler manufactured by The Daimler Motor Co., Ltd., Coventry & London. Supplied by Motor Power Co., Ltd., Regent Street London.

John Edward Douglas Scott-Montagu, KCIE, CSI, FRGS, AICE, AIME, MP – 2nd Baron Montagu of Beaulieu. Drove his Daimler 12 h.p. on the Trial, at the age of 34.

He was born in 1866; educated at Eton and New College Oxford. The young Montagu was interested in mechanical science and railways. His first wife was Lady Cecil Kerr, daughter of the 9th Marquess of Lothian, they married in 1889 and had two daughters. Montagu's first introduction to a car was a ride in a Panhard owned by Hugh Weguelin in 1897. Soon after, he purchased a 2 cyl. 6 h.p. English Daimler, followed by a 12 h.p. model which he raced at Paris/Ostend finishing 3rd to Rolls who was 2nd in the Tourist category, 1898. He had been an MP since 1892 [24 years old] and became the first M.P. to own a car.

Left:
No. A11 Daimler 12 h.p. entered by Hon. J. Scott-Montagu M.P. (P.H.H.)

No. A12 Daimler

6 h.p.
Owned by Henry Edmunds Esq.
Class C (price £300-500)
price £410 weight 18 cwts (petrol driven)
A 6 h.p. Parisian Daimler manufactured by The Daimler Motor Co., Ltd., Coventry & London. Supplied by Motor Power Co., Ltd., Regent Street London.

Mr. Henry Edmunds and **John Goody** drove this entry.

Right:
No. A12 Mr. Henry Edmunds 6 h.p. Daimler. (Photo: Argent Archer)

• No. A13 Daimler

6 h.p.
Owned by Ernest Estcourt, Esq.
price £472-10s-0d weight 18 cwts (petrol driven)

• No. A14 Napier

8 h.p.
Entrant W. D. G. Goff, Esq.
price £500 weight 23 cwts (petrol driven)

• No. A15 Phaeton

5 h.p.
manuf: Wilson & Pilcher, Westminster
Robert Mackay Wilson Esq.
price £400 weight 12 cwts. (petrol driven)

• non-starter on April 23rd 1900

No. A16 Ariel Tricycle

2¼ h.p.
Entered by A. J. Wilson Esq.
Class E (e)
price £84 weight 2¼ cwts (petrol driven)

Ariel Tricycle with 2¼ h.p. engine manufactured by The Ariel Motor Co., Birmingham, and the property of **Arthur James Wilson Esq.**, an experienced cyclist who had commenced motorcycling in 1898. He was stone deaf from childhood.

Left:
No. A16 2¼ h.p. Ariel Tricycle

No. A17 Panhard

12 h.p.
Entrant and driver Hon. Charles S. Rolls
Class D (price over £500)
price £900 (petrol driven)

A 12 h.p. Panhard manufactured by Messrs Panhard & Levassor, Avenue D'Ivry, Paris. The Honorable Charles S. Rolls saw it as his duty to support the Thousand Miles Trial, regardless of the expense. At this time Rolls was not associated with the motor trade, and he considered the Panhard the best marque available, although he is recorded as trying many other marques. He had already completed his personal market survey abroad of the best cars available; being well known on the Continent for having cars built to include his own specifications.

His car for the Thousand Mile Trial is quoted at a price of £900. The tyre bill for his chosen 12 h.p. Panhard on the Trial was in the region of £80.

Hon. Charles S. Rolls.
(*Contrib:* Tom Clarke)
At the time of the 1900 Trial the Hon. Charles S. Rolls was not yet 23. He must have been one of the youngest of the participants. Yet, for all the audacity and abandon of youth, he had been remarkably single-minded and mature in building up his motoring credentials. Serious and far from reckless though Rolls was he did have a small streak of showmanship. This and his youth and social status ensured that he caught the public eye.

Below:
Hon. Charles S. Rolls and his 12 h.p. Panhard. (Photo M. Grahame-White album, courtesy N.M.M. Beaulieu)

Left:
Hon. Charles S. Rolls (P.H.H.)

His courtesy title was new, resulting from his father's ennoblement in 1892. Though aristocratic, Rolls was not snobbish so that he had no difficulties mixing outside his social circle. He made extended travels in France during 1894/95 where he first encountered the car and began saving to buy one. At Cambridge he took up serious cycling and when he graduated in engineering in 1898 he equipped a large workshop at his parents' London home with machine tools.

Even before leaving university Rolls had begun moving in motoring circles. After meeting Sir David Salomons in early 1896 he had established sufficient credibility to meet visiting French and Belgian motor pioneers in July 1896 at the Hurlingham Club. His first car, a Peugeot, was purchased in October 1896. He joined the Automobile Club de France in July 1897 proposed by Baron Zuylen de Nyevelt, and the A.C.G.B.I. on 9 August 1898. Business plans included a proposal to make Duryeas in 1897.

Proselytising on the virtues of the car began after his Cambridge to Monmouth run in December 1896, and the display of his Peugeot in May 1897, with assiduous contributions to the motoring press. Further cars were purchased: in 1897 a Léon Bollée, De Dion tricycle, and an 1896 8 h.p. 4-cylinder Panhard; in 1898 a 6 h.p. and 4 h.p. Panhard, and Columbia electric; in 1899 a Peugeot 4 h.p., 8 h.p. Panhard, and he was also seen on a Lynx dogcart in May that year. In early 1900 he bought the car which was to bring him success in the 1900 Trial, a 12 h.p. Panhard racer.

His racing participation in these early years was modest, the Tourist Class of the Paris-Ostend race of August/September 1899, and the 1899 Paris-Boulogne race, but he won the Tourist Class of the Bordeaux-Biarritz race of October 1899. He then began in earnest to promote the forthcoming 1900 Trial and displayed his 6 h.p. Panhard in Bradford in January 1900, winning some prizes with it.

(T.C.)

A handwritten note has been discovered made by Hubert Egerton in the margin of his personal copy of(courtesy John Olorenshaw) "Vital to the Life of the Nation" produced by SMM&T 1946

"In the news at about 1898 was the Hon. C. S. Rolls, third son of Lord Llangattock, who, although not yet of age, was a keen autocarist. He owned at this period a Peugeot car which had been imported direct from France. By using it on the roads of the United Kingdom without having first paid ransom to the holders of the British rights to the patents, Rolls fell foul of the British Motor Syndicate and the case was taken to Court, where, to his indignation, judgment was given against him and he had to pay the owners of the patent rights the sum of £15."

Egertons' Margin Notes to above paragraph:

"I made the acquaintance of Charlie Rolls in the year 1898 – I well remember the Peugeot car here referred to – He also had a BOLLÉE three wheeler. There was a picture of him in the Bollée published in The Autocar *– I was his passenger on several occasions – and visited his home in Knightsbridge. I well rember waiting outside the Automobile Club with several other Members to see Rolls arrive on his 6 h.p. 2 cyl tube ignition PANHARD with WHEEL steering!! – He drove a 4 cyl 12 h.p. Panhard in the historic "1000 Miles Trial" (April & May 1900) and swept everything before him!*

Section II PRIVATE ENTRIES

• No. A18 Light Daimler

6 h.p.
Class B (price £200-300)
price £260 weight 11 cwts (petrol driven)
A 6 h.p. Parisian Daimler manufactured by The Daimler Motor Co., Ltd., Coventry & London.

Entered by Nevill Copland Esq

No. A19 Daimler

12 h.p.
John R. Hargreaves J.P.
Class D (price over £500)
price £800 weight 23 cwts (petrol driven)
A 12 h.p. Parisian Daimler manufactured by The Daimler Motor Co., Ltd., Coventry & London ran throughout but does not wish to claim records. Driven by **Otto Meyer** or **Cecil Grimshaw**.

No. A20 Empress Tricycle

2¾ h.p.
Entered by Herbert Ashby
Class E (a)
price £75 (petrol driven)
Herbert Ashby was on his Empress Motor Tricycle which was manufactured by United Motor Industries. 3, Rue Meyerbeer, Paris. It was his intention to go in to the motor trade, but this did not actually happen. He and his brother started a brick company in 1888. He was a keen mountaineer.

Left:
No. A20 Empress Tricycle entered by Herbert Ashby (Photo: Argent Archer)

Left:
Herbert Ashby

No. A21 Daimler

6 h.p.
Owner and driver Ernest Pitman Esq.
Class C (price £300-500)
price £400 weight 22 cwts (petrol driven).
A 6 h.p. Daimler manufactured by The Daimler Motor Co., Ltd., Coventry & London. Ernest Pitman contributed 2 gns to the prize fund. His mechanician was T. Weeks. His father Sir Isaac Pitman invented shorthand English and founded the Pitman Publishing empire. Ernest was a Country Member of the ACGBI, and owned the first car in Bath where he lived. He was also a keen aviator, owning a Voisin biplane. He had so many flying "incidents" that he flew under the alias of Mr. Theodore Beech to avoid publicity when he made (unscheduled) landings.

Right:
No. A21 6 h.p. Daimler entered by Ernest Pitman. (Courtesy J. Pitman)

Left:
No. A20 2¾ h.p. Empress Tricycle

● non-starter on April 23rd 1900

No. A22 Daimler

12 h.p.
Owner J A Holder Esq.
Class D (price over £500)
price £800 weight 19 cwts (petrol driven)

A 12 h.p. Daimler manufactured by The Daimler Motor Co., Ltd., Coventry & London. J. A. Holder was a Private Owners Representative on Competitors committee

Left:
No. A22 12 h.p. Daimler entered by J. A. Holder. (V.C.C. Archives)

No. A23 M.M.C. Phaeton

6¼ h.p.
Owned by Chas Cordingley
Class C (price £300-500)
price £435 weight 21¼ cwts (petrol driven).

A 6¼ h.p. MMC from the Motor manufacturing Co., Ltd., London & Coventry, **Robert Bunkall** is recorded as driving this entry 442 miles. Chas. Cordingley was responsible for the exhibitions mounted by ACGBI.

Left:
No. A23 Chas Cordingley's 6¼ h.p. M.M.C. Phaeton. (Photo: Argent Archer)

No. A24 Mors 'Petit Duc'

4 h.p.
Owned by Robert E Phillips
Class B (price £200-300)
price £280 weight 5 cwts

A 4 h.p. two seater.
Robert E. Phillips was on the ACGBI Committee

His car was supplied in this country by the Automobile Association Ltd., Holland Park Avenue, London W.

Robert E. Phillips born July 1855, and apprenticed to Davey Paxman & Co. Colchester Engineers 1872. Practised as a consulting Eng. & Patent agent 1889. Studied mechanical patents relating to motor vehicles.

Right:
Entry No. A24, Mors owned by R. E. Phillips

No. A25 Benz Ideal

3 h.p.
Entered by Mrs Louise Bazalgette
Class A (price up to £200)
price £175 weight 8 cwts

Supplied by Hewetson's Ltd of Dean Street Soho, London this Benz Ideal was the third Benz Ideal on the Trial and was entered by a friend of Henry Hewetson's, Mrs Louise Bazalgette, in the section for privately owned cars, **thus demonstrating the ease with which the car could be managed even by a woman. ...**

Louise Bazalgette was 49 in 1900. She had been a widow then for 15 years. She had married Major George Bazalgette who was over 20 years older than herself. Her husband was from the family that had made many fine contributions to Victorian England, mostly the work of Sir Joseph Bazalgette. He put his name to the Victorian sewer system of London, Thames Embankment, Hammersmith Bridge and other fine civil engineering achievements.

Louise was a very keen automobilist, and

was active in publicity for the movement. She was present at the Emancipation Run in 1896 from London to Brighton, (where she was photographed with her friend Henry Hewetson). She made news in *The Daily Mail* Aug 1899 under "The Autocar's Progress" which said: "Lady automobilists are increasing rapidly. The longest run so far made by an English lady has been achieved by Mrs Bazalgette who drove the other day from her house in Portman Square to Southampton."

Clarkson was her mechanician on the trip. (see also page 241)

Above:
Entry No. A25, Mrs Louise Bazalgette on her 3 h.p. Benz Ideal with Clarkson her mechanic. (Photo: Argent Archer)

No. A26 Daimler

6 h.p.
Clarence K. Gregson Esq & Percy Brennan
Class C (price £300-500)
price £450 weight 19½ cwts (petrol driven).

A 6 h.p. Daimler manufactured by The Daimler Motor Co., Ltd., Coventry & London. Clarence H. Gregson was a Private Owners Representative on the Competitors Committee. He and Percy Brennan shared the driving.

Left:
C. K. Gregson

Right:
Entry No. A26, 6 h.p. Daimler

No. A27 Daimler Mail Phaeton

12 h.p.
Entered by John R. Hargreaves J.P.
Class D (price over £500)
price £800 weight 29 cwts (petrol driven)

A 12 h.p. Daimler manufactured by The Daimler Motor Co., Ltd., Coventry & London. **ran throughout but does not wish to claim records** Driven by **Otto Meyer** or **Cecil Grimshaw.**

Left:
Entry No. A27 12 h.p. Daimler Mail Phaeton entered by John R. Hargreaves J.P.
(Photo: Argent Archer)

No. A28 Enfield Quad

2¼ h.p.
Entered by E. M. Iliffe, Esq.
Class E (b)
price £110-5s-0d.

Manufactured by the Enfield Cycle Co., Redditch,

Above:
Enfield Quad No. A28

Right:
No. A28 Enfield Quad 2¼ h.p. entered by E. M. Iliffe.
(Photo: Argent Archer)

Edward Mauger Iliffe (later Lord Iliffe) drove his 2¼ h.p. "quad" on the Trial. He was born May 1877, thus aged 23 at the time of the 1000 miles trial.

Sturmey wrote his book on travelling the length of the country in 1897 when his publishing partner was W. I. Iliffe of Coventry & London. He was William Iliffe J.P. and lived at Allesley, Warks., and Edward Mauger Iliffe was his son affectionately known as 'Thousand Miles Iliffe' (Hubert Egerton)

No. A29 Peugeot

7 h.p.
Owned by Mark Mayhew L.C.C.
Class D (price over £500)
price £600 weight 17 cwts
(*see also entry A4*)

Manufactured by Peugeot et Cie., Paris,

Said to have been driven 976 miles by **D. Haxton**

Below:
Mr. Mark Mayhew in his Panhard (A4).
(Photo: Argent Archer)

Section II PRIVATE ENTRIES

Left:
J. D. Siddeley
(P.H.H.)

No. A30 Daimler

6 h.p.
Entrant and driver J. D. Siddeley, Esq.
Class C (price £300-500)
price £472-10s-0d weight 17 cwts (petrol driven)

A 6 h.p. Parisian Daimler manufactured by The Daimler Motor Co., Ltd., Coventry & London.

John Davenport Siddeley CBE, FRAES – 1st Baron Kenilworth was born the same year as Scott-Montagu – 1866. He married Sarah Mabel Goodier of Macclesfield in 1893, and owned his first car, a 6 h.p. Daimler in 1899.

At the time of the 1000 Mile Trial Siddeley was Managing Director of the Clipper Tyre Co.

No. A31 Daimler

6 h.p.
Driven by Wm Exe (An alias for Claude Johnson)
Class C (price £300-500)
price £472-10s-0d weight 17 cwts (petrol driven)

A 6 h.p. Parisian Daimler manufactured by The Daimler Motor Co., Ltd., Coventry & London. Claude Johnson took part in the Trial himself under the name `William Exe', driving this 6 h.p. Daimler.

Right:
Claude Johnson founder member and first Secretary of A.C.G.B.I. portrait by Ambrose McEvoy.
(Courtesy Royal Automobile Club. E.B)

PARTS (Section III.)

CLASS A. PNEUMATIC TYRES.

A Set of

Clipper Pneumatic Tyres,

MADE BY THE

CLIPPER PNEUMATIC TYRE CO., LTD.,

CLIPPER MILLS, ASTON CROSS, BIRMINGHAM,

Fitted to a Parisian Daimler Car.

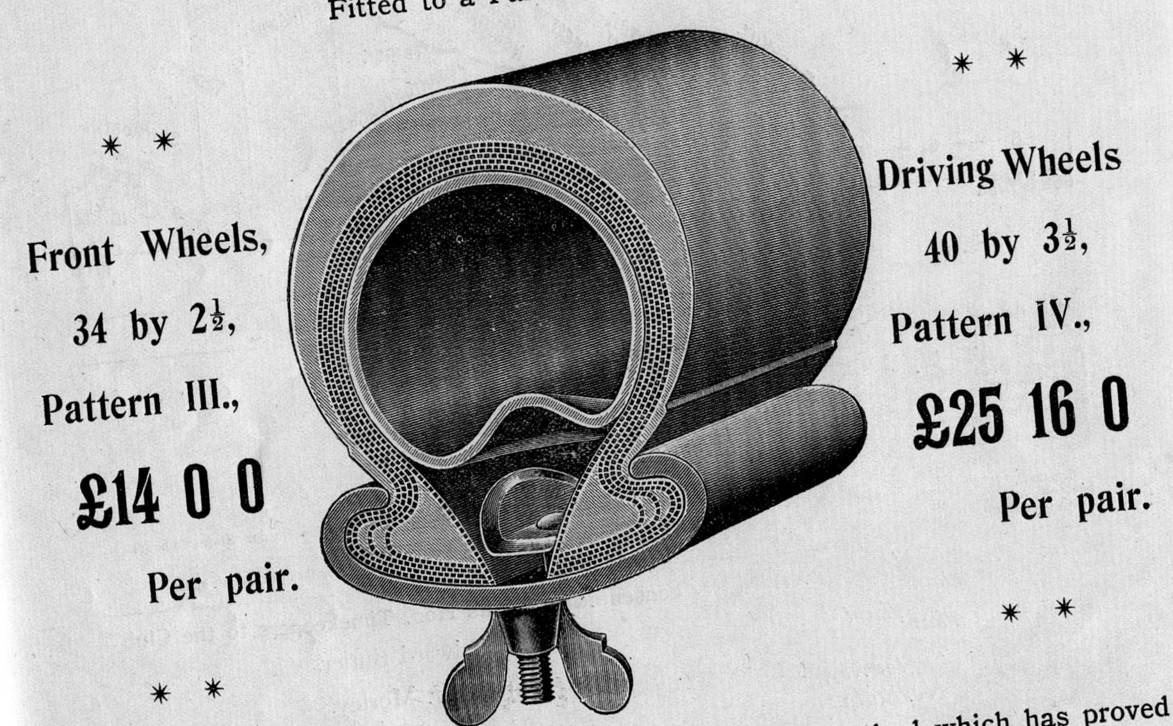

* *

Front Wheels,

34 by 2½,

Pattern III.,

£14 0 0

Per pair.

* *

* *

Driving Wheels

40 by 3½,

Pattern IV.,

£25 16 0

Per pair.

* *

Illustration explains attachment. This is the only method which has proved durable and reliable. CLIPPER TYRES are interchangeable with the leading Foreign Tyres.

Send for the Clipper Motor Tyre Catalogue, it is full of information relating to Pneumatic Tyres, and also explains why Clipper Motor Tyres are best for all forms of Automobile Cycles or carriages.

THOUSAND MILE TRIAL 23rd April 1900 Entrants

Section I TRADE ENTRIES

No	Make	h.p.	Entered by	Driver
1	Benz	3	Hewetson	Henry Hewetson
2	Benz	3	Hewetsons	A. J. Coles
3	Ariel quad	3½	Ariel Motor Co Birmingham	Mr. John W Stocks
4	Ariel trike with whippet	2¼	Ariel Motor Co Birmingham	Mr. Edwin S. Cheel
5	Locomobile Steam Carriage	2	The Locomobile Co of America	
● 6	MMC Balmoral Charbanc	12	Motor Manuf Co London & Coventry	
● 7	MMC Phaeton	12	Motor Manuf Co London & Coventry	
8	MMC Panhard	6	Motor Manuf Co London & Coventry	Mr. A. Burgess
9	MMC Iveagh Phaeton (Daimler)	6	Motor Manuf Co London & Coventry	William White
● 10	MMC 'Princess'	4½	Motor Manuf Co London & Coventry	
11	MMC 'Princess'	4½	Motor Manuf Co London & Coventry	
12	Motor Manufacturing Co's Tricycle	2¼	Motor Manuf Co London & Coventry	E. Buck
● 13	Ariel Panhard Voiturette	3½	Ariel Motor Co Birmingham	
14	De Dion Voiturette	3	De Dion Syndicate Ltd	Mr. Grierson
15	De Dion	3	De Dion Syndicate (Egerton)	Mr. Hubert Egerton
16	Gladiator	3¼	Motor Power Co London	Roland le Bars
● 17	Napier (*may not be ready*)	16	Motor Power Co London	
18	Endurance Car	5	Endurance Motor Co ltd.	
19	Orient Express	6	Automobile Association Ltd	
20	Simms Motor Wheel	2¾	Motor Carriage Supply Ltd	Samuel Rowbottom
21	Lanchester carriage	8	Lanchester Engine Co.	George Lanchester
22	Lanchester carriage	8	Lanchester Engine Co.	Archibald Millership
23	Brown-Whitney Steam Car	–	Brown Bros. Ltd	E. R. Banks
24	Marshall Carriage	5	Marshall & Co	
● 25	Déchamps	9	J. Burns Oxford St. London	
26	Peugeot	8	Friswell Ltd 18 Holborn Viaduct	Mr. Friswell
27	New Orleans	3	Burford van Toll & Co Twickenham	Mr. Astell
28	New Orleans	3	Burford van Toll & Co Twickenham	I. C. Forrow
29	Eureka car	2¼	Motor Car Co. Ltd	
30	Eureka car	2¼	Motor Car Co. Ltd	
31	M.C.C. Triumph	3½	Motor Car Co. Ltd	H. Farman
32	M.C.C. Triumph	3½	Motor Car Co. Ltd	R. Moffat Ford
33	Decauville	3½	Motor Car Co 168 Shaftesbury Ave	Frank Strange
34	Decauville	3½	Motor Car Co 168 Shaftesbury Ave	Jules Debois / M. K. Hales
35	Daimler	6	Daimler Motor Co Ltd	Mr. J. S. Critchley
36	Daimler	6	Daimler Motor Co Ltd	Mr. Richardson
37	Daimler Parisian	6	Daimler Motor Co Ltd	M. Grahame-White
38	Daimler Public Service Vehicle	9½	Daimler Motor Co Ltd	
39	Century Tandem Tricycle	2¼	Century Engineering Manchester	Ralph Jackson
40	Wolseley	3	Wolseley Sheep Shearing Machine Co Birmingham	Mr. Herbert C. Austin
41	International Victoria	3	International Motor Car Co London	Mr. Seyd
42	Hurlingham Voiturette	3½	London Motor Van & Wagon Co Ltd	
43	Phaeton	5½	London Motor Van & Wagon Co Ltd	
44	International Victoria	3	International Motor Car Co London	Mr. Cappellan
45	S.S. Carriage	5½	S.S. Motor Co	
46	Richard	7	Automobile Manufacturing Co London	French
47	Richard	7	Automobile Manufacturing Co London	W. C. Bersey / M. Berduil
● 48	Humber voiturette	3	Humber & Co Holborn Viaduct London	
49	Marshall	5	Marshall & Co Belsize Works Manr	Mr. J. J. Mann
● 50	Renaux Tricycle	3	Marshall & Co Belsize Works Manr	
51	Star Voiturette	3½	Star Motor Co	Messrs Lisle / Prew
52	Roots & Venables Oil Carriage	2⅞	Roots & Venables	
* 53	Wolseley Carriage	8	Wolseley Sheep Shearing Machine Co Birmingham	

● non-starter on April 23rd 1900
* non-starter on April 23rd 1900 but joined Birmingham, retired Manchester

THOUSAND MILE TRIAL 23rd April 1900 Entrants

Section II PRIVATE ENTRIES

No	Make	h.p.	Owner	Driver
● A1	Panhard	12	J. Ernest Hutton Esq J.P.	
A2	Panhard	6	Frank Butler	Frank Butler
A3	Panhard	6	T. B. Browne	T. B. Browne
A4	Panhard	8	Mark Mayhew L.C.C.	Mark Mayhew
● A5	Steam Car	12	Cyril Gooch	
* A6	Panhard	12	Alfred Harmsworth Esq	
A7	Daimler	6	Alfred Harmsworth Esq	Capt H. Langrishe
A8	not allocated			
● A9	Napier	8	Harvey du Cros jun	
A10	Napier	8	E. Kennard	S. F. Edge
A11	Daimler	12	Hon. J. S. Montagu	Hon. J. S. Montagu
A12	Daimler	6	Henry Edmunds	Edmunds / J. Goody
● A13	Daimler	6	Ernest Estcourt Esq.	
● A14	Napier	8	W. D. G. Goff Esq.	
● A15	petrol Phaeton	5	Robert McCay Wilson	
A16	Ariel Tricycle	2¼	A. J. Wilson	A. J. Wilson
A17	Panhard	12	Hon. C. S. Rolls	Hon C. S. Rolls
● A18	Light Daimler	6	Neville Copland	
A19	Daimler	12	John R. Hargreaves J.P.	O. Meyer / C. Grimshaw
A20	Empress Trike	2¾	Herbert Ashby	Herbert Ashby
A21	Daimler	6	Ernest Pitman	E. Pitman / T. Weeks
A22	Daimler	12	J. S. Holder	J. S. Holder
A23	M.M.C. Phaeton	6¼	Chas Cordingley	Robert Bunkall
A24	Mors Petit Duc	4	R. E. Phillips	R. E. Phillips
A25	Benz Ideal	3	Mrs L. Bazalgette	Mrs L. B. / Clarkson
A26	Daimler	6	Clarence Gregson	C. G. / Percy Brennan
A27	Daimler Mail Phaeton	12	John R. Hargreaves J.P.	O. Meyer / C. Grimshaw
A28	Enfield Quad	2¼	E. M. Iliffe	E. M. Iliffe
A29	Peugeot	7	Mark Mayhew L.C.C.	D. Haxton
A30	Daimler	6	J. D. Siddeley	J. D. Siddeley
A31	Daimler	6	William Exe	Claude Johnson

● non-starter on April 23rd 1900
* non-starter on April 23rd 1900, ran some sections only

Section III

Parts of Motor Vehicles entered by their Manufacturers or by their authorised agents.
P 1. Class A. A set of Clipper pneumatic tyres, fitted to a Daimler 6 h.p. carriage, No. 37.
Entered by the Clipper Pneumatic Tyre Co., Ltd., Aston Cross, Birmingham.

THE FIRST DAY'S RUN

MONDAY 23RD APRIL

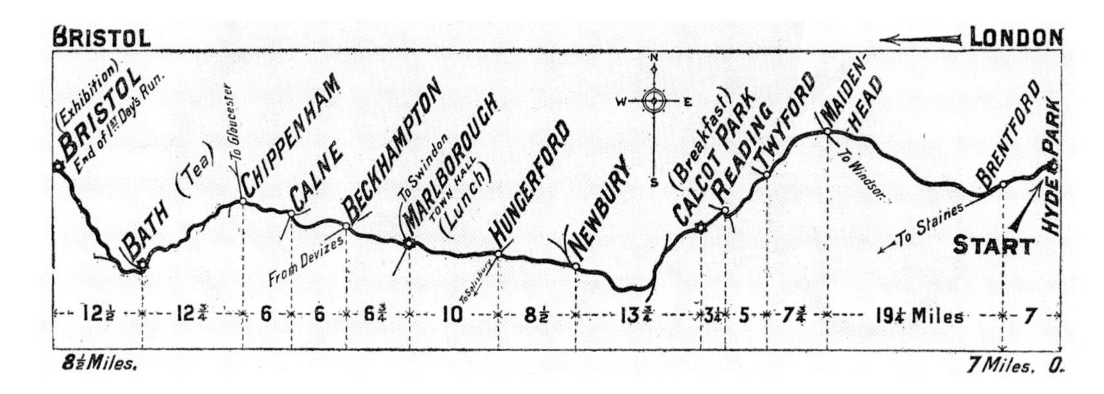

London to Bristol
118½ miles

AT THE EXHIBITION in the Agricultural Hall, Islington, the lengthy process of the examination and sealing was completed over the weekend of April 21st-22nd 1900. The Judges had inspected the cars and stamped various parts.

The Entrants had spent endless days planning. The cars had to be prepared (in some cases – built!) They also had to prepare themselves and their passengers to be on the road for 20 days. They packed on to the car whatever spare parts and fuel they could carry; and attempted to procure suitable clothing for the task ahead. Those who were cyclists (like S. F. Edge, E. M. Iliffe etc.,) knew what was necessary to keep out wind and rain. Others like Herbert Ashby who was a keen Alpinist must also have had clothing that would keep out the weather.

They had read with care the 205 page programme of instructions; and reserved their rooms, garaging and fuel, at the various stops. The logistics of each entrant's journey must have been daunting. In the wee small hours of the morning some doubts must have surfaced in the minds of our intrepid Autocarists. All was uncertain, including the weather.

It was amazing that as many as 64 of the original 85 entries appeared at the Start.

Contemporary reports tell the story best ...

The Start

BY AN OCCASIONAL EARLY RISER

Energy and early rising are characteristic of the motorcar and the motorist alike. Such was my reflection on arriving at Grosvenor Place shortly after six on Monday morning. I found a score of enthusiasts were already there, and cars were arriving simultaneously with the morning milk. The morning was rather dull, and a chilliness was in the air – not the chilliness that comes upon us at night, but that curious condition associated with unaired things – whether clothes or thoroughfares. Policemen were less stolid than usual, workmen lingered on their way to work, and milkmen glanced from the housemaids on the one side to the curiously-garbed creatures formed into chatty groups on the other. It was a sight such as is not often seen. In fact, it has never occurred before, and only early risers are destined to see such an affair in the future.

It was evident something unusual was about to take place. Sandwichmen stood in the gutter bearing aloft banners – journalistic licence thus

The Start at Grosvenor Place. April 23rd, 1900.
No. A2 Frank Butler (and his daughter Vera who accompanied him throughout) on his 6 hp Panhard.
No. A3 T. B. Browne's 6 hp Panhard.
No. A7 Alfred Harmsworth's 6 h.p. Parisien Daimler driven by Captain Langrishe. (Photo: Argent Archer)

honours the commonplace boards of the advertiser – with the device 'Class A,' 'Class B,' and so on through the first five letters of the alphabet. Close scrutiny revealed the fact that these letters were duplicated, and that each bore a further reference to Section I or Section II. On the pavement chalk marks were being made to indicate the positions to be assumed by the cars on their arrival, and from six to seven Mr. Lyons Sampson, Mr. H. J. Mulliner, Mr. C. Johnson, and other officials had a busy time in seeing that proper positions were occupied. Apart from the cars the greatest interest was taken in the raiment worn by the intending passengers, of whom there were about 200, with almost as many varieties of clothing, for certainly no two complete suits were alike. The headgear was equally varied and distinctive. One gentleman seemed to have distorted a flat piece of felt into some form resembling a cross between a billycock and a pie-dish, and was content. Others wore fishermen's caps: the majority were seen under leather caps of different shapes and styles, and only a few kept to the ordinary bowler. As to jackets, they ranged from leather to fur and back again, in varying gradations, from fur to leather. Evidently, there is no correct 'fashion' in automobile attire, and even the Frenchmen who came over as though prepared to journey to the North Pole did not wholly satisfy the popular fancy. Altogether it was a kaleidoscopic scene, as the strangely attired persons flitted about from one car to another, full of interest. Of course, all the prominent motorists of the country were there. Among amateurs the Hon. J. Scott Montagu, M.P., and the Hon. C. S. Rolls were recognised by the crowd, while a little crowd gathered around Captain Langrishe on Mr. Alfred Harmsworth's Daimler, Messrs J. A. Holder, J. Hargreaves, J. D. Siddeley, C. K. Gregson, C. Cordingley, E. Pitman, H Edmunds, R. E. Phillips, and T. B. Browne were early astir, as was also Mr. S. F. Edge, who was to drive Mr. Kennard's 8 h.p. Napier, and Mr. Frank H. Butler, the Hon. Treasurer of the Automobile Club, on his new 6 h.p. Panhard, having his daughter as one of the passengers. There were only a few ladies about, Mrs Mann and Mrs Friswell, with their respective husbands, and Mrs Bazalgette, on her own car, being the best known.

Right up to the stroke of seven cars were arriving, one electric cab having specially

honoured the occasion with its presence reminiscent of a score of others seen on London streets some months ago. Cyclists were plentiful and policemen polite, with the result that a clear way was made for the cars, which made a good show as they went round the corner of St George's Hospital. However new and novel may have been the appearance of the cars to the general public, the majority were all familiar to those who have faithfully followed the pages of *The Motor-Car Journal*. So far as I could see, the only vehicles that started, and which had not previously been seen were the new Georges Richard car, the Daimler public service char-à-banc (the latter having one of the few ladies taking part in the tour for a passenger), and the S.S. car, which had been kept as a kind of 'dark horse'.

The S.S. Motor Company's vehicle was a four-seated car, fitted with wheel-steering and detachable body. The engine is a single cylinder one of 5½ h.p., the transmission being effected by gear wheels. The vehicle is fitted with three speeds forward – 4, 10, and 20 miles per hour – and reverse motion.

Standing at the corner of St. George's Hospital, and closely wedged between a full round policeman and a fair cyclist, I saw only the cars as they sped by. First came Mr. Hewetson on his Benz; then Mr. Coles, even more at home on the road than on the stage; then, in rapid succession, came the rest of the vehicles in Class A, the only non-starter being the Humber voiturette and one of the New Orleans cars, which, however, strolled along later and made a good start all to itself. With only a minute's interval between, Class B followed the first fleet, and here the Princess cars and the Ariel Panhard voiturette were missing, the new S.S. carriage, the Renault cars (known in this country as the M.C.C. Triumphs), De Dion voiturettes, and the Wolseley and the Marshall cars – the latter driven by Mr. J. J. Mann – forming the rest of the contingent. Class C came along well, and proved one of the most attractive sections to the public, the number of passengers carried by most of the vehicles demonstrating the practical nature of the section. Mr. A. Burgess drove the Motor Manufacturing Company's 6 h.p. phaeton, and was closely followed by the Brown-Whitney steam car, which had attracted much attention during the exhibition at the Agricultural Hall. Hardly had I saluted Mr. Albert Brown and Mr. Banks, who were aboard, when some well-known cars rounded the corner almost together, only allowing one to recognise such well-known faces as those of Messrs. Friswell, Critchley, Pedley, and Richardson, all apparently setting out on their long pilgrimage with lightness of heart and ease of mind. The cheerfulness of the passengers was, in fact, very noticeable – a condition probably based on the thorough overhauling of the cars which had taken place in the preceding hours. So anxious were the owners of cars to have everything in a perfect state for the start, that some had stayed up through a good many hours of the night attending to mechanism and generally looking to their cars. Such devotion deserves success.

Alas! for the curiosity of the public. It overwhelmed several journalists on Monday morning, and despite the way in which the police backed on to frail toes and smiled pleasantly if caught in the act, the crowd pushed outward from the kerb. I lost the protection afforded by the cycle of the spectator already referred to, and while engaged in preserving equilibrium missed some of the quadricycles and tricycles that I had seen standing idly in Grosvenor Place half an hour before. I did not, however, miss the Daimler public service vehicle driven by Mr. Straker. Then followed in rapid procession the privately-owned vehicles whose owners have already been mentioned, Mr. Grimshaw driving the Daimler car of Mr. Hargreaves, and Mr. Johnson being in charge of the wheel on Mr. Exe's phaeton.

The long procession, which had only taken twenty minutes in passing, was brought to an end by Messrs. A. J. Wilson, H. Ashby, and E. M. Iliffe, the two former on tricycles and the latter on an Enfield quadricycle. One notable motorist was absent, and I turned round into Grosvenor Place to see if any laggards were about. There was the waggonette of the Thames Valley Motor-

Car Company full of baggage, and suddenly Mr. Mark Mayhew, L.C.C. came into view. He was rather late, but he was going well, and seemed likely to quickly overtake some of the earlier starters. After I had left the scene, yet another competitor appears to have put in an appearance and to have gone on the journey to Bristol.

Several vehicles were about which intended to go part of the way, these including the Delahaye; but Dr. Lehwess and Mr. Weigel were the most prominent on their Vallée racer, which doubtless regarded the course as rather tame. And when the cars had gone the crowd dispersed to its work, having had a new education and an object lesson in what will, in a few years, be regarded as quite commonplace, viz, the advantages of motor traction over horses. Not a car 'jibbed' at the start: every vehicle went off at the word command, and it was clearly demonstrated that if the motor-vehicle has come to stay, it has also come to go.”

The Motor-Car Journal, Wednesday, April 25th, 1900

The following is a complete list of the cars that started from Grosvenor Place:

SECTION I
(Cars entered by Manufacturer or Agent)

Class A

1	Benz Ideal
2	Benz Ideal
3	Locomobile Steam Car
16	Gladiator Voiturette
18	Endurance Car
19	Orient Express
27	New Orleans Car
28	New Orleans Car
29	Eureka Car
30	Eureka Car
33	Décauville
34	Décauville
42	3½ h.p. 'Hurlingham'
41	International Victoria
44	International Victoria
51	Star Voiturette
52	Roots and Venables

Class B

14	De Dion Voiturette
15	De Dion Voiturette
24	Marshall Carriage
31	M.C.C. Triumph
32	M.C.C. Triumph
40	Wolseley Voiturette
43	S.S. Carriage
49	Marshall Carriage

Class C

8	M.M. Co.'s 6 h.p. Phaeton
9	M.M. Co.'s Iveagh Phaeton
23	Brown-Whitney Steam Car
26	8 h.p. Peugeot (Friswell's)
33	6 h.p. Daimler
36	6 h.p. Daimler
37	Daimler Parisian
43	L.M.V. and Wagon Co.'s Phaeton, 5½ h.p.
46	Richard Car
47	Richard Car

Class D

17	16 h.p. Napier
21	Lanchester Carriage
22	Lanchester Carriage

Class E (a)

12	Motor Manufacturing Company's Tricycle
20	Simms Motor Wheel

Class E (b)

3	Ariel Quadricycle
4	Ariel Tricycle with Whippet attachment

Class F

38	Daimler Public Service Vehicle

SECTION II
(Privately owned Vehicles)

Class A

A25	Benz Ideal (Mrs. Bazalgette)

Class B

A24	Mors Voiturette (Mr. Phillips)

Class C

A2	6 h.p. Panhard (Mr. Butler)
A3	6 h.p. Panhard (Mr. T. B. Browne)
A7	6 h.p. Daimler (Mr. A. Harmsworth)
A10	8 h.p. Napier (Mr. E. Kennard)
A12	6 h.p. Daimler (Mr H. Edmunds)
A21	6 h.p. Daimler (Mr. E. Pitman)
A23	6¼ h.p. Motor Mfg. Co.'s Phaeton (Mr C. Cordingley)
A26	6 h.p. Daimler (Mr. C. K. Gregson)
A30	6 h.p. Daimler (Mr. J.D. Siddeley)
A31	6 h.p. Daimler (Mr. W. Exe)

Class D

A4	8 h.p. Panhard (Mr. Mark Mayhew)
A11	12 h.p. Daimler (Hon. J.S. Montagu, M.P.)
A17	12 h.p. Panhard (Hon. C. S. Rolls)
A22	12 h.p. Daimler (Mr. J. A. Holder)
A27	11 h.p. Daimler (Mr. J. Hargreaves)
A29	7 h.p. Peugeot (Mr. Mark Mayhew)

Class E (a)

A16	Ariel Tricycle (Mr. A.J. Wilson)
A20	Empress Motor Tricycle (Mr. H. Ashby)

Class E (b)

A28	Enfield Quadricycle (Mr. E.M. Iliffe)

A curious racing car appeared on the route that was not an official entrant. Driven by Dr. Lehwess it was in fact known as the 'slipper' due to its body shape. It had a 4 cylinder horizontal engine of 7,598cc. no gearbox provided, the engine being thought sufficiently powerful and flexible to avoid the need. Final drive by single wide belt to rear axle (Georgano)
(Photo: From Friswell Collection by kind permission of Peter Heilbron)

The Start at Grosvenor Place. April 23rd, 1900. No. A12 Henry Edmunds 6 h.p. Daimler; No. A21 Ernest Pitman's 6 h.p. Daimler and T. Weeks, his mechanician; No. A23 6¼ h.p. M.M.C. Phaeton of Charles Cordingley – Editor of *The Motor-Car Journal*. (Photo: Argent Archer)

" Scores of photographs have been taken, both from and of the cars and passengers. Unfortunately the light at the start in Grosvenor Place was so bad that our photographers, who were stationed on an overlooking balcony at Hyde Park Corner did not get a satisfactory picture of the commencement of the trip. Mr. Argent Archer, however, was more successful and took a couple of interesting views. Mr. Archer is accompanying the vehicles, and will probably have a splendid set of photographs as a souvenir of this important trip. "

The Motor-Car Journal, Wednesday, April 25th, 1900

The Automobile Club's 1,000 Miles Trial

"The First Day's Run
as viewed from Mr. Lord's Car.

We were still at breakfast when the throbbing hum of Mr. Lord's seven horse-power Peugeot was heard breaking on the stillness of the early – the very early – morning, and she ran over Hammersmith Bridge to pick us up and take us bag and baggage to Hyde Park Corner. It was very fresh as we flew through Kensington and past the almost tenantless barracks at Knightsbridge (*the soldiers were all at the Boer War*) for the spot appointed for the gathering of the cars which were to travel far and wide e'er they should be back again. When we reached Grosvenor Place we found the entered and accompanying vehicles backed against the kerbstone on the park side of the road facing St. George's Hospital, giving that spot the appearance of an open-air market for autocars. It wanted five minutes to the appointed time when we arrived at the start, and a slow prowl up and down the line, which stretched quite three hundred yards down Grosvenor Place, revealed many personal friends, club members, and otherwise, to say nothing of new cars galore entered for the great round. The A section led, A1, the privately-owned vehicles, followed, and the quadricycles, two in number only, and several tricycles completed the line. In such a state of preparedness were the whole arrangements that little time was available for greetings. Before we had time to look round Mr. Lyon Sampson had dropped the flag, and the start for the first great automobile tour ever made in England was under way. The crowd at the corner was wonderfully numerous considering the time, and the descent of St. George's Terrace was made through a narrow passage formed by early risers who had come out to see the show. Clouds of cyclists accompanied the column well through the suburbs. The continuous wood pavement to the far side of Hounslow, even to the parting of the ways for Bristol and Southampton respectively, made the running out of town quite comfortable, and our obliging car-owner ran through the cars and the crowds to give us halt at that famous road forking so that the cars might pass before us for enumeration. A few minutes and they were heading past in close formation and quite out of the starting order. Big Daimlers came hard on the wheels of panting

Left:
Mr. O. E. Lord's 7 h.p. Peugeot which accompanied the 1000 miles tourists throughout. (Photo: *The Autocar*)

Autocar map slips into their neat cases with transparent celluloid covers

voiturettes, a throbbing quad separated a public service vehicle from a twelve horse-power Panhard. Eurekas, Decauvilles, and similar small fry went scuttling by to the number of seventy-five cars in all, four motor tricycles, and nine quadricycles and two Werner bicyclettes, a woman driving one. A mile farther on the cars were crowded up at the outward metropolitan control, and here the much appreciated Autocar map slips in their neat cases with transparent celluloid covers were distributed to the drivers of each vehicle. The cars were loosed one by one from the control, and presently we sped after them. The Bath Road right away to Maidenhead was never in better condition, and cars ran easily over such excellent surfaces. At the ninth milestone from London No. 16, the Gladiator voiturette, was halted, and a mile or so short of Maidenhead Bridge we saw the M.C.C. Triumph, as the water-jacketed Renault is named, standing deserted on the road skirting a wood. The demand for toll at Maidenhead Bridge, and the consequent holding up of the line of cars, caused great excitement amidst Skindle's staff and such hippos as were around, but that was nothing to the stir we all caused in the town of Maidenhead itself, where the inhabitants seemed to be in our honour. The streets were lined, and the greatest interest was evinced in the controlled cars as they rolled through. On the steep hill out of the town up to Maidenhead Thicket we noted the Simms motor wheel stopped, but she started shortly after in pursuit, and travelled bravely until undone by the treacherous tram rail grease of Bath. Farther on we passed Mr. Hewetson soothing his Benz motor from the rear, and later the Hon. John Scott-Montagu went by with his twelve horse-power Daimler,

continued on page 111

Right:
Breakfast at Calcot Park, home of Mr. Alfred Harmsworth.
(Photo: Argent Archer)

37

1,000-Mile Trial. 39

MONDAY, 23rd APRIL, 1900.

LONDON to BRISTOL ($118\frac{1}{2}$ miles).

[For particulars of the Route, London to Bristol, *see* Vol. II. of the "Cyclists' Touring Club British Road Book, Route 1." Price to subscribing members of the C.T.C., *7s. 6d.* To non-members of the C.T.C. *12s. 6d.* net. Office: 47, Victoria Street, Westminster. *See* also the "Bath Road Map with Contour," *1s.*, or "Contour Road Book." Gall & Inglis, 25, Paternoster Square, E.C.]

CONTROL.—LONDON TO HOUNSLOW. 11 MILES.

NO PASSING ALLOWED.

MEET AT GROSVENOR PLACE, opposite Hyde Park Corner, at 6.30 a.m. Draw up against East side of the road by the Palace Wall in order of numbers, in various sections, as follows:—

First.	Section I.	Classes A, B, C, D, and F.
Second.	Section I.	Class E.
Third.	Section II.	Class E.
Fourth.	Section II.	Classes A, B, C, and D.

For correct order, *see* pages 33, 34, 35.

STOP. — Here STOP.

RECORD SHEETS must be filled in here (before starting).

8 m. p. h. for $4\frac{1}{2}$ m. — **START FROM GROSVENOR PLACE,** at 7.0 a.m. punctually, on Starters dropping red flags. Keep in same order. Speed 8 m. p. h. Route *viâ* Knightsbridge, High Street, Kensington, Hammersmith to the Tramway Station on the right beyond Hammersmith.

10 m. p. h. for $6\frac{1}{2}$ m. — From here the speed may be 10 m. p. h., but no passing is permitted. Pass through Brentford and Hounslow, and at lamp-post at point where road forks at end of Hounslow, take R road. R

STOP. — About six telegraph poles beyond Hounslow Barracks Railway Station, at milestone on L marked *"11 FROM LONDON; 6 TO COLNBROOK,"* STOP, as this is the end of the control, and vehicles will be re-started at 8.10 a.m., at 30 seconds' interval.

RECORD SHEETS must be filled in here.

R. A. for 6 m. — On receiving signal to start, PROCEED Right Away, observing the following Restrictions:—

After the milestone, *"16 FROM LONDON, 1 TO COLNBROOK,"* beware of level crossing.

1,00

LONDON TO BRISTOL *(contin*

8 m. p. h. through Colnbrook. — *ONE MILE FURTHER,* on e beginning of the control for Co Colnbrook.

R. A. for 3 m. — At the "Golden Cross" Inn PROCEED R.A. to Slough.

8 m. p. h. through Slough. — At milestone on L, *"20 M* for Slough, slow down to 8 m.

R. A. for 5 m. — At the milestone, *"21 MILE* PROCEED R.A. to Maidenhead

STOP. — Stop at Toll Gate, just be Beginning of control for Maiden

RECORD SHEETS m

6 m. p. h. through Maidenhead. — PROCEED at 6 m. p. h. in the other end of control until covering the distance between the

PROCEED up the hill, and

STOP. — Stop at the fork at the top c for Maidenhead.

RECORD SHEETS m

R. A. for about 7 m. — 14 minutes after entering M Twyford (7 miles), taking, $6\frac{1}{4}$ m.

8 m. p. h. through Twyford. — $\frac{3}{8}$ of a mile beyond the mile *6 MILES TO READING,"* the beg

R. A. to Reading, 4 m. — On leaving the Bridge over to Reading (4 miles).

About 1 mile after leaving T

10 m. p. h. — Under the Railway Bridge junction of the tramways, where tw

STOP. — At the cross roads, where Reading control begins here.

RECORD SHEETS mu

Starting a motor in the year 1900, the ears were very important to guide the adjustment of the controls. Very few of the Drivers would have been prepared for the experience of having to start their car in a noisy environment with other engines running nearby. Once they had got started, to travel in a group was an almost unique experience bringing fresh problems that they had hardly contemplated. The camaraderie was offset by problems of dust and balking.

LONDON TO BRISTOL (*continued*).

8 m. p. h.	PROCEED through Reading at **8** m. p. h.; turn **R** into Southampton Street, cross the river, and 200 yards on, turn to the **L** and proceed to the "Horse and Jockey" Inn on **R** at foot of the hill, the end of the control for Reading.	**R** **L**
STOP.	Here STOP, and be prepared to proceed 11 minutes after passing red flag.	
✕	**RECORD SHEETS must be filled in here.**	
R. A. for 2½ m.	Then PROCEED to the Lodge Gate of Calcot Park on **R**.	**R**
STOP.	Here STOP.	
✕	**RECORD SHEETS must be filled in here.**	
8 m. p. h. in Calcot Park.	PROCEED through the Park to Calcot House, the residence of Mr. Alfred Harmsworth.	
STOP. Breakfast	STOP for Breakfast, as Mr. Harmsworth's guests.	
	Then PROCEED to the other Lodge.	
STOP.	Here STOP, and be prepared to start at the other Lodge half-an-hour after arrival.	
✕	**RECORD SHEETS must be filled in here.**	
R. A. for about 13 m.	Then PROCEED for about 13 miles, keeping **R** at the fork in Thatcham about 9 miles on; and proceed to the Church on **L**, the beginning of the control for Newbury.	**R**
8 m. p. h. through Newbury.	Here slow down to **8** m. p. h. through Newbury.	
R. A. for 8 m.	At the fork, the end of the control for Newbury, take the road on **L** and proceed R. A. for about 8 miles.	**L**

ok, at "White Hart" Inn, on **R**, the
down to **8** m. p. h. to pass through

the end of the control for Colnbrook,

NDON," the beginning of the control
rough Slough.

N," the end of the control for Slough,

ad Bridge. Toll of *2d.* per wheel.

ed in here.

Cars will not be allowed to pass out at
elapsed, the time to be occupied in
. p. h.

top take **L**-hand Road. **L**

e Maidenhead, the end of the control

in here.

l be ready to PROCEED R. A. to
to **L** at fork. **L**

rked *"33 MILES FROM LONDON;*
ntrol for Twyford, slow to **8** m. p. h.

he control for Twyford, proceed R. A.

nd road at fork. **L**

slow down to **10** m. p. h. At the
e the **L**. **L**

ad crosses the high road, STOP.

in here.

Breakfast at Calcot Park, home of Mr. Alfred Harmsworth. (Photo: Argent Archer)

raising a column of dust behind him. At Twyford the school children lined the road, waving little flags, their fresh young voices greeting car after car with shrill cheers. What will they not be able to recount to their children of the antique road vehicles they saw long ago passing so soberly through their quiet village on April 23rd, 1900?

Folks were turning out in numbers now all along the route, small crowds of people being massed at every cross road. The road through Reading had been nicely watered, and once again we called a halt of our car to watch the other cars tackle the stiff rise of Reading Town. The Wolseley voiturette, the De Dion, the M.C.C. Triumph, and one of the Eurekas came up bravely; the new Lanchester waltzed up on her top speed, making nothing of the rise, as did also the big cars. The sight of Mr. Alfred Harmsworth's park gates were welcome indeed, and after making our bow to the most hospitable owner of that charming house and grounds, all the members of the party were more than willing to do justice to the recherché repast so generously provided by the one newspaper proprietor in England who has done all in his power to further the interests of automobilism. Giving the Peugeot a two-gallon drink of the spirit it most affects, and feeling like new men after our own repast, we were soon again heading westward, and ran through Theale and more cheering school children en route for Marlborough. Beyond Thatcham police officiousness in the shape of timing and booking began. Policemen were noticed at every milestone sitting in ditches, hiding behind hedges, timing and noting after the manner of police, and asking for the numbers of the cars as they passed. What will be the result of this objectionable and unnecessary behaviour remains to be seen. The criminal classes, if they only knew of this temporary absence of the police from their legitimate duty, would be making the most of this opportunity. We took the accurate timing of three cars over three of these miles, which are unreservedly at the service of the chief constable of Berkshire.

Mr. Cordingley's new car shed one of its Cannstatt vulcanised tyres shortly after he left Theale, and practically put that vehicle out of the running. The drop into Marlborough off the downs was most enjoyable, and that quiet and stately Wiltshire town was aroused from its chronic state of lethargy by the presence in its wide street of so many self-propelled vehicles. After Mr. Harmsworth's sumptuous

(Photo: Argent Archer)

breakfast, lunch was hardly necessary, and many of the cars halted only for a short time before leaving for Bath. The farthest westward we went the more numerous became the little knots of people gathered along the road, the whole of the inhabitants of Calne and Chippenham appearing to have turned out to see the cars pass through. Rain fell heavily just as Bath was reached, and made the running through that ancient city particularly difficult over the tramlines. Our Peugeot 'set to partners' in one place, turning squarely across the road, and going crab fashion for some distance to the wild astonishment of the onlookers unlearned in the manners of autocars when travelling over mud. Little incident for remark occurred on the road to Bristol, save that the Peugeot took the hill at Keynsham in grand style, and completed her little trip of 118½ miles as fit as when she left London.

Bicycling News, reporting on the first stage of the run from London to the lunch stop at Calcot Park, a few miles west of Reading, observed that Hon C.S. Rolls had positively adhered to his determination not to race, for he was a long way behind the leaders, notwithstanding the fact that his car could probably have easily beaten the crowd, and praised him for enduring the dust clouds raised by other competitors. But beyond Calcot it was another story, though the same paper had to admit that Rolls was 'the safest, though speediest scorcher of them all'. Between Marlborough and Bristol quite a race developed between Rolls' Panhard and Kennard's Napier driven by S. F. Edge – it was noted that neither crew stopped for tea on this stretch. ”

Breakfast at Calcot Park.
(Photo: Argent Archer)

The Autocar, Saturday, April 28th, 1900

“ Going through with the Baggage Train

Monster gatherings at unearthly early hours, where men have to come from all the quarters of London, are not, as a rule, remarkable for punctuality, so we thought we had ample time to spare when we got to Hyde Park Corner at five minutes to the appointed hour, but we were mistaken. The ballot for seats had given us a place on a New Orleans voiturette, and we had been congratulating ourselves on the excellent opportunity this would give us for a real test ride on this new and very interesting little car. But it was not to be. Only one New Orleans was there: the other, upon which, with Mr. Van Toll, we should have ridden, had had a dispute with a brewer's dray on the way down, with a damaged wheel as the result of the contretemps, and was for the time being non est. Whether appalled at the prospect of nearly fifteen stone as a make weight or not, we do not know, but Mr. Astill, who was in charge of the remaining one, found his spare seat 'engaged,' and as the order to start came within a few minutes, there was no time to seek a seat on another competing car, so that it looked very like being left altogether for a moment, when Van Toll helped us out of the difficulty by suggesting our going through with the baggage train, and giving us a seat on one of the Thames Valley Motor Co.'s Daimler covered vans, with which he was conveying sundry baggage, and acting as convoy to the voiturette. Needless to say, we accepted, and within a minute were off in trail of the speed cars, our ponderous machine with iron tyres on the drivers knocking out very close on a steady fourteen where the road was good, and, as we were unhampered by such things as checks and controls, 'getting a bit' every now and then, as the ardour of the sprinters was checked by the flag wavers. At the Hounslow control we found nearly all the larger cars in one big jam, waiting the permit to pass, as they had evidently exceeded somewhat the eight mile control pace, and were paying the penalty therefor. Few of the voiturettes were to be seen. They had evidently gone ahead, and, as there was nothing to prevent us, we wormed our way through the crowd of waiting cars and went ahead too. Soon there was a whirr and a whizz, and Dr. Lehwess – also 'out of control' – flew by on the Vallée 'shoe' in a cloud of dust, followed shortly after by Mr. Hargreaves on his new twelve horse-power Daimler, the first of the controlled cars to be 'let out.' A little later Jules Dubois, solus on a Decauville, was met smothered in dust, with three of the Motor Car Co.'s Victoria combinations following. They had overshot the Hounslow control, and were running back to get checked. Shortly after the twenty-third milestone, a Renault car (No. 31) was passed tenantless by the side of the road, and at Maidenhead, as elsewhere along the route, the people were out in crowds to see the cars. All cars were stopped on crossing the bridge, and, so far as our baggage wagon was concerned at any rate, mulcted in a charge of eightpence as bridge tolls, and some three miles beyond the town, at the commencement of a level straightaway piece of broad, almost deserted, highway, two palpably plainclothes policemen were seen standing, one on each side of the road, at a milestone, timing and checking the cars as they went by. So far as our slow coach was concerned, as we were only just topping twelve, a drop of the accelerator a couple of notches served to put us on the safe side. The corresponding checkers were located a mile and a half along the road, partly concealed in a knot of bystanders at a wayside inn.

Some thousands of people were out at Reading to see the cars, the streets being lined at both the controls and at the principal turning points within the town. Here the two Renault cars which had passed us just before

(Photo: courtesy N.M.M. Beaulieu E.B.)

stopped for petrol, and we passed S. F. Edge with the new Napier on the hill out of town, some trouble with a valve giving him a fit of the slows for the time being. The party had been timed to reach Calcot Park at 10.30, where Mr. Alfred Harmsworth, himself a member of the club, had invited all participants to the hospitality of breakfast, and it was exactly that hour to the minute as our baggage wagon entered the park gates, and ran on reduced speed through the fine old drive to the house. Here we found that the New Orleans voiturette had arrived first; indeed, it was just running out to proceed on the next stage of the journey as we ran in. The spacious court at the back of the house was crowded with cars, Mr. Harmsworth's own twelve horsepower Panhard and Columbia electric vehicles, looking very spick and span in their cleanness beside the dusty equipages of the visitors, being run out of their coachhouses for inspection. In the centre of all was a huge marquee, and here the entire party were right royally entertained to what was virtually a champagne luncheon, for which the forty miles drive through a decidedly cold atmosphere in the earlier hours of the morning had well prepared the appetites. Mr. Harmsworth himself did the honours of the day, and under the warm rays of a rapidly brightening sun the scene was a gay and interesting one. Cars continued to arrive and depart, and the Van Tollian pennant being shifted to another of his company's cars, an M.M.C. waggonette with a higher speeding, we started shortly before noon with the body completely packed with baggage and three on board. The weather was now gloriously warm and fine, and bowling over fine but dusty roads, amidst an interesting and ever-changing landscape, was exhilarating work, more especially as our new baggage waggon was rolling off her miles at a good eighteen, and making excellent running. A couple of miles out Mr. Cordingley was met, returning slowly on his M.C.C. Panhard, one of the German vulcanised tyres having come bodily off, and being, of course, unrepairable. From now on, so long as the good roads lasted, policemen were noticed at almost every milestone, checking the times and numbers of the cars as they came by. In one place a little man on an old-fashioned solid tyred tricycle – probably a local magistrate – was ostentatiously helping the constable, and at another we witnessed a glorious specimen of police time-

Above:
Mr. A. C. Harmsworth on his 12 h.p. Panhard. (Photo: *The Autocar*)

Richard Car with the Mayor of Reading (Photo: Argent Archer)

keeping, for we saw the man, when we were yet quite eighty yards from him, look at his watch, put it in his pocket, and then with notebook in hand he stepped forward as we drove by and coolly asked us for our number. Then, as we looked back, we saw him entering carefully the time and number which – as he seemed so anxious for one – we obligingly gave him. In every case the police had chosen those stretches of road where the autocarists would be most likely to travel fast – straight, broad, smooth highways, either level or downhill, and almost entirely destitute of traffic, and if summonses are issued, as it seems possible they may be in numbers, it will but prove the existence of an amount of crass prejudice and blind opposition to progress which we could not have believed to have existed in a civilised country, for we travelled over the whole route and saw no signs of furious or inconsiderate driving, and, at any rate over the routes chosen for the clocking operations,

Lanchester Gold Medal Phaeton driven by Archie Millership

speed travelling could not have caused the slightest danger or inconvenience to anyone. Once out of Berkshire, however, we found the Hants County police courtesy itself. They were freely stationed at cross roads to protect impinging lines of traffic, and here, as elsewhere, from end to end of the journey, the public were gathered at every point of vantage. At most of the cross and junction roads carriages were standing. In many cases vehicles were drawn up in fields, and cyclists and people generally were camping out on the roadside, some with chairs and camp stools and all the paraphernalia of a picnic, evidently out to make a day of it, and see all there was to be seen. We now began to get into hillier country, and the way the baggage wagon showed up some of the higher geared 'speed' cars on the rises was somewhat gratifying. Just through the entrance gate to Savernake Forest we found the two Lanchester cars, the larger one evidently in difficulties, and this proved to be the case, for subsequent enquiries elicited the fact that the casting of a valve gear bracket had broken, with the result that Messrs. Lanchester and Pugh, after pushing her the two and a half miles into Hungerford, left her there, and came on by train. After a stiff climb through the beauties of the forest, an immense expanse of country stretched away to the view beneath, with the town of Marlborough snugly nestling below, and down the long and steep incline, with motor out of gear, we swept at a soul-inspiring speed, and on into the market place at the foot, where the cars were grouped around the different hostelries, whilst their occupants enjoyed a well-earned lunch. Here a privately owned Locomobile steamer was showing off its paces for the delectation of the interested. When we got going again, our motor proved refractory, lamps going out, the pressure falling, and, after struggling up several rises, we stopped to investigate, to find that the dash down Marlborough Hill had sprung a weak joint in the copper back pressure pipe. Having discovered the cause, we repaired damages with a rubber strapping, and this held well until we had run down from the mound of Silbury, when the tube broke off short at the neck, causing us to lose pressure altogether. Enquiries for the whereabouts of solder and a soldering iron anywhere in the neighbourhood having failed we adopted the expedient of using a piece of rubber tubing, which we forced into the nut at one end, in place of the broken nozzle, and tied with a 2in strapping to the main pipe at the other, and this made a tight joint, with which we ran the remaining forty miles or thereabouts with no more trouble than a jolting out of one of the burners several times when running down slopes. Just beyond Chippenham a twelve horse-power Daimler was passed, taking in a fresh water supply, and then, after an exhilarating dash down the long slopes of the noted Box Hill, through a mizzling rain, we ran through the little village of Box, and at the foot of the descent out of that town found Dr. Lehwess with a tyre of the 'shoe' strewing the ground, the rubber cover having left the canvas, and finding it eventually beyond repair he completed the journey on the canvas. Although rain threatened, but little fell, though it was soon evident we had missed the brunt of the storm, for the roads right into and through Bath were soaked, and the greasy oolite surface made driving a matter of some anxiety, especially through the tortuous hilly and sett paved streets of the ancient city. Once clear of this place, however, we encountered dry roads again, though the recent watering of the tram rails in Bristol made safe driving a matter of delicacy and skill. At Bristol the local committee had a regular surprise packet for the cars in the way of a hill, for they took them to the exhibition building – the Drill Hall – by way of Park Street, one of the stiffest grades of the whole route. Here – at the top – as elsewhere through the city, the citizens were assembled in force, with the exception of

(Photo: P.H.H.)

some of the cycles, all successfully mounted the grade. We got in about 6.30, finding a couple of score of cars already there, the earliest arrivals including the Hon. C.S. Rolls, S.F. Edge, Jules Dubois, J.A. Holder, the Hon. Scott Montagu, and Mr. Astill, and the full list of testing cars housed by seven p.m., twelve hours from the start, being as follows: A17, A10, 34, A22, 3, A11, 26, 15, 4, 43, 27, 37, 16, 47, A30, A3, 44, A21, 40, A26, A24, 35, A16, 19, 46, A7, A31, 41, A2, A28, 32, 22, 22, 2, 14, 1, 9, 51, 12, 5, and 20, the latter – Simms motor wheel – turning up in a most dilapidated condition, having turned two complete

Left:
The Simms Motor Wheel $2\frac{3}{4}$ h.p.

somersaults, through incautious driving on the Bristol tramlines, bending both front axles, and knocking things about generally, though the driver came out clear each time and was unhurt. As we wended our way back to the hotel, Nos. 12, 8, 36, A27, and A29 were met fighting their way up the Park Street rise, and another visit to the hall at nine o'clock found further arrivals in the shape of A12, 52, 45, and A25. No. 23, the Brown-Whitney steam car, put in an appearance at 9.40, having been delayed a couple of hours at the start through a link of the chain breaking and going through the water tank and a loose joint at Hungerford, necessitating an hour's stop for repairs. About 10.30 Mr. Straker put in an appearance with No. 38, the Daimler char-á-banc, having had trouble with a broken induction valve, and a general choking up of his engine with dust. The two Marshall cars fetched home about 11.30, one having waited on the other, whose pump had broken up, Mr. Mann eventually getting in by the expedient of stopping up the pipe with rags, and filling up with fresh water every five miles, whilst the second New Orleans, which had repaired damages incurred before the start, ran in shortly after midnight. In all, including several non-competing cars, some seventy-six vehicles made the journey through. ”

The Autocar, Saturday, April 28th, 1900

At the Start

Jottings on the First Day's Run

Sir David Salomons, on his Peugeot car, was one of the interested spectators at the start at Hyde Park Corner on Monday last.

— o§o —

The Vallée shoe-shaped racing car, with Dr. Lehwess and Mr. Weigel aboard, attracted much attention at the start.

— o§o —

The four-cylindered Déchamps car which was entered was unable to complete, as M. Déchamps in driving it from Brussels to Antwerp on Thursday last on the way to London, unfortunately met with a serious accident which rendered him and the car *hors de combat.*

The Autocar, Saturday, April, 28th, 1990

En Route

“

Reading

Evidently automobilists cared more for breakfast than for biscuits, judging by the slight stop which was made. Doubtless the proximity of Calcot House, where Mr. Alfred Harmsworth had promised hospitality, was the cause.* Still they made a brave show, and although unfortunately one car seemed to be in trouble, the general impression made on the townspeople was distinctly good.

* Our correspondent is mistaken. The official programme only allowed a stop at Reading for the filling in of record sheets. – Ed. M.C.J.

Marlborough

Marlborough was *en fete* in honour of the automobilists, and the market place was thronged with spectators, inquisitive crowds inspecting the vehicles while their passengers were taking lunch. Particularly curious were the cyclists, many of whom had come from distant Wiltshire towns and villages to see the motor-cars. A very pleasing sight was a number of children, who waved Union Jacks with juvenile energy, whether in honour of St. George's Day or the motor-cars none seemed to know. Among the news brought by the first half-dozen cars was a report as to a defective casting in one of the cars having caused it to give out just before entering the town.

The Motor Car Journal, Friday, April 27th, 1900

Bath

The first arrival at Bath was the 'Orient Express,' and a dozen other cars turned up within the next half-hour. A splendid instance of how completely the cars can be controlled was given by one of the early arrivals, a lady being knocked down by a car, but getting up uninjured – in fact, the car had stopped before the lady reached the ground. In the amateur section, Mr. Ernest Pitman was among the first arrivals. Most of the tricycles came into the city in good style, although one rider coming up the steep above Cleveland Bridge had to make a second attempt, pedalling all the time, before he surmounted it. During the afternoon about half the vehicles passed through Bath. Somehow or other the idea was abroad in the city that the demonstration would take the form of a procession, and apparently some disappointment was felt as the cars came along in twos and threes instead of in regular review order.

Bristol

The most enthusiastic motorist ought to be satisfied with the reception accorded the vehicles in this ancient city. Hundreds of people crowded into the main thoroughfares leading the way to the Drill Hall. The Hon. C. S. Rolls and Mr. E. Kennard were the first arrivals at the Drill Hall, the third car to put in an appearance being a Décauville voiturette. Mr. Herbert Ashby on his 'Empress' motor-tricycle, Mr. J. A. Holder on his 12 h.p. Daimler, and the Hon. J. Scott Montagu were in the next batch of arrivals, and between 6 and 7 p.m. twenty-six cars had taken their positions in the hall, all bearing evidence of the dusty roads that had been encountered. The finish of the run of 118 miles was as stiff as anything encountered in the journey. Park Street having a steep gradient, but all the cars seemed to take it very well. According to the official records, twenty-four of the entries in the manufacturers and agents' section completed the entire journey at a speed up to the legal limit of twelve miles an hour. One, a 6 h.p. Daimler, made an average of eleven and a-half miles an hour, and two – the I.S.S. 5½ h.p. car, and Roots and Venables' 2⅞ h.p. car – at an average of eleven miles an hour. Shortly before ten o'clock the Brown-Whitney car arrived, having made the journey at an average speed of rather more than nine miles an hour. Among those who joined the party at Bristol was Dr. Stewart Irwin, of Fockington (Glos.), who came on his M.M.C. Panhard dogcart – a splendid vehicle, which recently climbed a hill of 1 in 6, about a mile long, with four passengers aboard. The following is the official list of vehicles completing the journey at a speed up to the legal limit:

- Nos. 1 and 2, Benz 'Ideals.'
- No. 4, 'Ariel' tricycle, with Whippet detachable trailer.
- No. 5, 'Locomobile' steam carriage.
- No. 8, Motor Manufacturing Company's 6 h.p. phaeton.
- No. 12, Motor Manufacturing Company's tricycle.
- Nos. 14 and 15, De Dion voiturettes.
- No. 16, Motor Power Company's 'Gladiator' voiturette.
- No. 19, Automobile Association's 'Orient Express.'

Crowds in the Drill Hall at Bristol
(Photo: Argent Archer)

1,000-Mile Trial. 51

BRISTOL,
TUESDAY, APRIL 24th, 1900.

A ONE-DAY

EXHIBITION

OF THE

MOTOR VEHICLES

TAKING PART IN THE

1,000-Mile Trial, organized by the Automobile Club of Great Britain and Ireland,

WILL BE HELD UNDER THE PATRONAGE OF

THE LORD MAYOR OF BRISTOL,

IN THE

DRILL HALL,

By kind permission of the Officer commanding the Volunteers.

ADMISSION—

On MONDAY EVENING, APRIL 23rd, to witness the arrival of the Vehicles, from 6.30 till 11 p.m. ... ... TWO SHILLINGS.

On TUESDAY, APRIL 24th—

From 12 o'clock noon to 6 p.m. ... ... ONE SHILLING.

From 6 p.m. until 10 p.m. ... ... SIXPENCE.

THE PROFITS WILL BE DEVOTED TO THE TRANSVAAL WAR FUND.

Vice Patrons:

Rt. Hon. Earl of Ducie.
Rt. Hon. Sir Michael Hicks-Beach, Bart., M.P.
His Honour Judge Austin.

The High Sheriff of the County.
Sir Chas. Wills, Bart.
J. D. Howell, Esq., J.P.

Committee for Local Arrangements:

Dr. Stewart Irwin.
Mr. C. H. Tucker.
" G. L. Wood.
" C. Kenyon Townsend.
" Sydney G. Turner.
" T. Holmes.

Mr. J. H. Dunn.
" R. H. Tucker.
" A. E. G. Way.
" R. Howard.
" C. D. Dowson.
" C. T. Coulsting.

Mr. C. M. Trotman.
" M. Ridler.
" C. R. Edbrooke.
" R. W. Wickham
" H. I. Spear.
" Dr. D. E. Bernard.

Hon. Sec, Mr. W. M. Appleton, Tyn-y-Coed, Hill Road, Weston-super-Mare.

D 2

No. 20, Motor Carriage Supply Company's 'Simms' Motor Wheel.
No. 22, Lanchester Engine Company's 8 h.p. carriage.
No. 26, Friswell's 8 h.p. Peugeot.
No. 27, Burford Van Toll's 3½ h.p. 'New Orleans' car.
Nos. 31 and 32, Motor-Car Company's 3½ h.p. 'Triumphs.'
No. 34, Motor-Car Company's 3½ h.p. Décauville.
Nos. 35 and 36, The Daimler Company's 6 h.p. cars.
No. 37, The Daimler Company's 6 h.p. Parisian car.
No. 40, Wolseley Company's 3 h.p. voiturette.
No. 43, London Motor Van and Wagon Company's 5½ h.p. phaeton.
No. 44, International Company's 3 h.p. Victoria.
Nos. 46 and 47, Automobile Manufacturing Company's 7 h.p. 'Richard.'
No. 51, Star Motor Company's 3½ h.p. voiturette.

Arrival of cars at Bristol Drill Hall (Photo: Argent Archer)

Privately owned vehicles did well, eleven obtaining certificates as completing the journey up to the legal limit of twelve miles an hour, two for eleven and a-half miles, one for eleven miles, and one for ten miles an hour, the latter being Mr. Mark Mayhew's 7 h.p. Peugeot, Mr. H. Edmunds' 6 h.p. Daimler, and Mrs Bazalgette's 3 h.p. Benz 'Ideal' respectively. The eleven most successful vehicles were:

No. A3, Mr. T. B. Browne's 6 h.p. Panhard.
No. A7, Mr. Alfred Harmsworth's 6 h.p. Parisian Daimler.
No. A10, Mr. Edward Kennard's 8 h.p. Napier.
No. A17, the Hon. C. S. Rolls' 12 h.p. Panhard.
No. A20, Mr. Herbert Ashby's 2¾ h.p. 'Empress' tricycle.
No. A21, Mr. Ernest Pitman's 6 h.p. Daimler.
No. A22, Mr. J. Holder's 12 h.p. Daimler.
No. A24, Mr. Robert Phillips's 4 h.p. Mors.
No. A26, Mr. C.K. Gregson's 6 h.p. Parisian Daimler.
No. A28, Mr. E. M. Iliffe's 2¼ h.p. Enfield quadricycle.
No. A30, Mr. J. D. Siddeley's 6-h.p. Parisian Daimler.
No. A31, Mr. Wm. Exe's 6 h.p. Parisian Daimler.

Although one of Mr. Mark Mayhew's cars came in on Monday, that gentleman did not arrive on his Panhard till Tuesday evening.

On Wednesday morning the departure of the cars attracted much attention, and the local committee certainly deserve credit. That Bristol's welcome was appreciated may be gleaned from the telegram sent to the Lord Mayor from Cheltenham on Tuesday, as follows:

'Cheltenham, 1.57 p.m.

'Automobile Club begs to thank Bristol for courtesy during recent visit.' ”

The Motor Car Journal, Friday, April 27th, 1900

Mr. Mark Mayhew

Cars on exhibition at Bristol. (Photo: Argent Archer)

“ On the Long Pilgrimage

by Observer

BRISTOL, MONDAY

After a busy day one hardly feels in the humour for sitting down and detailing the incidents that have made St George’s Day, 1900, memorable in the annals of automobilism. There has been plenty to interest those who have had the good fortune to be members of the pilgrimage, but to give a connected story of what Mr. Mark Mayhew calls a ‘drive’ would be well-nigh impossible. The cars have passed and repassed all day; reminding us very much of the fable of the hare and the tortoise, the occupants of the swiftly travelling cars smiling on those whose vehicles were of slower progress as they went ahead. But these tortoises have often been able to laugh in return as they have steadily pursued their way, ultimately finding the hare-like cars stationary by the roadside, their passengers attempting to play the part of the philosopher while waiting for the repair of a punctured tyre – or something equally annoying. One driver was seen calmly smoking his cigar while the axle of his car cooled after firing.

If I were asked for the dominant feature of the ride from London to here I should say, ‘Dust.’ It was everywhere, and we got more like millers as the day was gone through, until rain came after passing through Bath.

Leaving Hounslow we quickly came upon a ‘Star’ car by the wayside, and soon after passed a

Standing near Mrs Bazalgette’s Benz (left) Mrs Thorburn aged 76 (born c. 1824) and Miss Perry aged 86 (born c. 1814). One wonders what these ladies thought of the horseless carriages. (Photo: Argent Archer)

second vehicle. Between the thirteenth and fourteenth milestone the 'Endurance' car was left behind and before another two miles had been covered saw two 'Eurekas' and a 'Decauville' returning to town. Mr. A. J. Wilson then went ahead on his motor-tricycle, and I had the road practically to myself – save, of course, for the occupants of my car – until a level crossing was reached, where owing to the gates being shut, eight other vehicles were grouped. Starting very well together a veritable cloud of dust was caused – such a cloud as could be seen, felt, and chewed. It tickled one's eyes, settled on the tongue, and clung with glue-like tenaciousness to one's garments. Even the most highly polished leather suits received a whitened and chastened gloss, while fur coats and jackets became heavy with dust and sand. But that is one of the delights and novelties of motoring on a fine day on a good hard road. And so on till Colnbrook was reached, when the merry group broke up and each car became concerned only with its individual performances.

(Photo: Argent Archer)

So far the appearance of the roads had been quite as interesting to the travellers by motor-car as mere sightseers on foot. The whole countryside seemed to have turned out, and men, women, and children cheered the vehicles as they sped by. Evidently public interest had been fully aroused, and as much attention was given to the costumes as the cars. Before entering Slough two more cars were descried resting by the way, and the Twin Daimler of Mr. J.A. Hargreaves, driven by Mr. Grimshaw, was passed. As we neared the town several cars came into view, and just beyond Slough our car came up with the Daimler char-á-banc, having passed a De Dion voiturette and a Benz car while the Twin Daimler had gone ahead. Arrived at the toll-gate, Maidenhead, about a dozen cars were waiting to pass through, and Mr. C. Johnson came up driving a Parisian Daimler. In passing through this pleasant riverside town the wisdom of limiting speed was seen, as the cattle which happened to be about seemed rather restless at the approach of our cars. Shortly after leaving Maidenhead Mr. Jarrott went to the front, and Mrs Bazalgette, the only lady entrant came along. The Wolseley car, stationary in the road with a chain off, was an object of much solicitude. Going ahead of the Twin Daimler we passed Mr. Herbert Ashby on his Empress motor-tricycle on the thirtieth milestone, and then the Twin repassed us, and was seen no more till we got to Bristol in the evening. In the town of Reading two of the M.C.C. Triumphs were seen, but breakfast was ahead, and few stayed to inquire how they were getting on. From Reading the trip to Calcot Park was short and enjoyable, and there Mr. Alfred Harmsworth royally entertained his fellow automobilists. Leaving Mr. Harmsworth, the cars had a straight run to Newbury, from whence a clear eight miles spin took us to Hungerford, where the hilly roads became noticeable, the roads up to that point having been fairly level. About eight miles from Reading the new vulcanised flat rim of the driving wheel of Mr. C. Cordingley's new car split, with the result that he had to return to Reading on the first speed. The tyre being vulcanised on to the rim it was, of course, impossible to repair it on the road, and he had to return, ultimately getting to Bristol by train. Offers of assistance were made – but all, unfortunately, were unavailing.

By way of Beckhampton, Calne, Chippenham, and Bath we proceeded to Bristol, where cheering crowds welcomed the dusty motorists. ”

(Photo: Argent Archer)

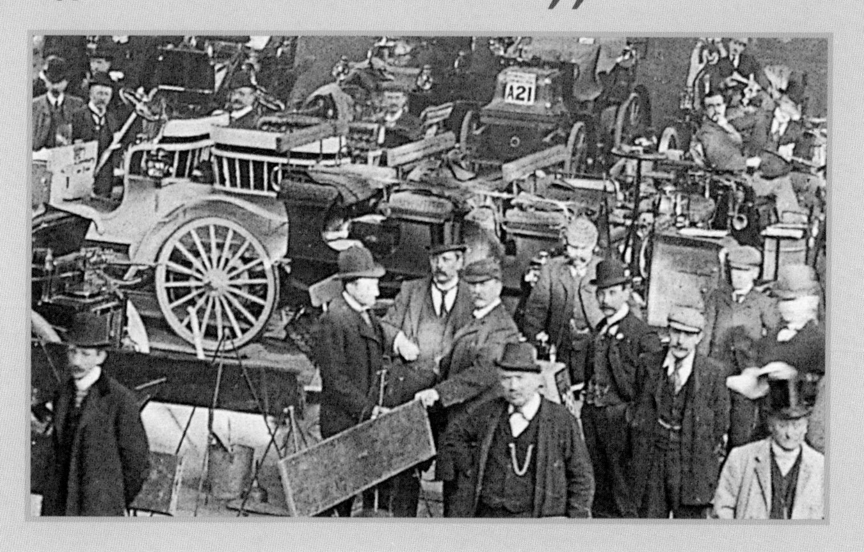

The Motor-Car Journal, Friday, April 27th, 1900

The Thousand Mile Trial participant had more than the whims of his motor car to deal with. The population and the police were very suspicious of the horseless carriages ...

“ Police Precautions

Very solicitous with regard to the progress of the vehicles were the police authorities whose interest in automobilism has been demonstrated in many ways. On the first occasion Toby, M.P., of Punch, mounted a motor-car he was delighted at the experience – the trees leaped by, the bushes were continuous along the hedges, and the air seemed fresh and free. His only regret was inability to hold converse with a figure he assumed to be that of a policeman – but who had disappeared ere he could dismount.

Not so on the present trip. With the deliberate speed at which the cars have progressed there has been every chance of clear discernment of the figures by the roadside; and among those figures policemen have been numerous. In fact, many of the law-abiding automobilists have never seen so many policemen in the course of a single day before. They have been ubiquitous, and although some have resorted to the Boer tactics of seeking cover of hedges from which to take observations, many, unlike the Boers, have come out into the open. One practical man, having regard to the exactitude of the law and his own personal comfort, had provided a chair and table with books and stationery, upon which were recorded the times of the cars as told by his Waterbury. It was an interesting sight, and although some feel honoured at this official recognition of automobilism, others deplored the kindly-intentioned care of the Automobile Club that had numbered the vehicles fore and aft. There was no dodging the eye of the law. One driver sought to escape the numbering process by rushing into the cloud of dust ostentatiously created by the preceding vehicle, but to no purpose. He went on: but the plate at the rear of the car gave his number, and with the help of the official catalogue identity will be disclosed, thanks to the amplitude with which every detail – even such little matters as names and addresses – has been attended to by Mr. Johnson and his staff.

There were other policemen less official in their equipment, but still taking times and numbers, and two or three laid on sloping banks with watches hanging from lower branches of shady trees, and notebooks in hand.

We do not know whether the police took snapshots, although such a procedure would have been extremely useful as evidence. ”

The Motor-Car Journal, Friday, April 27th, 1900

Also it seemed it was not all plain sailing for the Secretary, Mr. Claude Johnson concerning controlling the participants.

“ A Competitors’ Committee

On Tuesday evening an emergency meeting was called by Mr. C. Johnson, at the Drill Hall, Bristol, to consider the question of the co-operation of competitors with the members of the Club Committee taking part in the tour, and to advise the officials as to the exercise of the duties entrusted to them under the Club rules. Mr. E. Edmunds was voted to the chair, and it was decided that the committee should consist of three representatives of the amateurs and five representatives of the makers. The election resulted in the appointment of Messrs. Browne, Holder, and Gregson on behalf of the former section, and Messrs. A. Burgess, Critchley, Friswell, Mann, and Van Toll on behalf of the latter class.

The Exhibition

Bristol

To the first of the provincial exhibitions held in connection with the Trial the Lord Mayor of Bristol gave his patronage, and the officer commanding the Volunteers granted the use of the Drill Hall. Mr. W. M. Appleton was the local hon. secretary, and, favoured with fine weather, the exhibition proved a great attraction. Both on Monday evening and all day on Tuesday there was a capital attendance, and although some of the exhibitors would have liked to have received the certificates of their performance earlier than was the case, excellent arrangements were made. The scene about the hall on Tuesday morning was one of briskness and bustle, many of the cars being taken from the hall to be cleaned after the dust and showers of the latter stages of the first day’s journey. In the evening the band of the 1st V.B. (City of Bristol) Gloucestershire Regiment discoursed an excellent musical programme, and general praise was bestowed on the courtesy and willingness of those in charge of the cars to explain their working and their merits to visitors. Mr. Howard, a member of the Bristol local committee, had his motor phaeton on view, and as this has just done admirable work on Dartmoor, general interest was manifested in the vehicle. ”

The Motor-Car Journal, Friday, April 27th, 1900

Exhibition Bristol

Returning to the Drill Hall in Bristol up the steep ascent of Park Street, after cleaning on Tuesday, Mr. Stocks drove his quad up that hill without any assistance from the pedals, averaging quite ten miles an hour on the run up.

— o§o —

The exhibition of the trial cars at Bristol on Tuesday night was crammed to suffocation and from three to four thousand people must have passed the turnstile during the day. The Transvaal War Fund should therefore benefit considerably. Expenses had been cleared by 5 p.m.

Claude Johnson's work was starting to be appreciated

Notes on Organisation

The Official Programme

The programme provided for the entrants is a manual requiring much study and should train the mind in persevering endeavour, being a volume of more than two hundred quarto pages. On Mr. C. Johnson, the secretary of the Club, its compilation has added a weight of responsibility, and it must be gratifying to the committee and all concerned to see how singularly free from errors is the published work. The organising genius of Mr. C. Johnson is well-known, but on the present occasion he has eclipsed his former records. Every detail has been considered, and there should be no hitch on the journey; the only way in which the arrangements can be upset will be owing to the zeal of members in arriving much earlier than the appointed time arranged at the various stopping places.

Convenience of Controls

On opening the programme of the Trial the official list of controls appeared very formidable, but in active operation they have proved simplicity itself, causing practically no inconvenience. In fact, they have been distinct advantages, enabling the entrants to foregather every few miles and pass the time of day with each other, or indulge in good-humoured chaff at each other's personal appearance, or retail – with full play of the imagination very often – incidents on the way. Some of the drivers waited with some impatience the fall of the flags, wielded so well by those responsible for the controls, but all seemed willing to recognise the necessity of discipline. At Bath the impetuosity of one young gentleman driving a car was curbed for the rest of the tour by a useful lesson in 'making haste slowly.' He thought he would dispense with the fifteen minutes' allowance for tea, but on proceeding forward his control card convicted him, and he had to wait twenty-five minutes before receiving official permission to re-start – to say nothing of the mortification of seeing half a dozen other cars go on ahead.

For the exhibitions, certificates showing performance were prepared – from checkpoint data, etc.

Certificates

The value of the exhibitions to the manufacturing firms entered in the Trial depends largely on being able to show a good record to the people who visit the places of display early in the day – hence the necessity for the prompt and early issue of certificates to be affixed to the cars. Those responsible have very exacting duties, and it is hoped that all competitors will help the officials in every possible way so that the certificates can be placed on the cars early on the morning of each day exhibition.

Local Committees

A word of praise must be given to the local committees for the excellence of their arrangements in connection with the exhibition, controls, etc. On one or two occasions competitors and controllers have not always turned up at the identical moment, and while in some places the latter have waited for the former, at others the competitors have exceeded the controllers in punctuality. Still, everything seems to be working very smoothly, and when votes of thanks come to be accorded on the return to town, the local committees will well deserve any that are given to them. ”

The Motor-Car Journal, Friday, April 27th, 1900

Diary Notes, April 23rd, 1900

Mr. Cordingley's Car

About eight miles from Reading the failure of the tyres on the driving-wheels of Mr. C. Cordingley's car led to his return to Reading. Things had been going well when suddenly a loud noise and 'bump, bump' they went. The brakes were put on and it was discovered that one of the vulcanised flat rubber tyres had come straight away from the rim. At Reading telegrams and messengers were dispatched for a complete set of new wheels, Mr. Cordingley having had quite enough of those upon which he had relied. They were very cool, had not run three hundred miles and yet were in rags, pieces two inches in diameter having been stripped off. Leaving his car at some stables, the owner took train for Bristol, where he found thirty-six cars had arrived. A complete set of new wheels arrived on Tuesday, and these having been fitted, the car was driven to Bristol and the journey to Birmingham completed on Wednesday in good style.

A Daimler Carries the Standard

One of the 6 h.p. Daimler phaetons was driven by Mr. Percy Richardson, who had with him the Lord Justice Clerk for Scotland, and Colonel Magrath, an engineer, and a correspondent of the Standard. Everything went well, and the descent from Savernake Forest (where Mr. Pedley had his memorable drive through the snow) into Marlborough was accomplished with ease. At Marlborough our photographer took the snapshot given elsewhere – in which the gallant Colonel appears 'on guard.' The steep ascents after leaving Chippenham were all negotiated with confidence and the only incident occurred at the summit of Rowden Hill. There something connected with the water circulation went wrong, necessitating a stoppage of about an hour. Bristol was, however, reached at 7.10 p.m., only ten minutes after the appointed time.

Wayward No. 9

Pressmen will come to the conclusion that there is something uncanny about the Motor Manufacturing Company's 6 h.p. phaeton 'No. 9' in the official list. On that the Daily Chronicle representative had intended to journey as far as Carlisle, and Mr. J. H. Gretton, the chairman of the company, was also to be a passenger. Both these gentlemen were early at Grosvenor Place, but no No.9 could they see. They saw the last of the cars depart and the crowd disperse to go about its business; they then sought consolation in telephones and telegrams, and, after a while, took

Entry No. A23 Chas. Cordingley's M.M.C. Phaeton. (Photo: Argent Archer)

train to Reading. No. 9 had not been seen, but a telegram came to hand that it had left Hyde Park at seven o'clock. So, by common cab, they went to Calcot Park, and the first vehicle they saw was No. 9. Its time-sheet showed that it had started at 7.10 a.m., and that punctuality was more to be regarded than pressmen. But the character of the car was thoroughly redeemed, as it went from Reading to Bristol without any signs of distress, climbing hills with perfect ease. The thirty-two miles to Marlborough were covered in just under two hours. In all, the journey of 118 miles was performed in well under twelve hours, of which nine were actual running time. No real incidents occurred to call for graphic description, but variety was added to the drive by the way in which this 6 h.p. motor kept up for sixty miles with an 8 h.p. vehicle carrying two fewer passengers.

Dust was a problem
(Photo: Argent Archer)

Hills Surmounted

Newspaper correspondents have been loud in their praise of the motor-vehicle as a hill-climber, and, whatever they may say as the cars go north, their eulogy has been noteworthy. As one observant Pressman observed, 'No hill could have been negotiated by horses as was done by the cars, and no hills could have been descended safely by animals at the rate which the cars came down with ease.'

Little Cars Doing Well

While the success of the larger cars was freely anticipated there were misgivings as to some of the smaller ones that had entered; but up to Wednesday many of the little cars had done exceedingly well, and were 'going strong.' One car, belonging to Mr. Moffatt Ford and driven by a little French lad with an equally diminutive companion aboard, has been particularly noticeable. the nonchalant way in which the little fellows lean back perfectly at ease in what appears an animated bath chair is simply delightful, and they know how to manipulate the car quite as well as older and larger motorists, turning up betimes at the controls. At the same time it must not be overlooked that a few of the small cars were running somewhat irregularly on the first two day's runs. Probably they will settle down as the trip progresses.

On a Richard Car

A Passenger on the 5 h.p. Richard car, driven by M. Bertin records that the baptism of dust was undergone about a mile from Hounslow. At Calcot Park he arrived fifty minutes in advance of the appointed time, being third or fourth to put in an appearance. Newbury was reached at noon, and Marlborough afforded the opportunity for luncheon. The long descent of Box Hill was done in good style, and everything promised well until, two miles from Bath, the leather driving band became torn and an hour's stoppage was the result. Other cars passed in irritating fashion; but, once started again, the Richard car made good progress, and reached the ancient city of springs about half way in the procession of vehicles. Tea having been taken, the run was continued and Bristol was reached in good time.

Pneumatic and Solid Tyres

Very remarkable is the success attending the cars fitted with pneumatic tyres. There are a large number of vehicles so provided, and they are going along splendidly. Certainly some of the cars whose wheels are shod with solid tyres have envious passengers.

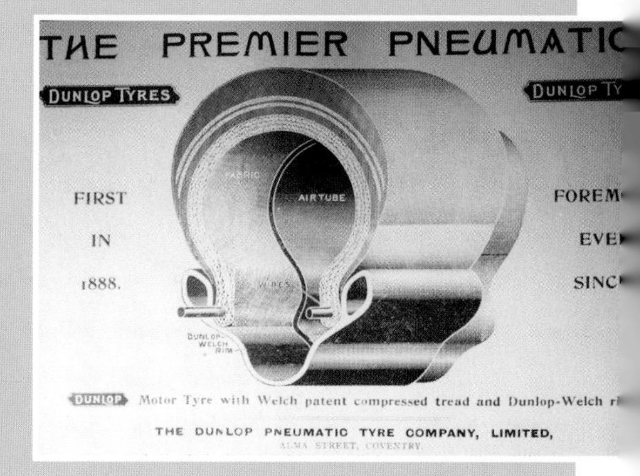

Miss Bacon's Mishap

Miss Bacon on her Werner bicycle was one of the first arrivals at Grosvenor Place on Monday, and was the first to reach Calcot Park. About half an hour's run from there, however, she came to grief, and reached Bristol by train late at night, her machine having been smashed on the Great Western Railway between Reading and Swindon Junction. Her battery gave out about two and a-half miles after leaving Calcot Park, so the lady rider pedalled back to Reading, and took the 2.25 train for Bristol. She paid 4s. for the carriage of her motor-bicycle, and got into the guard's van to take care of it, but the officials objected to her being in the van, and she got out at the next station. At Swindon Junction, where she had to change trains, the bicycle was handed to her with the lubricator broken, and it was supposed that on going round the curves into the station the machine was thrown down. But for the breaking of the lubricator a new accumulator could have been obtained at Bristol, and the journey continued.

The Daimler Parisian

One who had never before been on a motor vehicle drove on the Daimler Parisian with Mr. G. F. Pedley from Gloucester to Cheltenham, and had his preconceived notions as to the vibration and perfume attached to automobilism quite exploded. He writes: – 'The vibration which one fears so much on seeing the car standing still is entirely lost as soon as the start is made, and when a fair speed is attained nothing can exceed the smoothness with which the car runs. There is also very little smell, and in the hands of such a capable driver as Mr. Pedley the motor seems almost perfection. Of course the speed the 'Parisian' attained on her run from Gloucester to Cheltenham was limited to regulations, but once or twice she fairly flew along, giving one a good idea of her capabilities. Loaded as she was with three passengers and a quantity of baggage her performance was first-class, and she has so far run the tour through without the slightest mishap.'

New Orleans, No. 27
(Photo: Argent Archer)

On a New Orleans Voiturette

One of the New Orleans cars started very late on Monday and was a bit behind in getting forward on Wednesday morning. But it made capital runs and went from Bristol to Cheltenham without a stop, overtaking seven other cars which had started an hour earlier. It covered the distance of 42 miles in three and a half hours, or at the average speed of 12 miles an hour, one note-

(Photo: Argent Archer)

worthy characteristic being that most of the passing of other cars was done on the hills, which the voiturette took with ease, winning the praise of those on other cars, as well as proving satisfactory to its own passengers.

The first car into Newbury was that driven by Mr. S. F. Edge. The Hon. C. S. Rolls was second. At Bristol, these two were still leading although in reversed positions.

Almost Together

The Hon. C.S. Rolls arrived at Bristol just a minute ahead of Mr.. Edward Kennard. Their cars – a 12 h.p. Panhard, and a 8 h.p. Napier, respectively, had kept well together between Marlborough and their destination. We are glad to learn that the English-built car ran splendidly all the way – as did that of French make.

Traveller's Tales

Many have been the stories told in the hotels each evening and some of the yarns will attain considerable dimensions before Edinburgh is reached. One neat little story we heard was that of a fly-wheel falling off from the car going down hill and careering along ahead of the car 'on its own.' Another was that of an innocent pressman on a local paper who mounted a petrol car and asked where the electricity was stored. Many such anecdotes have been told over supper, and would form interesting reading could a complete collection be obtained.

Motor-Wheels and Tram Lines

Simms motor-wheel has no particular liking for tram lines, and apparently a deeply rooted antipathy to such common matters is a characteristic feature. Certainly the driver had an exciting time. At Bath the machine skidded on a tram line and turned completely over, the driver being thrown off. Fortunately the mechanism was only slightly damaged and the driver was able to put things right and continue his journey on the fine road leading into Bristol. But there again the tram lines brought him low, for the car turned completely over again, owing to the presence of a flanged tram line. He was, however, able to set up his machine again and reached the Drill Hall in time to secure the club certificate for having attained the legal speed of twelve miles an hour.

Samuel Rowbottom 'engaged in making small adjustment' on Simms Motor Wheel. (Photo: *The Autocar*)

Provincial Exhibition

On Tuesday we had a five minutes' chat with Dr. Lehwess, of the Automobile Association, who had spent the previous day on his Vallée racing car, with which he and Mr. Weigel had gone to Bristol. He was apparently well satisfied with the exhibition last week, (in London) not only with the arrangements made on behalf of exhibitors, but also with the business done by his association. So far as the provincial exhibitions about to be held are concerned he does not anticipate any of the exhibitors will do much business – although full of confidence as to the value of the Trial, in proving helpful to the automobile movement generally.

Pigeons and Sparrows

We had an interesting experience at Hounslow, when we came suddenly upon three pigeons in the road. They evidently did not notice our approach, for they made no attempt to escape. The car passed over them, and they flew out at the rear. Such an experience must have been a novelty to the pigeons. The Hon. Scott Montagu tells us he frequently has similar experience with sparrows, but unfortunately they do not seem to be keen judges of speed, and are frequently knocked down by the hood of his car. Such incidents have been rare this trip, and only one dog has been reported killed.

Climatic Changes

One of the greatest troubles on such a tour is concerned with the rapid changes of weather. These are frequent enough on an April day in one place, but when it is remembered that the journey from London to Bristol is practically 120 miles, and that a day's course on this Trial carries one from the West to the Midlands, and from the Midlands to the North, the difference is even more noticeable. Thus we start with a dull morning which seems full of rainy prospects, and as the hours pass get into a warmer atmosphere, until the heat becomes oppressive under great coats at noon. This may be succeeded by a sharp crisp afternoon, and followed by a bitterly cold evening. Such variations have already been seen and felt, and doubtless many more 'samples' of British weather will be experienced ere the Trial comes to an end.

Late Arrivals

Mr. J. E. Hutton arrived at Bristol about 10.30 p.m. on Monday night, having travelled straight from London. Unfortunately on entering the Drill Hall his radiator got broken. Another late visitor was Mr. Muhlenkamp, of Brighton, who travelled from Brighton to Bristol via London, on his 6 h.p. M.M.C. 'Princess' car. This car certainly went very well. At Bristol a Lanchester car also returned to the ranks, having been taken off the route for some adjustment. ”

The Motor-Car Journal, Friday, April 27th, 1900

“ Breakdowns Day 1

One of the new Parisian Daimlers, driven by Mr. Richardson with the Lord Justice Clerk of Scotland and Colonel McGrath on board, had the pump go wrong through the breakage of the actuating wheel. As luck would have it, they had a spare one on board, and were further fortunate in being close to the grounds of a gentleman who took pity on them and not only allowed them to bring the machine into his drive whilst they made the change in comfort, but entertained the passengers to tea during the hour's wait necessitated thereby.

Mr. Friswell broke the starting gear of his Peugeot at the first go off, and got over the difficulty by keeping his motor running the whole day during all the stoppages for meals and controls.

The Motor Car Co., Ltd., writes: 'In your interesting account of the first day's trip to Bristol of the cars entered in the 1,000 miles trial, you mention that our M.C.C. Triumph was discovered standing deserted on the road skirting a wood. Now, this will lead many to imagine that there was something wrong with this car, and that its driver had run away from it in disgust. It is a pleasure, therefore, to us to intimate that nothing whatever had happened so far to the car; it has gone the whole distance to Manchester in brilliant fashion, arriving there first of all voiturettes; and in the hill-climbing competition up Taddington Hill, two and a half miles of gradient averaging one in fifteen, it beat thirty other cars, seventeen of which had over double its horse-power. ”

The Autocar, Friday, 27th April 1990

Mr. & Mrs C. Friswell on 8 h.p. Peugeot. (Photo: Argent Archer)

The Peugeot Lion

“ End of first day’s driving

The Locomobile (Stanley) car made good running throughout the journey, and it is interesting to record used seven and a half gallons of petrol as fuel in two instalments, whilst she made water replenishments at Reading, Maidenhead, and Bath.

South Wales was represented by Mr. J. C. Morris, director of the Swansea Motor Omnibus Co., and Mr. W. M. Morris, of Pontypridd, the Daimler South Wales agent, who were more particularly interested in the performances of Mr. Straker's new public vehicle.

Incidents

Among the visitors at the exhibition at Cheltenham was Mr. J. W. Boughton, of St. John's, Worcester, who proceeded thither on his motor-car, which is said to be the only vehicle of the kind privately owned in the Faithful City.

Owing to the breaking of the chain of the Brown-Whitney steam car the water tank was perforated. Otherwise a better average would have been obtained on the run from London to Bristol.

Several cars skidded on the tram lines at Bath, where recent rain had made them greasy.

These two 'Local automobilist turn out in support'. Near Newbury, Lord Carnarvon drove over a part of the course on his Panhard car, and among other motorists observed near that town were Mr. and Mrs Neville Cross, of Inkpen, Berkshire.”

The Autocar, Friday, 27th April 1990

Two large Daimler Motor cars at Bristol. (Photo from Montague Grahame-White's album, courtesy N.M.M. Beaulieu)

BRISTOL TO BIRMINGHAM

WEDNESDAY 25TH APRIL

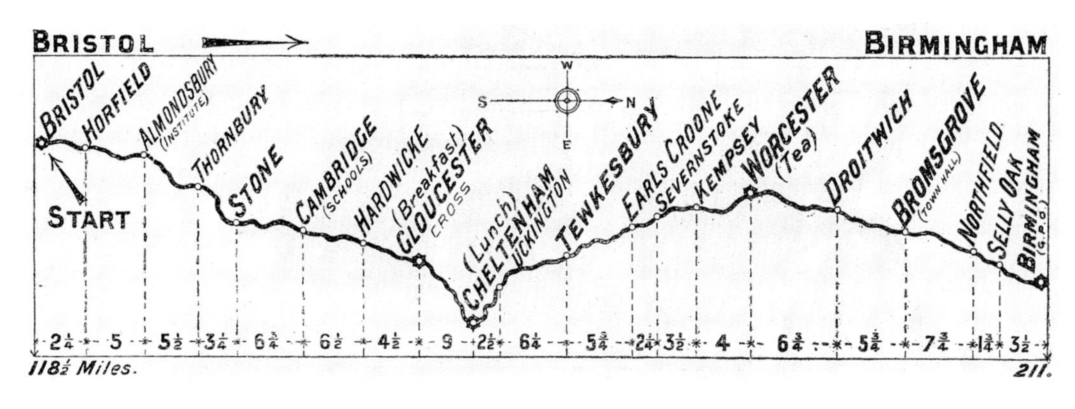

92½ miles via Gloucester, Cheltenham (3 hours Exhibition), Worcester

If the participants were ever in any doubt about the degree of control and organisation placed upon them by Claude Johnson in this endeavour they would have no doubt now. If they wished their car to be in the ratings they must knuckle under and obey the Rules. This was not a run in the country, but a serious motoring demonstration. On this crisp cold grey morning they set out with their gradient maps and their route cards. All was carefully marked, so they knew when to expect larger than average numbers of spectators. 7¼ miles out at Almondbury there was the Institute. 22¾ miles out, Cambridge with its schools; and 33¾ miles out the stop at Gloucester for breakfast! Then, 9 miles to Cheltenham, where a 3 hour Exhibition was mounted from 11.30 a.m. to 2.45 p.m., in the Winter Gardens.

Instruction to Participants

WEDNESDAY, 25th APRIL, 1900.

BRISTOL to CHELTENHAM (43 miles.)

[*See* "Cyclists' Touring Club Road Book," Vol. II., Routes 66, 124, 133, and 172; "Contour Road Book," 855].

START from Drill Hall, 7 a.m., in the order of arrival on Monday evening.

RECORD SHEETS must be signed ON LEAVING DRILL HALL.

N.B.—It is essential that the Record Sheets shall be signed, and control cards be obtained, each day at the Exhibition Building before starting for the outward control. Non-compliance with this rule renders the car liable to be disqualified for the day's run.

8 m. p. h. out of Bristol.

PROCEED at 8 m. p. h. to the outward control for Bristol. No passing permitted.

On leaving Drill Hall turn to left up White Lady's Road, following the trams for one mile, turn **R.** down Redland Park and follow on down Clyde Road, Redland Park Road, turn **L** just before reaching Railway Bridge down Tetland Road; on reaching tram lines turn **L** and follow tram lines up Gloucester Road to Barracks on **R.** Here the control for Bristol ends.

STOP.

HereSTOP.

RECORD SHEETS must be filled in here.

On Wednesday morning (Bristol) the departure of the cars attracted much attention, and the local committee certainly deserve credit. This was acknowledged by sending a telegram to the Lord Mayor of Bristol from Cheltenham:

'Cheltenham 1.57 p.m.

'Automobile Club begs to thank Bristol for courtesy during recent visit.'

Gloucester

In this ancient city great interest had been aroused, and there was considerable commotion in the streets as the vehicles made their way up to the Cattle Market, where they were drawn up in the horse stalls while the drivers breakfasted. Never before had such a sight been seen in any cattle market, and many of the leading owners of horses made careful inspection of the cars in their strange and unaccustomed quarters.

Cheltenham

It was really a holiday occasion at Cheltenham, and quite two thousand people had gathered near the Winter Gardens to see the arrival of the cars, which were manipulated with wonderful skill. Certainly a splendid demonstration of controlling power was given, and no fear of mishap seemed anywhere in evidence. Quite as much interest was shown in the departing procession, when 58 vehicles were counted.

The Motor-Car Journal, Friday, April 27th, 1900

Cheltenham Examiner.
GLOUCESTERSHIRE GUARDIAN, AND COUNTY ADVERTISER.

The Auto-Car upon its Trial

A THOUSAND MILES' TOUR
CHELTENHAM VISITED

'The Auto-Car upon its trial.' A Frenchman would be inclined to smile at the very phrase: he would say that as things go in this rapid age the motor-car is already, if not an old invention, yet one which has passed the precarious stage of infancy into that of well-established youth. It would not be admitted across the Channel that the practicability of the idea is any longer in doubt. Improvements, of course, there will be, but obviously if new mechanical ideas were never materialised and reduced to practice until all possible developments had been worked out on paper, there would be no progress at all. Has the auto-car advanced beyond the line which – perfection being still far ahead – separates the merely ingenious and promising idea from the reliably useful? The question has been affirmatively answered abroad and the Automobile Club of Great Britain and Ireland, by organising its Thousand Mile Run, seeks to extract a similar admission from British public opinion. It goes forth, then, upon its journey with something of missionary zeal; it aims to convert the unconverted, to arouse the indifferent, and to instruct the uninformed. It has a difficult task to fulfil.

Arrival at Cheltenham
Hubert Egerton De Dion (No. 15)
Percy Richardson Parisien Daimler (No. 36).
(Photo: Argent Archer)

So slowly do ideas penetrate into the mass of English society, especially in the lesser provinces, that probably many of the slumbrous towns and rural districts on the route of the trial are now realising for the first time that such contrivances as auto-cars really exist and that a revolution in road locomotion is promised – or threatened, according to individual point of view – in the not too distant future. As between England and France in this matter, there is becoming something more than differences in race and temperament. Added to the Gallic receptivity of mind, the material conditions are more favourable in the neighbouring country than our own. Every cyclist who has tried them knows that, speaking generally, the French roads are much superior to the English, while in Paris and the cities which look up to her as a pattern, the art of paving is correspondingly in advance of that which satisfies a more penurous, and less economical, municipal government here. It may be that some of the vehicles which have come out honourably in the French trials will hardly prove equal to the wear and tear of rougher tracks; and inseparably linked with the progress of what is called the 'Automobile Movement' in this kingdom is improvement in road making. The cyclist, who himself has not been without influence in this direction, ought to instinctively sympathise with the 'motist.' They have a common cause, and a common enemy in the existing generation of road surveyors.

The purpose of the present tour, which began on April 23rd and finishes on 12th inst., is twofold. It is desired, in the first place, to prove the capabilities of the various types of motor vehicles to stand the strain of a long journey through any kind of country, and in the second to familiarise the general public with the machines, and so give impetus to the 'movement.' That it is literally a movement may be gathered, not from our recent observation in Cheltenham, but in the phraseology of our enthusiastic contemporary, the Autocar, in recording the start from London. We read of the 'hum' of the seven-horse power Peugot [*sic*], which, breaking the stillness of the early morning while the representative of that Journal was at breakfast, took him up and 'flew' with him through Kensington; of how the big Daimlers came hard on the wheels of the 'panting' voiturettes, and a throbbing 'quad' separated a public service vehicle from a twelve-horse-power Panhard; while Eurekas, Decauvilles, and similar small fry 'scuttled past' to the number of seventy-five, and, when the big village had been left behind, and all were joyfully 'out of control', one car 'waltzed', another 'dashed', others 'hustled along' and another 'swept' onward at a speed which was 'soul-inspiring'. As may be judged even from this brief hint of the procession, the variety is not one of the least conspicuous features of the 'movement.' The vehicles vary greatly in size, price, and power – from the motor tricycle of 2¼ h.p., costing about £80, to the powerful 12 h.p. car for which as much as £1,600 is paid. They are divided into two sections, viz., those which are entered by the manufacturers and agents for business purposes, and those which are entered by private owners who are going through the trial for their own pleasure and satisfaction. The trial is not a race, as the judges will not consider, and the committee will not record, any speed in excess of the legal limit, which is 12 miles an hour on country roads (10 in Scotland) and eight in towns. But, of course, it is one thing to lay down rules, an another thing to get them acted upon; one thing to race officially, and another thing to race unofficially. There is no 'racing' but 'scorching of a competitive nature' means much the same, and the drivers would be more than human if they did not take – when 'out of control' – a more or less broad view of their opportunities. Already they would appear to have developed a good healthy antipathy to the police who evince a disposition to insist on the letter of the statute. Thus, beyond Reading, much disgust appears to have been excited by the fact that the functionaries of the Law were actually on the watch. 'The weather was now gloriously warm and fine' – to quote the account of the opening day's journey given by our enthusiastic contemporary before mentioned – 'and bowling over fine but dusty roads, amidst an interesting and ever-changing landscape, was exhilarating work, more especially as our new baggage wagon was rolling off her miles at a good eighteen and making excellent running. From now on, so long as the good roads lasted, policemen were noticed at almost every milestone, checking the time and numbers of the cars as they came by. In one place a little man on an old-fashioned solid-tyred tricycle – probably a local magistrate – was ostentatiously helping a constable, and at another we witnessed a glorious specimen of police time-keeping, for we saw the man, when we were yet quite eighty yards from him, look at his watch, put it in his pocket, and then with notebook in hand he stepped forward as we drove by and coolly asked us for our number. Then, as we looked back, we saw him entering carefully the time and number which – as he seemed so anxious for one – we obligingly gave him. In every case the police had chosen those stretches of road where the autocarists would be most likely to travel fast – straight, broad, smooth highways, either level or downhill, and almost entirely destitute of traffic; and if summonses are issued, as it seems possible they may be in numbers, it will but prove the existance of an amount of crass prejudice and blind opposition to progress, which we could not have believed existed in a civilised country.' So much for Berkshire; in Hampshire the police were either not visible or had no notebooks, and were 'courtesy itself' – an agreeable state of things which apparently Wiltshire and Gloucestershire reflected. There was, indeed a sinister rumour- the bare mention of which

1,000-Mile Trial. 59

CHELTENHAM,

WEDNESDAY, 25th APRIL, 1900.

A THREE-HOURS

EXHIBITION

OF THE

MOTOR VEHICLES

TAKING PART IN THE

1,000-Mile Trial organized by the Automobile Club of Great Britain & Ireland

WILL BE HELD UNDER THE PATRONAGE OF

THE MAYOR OF CHELTENHAM,

IN THE

WINTER GARDENS,

From 11.30 a.m. to 2.45 p.m.

ADMISSION - - - - - - - ONE SHILLING.

THE PROFITS WILL BE GIVEN TO THE TRANSVAAL WAR FUND.

Committee for Local Arrangements:

Dr. H. P. Fernald.	Mr. A. Meats.	Mr. F. Norman.
Mr. C. Wright.	,, Courteen.	,, F. J. Bennett.
,, W. Watts.	,, Morgan.	,, Stephenson Peach.
,, S. Dix.	,, Clark.	Dr. Abbott.

Mr. F. M. Bostock, 38, Lansdown Crescent, Cheltenham, *Hon. Sec.*

nearly caused cars and carists to simultaneously explode – that the visitors were to be personally conducted through Gloucester-shire precisely at a pace of twelve miles an hour, by a gentleman in buttons ordered North. Happily, however, for human life, this idea did not 'materialise', and on Wednesday's tour of the county it was pleasant, officially, as it would have been atmospherically if the genial weather of the earlier days of the week had been maintained.

Large crowds at anything like populous centres have been, and doubtless will continue to be, the order of the route. Cheltenham was not an exception and the 'coming of the motor car' was awaited with a great deal of interest. The time of arrival at the Winter Gardens [*a smaller version of the Crystal Palace behind what was to become the Town Hall*] had been entered in the official 'approximate time-table' as 11.40. An approximate time-table, like an approximate estimate, is apt to be – approximate. For this tour, which is not a race, the participants know brisk anxiety to be of mere time-sheets. It was about ten o'clock when the first of the cars – naturally and appropriately enough the 12 h.p. Panhard – passed Lansdowne Castle [*a recently demolished inn immortalised by a march by Holst*], where the Cheltenham control was placed, and whence to the Winter Gardens the avenues were soon alive with pedestrians and cyclists. The general expectation seems to have been that the arrival would have assumed the character of a procession, more or less corresponding in regularity to a circus. Quite otherwise the realisation. Taking one's stand by the flagman near the Whish fountain and looking down the long vista, one saw black specks in the distance looming larger and larger until the ear added its testimony to the eye, and the nose confirmed the evidence of both, that motors were motoring. Sometimes the intervals were many minutes long, and then it was with stimulated interest that the next arrivals were scanned as they flew, swept, dashed, bowled, scuttled or waltzed by, whichever verb may be preferred. In point of fact, the regulation town-speed seemed to be generally complied with, notwithstanding the temptations of the wide roadways of Lansdowne. Except when batches of three or four cars came along together, the crown of the road was invariably selected, and it would be interesting to know what the drivers of solid tyred machines thought of it. At the Gordon lamp, and thence down to the Queen's [*Hotel*], the crowds suggested Royalty, but their audible reflections did not. Scepticism struggled with faith, and faith would have had in some instances an easier victory but for the powerful ally which doubt found in the comical aspect of both cars and passengers. Of the vehicles, the more powerful, with their great locomotive looking lamps and enormous pneumatic tyres, had an air of strength which was by no means unimpressive. Some of the voitures or voiturettes , too, were not without a certain elegance of line which rendered them tolerable to the sight. But most of the medium powered machines, intended as the motor equivalent to a small wagonette, were quite aggressively and gratuitously ugly; and the strains of travel did not tend to mollify the outraged aesthetic faculty of the critical onlookers. As for the get-up of the travellers, words fail to describe the feeling of a person of ordinary sensitiveness on seeing a fellow countryman disguised as an Esquimaux and a Pantomime Demon rolled into one. The furs and oilskins, the sea boots and arctic caps, might pass, with a shiver; but when it came to Guy Faux [*sic*] masks and blue goggles, a cry either of suffering or derision – according to temperament – was forced from

continued on page 150

Cars on Exhibition at Cheltenham. Burrows (Club Steward) and Montague Grahame-White standing on 12 hp Daimler (*Foreground:*) Friswell Peugeot with St. John Nixon (aged 14) seated. (Photo: Argent Archer)

Winter Gardens
Cheltenham lunch stop.
Exhibition 25th April
1900. (*left:*) J. A. Holder's
12 h.p. Daimler.
(Photo: V.C.C. Archives)

Cheltenham

At Cheltenham the exhibition was held in the Winter Gardens, under the patronage of the Mayor, with Mr. F.M. Bostock as the local hon. secretary. Although the exhibition only lasted an hour or two, the takings at the gate amounted to £25, and as probably very nearly that amount was realised by the sale of the tickets, the War Fund should benefit considerably from the exhibition, which can certainly be described as a great success. Messrs. Clark and Morgan, motor engineers, at Clarence Parade, Cheltenham, had several cars on exhibition, and the large building, admirably adapted for the purpose, was the scene of much animation, many of the leading gentry of the district being present.

The Motor-Car Journal report of Cheltenham Exhibition

AUTOMOBILE CLUB
1000-MILE-TRIAL
A.22

Winter Gardens Cheltenham lunch stop Exhibition
25th April 1900. (*left to right:*)
No. A22, J. A. Holder's 12 h.p. Daimler
No. 46, 7 h.p. Richard car;
No. 19, 6 h.p. Orient Express;
No. A10, Edward Kennard's 8 h.p. Napier.
(Photo: V.C.C. Archives)

Winter Gardens Cheltenham lunch stop Exhibition 25th April 1900. (*right:*) 12 h.p. Daimler Phaeton driven by Montague Grahame-White. (Photo: V.C.C. Archives)

Cars leaving Exhibition Grounds Cheltenham
No. A27 John Hargreaves 12 h.p. Daimler Mail Phaeton.
Mrs Louise Bazalgette No. A25 waits while her
mechanician assists the starting of Henry Hewetson's
Benz. (He was the victim of bad fuel at this point).
(Photo: Argent Archer)

1
125

Procession of cars through Cheltenham.
(*Right:*) Clarence Gregson No. A26 on 6 h.p. Daimler
(*Centre:*) 4 cyl 12 h.p. Daimler owned and driven by Montague Grahame-White, with Burrows, Club Steward followed by No. 47 Richard.
(Photo: Argent Archer)

the lips. Hideous enough as an adjunct to male attire, the effect in the case of the two or three ladies who are going on the tour, was enough, as a man in the street phrased it, to 'startle the dead.' However, to the uncanniest of sights we may all grow accustomed in time, and, certes, motoring without a special protective dress is virtually impossible.

From 11.30 until 2.30 the cars were on view at the Winter Garden, which once more demonstrated its utility for the occasion of the kind; a better exhibition building the competitors will not meet with in their twenty days' spin. The vehicles were run in at the east gate, round the building to the open-air skating rink, whence access was gained to the interior. Within, the machines were arranged along the walls until their departure at three o'clock. A local Committee, of which Dr. Fernald was treasurer and Mr F. M. Bostock secretary (other members being Dr. Abbott, Messrs Stephenson-Peach, S. B. Dix, F. J. Bennett, C. Wright, F. M. Norman, W. Watts, A. Meats, Couteen, Morgan and Clark), had charge of the arrangements, and the opportunity was taken of swelling the war funds by charging a shilling admission. The exhibition was well attended, and the Mayor's fund has profited by the venture to a good extent. The patrons, the representatives of *The Autocar* noted, were 'a good class public' and this fact, coupled with the presence of half-a-dozen cars form the Cheltenham firm of motor engineers (Messrs. Clark and Morgan) must have given a promising aspect from the automobile point of view. Perhaps the town will justify these hopes. The smartest looking of the locally owned exhibits was that belonging to Mr. Arthur Dale, a 3½ h.p. car of the 'Benz' type, but containing several improvements in detail carried out in accordance with the owner's instructions. This car, by the way, is chiefly used in the ascent and descent of Leckhampton Hill. In wandering round the show generally, we had the good fortune to hit upon a gentleman who was willing to enlighten our darkness, and whose mind appeared to be refreshingly free from bias towards particular makes and manufactures. We gathered that the most up-to-date cars are those with vertical engines, placed in the fore part of the vehicle; by this arrangement noise and vibration are reduced, and cooling in more complete, and the result generally more satisfactory. The premier cars shown were, no doubt, the two French 12 h.p. (Panhard et Levassor, Paris) owned and driven by the Hon Chas. S. Rolls and Mr Alfred Harmsworth respectively. To the uninitiated eye, £900 seemed a long price for these cars, and, when to this is added a premium bringing up the cost to £1,600 or £2,000, it may be judged how greatly the demand exceeds the supply. The Panhard factories are turning out 75 a month. The English equivalent to the machine referred to is the 12 h.p. Daimler (Daimler Motor Company, Coventry and London), and which was represented by exhibits belonging to the Hon. John Scott Montagu, M.P., Mr. John R. Hargreaves, J.P., and Mr. J. A. Holder. Another of the privately-owned machines (also belonging to Mr. J. R. Hargreaves) was a Daimler mail phaeton of 12 h.p.: and in the manufacturer's section machines of equal, and in one case of 16 h.p., were entered. Amidst the variety already alluded to as characteristic of automobiles, there is one strong mark of family likeness. For the motive power, petroleum spirit is practically universal. There were but three exceptions in the exhibition: in one heavy oil was used, and the other two were the Stanley and Brown-Witney (American) steam carriages. Concerning the latter, there could be only one opinion from cursory observation. They were the neatest things shown, they run with the utmost ease and smoothness, and apparently had everything to recommend them. But they are thirsty creatures and require extremely careful driving. For practical purposes, manufacturers, both in this country and in France, have had recourse to petrol. Among the machines pointed out as specially worthy of notice was an 8 h.p. Napier (Motive Power Co., London), owned by Mr. Ed. Kennard, D.L., J.P., the husband of the novelist. This machine has two cylinders and thanks to being fitted with ball bearings, it did almost as well as the great Panhard. Many of the vehicles, such as the Parisian Daimler, are of 6 h.p., and below there are several types of light-carriage and voiturette, to carry two or three persons and of quadricycles and tricycles – in respect to which latter it was satisfactory to be told that the English make was the better on account of the weight being more evenly distributed.

Cheltenham Examiner (continued)

The departure from the Winter Garden, which was fixed for three o'clock but was somewhat delayed, was made in the presence of many hundreds of spectators, and the cars had to carefully thread their way through the Promenade to the 'control' on the Tewkesbury-road. One little mishap and only one there was: a terrier came to an untimely end opposite the New Club. The watches used locally by the honorary timekeepers (Dr. Abbott, Messrs. W. Turner, W. W. Whittard, E. F. Bick, G. D. Hawling, T. George, W. Hughes, G. Rudge, and Loveridge) were lent by Messrs. Furber and Son, jewellers, of Cheltenham.

Contributor: D Copson. Extract from the *Cheltenham Examiner,* 2nd May 1900

Photo from Montague Grahame-White's album. (Courtesy N.M.M. Beaulieu)

The Autocar reporter was allocated a place on a Wolseley voiturette. This was entry 40, driven by Mr. Herbert Austin. The car was entered by the Wolseley Sheep Shearing Machine Co. of Birmingham, and Herbert Austin was their Chief Engineer and Designer. It was 3 horse power, and an account of the days driving follows. (Herbert Austin went on in later years to found the Austin Company.)

Wednesday, 25th April
Autocar Reporter rides with Herbert Austin on the Wolseley

" The Second Day's Run

Wednesday, the second day of the tour, opened dull and lowering. The clerk of the weather thought seriously whether it should rain or be fine, and finally settled down to a cold grey day, giving a biting crispness to the air as the speeding motors rushed through. This until mid-afternoon, when the wind, shifting to the east, made it colder still, but a glorious sun shone out once more. As on the first day, the start was punctuality itself. Indeed, the cars filed out of the drill hall quite ten minutes before seven, and were then checked out in order on the road, though we think some little time might have been saved by checking them out ere they left the hall. For our own part we were located for the day on the Wolseley voiturette, driver Herbert Austin, and were pleased to have the opportunity of sampling this new and interesting machine. After a considerable wait on the top of the downs by the barracks, where the Bristol control ended and the cars were sent off at thirty second intervals, we got away. Although our little motor was not running at her best, according to the driver, she made good headway, and soon began picking up the cars in front, the first to be overhauled being the Stanley steamer, running slow, with a pair of dead flat pneumatics, and it was soon seen that the day would be one full of incidents in connection with the different cars, for ere the first mile had been finished No. 1 was in trouble, apparently with a burner, and in the next mile No. 14 was passed, also in temporary difficulties. One after another vehicles were overhauled or passed in more or less tribulation, till just on entering the control at Thornbury a Renault voiturette flew by us, the first to show us its back wheels. Once clear of the control, flying over splendid roads, though somewhat dusty, we again began to pick up on the motors in front, overhauling the Roots car thirteen miles out, then quickly picking up Mr. Astell on the New Orleans. Shortly afterwards Mr. Egerton was seen stranded at the bottom of a sharp incline, the tube of the petrol supply on his De Dion voiturette having shaken adrift, with the result of emptying his fuel tank. He had to remain for half an hour before a good Samaritan came to his aid. Mr. Pitman's Daimler was the next to be overhauled, and then we in our turn were passed at seventeen miles out by Mr. Ashby on his Empress tricycle. Several other cars were passed in quick succession between the nineteenth and twenty-seventh miles, during which period of the run the Century tandem tricycle, which had come down on the previous day and joined in the tour this morning, flew by us up a grade, going at a big speed. The two Renault cars were together, No. 32 apparently in difficulties, and the other acting as tender, a couple of miles out of Gloucester, which town was reached shortly after ten o'clock.

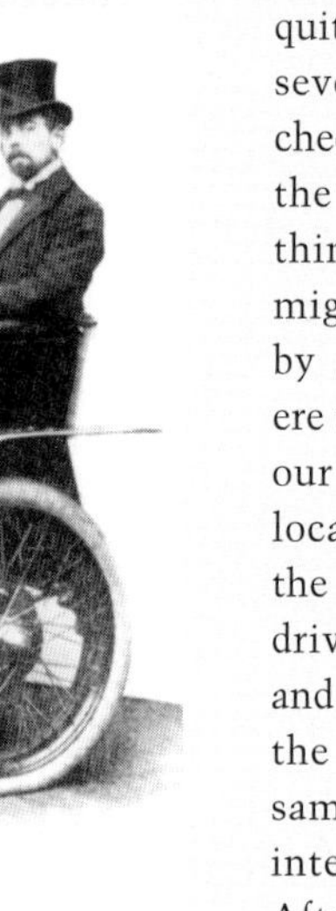

Herbert Austin on his 3 h.p. Wolseley

Here the programme said breakfast, and many of those who had started away without any were quite ready for it. The cars were stabled in the big stock sales yard which gave them excellent accommodation, and the opportunity of adjustments and repairs was taken by several, Mr. Edge being busy with the pump gear of his Napier, and the driver of our own vehicle adjusting a loose pin of the needle valve of the float, as well as oiling the steering, which had been very stiff. We may say here that the Wolseley car, whilst being a decided success for the first of a new type, behaved exactly as we thought she would, owing to a short wheelbase, the result being a tendency to swerving at high speed on down grades, together with considerable bumping when going into hollows and over crossings, owing to the seat being so immediately over the back axle, and we are pleased to learn that the new cars which are to follow the first will be both longer in the wheelbase and fitted with wheel-steering. The stiffness of our steering gear during the run to Gloucester made the slewing tendency more noticeable, but the attention it then received much mended matters. The run for the nine miles to Cheltenham was made without incident in good time, and here the cars were placed in the Winter Gardens, a building excellently adapted for the purpose, where they remained on show some four hours, and were inspected by a very interested and good class public. Petrol was required to be filled up before entering the hall, a good supply being on hand, and again the opportunity was taken for many adjustments and repairs, the driver of the Simms motor wheel, who had licked his machine into shape enough for running the previous day, making most of the opportunity, whilst our own driver found it necessary to make some adjustments to the reversing gear, which had got adrift, and in the end lost one of the screws in the thick grease at the bottom of the gear case, and, not being able to locate it, eventually decided, happily without any disastrous results, to take his chance of its getting into the gear. The cars were timed to leave Cheltenham at three o'clock, Mr. Straker, with the Daimler char-à-banc, turning up just as the procession was leaving, having broken a burner on the way. An annoying and very tedious wait was caused here by an excess of zeal in the management of the control, it being nearly 4 p.m. before the cars were fairly under weigh towards Birmingham. ”

The Autocar, Saturday, April 28th, 1900

The Autocar Reporter continues his account of his ride with Herbert Austin in the Wolseley. We pick up the story as he leaves Cheltenham ...

"AFTER GOING steadily and cautiously for a while, our driver began to recover his confidence, and the Wolseley was soon hustling along with the best of them, passing Mr. Butler making adjustments in Tewkesbury, and up the hill out of that place overhauling Mr. Cordingley, who had got new wheels fitted to his car, and got her through on the previous day in time to continue with the tour, also going by the Star, and one or two other cars, and then we found ourselves fairly amongst the vehicles of about our own class, and, what with passing and repassing, the Wolseley generally getting the best of it on the up grades, we enjoyed the experience of about as thorough a dusting as could be wished. Several more vehicles were noticed in difficulties on the way, and when we ran into Worcester there was a bigger crowd assembled than at any point previously encountered, the people lining the streets throughout the town four or five deep, and the cars having to enfilade through a narrow passage only just wide enough to admit them. A quarter of an hour stoppage for tea was scheduled here, but by the time we reached the Star, where arrangements had been made, the hotel yard of that hostelry was packed tight with cars, and the rest of us proceeded on our way to the outward control, after stopping for refreshments elsewhere on the way. The control here was at the bottom of a hill, and, when pulled up for checking, one of the now fairly numerous 'stranger' cars which chipped in during the day dashed into the back of Mr. Grimshaw's twelve horse-power Daimler, and gave it 'a good hard knock.' Mr. Alfred Bird turned up here on his Panhard, and his son on Mr. Holder's Stanley steamer, and driving over splendid roads, though considerably dusty, through very pretty country, we began, after a few miles of level running, the ascent of the Lickey Hills. Near the top our own troubles began, for the driving belt broke, necessitating a half hour's stoppage to adjust a new one, and then just at the foot of a splendid two-miles descent which we made at speed, an ominous sound portended tyre trouble, and a few minutes later it was plain that our near driving tyre had gone, so, mindful of the wheel, the car was slowed down to an eight miles pace, and so crawled into Birmingham through streets which for miles were packed to repletion with a seething crowd of humanity, nearly every individual unit of which made the wonderful discovery that our tyre was down, and promptly told us of it. We were by no means last, even in spite of this delay, for, having stabled the car in the Bingley Hall, where the cars were to be on exhibition on Thursday, we met several others coming in as we made our way to the hotel, and a later enquiry showed that the following had safely come through, though doubtless several more turned up at a later hour, or would put in an appearance next day, as a Victoria combination and one of the Decauvilles did on Tuesday. From enquiries made throughout the day, it was clear that for individual incident in connection with the cars, this day's run was very much fuller than that of Monday, quite the majority of the vehicles having had to stop at some time or other during the day for the purpose of adjustment or repair, the troubles, however, for the most part being of a trivial order. The following is a list of the arrivals at Birmingham up till 9.45 on Wednesday evening:

A30, 6 h.p. Daimler; A22, 12 h.p. Daimler; A17, 12 h.p. Panhard; A10, 8 h.p. Napier; A11, 12 h.p. Daimler; 46, 7 h.p. Richard car; A2, 6 h.p. Panhard; A4, 8 h.p. Panhard; A3, 6 h.p. Panhard; 35, 6 h.p. Daimler; 37, 6 h.p. Parisian Daimler; 22, Lanchester car; 26, 8 h.p. Peugeot; 19, 6 h.p. Orient Express; 15, De Dion voiturette; 14, De Dion voiturette; A31, 6 h.p. Parisian Daimler; 16, Gladiator voiturette; A23, 6.¼ h.p. Motor Manufacturing Co.'s phaeton; 9, Iveagh phaeton; 36, 6 h.p. Daimler; 47, Richard car; 1, 3 h.p. Benz Ideal; A7, 6 h.p. Daimler; 31, M.C.C. Triumph; 51, Star voiturette; 32, M.C.C. Triumph; 44, 3 h.p. International Victoria; 21, Lanchester making fresh start; 34, Decauville; 40, Wolseley voiturette; A24, Marshall car; A26, 6 h.p. Daimler phaeton; 2, Benz Ideal; A12, 6 h.p. Panhard; A21, 6 h.p. Daimler; 41, International Victoria; 27, New Orleans car; 49, Marshall car; 8, 6 h.p. phaeton; A25, Benz Ideal; 5, Locomobile steam car; 45, S.S. carriage; A28, Enfield quadricycle; 20, Simms's motor wheel; A20, Empress motor tricycle; 3, Ariel quadricycle; 4, Ariel tricycle Whippet detachable trailer; 39, Century tandem; A16, Ariel tricycle."

The Autocar Saturday, April 28th, 1900

7

BIRMINGHAM
THURSDAY 26TH APRIL

IN BIRMINGHAM the programme notes that 'Messrs. Mulliners, of Gas Street, Birmingham, have kindly made special arrangements for vehicles to be washed at their premises.' Another of Claude Johnson's myriad details.

So reducing their speed from 8 to 6 m.p.h. our tired and dusty autocarists followed the tram lines up Suffolk Street. At the top of the hill they turned left into Broad Street, from which on the right they entered King Alfred's Place and they came to Bingley Hall. Sixteen hotels were on the recommended list for this town, two of them (Cobden and Clark's) listed as 'temperance'; the others ranged from The Grand where 'Single bedroom in guest's portion of hotel, including lights, attendance, boot-cleaning, and bath (hot or cold, as desired), per night cost from 5/-': to the Granville where ditto cost 2/-. Meanwhile small bedroom in valets' wing, with lights and attendance per night 3/6 at the Grand but 1/6 at The Great Western. Dinner of soup, fish, joint or grill, sweets, cheese, bread and butter, and coffee, including attendance could be obtained for 5/- per person at The Grand, and 1/6 per person at The White Horse. If you required your car to be stored under lock-and-key, with supply of water and attendance, but not labour for washing of vehicle, this was available only at the Great Western and Shaftesbury Hotels for 2/6 per night. All these details, as well as the prices for various other meals and services were laboriously recorded in the Official Programme (price 6d) provided by Claude Johnson's organisation for every town of consequence that the Thousand Mile Trial passed through.

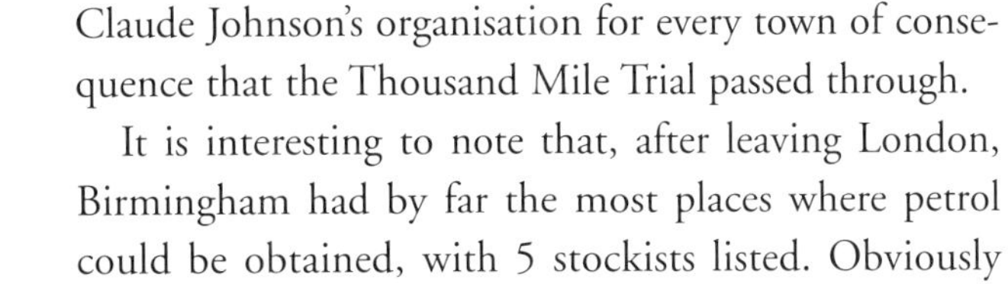

It is interesting to note that, after leaving London, Birmingham had by far the most places where petrol could be obtained, with 5 stockists listed. Obviously competition between petrol suppliers was beginning, because one supplier, a Williams & Son of Broad Street offered the cheapest petrol of the Trial at 1 shilling and 2 pence per gallon.

At Birmingham, the Yorkshire Post commented 'Rolls still forges to the front, no matter in what order the cars start.'

At Bingley Hall (By kind permission of The NEW RAPID CYCLE CO.), the one day Exhibition on Thursday 26th April 1900, was open to the public 12 o'clock noon to 6 p.m. admission one shilling, and 6 to 10 p.m. admission six pence. The profits to be devoted to the Transvaal War Fund.

Vera Butler

1,000-Mile Trial. 67

BIRMINGHAM,

THURSDAY, 26th APRIL, 1900.

A ONE-DAY

EXHIBITION

OF THE

MOTOR VEHICLES

TAKING PART IN THE

1,000-Miles Trial organized by the Automobile Club of Great Britain and Ireland,

WILL BE HELD IN THE

BINGLEY HALL,

By kind permission of The NEW RAPID CYCLE CO.

ADMISSION—
On THURSDAY, 26th APRIL, from 12 o'clock noon to 6 p.m. ONE SHILLING.
" " from 6 o'clock to 10 p.m. SIXPENCE.

THE PROFITS WILL BE DEVOTED TO THE TRANSVAAL WAR FUND.

The following Gentlemen at the invitation of the Club guaranteed the expenses of, and made all the necessary arrangements in Birmingham in connection with the Trial and Exhibition:—

Mr. A. J. Aldred.
" W. F. Ball.
" E. J. Banks.
* " Alfred F. Bird.
* " R. B. Bird
" J Blunn.
" J. Cnatwin.
" G. Cox.
* " G. W. Dawes.
" Broughton Dugdale, J.P.

Mr. Ralph Gilbert.
* " H. Berger Graham.
* " R. F. Hall.
" Inshaw.
" J. M. James.
* " F. W. Lanchester.
* " J. W. Price.
" Robert Price.
" Thos. Ratcliffe.

*Mr. Chas. Sangster.
" N. C. Siddeley.
* " J. W. Stocks.
" J. S. Taylor.
" Allan Whitfield.
" James Whitfield.
* " C. H. Palethorpe.
* " J. Holder.
* " J. T. Siddeley.

Mr. H. Berger Graham, Linden House, Gough Road, Edgbaston, *Hon. Sec.*

Those marked * are Executive Committee.

E 2

To stop over in Birmingham and have an exhibition was a bold step by Claude Johnson. Earlier that year as reported in *The Autocar* February 3rd, 1900, the Cycle and Motor Show at Bingley Hall had been a failure (described as a 'frost') with barely 50 people a day attending!

"As an example of what a complete 'frost' an exhibition in an enclosed hall can be, even with the attraction of autocars, no better instance can be adduced than the motor and cycle show which closes its doors at the Bingley Hall, Birmingham, to-day. In the first years of the inauguration of this function great success attended its efforts, but we have never looked upon it as more than ephemeral and a passing phase of the then existing cycle boom. The promoters have hoped that the declining support obtained from the cycle makers would be counter-balanced by the increasing support from the motor people, and, although they have secured some very good motor makers' patronage, and although it is plain that these exhibits form the principal attraction to those of the public who do attend, it is a striking instance of absolute failure. During the day scarcely fifty people apparently pass the turnstiles, though a few more come in in the evening when the band plays, and stage performances are given. In this case doubtless the weather and the war combined have had something to do with it, but that it is the last cycle and motor show of the kind held in Birmingham most people are imagining, and all people, including ourselves, hope."

The Autocar February 3rd, 1900

Despite previous bad experiences the Birmingham Exhibition was a success:

> **Birmingham**
>
> "With Mr. H. Berger Graham as local hon. secretary and a loyal committee, mainly composed of automobilists, the exhibition at Bingley Hall has introduced hundreds of Midlanders to the many varieties of automobiles. Not that such education was so urgently needed as at some other centres, for of the eighty-four vehicles entered in the Trial, thirty-five were manufactured in the Midlands, twenty-four of them at Coventry, the remainder hailing from Birmingham and Wolverhampton. Still, in the French and Belgian cars there was much to interest the crowds that attended, who showed their appreciation of recent advance."

The Motor-Car Journal, 1900

Above:
Special efforts were made at Birmingham including a map for the participants. From Montague Grahame-White's personal album. (Courtesy of NMM Beaulieu).

Left:
Mr. F. T. Bidlake on his tricycle.
(Photo: Argent Archer)

Tour Jottings

Thirty-five of the cars running in the trial are driven by chains, and thirty of the pairs of chains are Bramptons. This speaks well for one branch of English autocar manufacture.

— o§o —

Mr. F. T. Bidlake, who started to cover the whole round on a bicycle, succumbed to petrol at Birmingham, and continued the journey on a two and a quarter horse-power tricycle.

From Worcester the car of Messrs. Roots and Venables mistook the turning at Barbourne and went to Ombersley where the supply pipe for the oil was broken. Fastened to the back of a cart the vehicle proceeded to Droitwich where the necessary repairs were made.

— o§o —

En Route

BIRMINGHAM

Thursday last was rather a dull day in Birmingham, and at least one automobilist took the opportunity of the chance to run up to London. Late in the afternoon some stir was created by the unexpected arrival of Mr. Alfred Harmsworth's splendid 12 h.p. Panhard, which was driven in from Reading. At the exhibition in Bingley Hall the attendance was larger than was anticipated, and much interest was shown in the construction of the machines by the greater portion of the visitors, many of whom were manufacturers and others desirous of becoming acquainted with the mechanism of the various vehicles. From noon, when the exhibition opened, until the closing hour, ten o'clock, there was a steady inflow of visitors.

The official records concerning the run from Bristol to Birmingham, via Cheltenham (92½ miles), which took place on Wednesday last week – the roads being hard, but dusty; weather fine – show that the following motor-vehicles in the manufacturers' and agents' section completed the journey at a speed up to the legal limit of twelve miles an hour, namely:

Nos. 1 and 2, Benz 'Ideals.'
No. 3, 'Ariel' quadricycle.
No.4, 'Ariel' tricycle, with Whippet trailer.
No.7, Motor Manufacturing Company's 12 h.p. phaeton.
No.9, Motor Manufacturing Company's 'Iveagh' phaeton, 6-h.p.
Nos. 14 and 15, De Dion voiturettes.
No. 16, Motor Power Company's 'Gladiator' voiturette.
No. 19, Automobile Association's 'Orient Express.'
No. 20, Motor-Carriage Supply Company's 'Simms' Motor Wheel.'
Nos. 21 and 22, Lanchester Engine Company's 8-h.p. carriages.
No. 23, Brown-Whitney steam car.
No. 26, Friswell's 8-h.p. Peugeot.
No. 27, Burford, Van Toll's 3½-h.p. 'New Orleans' car.
Nos. 31 and 32, Motor-Car Company's 3½ h.p. 'Triumphs.'
No. 34, Motor-Car Company's 3½ h.p. Decauville.
Nos. 35 and 36, The Daimler Company's 6 h.p. carriages.
No. 37, The Daimler Company's 6-h.p. Parisian car.
No. 39, 'Century' Tandem Tricycle.
No. 40, Wolseley Company's voiturette.
Nos. 41 and 44, international Company's 3 h.p. Victorias.
Nos. 46 and 47, Automobile Manufacturing Company's 7-h.p. 'Richard' cars.
No. 49, Marshall and Company's 5 h.p. carriage.
No. 51, Star Motor Company's voiturette.

In the Section for privately-owned vehicles, the following completed the journey at a speed up to the legal limit:

No. A2, Mr. Frank Butler's 6 h.p. Panhard.
No. 3A, Mr. T.B. Browne's 6 h.p. Panhard.
No. A4, Mr. Mark Mayhew's 8 h.p. Panhard.
No. A7, Mr. Alfred Harmsworth's 6 h.p. Parisian Daimler.
No. A10, Mr. Edward Kennard's 8 h.p. Napier.
No. A11, the Hon. John Scott Montagu's 12 h.p. Daimler.
No. A12, Mr. Henry Edmund's 6-h.p. Daimler.
No. A16, Mr. A. J. Wilson's 'Ariel' tricycle.
No. A17, the Hon. C. S. Rolls' 12 h.p. Panhard.
No. A20, Mr. Herbert Ashby's 'Empress' tricycle.
No. A21, Mr. Ernest Pitman's 6 h.p. Daimler.
No. A22, Mr. J. Holder's 12 h.p. Daimler.
No. A23, Mr. Charles Cordingley's 6¼ h.p. Motor Manufacturing Co.'s phaeton.
No. A24, Mr. Robert Phillip's 4 h.p. Mors car.
No. A26, Mr. C.K. Gregson's 6 h.p. Daimler phaeton.
No. A28, Mr. E.M. Iliffe's 2¼ h.p. Enfield quadricycle.
No. A30, Mr. J.D. Siddeley's 6 h.p. Parisian Daimler.
No. A31, Mr. W. Exe's 6 h.p. Parisian Daimler. ”

The Motor-Car Journal, Friday, May 4th, 1900

De Dion Cells, 6/- each.

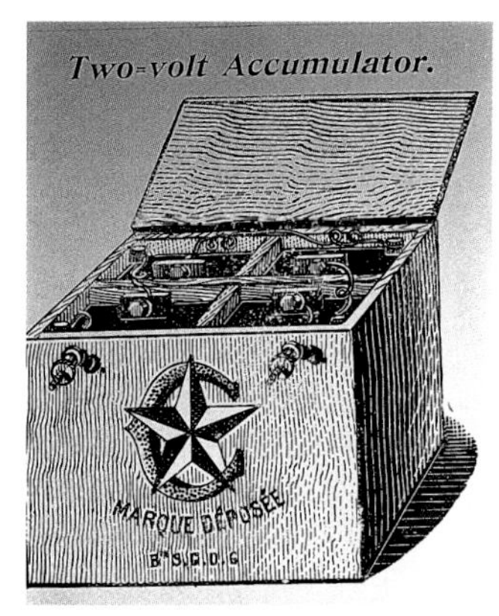

Two volt accumulator

Ampèremeter

BIRMINGHAM TO MANCHESTER

FRIDAY 27TH APRIL

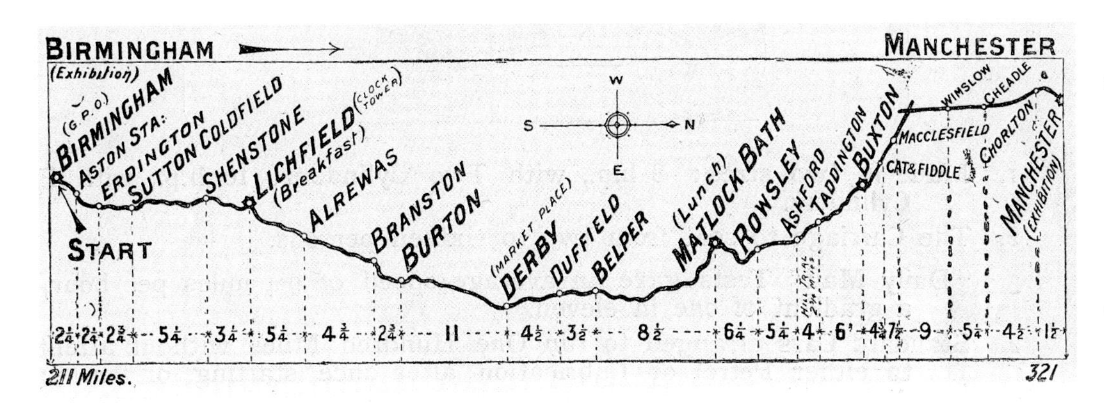

110 miles
Via Lichfield, Burton-on-Trent, Derby, Matlock Bath, Buxton, Manchester

THIS TIME the reporter from *The Autocar* found himself a seat upon Mr Alfred Harmsworth's 12 hp Panhard. The great man himself had driven up from Calcot Park as a visiting driver, so their ride was outside the constraint of record keeping and checking out at 'the controls'. They had a wonderful ride, leaving later than the compulsory early risers, and 'away on the wings of the wind in the finest and most beautifully sprung vehicle' the reporter had ever been on. Heady stuff indeed, and very exhalted company! His report of the day's run follows.

"The Automobile Club's 1,000 Miles Trial

Birmingham to Manchester

Friday morning, April 27th, was unpromising, and even wet in the early hours, so that when the cars came to start at seven – punctually again as usual – there was a light drizzle, and the always awkward tram rails of Birmingham were in about as greasy and dangerous a condition as it is possible to imagine. At the order to go the following cars quitted the Bingley Hall in the order named: A22, A17, A10, A16, A20, 4, 20, 39, 31, 44, 27, A30, 16, 8, 12, A26, A24, A21, 22, 34, 28, 47, 46, 3, 35, 33, A7, 9, 51, 36, 29, 30, 23, 38, 5, 26, 41, 24, A3, 49, 37, A31, 15, 52, A23, 40, 1, 45, A4, A28, A25, 2, 19, 53, 38, totalling thirty-nine cars of Section 1 and sixteen of Section 2. One or two of these had not finished the run with the rest on Wednesday, but had come in next day, amongst these being Mr. Grimshaw, who had got a new tyre fitted and driven up from Worcester the previous evening, and the larger Lanchester, which had been sent on from Reading by train and repaired, chipped in again. Mr. Hargreaves, too, on his new twelve horse-power Daimler, who had turned back at Calcot Park on Monday with faulty condensers, once more joined in. Needless to say, cautious and slow driving was the order of the day till clear of the trams, but in spite of all care the side-slips were numerous, several of the cars pirouetting round in marvellous fashion, whilst Mr. Grimshaw and Capt. Langrishe made excursions on the pavement and took a peep into the shop windows. As for ourselves, Mr. Alfred Harmsworth had driven through from Calcot Park the previous day, and gave us a seat on his twelve horse-power Panhard, which proved the flier of the party, and is without exception the finest and most beautifully sprung vehicle we have ever been on. Not being 'in control,' there was no occasion to leave so early, and we got away shortly before ten, and under skilful pilotage passed over the greasy tramlines without anything very alarming. And then away on the wings of the wind under a slight drizzle, but over dustless and finely-graded roads, romping gaily up Gravelly Hill and the steep rise through Sutton Coldfield, occasionally steadying for a restive or unattended horse, and eventually getting up with the tail end of the competing cars at Lichfield, one of the Georges Richard cars being the first to be overtaken just inside the control of that city. Just clear of the out control the Motor Wheel was seen with her driver making adjustments, and then we rapidly flew by the Orient Express and one of the Eurekas. We were now on the fine straightaway dead-level Roman road, and our car was given her head when the road was clear, rolling off close on forty at times, and travelling with a steadiness and smoothness which were delightful and exhilarating. Needless to say, the slower of the competing cars now began to 'come back' in quick succession. One of the New Orleans cars and Grahame-White's Daimler were passed close together making adjustments, and just entering Burton, Van Toll's M.M.C. Daimler baggage waggon, on which we journeyed to Bristol on Monday, was passed changing water whilst waiting on the second New Orleans, which had broken a spring and was repairing. No. 34 Decauville was passed halted about four miles out, and the S.S. carriage, No. 45, also in difficulties, a little further on. Then No. 21 – the larger Lanchester – hove in sight, travelling rather slowly. Next Mr. Mayhew's Panhard stopped by the roadside four miles out of Derby, and up a short rise a little later we flew by Mr. Butler's Panhard going well, overhauling the other Eureka just on the Derby control. As at most other places, the crowds were out considerably in the county town, and as we rolled gently down the hill approaching the town a private De Dion voiturette in front of us had a little difference with a small herd of cattle, and carried away part of her mudguards. We passed on through the packed and enthusiastic crowds, and slipped No. 32 on the outward control, overhauling Mr. Austin driving the Wolseley, and travelling in good style in full pursuit of the Daimler baggage waggon just outside Duffield. The Roots car was stopped on a hill outside, and going up the hill into Belper we ran by the Orient Express travelling well. At the top of the hill Captain Langrishe's and Mr. Johnson's vehicles were standing, the former's induction valves giving trouble, and the latter 'standing by.' Then we sighted the International Victoria going slowly, and overhauled the two Benz cars on the down grades of the Derwent Valley shortly after, having only just room to get by No. 29 Eureka, which had stopped in the middle of the road, and came up with No. 33 Decauville and the smaller Lanchester signing their control sheets into Matlock. Here the road dipped sharply on a curve, and was covered with greasy mud, necessitating the most careful driving, and we afterwards learned that several of the larger cars made some wonderful slides here, Capt. Langrishe (*driving Mr. Alfred Harmsworth's other smaller [6 h.p.] Daimler*) coming off worst, for, although going dead slow, he found himself heading straight into the cliff, with the result of a broken spring, which necessitated a call on a local coachbuilder for repairs. At Matlock all stopped for lunch, being divided up amongst the different hotels, many of the *chauffeurs* leaving their cars at the bottom of the hills rather than take them up the steep grades to the hotels. From the grounds of the Royal Hotel very fine views of the neighbouring hills were obtained, and looking down on the road below an overturned furniture van could be seen, this not being the result, as many surmised, of the horse being frightened by the cars, but simply because the poor animal was unequal to the task accorded it, and the load ran back and overturned.

After lunch we got under weigh, going cautiously over the steep and tortuous roads out of the town, many of which were greasy in the extreme, and on the last of these wet declines found a small crowd assembled round the wreck of No. 14 De Dion voiturette, which had side slipped, straightened, and broken off both front wheels, and was there is the roadway reclining on her nose. No one was hurt.❞

The Autocar Saturday May 5th, 1900

27th April
The Mayor of Lichfield invited the citizens to welcome the automobilists by decorating the houses on the line of the route with flags, etc.

Claude Johnson at Matlock control in 6 h.p. Daimler, lady passenger unknown – perhaps his wife.
(Photo: *The Autocar*)

By Observer

WRITING FROM MANCHESTER, FRIDAY NIGHT

"Early this morning we were astir getting the vehicles ready, and despite the early hour a good concourse of people saw us leave Bingley Hall and start on our way for Sutton Coldfield to Dr. Johnson's ancient city of Lichfield. Sir Francis Jeune not long ago reminded us of the worthy doctor's suggestion as to travelling in a postchaise, and as the reflection as to his feeling with regard to motor-cars is obvious I will not pursue Dr. Johnson any further, but continue the chronicle of my journey with the interesting statement that breakfast was indulged in at Lichfield. From thence to Burton we went along steadily and well, nothing of importance passing us on the way, but it was clear from the muddy state of the roads that rain had fallen during the night, and so we had a condition that had befallen us but once so far.

It was market day at Derby, and so we were cautioned to drive at nothing more than six miles an hour owing to that fact. Naturally the streets were abnormally crowded, and a quicker pace would have been both difficult and dangerous. Probably the only incident of importance – if such an affair can be deemed worthy of publication – was the attempt of a cow to enter a car: an adventure to be ascribed to the excitement of the animal's nerves and not to any idea of curiosity. Beyond Duffield the vehicles ran through the valley of the Derwent, and, passing through Bakewell to Macclesfield, permitted the tourists to enjoy a fine sample of Derbyshire scenery.

In the pleasant town of Matlock I took lunch – amid the most pleasant surroundings so far seen on the tour. Green hedgerows and long winding lanes may be the dream of the poet, but there is a pleasure and beauty of their own associated with the low stone walls that intersect the fields of Derbyshire, especially when there are hills to go up and hills to go down, giving one sensations of a peculiar and wonderful character. From Matlock to Bakewell was a grand run, and at all the corners on the way to Ashford little knots of people assembled to see the rather straggling procession. On the way out from Matlock an unfortunate accident occurred to one of the De Dion voiturettes, which had done very well in the early stages of the journey. The car had to cross a patch of stone, and this evidently proved a finishing touch to a latent flaw in the spindle of the near front wheel. The spindle snapped, and its fellow on the off front wheel followed suit, with the result that both wheels left the car, the fore part of which fell on the road. But that was a mere incident in the campaign, and the rest of the cars went on, little heeding the pieces. Sometimes cyclists would venture to outpace us, but gave up after a few miles. One venturesome rider came up too near our car, and was nearly knocked down as we suddenly stopped because of an obstruction in front. Why do men risk their lives for the little 'cover' they get from a motor-car?

At Bakewell there were some peculiar styles of roads. Deep ruts had been covered with dressings of macadam, and one sharp flint, more obtrusive than its low-lying fellows, played upon the tire of the Wolseley voiturette. Still the other cars went on, their passengers truly thankful at escaping without breakdowns the fearsome character of these treacherous roads. Probably one of the most delightful parts of the 'drive' was from Darley Dale to Rowsley, and not a few would have been glad to have turned into Chatsworth. But we were motoring, and motoring is not mere sightseeing. It is something more: some would say something less."

The Motor-Car Journal Friday, May 4th, 1900

Derby

In any case there would have been a crowd here, but the fact that it was market day and that some of the schools were closed in honour of St. George and Automobile Day, helped to swell the crowds. Some excitement was caused by restive horses, but all, even the police, were willing to acknowledge that excitement on that account was caused by the carelessness of the drivers rather than by the presence of the cars.

(Local News)

Matlock

Here, beneath the shadow of the High Tor, a great deal of interest was taken in the tour, and it was confidently predicted by many of the knowing ones that the cars would find the hills of Derbyshire too much. At the local schools the children had been given a holiday, and they, of course, cheered to the echo. The police gave every assistance, and the only matter that aroused concern was the upsetting of a furniture van in trying to get out of the way of one of the cars.

(Local News)

Lichfield c. 1900 (Courtesy J. Riddell)

204 — 1,000-Mile Trial.

THE IMPORTANCE OF GOOD SPEED IN HILL-CLIMBING.

THOSE who contemplate the purchase of, and to that end are seeking particulars of, a Motor Vehicle for touring purposes, should enquire carefully into not only its ability to mount hills but the **speed** at which it can mount hills. The results of the four Hill-Climbing Trials, which are included in the 1,000-Mile Trial, should be of considerable service for this purpose.

In order to illustrate the importance of a good speed on ascents, two examples are here given :—

EXAMPLE I.

A Race between two vehicles.

Course: (*a*) A mile up hill, (*b*) a mile down hill, and (*c*) a mile on the flat.

Vehicle A is capable of climbing the hill at 10 miles an hour, but is not permitted to travel more than 12 miles an hour at any point.

This vehicle accomplishes the course, as follows :—

1 mile up hill, at 10 m. p. h. = 6 min.
1 mile down hill, at 12 m. p. h. = 5 min.
1 mile on the flat, at 12 m. p. h. = 5 min.

Total ... 16 mins.

Vehicle B is capable of climbing the hill at only 4 miles an hour, but can run down hill at **60** miles per hour.

This vehicle accomplishes the course, as follows :—

1 mile up hill, at 4 m. p. h. = 15 min.
1 mile down hill, at 60 m. p. h. = 1 min.

But it is unnecessary for Vehicle B to complete the course, for in spite of the break-neck speed of 60 m. p. h. at which it has covered the second portion of the course, Vehicle A which has at no time exceeded 12 m. p. h. is a mile a-head, and has WON the race.

EXAMPLE II.

A race of 60 miles, one-third (the last portion, say) of the distance being up hill, the remainder down hill or flat.

Vehicle A ascends hills at 10 miles per hour, and down hill and on the flat travels at 12 miles per hour.

Vehicle B ascends hills at 4 miles per hour, and down hill and on the flat travels at 30 miles per hour.

RESULTS.—Vehicle A travels over the 40 miles flat and down hill at 12 m. p. h. = 3 hrs. 20 mins.
and 20 miles up hill at 10 m. p. h. = 2 „ 0 „

TOTAL ... 5 „ 20 „

Vehicle B travels over the 40 miles flat and down hill at 30 m. p. h. = 1 hrs. 20 mins.
and 20 miles up hill at 4 m. p. h. = 5 „ 0 „

TOTAL ... 6 „ 20 „

NOTE.—Vehicle B has travelled over two-thirds of the journey at **30** miles per hour as opposed to Vehicle A's 12 miles per hour. Yet Vehicle B loses by one hour.

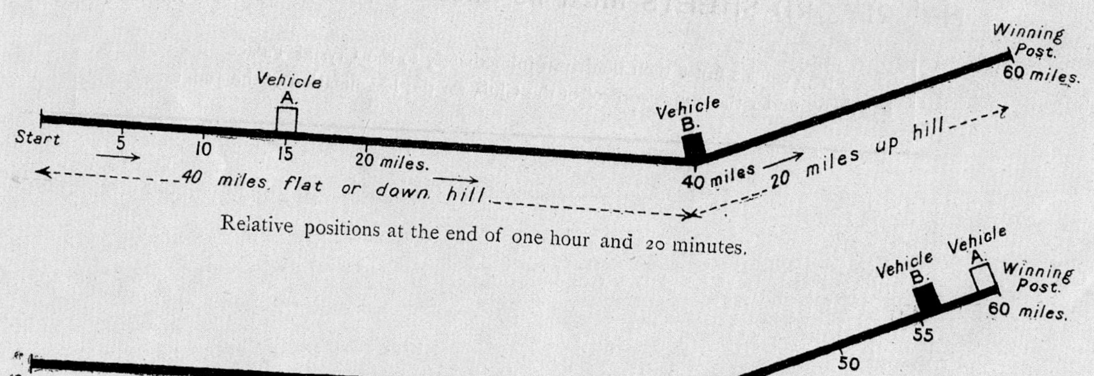

Relative positions at the end of one hour and 20 minutes.

Vehicle B. Vehicle A. Winning Post. 60 miles. 55 50 45 Start · 20 miles. 40 miles.

Relative positions at the end of 5 hours and 20 minutes, Vehicle **A** at winning post, Vehicle **B** 4 miles behind, a distance which it will take one hour to accomplish.

Friday 27th April
Matlock checkpoint
(*left:*) Brown-Whitney steam car entered by Brown Bros
(*right:*) Captain Hercules Langrishe driving Mr Alfred Harmsworth's 6 h.p. Daimler
(Photos: *The Autocar*)

1,000-Mile Trial. 79

HILL-CLIMBING TRIAL, No. 1.

THE HILL-CLIMBING COMPETITION

OF

TADDINGTON HILL (2½ miles).

STOP. STOP at foot of Hill, at the milestone marked "8 miles to Buxton."

RECORD SHEETS must be filled in here.

R. A. PROCEED at full speed nearly to the summit of Taddington Hill, 4,440 yards= 2·522 miles.

STOP. STOP at a guide-post on **R**, about 140 yards beforer eaching the summit.

RECORD SHEETS must be filled in here.

HONORARY TIMEKEEPERS:—

Messrs. WILLIAM BRAMWELL, WILLIAM GREGORY, GEORGE MORRIS, and FREDERICK OSBORN.

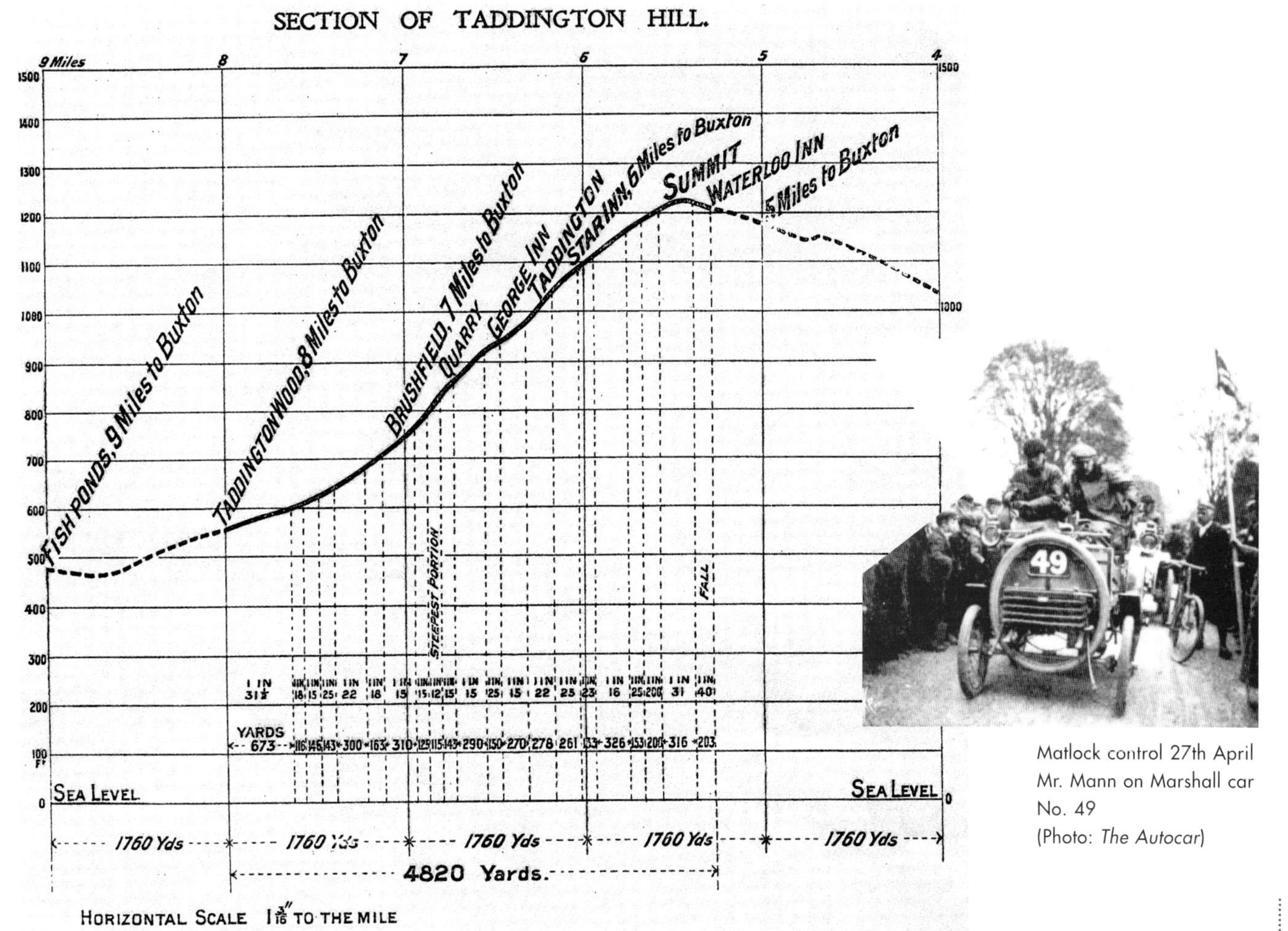

Matlock control 27th April
Mr. Mann on Marshall car
No. 49
(Photo: *The Autocar*)

1,000-Mile Trial. 79

HILL-CLIMBING TRIAL, No. 1.

THE HILL-CLIMBING COMPETITION

Returning to *The Autocar* correspondent riding in Mr. Alfred Harmsworth's 12 h.p. Daimler:

"Rapidly overhauling car after car, our vehicle running splendidly, the ascent of Taddington Hill, the first of the hill-climbing test gradients, was entered upon. Our car flew by the controls on the top speed, and we were wondering when the hill would commence when we encountered the weird sight of a cyclist apparently 'coasting' up hill, which at once showed the hill we were really on. Soon the road entered a magnificent winding gorge, rising steeper and steeper all the way, and the speeds were dropped to the second, below which it was not necessary to go. We simply romped up the hill, passing car after car, some going grandly and others labouring at the task, whilst two, including Mr. Critchley's Daimler, were stopped, having run out of petrol, and were waiting for the aid of some good Samaritan. We averaged the grade at about sixteen miles an hour, and the performances of the different cars in the competition over the two and a half miles gradient worked out as follows:

Ascent of Taddington Hill, 2.½ Miles

		Miles per hour
A16	Mr. A. J. Wilson's Ariel tricycle	18.9
A17	The Hon. S. C. Rolls's 12 h.p. Panhard	17.7
3	Mr. J. Stocks's Ariel quadricycle	15.13
A22	Mr. Holder's 12 h.p. Daimler	14.40
4	Ariel tricycle with Whippet trailer	14.40
A10	Mr. Kennard's 8 h.p. Napier	13.74
A11	The Hon. J. Scott-Montagu's 12 h.p. Daimler	11.19
5	Locomobile steam carriage	10.08
15	De Dion voiturette	10.08
A4	Mr. Mayhew's 8 h.p. Peugeot	10.08
40	Wolseley voiturette	10.08
20	Simms's Motor Wheel	9.45
26	Mr. Friswell's 8 h.p. Peugeot	9.45
31	Motor Car Co.'s Triumph	9.45
37	Daimler Co.'s Parisian	9.15
51	Star voiturette	9.15
A28	Mr. Edward Iliffe's Enfield quadricycle	9.15
22	8 h.p. Lanchester car	8.62
A30	Mr. Siddeley's Parisian Daimler	8.39
A24	Mr. Phillips's Mors Petit Duc	8.39
16	Gladiator voiturette	8.17
A3	Mr. T.B. Browne's 6 h.p. Panhard	8.17
A31	Mr. W. Exe's 6 h.p. Parisian Daimler	8.17
A29	Mr. Mark Mayhew's 7 h.p. Peugeot	7.74
32	Motor Car Co.'s Triumph	7.56
2	Benz Ideal	7.18
33	Decauville car	6.70
A25	Mrs Bazalgette's Benz Ideal	6.70
36	6 h.p. Daimler	6.55
47	Richard car	6.43
A12	Mr. Edmunds's 6 h.p. Daimler	6.43
27	New Orleans	6.30
34	Decauville	6.30
35	Daimler (stopped for spirit five minutes)	6.30
44	International	6.17
52	Roots and Venables	5.80
A26	Mr. Gregson's 6 h.p. Daimler	5.80
A2	Mr. Butler's 6 h.p. Panhard	5.69
9	Motor Mfg. Co.'s Iveagh phaeton	5.49
1	Benz Ideal	5.39
8	Motor Mfg. Co.'s 6 h.p. phaeton	5.29
41	International Victoria	5.29
49	5 h.p. Marshall car	4.94
23	Brown-Whitney steam car	4.56

The run down over firm roads to Buxton was fine, and we found a large crowd assembled on the top of the hill in the town. Here a little later on what might have been a serious accident occurred when a local reporter on a cycle was thrown by some dogs right in front of a car which ran over and smashed his machine, though he himself escaped unhurt. Then commenced one of the finest drives in the world, the run to Macclesfield, taking the tourists along a continuous upgrade for four miles to the solitary hostelry known as the 'Cat and Fiddle.' The road can be seen almost the whole of the way, and the progress of the cars, like flies crawling up a window pane, could be readily watched, a little moving

Left:
Mr. & Mrs Friswell (P.H.H.)

cloud of steam half way up resolving itself into Mr. Friswell's Peugeot when we overtook it a few yards from the top. The view from here and for the next few miles was grand, an expanse of hills stretching away below on every side, whilst the air was simply glorious, and we drank it in with the scenery as we flew along. And now began a run down right away into Macclesfield, mile after mile over moor and hill, always descending, with innumerable sharp stone-wall-bound curves, which required the best of steersmanship to negotiate. We 'floated' down at an exhilarating yet cautious pace, but some of the travellers reported somewhat exciting episodes, the most noteworthy perhaps being that of Mr. Rolls, whose attendant was shot out on one of the curves, followed by half the contents of the car, without, however, any damage being done. Not so fortunate, however, No. 45, the S.S. carriage, which, taking one of the curves at too great a speed, failed to negotiate it, dashed into the wall and smashed its axles.

During the last mile of the run the town of Macclesfield lay spread out like a map below, and on reaching the outward control we found we were up with the leaders, Messrs. Rolls on the twelve horse-power Panhard, S. F. Edge on the Napier, J. Holden on his new twelve horse-power Daimler, together with Messrs. A. J. Wilson, Stocks, Jarrott, and Harvey Ducros, jun., on quads and tricycles, being there held up by the control. Whilst waiting, Mr. Rolls came to our aid with a gallon of petrol, and we all got under weigh together. After holding back to avoid the dust thrown up by the leading vehicles we suddenly came across them backing round, having made a wrong turn, so we took the opportunity and slipped by, and never saw any more of them, eventually running into the Botanical Gardens, Manchester, at 4.45 with Mr. Hargreaves, who had come up in the last few miles, in

News report with regard to Hon. Charles S. Rolls

C. S. Rolls had an incident on the Cat and Fiddle Pass on the way into Manchester. Rolls took a corner too fast, decanting Poole, his mechanic, and some baggage. The damage done was slight, but Rolls was furious, and told the young man in no uncertain terms that if he fell out again, he would not stop to pick him up. It was probably this spill, rather than any actual fast driving, that aroused the animosity of the press against Charles, who for the next few years was frequently subjected to scathing comment.

John Hargreave's 12 h.p. Daimler. No. A27 from the album of Montague Grahame-White. (Courtesy N.M.M. Beaulieu)

attendance. Seventeen minutes later Mr. Holden's twelve horse-power Daimler turned up with the M.C.C. Triumph, No. 31, Mr. Siddeley's Daimler and Mr. Egerton's De Dion voiturette close up. Two minutes later Messrs. Rolls and Edge followed, and then Nos. 16, 4, and 3 filed in. Mr. Scott Montagu was the next to show up, followed by Mr. Mayhew's Peugeot, the latter having suffered delay with a broken exhaust pipe. Mr. Millership's Lanchester turned up smiling as usual, No. 37 Daimler followed with a punctured tyre, and reported delay from a pump stoppage. The Century tandem had been ridden the last seventeen miles on a flat driving tyre, and the Star had come through with a short delay for a broken chain. Mr. A. J. Wilson's tricycle and the Locomobile reported no mishap, as also did Mr. Cordingley's M.M.C. phaeton and Mr. Seyd's International, which arrived at 5.42. The Wolseley put in an appearance at six o'clock, having had a tyre puncture on the way, and the No. 2 Benz reported a stoppage through the cap coming off a valve spring. The larger Lanchester, after delay with a broken spring of the ignition gear, crawled in with the body split in two, and decided to relinquish the contest. The Motor Mfg. Co.'s Iveagh phaeton No. 9 and Mr. Johnson's Daimler Parisian showed up shortly after six with clean records, and Mr. Edmunds reported a half hour's delay to repair a broken accelerator wire. Capt. Langrishe followed soon after, his car looking none the worse for the Matlock experiences, and he was closely followed by Mr. R. E. Phillips's Petit Duc, the No. 1 Mors, and Mr. Edward Iliffe's Enfield quad, the latter puncturing a tyre at the very door, but reporting no other incident. Mr. Friswell's Peugeot was the next car in with Mr. T. B. Browne on his heels, the latter having had trouble with a faulty pump. The Richard car No. 47 reported a punctured tyre, and at the time of our leaving the hall Mr. Gregson's Daimler, Mr. Astell's New Orleans, Dubois on the Decauville and Mr. Mayhew's Panhard had also arrived. Others came in later, including Mr. Straker's Daimler char-à-banc at eleven but the Orient Express was reported hung up with a broken piston. ”

The Autocar Saturday, May 5th, 1900

News report with regard to Hon. Charles S. Rolls

At Birmingham, the Yorkshire Post was commenting that Rolls 'still forges to the front, no matter in what order the Cars start'.

C. S. Rolls progress in the 12 h.p. Panhard:

On Taddington the Panhard was off form, for it was beaten by A16. Wilson's Ariel tricycle; though in the eyes of the Automotor Journal 'Wilson was somewhat of a superman whose skill in pedalling is a factor in this case which an ordinary flabby mortal in like conditions would have to allow for'. His speed was 18.9 mph. to the Panhard's 17.7 mph. By contrast the Brown-Whitney steamer which had engaged Rolls's attention at the last Agricultural Hall Show staggered to the top at a speed of 4.56 mph.

A. J. Wilson Ariel Trike A16

The figures giving the speeds at which the cars running in the trials surmounted Taddington Hill form an interesting study. Mr. Wilson's time on his Ariel tricycle is extraordinary, but as the little two and a quarter horse-power motor was assisted by his skilful pedalling the comparison with the car speeds are of value. In fact, we think the old hero of Muswell, Knockmaroon, and many another steep, must have forgotten himself, and pedalled as though he were in one of the fierce athletic contests in which he shone in the early eighties. Anyway, his performance was a fine one.

MANCHESTER WAS a town of some considerable size. It boasted 33 hotels on the programme list (none of them Temperance), although pricing details are only listed for 10 of them. A room at The Grand could cost you up to 6/6, with 3/6 for a servants room. One could economise with a room at the Old Boar's Head or the Black Friars for 3/-, but they were here for 3 nights, so comfort could be considered more important! It is interesting to note that there were 3 places where petrol could be obtained. The normal price was 1/6 per gallon, but at Newton & Co in Blackfriars Strett (Agents for Messrs Carless, Capel & Leonard, and Anglo-American Oil) the price was 1/9 per gallon.

The Motor-Car Journal thought to record the reactions of the people of Manchester to the arrival of the motocars ...

"HOW THE CARS CAME INTO MANCHESTER

BY MANCUNIAN

As 'Fair Lancastria' prides itself on it being the case that, whatever its good people approve to-day, England will look upon with favour to-morrow – or something to that effect – we thought it might not be unprofitable to find out, as far as possible, what Manchester and district opinions on automobile matters were, as expressed by 'the man in the street.' With that end in view, therefore, we determined not only to keep our eyes upon the cars and their occupants, but to let our ears also do duty as we rubbed shoulders with the folks along the last two or three miles of the route from Birmingham to Cottonpolis.

The general impression of the expectant people, in the outlying districts, at all events, was that the cars would pass by a la a circus procession. A little 'Tommy' or a 'Mary Ellen' was stationed at the end of many a street, in order to 'Let muther know when thaay coom,' and the disappointment was very keen when the true condition of things was at length realised.

The little flags which were attached to the lampposts and elsewhere, and whose purpose was, of course, to indicate the route, and the turnings, and so forth, were a source of strange comment. Some thought they were significant of welcome and criticised it as a stingy display, and we actually heard one old lady informing her inquisitive little grandson that why the flags were of various colours was 'because it looked prettier.' But she was more correct in her conclusion that he might not have a blue one after it was done with. The last we heard of the colloquy was 'Will they send them to war, grandma?'

At the point at which we then stood it was the sense of hearing which first realised the approach of the foremost car, and 'expectation stood on tip-toe' until it hove in sight: and many and novel were the comments it and its occupants evoked. At short intervals, other cars went 'puffing' past, and strange were the names bestowed on the vehicles which in technical circles are designated voiturettes, phaetons, broughams, victorias, etc. The variety and colours of the cars called forth admiration or condemnation in accordance with the preferences and predilections of the critics, whose reasoning we sometimes thought was as unaccountable as the poetic gentleman who wrote, 'The reason why I cannot tell, I do not like thee, Dr. Fell.' Mr. Harmsworth's car, with its large expanse of burnished metal still shining through layers of dust, was on every side declared to be 'a perfect beauty,' and another car, over the destinies of which a lady presided, was gallantly acclaimed. And of course the inevitable khaki was there, and duly commented upon.

But if the cars came in for 'quizzing,' their occupants were treated in the same way, only more so. The 'Goggles' were subject to jocular remarks generally speaking, but one good-hearted dame sought to excuse their use in one case by hazarding the belief that the wearer had weak eyes. The hollows of the eyes of those who did not wear protectors presented the appearance of a comedienne's after a liberal application of belladonna.

As in the case of the goggles, so with the clothing; for the people did not seem to understand that when rattling along and cutting through the air at, perhaps, a score of miles an hour, it is absolutely necessary to be protected from the cold and dust; and therefore the wearing of leather and oil-skin coats, furs, wraps, Sou'westers, slouch hats, tweed caps with ear-flaps, and so on, was regarded less in the light of utility than as the eccentricity of automobile genius. But as the philosopher says that there's many an honest heart beats beneath a ragged coat, so beneath that ollapodrida of apparel were fashionable garments that saw their sartorial birth in Bond Street.

Here and there we noticed a disposition on the part of the drivers of horse-vehicles to be disagreeable, and in one instance such conduct necessitated the speedy stoppage of the motor-car, but this was so well accomplished that it earned the audibly-expressed admiration of the on-lookers. One amusing little episode we may here record. There was heard a shout of 'Here's a big 'un!' – but it turned out to be a steam roller that had just turned the corner.

At the junction of Barlowmoor Road and Seymour Grove, there was a fair concourse of people, anxious to watch the cars sweep round the curve; and so anxious was one British workman to impress the fame of the locality upon the occupants of a certain Daimler car he shouted (pointing to a marked spot on the wall), 'Hi, guv'nor, this is where Charlie Peace shot the bobby!'

It was really too inconsiderate of the powers-that-be to select that very day for re-macadamising the Old Trafford end of Seymour Grove. For some distance the entire breadth of the roadway was laid with rough new stones, and here and there were heaps of stones just deposited. A steam roller was also at work and blocking the traffic. The observations of the by-standers were not complimentary to whomsoever was responsible for the unfortunate choice of a day and hour to begin such drastic road repairing.

At the Deaf and Dumb Asylum, at the corner of Boyer Street and Stretford Road – a few hundred yards on being the Botanical Gardens, the goal of the motorcarists – a lot of the deaf-mutes were interested spectators, and even if one were not familiar with the finger language and display of pantomime, the lads' animated countenances were sufficiently indicative of their admiration. But chancing to know something of the manual alphabet, we asked one little fellow what he thought of a car that had just passed, and he replied, 'Goes very fast.' But the query, Would he like to have a ride on it? caused him to pout his lips and shake his head – whereupon several of his companions nodded and smiled, and tapped their fingers on their breasts, to signify 'We would.' Wise little boys!

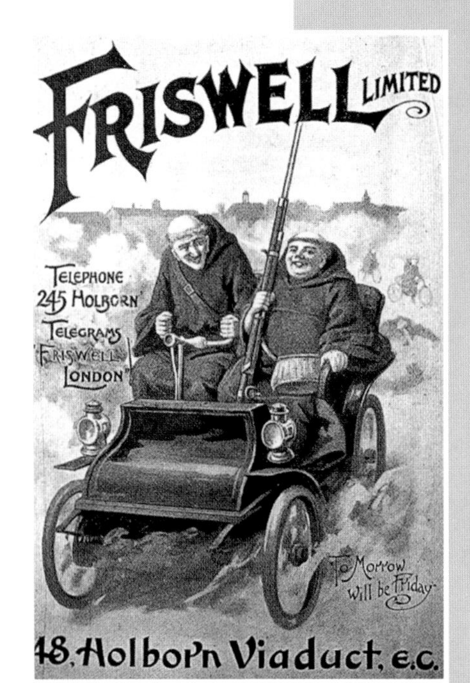

(P.H.H.)

By this time we are very nearly at the Botanical Gardens, which are in Old Trafford. The Gardens are too far from the city to have brought a big miscellaneous crowd, nor to say the truth are they popular with the proletariat – for which relief the pious inhabitants of the district often ejaculate 'Thank Heaven!'

The arrangements of the local committee seemed to be excellent. The carriage entrance to the gardens has an ugly centre stone against which the folded gates are bolted when shut; and an official was thoughtfully told off to warn the car-drivers to exercise due care. The way the steering apparatus answered was quite a theme of remark to those uninitiated into the mysteries of autocarism. After Mr. A. Heatly, the honorary timekeeper, had taken the necessary particulars, the cars entered the glass-domed buildings and took up their places for the exhibition on the morrow. And here parenthetically we may tell that we noticed a well-known gentleman cleaning up his car with all the affection with which a mother washes her first baby.

A long interval having elapsed without the arrival of a car, we cycled off to meet any belated ones. At Chorlton-cum-Hardy we saw one being dragged along by a 'growler,' and could not help thinking, 'Oh, what a falling off was there!' and indeed it looked as if there had literally been a falling off for the occupants.

Thence we wheeled towards Didsbury, past the Crematorium and Southern Cemetery – and an ominous place of buried hopes of getting in first it must have seemed to the occupants of a slow travelling car we met, but who were nevertheless bravely endeavouring to wear a look indicative of 'Oh, we might have been earlier if we had chosen!'

And now may the present writer make a suggestion? If it be that this 1,000-mile Trial has largely been induced by a desire to educate the public on the subject of motor-vehicles, would it not be well to select a halting place a few miles out of the large cities and towns visited, where all the cars would collect and thence travel at short distances apart? There would then be opportunity to make accurate comparisons and awaken the interest of those whose alliance with the movement would be very valuable. ”

The Motor-Car Journal, Friday, May 4th, 1900

MANCHESTER

SATURDAY 28TH APRIL

Arriving 27th April
leaving 29th April

MANCHESTER,
SATURDAY, APRIL 28th, 1900.

A ONE-DAY

EXHIBITION

OF THE

MOTOR VEHICLES

TAKING PART IN THE

1,000-Mile Trial organized by the Automobile Club of Great Britain and Ireland,

WILL BE OPENED BY

THE LORD MAYOR OF MANCHESTER,

AT THE

BOTANICAL GARDENS, OLD TRAFFORD.

OPENING CEREMONY AT 3 O'CLOCK.

ADMISSION—
SATURDAY, APRIL 28th, from 11 o'clock a.m. to 10 p.m. ONE SHILLING.

FRIDAY EVENING, APRIL 27th, anyone wishing to enter the gardens to witness the arrival of the vehicles may do so on payment of ... ... TWO SHILLINGS.

COMMITTEE F

(Being the Com

The following Gentlemen, in conjunctio
the necessary arrangements and guar

Mr. G. P. Dawson.
„ F. Gresham.
„ J. Lowe.
Hon. Sec., Mr. J. Hoyle Smith, Ma

Below: Crossing the tram-lines in Albert Square, Manchester c. 1900. (Courtesy J. Riddell)

We are granted some lovely insights into the prevailing attitudes by this account of some of the speeches made at the opening of the exhibition in Manchester by combining reports in *The Motor-Car Journal* and *The Autocar.*

“ The Exhibition at Manchester

Bristol, Cheltenham, and Birmingham having been favoured with exhibitions of the competing vehicles, it was only fitting that Manchester should also have its one day's display. Some have wondered why Liverpool was omitted from the itinerary; but it must be remembered that, thanks to the efforts of the Liverpool Self-Propelled Traffic Association, the maritime city is far more familiar with automobiles than the textile centre. And so the work of education was devoted to Cottonpolis. Our special correspondent describes elsewhere the reception accorded by the populace; and it is interesting to know that the commercial men and others of influence in the industrial world also gave heed to the coming of the motor-vehicle.

The Royal Botanical Gardens, in which the Exhibition was held on Friday last, presented an unusual sight as the cars were negotiated round and about the flower beds – an exercise that tested the capacity and skill of the drivers to a considerable degree. The exhibition was opened by the Lord Mayor of Manchester (Mr. Thomas Briggs). There was a large attendance at the opening ceremony, and great interest was taken in the fifty cars or more on exhibition. Mr. W.E. Rowcliffe, of Manchester, presided, and the Mayor of Salford (Alderman S. Rudman) was among those present.

The Chairman, before calling upon the Lord Mayor, said that in the near future something would be done in the form of power traction in regard to warfare. There could be no doubt that sooner or later mechanical power would supersede horses. There was and had been a gradual evolution of the battery for storing electricity, and so by degrees reducing the weight to such an extent that it would become a practical commodity. As soon as they were able to secure a battery which with a minimum amount of weight would take storage and run for a period of, say, ten hours, it might be reasonably expected that so soon would all large towns, within reasonable distance of each other, have their own electrical installation with charging stations. Electricity would perhaps be the most popular motive power. It was almost free from noise, had no smell or oscillation, was entirely under control of the driver, and not explosive. Therefore there was no risk to either life or limb, and one was enabled to go almost any distance.

The Lord Mayor said that on looking round the exhibition he had come to the conclusion that a great improvement had been made in the design of the cars. He believed, with the chairman, that the cars of the future would be run by electricity, but in the meantime oil and steam were found to be very satisfactory substitutes. If motorists intended, however, to have public opinion with them, they must be cautious and remember that other people had rights to the road as well as they. There was no doubt that motor-cars would prevent a good deal of cruelty to horses, particularly where long journeys had to be made. He was particularly pleased to know that the proceeds of the exhibition would be handed over to the local War Fund. They were distributing now about £1,000 a week in relief, and more would be wanted. As there was no telling how long the war would still last, it was important that the sum in hand, which now amounted to about £44,000, should be increased. He had great pleasure in declaring the exhibition open.

Mr. S. Okell, of the Manchester Automobile Club, proposed a vote of thanks to the Lord Mayor for extending his patronage to the exhibition. The resolution was seconded by the Hon. Jno. Scott-Montagu, M.P., who reminded the audience that as Manchester had been the birthplace of railways, so he hoped it would be equally progressive in the matter of automobilism. All the way from London to Manchester, via Bristol, nothing but goodwill had been shown to the motoring tourists throughout the country, the villages, and the towns. The Lord Mayor briefly returned thanks. In moving a vote of thanks to the Manchester A.C. for their ardent labours in the arrangement of the controls and their excellent preparations for the exhibition, the Lord Justice Clerk of Scotland said he came from the far north to London for the purpose of riding through Manchester to Edinburgh and back again to London on an autocar. If any of his friends had been told two years ago that he was going to do that they would have thought him quite mad. He thought that we

had dispersed that feeling now. It had been suggested that the position had quite changed during that time. If they had started on this expedition two years ago, they would have been received with the jeers of the grown-up population, and probably the stones of the younger members of the community. There was a sort of notion then that the autocar was a wild unmanageable animal, with wild men seated atop, whose sole purpose it was to break legs, or to knock ladies down and tear their dresses. He was very fond of driving, and had himself driven horses regularly for twenty years, nor would he give up his horses for anything, but that did not prevent him from taking interest in the new sport. The people in all the towns and villages stood far nearer to the cars when they passed than they would have done if the vehicles had been horse drawn.

The people saw at once that the autocars could be guided with safety, and the drivers knew what they were about, and machines would do nothing wrong unless the drivers were themselves wrong. That was not the case with horses. He was quite certain that horses had much more sense with regard to this matter than most of the rest of the population. They were led to suppose that the horse was an animal that could not understand the use of the autocar, and that the autocar when it came near any horses immediately set them into a state of tremendous alarm and excitement, which caused danger to themselves and those who were driving. He appealed to all on this expedition, and to the public in every place they had passed through, to confirm him in his statement that not one horse in 200 had taken the slightest notice of an autocar unless his driver, male or female, was nervous enough to excite the animal, and not leave him quietly to take things as they happened. They must have passed many thousands of horses during the last few days, and in very rare instances had they shown the slightest objection whatever – indeed, no one had done so, not even human beings, so far as he had seen. Certainly, horses were getting perfectly accustomed to motors, and they would know that to a horse the autocar was the greatest blessing that had ever been put upon the road. He thought the public had come to realise that this movement had come to stay. So far as the control of these self-controlled vehicles were concerned, which he had heard described as dangerous, he was prepared to allow any one of the cars they saw before them to be driven to within twelve feet of him at twelve miles per hour, and was confident that it would be brought to a dead standstill before it reached him. In proposing a vote of thanks to the Manchester Committee, he desired also to include all the local committees of the various places they had passed through, in all of which, without exception, the arrangements for their guidance and comfort had been without flaw.

The Hon. S. C. Rolls seconded the vote of thanks, and in the course of his remarks referred to the care exercised by all the drivers of cars throughout the run in strictly adhering to the legal limit of speed.

Mr. Henry Sturmey said he supported the motion as a member of the London club. The arrangements were perfect, and the crowds of people who turned out to watch the passing of the cars simply wonderful. The police from start to finish, excepting the constabulary of Berkshire, who had behaved idiotically, had done all in their power to assist, and had not in one single instance suggested that any car was travelling at twelve and a quarter miles per hour. Their action showed that in future they could be relied upon to exercise the powers conferred upon them by the light of common sense. In Manchester the arrangements for the entry of the city were so admirable that they had only to follow the flags and they arrived. With Mr. Adam Laidlaw's reply on behalf of the Manchester Club, the proceedings terminated.

For us the day closed with a very recherché little dinner given by Mr. Edmunds at the Conservative Club to a few of the party, at which, of course, 'petrol talk' was a feature of the hour. ”

The Autocar Saturday, May 5th, 1900

“ **A Festive Gathering**

On Saturday evening the members of the Automobile Clubs of Manchester and London were entertained at dinner at the Conservative Club at Manchester by Mr. Henry Edmunds, who is a member of both clubs. In toasting the Manchester Club, Mr. C. Johnson, secretary of the London Club, spoke with pleasure of its excellent arrangements in connection with the trials, and said that the place selected for the exhibition had been eminently satisfactory. ”

The Motor-Car Journal, May 1900

The Motor-Car Journal reviewed the first few days of the Trial with, after a few opening remarks, a review of the English weather so far ...

"The Automobile Club's 1,000-Mile Trial

This Trial is now in the second week of its progress, and the results, so far, have completely justified those who urged the Automobile Club to embark on the undertaking. Such a contest, conducted without the incitement of great rewards or large gains, must assure the public with regard to the future of automobilism in this country, and prove to all that mechanical traction on our country roads is rapidly passing beyond the experimental stage, and is destined to play an important part in the transit of goods and the conveyance of passengers in the Twentieth Century.

The weather has been favourable on the whole, although the dryness has revealed a quantity of dust on our roads, which even veteran drivers of horse-drawn vehicles could hardly have regarded as possible. Those who have taken part in the tour have certainly experienced a succession of varying climatic conditions that must have proved exceptionally interesting to those unacquainted with the differences in temperature which make themselves felt over a long stretch of country in our little island, and many will be the reminiscences they will have to tell when they return to town as to the trials and ordeals they have undergone.

The cars that did not run up to the legal limit of speed upon the Bristol to Birmingham run were: No. 2, eleven miles per hour; 5, nine miles per hour; 8, ten miles per hour; 21, no record; 24, no record; 27, eleven miles per hour; 28, five and a half miles per hour; 29, six and a half miles per hour; 30, seven miles per hour; 31, no record; 33, six miles per hour; 34, no record; 38, no record; 41, eleven miles per hour; 43, no record; 45, eight miles per hour; 49, eleven miles per hour; 51, ten and a half miles per hour; 52, two and a quarter miles per hour; A7, no record; A12, eleven and a half miles per hour; A21, eleven miles per hour; A25, ten miles per hour; A26, eleven and a half miles per hour."

Captain Hercules Langrishe carrying out maintenance on Mr. Alfred Harmsworth's 6 h.p. Daimler at Manchester

Right:
Mr. Hubert Egerton cleaning his de Dion Voiturette at Manchester

Right:
A day off. Messrs. Egerton, Edge, and Scott-Montagu
(Photos: *The Autocar*)

The Motor-Car Journal Friday, May 4th, 1900

The 1900 Trial and Manchester: how local motoring spurred the beginnings of Rolls-Royce

by Tom Clarke

The State of Automobilism in Manchester c.1900

On Friday, 27th April 1900, the Hon. C. S. Rolls was leading the Trial in his speedy 12 h.p. Panhard during the Birmingham-Manchester leg. From Buxton in the Derbyshire Peak District he reached the Cat and Fiddle pass (later a favourite spot for testing Rolls-Royce cars). But all was not well. T. B. Browne in his 6 h.p. Panhard noticed that Rolls was experiencing overheated brakes in this section of the run (Note 1). Perhaps as a result, Rolls managed to jettison his personal driver/'mechanician' Alfred J. Poole and some luggage whilst descending the twisting road, treacherous even today. Rolls was not best pleased at having to stop for him and Poole was to harbour a grudge over this incident for many years. Together again, they reached Macclesfield at the bottom and sped on through Alderley Edge towards Manchester. They entered the city on the Barlow Moor Road, through Chorlton-cum-Hardy (where Henry Royce had lived not long before) and on through Seymour Grove to their destination in Old Trafford. Rolls pulled up at 4.50 p.m. at the Royal Botanical Gardens. Some sources claim he was the first to arrive but *The Autocar* listed the first arrival as 4.45 p.m. and Rolls as 5.04, a further reason for Rolls to be grumpy with Poole. He was to know this area better from 1904 when he became part of the Rolls-Royce story.

This most celebrated of names in motoring history has held an endless fascination for researchers, particularly for the circumstances in which Rolls (1877-1910) met Royce (1863-1933). It is widely accepted that they were introduced by their mutual acquaintance Henry Edmunds (1853-1927) in Manchester on May 4th 1904, when the terms of their co-operation were broadly agreed. This meeting is well recorded and needs no coverage here. But it is also widely believed that the two men had not met before. A fresh look at this period, however, throws up the possibility that the 1,000 Miles Trial brought the men together earlier than thought. This was first suggested by Paul Tritton in his biography of Edmunds (Note 2). The Trial might thus have played its part not only in promoting the motor-car locally but a famous name in the motor industry as well.

The first impact of the planned Trial was the formation of the Manchester Automobile Club. An inaugural meeting was held at the Queens Hotel on 23rd November 1899. The Secretary of the Automobile Club in London, Claude G. Johnson (1864-1926), whilst making a circuit of the Trial route from 19th December 1899 to 5th January 1900 and thus seeing in Christmas and the century 'on the road', stayed overnight in Manchester on 20th December for the next meeting. This was the first official meeting of the Manchester Automobile Club as a branch of the A.C.G.B.I. Here Johnson met the Club's members who would be arranging the Trial's local routes and exhibition. Johnson's assistant on the reconnaissance run was Montague R. Grahame-White (1877-1964), supplied by the Daimler company and later a designer of some Rolls-Royce bodies.

Motor-car manufacture in Manchester

How familiar was Royce with the motor-car at the time of the 1900 Trial? This would be a factor in determining Royce's motivation by 1900 and the likelihood of his interest in the Trial. Manchester where he worked was then hardly full of motor-cars, foreign or locally-made. However, many ventures were springing up although none that would later threaten Coventry's position as the centre of the motor industry. Through his business contacts, and magazines, Royce would have become aware of the fascinating developments occurring in Manchester, some virtually on his doorstep. Many of these new makers required bicycle-type chains and a world famous maker of these was local, Hans Renold. Royce had assisted Renold on manufacturing problems with his new roller chains requiring accurate layout and press work. The New Two Speed Gear Co. of 81 Bridge Street, Manchester, makers of *'Reilly & Haigh's two speed gears for cycles, motor cars and all horseless vehicles'* by February 1897 were clearly hoping to supply the infant motor industry. William Reilly's most famous bicycle gear was patented to Sturmey-Archer because of Reilly's obligations to Haigh but a connection to Royce arises from the prototype being made in his works!

The first car made in the city was claimed to be the single Holland example, made in nearby Longsight ca 1895 by Frank Holland, an electrical engineer, and his brother William both of the Rowsley Arms Hotel, 48 Rowsley Street, Beswick. It was designed for them by the patent engineers R. James Urquhart & Bolle at 57 Deansgate (i.e. Barton Arcade in central Manchester where several cycle and motor factors were soon to be found). With a tubular steel frame and walnut body by Cockshoot it was said to have two cylinders of 6" and a tin carburetter (Note 3).

Below:
Entry No. 24, 5 h.p. Marshall Carriage

Also active in 1895-96 was F. Clarke of New Moston in Manchester. He made a two-cylinder engine bolted onto a bicycle wheel. Measuring 2¾" x 6" and geared 1:1 it propelled the bicycle in a series of jerks when tested in August 1896. The device was displayed in 1912 when the short-lived museum of historic vehicles was formed in London.

And there was also the Marshall (*'on the lines of the 3½ h.p. Benz'* which started life as a Benz-based French Hurtu, and later became the Belsize), made at Belsize Works, Clayton from early 1899. Marshall & Co. had bought the Belsize Cycle Company's works in 1897 and began their experiments. Two Marshalls completed the 1900 Trial and the make will figure again in this survey. By late 1901 the 12 h.p. Belsize was being made.

In 1897 John Edward Thornton (1865-1940), who was well-known for his Thornton-Pickard camera company in Altrincham, established the Thornton Motor Co. Ltd. at Worsley Mills off Egerton Street in Hulme. This was very close to Royce's own works and here Thornton made at least two Thornton three-wheel forecars by 1900, using an engine to his own design (Note 4). Another three-wheel forecar was the Century Tandem air-cooled 2¾ h.p. in 1899 made by the talented Ralph Jackson and Arthur Firth of the Century Engineering & Motor Co. at Oakfield Road, Altrincham (coincidentally the street where Thornton lived). This later became the well-known three-wheel Eagle Runabout from 1903 (Note 5). Rolls competed against a Century at the Sheen trials of 28th July 1900 and one also completed the 1900 Thousand Miles Trial.

George Hindle was a well-known owner of a single-cylinder Imperial, made by W. Turner's cycle shop at 291 Stretford Road (very close to Royce). By 1900, now known as the Imperial Autocar Manufacturing Co. Ltd. of Erskine Street, Hulme and later at Rusholme until 1905, a 7 h.p. tonneau was in preparation for the February 1901 Show. Also near Royce was the Trafford Motor Co. at Christ Church Sq., Hulme. From at least 1901 they made bodies and wheels for cars. Other companies announced their plans but subsequent developments are sketchy. For example, in February 1899 it was announced that Baxendale & Co. of Miller Street in the city were to make motor tricycles. And *The Autocar* for 27th May 1899 revealed that Sir W. H. Bailey & Sons of

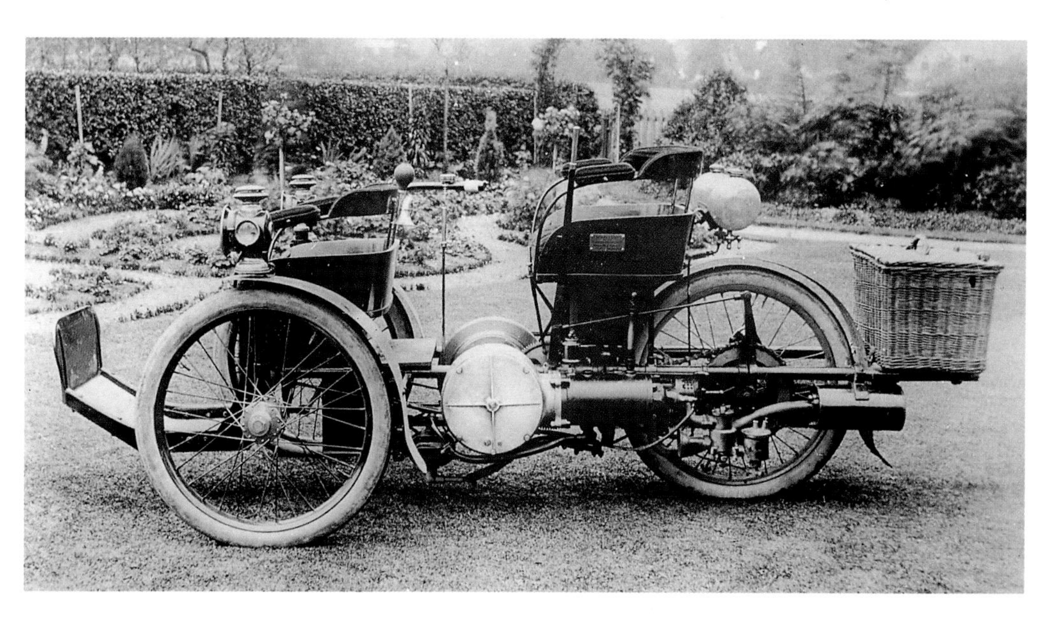

Right:
Another car Royce might have seen in Hulme and on the Manchester-Knutsford road, J. E. Thornton's 1900 Thornton forecar photographed at his home 'Rokeby, Oldfield Road, Altrincham. High-quality Thornton-Pickard cameras might even have been in use in Royce Ltd's photographic department. (Courtesy of Doug Rendell)

Bridgewater Canal Works in Salford were to make motors.

A slightly less early car was the Turrell from late 1900. This was a 7 h.p. 2-cylinder horizontally-opposed, based on the Accles-Turrell of Perry Bar, Birmingham, and with what J. O. H. Norris of Cockshoot recalled as a 'comic' gearbox. Charles McRobie Turrell, the engineer and insurance consultant formerly with the motor monopolist Harry Lawson and the Coventry Motor Co., formed Accles-Turrell Autocars Ltd. in January 1900 at Brown Street, Manchester. Pollock & Macnab Ltd. in nearby Ashton-under-Lyne were the actual makers until Thomas Pollock branched into other engineering with J. G. Accles. By 1902 the Turrell was being made in Manchester by the Autocar Construction Co. Ltd. of Openshaw and called the Hermes. It was now a 15 h.p. 2-cylinder with four speeds. The company also sold the Saracen 5½ h.p. steam engine and an agent, John L. Sardy, operated in London.

Two local industrialists, Frank J. Gresham and Harry Gresham of Gresham & Craven crane makers, had an experimental chassis built in 1901 called the Heatley-Gresham, designed by H. Heatley of London. It was fitted with Cockshoot's first motor body (number 6356), a rear entrance tonneau. (However, a claim is also made that Cockshoot's first body was on the 1895 Holland car, see Note 3.) Apart from Rolls-Royce the best known motor-car maker associated with Manchester was Crossley, also known as stationary engine makers. Their motor-cars did not appear until February 1904, outside the period being covered here.

The first actual car in the city regardless of origin was claimed to be a French-made Cambier for J. H. Pemberton ca 1897. At the same time an 1896 Lutzmann from Lancashire was known in the city owned by Charles C. Goodwin. It was used to sell Mother Shipton's soap (Note 6). The law was alert to these local curiosities and thus the first prosecution was made for speeding. John Wilkerson of Quay Street was fined two shillings and sixpence plus costs for his offence of 18th January 1898. To make matters worse his car carried advertisements for a pantomime at the Theatre Royal! In November 1898 Mr. Courtis, the driver of the dubious U.S. inventor Edward J. Pennington, was acquitted of dangerous driving.

Not far away in Oldham Fred Rothwell, of the cycle maker Eclipse Machine Co., imported a 1½ h.p. Benz 'Velo' (no.510) from Mannheim

in April 1897. At the 1st Manchester Cycle and Motor Show in late 1897 it is said a Rothwell was displayed alongside another make. It was certainly not shown in June that year at the Royal Agricultural Society show at Old Trafford which *The Autocar* variously records with an Anglo-French Autocar and lorry (or four Roger-Benz vehicles), and a Leyland van. The Rothwell was designed in co-operation with Pennington (who proposed a car club in Manchester as early as February 1899). The car was rope driven through the front wheels, with wooden pulleys, and was a failure for Rothwell. But Pennington showed this platform-based car in London, in late 1898, as his 'Victoria'. Rothwell survived to make far better models by 1904. During 1905 A. J. Adams became their designer, having left Royce Ltd. where he had been draughtsman for the first Royce cars (Note 7). Also in Oldham the first Bradbury car was noted in *The Autocar* for 29th October 1898 though it is likely to have been a motorcycle.

Commercial use of cars was begun in March 1898 when the John Heywood Co., and the Sutton Co., used them for goods deliveries. Racing too caught on and a dirt track at Fallowfield saw a competitive event between D. H. Simpson on a 1¾ h.p. Peugeot motorcyle and C. G. Wridgway of Chorlton-cum-Hardy on a Phébus 2¼ h.p. tricycle (Note 8). Wridgway worked locally for Griffiths Cycle and then joined Pennington & Baines in Manchester to become a well-known car promoter before working in the U.S. from September 1900.

Inevitably accidents occurred. *The Autocar* for 1st July 1899 noted an accident in Altrincham in which George Barnes, driving the Bond's Soap van from Salford, was injured after the steering linkage broke. Luckily unscathed were some ladies on board, which was not commented on by the press! The following prosecution was eventually withdrawn because of Barnes's injuries.

Such was the industrial side of the Manchester motor scene as Royce might have known it. His own motor experience had actually begun several years before, far from Manchester.

Royce crosses the Channel

A route back to the early days of Royce's motoring knowledge comes through a James Peter Whitehead (1860-1932) about whom P. E. Jenkins wrote some recollections in the Manchester Guardian in 1963. Whitehead was a Manchester engineer and manufacturers' agent specialising in textile machinery. On one occasion he was visiting a Continental customer and noticed some excellent Royce electrical equipment in use, a name he was unfamiliar with. Back in Manchester he hurried to find Royce's workshop and arranged to sell a variety of Royce equipment as an agent. Whitehead and Royce's partner Ernest Claremont (1863-1922) became friends and in 1893 Whitehead came to live in the same street as Royce in Chorlton-cum-Hardy, around the corner from Claremont's house. In 1894 he was called upon to invest in F. H. Royce & Co. Ltd., buying 500 shares from Royce and Claremont and becoming a director soon after (Note 9).

Around this time Royce went with Whitehead to Mulhouse in Alsace, eastern France, which was under German control 1871-1918 and where Whitehead had arranged a meeting with his local agent. The area was significant in the textile industry with many mills and dyeing works. It is not clear what the reason for the journey was but promoting textile equipment and Royce's electrical range is likely (Note 10). The Mulhouse visit must date from the mid to late 1890s. In any event, Whitehead's French agent turned out to be an early automobilist. He was certainly a rarity as there were only 125 cars in the whole of France by 1893. Over the next few days the agent's car was used to take the three men on visits to local factories. On one run they had the inevitable close shave with a haycart which rather unsettled Royce. He told Whitehead he would not ride again in such contraptions and walked back to town.

By January 1904 Whitehead's business was big enough, now with several associates, for the formation of a trading company. Luckily its records have survived in Manchester, enabling a vital name to be added to the Mulhouse visit. The main English company formed was Whitehead, Sumner, Harker & Co. (196 Deansgate, Manchester). Its Mulhouse branch was Prêcheur, Sumner & Co. which controlled activities in France, Portugal, and Italy. The founder, Julien Prêcheur, is thought to be the agent whose car Royce experienced about ten years earlier. And it is likely he was also the new member of the Automobile Club de France listed in 1897 as *'Julien Pêcheur [sic], vice-consul for Greece (Hérault)'* (Note 11), Greece being a country served by Prêcheur's company. Historian Malcolm Jeal has suggested that for the mid-1890s a Daimler-engined Peugeot (the first make Rolls owned) could have been the car that Prêcheur owned. It was able to carry three men and was made not far away at Valentigney, later at Audincourt. Sadly, Peugeot records do not show Prêcheur's name although his ownership might have been secondhand. Another possibility is Panhard, and of course the German make Benz in view of Mulhouse then being within Germany. Prêcheur left in 1913 and his salesman Georg Roellinger took over. He too might have been on the scene during Royce's visit (Note 12).

Soon after 1899, when Royce's company was floated as Royce Ltd., Whitehead ceased to be a director and lost regular contact with Royce although he retained his investment. He met Royce again when the first Royce car was being designed in early 1903. Whitehead claimed Royce now told him he was so impressed by the saving of time in Mulhouse when the car was used that he thought he should make his own!

Whitehead later got into business difficulties and in March 1915 was helped with a loan from Royce and Claremont of £400. He ended his association with the export agency companies, latterly part-time, in August 1916. Royce and Claremont went further – they found Whitehead a position at Rolls-Royce in Derby as head of Supplies Dept. (He was Chief Purchasing Agent, from at least 1913 until after 1929, although until 1916 he still travelled on behalf of his former agencies). It seems likely a debt of honour was being redeemed for the early work Whitehead had done as a director in promoting Royce's wares and, unintentionally, giving him his first experience of a motor-car. Perhaps it was this that turned his mind towards car manufacture. Whitehead died in May 1932. As for the reason Royce entered motor manufacturing, the Rolls-Royce historian Michael H. Evans emphasises that the economic downturn from 1902 caused Royce to wonder what new product he could make that utilised his two skills – mechanical engineering from his cranes, and electrical engineering from his many other products. The motor-car beckoned.

The exhibition

Royce's decision to become a motorist and later a maker was surely a result of various influences: his earlier experience in France, news of Edmunds' motoring forays in the late 1890s, local cars seen in Knutsford where he now lived and others in Manchester, the economic situation, and finally the April-May 1900 Thousand Miles Trial itself. At the Royal Botanical Gardens, Old Trafford, in the Palm House built for the 1887 Jubilee exhibition, about fifty cars were displayed on Saturday 28th April from 11 a.m. to 10 p.m. Viewers were permitted to come on the Friday night for two shillings, and on the Saturday entry cost one shilling with a reduced price of sixpence after 6 p.m. The Sunday was a free day for the drivers. On Monday the 30th two omnibuses took many of the participants from their hotel in Piccadilly to Old Trafford and the 54 surviving cars then started north via Bolton. They left Manchester by the swing bridge over the Ship Canal, through Salford, and on to Pendleton.

(The Gardens were on the main Chester Road, now the A56, immediately opposite the entrance to Trafford Park which was gradually being filled as an industrial estate, and less than a mile from Royce's factory at Cooke Street. The Palm House was on the Talbot Road side of the Gardens, close to the present day Old Trafford Cricket Ground. Royce did not show his electrical wares at the inaugural exhibition for the 1887 Jubilee but would have gone to see the extensive electrical lighting used and other exhibits. The Palm House had also seen four annual motor exhibitions by 1900 and, with Royce's sense of curiosity, it can easily be imagined that he visited some of these events as well. The last, the 4th Manchester Motor Show, had been held from 16-24th February not long before the Trial, and the Manchester Cycle & Motor Show competed with it from 9-17th February at St. James's Hall. Around 1907 the Gardens became White City amusement park. The area has now been totally redeveloped.)

Amongst the many well-known Trial participants was Rolls friend Henry Edmunds. An acquaintance of Royce, with an incredible knack for bringing people and ideas together, he was connected to Manchester through business. He stayed in the city regularly to fulfil his duties as managing director of W. T. Glover & Co., cablemakers in Salford, on the other side of Manchester's River Irwell. Another director was Ernest Claremont of Royce Ltd. (In July 1901 Royce Ltd. began to build new crane

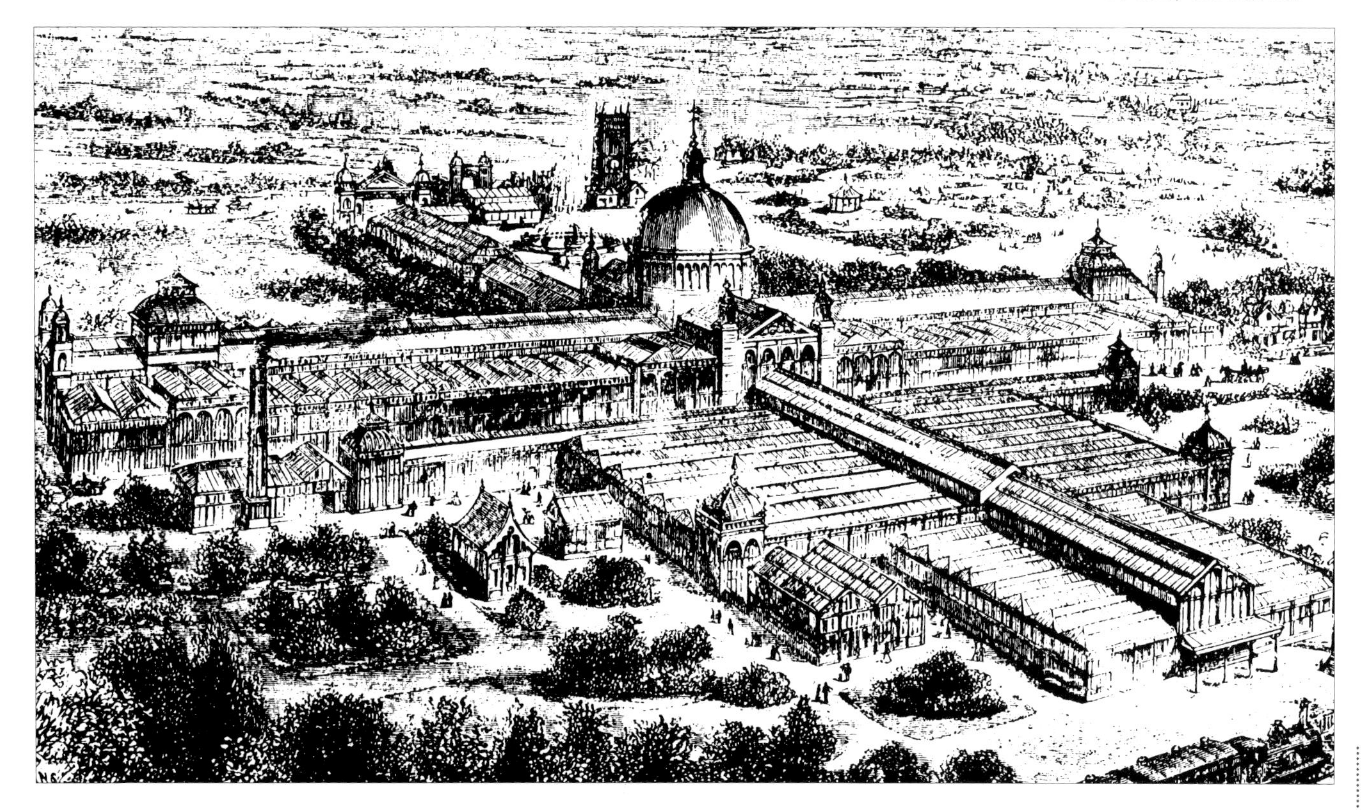

The Exhibition building at the Royal Botanical Gardens, Old Trafford.

works, opposite the equally new Glover works, in Trafford Park although these were not occupied until early 1902.) In addition, Edmunds was a member of the Manchester Automobile Club which now had fifty members (Note 13).

Given Edmunds' Manchester connections and Trial involvement it would not be unreasonable to think that he arranged for Claremont and Royce, rising local industrialists, to visit the displayed cars. They might also have noticed the advance and progress reports of the Trial in the local press. Both Royce and Claremont went by train to their work in Cooke Street, Hulme. On the way from their homes in Knutsford the train stopped at Old Trafford station. It would be amazing if neither had alighted here and 'popped in' to see the cars. They could just as easily have walked from their works. Royce in particular was much more open to the new ideas the exhibition represented.

The local organisers of the exhibition had made lavish plans. The Lord Mayor of Manchester, Thomas Briggs, opened the show on Saturday at 3 p.m. His remarks were favourable to motoring, hoping electric vehicles would prevail and calling for considerateness by motorists. Loud applause followed his references to the Boer War which daily filled all the local newspapers. Proceeds from the exhibition were to go to the local War Fund. The motions of thanks included one from the Scottish Lord Justice J. H. A. Macdonald which Rolls seconded. Some reports claim eighty-two cars at the exhibition. This would imply about thirty local vehicles augmenting the display or perhaps just parked around the Gardens. The journalist Sam Lomax, who in 1948 wrote the history of Manchester motoring with John Norris, 'gate crashed' the Trial exhibition on his 2¾ h.p. quadricycle (Note 14).

With the late closing of the Saturday exhibition the main participants must have moved on for dinner, leaving others to explain the cars to the evening visitors. As an enthusiastic proselytiser for the motor-car Rolls would have played his full part during the day. That evening Edmunds gave a small 'recherché' dinner party in the city for several participants and local club members. Early reports claimed this was held at the Conservative Club but it was in fact changed to the Queen's Hotel. Though Royce later joined the Manchester Automobile Club, during 1903, he is an unlikely fellow diner. Edmunds might also have taken charge of Rolls on the Sunday to fill in the free day although motor maintenance must have been a strong option. Unfortunately, Edmunds' memoirs only describe the formal meeting he arranged between Rolls and Royce in 1904 and not any social gathering in 1900.

The growth of local motor clubs

At the exhibition the Lord Mayor had been assisted by the Chairman of the Manchester Automobile Club, W. E. Rowcliffe (owner of a Century forecar and later a 9 h.p. Clément registered M-9). Newspapers gave credit to the local members who were backing the display with £3.3s.0d each: H. M. Addey, J. Butterworth, George Pilkington Dawson of Prestbury (a railway engineer with a Benz International 5 h.p. dogcart, part-exchanged in January 1901 for Rolls's 1899 8 h.p. Panhard), C. Featherstone, Frank James Gresham, J. Harvey, J. Leeming, James Lowe, Benjamin Marsden, Samuel Okell, Victor F. O'Neill (6 h.p. Daimler), Daniel H. Simpson, T. Taylor, Rupert Williamson (5 h.p. Marshall), A. L. MacKillop as Treasurer (later company secretary at Arrol-Johnston Ltd.), and Secretary J. Hoyle Smith (managing director of Marshall & Co. who ran a Renaux 3½ h.p. quad made by Marshall). Rowcliffe's office at 37 Cross Street served as the Club's headquarters.

In addition to the backers the local Club's thirty-eight inaugural members and their cars are interesting. Some had useful connections and Royce would come to know some of them after he joined: John Harvey (motor agent, and perhaps the eponymous contributing editor to the journal *La Locomotion Automobile* in France after 1894), Adam Laidlaw (10 h.p. Daimler later registered M-59), J. J. Mann (a director of Marshall & Co. and a participant in the 1900 Trial on a 5 h.p. Marshall), Walter Featherstone (an engineer and city councillor who had tried a Pennington and announced in *The Autocar* for 5th November 1898 that he intended to make a car), Sydney Norris (of carriagebuilder Cockshoot, later Rolls-Royce agents), F. E. Baron (6 h.p. Daimler), W. L. Bodman, C. T. Brown, John Cooke, A. J. King, J. J. Marsden (a shareholder in F. H. Royce & Co. Ltd.), R. Marsden, S. Marsden, Thomas Myers, R. E. Platt, J. T. Simpson (previously Mayor of Halifax), W. H. Taylor, F. Eckersley, John E. Thornton (the inventor described earlier), Dr. R. M. Marshall, E. Mellor, Ludlow P. Perkins, and W. le P. Webb.

Sam Okell's 1897 Hurtu built in France, 3½ h.p. air-cooled Benz engine. Photographed at Okell's home, 'Overley', Langham Rd., Bowdon, Cheshire. It was probably this car Okell used for the 1900 Trial Exhibition. (Courtesy of Mrs. C. Okell-Jones)

Other interesting members were Gresham's friend Frederick Smith of 'Dunham Lawn', Bowdon who ran a Benz in the 1890s. He became chairman of the M.A.C. in October 1904 and was later a Rolls-Royce owner (Note 15); Dr. Marshall of Newton Heath bought a troublesome Benz from the local agents in November 1898 and by late 1900 had resumed using his horse and a bicycle on his rounds!; Daniel Simpson ran a tricycle and, with his partner Bodman, operated Simpson-Bodman of Pomona Engine Works, Lund Street, Cornbrook where steam lorries were made. By August 1900 Bodman had left for the U.S.A. but he left behind an active company (Note 16).

A final look at one member's cars reveals the rise of what became the third major Manchester maker, Belsize. According to family recollections Samuel Okell (1838-1932) of 'Overley', Langham Road, Bowdon, whose second wife was the artist Mary Lever Burdekin, was determined to have a car in time for the abolition of the 'Red Flag' Act. Accordingly he went to the Paris Exhibition in 1896. There he saw a Hurtu which was ordered via London and delivered to Manchester by rail some months before the November 'Emancipation Run'. It was fitted with a 3½ h.p. air-cooled Benz engine and it too could claim to be the earliest car in the city and probably Cheshire as well. However, this model only became available from late 1897 so it seems Okell must have purchased his first car after and not before the Emancipation Run of 1896 as claimed. He soon replaced this car with a Marshall copy of the Hurtu having a water-cooled Benz 6 h.p. horizontal engine. The Hurtu air-cooled 3½ and then the 5 h.p. were first made under licence by Marshall of Manchester from early 1899 followed by the water-cooled 6 h.p. from late 1900.

The Marshall copies of the Hurtu could have been inspired by Okell's first car but a 1907 report on the company (in C. S. Rolls's cuttings books, original source unfortunately not known) noted Marshall's connections with French engineers resulting from their exports to France of mutoscopes. As the Hurtu was rear-engined, and belt-driven, the Marshall copy was already behind the times. In addition, the French 3½ h.p. Renaux tricycle was being made by Marshall by 1900.

In late January 1900 at the Grand Hotel a rival organisation, the Manchester Motor Club, was formed with about twenty-five to thirty members. Ten members formed an inaugural committee: J. A. Bennett (Phébus-Aster 2¼ h.p. quadricycle), T. W. Grace, J. M. Hewitt (of Turrell cars), H. Johnson, A. E. Jones, J. W.

Jones, W. Kenyon, H. M. Lee, John Newton (associated with several motor ventures in the city), Thomas Pollock Jr., R. H. Carlisle (of agents Bennett & Carlisle) as treasurer, and Walter Cawood as secretary. The Club was *'open only to autocar owners'* and seems to have concentrated on the sporting side (Note 17).

And so to the first car

Royce rejected, if he even considered, the local Marshall although his partner Claremont had a tangential link – his mistress from 1899 was Clara McKnight, sister of George Walter McKnight the chief designer at Marshall! Belsize, as Marshall had become, soon after employed another ex-Royce designer, one George Tilghman Richards. Royce probably rejected another new Manchester make when his second French car was purchased. This was the Horbick produced in Pendleton from 1902.

Royce's first 'car' was a De Dion Quad purchased around 1900. The 'Acme' and 'Convertible' models had a front seat for one passenger. Manchester's first motor agency, established by 1898 as the Manchester Motor Corp. of 1 Victoria Bridge Street, Salford, seems at first a likely source. Its founder was C. B. Nixon, later of Leyland Motors, and by 1900 it was owned by John Harvey. Their agencies were for Benz and Panhard according to their sign but M.M.C., Allard (later Rex), Hurtu, Decauville, and Pennington were also known. But their records did not list any sales to Royce although petrol sales to the 1900 Trial participants did figure prominently (Note 18). Also trading by 1900 were the Griffiths Cycle Corp and the Cycle & Motor Co. Ltd. at Oriel House, 19 Deansgate and 1-3 St. Mary's Gate with Frank Hutchinson as manager. There were, however, two even more local possibilities for Royce.

The first was at the bottom of Blake Street, Hulme, where Royce's original 1884 workshop was situated. Here, at 219 Stretford Road, the ironmonger and cycle and motor-car factor F. D. Nawell ran his business. Moreover, Royce rented a stable workshop from him in Blake Street. He sold Premier cycles and exhibited at the 3rd Cycle and Motor Show at the Royal Botanical Gardens from 17-25th February 1899 with a motor tricycle and 4-wheel multi-cycle International Motor Carriage 'Modèle de Luxe' (Note 19). Nawell was also a source for petrol and was listed with two others in the 1900 Trial Programme as a source. This provided a further opportunity for Royce seeing (and hearing!) the visiting cars because

Sam Okell's late 1900 or early 1901 Marshall 6 h.p. based on a Hurtu, a dos-à-dos built by Marshall (later Belsize) of Clayton, Manchester. Photographed at Okell's home. His son Arthur Percival Okell (1865-1959) at the tiller with Granny Coleby alongside, Grandfather Coleby behind and Miss Amy Coleby (Okell's fiancée) beside him. The photograph dates from after June but before October 1901 by which time the engaged couple were married. Note the front radiator. Royce would have seen this and the earlier 5 h.p. Marshall models around Manchester. (Courtesy of Mrs. C. Okell-Jones)

The Manchester Motor Corporation at 1 Victoria Bridge Street, Salford ca 1899/1900 and believed to be the first agency in the city. From the left: 1897/8 Benz 5 h.p. dos-à-dos; 1899 Orient Express or Benz Ideal 5 h.p. dogcart; an Allard; 1899 Benz Velo Confortable; 1899 Decauville voiturette with kicked up rear wings; Benz Velo dogcart with C. B. Nixon, founder of the Manchester Motor Corp., later owned or managed by John Harvey. In the show window behind a motor tricycle can be glimpsed; far right, Benz Velo Confortable. (Courtesy of Roy Brooks. V.C.C. gazette 'Veteran Car' Oct. 1997 p.97)

MOTOR CARS

ENQUIRE for special prices for Allard, Benz, Decauville, Argyll, Star, Panhard, Hurtu, and other Cars; also Quads and Tricycles. Large Stock of HIGH-CLASS MOTOR CARS to choose from at our Show Rooms.

ANY MAKE OF CAR PROCURED AT SHORT NOTICE.

THE MANCHESTER MOTOR CAR CORPORATION,
VICTORIA BRIDGE, MANCHESTER.

Nawell was the closest petrol supplier to Old Trafford where the cars were housed.

A recollection of Royce includes his regular avoidance of a police speed trap on the road to Manchester. A policeman at Bowdon would record the time of Royce's appearance but this was always noticed. Royce then stopped by St. Margaret's Church at Dunham Massey, farther down the road, and lit his pipe. After some time he would continue through Altrincham and on to Sale where the next policeman, Inspector Ennion, recorded Royce's time through the town. This invariably gave a legal speed for the distance covered! One of the policemen of the area, the suitably-named Sgt. Bratt, was once overwhelmed on the Knutsford Road by 740 speeding cyclists in twenty minutes which rather puts a single motor 'scorcher' to shame.

In Knutsford Royce would have known the earliest local cars: in 1899 Alan de Tatton Egerton, M.P. (from 1902 3rd Lord Egerton) of Tatton Park with his first car, an 1897 Benz 3½ h.p. (registered M-1 only years later and later still honoured with an overhaul by Rolls-Royce Ltd. at Crewe!), Mr. Leicester-Warren of Tabley Hall with the second car (of unknown make), a steamer owned by the Rev. Arthur Guest of Lower Peover from 1900, Frank J. Gresham with his 1899 3½ h.p. Hurtu painted green and red although it was probably the Marshall copy. In 1900 he acquired a De Dion voiturette. And a car owned by a local doctor.

Royce's partner Claremont, and their doctor Theodore Llewellyn Fennell in Knutsford, also bought Quads at the same time as Royce. A designer who worked under Royce later recalled that he referred to 'Jubilee' in connection with this vehicle or that of his friends, perhaps a name resulting from the 1897 Diamond Jubilee. Rolls owned a De Dion tricycle from 1897 whilst at Cambridge (he still had it in late 1900) and Edmunds had one with a trailer in 1898. Was a Quad their recommendation to the Manchester novices?

Although some of the evidence is anecdotal and even speculative it is at least possible that Rolls and Royce became aware of each other during the 1900 Trial, with only the Royce car finally creating the conditions for a formal business meeting in 1904. In so many ways the 1900 Trial foreshadowed Rolls-Royce: it was organised by Claude Johnson, the Company's first managing-director and years later called the 'hyphen' in Rolls-Royce; it was underwritten by the press baron Alfred Harmsworth who, as Lord Northcliffe, was a major force behind the scenes at Rolls-Royce (and who drove the 1900 Trial's Birmingham to Manchester leg, staying overnight on Friday 27th April); it was 'won' by the Hon. C. S. Rolls the co-founder of the marque; and it exhibited participants' cars in Manchester, birthplace of Rolls-Royce, only a short distance from Royce's first two factories. Who knows, on May 4th 1904 Rolls and Royce might even have recalled their earlier meeting during the 1900 Thousand Miles Trial exhibition in Manchester.

Notes

1. V.C.C. *Gazette* Dec. 1945 p.265.
2. Paul Tritton. *'The godfather of Rolls-Royce: the life and times of Henry Edmunds...'*. London: Academy Books, 1993.
3. Manchester Evening News 3 Oct. 1925 p.7, & 14 May 1968; V.C.C. *Gazette* Spring 1969 p.341 (also mentions Cockshoot body).
4. David A. Davies. *'John Edward Thornton: a forgotten Mancunian'* in Manchester Region History Review v.11 no.2 1988/89 p.21-4; Douglas Rendell. *'The Thornton-Pickard story'*. Prudhoe, Northumberland: Photographic Collectors' Club, 1992. 52p; T. C. Clarke. 'From cameras to cars' in *Veteran Car* no.266 June 1999 p.19-23.
5. R. J. Wyatt. 'The Eagle Engineering & Motor Co. Ltd.' in *Old Motor & Vintage Commercial,* 1962 p.105-109.
6. The Lutzmann passed from Goodwin to Eric Berry in Southport, 1948, and later to Mr. Bradshaw of Loxhams Garage. It is now preserved in Jersey.
7. J. H. Schofield. *'The Rothwell car'*. Oldham Local Interest Centre, 1978. (Oldham Studies no.1).
8. *The Autocar* 26 August 1899 p.755.
9. Tom Clarke. *'Ernest Claremont: a Manchester life with Rolls-Royce and W. T. Glover & Co.'* Sale: Hulme Press, 1995.
10. Royce's 1894 catalogue *'Electric transmission of power'* mentioned the advantage of electric motors over steam power in mills where machinery was separated in scattered locations.
11. *La Locomotion Automobile* 10 June 1897 p.275.
12. Manchester Central Library, Local Studies Unit: Archive M559 Sumner, Harker & Co.
13. *Automobile Club Journal* 1899, 1900 p.89-90.
14. Sam Lomax and J. O. H. Norris. *'Early days: memories of the beginnings of automobile engineering in south Lancashire and Cheshire'*. Manchester: Cockshoot & Co., 1948. 47 pages.
15. *Early & Late* (VSCC) no.31 Apr. 1967 p.111-115.
16. *The Autocar* 5 Mar. 1898 p.146, 2 June 1900 p.529.
17. The Autocar 3 Feb. 1900 p.98.
18. The records for this company survived with Harvey's son Luther Fletcher Harvey of Bowdon (trading at 225-7 Deansgate and later 6 Chapel Street, Salford) until at least his death on 27 September 1947. See also Lomax & Norris above.
19. If Royce went to the Show he would also have seen: F. Bullock, a wire wheel specialist of Strangeways, with a motor-car on his stand; the Bracegirdle Cycle Co. (Mercury Cycle works, 56 Alexandra Road) with an Allard motor tricycle *'with De Dion principle'*; William Prince (The Wheeleries, 198 Stretford Road near Cooke Street) with a Beeston motor quadricycle; and M.M.C. (of 40 Holborn Viaduct, London) with 'three handsome motor cars...and...well built reliable motor tricycles'.

Acknowledgements

Mrs. Joan Williamson, Librarian of the R.A.C.; Mrs. C. Okell-Jones, Altrincham; Mrs. Joan Leach, local historian of Knutsford; Manchester Central Library; Malcolm Jeal and Mrs. Elizabeth Bennett of the V.C.C. for abetting my interest.

MANCHESTER TO KENDAL

10

MONDAY 30TH APRIL

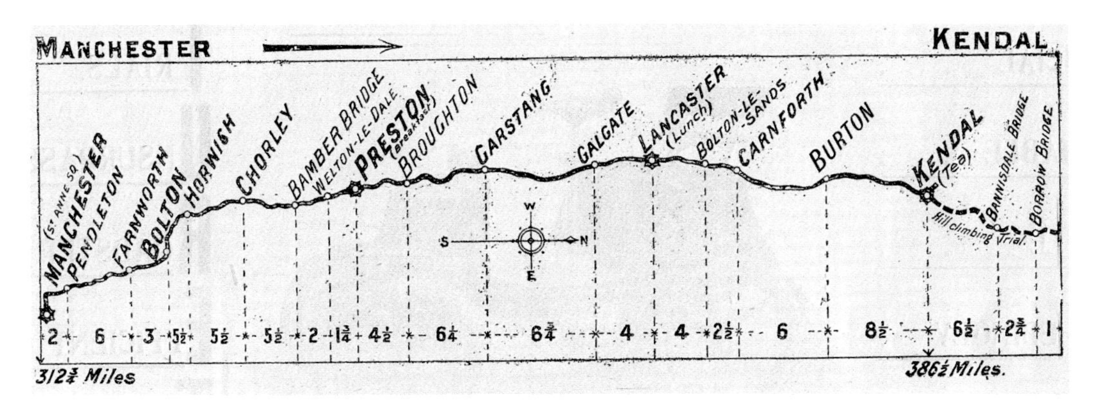

73¾ miles
Via Bolton, Chorley, Preston, Lancaster, to Kendal.
Evening optional Hill-climbing trials on Shap Fell

STRICTLY TO the letter of Claude Johnson's instructions, which by now had the firm respect born of experience as to their reliable and detailed content, the Participants readied themselves early on the Monday morning April 30th 1900. They had experienced a wet Sunday in Manchester for their day off (somewhat fostering the legend that it always rains in Manchester), and as they gathered outside the Botanical Gardens, Trafford Park, they prepared to proceed in a line for the 30 miles to Preston, not exceeding 8 mph, behind a lead car. 'Cars will not be allowed to pass each other or to run abreast'. Considering the wet conditions this was a wise ruling. The road was through the industrial areas, and paved with Lancashire 'cobbles', a kind of granite setts, which were bumpy and dangerously coated with grease where there was paving, but mostly rough surfaces. Mr Scott Montagu's Daimler was the pace car, although he did actually loose his way at some point. The Autocar reporter had a seat on Mr. Critchley's 6 hp Parisian Daimler number 35.

The County Surveyors

Almost without exception the county surveyors have given excellent facilities to the motorists, and their practical appreciation of the new movement has been well demonstrated. On the cars leaving Manchester the county surveyor for the Salford Hundred had a seat on Mr. Montagu's car as far as Horwich, and directed the driver at the difficult points of the route, and another county surveyor accompanied the car to Kendal.

The Motor-Car Journal, Friday, April 27th, 1900

Mr. J. S. Critchley was the Manager of Daimler Motor Works. The Daimler Motor Co Ltd had premises in Shaftesbury Avenue, London; and the works in Coventry. Mr. J. S. Critchley claimed that throughout the Trial no parts were replaced and no failures to report on his car. It is to his credit that 12 of the 13 Daimlers under his supervision were successful.

Number 35 was painted a khaki colour, which must have proved very 'serviceable' in the prevailing conditions. Breakfast was taken in Preston after this tedious 30 mile drive. Claude Johnson must have had some concerns here, as the instructions state that during breakfast the cars could stand in the Market Square, but must 'be left in charge of a responsible and qualified person.' The story is best told in *The Autocar* reporters' own words ...

Manchester to Kendal

"Promptly to the minute of seven the cars left Manchester on Monday morning, 30th April, having first been ranged in proper order by the roadside outside the Botanical Gardens. It was cold and raw, with a promise of wet, and, after the copious rain of the previous day, the stone-setted streets over which we had to travel were in a somewhat slippery condition, though in not anything like the condition of the Birmingham tramways. Our route lay for thirty miles as far as Preston; in fact, through a continuous succession of busy manufacturing towns and villages, all for the most part paved with the universal Lancashire 'cobbles,' and in order to minimise the chance of accident Mr. Scott Montagu's car was requisitioned as a pilot car to lead the way, and set the pace, the whole thirty miles being, in fact, one continuous control, no car being allowed to pass another, and all therefore coming through virtually in procession at a steady and moderate pace. For our own part we found a place for the day on a khaki coloured six horse-power Parisian Daimler, driven by Mr. Critchley, and, through a mistake at the outset on the part of the pilot car, we found ourselves running sixth, almost at the head of the procession. For almost the entire thirty miles we bumped over bad roads and crawled through dense throngs of factory hands and children, being led through Farnworth by a man on horseback. Passing through Bolton, a local Benz chipped in, but retired to the roadside almost immediately with a broken belt, and a local Stanley steamer was also seen. All the way we had in our immediate front the Star running steadily and well, and the Locomobile (Stanley) steamer doing ditto. This gave us an opportunity of observing her action, and she struck us as being well balanced on her springs, and running with great steadiness, but she smelled somewhat, and we got the full benefit of it, her uptake being almost on a level with our noses. Preston was reached by the leading car at 10.50, Messrs. Coulthard's steam lorry, together with Messrs. Norris and Toulmin of that firm, being on hand to welcome the travellers. A short stoppage for breakfast was made here, and then the twenty miles run into Lancaster was made in excellent time over roads of the best, almost level, and just nicely free of dust, without being heavy in running, some very interesting little speed tests between Nos. 29, 15, A30, and our own car *en route* serving to enliven the journey, and the leaders arrived at the Lancaster control, only to find themselves too early for the officials, who kept them nearly twenty minutes waiting for them. Whilst waiting, the more tardy ones arrived and formed up in line, some bringing the news of an unfortunate accident to the Star, which had broken a front axle, and placed herself *hors de combat*, happily without danger to her passengers. After a very hurried and insubstantial lunch at Lancaster, the cars filed out for the destination for the day – Kendal, the twenty miles to which town were accomplished in good time over roads which were dry and dusty, so that as we got in a ruck of cars travelling at almost our own pace we were soon as dusty as millers. On arrival, the cars were housed in the Market Hall, and were on exhibition during the evening, after the cars returned from the climbing of Shap Fell."

The Autocar, Saturday, May 5th, 1900

Entering Preston – note the cobbles (Photo: *The Autocar*)

Children and Motor-Cars

"So deep has been the interest aroused in the Trial that in most of the schools along the route in Derbyshire and Lancashire work was suspended in the morning or afternoon to allow the children to see the automobiles. Doubtless the occasion will be regarded as a great event, and certainly the action was well calculated to get the motors 'talked about.'"

The Motor-Car Journal, Monday April 30th 1900

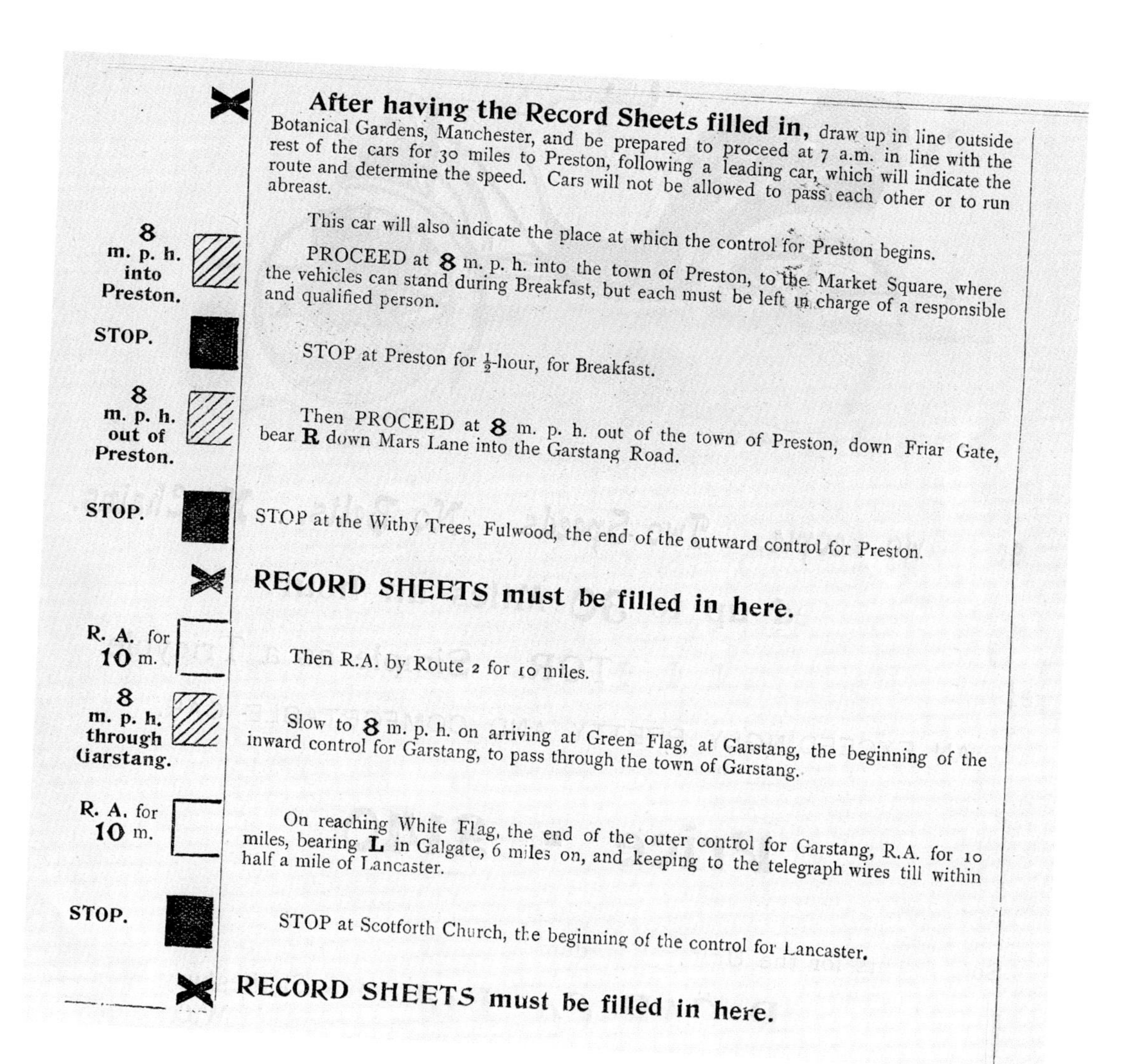

After having the Record Sheets filled in, draw up in line outside Botanical Gardens, Manchester, and be prepared to proceed at 7 a.m. in line with the rest of the cars for 30 miles to Preston, following a leading car, which will indicate the route and determine the speed. Cars will not be allowed to pass each other or to run abreast.

This car will also indicate the place at which the control for Preston begins.

8 m. p. h. into Preston. PROCEED at **8** m. p. h. into the town of Preston, to the Market Square, where the vehicles can stand during Breakfast, but each must be left in charge of a responsible and qualified person.

STOP. STOP at Preston for ½-hour, for Breakfast.

8 m. p. h. out of Preston. Then PROCEED at **8** m. p. h. out of the town of Preston, down Friar Gate, bear **R** down Mars Lane into the Garstang Road.

STOP. STOP at the Withy Trees, Fulwood, the end of the outward control for Preston.

RECORD SHEETS must be filled in here.

R. A. for **10** m. Then R.A. by Route 2 for 10 miles.

8 m. p. h. through Garstang. Slow to **8** m. p. h. on arriving at Green Flag, at Garstang, the beginning of the inward control for Garstang, to pass through the town of Garstang.

R. A. for **10** m. On reaching White Flag, the end of the outer control for Garstang, R.A. for 10 miles, bearing **L** in Galgate, 6 miles on, and keeping to the telegraph wires till within half a mile of Lancaster.

STOP. STOP at Scotforth Church, the beginning of the control for Lancaster.

RECORD SHEETS must be filled in here.

" One good thing which the Automobile Club tour is doing – a feat which in the Manchester district is regarded as bordering on the miraculous – is to soften the asperity of the police towards the movement, and to convert them into friends. The *Manchester Evening News* states that along the route constables were numerous, but, instead of hiding behind trees, at bends in the road, or waiting for the unwary scorcher at the foot of hills, they were in the middle of the roads at crossings waving flags and directing the motorists which way to take. Their politeness was commendable, and the most astonishing thing of all was that when the cars reached a speed of twelve and a quarter miles an hour the police looked on with admiring approval. Truly, wonders will never cease. "

The Autocar Saturday May 5th, 1900

Lancaster

" The presence of the motor-cars at Lancaster attracted a good deal of attention. Very few were much behind the scheduled time. The roads from Preston were in excellent order, and the journey was made with ease and comfort. The police arranged the route so that the cars passed through several streets instead of passing straight through the town, and the parade created a good deal of interest. The party stayed over an hour in the town, and lunched at the King's Arms Hotel, the cars meanwhile being on exhibition in Parliament Street, where an interested company inspected them and made various inquiries. One or two cars needed re-adjustment, but there were no causalities requiring serious repairs, and the ease with which sharp corners were negotiated in the progress through the town was remarkable. "

The Motor-Car Journal, Monday April 30th 1900

" Lancaster was put in greater sympathy with the tour and the automobile movement in general by reason of the fact that the previous day to the automobilist's visit one of its most respected citizens had breathed his last, his death being caused by the unaccountable shying of a horse. We refer to the death of Mr. Frank Bicknell, the business manager of the Lancaster Standard. Six others sustained more or less serious injuries. The lamentable affair occurred within the grounds of Col. Foster, M.P., the member for the Lancaster Division. "

The Autocar Saturday May 5th, 1900

MOTOR VEHICLE, No. 34 (Section I.)

THE DECAUVILLE.

To SEAT 2, with small Seat for occasional party.

THREE SPEEDS. NO BELTS. NO CHAINS.

Speed up to 22 Miles an hour.

MOTOR $3\frac{1}{2}$ h.p. Started from the Seat.

MAGNIFICENT HILL-CLIMBER.

Sole Agents for the United Kingdom—

THE MOTOR CAR Co., LTD.,

168, Shaftesbury Avenue, London, W.C.

GOOD AGENTS WANTED.

HILL CLIMBING TRIAL, No. 2.

HILL-CLIMBING TRIAL (OPTIONAL)

OF

SHAP FELL (7¼ miles and 1⅜ miles),

Monday, April 30th, 1900, at 4.15 p.m.

The Hill is on the North side of Kendal, and is shown on the "Contour Road Book," No. 161 N.

The vehicles will assemble at the Fish Market, at 4.15 p.m.

RECORD SHEETS must be filled in here.

Proceed to Mint Bridge, one and a fifth miles from the Fish Market.

STOP. STOP at Mint Bridge.

RECORD SHEETS must be filled in here.

The vehicles will be started from the Mint Bridge, at 4.30 punctually, in the order of their arrival at Kendal, at 30 seconds' intervals.

Proceed up Shap. PROCEED at full speed up Shap Fell.

N.B.—No car will be allowed to pass another car on the down gradients of the ascent.

STOP. STOP 7¼ miles from the start, at the top of a steep descent just before Huck's Bridge.

(NOTE.—Huck's Bridge is the bridge shown on Contour, on page 105, by the "Bay Horse" Inn.)

RECORD SHEETS must be filled in here.

Proceed at slowest possible speed. On the signal being given by the timekeeper, PROCEED down the hill at your slowest possible speed till you reach the timekeeper at the bottom. This is a test of brake-power—records will be kept—so the slowest possible speed is desirable.

R.A. to the summit. Your time will be taken at the bottom of the descent, but you need not Stop, but PROCEED at full speed to the summit, 1⅜-miles on.

STOP. On arriving at the summit, STOP.

RECORD SHEETS must be filled in here.

HILL CLIMBING TRIAL, No. 2 (*continued*).

Then go on and turn round, and place your car close up on the near side in such a position as not to interfere with competing cars, and wait there till all other cars have arrived at the summit and the signal is given to descend.

During the descent into Kendal, no car is to pass another car, under pain of disqualification from the whole of the Trials, unless the driver of the car in front signals to pass.

No account is taken of the time occupied in descending the hill in calculating the averages, unless more than 1½-hours is occupied, when the excess will be added to the running time of the day; this is provided so that time apparently spent on the descent may not be devoted to repairs.

Return direct to the Market Hall.

Stop.  Here STOP.

RECORD SHEETS must be filled in here.

Vehicles must be taken into the Exhibition building immediately and allowed to remain there until 6 a.m. the next morning.

Shap Fell – the worst hill in England

Monday April 30th was a short days motoring (73¼ miles) with a sting in the tail! Participants were supposed to arrive in Kendal in time for tea (4.30 p.m.); and then an optional Hill Climbing Trial up Shap Fell (10 miles) was billed for the early evening. Hill climbing was a challenge to motorcar makers, and they were keen to display their prowess in this competitive set-up. The grades were continually changing, and if any driver missed a gear his car came to a stop and he would invariably have to coast backwards some distance before starting again. The gradients were well documented, and a great deal of home-work before starting would surely pay off. The surface was poor, and the gradients long, as can be seen from the map below.

Twenty seven of the Participants decided to climb Shap Fell. Nineteen were from the manufacturers entries, who were of course more commercially aware of the benefits of good results for potential sales. Having said that, some of the private (Amateur) class were also keen to prove their cars, Herbert Ashby's Empress tricycle (A20), Hon. C. S. Rolls' in his 12 h.p. Panhard (A17), Frank Butler's 6 h.p. Panhard (A2), Mark Mayhews 8 h.p. Panhard (A4) and his 7 h.p. Peugeot (A29) (quite a sporting Gentleman), T. B. Browne's 6 h.p. Panhard (A3), J. S. Holder's 12 h.p. Daimler (A22), and Ernest Pitman's Daimler (A21).

The story of this Hill Climb is well documented.

C. S. Rolls progress on Shap was 27.5 mph., according to some accounts the best ascent though others credited an Empress tricycle with a better performance. This speed seems almost incredible by the standards of 1900, and in fact represents Rolls's time over the total observed section of seven and a half miles: over the stiffest part of the climb he recorded a still creditable 17.71 mph.

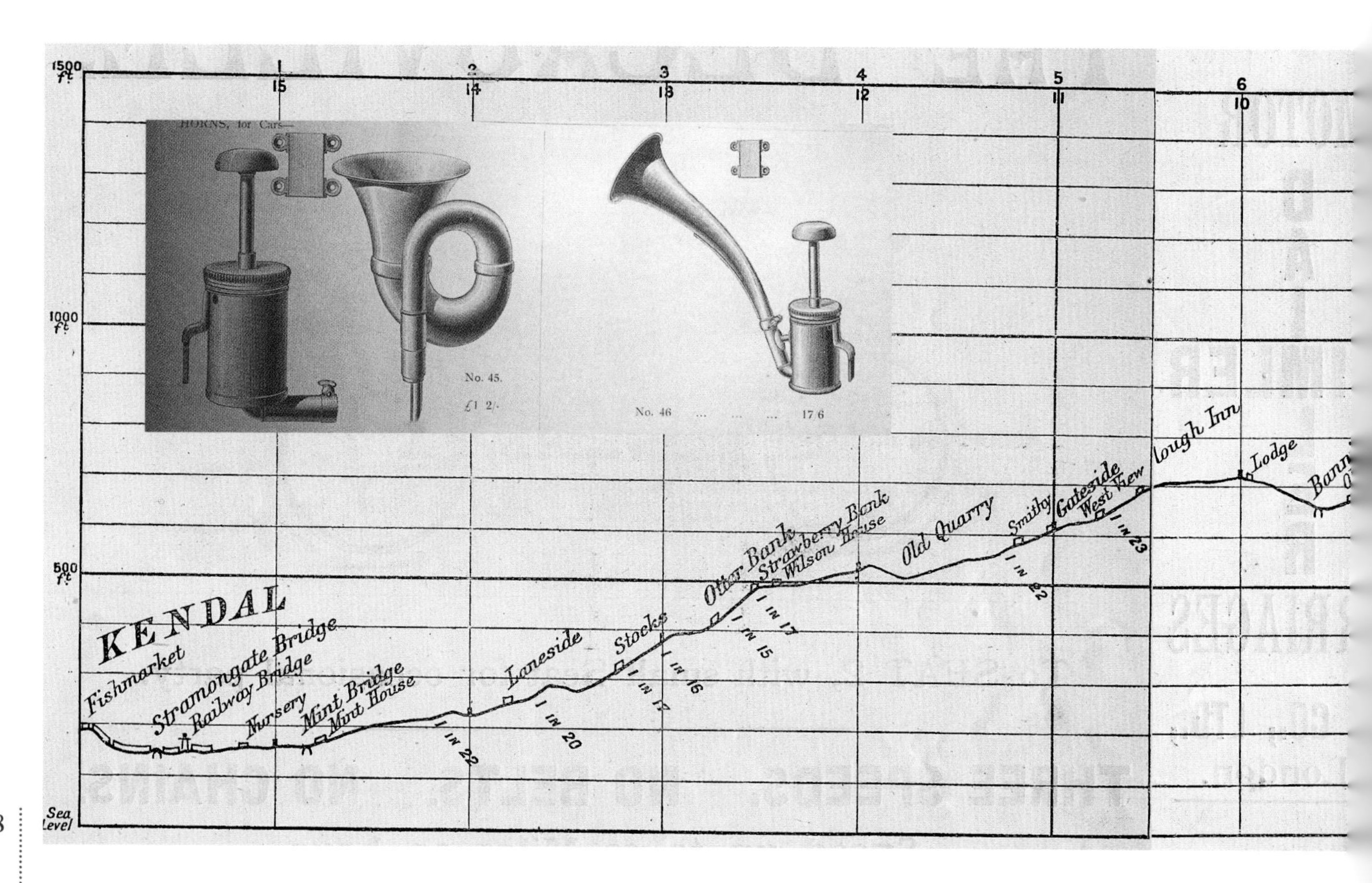

“The Climbing of Shap Fell

For this trial, which was optional, some twenty-seven cars elected to compete. We went up in Mr. Johnson’s car, taking the long ascents well, and getting off at the bottom of a steep ten per cent descent, a little over eight miles up. The descent was made the scene of a brake test, all cars having to go down dead slow, and stop at the bottom, and then go on for the last and steepest part of the rise. With the exception of Mr. Astell’s New Orleans, which stopped half-way up the first ascent from here, but started again on the hill, and finished the journey, all the cars successfully accomplished the ascent.

The times and average speeds up the steep portion from Bay Horse Inn to the summit, one and threequarter miles, were:

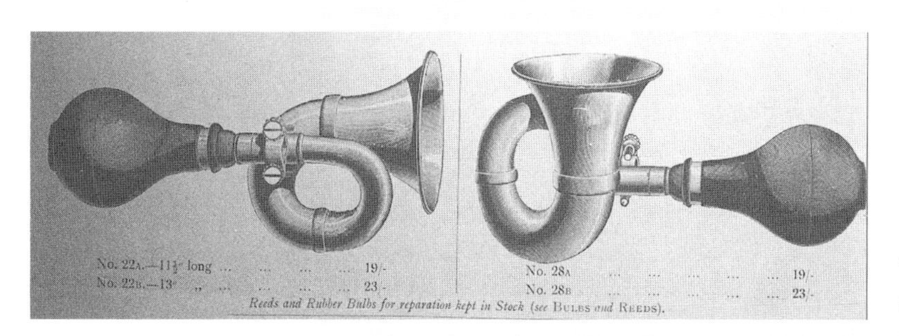

No. of Car	*Miles per hour*	*Description*	*m. s.*
A20	14.48	Empress motor tricycle	5.20⅖
A17	13.29	12 h.p. Panhard	5.59
A2	8.5	6 h.p. Panhard	9.15
4	8.85	Ariel tricycle and trailer	9.45
A29	7.58	7 h.p. Peugeot	10.17
15	7.58	De Dion voiturette	10.25
14	7.58	De Dion voiturette	10.27⅖
5	6.37	Locomobile	12.20
40	6.12	Wolseley voiturette	12.53
32	6.12	M.M.C Triumph	13.4
35	5.12	Daimler	13.33
A3	5.68	6 h.p. Panhard	14.12
A4	5.31	8 h.p. Panhard	14.50
A22	5.31	12 h.p. Daimler	14.52
8	4.82	Motor Mfg. Co.’s 6 h.p. Phaeton	16.18
2	4.82	Benz Ideal	16.23
22	4.82	Small Lanchester	16.35
27	4.42	New Orleans	17.39
49	4.54	Marshall	17.42
24	4.42	Marshall	18.0
A21	4.42	Daimler	18.6
36	4.42	Daimler	18.10
9	4.42	Motor Mfg. Co.’s phaeton	18.11
25	3.75	Déchamps	20.44

The above times and averages are for the most trying portion of Shap Fell, the steep being taken after the cars had climbed 840 feet in seven and one-third miles. The times were taken by Messrs. Henry Sturmey and Harry J. Swindley (hon. official timekeeper A.C.G.B.)

From the top the views over hill and dale were magnificent, and the air, though cold, exhilarating, whilst the run down to the bottom was simply splendid.”

Owing to an error in the transcription of numbers, and subsequent elaboration of our report, we included the Déchamps car as figuring at the bottom of the list of cars which ascended Shap Fell. Needless to say, this is incorrect, for, as already reported, the Déchamps car was smashed up on the Continent on its way to London, and did not take part in the trials at all.

The Autocar Saturday May 5th, 1900

Left:
Year 2000, the same spot on Alice Howe facing Bannerigg that was (***below)*** passed over by Mrs Louise Bazalgette on her Benz (A25) in 1900
(Photo courtesy Eric Dobson)

Above:
Mill Bridge – the start of the Dunmail Hill-Climb

Above right:
Dunmail Cairn at the top of Dunmail Raise marking the Cumberland/ Westmorland border.

Right:
After Dunmail summit – the old road at Thirlmere
(Photos Gowan Coulthard)

KENDAL TO CARLISLE 11

TUESDAY 1st MAY

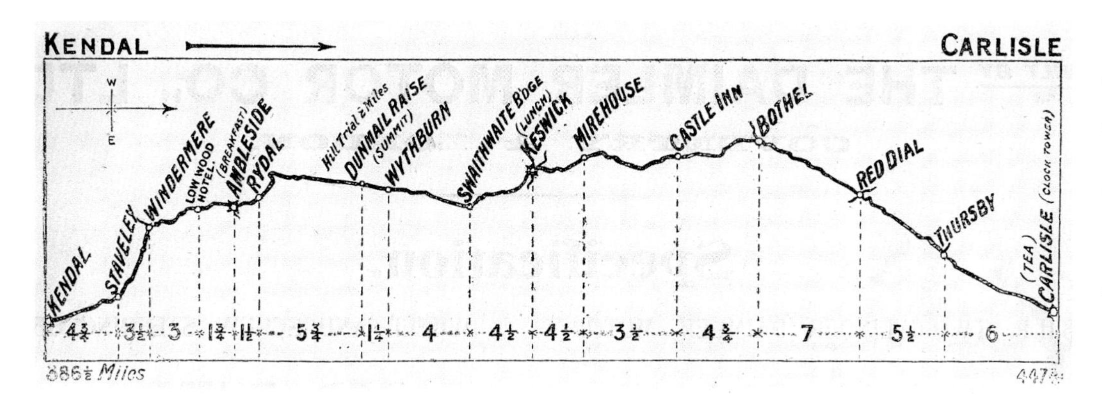

61½ miles
Via Hill-Climbing Trial on Dunmail raise 1¾ miles, Bothel, Keswick to Carlisle,

PARTICIPANTS HAD breakfast in Kendal, so they were permitted a later start of 9.30.a.m. This was appreciated by even the earliest of risers 'for the Trial is proving something more than a lazy holiday'.The road was slow, marked at 6 mph through Staveley, and on to the summit of Bannerigg. Here the decent had very sharp corners and was very precipitous; vehicles were not allowed to pass each other on the down gradient until after passing over Troutbeck bridge. The road was leading them to the Dunmail Raise, and the third Hill Climbing Competition. It was stunning countryside, and *The Autocar* reporter rode with Claude Johnson in his Daimler. His account takes us through the day, including the Ascent of Dunmail Raise.

"Kendal to Carlisle

The drive on Tuesday from Kendal to Carlisle, although only sixty-two miles in length, was by far the finest yet experienced on the tour. This day, for the first time, the start was not until 9.30, but, as we wished Mr. Swindley to check the timing on the hill-climbing contest we took a seat on Mr. Johnson's secretarial conveyance (six horse-power Parisian Daimler), and started at 8.30, so as to be there before the speed cars. As we were leaving the first car we espied was the Star, which Messrs. Lisles and Prue had got running again in the early morning, having had a new forecarriage sent on from the works. The road rose by a succession of more or less steep stretches, until the summit of Bannerigg was reached, from which a glorious peep into the hills and valleys of the Lake District was obtained, and then, as we 'floated' rapidly down on the brakes into Windermere, and speedily sped alongside the borders of that exquisite lake, recollections of our last visit to the place crowded on the mind. But the aspect was very different from that damp, wild, and misty peep we got of the lake on that November morning three years ago*, when, with memories of our frantic dive down from the Kirkstone into Ambleside fresh in our mind, we were only anxious to leave so uncompromising and fateful a place in the rear. Now all was glorious sunshine, which lit up the delicate setting of the lake in woodland glade and mountain crag,

Mark Mayhew's Panhard (Photo: *The Autocar*)

Right:
House of Correction Hill, Kendal, Westmorland 01.05.1900. No 9 M.M.C. Iveagh Phaeton.

These three photographs are courtesy of Margaret Duff Collection and researched by Gowan Coultard.

Left:
Competitors in the Automibiles Clubs' 1.000 Miles Trial pausing at Green Road, Kendal after ascending House of Correction Hill. 01.05.1900.
No. 1 Henry Hewetson's Benz Ideal followed by Mrs Louise Bazalgette with Clarkson on No. A25 Benz Ideal.

Right:
Competitor (unknown) – open road on a hill approaching Windermere. This scene is much the same as it is today.

with a colouring so exquisitely beautiful as to fill the soul with joy, and cause regrets at every turn of the tortuous road that the rapidity of our mode of transit, and the urgency of our mission, rendered it impossible to linger on the scene. Soon we were in Ambleside, where a locally owned Benz and a Stanley steamer put in an appearance, and gave us a welcoming toot on their horns, and then by beautiful Rydal Water, past Wordworth's house and favourite rock, and speeding by with never a halt, our motor running splendidly, we passed beyond the confines of this gem of the mountain crown, and as quickly skirting Grasmere, found ourselves at the Mill bridge, at the foot of the 'Raise,' with not a trace of the fliers in the rear, whom we had expected to overhaul us several miles behind. Cyclists in scores had been passed on the road, all bent Raisewards, and now we found every point of vantage on the steep banks containing the road occupied by sightseers numerously armed with cameras. Starting at once with four on board, Mr. Johnson put his car at the hill, and, steadily surmounting the various gradients without trouble, at last came to the *pièce de résistance* of the trial, the two hundred yards or so of one in eight and a half, the top of which was thickly thronged with spectators. Steadily the car took it, and, after giving us a few moments of doubt as to whether she would get up with her full load, settled the matter by going ahead without a hitch. From this point the hill presents no difficulties, and the higher speeds being brought into requisition we finished at the top in 12m. 42s., and then waited for the rest.

The view from the summit was glorious, with vistas of the country we had just left on the one side, and with Thirlmere stretching away below on the other, and the air most invigorating and clear. The small knot of people on the top gradually increased as the day wore on, and soon the competing cars hove in sight, were checked and passed down on the other side, the results of the competition being shown below, the figures for average pace given being worked out per half minute, as shown in the official guide:

Times recorded for the ascent of Dunmail Raise
(This is 3013½ yards from centre of Mill Bridge to summit, including gradients of 1 in 8½, 1 in 11, 1 in 12 and varying.)

No. of Car	*Description*	*Time occupied m.s.*	*Rough average per hour miles*
A17	Hon. C. S. Rolls 12 h.p. Panhard	5.49	17.06
A28	Mr. E. M. Iliffe's Enfield quadricycle	6.15	17.06
A20	Mr. Ashby's Empress tricycle	6.36⅘	15.80
3	Mr. J. W. Stock's Ariel quadricycle	9.27	10.8
A29	Mr. Mayhew's 7 h.p. Peugeot	10.32⅖	9.79
14	Mr. Roger Fuller's De Dion voiturette	10 34	9.79
5	Locomobile steam car	10 39⅗	9.79
A22	Mr. J. A. Holder's 12 h.p. Daimler	10 45	9.33
31	M.C.C. Triumph	10 47⅖	9.33
A30	Mr. Siddeley's 6 h.p. Daimler	11 10	9.33
26	Mr. Friswell's 8 h.p. Peugeot	11 21⅘	8.92
53	8 h.p. Wolseley	12 13⅘	8.55
37	Daimler Parisian 6 h.p.	12 20⅗	8.22
A3	Mr. T. B. Browne's 6 h.p. Panhard	12 31⅕	8.22
12	M.M.C. tricycle	12 41⅘	8.22
A31	Mr. Johnson's 6 h.p. Parisian Daimler (four passengers)	12.42	8.22
46	7 h.p. Richard car	12.47	7.9
35	Mr. Critchley's 6 h.p. Daimler	13.7⅕	7.9
A24	Mr. R. E. Phillips's Petit Duc Mors	13.10⅕	7.9
40	3 h.p. Wolseley voiturette	13.13	7.9
16	Gladiator voiturette	13.16⅖	7.67
4	Ariel tricycle with trailer	13.28⅗	7.67
23	Brown-Whitney steam car	13.34⅕	7.67
45	5½ h.p. S.S. carriage	13.0⅖	7.33
34	J. Dubois's 3½ h.p. Decauville	14.30⅖	7.08
A12	Mr. Edmund's 6 h.p. Daimler	14.38	7.08
22	Mr. Millerchip's 8 h.p. Lanchester	14.44⅗	6.84
A10	Mr. Edge's 8 h.p. Napier	15.6⅗	6.84
2	Mr. Cole's Benz Ideal	15.16⅖	6.64
A26	Mr. Gregson's 6 h.p. Daimler	15.18	6.64
27	Mr. Astell's New Orleans	15.36⅖	6.64
36	6 h.p. Daimler	15.48⅘	6.41
A2	Mr. F.H. Butler's 6 h.p. Panhard	16.1	6.41
A21	Mr. Pitman's 6 h.p. Daimler	16.47⅖	6.04
44	3 h.p. International	17.18⅗	5.86
47	7 h.p. Richard car	17.23	5.86
49	5 h.p. Marshall car	17.42⅖	5.86
8	6 h.p. M.M.C. Panhard	17.43	5.86
41	Mr. Seyd's International	18.21	5.55
29	Eureka Car	18.54⅘	5.4
A11	Hon. John Scott Montagu's 12 h.p. Daimler	19.20	5.26
9	Mr. Burgess's 6 h.p. M.M.C. Panhard	19.25⅕	5.4
33	Decauville	20.3⅗	5.01
A16	Mr. A. J. Wilson's Ariel tricycle	20.6⅖	5.13
1	Mr. Hewetson's Benz Ideal	20.30⅖	5.01
28	New Orleans	21.54⅘	4.66
A7	Captain Langrishe's 6 h.p. Parisian Daimler	22.6⅖	4.66
A4	Mr. Mayhew's 8 h.p. Panhard	35.28	under 4
20	Simms's Motor Wheel	34.25⅗	4 ”

The Autocar, Saturday, May 5th, 1900

* The reference to 1897 gives away the anonomous author's name. It is in all probability Henry Sturmey (Editor of *The Autocar*) refering to his epic journey described in his book *On an Autocar – Through the length and breadth of the land* a tour of 1,600 miles, from John O'Groats to Land's End, London and Coventry, which Henry Sturmey did in his Daimler accompanied by Richard Ashley from the Daimler Co., in October 1897.

“The others which took part in the day's run either failed to arrive in time or to reach the top before the timekeepers had left their situations. The times recorded above were taken by Messrs. Henry Sturmey and Harry J. Swindley, of *The Autocar*, official timekeepers National Cyclists' Union. By noon all the above recorded contestants had passed over the hill, and we once more sounded the 'all aboard' and sped on to Keswick for lunch.

The Keswick (inward) control – No. A11 John Scott-Montagu's Daimler, 1st May 1900. (Photo: *The Autocar*)

Up to now the run had been devoid of incident, save that Mr. Edge had suddenly found his clutch fail on a hill, and, not being ready with the sprag, his eight horse-power Napier had made a record trip backwards for one hundred yards or so, happily without mishap, although the cargo emptied themselves in double quick time. Now, however, the incidents became numerous, and our trailing of the crowd gave us an opportunity of discovering them. We had scarce got well to the level of Thirlmere, and were skirting its beautiful waters along an excellent road, when we came across Mr. Edmunds's car with a broken spring, and a hole in the adjacent wall. Close by Mr. Grahame-White was wrestling with an obstinate exhaust valve, whilst round the next corner Mr. Siddeley had his car jacked up and was replacing a tyre, enquiry eliciting particulars of what has been, we believe, the only accident of the tour up to now. It seems a led horse had suddenly and without warning backed right in front of the car when it was only a yard or two from it, with a result which was disastrous to both parties, for the shock had sent the car into the wall at the side of the road, and smashed in a spring and the front of the car, as well as displacing a tyre, whilst the blow broke the horse's leg, and the poor beast was led into a neighbouring field to await its doom. A little later on the Stanley steam carriage was passed with a broken chain, and visions of horse haulage flitting before the driver's eyes. The Century tandem shot by us, but stopped on the next hill, and our friends of the Star were also passed at the same spot walking their machine. The steep declines into Keswick were carefully and successfully negotiated the while the ever changing view was absorbed to the full.

Apology May 12th

In our last issue we stated that by Thirlmere we passed the Stanley steam car with a broken chain and her driver contemplating the question of horse haulage. This was a typographical error. The mishap referred to occurred to the 'S.S.' carriage of the S.S. Motor Co., and the printers took it into their heads that S.S. was a contraction, and so expanded it into 'Stanley steam' car, which up to the present has gone through with a whole chain.

Upon getting under weigh after lunch, our motor was again running splendidly, and, after enjoying (?) its dust for awhile, Mr. Critchley's car was overhauled. Then a Eureka was seen stranded by the roadside, and the Century tandem shortly after repeated its performance of the morning. The Brown-Whitney steamer was seen by a roadside stream taking on a fresh supply of water, and then the roads for some miles rapidly deteriorated, being loose with several steep rises and bare uninteresting scenery. Mr. Bersey's Richard car was 'pipped' on the top of a hill, and Van Toll with the baggage waggon was seen struggling with a motor suffering from a leaky joint. Mr. Butler was stopped at the foot of a slope with lamp troubles, and the Orient Express discovered at the top with the end of the countershaft broken off, and her driver gone in search of assistance behind a 'hay motor.' A mile or two farther on we entered a mining village, meeting many begrimed toilers on their way home from work, and here a Leyland steam lorry was passed engaged in its daily task.

Then we once more ran out on the main road, and rapidly gliding over a broad superb surface with several sharp gradients began overhauling cars in quick succession, simply flying up to the No. 8 car of the Motor Manufacturing Co. at the top of a hill taken with a rush down the approaching dip as a first go off. Fourteen miles from Carlisle Mr. Ashby was passed with the gear pinion of his

No. A12 Henry Edmund's 6 h.p. Daimler had an accident hitting a wall by Thirlemere Water – see *The Autocar* report. (Photo: *The Autocar*)

tricycle 'gone,' and next we came in for a little venture ourselves. In front of us, at the foot of a long decline, we saw a hill about as steep as nay on the route. We were going at a big speed, with Mr. Coles and Mr. Friswell well in front. Keeping going, we shot up the hill like lightening, and dashed up alongside the two, but the gear not changing readily stopped the motor, and we were only just in time to catch her on the sprag. By the time we had reached the top the others were a long way in front again. No. 41 was next given the go-by, and Messrs. Coles and Friswell passed to the rear a mile later, when the Brown-Whitney steamer came by up the next hill like an arrow from a bow, and, keeping just in front, gave us her dust for a mile or two, until again running short of water she let us go by on a rise. Mr. Astell was the next to heave in sight and pass beyond our ken, and the M.M.C. tricycle was seen by the roadside adjusting. The Marshall car, No. 49, was then passed on a straightaway mile of road, and then Mr. Pitman given the go-by, and we ran on to Captain Langrishe's tailboard at the Carlisle control, which was reached at 3.20, after a simply grand run. The cars were stabled in the Fish Market and placed on exhibition during the evening, the 'show' being excellently patronised by the public, the greatest interest being evinced here as at every point of the route.

There were quite a dozen private motor-cars at Dunmail Raise, in addition to those engaged in the Trial, the smartest being the steam car belonging to Mr. Buxton, of Sawrey, in Lakeland. ”

The Autocar, Saturday, May 5th, 1900

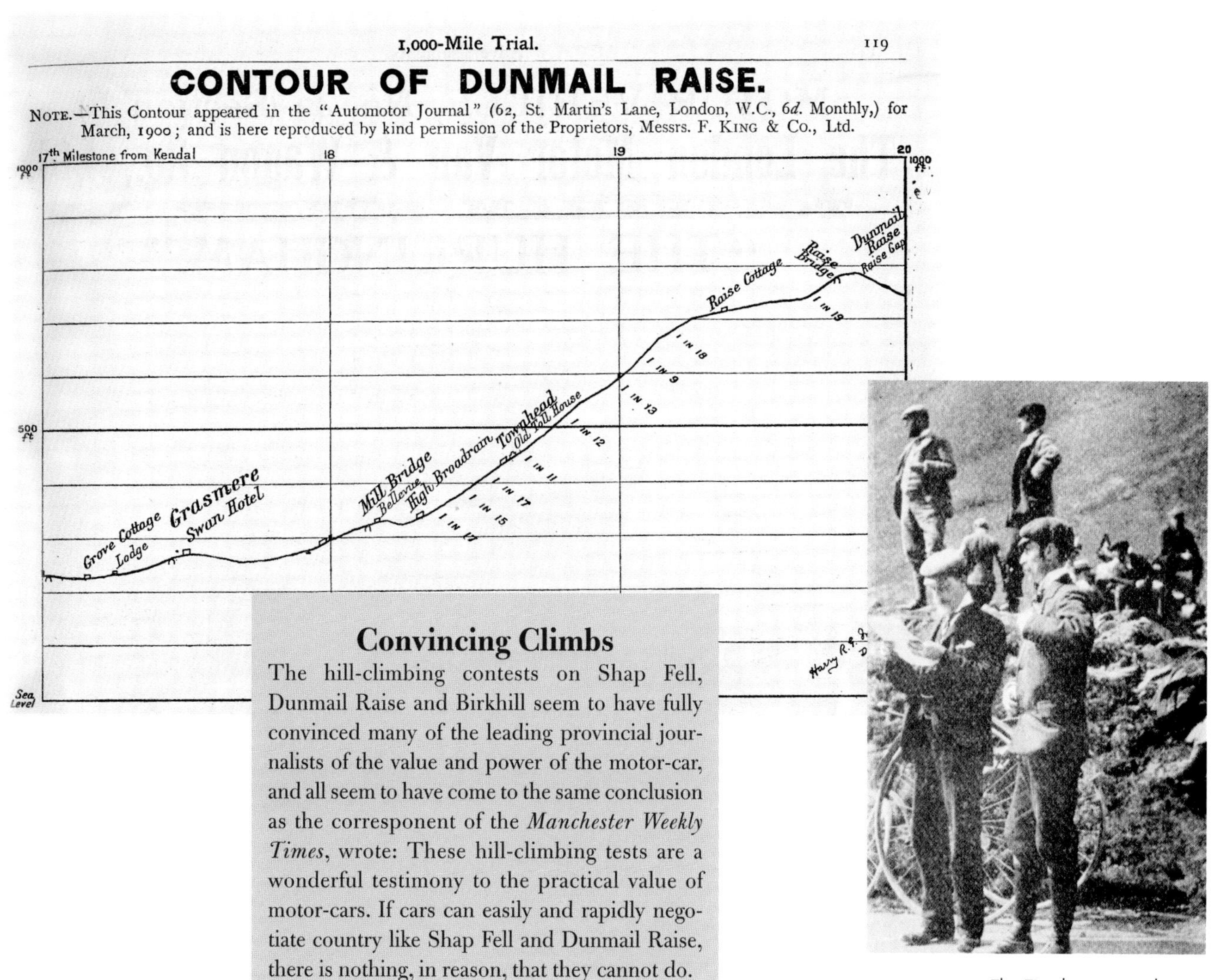
1,000-Mile Trial. 119

CONTOUR OF DUNMAIL RAISE.

NOTE.—This Contour appeared in the "Automotor Journal" (62, St. Martin's Lane, London, W.C., 6*d.* Monthly,) for March, 1900; and is here reproduced by kind permission of the Proprietors, Messrs. F. KING & Co., Ltd.

Convincing Climbs

The hill-climbing contests on Shap Fell, Dunmail Raise and Birkhill seem to have fully convinced many of the leading provincial journalists of the value and power of the motor-car, and all seem to have come to the same conclusion as the correspondent of the *Manchester Weekly Times*, wrote: These hill-climbing tests are a wonderful testimony to the practical value of motor-cars. If cars can easily and rapidly negotiate country like Shap Fell and Dunmail Raise, there is nothing, in reason, that they cannot do.

The Motor-Car Journal

The Timekeepers at the top of Dunmail Raise (Photo: *The Autocar*)

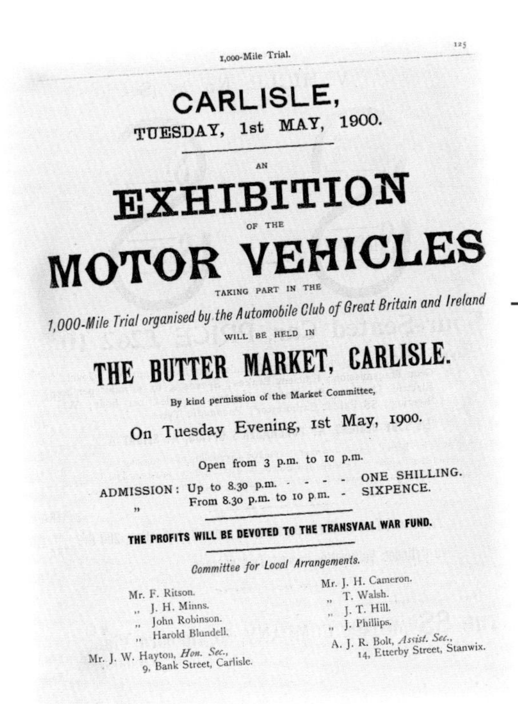

1,000-Mile Trial. 125

CARLISLE,
TUESDAY, 1st MAY, 1900.

AN

EXHIBITION

OF THE

MOTOR VEHICLES

TAKING PART IN THE

1,000-Mile Trial organised by the Automobile Club of Great Britain and Ireland

WILL BE HELD IN

THE BUTTER MARKET, CARLISLE.

By kind permission of the Market Committee,

On Tuesday Evening, 1st May, 1900.

Open from 3 p.m. to 10 p.m.

ADMISSION: Up to 8.30 p.m. - - - - ONE SHILLING.
" From 8.30 p.m. to 10 p.m. - SIXPENCE.

THE PROFITS WILL BE DEVOTED TO THE TRANSVAAL WAR FUND.

Committee for Local Arrangements.

Mr. F. Ritson.	Mr. J. H. Cameron.
,, J. H. Minns.	,, T. Walsh.
,, John Robinson.	,, J. T. Hill.
,, Harold Blundell.	,, J. Phillips.
Mr. J. W. Hayton, *Hon. Sec.*, 9, Bank Street, Carlisle.	A. J. R. Bolt, *Assist. Sec.*, 14, Etterby Street, Stanwix.

After such a full day there was some concern that no cars would appear at the Butter market Carlisle for the Evening Exhibition 1st May 1900. Open from 3 p.m. to 10 p.m., admission was one shilling up to 8.30 p.m. and sixpence from 8.30.to 10 p.m. In order that the people of Carlisle should have something to see, Claude Johnson's instructions to Participants has the following stern note:

> **SPECIAL NOTICE**
>
> In order to secure a proper display of vehicles at the Carlisle Exhibition, vehicles on their arrival must proceed straight to the Exhibition, and remain there until 6 a.m. on Wednesday Morning, when they may be removed for cleaning from 6 a.m. until 9 a.m. Breakfast will be taken at Carlisle, on Wednesday Morning, and the start from the Exhibition Building will take place at 9.30 a.m.

So, no preparing the car for the morrow. Some people had to be up very early the next morning to clean and fettle for the run to Edinburgh on May 2nd. This could have been helped by the fact that Carlisle had 14 hotels listed; six of them were temperance (no alcohol); but not helped by the fact that there was only one place where petrol could be obtained. This was F. Ritson the Chemist. At 1 shilling and 4 pence a gallon this poor Chemist must have been under some considerable pressure, bearing in mind that some 250 Gallons of Petroleum spirit was estimated to be required.

May 1st 1900. Cars waiting at the Carlisle control (Photo: *The Autocar*)

Carlisle

The counter-attraction of the local spring race meeting robbed the arrival of the cars in Carlisle of a good deal of the interest they would otherwise have excited; but even as it was, hundreds of spectators turned out to watch the entry of the party into the Butter Market, where the vehicles remained on exhibition during Tuesday evening. After the first of the cars arrived, every few minutes a fresh vehicle turned the sharp corner into the market entrance, and fifty-five cars were counted during the afternoon. The weather enjoyed on the way was brilliantly fine, but the begrimed appearance of both cars and occupants showed clearly how dusty the roads had been. The beauty of the scenery of the Lake district came as a revelation to the foreigners who are of the company, and scores of snapshots were secured during this part of the journey. ”

The Motor-Car Journal, Tuesday May 1st 190

“ Mr. Rolls' incident

The drive from Keswick to Carlisle on Tuesday was a fine and a fast one, the roads being excellent and practically devoid of traffic. Most of the cars made excellent running and came through well. A few of the incidents are noted elsewhere, but the two leaders also had an interesting time, Mr. Rolls puncturing a tyre with half of a racing horseshoe, making a record repair in thirteen minutes, and then finding the front of his car on fire when he came to restart owing to a burner nut shaking loose. This was quickly put out, and then, *mirabile dictu*, out came a pot of white paint and the scorched finish was restored to its original tint. Mr. Edge's adventure is referred to elsewhere. ”

The Autocar

It is interesting to note that Hon. C. S. Rolls was prepared for nearly any eventuality.

Messr. Lord and Swindley on the 7 h.p. Peugeot which followed the trials throughout as a non-competing car. The car is the property of Mr. Lord (Photo: *The Autocar*)

" DIARY from Birmingham to Carlisle

WRITTEN BY MR. H. J. SWINDLEY

The A.C.G.B. 1,000 Miles Test

As seen from the seat of a 7 h.p. Peugeot

The skies were ashen and drear when we left the Grand Hotel to count the competing vehicles out of Bingley Hall, where they had spent the previous day, and made motor cars of all degrees fifty-four in number as they ranged themselves in line. The exit from Birmingham was rendered a trifle perilous by the watered tramlines, but such sideslips as did occur were not serious after all, save for the hero who guides the fortunes of the Simms Motor Wheel, who, I was informed, slithered badly in New Street, but he is in Carlisle to-night as I write, and right well has he done. Our cream-coloured Peugeot began to get through the cars at Sutton Coldfield, where up the stiff hill there was a great clash and clanging of changing gears. The roads away to Lichfield were both greasy and holding, and rain threatened from time to time. Beyond the cathedral city, when the long line of cars were running free along the old British way of Icknield Street, the rain fell in a fine drizzle, enough to damp one's outer garments, but by the time Burton was reached the dull grey clouds were breaking and the blue was peeping through. Both Lichfield and Burton's streets were lined with enthusiastic onlookers, and the chauffeurs were well received, although the goggles worn appeared to amuse the crowds, likewise what they called the 'woolly bear' coats affected by a few drivers. Beyond Burton the cars passed over the fine straight road of Ryknield Street, another British way, and the legal limit was as usual strictly adhered to. Derby was all agog to see the cars, and had the authorities but restrained their watercarts for the nonce we should the more fully have appreciated our reception. Derby past, the country grew prettier and more difficult, but the grand scenery more than compensated, for were we not running up the valley of the famed Derwent and the High Tor of Matlock, and the famous dales, or some of them, were ours to view. The crux of the day's performance, however, was the climbing trial of Taddington Hill, a section of which, with its varying gradients shown, appears in another place. Before we reached the bank we enjoyed what was to us the finest sight of the day. Our Peugeot was doing her best up a fair grade when we heard a faint toot-toot down the valley. A glance back showed us that the sound proceeded from the horn of the grand twelve horse-power Panhard belonging to Mr. Harmsworth. In shorter time than these words are written the toot-toot sounded again directly behind us. The road was straight, naked, and desolate. There was nothing to stop her. With a crish of whirling wheels, a wild flash of plated work, the deep hum of her flying engines, she was past and gone with a just perceptible wave of hands from our editor aboard and Mr. Harmsworth sheltering behind his broad shoulders. No sight but that of the Flying Dutchman westward bound, twenty miles out from town, and in a hurry too, ever approached it. The upgrade, which necessitated our third, and hard put to it at that, this powerful car de luxe was taking on her top speed, and flinging the miles behind her. It was Birmingham to Manchester with no thought of the intervening distance. Her dust fell upon us for miles after.

The results of Taddington are given elsewhere. It is a steep climb, which our Peugeot accomplished in 13m. 58s. = 10.79 miles per hour, a most creditable performance. The remaining features of the day's run were the climb from Buxton to the Cat and Fiddle Inn on the summit of Macclesfield Forest, which is no forest, being treeless, and the long, steep, and winding descent into Macclesfield, where the really awful corners made many a passenger sit tight and grip with his toes. Also the run into Old Trafford, which was by way of a 'progress,' police guarded and very gratifying, though we could have done with better road surfaces.

Monday

After a two days' sojourn in Cottonopolis, last Monday at seven saw us upon the road to Preston, Lancaster, Kendal, and the climb up famous Shap. Anything more unpleasant than the run for the first thirty miles out of Manchester we do not want to experience. Holey greasy setts, varied and striped with tramlines, and frequently accompanied by a side-slip of the eviliest macadam make us wonder if the Manchester A.C. will ever drive their vehicles northwards by this abominable route. It may be a road after the horse-hauled lorryman's own heart; it is no place for automobiles. Never had any poor autocars such a shaking up, and we marvel that many did not there and then emulate the passing of the wonderful one-horse shay. It speaks volumes for them all that they reached Preston whole and with their wheels still pertaining to the circular. Beyond the last named town, where a halt was called for breakfast, things vastly improved, the country grew sweet and beautiful to gaze upon, and that thirty miles of villainous highway was almost forgotten. At Garstang the whole population was out motor-gazing, and Lancaster further on was treated to a processional entry. The majesty of this was marred, however, by a threading of by-streets, owing to the building of a new bridge, but the Lancastrians enjoyed it all the same. Nothing beyond the contemplation of beautiful ranges of hills to the east, and condolation with Mr. Lisle on his bad luck in suffering from a broken near steering wheel spindle, and congratulating him on an escape from what might have been a very bad accident, distinguished the remainder of our run into Kendal, which was literally *en fête* to receive us. With but little delay we made for Shap, and timing the Peugeot up the one and threequarter miles shoot from the Bay Horse Inn at Huck's Bridge, made her do 12.52 = 6.12 miles per hour, a good effort. All Kendal seemed to strew itself up and down the long climb of ten miles, and took particular interest in the flying return of the competing vehicles. The recollection of that ten miles coast will long remain with us. In parts it resembled aerial-flight as near as might be.

Tuesday

All on a bright May morning, the cars wound out of Kendal to tackle the precipitous steep of Dunmail Raise into Cumberland, and to flit by the placid deep blue waters of lovely Lakeland midst the swelling bosoms of the everlasting hills to 'merry Carlisle.' The country far and wide was up and out for the hill scaling by motor car. Excursions had been arranged by brake owners, and the Furness Railway Co. ran special trains. We dare not suggest the number of the people who gathered all up and down the hill. There were thousands, and every owner of an autocar within twenty miles had wound up his engine and come along. That some of the entered cars did so well, and that all from the twelve horses to the three horse-power New Orleans voiturette got up and over this mighty bank in earnest of what may confidently be expected of self-propelled traffic in the future. Forty-five cars were put at and surmounted this terrible hill with its one in 8.6 gradient.

The climb over, there remained the run by Liverpool's thirst quencher, Thirlmere, which in all its early spring beauty suggested no such utilitarianism through Keswick, past frowning Skiddaw, by a narrow and roughish road to Bothel, whence the run to Carlisle on the Cockermouth and Carlisle road was pleasantly made. Nought marred this but the unfortunate horse accident sustained by Mr. Siddeley, which is referred to elsewhere. Carlisle, full of race-going folk, welcomed us right heartily. The cars were displayed for the evening in the Butter Market, and crowds paid to see them. ”

The Autocar, Saturday, May 5th, 1900

On Dunmail Raise there was a good crowd watching the struggles of the cars up the steeper parts of the long stretch. If they had expected to gaze upon failures they must have been disappointed, for all but two of the vehicles were timed up the ascent.

C. S. Rolls progress:
On Dunmail Raise Rolls tied with Edward Iliffe's Enfield Quad for first place with a speed of 17.6 mph.

May 1st 1900. Hon. C. S. Rolls restarting after climbing Dunmail Raise. (Photo: *The Autocar*)

During the day they saw snow on the crags, and were up amongst the clouds, where the moisture probably affected the cars that had belt transmission.

"There is a level crossing on the railway between Kendal and Windermere, about a mile south of Staveley, which should receive attention at the hands of the Automobile or the Cyclist's Touring Clubs. It is situated half way up a fairly steep hill, and the autocarists and cyclists descending come upon it suddenly round a bend. We do not know how the other cars fared, but the one in which we travelled jumped off all four wheels twice in crossing the metals. If there had been anything to go it would have gone then. Perhaps Mr. A.W. Rumney, of the C.T.C., will give this danger to traffic his attention."

The Autocar, Saturday, May 5th, 1900

Carlisle Express

5 May The Trial of Motor Cars. The Journey through Carlisle.

'The motor-cars and other self-propelling vehicles taking part in the 1,000 miles trial reached Carlisle on Tuesday afternoon, the day's run having been over the roads from Kendal to the city *via* Keswick and Bothel. The weather in the morning was delightful. The atmosphere was remarkably clear and Lakeland was in one of the most charming aspects, Windermere, Grasmere, Thirlmere, Derwentwater and Bassenthwaite Lakes being presented to the visitors with all the added beauty of early spring and a typical May Day. The hills too were beautifully clear, with here and there white fringes on the heights and patches of snow in the sheltered parts, to which much of the invigorating freshness of the morning was due.

Kendal was left at 9.30 a.m. and the journey to Keswick, a distance of 30 miles, was performed in a remarkably short time. The probable hour of arrival in Keswick was given in the programme as 2.10 p.m. Great therefore was the astonishment when the Panhard driven by Hon. C. S. Rolls, preceded by a couple of tricycles, swept into the town a few minutes after twelve o'clock 1 and drew up in the Market Place. Close in its wake was Mr. Kennard's 5 h.p. Napier, which since the trial commenced has run Mr. Rolls' Panhard close for the honour of finishing the day first. Others quickly followed and in the market place there was soon a large collection of vehicles with the travellers standing round dressed in dual-covered oil capes or furs. The remarkable control which the drivers had of the machines was the subject of general comment. They swung round the street corners and took their places in the Market Place with marvellous precision and were brought to a standstill with an abruptness that was scarcely conceivable.

Dunmail Rise had proved a severe test of the powers of the machines but none of them totally failed to get over. Mr. Rolls Panhard went up at a swinging pace and reached the top with four passengers on board. The small American steam car climbed the hill in an astonishing way, and the 3 horse power Benz cars of German make also performed well. Some of the cars with four passengers were unequal to the task, their passengers having to dismount and this was the experience of many of the smaller machines and tricycles. Nine of the competitors had to unload in this way one or all of their passengers. After the hill climbing competition the cars descended from old Keswick road, and swept round Thirlmere on the newer and better road. It was along this stretch that an accident occurred to Mr. Siddeley's car which might have had serious consequences. A horse had been taken out of the shafts of a cart and was being held by the bridle parallel to the direction of the road. Just then a car came up, the horse swerved sharply round and came into collision with the front spring of the car, which was broken by the impact. The horse's leg was also fractured and the animal had to be destroyed. The occupant of one of the cars produced a revolver, and offered to put the animal out of its misery, but the owner would not allow it to be shot until it had been valued in order that he might lay a claim against the driver of the car with which it collided.

The early arrival of the vehicles at Keswick upset the local arrangements and the local committee endeavoured to delay the departure until 2.35, the time mentioned on the programme, but the machines were not required to stay more than an hour after entering the Keswick control, and about one o'clock, the hour of stoppage had elapsed, the cars proceeded towards Crossthwaite on their way to Carlisle, raising clouds of dust as they departed. Just outside Keswick Mr. Youdale, of Cockermouth, took cinematograph photographs of the machines as they passed. Several cyclist endeavoured to accompany them, but were quickly outpaced. Meanwhile fresh arrivals were drawing up to the Market Place, and the odd vehicles were turning up until three o'clock.

Mr. Kennard's Napier at the Carlisle Control. Mr. S. F. Edge at the helm. (Photo: *The Autocar*)

The first breakdown of any consequence on the journey from London to Carlisle occurred at the bottom of a small hill between the Castle Inn, Bassenthwaite and Bothel, when the main axle of a powerful looking car suddenly snapped. At the same moment Mr. Taylor Scott happened to be driving past and at once stopped to render assistance, but it was immediately seen that nothing could be done there, and the owner was driven to Bassenthwaite to catch a train to Carlisle, his enthusiasm leading him to decide to telephone the makers in London to send a man by the first train with a new axle in order that he might catch his companions at Edinburgh. In the meantime his ill-fated machine was left on the roadside in charge of a German companion unable to understand a word of English, until a horse and cart could be dispatched from Carlisle to drag it back.

On the journey from Keswick to Carlisle there were large gatherings of people at such places as the Castle Inn, Bothel and the Red Dial where several roads converge; in fact the Castle Inn, Bassenthwaite presented quite a gay appearance with a large crowd of ladies and gentlemen, who had arrived in carriages and bicycles from various parts of the Lake District.

The first of the 'automobiles' reached Carlisle about half-past two, having travelled over 31 miles in and hour and a half. This was the Napier owned by Mr. Kennard, which had also been the first to arrive at Manchester and on the other days of competition had been second to the Hon. C. S. Rolls' Panhard. An Ariel Tricycle and an Ariel Quadricycle came next and other machines followed at intervals. The Hon. C. S. Rolls' Panhard was considerably in the rear having had a punctured tyre soon after leaving Bassenthwaite. There were 56 of the vehicles which started the tour still running, but in addition to these four baggage cars and four others not mentioned in the programme reached the city during the afternoon, and another arrived during the night. Two of the machines which started from Kendal, viz. Mr. Mark Mayhew's 8 h.p. Panhard (No. A4) and the 16 h.p. Napier (No. 17), failed to turn up (*This car never started*). The other machines were exhibited in the evening in the Butter Market. A charge was made for admission and the proceeds were handed over to the Transvaal war Fund. There was a fairly large number of spectators. Early on Wednesday morning the machines were got ready for the road again, and the Market was left between 9 and 10 o'clock. The vehicles proceeded via Market Street, Peter Street and Corporation Road to Stanwix, and kept up a fair speed until the Glasgow road at Kingtown was reached. After making a stop for the marking of record sheets the journey was resumed in earnest, Edinburgh being the destination. A large crowd assembled at the Market to witness the departure. Both sides of Eden Bridge were also lined , and many people stationed themselves on Stanwix Bank to see the machines climb the hill.'

“ ANOTHER PARTICIPANT’S DIARY

Reflections at Carlisle

By a Worldling

It is Tuesday evening. Those of us who have survived the hills of the North have tasted of the hospitality of Carlisle, and have found it not wanting in any respect. The smoking room of the County Hotel has been turned for the moment into a *chauffeurs' tabaks-parlement*, where we have laughed over the disasters of our friends, and boasted of our deeds of 'derring do,' till the rafters – if there are such things in modern hotels – rang with wondrous tales of hill-climbing and mirages that have set at naught the principles of dynamics to which we were trained in our school days.

That of which we have been talking the most is the wonderful performance of Mr. S. F. Edge on his Napier car. On one of the hills between Keswick and Carlisle – I speak only from hearsay – he missed his change of speed, and owing to the faulty arrangement of his brake, began to travel backwards at about twenty miles an hour. With that presence of mind which is his chief characteristic he told Mr. Kennard and young Mr. Cusens to jump from the car, and steered her backwards on to the upward grade behind him (*Young Mr. Cusen was the 14 year old St. John Nixon*). Two or three minutes of adjustment and all was well again, and the twelve miles an hour or thereabouts, which the car subsequently developed, brought him first into Carlisle.

The hill-climbing competitions have been a bit trying to the nerves and tempers of many of us. I never felt so angry in all my life as when I was running the gauntlet of a thousand or so cameras on slow speed. At the top of Dunmail, whizz past me went Mr. Ashby on his tricycle, but I got little consolation when Mr. A. C. Edge, Mr. Stocks, and an Ariel quad came by, all three walking up the steeper part. By the way, their machine has got the best record after Mr. Rolls' Panhard, which is, of course, much faster up hills, and which, I regret to see, is credited with a pace above the legal limit.

What surprises me more than anything is the way in which the small fry are getting through. I passed a boy gazing sadly on a Victoria Combination that, he said, had something wrong with its 'innards,' ten miles from anywhere on the Cat and Fiddle road, and yet that same youth smiled encouragingly on me to-day as he sailed past me at Bassenthwaite, where I had stopped for some small repair. Two cars were incapacitated to-day by broken countershafts, but I hear that some lightning repair work has been done, and that they will be on the road again to-morrow. A Star car, which we all thought was a corpse, turned up again smiling to-day, and there are similar illustrations hourly of the fact that the dead automobile is as rare a bird as Sam Weller's dead donkey.

The nicest place we have stopped at yet is Kendal, where we slept, or tried to sleep, last night. I regret to say it was all trying in my case, because my room, in a perfectly delightful little hotel called the Dolphin, was opposite a church with a clock. There is nothing particularly unusual about that, but as luck would have it the machinery working the chimes had broken down, and the ringing of them had been entrusted to some fiend who amused himself by playing patriotic tunes all night. Nobody seemed to have heard them but myself, so I must add that the Dolphin is a temperance hotel. From an aesthetic point of view the tour is not a success. Covered with dust and dirt, on cars laden with petrol and oil cans, spare tires, &c., we must appear singularly unprepossessing to the thousands of people who daily watch our flight. I wonder if they understand that a superlative degree of uncleanliness is not necessarily part of the price to be paid for the delights of automobilism, and that the *chauffeur* is sometimes clean. I am personally rather worried by noticing that girls, who under other conditions would turn their eyes away from my masculine gaze, now stare at me with a boldness which is only made the more disgraceful by the inevitable giggle which accompanies it. Am I a freak that I should be treated in this way?

Nearing the border

Carlisle, Tuesday

At the time of writing the Automobile Club's educational course in the geography of our own country (as we may not unfitly term the 1,000-mile Trial) is still in progress. Up to the present our total cumulative mileage tots up to 447¾ miles, and we rest to-night in the fair city of Carlisle, only eighteen and a-half miles short of the Scottish border. Not, mark you, that we are so many Dr. Syntaxes in search of the picturesque. Neither, on the other hand, are we (or at the least of it should we be) motor scorchers emulative of pace. Ours are aims of another sort: to form a kind of perambulating object-lesson in the appearance and capabilities of motor-cars in those benighted regions that do not already know them well, and to collect a mass of carefully-noted data for the use of the Automobile Club and for the industry in general.

When we have finished this pilgrims' progress, and the long story of our several and collective doings is duly digested, we shall be certificated, medalled, and bonused until we shall scarce be able to recognise ourselves. We shall not, like the hymn-singers, at the end of our journey wear a crown in the New Jerusalem, but we (or those among us who are in the industry) will be able to sport things almost as pretty and a great deal more useful. We shall, that is to say, be enabled to show the would-be motorists, shivering on the brink of automobilism, and yet afraid to make the change from the horsed to the horseless vehicle that we can climb gradients of 1 in 9 for three weeks on end; that we can descend pitches of equal steepness at very much less than a walking pace if we want to do so; and that 'from morn to dewy eve,' as the poet remarks, we can urge the flying wheel, coming up dusty, but smiling, at the end. There may have been those who, hearing of this 1,000 miles or so of travelling, have waited to hear of early break down by wholesale. If such there were, they are disillusioned by now. As Mr. W.S. Gilbert says, in the 'Mikado':

'Perhaps you suppose this throng
Can't keep it up all day long.
If that's your idea you're wrong.'

The throng (or most of them) have kept it up all day, and for nine days up to date. That is to say, of the sixty-four actual starters, fifty-five had actually arrived at the Butter Market, Carlisle, up to 8 o'clock this evening, a very small wastage when one considers the severe tests of endurance which the eleven miles of uneven granite setts between Manchester and Preston and the trying hills of the Lake country have imposed. The nine cars that are missing may, indeed, be arriving even now, for we have no official pronouncement of their final dropping out, and even if they do not keep the twelve-mile record throughout, those of Section I. are still eligible for the £10 *Daily Mail* premium, to be awarded to those which perform an average throughout of five miles an hour.

But what of the tour from Friday last? Friday seems a long way back, so far have we come and so varied have our experiences been. The seven o'clock start from Birmingham on that morning was duly made amid cold and lowering weather, so that when we reached the end of the long Birmingham control at Sutton Coldfield, 7¼ miles out, and had, in accordance with official regulations, to stop there for the due filling in of cards, there were not a few who, shivering in the blasts that swept across the open country at that point, found Sutton Coldfield well named. Thence to Lichfield, where those of us who had not breakfasted employed the half hour's stop for that meal in stoking the human machine. There is a Cathedral at Lichfield, but few or none saw it. At nine o'clock we all pressed on to Burton-on-Trent, and thence to Derby and Matlock. Here the coy and fitful sun at length condescended to shine, and rendered the luncheon – threequarters of an hour – pleasant. Also, which was more important, it showed off the assemblage of cars to advantage before the crowds which gathered out of curiosity and stayed to admire. We have marched onwards since 1896, and no one can deny the taste and real beauty of many of the cars in this representative assemblage. Happily, we had little dust this day, and were not so travel-stained as on the phenomenally dusty trip from London to Bristol. Here, therefore, the neat finish and handsome painting of the big carriage-built cars were well in evidence. Of the fourteen English and Parisian Daimlers, the seven Panhards, the numerous Benz's, Peugeots, Napiers, and De Dions, many are finished in light and cheerful hues, and were much admired by the knowing ones. Of course Section II., the A, or amateur's class was chiefly in evidence in this respect. A2, Mr. Frank H. Butler's 6 h.p. Panhard, is a daring but successful 'confection' (as the milliners say) in pure white upper body and sealing-wax red lower frame and wheels. Then there is Mr. T. B. Browne's A3, Panhard, which reminded some old stagers of the old mail coach days, with its post-office red wheels and black and red body. Mr. Alfred Harmsworth's A7, a Parisian Daimler, is a quiet shade of green. Several cars are painted

Mr. Alfred Harmsworth's 12 h.p. Panhard which took part in some sections of the Trial. (Photo: *The Autocar*)

in a slate or French grey colour, which does not betray the dust, including A17, the Hon. C. S. Rolls' 12 h.p. Panhard; A22, Mr. Holder's 12 h.p. Daimler; and A31, the Secretary's 6 h.p. Parisian Daimler. One in Section I., a Daimler, No. 36, is of the same hue. These do not exhaust the pretty colours. Section I. has in No. 27, a New Orleans car entered by Messrs. Burford, Van Toll and Company, a charming finish in gamboge; a Daimler in light brown; two or three more Daimlers in blue-green; a Richard car (No. 46) in black and crimson lake; and two Marshall carriages in yellow and black. To return to the A class, No. 19, Mr. Hargreaves' big yellow and black Daimler, looks among the smartest.

Of course, with this long tour before us, we go somewhat heavy laden with luggage and with spare odds and ends that may be needed on the journey. For instance, the extra tires carried by many of the cars, which, slung on behind, perhaps detracted from our neatness to the rear view, and looked oddly like lifebelts. Fortified with lunch, for the climbing of Taddington Hill, that 4,440 yards of varying gradients ranging from 1 in $12\frac{3}{4}$ to 1 in 200, we did it with ease; passing, half way up, that treacherous bend by the roadside quarry where two brakeless cyclists descending with the wind at their backs were killed at Eastertide. We looked at the spot with interest, and, thinking of the much steeper descents before us, in Cumberland, dwelt with satisfaction upon the fact that every motor-car is provided with a plenitude of powerful and reliable brakes, calculated to safely bring a car to a standstill within six or seven yards. Tea at stately Buxton, and thence to the ascent among the Derbyshire limestone crags up to the wind-swept 'Cat and Fiddle' Inn, supposed to be the highest situated inn in England. Manchester, at the end of the day's run, was reached by the foremost cars about 5.30 p.m. Hitherto we had come through enthusiastic crowds, but Manchester and its neighbourhood were strangely apathetic. No cheering school-children as of yore, no crowds, and few locally-owned cars to meet us. We drove into the Botanical gardens at Old Trafford, where the public exhibition of cars took place that evening, and on the next day, Saturday. It was, after all, well attended, and by crowds of well-dressed Manchester people. An odd thing is that go-ahead, shrewd, business-like Manchester has not yet taken up with the motor-car movement, and up to our advent horseless vehicles had been rare in her streets. Even the Lord Mayor of Manchester, who officially declared the exhibition open, patronised and chid us a little. Speaking to one of us, a Manchester man (one always speaks of 'Manchester men,' just as one always says 'London cockneys,' 'Paisley bodies,' and 'Yorkshire tykes') let the secret out. 'Manchester,' he said, 'always like to be first in any enterprise, and if she *isn't* first, won't take it up afterwards with a good grace.' So there you have it!

Sunday was kept quietly, and rain made the day somewhat dismal; but Monday made amends, even though the roads were greasy and the setts already mentioned from Manchester, through Pendleton, Horwich, Bolton, and Preston made our pilgrimage somewhat penitential, by reason of jolting. Happily, we all came through without a smash, which incidentally proves the good workmanship of motor-cars in general, for no more cruel test than this could be applied. Fortunately for me who rode, the setts came to an end at Preston, and the roads for the rest of the day were perfect. Popular enthusiasm began again at Bolton, and continued with us for the rest of the day, through Lancaster, where a halt was called for lunch, right away to Kendal, our stopping-place for the day's run, where the whole town made holiday to witness our arrival and to visit the evening exhibition. We arrived at various times in the afternoon, and twenty-nine cars afterwards took part in the optional climbing of Shap Fell, which involved an out-and-home run from Kendal of twenty miles. It is a ten-miles climb up to the bleak expanse of Shap Common, 1,400ft. above sea-level, with gradients of 1 in 10, 1 in 13, 1 in 15, and so on, down to 1 in 25, with an intermediate descent of 600 yards from Huck's Brow to Huck's Bridge, with a gradient of 1 in 10, which had to be descended as slowly as possible. This involved practically restarting from a stop at the bottom, where an immediate ascent of 1 in 11 faced the assemblage. That the cars did it bravely is excellent testimony to their powers; but it entailed hard work upon the $2\frac{1}{4}$ and 3-h.p. engines of the motor-tricycles, and upon their riders, who aided their machines by pedalling up. We were all glad to descend again from the bleak plateau at the summit, and came back to Kendal helter-skelter.

Starting this (Tuesday) morning from Kendal at 9.30, we had the compulsory hill-climbing of Dunmail Raise on our itinerary. We came to it by way of Windermere, whose waters looked a cold steely blue in the chary sunshine of this back-

ward spring, by Ambleside, and by romantic Rydal Water. Dunmail Raise is a 1¾ mile climb, with successive gradients of 1 in 17, 1 in 15, 17, 11, 12, 13, 15, and then to the trying stretch of 166 yards of 1 in 8½, after which it eases off to the summit. The official times are not yet issued (at this time of writing), but nearly all, it is understood, successfully negotiated the Raise. Thence by Thirlmere and its rock-girt road, followed by a steep and large drop into Keswick, we arrived early at Carlisle, the first to reach here being Mr. S. F. Edge, driving A10 and the Ariel tricycle, with the Whippet detachable trailer, at the same moment. Carlisle is in the thick of a race meeting, but the evening exhibition in the Butter Market has been exceedingly well attended. To-morrow we run to Edinburgh, our most northerly point, starting, thank goodness, at 9.30 a.m., instead of the more usual 7 a.m., a time when the world is not yet properly aired, and when, at this season, and in these northern latitudes, the air still bites shrewdly.”

The Motor-Car Journal, Friday, May 4th, 1900

THE MOTOR CAR TOUR, The Visit to the Lakeland

We have the assurance of several of the chief motorists taking part in the Automobile Clubs', 1,000 miles trial London to Edinburgh & back that no portion of their progress up to Wed. had proved half so charming as their run through Lakeland to Carlisle.

Many were south countrymen and some were foreigners who had never visited the English lakes before; and all were loud in their admiration of the beautiful lakes and dales and snug lying villages encompassed by the grim cold hills which form one of the endearing features of the County, therein created a lasting impression on most of the visitors who expressed their thanks to the committee general and local who had planned this memorable tour through the Lake District. All the same they 'did The Lakes' much as the American does who pays a flying visit across the to the Mother country to see all that is worth seeing and scoots through the Lakes without a stop satisfied that he has whipped off all the cream.

After Dunmail Raise the left bank of Thirlmere was taken and the ride to Keswick,with the numerous awkward corners and bridges was one requiring skilled attention of the drivers. They were not expected to Keswick till after two o'clock, but there was whisper that some of the party would like to attend Carlisle Races that day, and the scheduled times were not adhered to. It is certain that one or two of the cars which met with temporary disablement took a longer time than the maximum legal limit required. We have reason to believe that one of the cars containing a couple of adventurous motor-cyclists were so tempted by the excellent road before them that they did the 30 miles in one hour and ten minutes and though for the mile thence to Carlisle another ten minutes was added to the time of every vehicle.

One dust begrimed party on stopping at the Raffles Control/Check gleefully inquired as the time was checked 'Had we come up to the legal limit?' He knew well that he had been travelling some portions at the good road at the rate of 30 mph. The school children had been given holiday and lined the route at different villages and the inhabitants came out and gave them all a hearty greeting.

There were several ladies & most of them were heavily veiled & wrapped to keep out the dust & cold. The men wore leather or moleskin jackets & most of them wore large spectacles; their faces were black with grime & dust and their backs were white from the same cause it was the speed that did it and the wind which being behind them may have had something to do with the extra pace that was travelled. What struck the spectators was the noise & the vibration on each machine when it pulled up it seemed quite alarming and appearing in the case at the lighter machines of shattering them to pieces. A big car that went by steam was noteworthy as making the least noise but it left a trail of steam behind it coming from underneath the car. At Carlisle the cars were displayed in the New Market where a charge was made for their exhibition and the proceeds were donated to the War Fund.

Extracts from the report of: '*The Patriot*' Carlisle 04. 05. 1900.
(contrib: Gowan Coulthard)

CARLISLE TO EDINBURGH 12

WEDNESDAY 2ND MAY

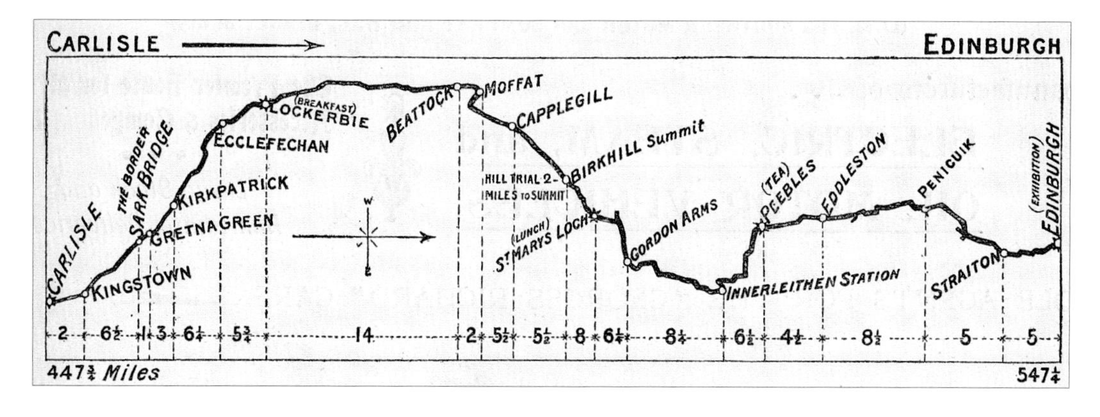

100 miles
Via Beattock, Moffatt (including Hill-Climbing Trials Moffatt to Birkhill 2 miles), Gordon Arms, Peebles, Edinburgh

THE CONTOUR map for May 2nd resembles the shape of a mountain, and this was a baptism of fire entering Scotland. In fact 40½ miles out, was the Hill-climbing Trial No. 4 on Birkhill. The instruction was 'after Record Sheets have been filled in, PROCEED at full speed up the hill for 2 miles to Birkhill Summit, which is at the milestone (obliterated) opposite a cowshed, after a cottage at the top.' The last few yards are marked as 1:11, which must have been a daunting sight after the steady climb. The programme has a helpful table saying that if you have taken 6 minutes you will have averaged 20 mph; and if you have taken 30 minutes you have averaged 4 mph; with every minute in between. So the pocket watch could be useful here!

The speed limits to be observed in Scotland were 10 mph out of town (against 12 mph in England).

HILL-CLIMBING TRIAL No. 4 on Birkhill

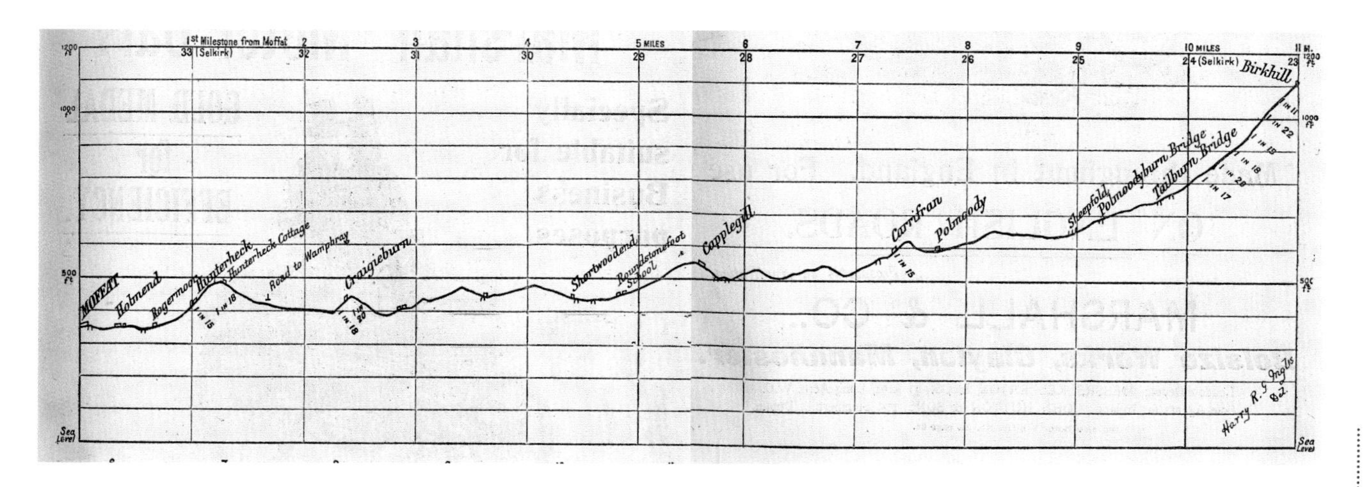

AVERAGES.

Vehicles which have accomplished the ascent of two miles in :—

6 minutes will have made an average of	20 m. p. h.	16 minutes will have made an average of	7·5 m. p. h.
6½	18·4	16½	7·2
7	17·1	17	7·0
7½	16	17½	6·8
8	15	18	6·6
8½	14·1	18½	6·5
9	13·3	19	6·3
9½	12·6	19½	6·1
10	12	20	6·0
10½	11·4	21	5·7
11	10·9	22	5·4
11½	10·4	23	5·2
12	10·0	24	5·0
12½	9·6	25	4·8
13	9·2	26	4·6
13½	8·9	27	4·4
14	8·6	28	4·3
14½	8·2	29	4·1
15	8·0	30	4·0
15½	7·7		

12

Carlisle to Edinburgh

(By Telegram)

Dull and lowering with a strong cool-wind, and a promise of wet, was Wednesday morning, when *The Autocar* representatives, having undertaken the timing of Birkhill, left Carlisle with five aboard Mr. Johnson's car at 8.17. With roads just dry, we made our miles over splendid gradients well under three, and were nearing Beattock when rain came down and rendered the surface slippery, so we slowed down, and ran steadily on to Moffat. Then we took the road for Birkhill, Rolls and Edge passing within a mile of the foot, at which point they waited while a heard of shaggy cattle stood around and gazed at the strange sight. Dropping Mr. Swindley at the bottom to time the starts, we set out for the two miles' going up, four aboard, in 14.43.

The rain had ceased, but the wind blew cold and strong straight up the hill, giving practically no radiation to the motors, and during our four hours' vigil at the top the cars finished one by one, with the following averages to their credit: A17, 16.0; 3, 13.3; 4 and 12, 12.6; A28, 12.0; A10, 11.5; A22, 26, 39, 5, and 14, 10.9; 11, 10.4; A29, 10.0; 31, 9.6; 23 and 27, 8.9; A3, 34 and 40, 8.6; A31, 8.2; 37, 15, and 51, 8.0; 27 and 22, 7.7; 46, A20, and 16, 7.5; A30, 7.0; 35 and A16, 6.8; A7, 2, and 36, 6.6; 8, 6.5; 9 and 49, 6.3; 1, 6.0; A2, 5.7; 47, 5.0; A21, 4.8; A23, 4.6; A26 and 44, 4.1. A. J. Wilson, whose current had given out, finished dead beat at the top. Several cars and all the single driven tandems shed passengers; the steamers came up hidden in a smother of steam, the Whitney running out of steam twice, and only just crawling past the post, then waiting to pump water into boiler. Cordingley stopped twenty yards from top, and was pulled over the line by the shepherds' by main force. As the day advanced, it became finer, and the roads soon became dry once more. St Mary's Loch gleamed in the sun, and the run down was splendid. Full justice was done to lunch at Rodono's Hotel. Wilson was passed, stranded for lack of current, a few miles on, and then a long climb and magnificent descent over wild and bleak country took us into Peebles, where several cars were waiting for tea. No. 16 was passed adjusting just beyond control, and the run of twenty-three miles into Edinburgh was made over magnificent roads in excellent time. Our car arrived at the Waverley Market shortly after seven, to find most of the rest already safely housed. A day of varied experiences, but a decided success. ”

The Autocar, Saturday, May 5th, 1900

What the Newspapers said

The Scotsman

3rd May The Thousand-Mile Motor-Car Trials

'The last stage of the outward run from London to Edinburgh in the great 1000-mile motor-car trials was accomplished yesterday when the 52 vehicles which have survived all tests so far made the journey from Carlisle to the Scottish capital. At half-past nine in the morning, when the cars set out from Carlisle, the prediction of a pleasant day's run would have been at once hazardous and thankless. The air was chilly, the sky was deeply overcast, and the distant hills were hidden in mist. In less than an hour from the start the procession struck a drizzling rain, and an outlook even more bleak than before, and every mile traversed brought into view roads more muddy than those left behind; but towards midday the sky cleared wonderfully and the latter half of the day's trip was actually run in brilliant sunshine and in not a little dust. The character of the track was quite as mixed as was the weather. While there were numerous stretches of straight and level highway such as are the delight and the enchantment of the 'motorist', there was, on the other, hand mile after mile of the sinuous and ascending turnpike for which the motor-driver has just as little affection as has the cyclist. For that very reason yesterday's journey was admitted to be one of the best tests of endurance which has been encountered since the tour was entered upon. There was another respect in which the ground traversed yesterday differed from all that had preceded it. Taken all over, it led the company through, perhaps, the most sparsely populated districts they had yet seen. Miles of country were passed through without a single human being coming within view; and that 'bête noir' of the motorist, as of the driver of any mechanically propelled vehicle, the restive horse, cropped up only at long intervals.

For yesterday's section of the tour, from Carlisle to Edinburgh, a representative of *The Scotsman* was fortunate enough to have a seat reserved for him upon the 12-horse-power Daimler (manufactured by the Daimler Motor Company, Coventry and London) with which Mr. J. A. Holder, of Birmingham, has all along been taking a not inconspicuous place in the 'A' class of the contest – that reserved for privately-owned motor vehicles. In common with some others engaged in the tour, this is the sort of machine upon which the novice in long-distance autocar running might trust himself without the least trepidation – the sort of machine that can climb a stubborn or shape its course down a not too facile descent with equal success and safety. The sensation of bowling along the Queen's highway at perhaps twenty or thirty miles an hour, without the protection of a weather board, probably strikes the timerous or nervous individual as at first more peculiar than pleasant. The eyes smart and water as the direct result of flying through the atmosphere – perhaps against a contrary wind – at such a pace; and there is, to begin with, an involuntary tendency to 'hold on' as a brae is being descended or a nasty curve is being rounded. The surprising thing is the rapidity with which suchlike untoward sensation pass off. The eyes in a short while become habituated to the swish of the air, and very soon the amateur voyageur feels quite comfortable and happy bending forward or leaning over to the inside of a curve, just as if he had been brought up to this sort of thing from infancy. The appetite for speed actually grows by what it feeds on; and the novice in motoring would fain plead with the driver after a time to put on another mile or two onto the pace 'just to see how it feels.' Motoring has all the exhilaration and more of cycling without the labour of pedalling. Talking of cycling, it was most striking to note the ease with which the cars yesterday passed on the road cyclists who were pedalling for all they were worth. That is the retribution which has overtaken the cyclist for the lofty scorn with which he has hitherto been accustomed to regard everything on the high road, so far as pace is concerned.

As has already been indicated, Carlisle was left yesterday morning about half-past nine o'clock. Hundreds of people watched the departure of the cars from the Butter Market, and hundreds more witnessed the send-off from the confines of the town a quarter of an hour later. All through the day's run the leading cars ran far in advance of the approximate times set down in the official time-table. The 21½ miles to Lockerbie were covered in an hour and twelve minutes. At every village on the way the populace turned out to see the cars pass northward and at Lockerbie itself everybody in the town seemed to line the route. At Moffat, which was gained about a quarter to twelve, or at a mean speed from Carlisle onwards of well nigh twenty miles an hour, the same thing happened. The route was thickly lined by inhabitants, and there, as elsewhere, the voyageurs evoked many a hearty cheer. At Moffat Market Place, the cars doubled somewhat on their track, and made for Capplegill, in order that the ascent to Birkhill Summit might be made the occasion of a hill climbing test. The winding and uneven nature of the road for the nine miles which lay between Moffat and the official hill-climbing test were in themselves a very fair test, but at the ninth milestone beyond Moffat the cars were brought to a temporary standstill as they arrived, and were then timed as they set out upon their still stiffer task. As a rule, the times made upon the ascent were surprisingly good, considering the heavy condition of the road. The hill-climbing test over, the cars set out upon their spin to St. Mary's Loch. By this time the weather had quite cleared up, and the loch itself and the hill ranges right and left, through which it is approached, looked their best in the serenely transparent atmosphere that enveloped them. The Rodono Hotel was reached a few minutes before one o'clock, and here a halt of three-quarters of an hour was called in order that lunch may be partaken of. Mounting their cars once more, the members of the party set out by way of the Gordon Arms for Inverleithen, which was passed about half-past two amid the cheers of hundreds of bystanders. Little more than a quarter of an hour later the advance party of the train of vehicles found themselves in Peebles, where half-an-hour was allowed for tea. At a quarter past three or thereby the last stage of the journey to Edinburgh was entered upon by way of Leadburn, Penicuik, and Liberton.

The Scotsman

Peebles ¼ hour compulsory STOP will be made for Tea

Peebles News and County Advertiser

5th May Motor Car Visitation

'On Wednesday afternoon hundreds lined the Eastgate to witness the arrival of the motor cars which have been doing the one thousand mile test race from London to London. The original plan was that the cars had to arrive at Peebles at about 6 p.m. with a stoppage of 15 minutes, but that was departed from, and the first car passed through the burgh at 2.30 and at intervals up to 8 o'clock in the evening when 54 had passed through the town. The parties in the cars presented a travel-stained appearance, being covered with dust, and the cars as thought hey had been engaged besieging mud hovels. There were tricycles, and low-seated as well as high-seated motors. The highest priced car arrived first in Peebles – A17 owner the Hon. C. S. Rolls, 12 h.p. and valued at £900. The cars ranged from £180 to £900, and the tricycles from £120. The time of the cars was taken by Mr. George Bridges and Mr. Thomas Russell, and after a delay proceeded to Edinburgh where there was to be an exhibition.'

Lord Kingsburgh on a Daimler at Edinburgh. (Photo: Argent Archer)

Arrival in Edinburgh

The first of the cars reached the southern boundaries of Edinburgh considerably before schedule time. So unexpectedly early did they come, indeed, that a halt had to be called at Nether Liberton pending the appearance of the timekeepers. At this point the drivers had their cards marked and returned to them, prior to continuing the 2 miles to the Waverley Market. For that distance fifteen minutes were allowed, being at the limited rate of eight miles an hour. As showing the growing popularity of the latest means of locomotion, large crowds of citizens turned out to witness the entry of the travellers. The spectators began to assemble shortly after four o'clock. By five o'clock the thoroughfares right out from Tron Church to the top of Minto Street were pretty thickly lined by people, the assemblage at various points being augmented by hundreds of workmen ceasing their labours for the day. At the top of Waverley Bridge, the junction of Princes Street and the North Bridge, the South Bridge and the High Street, and a little beyond the University the crowds were largest. Evidently much interest was taken in the arrivals, and from half-past six to eight o'clock or thereabouts thousands of onlookers crowded the streets and the corners mentioned. As the majority of the motor cars came in, at intervals of five minutes or so, a heavy vehicular traffic was in progress, and the police had not a little difficulty in keeping an open track. During the latter part of the evening the gathering of spectators was particularly dense at the upper end of the Waverley Bridge. Here the timekeepers were stationed for the final stage of the journey, and while their duties were being discharged opportunity was afforded of seeing the cars. Of the total of 52, the first arrived at 4.15 – car A19, a Daimler, owned by Mr. J. R. Hargreaves J.P. Others came in at short intervals up to about nine o'clock. Several of the travellers came in for a considerable amount of notice on the part of the spectators, the Lord Justice Clerk, for example, who rode on car 36, a Daimler, in the company of Colonel Magrath, R.H.A., reached the terminus at 6.48, being loudly cheered. On arrival at the market the cars took up the stances allotted to them, running from the western to the eastern end of the building. One and all bore traces of the dusty and dirty character of the roads that had been traversed, and a number of them, before being stalled for the night, were taken away and cleaned. An exhibition of the vehicles is to take place this afternoon, and will be opened at one o'clock by the Lord Justice-Clerk. Among other attractions there are to be obstacle races and also an exhibition of motor driving by Mr E.J. Coles', who recently performed at the Alhambra Theatre, London. The band and pipers of the Gordon Highlanders will play during the afternoon and evening. The cars will leave early tomorrow morning and proceed to Newcastle-on-Tyne by way of Berwick.

The Scotsman

27th April Motor Car Contest. British Tour of 1000 Miles

'Of the many possible infringements which render the competitors liable for disqualification of their vehicles, that of failing to show consideration to drivers of restless horses is one of those upon which most stress is laid.'

Berwick Advertiser

Only nine vehicles succumbed in the first 500 miles of the Trial, and of these three were experimental cars.

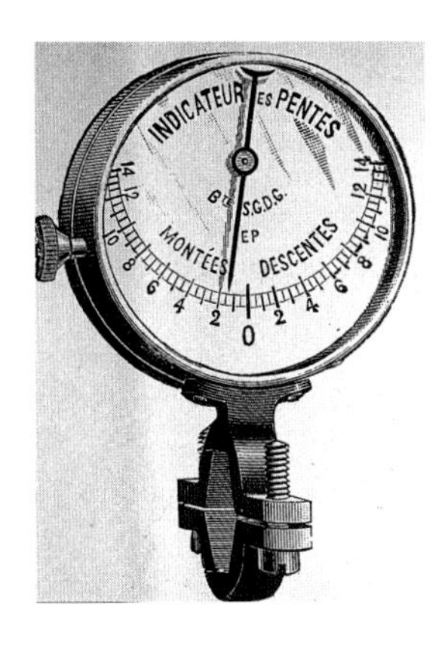

Gradient meter (PHH)

1,000-Mile Trial. 141

EDINBURGH,
THURSDAY, MAY 3rd, 1900.

A ONE-DAY
EXHIBITION
OF THE
MOTOR VEHICLES
TAKING PART IN THE
1,000-Mile Trial organized by the Automobile Club of Great Britain,
WILL BE HELD IN THE
WAVERLEY MARKET,
By kind permission of The Right Hon. MITCHELL THOMSON, Lord Provost, the Magistrates, and Town Council.

ADMISSION—
On WEDNESDAY EVENING, MAY 2nd, to witness the arrival of the vehicles until 11 p.m. ... ... TWO SHILLINGS.
On THURSDAY, MAY 3rd, from 12 o'clock noon to 10 p.m. ONE SHILLING.

THE PROFITS WILL BE DEVOTED TO THE LORD PROVOST'S TRANSVAAL WAR FUND.

The Committee for Local Arrangements,
Being the Committee of the Scottish Automobile Club, guaranteed the expenses and made all the necessary arrangements in Edinburgh in connection with the Trial and Exhibition.

Norman D. Macdonald, Esq., Advocate (Chairman).

Edwin Adam, Esq., Advocate.
James Burns, Esq.
Dr. Blair, Jedburgh.
W. H. Cox, Esq.
Isaac Connell, Esq., S.S.C.
Patrick Drummond, Esq.
T. R. B. Elliot, Esq.
John Harper, Jr., Esq.
J. H. Irons, Esq.
John Macdonald, Esq.
T. R. Outhwaite, Esq.
F. P. Pullar, Esq.
J. H. Paterson, Esq.
W. L. Sleigh, Esq.
H. A. Salvesen, Esq.
Thomas Symington, Esq.
John Stirling, Esq.
Dawson Turner, Esq., M.D.
John Wilson, Esq.

EXHIBITION AT EDINBURGH

THURSDAY 3RD MAY

“ Edinburgh

The local time-keepers were taken by surprise, and the occupants of the first few cars had to wait awhile. The first car to arrive was a Napier motor, driven by Mr. S.F. Edge. The next, a 12-h.p. Panhard, driven by the Hon. C.S. Rolls, passed the red flags a quarter of a minute later. The others arrived as follows:- Ariel tricycle with Whippet trailer for extra passenger, E.S. Cheel, driver; Daimler Parisian, driver G. White; Mr. J.A. Holder's 12-h.p. Daimler; Mr. Mark Mayhew's 7-h.p. Peugeot, driven by D. Haxton; Mr. J.W. Stocks on his Ariel quadricycle; Mr. E. Buck on the Motor Manufacturing Company's tricycle; the Hon. J. Scott Montagu, M.P., on his 12-h.p. Daimler; Mr. Friswell on his 8-h.p. Peugeot; Century tandem tricycle driven by S. Begbie; and Mr. T.B. Browne's 6-h.p. Panhard. As one car after another passed along, occupants, and everything white with dust, no little stir was occasioned, and all along the route to the Waverley Market soon became crowded. The 'inward control' at Liberton Brae were Messrs. A. Alexander, of the Cyclists' Touring Club, and W.L. Sleigh, of the Scottish Automobile Club; while the 'outward control' with the white flags at the Bridges were Messrs. Normand Macdonald and John Macdonald. At the Waverley Market the cards were obtained from the drivers, and a note of the time of their arrival at the Market taken, and the card signed by the timekeeper there. An exhibition of the vehicles took place within the Waverley Market yesterday (Thursday), among the attractions announced being an exhibition of motor driving by Mr. E.J. Coles, who recently performed at the Agricultural Hall exhibition. ”

Motor-Car Journal

Edinburgh Exhibition

The exhibition of motor cars in the Waverley Market Hall, Edinburgh, was formally opened by Lord Kingsburgh in the presence of a goodly company of spectators, who before the opening time had an opportunity of inspecting the vehicles, and of expressing surprise at and appreciation of the variety and construction of the motors. The audience included a number of Edinburgh Town Councillors and others. Lord Provost, Mitchell Thomson, at the outset, welcomed the motor-carists to Edinburgh, and predicted that in a few years they would see motor-cars running very frequently on country roads. He could not say that he liked them very much in cities, more especially when they ran too quickly: that was a thing that they, representing the people of Edinburgh, rather objected to. It said a great deal for the cars that they had reached the turning-point of their journey without any serious accident, and he complimented them, especially upon their hill-climbing records. With regard to the question of safety, he remarked that the driver of a motor-car had his machine under much greater control than the man driving horses. The Hon. J. Scott Montagu, M.P., and M. Berduil, a member of the Automobile Club of France, returned thanks for the Lord Provost's welcome. Lord Kingsburgh, in declaring the exhibition open, gave his opinion, as an unbiased spectator, of the trial run. He had been himself surprised, he said, to see the extraordinary power the cars had of climbing hills, in some cases the gradients being something like one in eight, and in others, for short distances, one in seven. Some of them, he also mentioned, mounted Shap Fell and Dunmail Rise at something like seventeen miles an hour. Speed was a very difficult question to enter upon. One thing he asked them to consider was whether it was not true that the question of speed and safety did not depend so much upon a named speed for all roads as on the capacity of the vehicle to be easily steered and to be easily stopped. One of the vehicles going twelve or fourteen miles an hour could be pulled up absolutely in its own length. That was an element of safety which they knew very well was not attainable with horses. Having spoken of the cordial welcome received from all classes on the route, particularly from the older generation, his Lordship said they had reason to congratulate themselves on escape from accident, and he could almost prophesy that in the return journey there would be no serious accident that could be attributed in any way to the motor-car. Automobilism was not only a sport, but a means of locomotion very much wanted in the country. He was quite sure that as soon as County Council authorities knew the capabilities of motor-cars they would have an alteration in the road regulations. Treasurer Cranston proposed a vote of thanks to Lord Kingsburgh, who in turn moved a vote of thanks to the Lord Provost for his presence. In the course of the Thursday the show was visited by large numbers of people, and the greatest interest appeared to be manifested in the different exhibits. During the evening the attendance was fully 5,000. Attractive music was provided by the brass and pipe bands of the Gordon Highlanders, and Mr. E. J. Coles gave a display of expert driving.

During the exhibition at Edinburgh the cars of the Edinburgh Motor-Car Company and several of the competing cars were driven round the Market Place, and afforded many people an opportunity for a spin. ”

The Motor-Car Journal, Saturday, May 12th, 1900

Edinburgh the turning point of the Trial

It is hard to imagine the emotions of the travellers on arrival at this fair city. The programme lists 2 whole pages of hotels, but not many at 'luxury' prices. A room at the Adelphi could be 3/- with a bath 6d or 1/- extra (depending one assumes upon whether it was cold or hot). Perhaps the more wealthy participants would have let their eye travel further down the alphabetical list, and could be found at the Royal, Royal British or Rutland Hotels, where a room would cost 5/- upwards. Strangely enough for a city boasting 50 listed hotels there were only 3 places where petroleum spirit could be obtained, an indication of how small local demand must have been in 1900.

Mr. & Mrs Friswell on their Peugeot (Photo: *The Autocar*)

The Exhibition in the Waverley Market was open Wednesday evening, from arrival to 11 p.m. at a premium price of 2/- admission. Strangely enough, on the Thursday the Exhibition opened at 12 noon, giving a whole morning for work upon the cars!

Fifty one of the 64 starters reached this point and they are listed below:

A10 8 h.p. Napier, Mr. Ed. Kennard, D.L., J.P., driven by Mr. S. F. Edge.
A17 12 h.p. Panhard, the Hon. S. C. Rolls.
A22 12 h.p. Daimler, Mr. J. A. Holder.
26 8 h.p. Peugeot, driven by Mr. C. Friswell.
6 h.p. Daimler Parisian, Mr. M. Grahame-White.
A24 Mors Petit Duc, Mr. R. E. Phillips.
2 Benz Ideal, Hewetsons Ltd., driven by A. J. Coles.
46 Richard car, French driver and crew.
47 Richard car, French driver, M. Berduil passenger.
A2 6 h.p. Panhard, Mr. F. H. Butler.
9 Motor Mfg. Co.'s 6 h.p. Iveagh phaeton.
A7 6 h.p. Parisian Daimler, Mr. A. C. Harmsworth, driven by Captain Langrishe.
A11 12 h.p. Daimler, the Hon. Jno. Scott-Montagu, M.P.
14 De Dion voiturette.
49 5 h.p. Marshall car.
35 6 h.p. Parisian Daimler, driven by Mr. C. Critchley.
A30 6 h.p. Parisian Daimler, driven by Mr. J. D. Siddeley.
A3 6 h.p. Panhard, driven by Mr. T. B. Browne.
A21 6 h.p. Daimler, driven by Mr. Ernest Pitman.
A20 Empress motor tricycle, Mr. Herbert Ashby.
A26 6 h.p. Daimler, driven by Mr. C. H. Gregson.
12 Motor Mfg. Co. tricycle, ridden by W. Buck.
41 3 h.p. International Victoria, driven by Mr. C. Seyd.
34 3½ h.p. Decauville car, driven by Jules Dubois.
28 3 h.p. New Orleans car.
15 De Dion voiturette, driven by Mr. C. Egerton.
44 3 h.p. International Victoria, driven by Mr. H. Capellan.
16 3¼ h.p. Gladiator voiturette, driven by M. Farman.
51 3½ h.p. Star voiturette, driven by Mr. Lisle.
4 Ariel tricycle, with Whippet detachable trailer, driven by Mr. E. S. Cheel.
1 3 h.p. Benz Ideal, driven by Mr. Hewetson.
A31 6 h.p. Parisian Daimler, driven by Mr. W. Exe.
27 3 h.p. New Orleans voiturette, driven by Mr. Astell.
8 Motor Mfg. Co.'s 6 h.p. phaeton, driven by Mr. Burgess.
24 5 h.p. Marshall car, driven by Mr. Mann
3 3⅛ h.p. Ariel quadricycle, driven by Mr. J. Stocks.
A12 6 h.p. Daimler, driven by Mr. H. Edmunds.
A29 7 h.p. Peugeot, Mr. Mark Mayhew, driven by H. Haxell.
A27 12 h.p. Daimler, driven by Mr. J. R. Hargreaves.
5 The Locomobile steam car.
31 3½ h.p. M.C.C. Triumph.
31 3½h.p. M.C.C. Triumph.
A28 Enfield quadricycle, driven by Mr. E. M. Iliffe.
A25 3 h.p. Benz Ideal, Mrs Bazalgette.
40 3 h.p. Wolseley voiturette, driven by Mr. H. Austin.
39 Century tandem tricycle, driven by Mr. Jackson.
36 6 h.p. Daimler, driven by Mr. Richardson. (This car conveyed the Lord Justice Clerk of Scotland and Colonel McGrath all the way from London, and they are returning in it.)
23 Brown-Whitney steam car, driven by Mr. Blake.
38 9½ h.p. Daimler public service vehicle, driven by Mr. Straker.

The above is not in sequence of arrival.

Dietz tubular driving lamp
(P.H.H.)

The 20th Century Tandem lamp
(P.H.H.)

49
24
2
27
3
185
39
33

Arrivals at Edinburgh taken on May 2nd
– Waverley Market detail:
(*Extreme right:*) George Lanchester on Lanchester No. 21;
H. Hewetson with Jules Dubois on Decauville No. 34
Mrs Bazalgette and friend on her Benz No. A25
(Photo: Argent Archer)

"For the most part the cars arrived well to time and without mishap, but the Daimler char-a-banc was towed in by the baggage waggon next day with a broken crosshead and the piston jammed in the cylinder and a leaky cylinder head, and did not put in an appearance at the Waverley Market at all, but went to Stirlings' motor works for repairs. Here also the Brown-Whitney steamer found its way on Thursday morning, it having been discovered upon overhauling that one of the crank bearings had come adrift and knocked out a cylinder head. Late on Thursday evening Mr. A. J. Wilson, minus machine, made his appearance at Edinburgh, and told a lugubrious tale of spent batteries and a broken crosshead pin in the cylinder, which had been grinding grooves in its surface all day and generally deranging its internal economy, the while Mr. Wilson spent many a horse-power of muscular energy in assisting the operation. He had reached the Gordon Arms at the head of St. Mary's Loch at 10.30 the previous night, and had sent his machine home by train, his weak knee having given out, as well it might. (*See the story which follows*).

The Waverley Market, where the cars were stabled, made a fine place for an exhibition, and the building was thronged throughout the day by considerable crowds, the people of the city generally taking great interest in the proceedings. Several of the cars were driven round the show and put through some somewhat startling evolutions at times, and, indeed, as much rapid running was indulged in virtually right among the people it speaks well for the ease of management of motor vehicles that no accident occurred. Coles, at the request of the Lord Chief Justice Clerk of Scotland, railed off an enclosure and gave his exhibition of driving and controlling the Benz car three times during the day. An excellent band performed during the day, as well as a pipers' band from one of the Highland regiments.

Punctually at one o'clock the Lord Provost of Edinburgh, accompanied by the Lord Justice Clerk, the Hon. Jno. Scott-Montagu, M.P., Claude Johnson, and other gentlemen, mounted on the bandstand, and attention having been called by several trumps upon a cyclorn, Lord Kingsburgh made a few remarks, as chairman, and asked the Lord Provost to open the exhibition. The chief magistrate of Edinburgh tendered a very hearty welcome to the Automobile Club and all who had taken part in the run from the South, and in referring to the presence of a prominent member of the Automobile Club of France, touched upon the commanding lead which the French had taken in automobilism, but hoped that the time would not be long before the British were abreast of them. He confessed to having read with interest the various accounts of the successive day trips the competing cars had made, and referred to the excellent run made on the previous day from Carlisle to Edinburgh. He admitted that the driving and control of the cars as they entered and moved about the city had astonished him beyond measure. The Lord Provost concluded his remarks by repeating his welcome, and regretting that the stay to be made by the club in Edinburgh was so brief. In returning thanks on behalf of the club, the Hon. Jno. Scott-Montagu, M.P., touched generally

Lord Provost of Edinburgh opens Exhibition (Photo: Argent Archer)

upon the details of the trial, its aims and ends, and referred to the practical acquaintance the Edinburgh people had already made with automobilism.

Lord Kingsburgh then gave a brief reflex of his experiences since he had left London with the cars, and testified to their speed, control, and management in similar terms to those he had employed at Manchester. His Lordship laid special stress upon the hearty welcome the club and their friends had received throughout the length and breadth of the country, and particularly from the oldest inhabitants, who might have been expected to regard motor cars with a prejudiced eye. He also remarked upon the fact that over fifty cars had travelled over five hundred miles, carrying nearly one hundred persons without any accident to life or limb. A vote of thanks to Lord Kingsburgh, proposed by the Secretary of the local committee, closed the ceremony.

Taken altogether our stay in Edinburgh was a great success, and as this brought us to the completion of one half of the tour it is a matter of congratulation that so many cars have successfully come through the journey so far and with so little in the way of mishaps. ”

The Autocar, Saturday, May 12th, 1900

The Scotsman

The Scotsman had more to say about Edinburgh's reaction to the motor-car and the Lord Provost's speech.

4th May The Thousand-Mile Motor Car Trial. Exhibition of cars in Edinburgh

'The competitors in the thousand-mile trial of motor cars promoted by the Automobile Club, having completed their northward journey, spent yesterday in Edinburgh, and an exhibition of the fifty-two vehicles remaining in the run took place in the Waverley Market. The trial has so far excited much attention on this side of the Border, not only among sportsmen and mechanics, but also among the general public, and yesterday many people turned out to inspect the cars. All day there was a large and interested gathering in the Market. Trial runs of several vehicles were a source of considerable interest and a series of obstacle races and a display of clever motor car driving by E. J. Coles were additional attractions. The brass and pipe bands of the Gordon Highlanders played selections. Shortly after one o'clock, the Right Hon. J. H. A. Macdonald (Lord Kingsburgh) formally declared the exhibition open. Accompanying his Lordship to the platform were Lord Provost Mitchell Thomson, the Hon. J. Scott Montagu, Sir Andrew McDonald, Treasurer Cranston, Mr. John Wilson, Mr. Edwin Adam, Mr. Norman Macdonald, and Mr. Johnson, secretary of the Automobile Club.

The Lord Provost, in bidding the visitors welcome to the city, said it might be invidious to mention names, but there was one gentleman he would like to refer to – M. Bourdil, who had come from France. (Applause.) From what he had seen in the south of France, a much greater interest was taken in this method of locomotion than what was the case in this country, but he ventured to predict that in the course of time people would be educated up to the point of adapting themselves to that kind of traction, and that in the course of a few years they would see automobiles very frequently on their country roads. He could not say he liked them very much in their cities, more especially when they were running too quick. That was a thing that they, as representing the people of Edinburgh, had rather an objection to. They had seen in recent years various kinds of trials of strength with regard to locomotion between Scotland and London. Some time ago there was what might be called the wheelbarrow craze, when a man trundled a wheelbarrow all the way from John O'Groats to Land's End. Two or three years ago they had a competition on the railways between the East and West Coast routes, as to which could do the journey quickest between London and Aberdeen. It said a great deal for automobile cars that they had arrived in Edinburgh, the turning point of the journey, without accident of any serious kind. In the newspapers they had read with interest the progress they had made northwards. Especially did they note with interest and satisfaction the remarkable record that they made in climbing steep hills at the rate of from fourteen to seventeen miles an hour. (Applause.) He believed that the people on the country roads only recently were rather aghast when they saw one of these cars coming along the road, in case of accident, but there was no reason why they should be so, because, as they would very soon get to know, the driver of an automobile car had his machine under much greater control than a man driving a horse. (Applause.) He hoped their stay in Edinburgh, which, unfortunately, was very short, would be happy, and that they would have a prosperous and successful run back to the capital of England. (Applause.)

The Hon. J. Scott Montagu, on behalf of the competitors, acknowledged the Lord Provost's welcome to Edinburgh. He was sure that in Edinburgh they only wanted to know more of the movement to take it up enthusiastically. He quite agreed with the Lord Provost that the speed of cars should be limited in cities to a rate that they would be able to stop and turn with the greatest possible ease. If the same pace was allowed them as horse-drawn vehicles, they need be in no trepidation on the point of safety. (Applause.)

M. Bourdil, addressing the gathering in English which, he said, he had mostly learned in Australia, thanked them on behalf of the Automobile Club of France and the French competitors generally for the welcome they had received in hospitable Scotland. He would be very glad to make known the progress made in this country to his fellow-countrymen and also to his club, and hoped sincerely that the international competition would promote the coming industry and also the friendship of the two great industrial countries. (Applause.)

Lord Kingsburgh, in declaring the exhibition open, gave his opinion, as an unbiased spectator, of the trial run. He had been himself surprised, he said, to see the extraordinary power the cars had of climbing hills, in some cases the gradient being something like one in eight, and in others, for short distances, one in seven. Some of them, he also mentioned, mounted Shap fell and Dunmail Rise at something like seventeen miles an hour. Speed was a very difficult question to enter upon. One thing he asked them to consider was whether it was true that the question of speed and safety did not depend so much upon a named speed for all roads as on the capacity of the vehicle to be easily steered and to be easily stopped. (Hear, hear.) One of these vehicles going twelve or fourteen miles an hour could be pulled up absolutely in its own length. That was an element of safety which they knew very well was not attainable with horses. Having spoken of the cordial welcome received from all classes on the route, one thing that struck him, he said, more than another was that they had the heartiest welcome from the oldest people. The true reason for that, he thought, was that these old people were young in the days when railways were coming into use in this country, and he had no doubt many of them saw shaking heads, the grumbling, the complaints, and the evil prophesying of their fathers and mothers about the introduction of these hated things. Commenting next on the absence of accident to life or limb, his lordship said that any breakdowns of cars were due, not because the motor machinery had been at fault, but because the coachbuilder had not understood the proper strength of wheels, axles, and springs to provide for such vehicles. His own belief was, though one never liked to prophesy, that he would ride to London and complete the thousand miles without any serious accident that could be attributed in any way to the autocar. Automobilism was not only a sport, but also a means of locomotion very much wanted in the country. He was quite sure that as soon as County Council authorities knew the capabilities of autocars they would have an alteration on the road regulations.

Treasurer Cranston proposed a vote of thanks to Lord Kingsburgh, who in turn moved a vote of thanks to the Lord Provost for his presence.

The cars will leave Edinburgh on the return journey at seven o'clock this morning. The following is the day's itinerary: – Haddington, 8.25 a.m.; Dunbar, 10 a.m.; Berwick, 1 p.m.; Belford, 3.5 p.m.; Alnwick, 4.20 p.m.; Morpeth, 6 p.m.; Newcastle, 7.35 p.m.'

“Half-way on a Motor-Tricycle

Mr. A. J. Wilson has had a wide experience of motor-tricycles. In fact, he has written a book about them; and doubtless, in the next edition, will be able to add an interesting chapter on his experiences during the 1,000-mile Trial. His ride on the Ariel motor-tricycle was not wholly a pleasant one. After carrying him splendidly to Manchester, the machine began to jib en route to Kendal. At Kendal he spent four hours in the morning wrestling with the motor. As the dovetailed ends of the piston rings were broken, he put new ones in and started for Carlisle. But the jibbing continued, although cautious riding was indulged in. Ultimately he sat down and took out exhaust valve, got some knife polish, and ground valve in. Joy! for five miles; then woe, shoving, and regretting that he had never been satisfactorily taught how to swear. Anon she bumped anew, and he went gaily on for a few miles, when suddenly some petrol spurted up through the chimney, and then air came – puff,

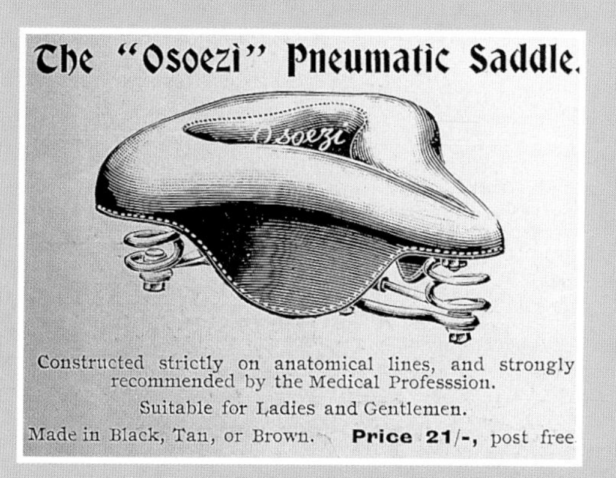

The 'Osoezi' pneumatic saddle (PHH)

puff, puff! he stopped, opened the valve chamber, and found the split pin of the inlet valve in fragments and the valve spring dancing about. Putting in a new split pin, he resumed the trip, went the last few miles at top speed, and finished the day in peace with all the world, thinking that all his sorrows were at an end.

On the Wednesday he carefully lubricated and tested everything before starting from Carlisle. The machine's behaviour began with a series of dying-away evolutions, which Mr. Wilson ascribed to a combination of bad petrol, moist air, and weak sparking. Once, after she had stopped dead, he sat down on the roadside, occupied exactly two hours taking the engine down and re-fitting, examining all contacts, putting new trembler and platinum screw, and so on. Then he had to shove the machine up Birkhill. After lunch the machine resumed, alternate flying free and dying away, with occasional jerky stops. Messrs. Sturmey and Swindley wanted to tow him, and then Mr. Cordingley came along, and seeing how impossible it was to move the trike (the wheels were almost locked), insisted on towing him. They got a rope, and the tricycle was towed for a mile or so; then at a sharp corner Mr. Wilson had to let the rope go; the machine instantly stopped dead, and he turned back and ran down hill to a little roadside hotel. There he sat down again, and proceeded in a vein of calm and philosophic contentment to take the whole concern to pieces. he resolved the affair into its primitive components, examining everything minutely. 'Eureka!' The cylinder was scored by two deep parallel lines, about half an inch apart. Searching for the cause he found it. The bolt which joins the piston to the top of the piston-rod should have a split pin through its thin ends, to prevent it turning round. There was no split pin! Some fragments of steel were all that remained of it. Consequently the bolt had been turning round; when it rested for a time in one position, all was well; but when it turned a quarter round, its edges scraped against the cylinder, causing a jambing action which stopped the up-and-down movement.

He had no spare split pin, so tried to obtain a suitable nail, failing which he selected a spare screw and laboriously filed it down to the correct size to jamb in the place of the split pin. he had also a new piston in his bag, and as the three new rings (put in only the previous day) were already broken, he determined to fit in the new piston. But the new piston was without a split pin; hence he had to make a substitute by filing down a screw.

It took just three hours to complete this job, and he started off before dark, hoping to get past a certain dangerous hill in daylight. But whether it was now only the bad petrol and feeble sparking, or whether his improvised pin had worked out or not, is not known. Certain it is that three miles was the limit of his run, and then he did another mighty shove uphill, stopping to rest now and again – alone in the midst of lofty rolling hills that would be entrancingly admirable under ordinary circumstances. When he got to the 'dangerous hill' he found that it was no great shakes; and the rapid descent warmed up the petrol, so that the machine bumped fairly well until he ran into Innerleithen.

The last we heard about the matter was that Mr. Wilson had decided to take the machine to Edinburgh by train, send it to Birmingham, and return to London as a passenger – by train or motor-car.”

The Motor-Car Journal, Wednesday, May 9th, 1900

EDINBURGH TO NEWCASTLE-ON-TYNE

FRIDAY, 4TH MAY

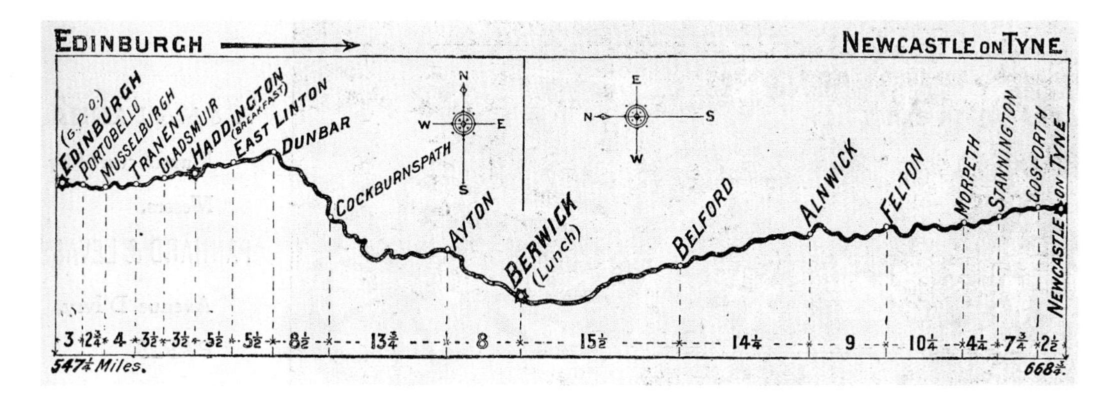

121½ miles

The Autocar reporter had a comfortable seat protected from the weather in a Lanchester driven by Mr. Millership.

" Going South – Edinburgh to Newcastle

Friday morning, May 4th, was not promising. Decidedly otherwise. Wild, ragged-looking clouds swept across a cold grey sky on the wings of a south-westerly gale. The streets were wet, and considerable rain had fallen in the night, with ample promise of more to follow, when, prompt to the minute of 7 a.m., the Hon. C. S. Rolls on his big Panhard headed out of the Waverley Market en route for Newcastle and home. Over the seven miles of tram rails to Levenhall, the end of the Edinburgh control, the cars slowly wended their way in a long procession, some of them skating and sliding uncomfortably on the wet sets as they bumped and shook over the, in places, vile surfaces, and our French friends on the two Georges Richard cars, who had donned their goggles, came in for no end of critical observation in broad Scotch from the numerous *gamins* and older people who, even at this early hour, had assembled to witness the passage of the cars. For ourselves, we were snugly ensconced beneath the hood and behind the folding dashboard of the Lanchester car, with Mr. Millership in command (*see below right*), and so long as we skirted the Forth with the wind more or less aft we kept the hood up and travelled in peace and comfort the while we watched the occupants of other cars struggling with refractory wraps and headgear and experiencing other discomforts of a minor character. The Edinburgh control ended at the foot of a stiffish upgrade, and the cars were 'slipped' as usual at half-minute intervals. When our turn came – we were tenth on the list – we shot away splendidly, and passed both Georges Richard cars, which were in front, before we reached the top, and going on for a mile or two, over excellent road

Facing the gale out of Edinburgh
Nos 46 and 47 Richard cars;
(*Third from right:*) *The Autocar* reporter rode in Lanchester Carriage No. 22 with Archie Millership
(*Fourth from right:*) No. A7, Alfred Harmsworth's 6 h.p. Daimler driven by Captain Langrishe.
(Photo: Argent Archer)

AUTOMOBILE CLUB
1000 MILES TRIAL
46

Above:
No. A11 Hon. J. S. Montagu's Daimler; No. 49 Marshall driven by J. J. Mann (Photo: Argent Archer)

surfaces, we travelled at an even steady pace, going up hill at about the same speed as on the level, and then we learned that the car had been geared down to a sixteen miles top speed for the tour, with the object of keeping together with her more bulky consort, so that, whilst she had no speed on the level, her eight horse-power engines took her up the grades without feeling them. The running was very steady and easy, and provided comfortable travelling. At Haddington half an hour was allowed for breakfast, and the sun struggled through the clouds the while the wind increased. We dropped our hood, and soon after getting under weigh one of the cylinders, which had previously shown signs of missing fire, continued to do so intermittently, with the result that our speed was greatly reduced, car after car passed us, we got more whiffs of petrol than were pleasant, and we had to use the low (six miles) gear on many of the hills. The gale had now considerably increased, and was dead in our teeth, and at times howled with such vehemence through the trees and telegraph wires adjacent to the road as to completely drown the beating of the engines.

Car after car passed us, and we stopped and changed an igniter, without, however, any better results, so we stopped again and changed the other, and, as this made but little

Right:
Gladiator Voiturette, Haddington Control (Photo: *The Autocar*)

difference, we had perforce to be content with our ten or eleven miles per hour, which, after our faster travelling of previous days, seemed a wretched crawl, more especially as the roads were broad, smooth, and dry, and, for the most part, excellent for speed travelling. What we lost in pace, however, we gained in comfort, and as at times the car took fits of fair travelling we managed to keep up our average for the day. Soon after leaving Haddington we passed Mrs. Kennard on her Dion voiturette apparently in difficulties with the pump. She went by during one of our above-mentioned stoppages, but was again in difficulties a few miles later, and we subsequently learned was obliged to stop and wait the arrival of a new pump, coming on again next day. Mr. Fuller's voiturette No. 14 apparently suffered from the same trouble, for no trace of it could be found on our arrival at Newcastle, and it did not make its appearance next day.

The Wolseley car was seen in difficulties with tyre troubles early in the day, and we subsequently learned her pneumatics had punctured four times during the day. The road to Berwick several times brought the tourists to the coast, and the last few miles took us up by a steady climb to the top of high cliffs, where the wind whistled and howled, and at times almost stopped the smaller cars, and the

Left:
The International at Haddington Control (Photo: *The Autocar*)

wide expanse of the wind-swept North Sea, covered with white-tipped waves – with here and there an ocean tramp burying her nose in the seas and ploughing a way through the murky waters in the teeth of the gale – spread out like a map before us. Our car was just now going well, and we had passed several cars up the hill. On the long run down into the little border town of Berwick, ensconced in a hollow below, we passed No. 28 New Orleans car with the motor bonnet off, and found rough but ample accommodation for lunch in the town, where a knot of cars closely surrounded by curious onlookers were assembled.

Just outside Berwick, Mr. Astill was stranded with the batteries of his New Orleans run out, and waiting for Van Toll with the baggage waggon, which carried a fresh set. The road via Belford to Alnwick provided excellent running, though we were not able to avail ourselves of it to any great extent, but murmuringly pursued the even tenor of our way. The Hon. J. Scott-Montagu – who had waved us from an express train earlier in the day and who had joined his car at Berwick – was passed with a punctured tyre, whilst Mr. Burgess's car (No. 8) and Mr. Richardson's (No. 36), with the Lord Justice Clerk and Col. McGrath on board, were passed in difficulties with refractory lamps, and shortly before reaching Alnwick Mr. Hargreaves on his twelve h.p. Daimler flew by us at a big speed, having left Edinburgh at nine. Soon Alnwick Castle with its picturesque surroundings was sighted, and we found a policeman stationed at the top of the very dangerous twisting descent to the river and bridge, with instructions to each car to take it cautiously. Just clear of the town we came across Mr. Hargreaves by the side of the road, and found he had had a somewhat exciting experience, for, not noticing the turn at the top of the hill, he had overshot the mark, and on backing down to the corner had found his brakes would not hold, so, in order to avoid a rapid dash down the hill backwards, he had, with great promptitude, backed into a wall and carried away a mudguard and swivel pin of the brake gear. This was soon put right, and he passed us again ere we were many miles on our way. Approaching Morpeth Mr. Butler was passed with a punctured tyre, and, indeed, punctures seem to have been very plentiful during the day's run. The Century tandem was in difficulties with its pump, and a few miles later on a haycart was seen overturned in a ditch, its horse having apparently endeavoured – unsuccessfully – to take it over a hedge into the neighbouring plantation. 'Who upset the haycart?' we queried, and subsequently ascertained that the Ariel tricycle and Whippet trailer (No. 4) were the innocent cause of the

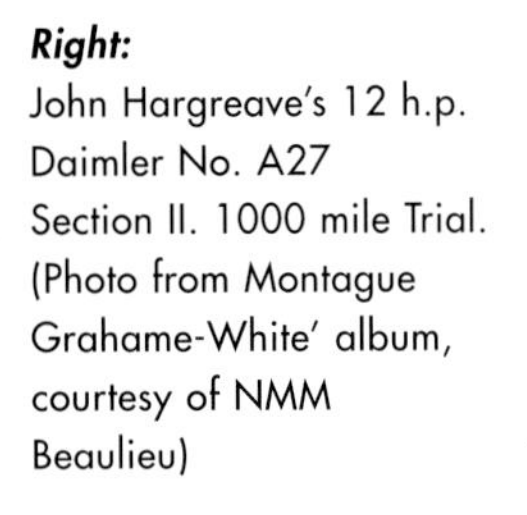
Right:
John Hargreave's 12 h.p. Daimler No. A27 Section II. 1000 mile Trial. (Photo from Montague Grahame-White' album, courtesy of NMM Beaulieu)

Left:
Montague Grahame-White
(Photos: Argent Archer)

mishap. They met the outfit. The driver held up his hand. They stopped immediately, but the horse had already got away, with the result related. As we approached Newcastle our motor ran better and better until, by the time the control was reached, we were doing as well as ever. There were not by any means so many people out to greet us here as at other places, which is, however, accounted for by the fact that seven p.m. had been announced as the hour of arrival, whereas it wanted a quarter to that hour when we reached the Cambridge Drill Hall, where we found fully three-fourths of the cars already arrived, Mr. Rolls and the leaders having got in by half-past two!

Enquiries concerning the day's run elicited the fact that the remaining Decauville, driven by Jules Dubois, had suffered delay through the breaking off of the end of the sparking plug in the cylinder. Mr. Richardson's car ran out of petrol a few miles from home, and found a good Samaritan in Mr. Lord, whose Peugeot had been itself delayed with pump troubles. Mr. Seyd's International finished with the loss of two lubricators, Mr. Montagu had been delayed by four punctures, and Mr. Iliffe's tandem had suffered from lack of compression, due to a washerless sparking plug. At 8.30 the visiting automobilists were formally received by Admiral Cleveland in the mess room of the Drill Hall, light refreshments were provided, and the visitors had the felicity of hearing a performance on the Northumbrian bagpipes, instruments deserving of wider recognition. Shortly after nine the toot of a horn and the throbbing of a motor outside told of a new arrival, and Grahame-White, whom we had seen stopped in Morpeth, turned up. He had had a strange adventure, the relation of which stamps him as one of the most resourceful and daring autocarists of this country. Whilst ascending a steep hill on the bottom speed he had got out of the car for a moment, and handed over the steering gear to his passenger, who promptly ran the car into a ditch, with the result of a fracture of the bracket holding the bottom of the steering post in place. This rendered the steering gear useless, and to add to his troubles he met with four punctures ere he reached home, which he did by the novel and daring expedient of standing on the step and steering the car with his foot on the axle of the right-hand front wheel, the axle being polished and the instep sole of his shoe nearly worn through in the operation, for he had travelled in this way no less than fifty-four miles, and, but for the before-mentioned punctures, would have averaged his twelve miles per hour at that. A few minutes after Mr. White's arrival, the Stanley steamer turned up. She had travelled through without accident, but had found the wind, and particularly the following wind at the start, most trying to her firing system. Her fires were continually blowing out, and Mr. Searle had to relight them at least thirty times during the journey. Shortly after ten, as we were leaving the hall, another belated traveller arrived in the shape of Mr. Mann with the Marshall carriage (No. 49), who related the story of the breaking of one of the bolts of the connecting rod bearing, with the jamming of the piston into the cylinder head as the result, together with further trouble with his water-cooling gear, the cause of which had at last been discovered in a pipe stopped up with solder, causing a steam lock. During the day Mr. Edmund's Daimler, which had repaired its broken spring at Kendal, also arrived, having come across from Kendal direct, whilst we learned that the Orient Express, after having repaired its broken countershaft at Kendal, had made an attempt to get on to Edinburgh, but a collision with a cow had caused its occupants to relinquish the trial and return with the car by train to London. ”

Below:
Leaving Edinburgh Control. Mr. Mann in his Marshall car No. 49 (not with his wife although she usually accompanied him)

Below:
Hon. John Scott-Montagu's Daimler No. A11 – but who is driving? The chauffeur turns away from the camera. John Scott-Montagu had waved from a train and joined his car at Berwick. (see *The Autocar* report)

The Autocar, Saturday, May 12th, 1900

The Motor Car Journal reporter sent in a telegraphed report from Newcastle, Friday, May 4th

"Newcastle, Friday, May 4th

It was not a very grand morning for our 122 miles run to the Tyne. The sky above Edinburgh was shedding teardrops as we left, and the roads were greasy and treacherous. As Arthur's Seat faded in the distance the weather cleared and the sun came out, revealing a beauty of landscape that must have delighted every passenger. Every town and village showed an interest in our progress. Portobello contributed its throng of fisher-folk and seaside residents; Musselburgh was awake to the interest of the occasion; and all the population of Tranent and Gladsmuir turned out in welcome. And right hearty the welcome was, everywhere. The elder people saluted pleasantly, even the stolid fisherman, taking the 'cutty' pipe from his mouth to wave it in token of his goodwill. As for the children, they went fairly wild with joy, cheering with a shrill treble that was the true keynote of delight. It was a veritable triumphal procession. But nobody had broken bread that morning; the rushing through the sea-scented air was appetising; and a halt at Haddington gave an opportunity to a hundred hungry people to fortify themselves against the hours to come.

As we entered the Haddington burgh control a strong breeze was blowing, slightly favouring the motorists, and the weather was fine, the roads being free from dust. Breakfast having been taken the journey resumed. At Haddington the motor-cars had got some distance into rural districts, but on setting out for Dunbar the sea coast soon came into view once more. It was kept in sight until after passing Cockburnspath, where the road again diverged in the direction of Grant's House, Houndwood, and Ayton, till Burnmouth was reached, when the German Ocean was once more sighted until Berwick was reached. The road gradually improved through Dunbar and Cockburnspath, where a hill with a nasty triple turn had to be negotiated, with plenty of grease at the corners. The countryside was now so sparsely populated that speedy travelling was both comfortable and safe, and good time was made to Berwick, 58 miles from the start.

Luncheon being partaken of, a start was made for Newcastle, and the run was quite uneventful. Among the minor troubles was the snapping of the driving chain on Mr. Edmund's car, which rather delayed his progress. Most of the people were ready for tea in Morpeth, and after that there was a clear run into Newcastle, which most of the cars reached well within the scheduled time.

Berwick-on-Tweed

The arrival of the cars in Berwick created considerable interest, and their advent to the town was keenly awaited by a large number of persons. It was scarcely anticipated, however, that the vanguard of the motorists would reach Berwick at the early hour they did. The Hon. C.S. Rolls' car was the first arrival. A couple of minutes later two more arrived, and they belonged to private owners. They were Mr. J.A. Holder's 12-h.p. Daimler and Mr. C.E. Kennard's 8-h.p. Napier. As three-quarters of an hour was allowed at Berwick for luncheon plenty

Left:
On the road out of Edinburgh (*left to right:*)
No. 28 New Orleans 3 h.p. who had a problem just outside Berwick.
No. 15 Hubert Egerton driving the De Dion 3 h.p. Grierson (his companion appears to have a cold).
No. 44 International Victoria 3 h.p. driven by Mr, Cappellan.
No. 16 Gladiator 3¼ h.p. driven by M. Farman.
(Photo: Argent Archer)

of opportunity was given the many interested spectators to examine the cars. After a short interval the motors began to arrive in more regular order, and continued to do so until after two o'clock. At the dinner hour there was a very large gathering of people in High Street. Although some inquired into the working parts of the motors, the majority were content to witness their arrival and departure, and many expressions of satisfaction were heard at the easy way in which they were turned or drawn up. The Head Constable (Mr. Nicholson) and several of his force ably kept the course where the crowd was thickest, and directed the motorists, while the work of timekeeping was most efficiently performed at the red flag control by Messrs. S. Oliphant and T.W. Boal; and at the white flag control by Messrs. W.M. Mather and W. Allan Caverhill. The inward control was near the cemetery gates on the North Road, and the outward control beyond the Tweed Saw Mills, a distance of one and a half miles. With the exception of a motor-tricycle and one car, all got safely away, the two exceptions having slight breakdowns, which necessitated their remaining for some time for repairs. ”

The Motor-Car Journal, Saturday, May 12th, 1900

The *Berwick Advertiser* carried the following report:

Friday, 11th May The Thousand Miles Motor Car Trial. Run from Edinburgh to Newcastle.

'After being exhibited in the Waverley Market for a day 49 of the 52 vehicles remaining in the 1000-mile motor car trial left Edinburgh on Friday morning on the return journey to London. The weather was not of the most favourable character, being showery, with a strong south-westerly breeze; but in spite of that, and the early hour of the start – seven o'clock - there was a fairly large gathering of spectators at the Market entrance, and in Princes Street, to see the travellers off. An hour or so previous to the cars starting, the market presented a somewhat animated and unusual scene. The car drivers and assistants were busy getting their machines ready, filling the oil tanks, and inflating the tyres, while the passengers were all excitement, getting their belongings properly packed into the vehicles and attending to other preliminaries. There was no set order for the cars going away, each being allowed to start whenever ready immediately after seven o'clock but 30 seconds had to elapse between the departure of each car. In a very short time the vehicles had cleared off, and soon were out of sight on their way by Portobello and Musselburgh to Haddington.

The novelty of the sight of so many motor cars on the road attracted crowds of spectators at every point of advantage all along the route from Edinburgh to Newcastle, on the first part of which – from Modern Athens to Berwick – a representative of the 'Advertiser' was, by the courtesy of the local secretary at Edinburgh – Mr. F. M. Norton – allowed to accompany the motorists on No 49 car, belonging to Messrs Marshall and Co., Belsize Works, Manchester, which was worked by a representative of the firm, whose machines are entirely of English manufacture. That there should have been so many vehicles able to compete in the second stage of the trial was a surprise, even to experts, for numerous specimens were admittedly not specially constructed to stand the test of a tour over some of the most trying portions of the United Kingdom. The drivers and owners of the cars were not less diversified in appearance than their vehicles. Clad in a variety of outfits, in leather caps, loose-fitting oilskin coats, and overalls, and gigantic goggles of different colours and patterns – designed to protect the eyes from dust, cold, wet, etc. – they certainly are not prepossessing. Assuming that one is properly equipped for the journey, nothing could be more exhilarating. The cars travel so quickly that the scene is ever changing, and the care which has to be exercised in negotiating sharp turns and declavities, not to speak of stray dogs or fowls and venturesome juveniles, keeps the mind constantly on the alert.

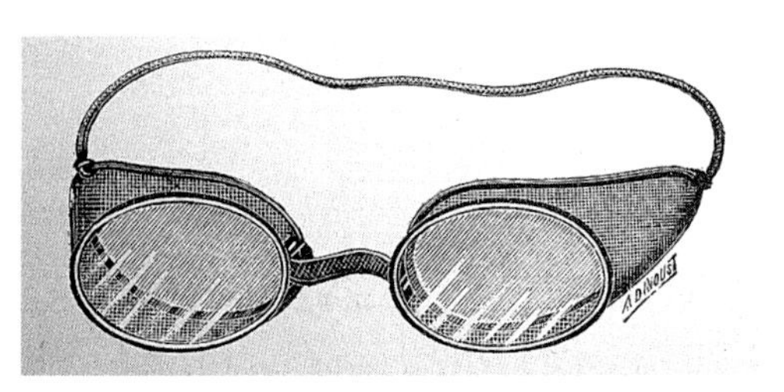

Shortly after starting from Edinburgh the weather cleared up and the sun shone out, but the wind from the south-west increased to a gale, and blew from the roads, which rapidly dried, showers of blinding dust right in the faces of the motorists. This hampered the cars in their attempts to climb the hills, reducing their pace on the level, and, in some instances, necessitating such unusual consumption of fuel that the drivers found they had exhausted their stock before the run finished, so that several stoppages occurred on the road between Edinburgh and Berwick owing to this and other causes, such as breakdowns, which, however, were, in most cases, soon remedied. The high wind and temporary casualties account for the long periods that the lighter cars took to traverse the 122 miles – one of the most extensive trips during the trial.

One of the pleasantest parts of the journey was that between Edinburgh and Haddington, which was effected in the freshness of the early morning before the heat of the sun had had time to dry the roads, and the gale had risen to its height to raise the dust. Edinburgh was just beginning to divest itself of the grey mist which enveloped it, and Arthur's Seat, towering over the picturesque city, was disclosed in all the beauty of its spring verdure. Pleasing as the prospect was to the west, it was not less attractive to the east, for there the Firth of Forth was

A Daimler dogcart
(Photo: Argent Archer)

sparkling in the light of a few glints of sunshine which had pierced the clouds, and towards the horizon the famous Bass Rock was dimly outlined. There was a stay at Musselburgh for the record cards to be overhauled and we proceeded without halt to Haddington, where opportunity was afforded for getting breakfast. Half an hour was spent in the burgh, the various machines being viewed with much interest by crowds of townspeople. Those who had travelled with the cars from London to Edinburgh stated that the road from that city to Newcastle was the only part of the journey which skirted the coast line for any distance, and the passengers were charmed with the country through which they passed for several hours after leaving Edinburgh. At Haddington the motor cars had got some distance into local rural districts, but on setting out for Dunbar the sea coast soon came into sight once more. It was kept in sight until after passing Cockburnspath, where the road again diverged in the direction of Grant's House, Houndwood and Ayton till Burnmouth was reached, when the German Ocean was once again sighted until Berwick was reached.

The greatest interest was manifested in the trials en route. Every village and hamlet appeared to have turned out its entire population to witness the cars go by, and to the young people especially the vision of the vehicles dashing along, sometimes at breakneck speed, was a source of much wonderment. When a town of any size was reached, large crowds lined the main thoroughfare, not infrequently the motorists were given a cheer as they passed. The elders smiled or waved their hands; the juveniles cheered vigorously. That was the order everywhere, either in the more populated districts, or sparsely inhabited regions which lie between Cockburnspath and Berwick. It must be said that perfect arrangements had been made to assist the drivers of vehicles all the way from Edinburgh to Newcastle. Dangerous hills were plainly pointed out, and special means were taken at cross roads to direct the vehicles aright. The cars left Edinburgh in something like procession order, and many kept well together until Haddington was reached. During the run of about 40 miles from Haddington to Berwick, however, the vehicles got so widely separated that it happened occasionally one did not catch a glimpse of any other vehicle for miles at a stretch.

By three o'clock in the afternoon all the cars except four which had lagged behind owing to accidents had resumed the journey south. Leaving Berwick the wind had now decreased, and the roads had greatly improved, but the country became much more hilly. A large number of people assembled at Belford to see the Automobile Club run through without any serious accident, although one boy had a narrow escape through one of the men in charge of the one of the cars trying to play tricks. A horse took fright also upset a cart, but no serious damage resulted. The first to pass through was a Panhard, 12 h.p., belonging to Hon. Chas. S. Rolls. It passed Belford at 12.12 p.m. and arrived in Newcastle at 2.49. The heaviest hills met during the day were encountered some miles before reaching and also after leaving Alnwick. At Morpeth a stop was made for tea. The first three cars to arrive in Newcastle were privately owned cars. A17 reached Newcastle at 2.49, A22 at 2.51 and A10 at 2.52. No others put in an appearance within the next two hours. At the expiration of that time there was a general arrival. The cars proceeded to the Cambridge Hall, where an exhibition was held on Saturday, and on Monday the journey was resumed. Twenty-nine of the cars, twelve privately owned and several belonging to manufacturers, reached Newcastle within the twelve miles an hour limit. Admiral Cleveland, chairman of the local committee, held a reception of members of the club and their friends. The arrival of the cars was watched by highly interested crowds.'

Berwick Advertiser 11th May 1900.
Contrib. D. Copson

A smart repair has been reported from Alnwick, where a driver discovered that a valve had broken, and that a piece of it had fallen into the cylinder. He disconnected all the parts, took the cylinder apart, refitted it, and was moving again in less than twenty minutes.

MEMORABLE MORPETH.

As the cars passed through Morpeth on the run to Edinburgh a local policeman called out "No smoking allowed" to those who happened to be enjoying the fragrant weed on any of the cars.

The incident recalls the fact that an automobilist was actually fined some time ago at this very place for smoking while on his car, though under what Act the charge was laid it would be interesting to know. A can of petrol uncorked is a source of danger, but petrol encased in the engine is another matter.

Left:
Friday 4th May. One quarter of an hour stop for tea at Morpeth 14 miles before Newcastle on Tyne. Press-cutting from Montague Grahame-White's album by kind permission of N.M.M. Beaulieu.

Mr. Shrapnell-Smith, the hon. sec. of the Liverpool Self-propelled Traffic Association, proved himself an expert pump repairer on Friday last. Short of a washer, one was improvised out of a halfpenny piece!

A Splendid Feat

Mr Grahame White, driving a Parisian Daimler, had an adventure on the run from Edinburgh to Newcastle. It appears that when seventeen miles north of Alnwick, on a quiet bit of road, he yielded to the request of one of his passengers to be allowed to try a hand at driving. The result was that the said novice turned the car into the ditch, and the effect of this little contretemps was to break the bracket of the steering gear. There were still fifty-two miles of road to cover, but Mr. White was in no wise daunted, and conceived the idea – which he carried to a successful issue – of steering the car with his foot. Standing on the off step with his left foot, he kept his right on the hub of the off front wheel, and, by pressure only, he guided the car the whole way to Newcastle. What is still more wonderful, he averaged ten miles an hour for the fifty-two miles, and, as the road included several steep hills, two or three 'controls,' and a compulsory stop of a quarter of an hour for tea at Morpeth, he must have travelled at a good speed at several stages of the journey. ”

The Motor-Car Journal Saturday, May 12th, 1900

Trial Notes Montague Grahame-White

4 cylinder 12 h.p. Daimler from 1899 purchased from the Hon. Evelyn Ellis. Driven by M.G-W from London to Bristol on 1000 miles Trial. From the album of Montague Grahame-White courtesy NMM Beaulieu.

WHICH CAR DID Montague Grahame-White really drive? As was revealed at the start, when Claude Johnson was planning the Trial and Montague Grahame-White accompanied him, M.G-W was part of the Daimler team. On the actual trial he started out in a 4 cylinder 12 h.p. Daimler from 1899 which was purchased from the Hon. Evelyn Ellis. This car features in his private photograph album, and the picture is reproduced here courtesy of the National Motor Museum, Beaulieu.

The accompanying notes clearly state that this car was driven by M. G-W from London to Bristol on the 1000 miles trial. A famous photograph was taken of this car in the 'procession of cars through Cheltenham' (*see right*); but it does not bear a trials number. He is accompanied on this occasion by Burrows, the ACGBI Steward.

Another photograph in M G-W's album complete with 'Notes on 1000 Miles Trial 1900' explains why No. 37 in the programme was described as Daimler 'Parisian' 6 h.p. entered by the Daimler Motor Co in Section 1 Class C.

His notes tell us beside the photograph

The first 'Parisian' 6 h.p. Light Daimler No. 37 driven in the 1000 miles Trial by M. Grahame-White & awarded First Prize in Section 1, Class 'C'. Gold Medal

In Section 2, Class 'C' a similar car driven by Mr Claud(e) Johnson won a silver medal.

Weight 17¼ cwt. Improvements included. Pneu tyres, side gear levers, aluminium gearbox and base chamber, lower frame and lighter coachwork, new design of bonnet, sight-feed lubrication. Larger wheel steering.

(These notes are handwritten and signed G.W.)

6 h.p. Parisian Daimler driven by Montague Grahame-White in the 1000 Mile Trial as No. 37. (Courtesy of N.M.M. Beaulieu)

The question arises, why did Montague Grahame-White complete the first two days in his old Daimler? Was someone else driving the 'Parisian' Daimler No. 37 on April 23rd 1900; or was it not there at all and started its Trial after Cheltenham?

Certainly *The Autocar* reports under records of daily running that:

'No. 37. (Daimler Parisian) Full avs. On first seven periods, 10 mph on 8th. Full aves. to finish.' and under recorded mishaps:

'No. 37. (Daimler Parisian, driven by Mr. Grahame-White.) Delay caused between Edinburgh and Newcastle by breakage, through collision, of steering gear worm bracket. On Shap burners went out owing to clogging of pressure valve.* Stop also between Edinburgh and Newcastle for water in petrol.

When his adventure, concerning the novice driver taking the controls 17 miles north of Alnwick on Friday 4th May 1900 to try their hand at driving, (we are not told who it was); the resultant arrival in the ditch and breaking of steering bracket was solved by the ever resourceful Montague G-W by driving 52 miles with his foot on the front wheel to steer. This would not have been possible in the larger 12 h.p. Daimler, and neither would he have suffered 4 punctures in the old car as that ran on solid tyres. (The new light Daimler you will note had the improvement of pneu tyres).

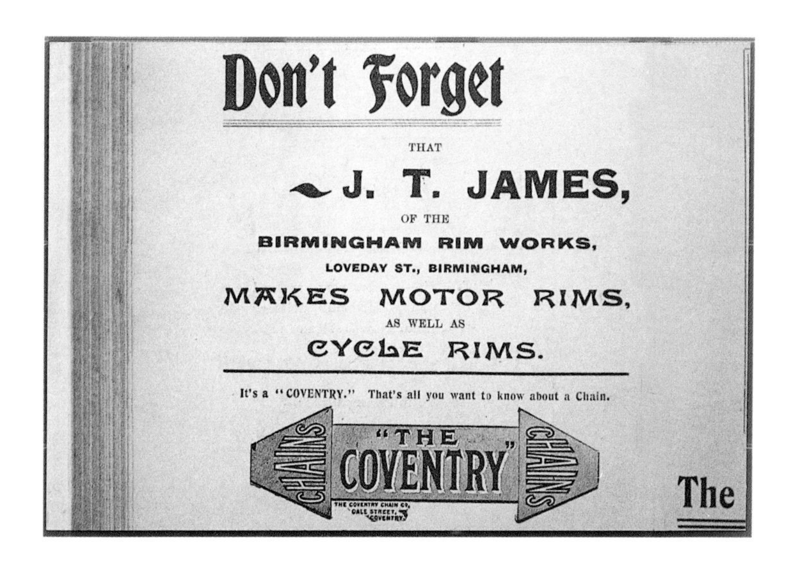

So, by his own admission he changed Daimlers after Bristol. The Judges must have been aware of this; yet the Daimler Parisian No. 37 was awarded First Prize and a gold medal in Section 1 (Trade Entries) Class C (selling price between £300-£500).

*This explains why there is no record for this car in the second section of the Shap hill climb.

EXHIBITION AT NEWCASTLE-ON-TYNE

SATURDAY 5TH MAY

Important people at Newcastle aligned in front of framed photographs of motor-cars

“ Newcastle

The motor-vehicles were on exhibition on Saturday in the Cambridge Hall, Newcastle. There was an influential gathering at the opening ceremony, over which Admiral Cleveland, director of Palmer's Shipbuilding Company, presided. The Mayor (Mr. Riley Lord), who attended to open the exhibition, was accompanied by the Mayoress (Mrs. Albert Lord), and amongst others present were the Hon. John Scott Montagu, M.P., Mr. Mark Mayhew, L.C.C., Colonel Palmer, Captain Chapman, Alderman Sutton, Alderman Sanderson, Alderman Winter, Councillors Thomas Cairns, Dr. Mason, John Beattie, R. Flowers, Wardbill, Ross, Kenshaw, Mr. J. R. Roberts, Mr. Richd. Welford; Mr. C. Johnson (secretary of the Automobile Club), Mr. William Philipson, and Mr. Rowland Barnett, hon. secretary of the local committee; Mr. Young, and many others. Letters of apology and regret for non-attendance were received from Earl Grey, Sir Benjamin Brown, Mr. Watson Askew-Robertson, and others. The Mayor, in opening the exhibition, said he was very glad to welcome the Automobile Club to this great engineering centre – probably the greatest engineering centre in the world. He reminded his audience that this was the birthplace of George Stephenson, and the locomotive, and added that railway engines were still built in Newcastle. It was the characteristic of Englishmen to peg away till they were successful, and he hoped the British

1,000-Mile Trial. 153

NEWCASTLE-ON-TYNE,
SATURDAY, 5th MAY, 1900.

A ONE-DAY

EXHIBITION

OF THE

MOTOR VEHICLES

TAKING PART IN THE

1,000-Mile Trial organized by the Automobile Club of Great Britain,

UNDER THE PATRONAGE OF

The Right Worshipful the Mayor of Newcastle-on-Tyne,

WILL BE HELD IN THE

Cambridge Drill Hall, Northumberland Road.

ADMISSION—

On FRIDAY EVENING, MAY 4th, to witness the arrival of the vehicles until 11 p.m. ... ... TWO SHILLINGS

On SATURDAY, MAY 5th, from 12 o'clock noon to 10 p.m. ONE SHILLING.

THE PROFITS WILL BE DEVOTED TO THE TRANSVAAL WAR FUND.

Committee for Local Arrangements.

The following Gentlemen, at the invitation of the Club, guaranteed the expenses of and made all the necessary arrangements in Newcastle-on-Tyne in connection with the Trial and Exhibition:—

Mr. J. W. Ellis.	Mr. T. Toward.	Mr. R. A. Young.
,, Rowland Barnett.	,, Justice Bruce.	,, Herbert Rowell.
,, W. Dunn.	,, C. W. Mitchell.	,, J. Duncan Hodgson.
,, T. R. Goodwin.	Admiral Cleveland.	,, Henry Maxson Wilson.
,, F. G. Lundi.	Mr. Scoby Smith.	,, W. C. Cockburn.
,, W. Philipson.	,, J. S. Comrie.	,, W. B. Kirsop.

Hon. Secretaries:—Mr. W. Philipson and Mr. Rowland Barnett.

Hon. Treasurer:—Mr. J. W. Ellis.

Hon. Press Secretary:—Mr. R. A. Young, Conservative Club Newcastle-on-Tyne.

manufacturers of motor cars would not be behind those of America and the Continent. The object of the Automobile Club, as he understood it, was to show what had been accomplished up to the present time and to encourage the use and develop the manufacture of these cars. He was glad to see that they laid down stringent instructions to abide by the regulations of the local authorities over whose roads they might pass on their tour. In conclusion, he hoped the members would be interested in their visit to Newcastle. This, he remarked, was one of the oldest towns in England, but, old as it was, he assured them it did not feel in any way aged, for the spirit of enterprise and progress was just as keen as amongst its younger rivals. He had very great pleasure in declaring the exhibition open, and wishing it every success.

A21 Ernest Pitman's Daimler at Newcastle. (Photo: Argent Archer)

The Hon. John Scott-Montagu, M.P., on behalf of the Automobile Club, returned thanks for the cordiality of the reception accorded to it in Newcastle. Throughout the tour, he said, the Club had been welcomed with open arms everywhere, and there had been a remarkable cordiality displayed in the various villages through which they passed. In the neighbourhood of George Stephenson's birthplace, he felt sure a more than usually intelligent interest would be excited in the motor-vehicles. The object of the club was to demonstrate that the manufacture of these cars had reached a stage when they might be considered thoroughly safe, reliable, and trustworthy in the varying conditions of road, wind, and weather, and that object, he thought, was being achieved in the present tour. Mr. Mark Mayhew moved a vote of thanks to Admiral Cleveland for presiding. He said the success of the present tour heralded the dawn of a new day for the motor-car industry. Admiral Cleveland, in reply, said the thanks of the club were rather due to the two local hon. secretaries, Messrs. Philipson and Barnett, and to Mr. Johnson, the secretary of the Automobile Club. There could, he said, be no doubt that the result of this 1,000-mile Trial was proving a great triumph for the motor-car. He was particularly struck, on watching the entrance of the cars into the hall on Friday night, to notice the skilful way in which they were manoeuvred. The term 'handy man' which had lately been applied to the blue-jackets was, he thought, one which the drivers of the cars had thoroughly earned. Afterwards the Mayor and Mayoress proceeded on a tour of inspection of the vehicles. The proceeds of the exhibition were devoted to the Reservists' Fund.

The Mayor of Newcastle opening the Exhibition (Photo: Argent Archer)

Coles to Newcastle

After a fortnight's hard travel – for it is becoming increasingly clear that this trial is no mere holiday jaunt – the spirits of the automobilists are still maintained, and jocularity has prevailed despite the weariness of the flesh with which some of the wayfarers have been seized. Many conundrums have been asked, and some still await solution. One of the riddles which was solved on the banks of the Tyne came from no less a personage than the Lord Chief Justice Clerk of Scotland, who asked Mr. Hewetson why one of his Benz cars was like a popular proverb, and himself gave answer, 'Because it is taking Coles to Newcastle.' ”

The Motor-Car Journal, Saturday May 12th, 1900

Arrival of the cars at Newcastle Drill Hall. Centre is No.41 International Victoria and above centre Mrs. Louise Bazelgette is visible next to Henry Hewetson with Clarkson her mechanician standing nearby. (Photo: Argent Archer)

“

The Exhibition

The Cambridge Drill Hall at Newcastle is the smallest building which has yet been used for this purpose, so much so indeed that when the fifty odd cars which were exhibited there were arranged in close set rows there was but a narrow gangway for the accommodation of the public. The interest, however, was great, and by six o'clock the whole of the catalogues had been sold out.

At midday the opening ceremony was performed by the Mayor of Newcastle, who, accompanied by the Mayoress, was supported by Admiral Cleveland, the chairman of the local committee, the Hon. Jno. Scott-Montagu, M.P., Mr. Mark Mayhew, L.C.C., Alderman W. Sutton, Colonel A.S. Palmer, Mr. A.M. Palmer, Captain Chapman, and others. Letters of regret for absence were read from Earl Grey, Sir Benjamin Browne, etc.

In declaring the exhibition open, the Mayor said he was pleased to welcome the Automobile Club to the great engineering centre of Newcastle. He thought that in what was probably the greatest engineering city in the world,

they might expect sound mechanical criticism of their cars. He was pleased to welcome them to the city, and wished their tour would close as successfully as it had commenced.

The Hon. Jno. Scott-Montagu, M.P., returned thanks for the great cordiality with which the club had been received in George Stephenson's birthplace. He thought they might feel sure of a more than usually intelligent audience there. The object of the club was to demonstrate that the manufacture of these cars had reached a stage when they might be considered thoroughly safe, reliable, and trustworthy in the varying conditions of road, wind, and weather, and that object he thought was being achieved during the present tour. Mr. Mark Mayhew moved a vote of thanks to Admiral Cleveland for presiding. he was sure the success of the present tour heralded the dawn of a new day for the motor car industry. In replying, Admiral Cleveland paid well-merited testimony to the energetic labours of the local secretaries, Messrs. W. Phillipson and Rowland Barnett, and also spoke in admiration of the great organising ability displayed by Mr. C. Johnson, the secretary of the club. He was sure the programme had been a great success. Autocars were no longer a phantom, but a reality. They had come to stay, and would in the near future be widely adopted, provided the cost was not made excessive by wholesale monopolies and patents. (Hear, hear.) The term 'handy men' which had lately been applied to the Naval Brigade might well be shared by the members of the Automobile Club. The gallant Admiral's speech closed then proceedings, and the Mayor and Mayoress then made a tour of inspection amongst the cars, Mr. Johnson acting as cicerone.

During the afternoon the Brown-Whitney car put in an appearance, having repaired damages at

Edinburgh, left the city the previous day at four p.m., and stayed the night at Berwick. As with the Stanley car, she had experienced some difficulty with her fires when travelling in the wind, and had journeyed most of the time with only half her burners going, so that she could only proceed at a very moderate pace. ❞

The Motor-Car Journal, Saturday, May 12th, 1900

Drill Hall Newcastle.
No. A20 Empress Trike; No. A24 Mors Petit Duc (*left:*)
No. 15 De Dion Mr. Egerton; No. 1 Benz Hewetson;
No. 46 Richard; No. A28 Enfield Quad and
No. 16 Gladiator.
(Photo: Argent Archer)

Mrs Louise Bazalgette

Louise Bazalgette seated on an Arnold car – London to Brighton 1896

LOUISE BAZALGETTE had been attracting attention as a Lady Automobilist for some time. Even so, it must have been somewhat daunting to be the only Lady Entrant in the Thousand Miles Trial of 1900.

Born Louise Seville c.1851 she married George Bazalgette, whose father, Jean Louis Bazalgette was a tailor's son from Ispagnac, in the Gorges du Tarn, Cervannes, France. George's father travelled to the Americas where he became a rich young man, and at the age of 25 settled in England, setting up a business in textiles. He was rich enough to lend huge sums to the Prince Regent, owned a stately home in Surrey, and moved in 'High Society'. The 12th child from his second marriage was George Bazalgette (b. 1829). This was a large Victorian family, and George's cousin was to become Sir Joseph Bazalgette engineer, famous for his work creating London's sewerage system, the Victoria Embankment, Hammersmith Bridge, and other projects.

George served in the British Army, Royal Marines Division, and distinguished himself in the 1857-8 China Expedition, being awarded a medal with clasp after the assault and capture of Nantow. This was followed by particular distinction in Canada/ N.W. USA border areas where he held a fort on the west coast (San Juan Island in Puget Sound), and where he remained keeping the peace for 7 years. In 1870 as a Captain, he was recruiting at Exeter, and in 1872 he retired on full pay with the rank of Major.

George died in 1885, leaving Louise widowed at the age of 35. There were no children.

Louise was interested in the automobile from the very beginning. In 1896 a photograph of the First London to Brighton Run shows Louise sitting upon an Arnold car that bears the name A. Cornell, Tonbridge. (Arnold cars were built at East Peckham, Kent by William Arnold who imported a 1½ h.p. Benz in 1895, and made cars to a similar design using his own engines.) The driver of the Arnold car looks very like Charles Friswell, and standing beside the car is Henry Hewetson.

Henry Hewetson claimed to have imported the first car (a Benz) into England. Later research disproves this claim, but he was certainly amongst the very early enthusiasts in Britain, and a picture of Henry Hewetson out driving his early Benz about 1897 (*see* page 63) shows Louise Bazalgette accompanying him.

After she was widowed Louise lived in an area of London not far from Henry Hewetson's Benz Showroom. By mid 1898 she owned her own 3 h.p. Benz, (supplied by Hewetson's), and she had a succession of models from the same source. Hewetson, as a car salesman, was keen to demonstrate his cars to a new potential market.

Louise became involved with Viscountess Harberton, President of the Mowbury House Cycling Association rational dress group. The objectives of the Rational Dress League were:

1. To promote a dress-reform whereby Ladies may enjoy outdoor exercise with greater comfort and less fatigue.
2. To advocate the wearing (particularly for Cycling) of the Zouave or Knickerbocker Costume, as adopted in France, Germany and America

Louise was guest speaker at a meeting at Lady Harberton's home, held in her drawing room at 108, Cromwell Road, on October 20th 1898. It was billed as a preliminary meeting of the proposed Ladies Automobile Club, and Ladies interested in motors were invited to attend, to see whether the time had come to form such a club. 'All intelligent women should be interested in the new mode of locomotion, and attend the Meeting.'

The report of the meeting:

Lady Motorists

by Mrs. Bazalgette

Having been asked to speak at this meeting I do so in the hope that our gathering will lead to the formation of an Automobile Club the membership of which will be open to ladies as well as gentleman, where ideas can be exchanged – ideas which may be a source of benefit and information concerning the use of motor cars to all those interested in the new pastime. I use the word 'pastime' advisedly, in preference to 'industry', as I myself have little experience of automobilism except as a pleasure giving the pursuit. The time surely has passed for gentleman to object to ladies participating in their sports. As I have owned and driven a Benz car for some three months, I have been especially asked to speak about Lady motorists, and I think I can give the result of my practical experience, and present details that may be useful and interesting to those ladies and – may I dare say? – gentleman who want to know something of the subject. My experiences may not be considered to be wide, for I have only driven a Benz Ideal and a Victoria, yet there are many gentleman as well as ladies who have not progressed so far, and it is to them more especially that I address myself.

Before one can enjoy motoring as a pastime, one must have one's own carriage, and I should recommend the purchase of a small, inexpensive car of good make. Any well-built carriage would do for the first performance of an amateur, although its speed may be low, for it is generally undesirable to learn to drive on a vehicle constructed for great pace. I have studied automobiles of almost every description for some three or four years, so I have something to say concerning them. I have travelled a great deal in my own car, and enjoyed more of the country than I at one time thought possible. I generally do some 10 to 14 mph visiting such places as Southsea, Brighton, Southampton, Bedford, Norwich, and I have run swiftly on the high roads and wandered through the lanes of Kent, Oxfordshire, Warwickshire, Berkshire, Buckinghamshire, and Essex.

It is possible to drive a car with very little knowledge of machinery, if you have a skilled mechanic with you to help in case of a breakdown; but the Lady motorist is in a much more happy frame of mind during her travels if she herself possesses knowledge of the mechanism of the automobile. It is so much more enjoyable to really study and understand everything concerning the car so that you take an interest in it. You must not imagine that it is possible for any Lady to acquire sufficient knowledge of the working parts of the driving machinery in a few days, or even months, but they should have the opportunity of studying. This is one of the main objects of the club we hope to form.

Many things may happen *en route* that may tax even the ingenuity of the expert, for some slight adjustment may be necessary, and the trouble must be diagnosed before the operation can be performed. The Lady motorists should at least know something about 'short-circuiting', 'back shot', 'compression' – as the doctor knows of a defective nervous system. She should be able to detect whether the bearings are becoming heated, or the belt is slipping, for if it does it will have to be shortened and a process of shortening is, to my mind, not beyond on the powers of a woman.

Why the pastime of motoring is so interesting is that there is always something to be learned concerning the mechanism of the car. Some experts maintain that no Lady cares to start the driving wheel. Why not? The operation is perfectly easy – it requires skill rather than strength, very little force is necessary.

I have driven my car some two thousand miles, and had been most fortunate in not having experienced any mishap. Yet the sceptics tell us of the dangers of the automobile! But accidents may happen to the most expert and careful driver, for there is still much jealousy and prejudice to overcome. These however are only temporary, for the day will come when England will follow the lead of other countries, and horseless vehicles will be seen here, there, and everywhere-and probably nothing else!

That a great impulse will shortly be given to automobilism no one doubts; but, like the boom in connection with cycling, it will not come until ladies take up the pastime; and the new club, the formation of which we have met to suggest, will do much to attain this end. ”

Paper read at Lady Harberton's house
20th October, 1899

The Motor-Car Journal, Friday November 3rd 1899

NEWCASTLE TO LEEDS

MONDAY 7TH MAY

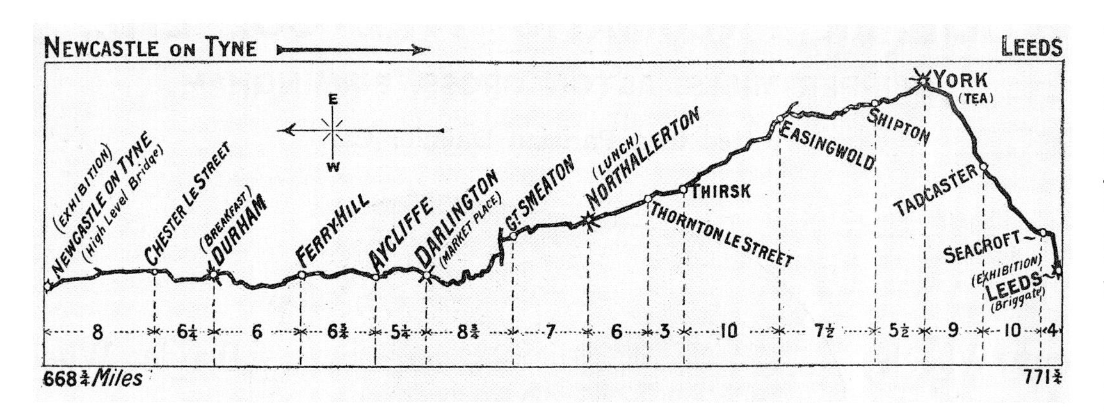

103 miles via Durham, Northallerton, Thirsk, York (Exhibition at York), to Leeds (Exhibition at Leeds)

ONCE AGAIN *The Autocar* reporter is riding in the 'Khaki' Daimler ...

Newcastle to Leeds

Monday morning, May 7th, was not promising in Newcastle. It had been raining all night and the better part of the previous day, and heavy and perhaps, greasy roads were a certainty. By seven o'clock, however, when, as usual, the start was made, the sun was making fitful efforts to show itself.

There was a busy scene outside the Drill Hall when we arrived, cars were loading up with petrol from huge waggons containing the supply, others were adjusting and tightening up generally, and a couple were busy repairing tyres. Amongst the starters Mr. Straker with his Daimler char-a-banc was on hand, having got into Newcastle the previous evening after having practically rebuilt the engine – new cylinder head, pistons, connecting rod and vaporiser – and one of the Eurekas (No. 29) was also there, having 'trekked' across from Carlisle the previous evening. She was in a most dilapidated condition, with mudguards carried away and smothered in mud, and her driver was not much better; but, full of philosophic pluck, was solemnly preparing to undertake the labours of the day with what could but be none too rosy a prospect before him. Once again we found a place for the day on Mr. Critchley's khaki-coloured Daimler, and the cars filed away to the outward control. Our back seat was occupied by a third passenger in the shape of a local pressman, who distinguished himself early by dropping his bag in the haymarket. At the foot of the hill a large locally-owned Benz was in difficulties, and as we passed on to the High Level Bridge across the river – for which a toll of 4d. was levied upon our vehicles – 'the banks of coaly Tyne' on either side were hidden in a thickening and impenetrable mist, and we slithered and slid over the vilest of stone-paved roadways in the rear of a long line of

Above: Mr. Friswell repairing a puncture which was not a puncture at all. (Could it be something to do with Mrs. Friswell's luggage?)

Bottom left: A raid on the petrol supplies at Newcastle

Below: John Stocks repairing tyre on Ariel Quad at Newcastle (Photos *The Autocar*)

No. 39 Century Tandem
(Photo: Argent Archer)

other cars. Suddenly one on ahead took a slide. It was Mr. Siddeley's Daimler, and it crushed the Century tandem, which was following and tried to get by, up against and on to the kerbstone, and badly buckled one of the steering wheels. This was not a promising beginning, and we put on our macintoshes as we waited at control, for the weather was gathering, and there was a thickening smother of mist which covered the hills and hid the valleys in gloom. Mr. Phillips's Petit Duc Mors was in front of us and stranded twenty yards from control with a chain off, which operation it repeated several times during the day. As for the khaki Daimler she was in the best of humours, and pulled and tugged her way through the mud, her solid tyres for once during the tour getting the pull over her pneumatic-tyred sisters, and during the first part of the day she went by all other equal-powered cars she encountered on the journey. Soon it rained, and at the foot of a steep hill a couple of miles out we passed Mr. Egerton's De Dion voiturette in difficulties. Later, when running into a little mining village, with No. 16 on our quarter, we encountered a big dog. The animal was first indifferent, then aggressive, then – when too late – repentant. That dog got the worst of the encounter. We were sorry for him, but it was his own fault. If he survives the shock he may have more respect for autocars in the future. Still doing 'a solid sixteen' up the long slight grades in the mud, we speedily overhauled No. 46 Georges Richard car going slow, then Mr. Mayhew's eight horse-power Panhard was sighted in temporary difficulties with refractory lamps, and Captain Langrishe was overtaken at the control of Chester-le-Street, the while he essayed the task of dispersing a drove of donkeys without running over them. Within the town, the private Benz we had seen in Newcastle, and which had passed as we waited in control, was in trouble again, and Mr. T. B. Browne's six horse-power Panhard was given the go by as we left the town. Here our passenger turned rusty. The rain was descending dismally, bags and petrol tins encumbered his feet, and his hands were occupied in the endeavour to keep a hard hat from harm whilst his efforts to arrange the rug were not successful – he was evidently 'all thumbs' – certainly he was not happy, and when Mr. Browne directed our attention to the perilous propinquity of his rug to our chain, and Mr. Critchley suggested he should give an eye to it, his overburdened soul outpoured. He consigned the car and all its belongings to Hades and confessed with multitudinous adjectives that he was sick of the whole proceedings, but he failed to see the point when it was suggested that there was nothing to prevent his walking if he so preferred. We changed him for Mr. Gregson at the next control. Evidently he was no autocarist. Up the hill out of Chester we steadily mowed down Mr. Hewetson, Mr. Millership, and Mr. Siddeley, the while Mr. Mayhew's eight horse-power Panhard went by. Mr. Butler, overtaken next, was not travelling well, and we overhauled in quick succession Mr. Gregson's Daimler and Mr. Cordingley. Mr. Pitman, travelling steadily as usual, was the next to heave in sight, and No. 9 was overtaken at the Durham control. Rounding the bend in the road as we entered the town, the fine old castle commanding the river, with the beautiful cathedral in the background, made an impressive picture, the latter almost lost in atmospheric haze. It had ceased raining by the time we reached our halting place for breakfast, and the opportunity was taken to stow waterproofs and make things snug. We did not need them again during the day.

On getting under weigh once more, we passed the International No. 41 with the passenger walking up the hill, and the Star was stopped a little later on. Some three miles out we crossed the river and commenced the ascent of a long gradient, the first quarter-mile of which was very steep. We went up it without difficulty, but Dubois had both his passenger and himself out of his Decauville in front of us, and Mr. Friswell, to our rear, missed his gear and carburation and came to a momentary halt, whilst the No. 47 Richard carriage was collared tacking to and fro across the road, the while Mr. Ashby brought his tricycle by in grand style. Once over the worst part the Richard came again, and, overtaking Dubois on the long slope which followed, the three cars ran level for quite a while, but both the others eventually fell away to the rear, and Dubois stopped with his sparking gear adrift. The climb into Ferry Hill was a stiff one, and we still further increased our lead on No. 47, which was running better than at any previous day of the tour.

Left:
Refractory lamps – meaning the hot tubes that ignite the fuel to drive the pistons, will not stay alight. Seen here – two hot tubes being heated by the burners on an 1899 Peugeot.
(Photo: Elizabeth Bennett)

Three miles later a *posse* of plain-clothes constables were observed timing the cars and taking their numbers, and we sighted another car a good way in front, and after a long chase we came up with it and passed it at the top of a hill three miles from Darlington, it proving to be Mr. Burgess's No. 8 M.M.C. Panhard, which too, was going excellently. Darlington was reached at 10.15. It was market day, and the streets were packed, whilst the numerous picturesque grounds around many of the private houses in the neighbourhood were lined with spectators. Much traffic was encountered as we left the town, but no difficulty was met with at any time, and we soon overtook a local Benz pursuing the even tenor of its way with a fine retriever lying contentedly stretched out on the top of the motor box behind. The little party made a very interesting group. The pretty little village of Croft with its Spa was next traversed, where Mr. Baron was seen with the lamps of his Daimler in difficulties, and a little later No. 12 tricycle was undergoing adjustments in a farmyard by the roadside. Then a grouping of cars and figures on ahead told of trouble, and Mr. Edge's Napier was seen repairing tyres with Mrs. Kennard and her voiturette in attendance. They had travelled some miles before they discovered it, and the inner tube was all to bits. That repair occupied an hour, but they were only five minutes behind us at Northallerton, into which place Mr. Friswell overtook us. here we lunched at the Golden Lion, and Mr. Hutton, who had abandoned his twelve horse-power car and was now at home, was met on a Creanche voiturette. Five miles from Northallerton, first Mr. Mayhew and then Mr. Edge went by us, and we ran into Thirsk to find a fair in progress, whilst No. 47, as usual, ignored the control regulations and, flying through the town, got up on our back wheels in the middle of it, but was in difficulties ere we left the town. The roads were now getting drier, a brisk wind having sprung up and dispersed the clouds, giving us a warm sun and very pleasant travelling. Mr. Browne was sighted far away in the rear on a long straight piece of road, and after a long stern chase he overhauled us five and a half miles out, and we in our turn, after another long chase, mowed down car No. 29 eight miles from York. The roads from Thirsk to York are level, though somewhat bumpy, yet afforded good running, and excellent progress was made. The fine cathedral was sighted some miles before we reached the city, and crowds of people were out on the roads to meet us. There were photographers galore, including a cinematographer, who 'wound off' the progress of the cars as they came along. ”

The Autocar, Saturday, May 12th, 1900

Left:
No. A20 Empress Tricycle
Herbert Ashby

"The eight horse-power Napier ran for some five miles on Monday on a deflated near side driving tyre. Mr. Edge from his seat on the offside diagnosed a deflated tyre long before he stopped, but was assured by his passengers for some time that the tyre was all right."

Edge repairing a puncture on the road (photo: *The Autocar*)

"The trials and tribulations of the baggage waggon' would make good reading. The Daimler waggonette used for this purpose by the company was one of the best cars on the run, and her driver and his car were the 'handy man' of the party. In connection with Mr. Straker's break-down with the char-à-banc she did good service, standing by the big car all the way from Moffat to Edinburgh, and practically towing the char-à-banc forty-six miles through the night. The larger car required constant fresh supplies of water, and the drivers tell weird tales of tramping over the moors with lamps and canvas buckets in search of the necessary fluid, the while floundered knee deep in bog holes, and otherwise enjoyed themselves at two o'clock in the morning. They got to Edinburghat 6.30 a.m. on Saturday, and then worked practically day and night on repairs, doing another night journey to Newcastle, during which their water-hunting adventures were repeated, and reaching the Tyneside capital at four on Monday morning, in time for a clean up for the start at seven. History records that the driver of the baggage car slumbered on his seat during the run to Leeds, and narrowly escaped an upset, and who can wonder at it? Needless to say, the day's rest arranged for at Leeds came as a welcome break in the monotony of work to at least one of those engaged in the tour."

The Motor-Car Journal

C. S. Rolls' progress from Darlington through Yorkshire on the southward leg was almost indecently rapid, and at Bradford, where school children turned out to cheer the cars, any thought of a speed limit had manifestly been forgotten.

Yorkshire Post

"Some of the northern industrial establishments, like the Darlington Forge, allowed their men an hour off to see the vehicles."

The Motor-Car Journal, Saturday, May 12th, 1900

The Autocar, Saturday, May 12th, 1900

"Newcastle to Leeds Monday, 7th

Capt. Chas. H. H. Nugant, R.E., and Lieut. Harwood, R.E., deputed by the War Office, rode from Durham to York on the Hon. J. Scott Montagu's twelve horse-power Daimler, and expressed themselves highly satisfied with the trip."

"The grease encountered in the early part of Monday's run was truly awful, and it speaks volumes for the skill of the drivers that no serious accident happened.

— o§o —

Pumps and punctures were the chief sources of trouble during Monday's trying and lengthy run. There is scope for the inventor in connection with the production of a really reliable and simple circulating pump for water-cooled motors."

Durham Cathedral

Monday 7th May – story of the day as seen by an unnamed participant reporting for *Motor-Car Journal*

" Leeds, Monday Night

After a rest we were off again in good time this morning. Certainly the outlook was not promising. There was a general dullness, and hardly were we in the street when the rain – a hard and biting rain – commenced. Not only were the elements above unkindly, but the roads were bad, an uncomfortable thought in connection with the length of the run and the long stay to be made in York.

Still, there is nothing but to start, and to try, when the Automobile Club goes on tour and fifty-one automobiles set forth, to achieve the distinction of success. But the climatic conditions were not the only drawbacks. One of the burners of my car soon gave trouble, and we had to draw aside – waiting in a heavy downpour of rain till deliverance came. The stoppage gave us opportunity for observing the mishaps of other people. Between Newcastle and Durham the roads were heavy, very heavy. Mr. Siddeley discovered that when he experienced a side slip on the greasy tram lines and his car was turned completely round. Immediately to the rear was the Century tandem, which ran into the pavement and struck one of the wheels of the Daimler Parisian. The former got the worst of the encounter, its wheel being buckled.

Through Chester-le-Street we went, and on to Durham, accompanied by a very substantial downpour of rain, which made the roads thick and sticky with mud. There was no dust now; and the respective disadvantages of rain and dust compared may form a topic for discussion at some later date. Breakfast was indulged in at Durham, a city of proud eminence, with a lovely old cathedral, whose glories would have been appreciated had the weather been otherwise. As it was, the glorious pile was enveloped in a thick mist, and breakfast was the only thing that interested us in Durham. The streets of the city are narrow and tortuous with many difficult rises, and were in a very greasy condition.

A fresh start being made, we came upon some very short and steep inclines. These came upon us with almost startling suddenness, causing us to drop from fourth to first speed straight away. On Ferry Hill, the Daimler of the Hon. J. Scott Montagu, which has done splendidly, required a little coaxing – it too, regarding the state of the roads as abnormally heavy, even for its fine constitution and good running powers. Leaving Wycliffe the roads showed a slight improvement on towards Darlington, where it appeared that all the population had turned out to greet us. The only passage for the cars was in the centre of the single greasy lines of tramways, and that no accident took place was a tribute to the skill of the drivers and the reliability of the cars, which should appeal to all who saw the way the vehicles were handled. In Darlington there are some awkward corners, that at Blackwellgate being probably the worst. In turning the corner near the Fleece Hotel, Mrs. Bazalgette met a horse and conveyance just ahead. She slowed, and did her best to clear, but failed, and jostled a lamp-post. Several standing by at once came to the rescue, and giving a turn of the head of the little car sent it on its way again.

Mrs. Bazalgette preparing to start her Benz – Newcastle (Photo: *The Autocar*)

The weather had up to Durham been somewhat of a 'Scotch mist,' but by the time Darlington was reached matters had improved; while on to Northallerton, where a halt was made for lunch, the going was excellent, and the sun glanced out for a second or so at pretty long intervals. In the Thirsk and Northallerton districts the scenery was very enjoyable, and, indeed, the same may be said of the journey right into York.

There was little excitement on the way, and my car was pulling grandly until within three miles of Northallerton. Then trouble with the burners began again, and within a mile it was necessary to get down eight times to attend to them. The driver of one or two cars that were close together, and each trying to get to the control first, failed to apply his brakes on a greasy road and skidded, travelling up a bank. Fortunately no damage was done to man or machine.

Luncheon was taken at Northallerton, and that meal being over, the rain ceased, but unfortunately the weather continued dull and threatening, and there was too much mud on the road to be pleasant. Mr. E. J. Hutton, J.P., whose misfortunes with his four-cylindered Panhard car are well-known, was at Northallerton with his new Creanche electric car. After the halt there was more greasy running as far as Thirsk. For company for some miles we had the Lanchester car, No. 22. On the level we were easily faster, but up hill the Lanchester car was two or three miles ahead, and the consequence was we were passed and repassed nearly the whole of the way, as the road was very hilly. The Wolseley car was frequently in our company during the next stages of the journey, but suffered from innumerable punctures, as have several cars with pneumatic tires. Mr. Johnson, too, has had rather a bad experience, puncturing several times.

Driving through Thirsk was no careless matter, as the market square was about as closely packed with people as any passed through during the whole course of the tour, a fact due to the hiring fair in progress, and not wholly associated with the coming of the cars. We met some very antiquated-looking vehicles drawn by horses going to the hiring fair, where merry-go-rounds seemed the leading feature – so far as our rapid observation revealed. The road improved slightly through Easingwold and Skipton, and at length we arrived at York, where each vehicle was detained an hour and a half in the grounds of the Railway Hotel for the purpose of the exhibition. The cars were released in order of their arrival, and there were about twenty of them in the grounds at one time. Great crowds had gathered in the picturesque old city, and the advent of the cars created much commotion. There was quite a fashionable gathering at the exhibition, and the whole proceedings were of the nature of a picnic. Many of us would have preferred to stay in York, but the programme had to be obeyed.

Exhibition at York
(Photo: *The Autocar*)

When York was left behind dry roads were entered upon for the first time, though the surface quality was otherwise none too satisfactory, especially after Tadcaster had been passed. The Napier car punctured badly outside Northallerton, and was overhauled by Mr. Holder's Daimler, but the latter had to change a burner outside York, and entered Leeds only just in front of its friendly rival.”

The Motor-Car Journal, Saturday, May 12th, 1900

1,000-Mile Trial. 163

YORK,

MONDAY, 7th MAY, 1900.

A ONE-HOUR

EXHIBITION

OF THE

MOTOR VEHICLES

TAKING PART IN THE

0-Mile Trial organized by the Automobile Club of Great Britain and Ireland,

WILL BE HELD IN THE

GARDENS OF THE RAILWAY HOTEL,

By kind permission of the Hotel Committee of the North-Eastern Railway Co.

ADMISSION from 2 p.m. - - - ONE SHILLING.

Every Vehicle will remain on Exhibition for about 1½ hours from the time of its arrival.

THE PROFITS TO BE GIVEN TO THE TRANSVAAL WAR FUND.

Honorary Committee.

Capt. the Hon. Cecil Duncombe, J.P.
Ernest Beckett, Esq., M.P.
J. Cleghorne, Esq.
F. Pease, Esq., J.P.
J. B. Dale, Esq., J.P
Capt. Vyner, J.P.
Hon. Sec.: G. Dent, Esq.

L 2

York Railway Hotel
gardens Monday, May 7th
(Photo: *The Autocar*)

The Autocar correspondent takes up the story

“ Exhibition at York

At York the cars were run into the fine grounds of the Railway Hotel, where they were on exhibition for one and a half hours after their arrival, and a considerable crowd of fashionably-dressed people thronged the enclosure. We found Nos. A17, A22, 4, 31, A20, A10, A4, 26, and A3 had arrived in order named, and at 2.15, when Mr. Rolls was sent away on the continuation of his journey, Nos. 47 and A29 had also come in. Our turn to depart came at 3.30, by which time cars Nos. 8, A30, A7, A11, 3, 34, 9, A24. A21, 37, 40, A23, 15, A26, 36, and 22 had put in an appearance. From York to Leeds the twenty-three miles of roads afforded for the most part good travelling, though the constant repairing of the surface in patches caused the car to dip and jump a great deal. The dry roads, the bright sun, and the cool breeze made travelling very pleasant, and the miles were rolled off in good order. We had an additional fourteen stones on board in the shape of a genial Leeds pressman, and the added weight and drier surface told when No. 47, which we had beaten in the morning, came by – with three passengers only instead of four, as earlier in the day. Mr. Mayhew's seven h.p. Peugeot also overtook us six miles out of Leeds, but we 'got our own back' after a couple of miles' running, when we passed her at the top of a long gradual rise, and after following us for a mile she stopped, with her governor springs off. Two local cars – a Benz and a Marshall – came out to meet us, and the last few miles into the town the roads were vile, and gave us a terrible bumping. The control began at the tram terminus, and the passage through the town was thronged with people, children innumerable and of the wildest and most reckless character greeted us in thousands on the outskirts, and as the centre of the town was reached we passed through a closely-packed lane of people the police at times having considerable difficulty in forcing a clear way for the cars, which were stabled in the Artillery Drill Hall, Fenton Street, a good mile and more away from the centre of the town and our hotels. We reached the depot at five o'clock, eleventh for the day's run, Mr. Rolls's Panhard having, as usual, finished first, an hour and a quarter earlier in the day. Mr. Cheel, with the Ariel tricycle and trailer, came next, with both lubricator and petrol connections gone, and makeshift substitutes of rubber tubing doing duty instead. Mr. Holder's twelve h.p. Daimler followed, and reported a slain fowl and a very narrow escape from what might have been an ugly smash, when a horse and cart backed right across the road and blocked their way at the foot of a hill, down which they were travelling somewhat quickly. It was too slippery under wheel to make it safe to apply the brakes hard, so they took the only other alternative to running into the cart, and charged a high footpath, grazed the edge, and just bent back their off mudguard as they brushed past the tail of the cart. Mr. Edge on Mr. Kennard's Napier had been delayed by the puncture above referred to, and was followed in by the M.C.C. Triumph (No. 31), Mr. Mayhew on his eight h.p. Panhard, Mr. Ashby's Empress tricycle, Mr. Friswell's seven h.p. Peugeot, Mr. Browne's six h.p. Panhard, No. 47 Richard carriage, and ourselves. Mr. Mayhew's

York Monday, May 7th. Boys selling *The Autocar* were a feature of every show throughout the 1,000 miles tour. Notice the flag shown in bottom right-hand corner. (Photo: *The Autocar*)

Peugeot, Mr. Burgess's M.M.C. Panhard (No. 8) – which has been running well all day – and Mr. Stocks on the Ariel quadricycle got in before 5.30. Mr. Siddeley, Mr. Scott-Montagu, Dubois on the Decauville, the M.M.C. car (No. 9) and Mr. Phillips's came in in the next quarter of an hour, Mr. Montagu reporting ignition troubles in the earlier part of the day. He had started late also, having been delayed doing good motor missionary work in influential quarter in the neighbourhood. By eight o'clock Nos. 15, 22, 16, 36, A21, 14, A7, A23, A26, 1, 2, 40, 37, 39, 5, 49, A28, A2, A12, 32, 27, 41, 12, 44, and 38 had arrived, all recording good runs devoid of untoward incident, save the International car (No. 41) – Mr. Capellan, who was driving, having been suddenly taken with a fit and broken a blood vessel, the car in the meantime running into the bank. Happily, Mr. Seyd, with the other International car, was not far behind, and after a rest the patient was brought safely in, and went back to London next day by train. The Century tandem, which had had seven spokes started in one wheel by the collision in Newcastle, had been made rideable by taking four spokes out of the other wheel and putting into the damaged one, and after the necessary delay she was got through in good time, and proper repairs carried out next day. The Wolseley car reported two more punctures of her pneumatic tyres. Mrs. Kennard also brought her De Dion voiturette through in good time, but minus a mudguard carried away by a collision with a lamppost in Northallerton (*It is strange that both lady drivers were reported to have collided with lampposts on this stretch – perhaps the first report relating to Mrs. Bazalgette was an error?*) Mr. Hargreaves with his two twelve h.p. Daimlers, the second driven by Mr. Meyer (late of the Daimler Co.), and who had not started till eleven from Newcastle, ran in at 8.20, and Mr. Johnson, about whose fate some really startling rumours were current at York, turned up at 9.15, having had no end of trouble with a punctured tyre. A jagged piece of iron had got in and worked round inside, injuring the air tube in many places, and as fast as one puncture had been located and repaired another developed, necessitating, of course, another stoppage and doing all the work over again. This had occurred nearly a score of times, which amply accounted for the delay. The Marshall carriage (No. 24) got in at 9.30, and as we wended our way back to our hotel we met Mrs. Bazalgette, who had encountered ignition troubles, steadily ascending the hill to the Hall.

The Exhibition at Leeds, which opened at noon on Tuesday, without, however, any formalities, was well patronised throughout the day, and a considerable number of well-dressed people were present, who took a decidedly intelligent interest in the cars and their construction. ”

The Autocar, Saturday, May 12th, 1900

— o§o —

“ The Mayor of Leeds was not influenced by the examples set him by the Lord Mayor of Manchester, the Lord Provost of Edinburgh, and the mayor and mayoress of Newcastle. His engagements precluded him from opening Tuesday's show in the Artillery Drill Hall. ”

— o§o —

NEWSPAPERS WERE BY now very much aware that the Trial was a newsworthy item. Many column inches were dedicated to their progress, and Claude Johnson's precaution of contacting all the local newspapers as well as telegraphing reports to the 'National' or London papers was paying dividends.

The Yorkshire Post May 8th 1900 described the proceedings of the day in the usual detail, adding that on arrival in Leeds the Hon. C. S. Rolls had to have 19 minutes accorded as lost by reason of a wait for the time-keeper at the top of York Road for the Leeds inward control.

They say that 'roughly half the machines whose travel stained appearance excited such curiosity are of English Manufacture. Their present condition and performance en route conclusively prove that the English manufacture is rapidly making up the somewhat considerable gap which last year existed between the best products of English and French firms.

It is a little surprising to find that steam had only one solitary representative, the whole of the other 49 being driven by petroleum vapour.

Many of the cars gave evidence of having been much bothered with the tyre puncturing nuisance, and others were equipped with solid tyres. Very little difference is felt in the riding comfort between thick solid and air tyres, but it is said that the difference in the wear of parts through vibration is very much greater in the case of solid tyred wheels.'

The *Leeds Mercury* May 9th 1900 stated 'There will always be cranks who will drive horses, and I think I shall be one of them.' There was one car (they said) in the Exhibition at Leeds which cost £1300*, which to the bulk of the visitors seemed apalling. In general their report was more hostile than most.

* This price was applied to a Napier that was not ready at the start

Darlington and Stockton Times

12 May The Motor-Car Tour

Continuing their 1,000 miles motor vehicle trial, members of the Automobile Club on Monday journeyed from Newcastle to Leeds after spending the week end in the former town. About ten minutes past seven the main body moved down Northumberland-street, and after crossing the High Level Bridge they were soon clear of Gateshead and making capital pace for Durham. The mud, however, seriously affected the smaller cars. By ten o'clock the main body were in the Cathedral City, and there half-an-hour was spent for breakfast. These minutes were used to advantage, and then a move was made in the direction of Darlington. Along the whole route a capital record was kept of the times of the various machines, the space allowed for the stoppages, as per the programme, being rigidly adhered to by the conductors, who were stationed at various points on the road.

Darlington

Large crowds lined Northgate, Prebend-row, Blackwellgate, and Grange-road for the purpose of seeing the cars pass through the town. Half-past ten was the time stated on the programme for arrival at Darlington, but before that hour several cars came buzzing through. The control for Darlington was supposed to begin at St Paul's Church, but little heed appeared to have been paid to these instructions. True, a fairly long string of cars and tricycles passed through at about eleven, and they presented a spectacle, indeed, occupants and cars alike being besmeared with mud. Although the streets in places were very crowded it being the second hirings, yet the cars travelled at a very fast rate were cleverly handled and threaded their way remarkably well through the traffic. Blackwellgate corner is not an ideal place to negotiate and one of the cars, driven by a lady, in turning near the Fleece Hotel met a horse and conveyance just ahead. She slowed, and did her best to clear, but failed, and jostled a lamp-post. Several standing by at once came to her rescue, and giving a turn to the head of the horseless carriage sent it on its way rejoicing.

Northallerton

Northallerton was the scene of great animation on Monday, on the occasion of the arrival of the motor cars and cycles on the 1,000 miles trial trip in connection with the Automobile Club. The first car to arrive was at 10.30 a.m., and by about 2 p.m. about 50 had arrived. They reached the town one after the other with irregular intervals between them, and drove up to the front of the Golden Lion and adjoining houses. There was a large crowd of people, including many visitors from a distance, to see the novel spectacle. All the cars and most of the occupants, with waterproofs and overalls, presented a mud-bespattered condition, the roads being moist. The control exhibited over the machines – the suddenness with which they arrested while going at a good speed, and the way they were guided to a nicety, elicited general admiration. What with the arrival and departure of the cars, the crowd was kept in a lively state of motion from one point of interest to another. As the riders arrived they adjourned in the Golden Lion Hotel, where a capital lunch was provided by Mrs Bennett and partaken of by 150 of the visitors separately, and several of those declared it was the best spread they had had on the road. There were 53 cars told off from the Golden Lion to depart on the road to York. One of the vehicles had a temporary break down in the town.

Thirsk

On Monday the motor cars passed through Thirsk from Northallerton, en route to York and Leeds. Excellent police arrangements had been made by Inspector Cook, who succeeded in keeping the road clear through the Market Square, it being no easy task seeing it was market day, and in addition the principal day of the May-day Statutes, and save an accident (which is reported in our columns) to the Vicar of Kilburn, nothing serious occurred, and this did not happen in a busy portion of the town, but in a comparatively quiet part of the route, viz. Inghram-gate, some distance away from the throng, which happily was not attended with any serious results as far as could be ascertained, when our parcel was dispatched. The first of the cars passed through Thirsk about 12 at noon and at the eve of the afternoon all had arrived. They one and all bore evidence of the dirty state of the roads in the north, for both cars and their occupants were liberally bespattered with mud.

Darlington and Stockton Times

The Evening Press, York. 5 May The Motor Car Tour

Amongst the timekeepers was a Mr. James Schumacher. No cars would be allowed to leave the city until they had spent at least 1½ hours in the exhibition outside the Station Hotel.

Exhibition at Leeds Tuesday May, 5th

After a long day's travelling (in, as it turned out, very unpleasant wet weather) and with the added delay of a compulsory 1½ hours Exhibition at York, many Participants found themselves arriving late at Leeds. Claude Johnson was aware that this might happen, and was very strict that the cars must be on display for the paying public to see.

Hence the ruling in the instructions:

> **SPECIAL Regulations for Leeds**
>
> **No Passes Out from the Leeds Drill Hall for cleaning will be issued until Tuesday 8th May, and they will not then be issued before 6 a.m. or after 8 a.m. Vehicles must therefore be taken out for cleaning by 8 a.m. on that day.**
>
> **No Passes Out for cleaning will be issued at Leeds on Monday, 7th May.**

Captain Langrishe drove Miss Irene Vanbrugh about Leeds on Tuesday in Mr. Harmsworth's Parisian Daimler, and the charming and talented actress expressed herself delighted with the experience.

On Monday 7th in Leeds the public could pay 1/- to see the cars arrive, and on Tuesday the Exhibition was open from noon to 10 p.m.

Leeds had 19 hotels listed, but only two places where petrol could be obtained. It is interesting to see that the price of petrol here was amongst the cheapest at 1s. 2d per gallon; while during the morning of that day petrol was available passing through Thirsk at the most expensive price quoted of 2/- per gallon. As it was possible to have a room in an Hotel, say in Carlisle, for 1/6 per night, this puts the cost of petrol into context

The second week's diary from another reporter appeared in *The Autocar*. His story from Carlisle to Leeds.

"

The A.C.G.B. 1,000 Miles Test

As seen from the Secretary's and Mr. Lord's Car

By H. J. Swindley

Wednesday was something of a red letter day in the course of the big round, for it was the day upon which the surviving cars would cross the border into Scotland, and indulge in the compulsory trial up Birkhill at the head of Moffat Water. It was an order that Mr. Henry Sturmey and the writer should time the climbs up this hill, so it became necessary for us as well as for the secretary to leave at 7.30 a.m., instead of 9.30 a.m., which was the time appointed for the crowd. For the first time our faithful Peugeot played us false, or rather the late rising habits of the Carlisle shopkeepers made it impossible to effect a minor repair in time. Consequently Mr. W. Exe's six horse-power Parisian took out a very heavy load, consisting of her owner, his wife (*It is interesting to note that Claude Johnson's wife was on the trial*), Mr. Sturmey, the writer, and a mechanician.

The writer occupied the seat usually affected by the mechanician, or, indeed, anyone who desires to save the car windage, and was alternately trodden on by his august editor, and pinched hard by the clutch pedal. Nothing but cheerful conversation distinguished the few remaining miles run on English soil; the road was somewhat heavy, and the meteorological outlook by no means promising. Under favourable conditions this road away to Lockerbie would make a fine autocar racecourse, for, with one or two exceptions, the bends are very gradual, and straights of considerable length abound. The Parisian fairly jumped into Scotland, for the bridge over the River Esk, which forms the boundary between the kingdoms, has the true *dos d'âne*. The attitude of the country folks towards the autocarists almost as soon as the border was passed differed considerably from that noticed further south. The people exhibited little enthusiasm, but much interest, and a good deal of respect. The men would frequently raise their hats in quite a French manner, while the women, particularly the old women, waved kindly welcome. The children, even the massed school children, did not cheer. Only their eyes, big with curiosity, showed how novel and strange the sight of this grey rolling monster of the road appeared to them. The sight of Fenton's steamboat on the Clyde was no stranger to their forbears than the aspect of the Parisian as she swept by to these wonder-struck boys and girls. The day's run had been well noised abroad, for, although full an hour and a half early, the people were already out and watching at all points of vantage

Leaving Moffat, and turning westwards, the charming part of the day's run began, for in a mile and a half we had entered the vale of Moffat Water, and were making for the ninth milestone, which was the place appointed for the start of the Birkhill trial. The rain of the previous night had made the going very heavy, and the sharp turns and twists in the narrow road required careful driving. Eight miles out from Moffat, Rolls's car was heard tootling sadly through the mist, but she was soon past and gone, though a halt must be called a mile further before the mighty twelve could be set at the bank.

We were dropped at the appointed spot, and quickly left alone in this lonely gorge, with the clouds a few feet only overhead, and no companionship but that of a score of Highland cattle, who showed an embarrassing desire to investigate the red control flag at a run. However, cars began soon to arrive at unequal intervals, steaming gloriously from the stiff pull-up from Moffat, and glad to halt to cool their engines and replenish tanks with pails and buckets from the rushing Moffat Water. One by one they were dispatched upon their way up the hill. Mr. Montagu arrived with Lady Montagu and a friend on their car, her ladyship being a keen automobilist, and anxious to make good time up the hill. Nearly all halted; only two cars took the hill in their stride. Occasionally we were alone for a considerable time, no car appearing, and the one lately dispatched being right out of sight, the Highland cattle would return and solemnly contemplate the red flag. But each time, and before they quite made up their minds to play toro with us in a lonely Scotch pass, a car came to the rescue. At last we too left in the cream Peugeot, and the shaggy brutes' opportunity was gone. The day had improved with the roads, and after a grand run to St. Mary's Loch, lunch, and a finer run yet by Yarrow Water, and down the wild slopes of Paddy's Slacks to Innerleithen, where the school children had had a half holiday on our account, and the shopkeepers had closed their shops to honour the cars, the way was taken to Peebles through Eddleston, and Penicuik to the northern Athens, where, intermittent as the arrival of the cars was, large crowds of sightseers gathered to witness their arrival.

Sixth Day

Once clear of tramlines and the setts of Portobello, the road from Edinburgh to Haddington was found in excellent condition. While running due east towards the latter place, the strong southerly wind aided rather than impeded most of the cars, which made good time over the first stage, where breakfast awaited them. At the end of the Edinburgh control the writer marked down forty-eight cars as quitting, but the Brown-Whitney steamer and the Daimler public service car were still to come. Whilst in Haddington, awaiting breakfast, we had an interesting conversation with a local medical man, who is keenly interested in automobilism, and intends shortly to substitute an autocar for his horses and carriages. Like most unsophisticated people, he was much exercised as to the choice of a car for his work, but if he buys as we advised him, he will not go far astray. Shortly after leaving Haddington, the Peugeot pump began to worry, with the result that we saw little but the tail-end of the run for that day. We lost a good deal of water by steaming, and more by leakage, so that we were afforded many excellent opportunities of studying the peasantry of the countryside through the medium of requests for buckets of water. Our unhappy friend Lord crawled under that car many times in the course of the day, but the Peugeot not carrying the outfit of an Elswick works, his repairs were unfortunately somewhat temporary. We became quite artists in gauging the willingness of the cottager to supply water by the bucket, and in one case were left by a kindly soul in charge of a

Highland cattle

two year old baby, who stiffened with terror and yelled continuously, while she sought the precious fluid at a spring some hundred yards in rear of her dwelling. We passed both Mr. Hargreaves's car and the Gladiator voiturette with punctures, but our pump laid heavy on our souls, and sympathy was at a premium. Midway between Haddington and Dunbar, on top of a hill, and Lord once more grovelling under the vehicle while the leak from the pump trickled steadily into his left eye, announced in heart-breaking tones that the quarter-inch nut securing the pump had gone. There was no other, and despair was seizing us for her own when a Marshall car came up the hill, and we hailed them on the subject of quarter nuts. Yes, they had one, was the reply, but, nevertheless, they went right away, so that to this day we marvel whether that driver thought that our query re quarter nuts was an automobilist's way of asking after his health. But aid came from a most unexpected quarter, from none other than a baker, who offered us quarter nuts from his splashboard brackets, and was quite willing we should take every quarter nut he had. We took two. Generous baker, may his yeast never turn sour, and his bread be always light. We were very late into Berwick, and Lord, being insatiable in the matter of mechanical faking, preferred changing his countershaft pinions for others two teeth better rather than lunching. Certainly it improved the running of the car immensely, the cut-outs being less frequent, and the travel more comfortable than ever. On the level the Peugeot was at least fifteen seconds per mile faster by reason of them. But the pump still leaked, and we still fetched and carried water for that thirsty heated engine. From Berwick to Newcastle the wind was a dead nose-ender, and in coasting it smote one upon the face with vicious force. Between Alnwick and Morpeth we began to run into the tail-end of the sluggards, and passed Grahame-White steering a Parisian Daimler with his right foot on the projecting axle box. He had relinquished the steering of his car for a brief moment to his passenger while he attended to some trifling matter, only to find himself the next instant in the ditch with a broken steering bracket, and no means of repairing it. The passenger then deserted him, going on on another car, and while his mechanician drove White stood with his left foot on the step and the hollow of his right foot on the axle box, as mentioned, guiding that car up hill and down dale for fifty-four miles. Three or four miles out from Gosforth we passed Lord Kingsburgh and Colonel McGrath stranded by the roadside for petrol, but luckily we had a spare half-gallon. Notwithstanding that faithless pump, we had got through well before the snails, and were not sorry to find ourselves on the banks of the coaly Tyne.

Seventh Day

The show day at Newcastle had been made use of by enlisting the skill of a craftsman of 'the greatest engineering city in the world' to settle that pump. But again our luck was out, for hardly had we cleared the high level bridge and struck the Gateshead shore than a hundred voices, more in glee than regret, informed us we were punctured. And we were. But after pumping up we drove to the top of the steep hill only to find when we reached the top that the pump was at it again.

Again we made cottage pilgrimages with that pail, and we fetched Chester-le-Street just as the precious handiwork of the Newcastle skilled artisan petered out, and the pump spindle went at the shut. But seven miles of 121½ were won, and not another mile could we make unless we could find a man to turn us a new spindle. But our luck was in in this matter, for we presently lighted on a smart cycle and general engineer, H. Shield by name, who in the course of some three or four hours made us a new spindle which served admirably. We took the opportunity of changing our punctured air-tube, the Michelin cover coming out of the rim with wonderful ease, and all being in order were under weigh again at half-past one with 114½ miles before us to Leeds if we went via York. But we selected the direct Northallerton, Boroughbridge, and Wetherby route instead, and halted half an hour for a brief survey of Durham's mighty fane. Two miles south of Darlington that wretched pump pumped no more, and Lord again retired beneath the car, while we started the weary bucket business once again. The little ¼in. nut with its left-handed thread had, in the hands of the skilful repairer, become a ⅜in. nut with a right-handed thread, which after a time unscrewed itself. The pump had to be taken to pieces, the nut screwed up, and the thread savagely burred. Mercifully this was the end of our troubles, and with fairly favourable grades we ran grandly for the rest of our journey. Halting for tea at Boroughbridge, we were told that the cars had scored a holocaust of victims in passing through Thirsk, where it was market and hiring day combined, and that several people had been injured by the colliding of two horse-drawn vehicles, the animals having been scared by the cars as they passed. Another sad case of uneducated horses, but when we arrived at Leeds none of the tourists were aware of the catastrophe. Happy is the autocar ride that has no history, and happy was the remainder of our run to Leeds with just one more bucket loan at Wetherby, where we stopped to light our lamps. Notwithstanding all our woes of the early part of the day, we reached our objective by a quarter-past nine thankful that nothing worse had befallen us. As we close this our friend Lord enters to inform us that now he has done that pump. So may it be, for it is yet a far cry to London town.”

The Autocar, Saturday, May 12th, 1900

“Tribute was paid by the Leeds journalists to the way in which the cars romped into the drill hall at Leeds. ‘Even a big Daimler car,’ said one, ‘built to carry eleven persons, dashed round the hall like an infuriated monster, but was brought up within an inch of the space allotted to it.’

Leeds Exhibition

On Tuesday, there was a one-day exhibition at the Artillery Drill Hall, Fenton Street, Leeds, by permission of the officer commanding the 1st West Riding Volunteer Artillery. There was a large number of visitors to see the motor-cars taking part in the Automobile Club's trial tour. Some there were who understood the means of propulsion used in varying forms in connection with the cars, but for the most part the people who walked between the rows of vehicles were merely attracted by curiosity, and the art of the coachbuilder was more to them than the engines and the gearing. The scene was a busy one throughout the day, attendants being busily employed in making good defects that had shown themselves during the journey from Newcastle, and in cleaning and preparing for the seventy-four miles run to Sheffield on Wednesday.

Darlington

The unusual sight of a string of motor-cars passing through Darlington caused quite a flutter and thrill of excitement in almost everybody's mind. The ordinary spectator had been led to believe that at 10.30 prompt, with a blowing of horns, the whole of the cars would perform a triumphal march through the town, and that the traffic would be suspended in certain streets for their benefit. Earlier than that hour the footpaths in Northgate, Prebend Row, and Blackwellgate were lined with people who had the pleasure of seeing a car in every fifteen minutes pass along. At about 11 a.m. a string of cars and tricycles came through mud-besmeared, and owing to the wretched weather presenting altogether a sad spectacle. None of the cars stopped at Darlington, but passed through smartly on their way to Northallerton, where luncheon was awaiting for them. By noon forty-five cars had passed through Darlington. The tricycles caused a lot of amusement by the manner in which they buzzed through the town at full speed, and yet threaded their way carefully amid the traffic in the centre of the town. The control for Darlington began at St. Paul's Church, and ended at Parkgate, George Road, and at that point they went straight ahead at will. Mr. J. W. Morley acted as time-keeper at Darlington, and the police attended to the traffic in a masterly manner.

York

There was a great crowd to welcome the vehicles and their passengers, and considerable interest was taken in the exhibition. Two hours' halt was made while tea was taken, and judging from the fashionable assembly in the hotel grounds, many of the leading county families were represented.

Leeds

A real Yorkshire welcome was accorded the cars and their riders as they came into Leeds, the Hon. C. S. Rolls leading. Those who have followed the reports of the Trial have seen how he has occupied a good position right through the contest, and the Leeds people were naturally interested in the personality of the famous chauffeur. He got in a few minutes before time. The Ariel tricycle with Whippet detachable trailer

Illness of Mr. Cappellen

All engaged in the Trial regret the sudden illness which has compelled Mr. Cappellen to return to town. He has been driving an International, which has travelled very well throughout the tour. When within six miles of the Leeds control he suddenly fell forward in a fainting fit. Fortunately he was only driving on the first speed at the time and although the machine went up a bank it did not turn over. Mr. Cappellen rallied sufficiently to take the machine into Leeds, but had to leave for London the next day. Mr. Billings is now driving the car.”

The Motor-Car Journal

was a quarter of an hour behind, and then came a Daimler 12-h.p. motor car and an 8-h.p. Napier, closely followed by the usual leading cars. For more than four hours after the first had made its appearance the cars kept arriving at short and long intervals, the last to turn up being a 7 h.p. Richard car. The fact that there was not a regular continuous stream of them robbed the scene of some interest, but it was apparent none the less attractive to the bystanders.

The great majority of the cars, it was stated, had accomplished the twelve-miles-an-hour average in the course of the day.

The official records concerning the run from Newcastle to Leeds show that the following vehicles completed the journey up to a speed of twelve miles an hour. We have not followed the division into amateur and manufacturers' sections in order that the cars could be arranged in the order of their running time.

Princes Street East Edinburgh

Royal Borders Bridge, Berwick-on-Tweed

Alnwick (Photos: courtesy J. Riddell)

The first thirty cars to arrive were:

A17	Hon. C. S. Rolls's 12 h.p. Panhard
4	Ariel tricycle and Whippet trailer
31	M.C.C. Triumph
A22	Mr. J. A. Holder's 12 h.p. Daimler
A10	Mr. E. Kennard's 8 h.p. Napier
A4	Mr. M. Mayhew's 8 h.p. Panhard
26	Friswell's 8 h.p. Peugeot
A20	Mr. Ashby's Empress tricycle
A3	Mr. T. B. Browne's 6 h.p. Panhard
47	Richard car
35	6 h.p. Daimler
A29	Mr. M. Mayhew's 7 h.p. Peugeot
A11	Hon. J. Scott Montagu's 12 h.p. Daimler
3	Ariel quadricycle
A30	Mr. J. D. Siddeley's 6 h.p. Parisian Daimler
8	Motor Manufacturing Company's 6 h.p. phaeton
A24	Mr. R. E. Phillip's Mors Petit Duc
9	Motor manufacturing Company's 6 h.p. Iveagh phaeton
16	Gladiator voiturette
34	Decauville car
15	De Dion voiturette
36	6 h.p. Daimler
14	De Dion voiturette
22	Lanchester car
A21	Mr. E. Pitman's 6 h.p. Daimler
A7	Mr. A. Harmsworth's Parisian Daimler
A2	Mr. F. H. Butler's 6 h.p. Panhard
2	Benz Ideal, 1900 pattern
A23	Mr. C. Cordingley's 6¼ h.p. M.M.C. phaeton
A26	Mr. C. K. Gregson's 6 h.p. Daimler ”

The Motor-Car Journal, Saturday, May 12th, 1900

LEEDS TO SHEFFIELD

WEDNESDAY 9TH MAY

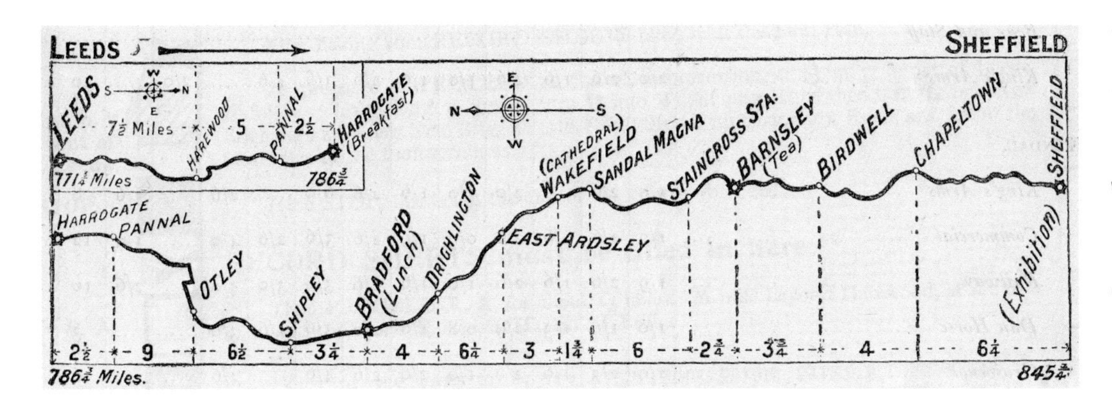

74 miles via Harrogate, Bradford, Wakefield, Barnsley, to Sheffield

MAY 9TH FINDS *The Autocar* reporter on Mr. T. B. Browne's 6 h.p. Panhard. The weather had deteriorated even further ...

Mr. T. B. Browne on his 6 h.p. Panhard. (Photo: Argent Archer)

“ Leeds to Sheffield

For roads and weather Wednesday last week was the worst day yet experienced. Although no actual rain fell during the run, it had been raining all night, and continued to do so till a few minutes before seven, when the start was made from the Drill Hall. Our run for the day was made on Mr. T. B. Browne's six horse-power Panhard, and, starting somewhat late from the hall, we found a long steady climb of about three miles over stone paved roads of the roughest description. Cars appeared to be early in difficulties, and long ere the outward control was reached the Daimler *char-à-banc* was left by the roadside; Mr. Friswell was passed with a burst ignition tube, and Grahame-White with lamp troubles. Mr. Mayhew's Panhard was wrestling with the same difficulties; the Stanley steam car was apparently chain adjusting, whilst Nos. 41 and A29 were also for the moment stationary. The Brown-Whitney steamer did not start with the rest, having only just got in, covered with mud. The wait at the control was a cold one, and a raw, damp wind blew with considerable strength right in the teeth of the autocarists, who, with every wrap they could muster, prepared to face it. Beneath the wheels the roads were thick with slippery mud, and in many places 'rough' was hardly the word for it. As the cars left one by one *en route* for Harrogate, Mr. Browne drove carefully, as the occasion dictated, and we had scarcely got under weigh ere Mr. Cordingley was discovered 'adjusting,' and at the foot of the next hill Mr. Farman, with car 31 well on the footpath, was busy tyre repairing with his lady passenger much interested in the operation. The grades were long and heavy, both up and down, and on the next ascent Mr. Friswell showed us his back wheels, whilst the International car No. 44 was passed near the top with the passenger walking. The long and winding descent to the valley of the Wharfe was slippery in the extreme, and whilst some flew it at a fair speed, others, including ourselves, took it steadily on the brakes. At the bridge over the river Grahame-White passed us with four up and a tyre binder worn nearly through, and No. 33 Decauville – which had 'chipped in' again – was stopped at the tenth milestone. Up the next long climb Mrs. Bazalgette was passed, going steadily up with the boy walking, whilst J. W. Stocks and his tandem, also minus passenger – for whom he had to wait – slipped by us. We were now nearing Harrogate, and overhauled the Lanchester on a long decline, at the end of which we had to face the ascent of Humphrey Bank, a well-known 'teaser' for cyclists. As we commenced the climb Stocks and the tandem came up with a dash, but were quickly stopped, and had to finish on their feet, whilst the No. 28 New Orleans was also passed, and No. 27 of the same make pegged steadily away in front, and actually beat us up the hill. The local chauffeurs evidently knew where to expect the fun, if there was any, for a Benz and a Mors were anchored at the worst corner, and we understand that several of the cars had their work cut out to take the climb, Mr. Butler in particular making several fresh starts before he reached the top. Nos. 27 and A26 were overtaken at the control, and then the cars ran steadily through the town to the gardens of the Victoria Baths, where they remained for

Right:
Harrogate – Wednesday, May 9th
(Photo: *The Autocar*)

A One Hour's Exhibition

the while their occupants regaled themselves with breakfast at the neighbouring hotels. The place was packed with an eager

---

“ Motor-Car v. Train

Will it be credited? The Hon. C. S. Rolls has been going at a high speed along a quiet country road. It is reported that between Otley and Guiseley his car had a neck-and-neck race with a North Eastern express for three or four miles. The train then made a detour through a tunnel, whereas the road was straight, and when the train came through the car had forged ahead. ”

The Motor-Car Journal,
Saturday, May 12th, 1900

crowd, and, on getting away, we retraced our steps for some miles, and once more regained the valley of the Wharfe, the run up which, had it been finer, would have been most beautiful, but everything was hidden in mist, and heavy damp-laden clouds were scudding wildly across the sky. No. 47 Georges Richard car followed us out of the town, and for several miles ran us closely, our car going ahead on the upgrades, and the Frenchman taking descents rapidly, if not recklessly – considering the grease – and picking up again. Before we changed our road Mr. Mayhew's Peugeot was met with the rider of No. 12 tricycle on board, and his machine was seen by the roadside a mile further back. He was en route for the town for the means to effect repairs. A few miles further on, at the foot of a sharp decline, a block was observed, and it turned out to be Mr. Meyer with car A27, who was stopped by a fallen horse, and a small string of cars soon gathered up behind her. Mr. Johnson's car in front of us took to waltzing round a corner, and inculcated caution in both of us, and Mr. Cordingley, who had cut off a corner and missed Harrogate altogether, was again found in trouble. He afterwards finished by train, leaving his car to come on as best she could. On the long hill approaching Shipley Mr. Phillips reported his Petit Duc going badly as we sailed by, and car 47, which had got in front, was finally overhauled at the top, Stocks and the tandem flying past us as we did so. Mr. Coles had been in front of us for several miles with the hood of his Benz up, and was overtaken here, whilst Mr. Burgess was stopped in the town with a punctured tyre. The road through here and right into Bradford was bad in the extreme, the paving being very rough, and we bumped our way to the Town Hall, where the cars were ranged up in double line for

A Three Hours' Exhibition

a 'free show,' as at Harrogate, and not, we fancy, of very much value, as the cars were so besieged and hemmed in by a seething crowd that people who really wanted to inspect them had very little opportunity of doing so. The police arrangements throughout the town were of the very best, and were most complete. Here we lunched, and got away shortly before two p.m., the departure being commenced, as at Leeds, by another two miles ascent of vile roads, during the course of which Capt. Langrishe was passed with his lamps out. There was a long and bitterly cold wait on the top of the hill at the outward control, and then No. 47 again 'took us on' as before, and was for most of the run somewhere in our vicinity. The roads now improved in places, and here and there some really fine running was encountered, the surface rapidly drying in the strong wind which blew. Mr. Coles was passed shortly after the start, and Mr. Ashby on his tricycle slipped by on a hill. No. 9 was experiencing lamp troubles near Drighlington, and Grahame White's Daimler was doing ditto just out of Wakefield, at the control into which town Mr. Lisle, with the Star, was overtaken with both back wheels wobbling considerably, having experienced a bad side-slip in Bradford, which had broken several spokes in both wheels. Some to and fro running now ensued between us and No. 47 and Mr. White, who had got up to us in the control, and they both shortly after went ahead, and were no more seen, whilst Mr. Mayhew's Peugeot was in trouble outside Barnsley with a burst ignition tube. At Barnsley another compulsory stop for tea for those who desired it was made, and, getting under weigh once more at the bottom of a long hill, Mr. Van Toll was passed with the baggage waggon, whilst close by a strange sight met our gaze, for, buried up to her axles in soft soil, and standing upright on all fours, with a gang of men digging her out, was a traction engine in a garden five or six feet below the road, whilst twenty feet of demolished stone wall told its own tale. On the long upgrade following this, No. 14 De Dion flew by at a tremendous pace, but at the next ascent a couple of miles further on she was seen struggling to the top with her passenger on the run, and she stopped altogether as we skittered past, Mr. Gregson's Daimler going by at the same time. At Chapeltown what was probably the steepest hill of the whole journey was negotiated, but as a descent, and not a climb. It was long and very steep, and covered thickly with slimy mud. We went down slowly with all five brakes hard on, and the smell of burning wood both from our own car and from that of Mr. Pitman just in front told the tale of the strain on the brake blocks. No hill better deserves the red danger-board

Barnsley

It had been understood in the town that the automobiles would reach Barnsley between 4 to 4.30 o'clock, and arrangements were made for them to stay a few minutes at the Kendray Market, where the people taking part would be welcomed by the Mayor (Alderman Wilkinson). Chief Constable Butler had arranged for the regulation of the traffic, but some of the cars stopped, some did not, and the arrangements unfortunately came to nothing, no demonstration of any kind being made. ”

The Motor-Car Journal,
Saturday, May 12th, 1900

In the Drill Hall ,
Sheffield
(Photo: Argent Archer)

AUTOMOBILE CLUB
1,000 MILES TRIAL
27
AUTOMOBILE CLUB
1,000 MILES TRIAL
44
AUTOMOBILE CLUB
1,000 MILES TRIAL
15
39

Right and bottom right: From Montague Grahame-White's personal album. (Courtesy NMM Beaulieu)

which the National Cyclists' Union has considerately placed at the top. At the bottom Capt. Langrishe was in trouble with his back pressure pipe gone, and he was patching it up to get in – which he eventually did – with a piece of leather and a bootlace. Mr. Pitman was passed shortly before entering the Sheffield control, and then ensued another long crawl through the town over paved roads to the Norfolk Drill Hall, an excellent place for the show which was arranged to be held the next day, and by 5.45 the following had registered in: A17, 4, A10, A22, A20, A4, A30, 34, A19, 26, A27, 35, A11, 16, 3, 37, 15, 40, 36, A29, 47, A3, A21, A31, A7, 9, 51, 1, 14, A28, 2, 31, and 12, the latter having experienced no end of troubles through the day, but sticking to it gamely, getting his machine through in average time. By 7.30, A2, A24, 44, A26, 8, A12, 46, 27, 33, 39, A25, 41, 32, and 38 had arrived, and the Stanley steamer was reported left five miles out at Birdwell with a ball bearing which persisted in locking itself. Save for a narrow escape of a smash caused by the sudden appearance of a team of three horses right across the road experienced by A28, which was only prevented by Mr. Iliffe chancing a wall, and just scraping through at the last moment, all the cars, with the exception of the incidents recorded, appear to have had successful and uneventful runs.

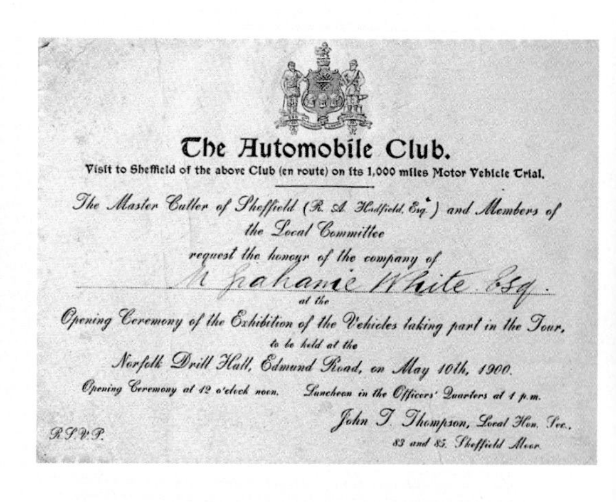

The Automobile Club.

Visit to Sheffield of the above Club (en route) on its 1,000 miles Motor Vehicle Trial.

The Master Cutler of Sheffield (R. A. Hadfield, Esq.) and Members of the Local Committee request the honour of the company of M Grahame White Esq. at the Opening Ceremony of the Exhibition of the Vehicles taking part in the Tour, to be held at the Norfolk Drill Hall, Edmund Road, on May 10th, 1900.

Opening Ceremony at 12 o'clock noon. Luncheon in the Officers' Quarters at 1 p.m.

John T. Thompson, Local Hon. Sec., 83 and 85, Sheffield Moor

R.S.V.P.

Cleaning at Sheffield (Photo: *The Autocar*)

The Cars at Sheffield

Whether it was that the time of arrival had not been fully known, or whether it was by reason of apathy, we do not know, but Sheffield presented a remarkable lack of autocar enthusiasm – as evidenced by the public in the streets of the city as the cars came in – when compared with the way in which the tourists had been received in other towns. True, at certain points small crowds assembled, but the closely-packed lines of spectators through which the cars had wended their way upon their arrival in other places were conspicuous by their absence. The same apathy was also apparent at the exhibition on the following day, the numbers attending this being strikingly small when compared with the packed enclosures elsewhere. The reception, however, of the visitors by the general committee and those more directly interested in the movement was the best which had yet been experienced, all taking part in the trial being entertained to a very excellent luncheon in the officers' mess room at the Drill Hall on Thursday evening, the exhibition having first been briefly opened by Mr. R. A. Hadfield, the Master Cutler of Sheffield, the proceedings, which were short, being as follows:

The chairman of the energetic and enthusiastic local committee, Mr. Reynolds, who is a most ardent automobilist, and the owner of a

THE AUTOMOBILE CLUB.

LUNCHEON

GIVEN IN THE DRILL HALL, EDMUND ROAD, BY THE MASTER CUTLER OF SHEFFIELD (R. A. HADFIELD, ESQ.) and MEMBERS OF THE LOCAL COMMITTEE,

In honour of the Visit of the Members of the Automobile Club of Great Britain to Sheffield, on their Thousand Miles trial run, May the 10th, 1900.

Left:
The Master Cutler opening the Exhibition at Sheffield. *(Photo: The Autocar)*

Daimler car, took the chair, and called upon the Master Cutler to declare the exhibition open. In doing so, the Master Cutler expressed the pleasure it gave him and his fellow citizens to welcome the Automobile Club to Sheffield. They recognised that the object of the tour was a very important one, inasmuch as it was an effort to bring prominently home to the public the practicability of automobilism. He thought the club were doing excellent work in fostering this new industry, bit he hoped that in connection with it they had seen the last of over-capitalisation. He could on his part perceive many advantages in connection with automobiles, and no real objections against them. The Master Cutler briefly referred to the lead the French had obtained in the manufacture of self-propelled carriages, but trusted British makers would now not lag long behind them. He thought, too, that automobiles would have a great bearing on questions of military transport. he assured all the makers present that Sheffield was always ready to supply the best material for the construction of such machines as he saw around him. He had great pleasure in declaring the exhibition open. The Hon. Jno. Scott-Montagu, M.P., briefly returned thanks on behalf of the hearty welcome the club had met with, and the company then adjourned to luncheon in the officers' mess room, at which the club members and others were the guests of the Master Cutler and the local committee. After a most recherché repast, the Master Cutler, who occupied the chair, and who was supported by Lord Wharncliffe, the Lord Justice Clerk of Scotland, the Hon. Jno. Scott-Montagu, the Hon. C. S. Rolls, Colonel McGrath, Mr. Henry Sturmey, and others, gave the usual loyal toast, which was duly honoured. he followed this with the 'health of

1,000-Mile Trial. 179

SHEFFIELD,

THURSDAY, 10th MAY, 1900.

A ONE-DAY

EXHIBITION

OF THE

MOTOR VEHICLES

TAKING PART IN THE

1,000-Mile Trial organized by the Automobile Club of Great Britain,

WILL BE HELD IN THE

NORFOLK DRILL HALL, REDMUND ROAD.

ADMISSION—

On WEDNESDAY EVENING, 9th MAY, to witness the arrival of the vehicles until 11 p.m. ... ... TWO SHILLINGS.

On THURSDAY, 10th MAY, from 12 o'clock noon to 10 p.m. ONE SHILLING.

THE PROFITS WILL BE DEVOTED TO THE TRANSVAAL WAR FUND.

General Committee.

The following Gentlemen, at the invitation of the Club, guaranteed the expenses of and made all the necessary arrangements in Sheffield in connection with the Trial and Exhibition:—

E. P. Reynolds, Esq., Ashdell Grove, *Chairman.*
R. A. Hadfield, Esq., *Master Cutler*, Parkhead House, Sheffield.
Alderman George Franklin, J.P., Broomfield, Sheffield.
B. J. Cocker, Esq., Westbourne Rd., Sheffield.
C. D. Leng, Esq., Sandygate, Sheffield.
W. St. Q. Leng, Esq., Stand House, Sheffield.
G. Ernest Branson, Esq., Westbourne Road, Sheffield.
Alleyne Reynolds, Esq., Riverdale, Sheffield.
F. C. Askham, Esq., Ranmooncliffe, Sheffield.
Arthur Davy, Esq., Paternoster Row, Sheffield.
John B. Gunstone, Esq., Steade Rd., Sheffield.
Charles Hansell, Esq., Montgomery Road, Sheffield.
H. M. Pashley, Esq., Ecclesall Road, Sheffield.
E. Frost, Esq., Hillsbro', Sheffield.
E. H. Hill, Esq., Victoria Road, Sheffield.
Harold Hill, Esq., Victoria Road, Sheffield.
J. T. Thompson, Esq., *Hon Sec.*, 83, Sheffield Moor, Sheffield.

M 2

the Automobile Club,' and referred again to his own great belief in the future of automobilism. He noted with pleasure the presence of M. Bourdil, of the A. C. de France, and took the opportunity of wishing success to the Paris Exhibition. While admiring the excellent performances of Mr. Rolls's French car, he was delighted to hear that an English-built vehicle – the Napier – had done so well. As the representative of the industries of a great city, he was delighted to welcome the club amongst them. Electric traction had done great things for Sheffield, and he was sure that autocars would yet do more. The Lord Justice Clerk then returned thanks on behalf of the club in one of those truly felicitous speeches, which have not been the least interesting feature of the 1,000 miles tour. Lord Wharncliffe, in responding for the visitors, testified to his belief in the future of automobilism, and his admiration of the work the club was engaged in. ”

The Autocar, Saturday, May 19th, 1900

The Motor-Car Journal extended their account of the speeches thus:

“The chairman proposed 'The Visitors and Success to Automobilism.' he complimented Mr. E. P. Reynolds on having done much to introduce automobilism into Sheffield, and was glad that the car he rode was entirely of British construction, and that the body was produced by a Sheffield carriage maker. The Napier car was doing good work, and for practical work, such as hauling loads, the British cars were coming out a long way ahead of their rivals. As representing the industries of that great city, he was delighted to see so many of those who were helping to introduce what he believed would be an enormous industry in the future. The manufacture of automobiles, he expected, would progress in the same way as the manufacture of cycles had progressed during the last ten or twelve years. Acknowledging the presence at the table of some French automobilists, Mr. Hadfield paid compliments to the manufacturers of France on their splendid enterprise in taking up the automobile movement, but at the same time he expressed the hope that before long we in England would not need to go to our neighbours on the Continent either to learn how to build motor-cars or how to appreciate their advantages.

The Lord Justice Clerk of Scotland responded in a humorous speech. He remembered the early days of the first successes of railways in this country, and could recollect incidents very similar to incidents which were happening now, and he believed that if moderation was practised automobilism would soon be looked upon as being as much a matter of course as railway travelling. Nowhere did automobilism receive such a welcome as in the villages, from old people, who remember the early days of railways, and, knowing how the predictions with regard to their dangers were falsified, had open minds on the subject of new means of travelling. he remarked that Sheffield was one of the places which petitioned in the early days against a railway which would come within ten miles. As to the cars which had fallen behind in the Trial, he divided them into three classes: those belonging to amateurs, who were dissatisfied with the speed attained; those which suffered from broken axles or wheels, through no fault of the art of automobilism, but because the coach builder and the engineer had not yet got to work together; and those which had actually broken down through the motive machinery being in an unsatisfactory condition, which was not to the credit of automobilism. if they got through the trip without doing serious injury to any human being, it would be a great thing in favour of automobilism. Horses soon grew accustomed to the cars, and he believed that the future of the autocar was not limited to sport, but it would provide a highly economical mode of land transport, and also of military transport, such as the world had never seen.

The Earl of Wharncliffe, who also responded, alluded to the usefulness of motor-cars to doctors, who were liable to be called up hurriedly in the night. if the stories he had heard as to the speed of the riders on the previous day were true, he was afraid he would have the pleasure of meeting some of them at Barnsley next Wednesday, but he had no doubt the West Riding police had exercised an amiable discretion in the matter. The exhibition had given a good deal of pleasure and instruction to the visitors.

The Hon. J. Scott Montagu, M.P., proposed 'The Press,' to which Mr. R. H. Dunbar and Mr. J. Derry responded, the former saying that the Press wished the movement all the success it deserved, and that the members of the club were pioneers in what would be a remarkable accession to the pleasure, the comfort, the convenience, and the business facilities of a great nation.

Mr. Mark Mayhew, L.C.C., proposed 'The Chairman and the Local Committee,' to which the Master Cutler, Mr. E. P. Reynolds, and Mr. J. T. Thompson responded. ”

The Motor-Car Journal, Saturday May 12th, 1900

"These proceedings over, the assembled party once more foregathered amongst the machines, and notes were compared as to the previous day's running. Mr. Butler's white Panhard we discovered quietly ensconced in the riding school amongst the guns *(see below)*, which had been placed there to make room for the cars in the main hall. here, with the assistance of Gadsden, one of the Daimler men, the motor was taken all to pieces, and after some hours' work it was found that the cause of the poor running throughout the trial had been the wearing down of one of the lift pins of a valve, which prevented the free action of one cylinder. The piston rings had also worked round so that their apertures coincided, and loss of compression resulted. These things were put right during the day, and subsequent events proved that the cause of the trouble had been at last properly located. In addition to the cars previously recorded as having arrived by 7.30 the previous evening, several others had put in an appearance by the time the exhibition opened, amongst them the Marshall car of Mr. Mann, who had experienced a six-hours' delay in making a new joint for the water jacket of his motor, which had 'gone' at Wakefield. The Brown-Whitney steamer had been 'held up' for general overhauling at Thirsk the previous day, and it only got into Leeds in the early hours of the morning, so had not left that point until 3 p.m., consequently was also very late in arriving at Sheffield. the Lanchester car got in at 5 a.m., having been delayed by the fracture of a bush in the valve gear, eventually getting in with an improvised one made for the occasion, replacing it during the day with a new one sent from the works in response to a wire. The Eureka car got in shortly after midnight, and her driver, unable to get rooms at that hour of the night, slept on the floor of the hall. Mr. Seyd reported having carried away a lamp bracket by collision with a tram-car entering Sheffield, and Mr. Begbie with the Century tandem, who also got in late, reported further tyre troubles, and, as the result of the collision in Newcastle, a badly-twisted frame, which caused the motor to work slightly askew in one direction with the pump acting ditto in the other; pump trouble also thus, not unnaturally, being a further source of difficulty."

The Autocar, Saturday May 19th, 1900

"The attendance at the exhibition during the day was very satisfactory. If there is any balance of profit it will be handed over to the Lord Mayor's War Fund. During the afternoon many of the visitors, on the invitation of the Master Cutler, inspected the works of Hadfields, Limited. The Earl of Wharncliffe enjoyed a ride through the city on one of the motor-cars. In addition to the forty-seven vehicles turned in at the Drill Hall on Wednesday afternoon, several others arrived at a later hour.

Five cars entered by the Motor Car Company have gone safely through the Trial, and all were at the exhibition at Sheffield – they having thus covered 855 miles."

The Motor-Car Journal, Saturday May 12th, 1900

...e engine of Mr. Butler's ...nhard being stripped ...own amongst the guns in ...e Riding School, ...effield. ...hoto: *The Autocar*)

"## Exhibitions

A General View

Several important exhibitions have been held this week, and the appearance of the cars as they stood in the hotel grounds at York, or the market square at Bradford, must have impressed thousands of people. One versatile journalist has suggested that the inscription 'These are they which came out of great tribulation' should have been placed over the halls at Edinburgh, Newcastle, Leeds, and Sheffield, in which the cars have been assembled together, and certainly the latter stages of the journey seem to have made the notion not inappropriate. the local war funds must have benefited to a very material extent, and even at Bradford, where the cars were on exhibition in the street for three hours, a street collection was made among the onlookers in aid of the Mayor's War Relief Fund. Over £100 was taken at Edinburgh, and the exhibition at Newcastle was equally successful from a financial point of view."

The Motor-Car Journal, Saturday May 12th, 1900

The story of the Gold Medal Lanchester –

Driven by Archie Millership who had problems at Bradford and also on the last day: told by George Lanchester.

So far Archie's car had behaved like a little lady and indeed she went without a hitch up to Edinburgh, through the Scottish section and down the Eastern section to Bradford, where a spot of bother occurred ... In the market square in Bradford where the cars were parked I found Archie bent low amongst the valve-gear, looking sorely worried. I asked, 'Can I do anything to help you?' and got a vicious dig in the ribs from his elbow and a curt 'Get out'.

He thought I was one of the crowd trying to be funny. We soon found that a choked oil-pipe had caused the cams to seize up solid in their bearing. In a couple of hours we had removed all the damaged parts and taken them to a local engineering shop – I think it belonged to one Fred Turvey. His boiler was being cleaned so there was no power available, but he let us have the run of his lathe and tools. Archie provided the power by pulling the belt round while I turned new parts. The tools were very primitive and I was only able to make a jury-rig; but we telegraphed to the Works for new parts to be delivered to us at Leicester. We had a trouble-free run there and stripped down again and completed the job properly.

In the final stages of the Tour from Northampton to London, which we did without stopping the engine, we found ourselves dozing at the tiller, so we took 2-hour spells. We arrived in London very tired and left our car in the street. Archie got up at 5.30 the following morning and drove the car to the Crystal Palace where the Tour ended with an Exhibition.

This annoying mishap spoilt the car's clean sheet, which it had maintained until the Bradford stage; it also made it impossible to take part in the Speed Trials at Welbeck. Unfortunately haste and fatigue led to the new parts being wrongly assembled at Leicester, so that the exhaust valve of the affected cylinder was opening on the firing stroke; this meant more delay as the job had to be done again, and the final run from Northampton to London was made at an average speed well above the legal limit.

With one car withdrawn and the other with a clean sheet for two-thirds of the Trial, the Lanchester record was at least as honourable as those of Wolseley and Napier. But because of bad reporting and the drawing of wrong conclusions, the contrary impression prevails. To quote from Pomeroy and Karslake: 'Apart from these mishaps the Lanchester was lamentably slow. In spite of its supposed 8 h.p. it was slower up all the hills than the little 3½-hp Wolseley.'

This is clearly unjust. In the first place the engine of the 3½-hp Wolseley, which had a bore of 4½ inches and a stroke of 5 inches, was described by the makers a little later as 'giving off over 5½ hp on the brake at 750 r.p.m.', and the Wolseley was certainly not faster on all the hills, whilst its maximum speed on the level was little more than 20 mph against the Lanchester's 30 mph. The Wolseley was between 1 and 1½ miles an hour faster on the optional test hills, which are the only ones for which accurate comparable figures are to be had, simply because of these gradients the Lanchester was reduced to its low gear whereas the Wolseley had the advantage because, though in many respects a rather primative machine, it was equipped with a 3-speed gearbox. Even at that early date Austin's notoriously strange choice of gear ratios was apparent, for it is said by St. John C. Nixon, who has driven the car, that it cannot 'pull' top gear except on a dead-level or downhill road. Most of the Wolseley's running was done on its second speed, which was low-geared enough to take gradients of about 1 in 9 at 9 or 10 mph. By contrast the Lanchester's maximum speed in its hill climbing gear was about 8½ mph. Every writer who has dealt with the 1,000 Miles Trial in the past has neglected to take gear ratios and power-to-weight ratios into account.

Despite the admitted shortcomings of a 2-speed gearbox, the Lanchester had no difficulty in outstripping the Wolseley and many more powerful cars on give-and-take roads. An observer riding in one of the 12 h.p. Daimlers said: 'For company for some miles we had the Lanchester car. On the level we drove faster but uphill the Lanchester was two or three miles ahead.' He presumably meant 2 or 3 mph faster. It has also been unfortunate for the Lanchester's reputation that some tables of results, and observations on the Trial, published by Worby Beaumont in his monumental (but not infrequently tendentious) *Motor Vehicles and Motors,* which appeared late in 1900, give a bad impression of the Gold Medal Phaeton's performance.

Extract from Lanchester Motorcars. A. Bird and F. Hutton-Stott

Above:
Frederick Lanchester at the tiller of the Lanchester Gold Medal Phaeton that ran in the Thousand Mile Trial 1900 as Entry No. 22. His brother George is the passenger.
(Photo: V.C.C. Archives)

SHEFFIELD TO NOTTINGHAM

FRIDAY 11TH MAY

82½ miles via Worksop, Lincoln, Nottingham including Welbeck Park Speed Trial

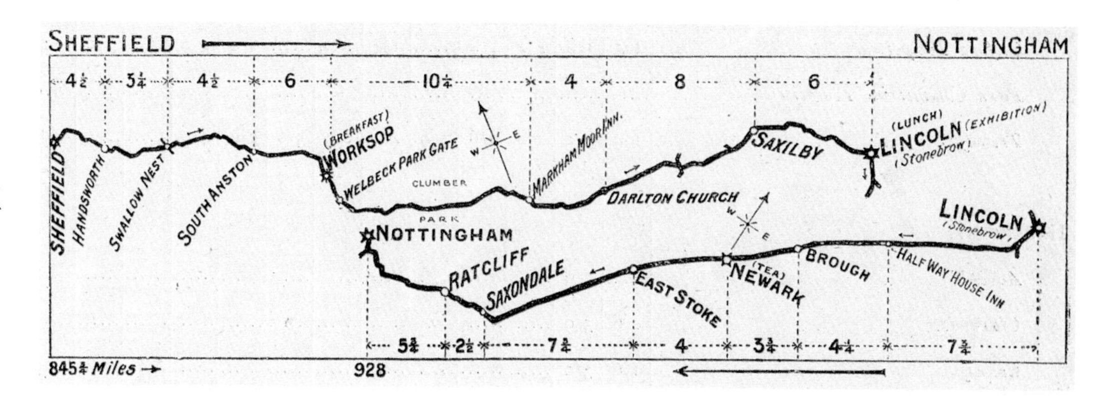

THE PARTICIPANTS were now firmly focusing on finishing the Trial; but today there was another exciting prospect on offer – a speed trial on private land at Welbeck Park. It must have been a tantalising choice – risk damage to the car at this stage in exchange for speed and glory. Several Trade entries and smaller cars played safe and did not participate. Meanwhile, the more adventurous drivers detoured to Welbeck Park.

“ Sheffield to Nottingham and the Speed Trials at Welbeck Park

Friday, May 11th, was not an attractive day so far as weather was concerned. Still it might have been worse. No rain fell but no sun appeared to warm the air, which was distinctly cold with a touch of the east in it. The absence of brightness was regrettable, as much very beautiful scenery, especially through Welbeck Park, was passed through. It was arranged that those cars entered for the speed trials should leave at an earlier hour than the touring vehicles, as a detour of some twenty miles would be taken to reach the appointed spot, the speed trial taking the form of a measured mile with flying start out and another home, the mean time of the two trials being taken, and for this purpose, by the kind permission of His Grace the Duke of Portland, a section of road within the confines of Welbeck Park had been selected and measured by the local surveyor. Our mount for the day was with the Hon. J. Scott Montagu on his twelve horse-power Daimler, No. A11, and, leaving a few minutes after seven, with Sir William Leng as passenger, we encountered exceedingly bad roads to start with, beginning with a long and steep climb out of Sheffield, in the course of which we passed Mr. Iliffe's tandem in difficulties with a split bearing cone, and after leaving the red control at a bridge at Handsworth, which cleared us from Sheffield, we all dismounted to take the car over some newly-laid stones, as a protective measure for the tyres. One or two very steep pitches were negotiated successfully, and after passing Mr. Cordingley, and with one short stoppage to relight a lamp, we traversed Worksop and arrived at the fine gates of Clumber Park, turning into which we ran some miles over the most perfect roads imaginable, and through exquisite scenery to the abbey, passing which we wended our way through several miles of lovely driving over a considerably winding and picturesque route. Finding Captain Langrishe stranded in a glen with pump trouble, we lent him our engineer, and proceeded another mile or two to a farm within a half a mile of the spot selected for the contest. Here we found Messrs. Rolls, Holder,

NOTE — An optional Speed-trial at Welbeck Park has been organised by kind permission of His Grace the Duke of Portland. The number of vehicles pemitted to take part in the trial will be limited, and owners wishing to enter their vehicles should communicate in writing with the Secretary at the Great Cenral Hotel, Sheffield, not later than 8 a.m., on Thursday, 8th May.

Official Programme

Stripping cars for action at Welbeck Park Speed Trial (*right:*) Hon. C. S. Rolls on 12 h.p. Panhard (*centre:*) Mr. Lord and his 7 h.p. Peugeot (not officially competing) (*left front:*) Hubert Egerton stepping off his De Dion. (Photo: Argent Archer)

Welbeck Park Speed Trial ready for the start (*left to right:*)
No. A3 T. B. Browne at the wheel of 6 h.p. Panhard.
No. A10 S. F. Edge at the wheel of 8 h.p.Napier, St. John Nixon in his mechanician seat and owner Mr. E. Kennard standing by the side.
No. A11 John Scott-Montagu on his 12 h.p. Daimler.
No. A2 Frank H. Butler on his 6 h.p. Panhard. Slightly behind, No. A22 Mr. J. A. Holder on his 12 h.p. Daimler.
No. A17 Hon. C. S. Rolls on his 12 h.p. Panhard,
Behind C. S. Rolls is Mr. Herbert Austin and his Wolseley and behind No. A11 are Messrs. Cheel and Newton with the Ariel Tricycle with Whippet Trailer.
(Photo: Argent Archer)

A.2
A17

Egerton, Kennard, and others waiting for us, the other entered cars coming up shortly after. Most of the owners were busily engaged in stripping their vehicles of such trifling accessories as back seats, and clearing out impedimenta in the way of petrol tins, bags, spare tyres, and other such-like items, and after checking our watch with that of Mr. Swindley, who, with us, was to act as official timekeeper, and accompanied by Lord Kingsburgh and Mr. F. T. Bidlake, who were acting as checkers upon our times, we wended our way upon the secretary's car to the trysting place, dropping Messrs. Swindley and Bidlake at the starting point, and going on to the other end of the mile ourselves. The course selected was almost straightaway, with a slight curve in the centre and a continuous rise – in one place fairly sharp – all one way, so that whilst the trial in one direction was steadily uphill, that in the other was as continuously down. Mr. Johnson having returned to the starting point, the cars were got off at half-minute intervals, and it was not many minutes before Mr. Rolls's Panhard flew by at a big rate. A minute later came the Napier, with Mr. Mayhew's Panhard following after. Then came Mr. Montagu, closely followed by Mr. Cheel's tricycle and trailer, which had picked up so much of the half-minute allowance on the big car that when the latter, not knowing of their proximity, stopped rather suddenly, there was nearly a collision, the tricycle just squeezing by between the front of the car and the hedge. We were then treated to quite an interesting finish, Mr. Browne's Panhard, Mr. Egerton's De Dion, and the Gladiator No. 16 making almost a tie of it, finishing within fractions of a second of each other, at one point of the course the Gladiator pulling out on to the grass to get by, but falling back again. No other special incident occurred in the run, and when Mr. Lord's Peugeot was brought up, the cars were turned and started on their downward journey, this time with minute intervals to avoid complications, and it was a rare sight to see the pace got up by some of the larger cars, especially that of Mr. Rolls, which flew the mile at better than forty-two and a half miles per hour. The times recorded by the various vehicles entered for the trials were as follows:

Placing	*No. of Car*	*Description*	*Time uphill*		*Time downhill*		*Meantime*		*Average hour of meantime*	*Average per hour of down hill time*	
			M.	*S.*	*M.*	*S.*	*M.*	*S.*			
1	A17	Hon. C. S. Rolls's 12 h.p. Panhard	1	46⅘	1	24¾	1	35⅗	37.63	42.55	
2	A4	Mr. Mark Mayhew's 8 h.p. Panhard	2	17⅗	1	45⅘	2	1⅗	29.60	34.02	
	A10	Mr. Kennard's 8 h.p. Napier	2	16	1	47⅖	2	1⅗	29.60	33.51	
3	4	Ariel tricycle with Whippet trailer	*2	11⅕	1	53⅕	2	2⅕	29.45	31.80	* Both riders pedalling
4	A22	Mr. J. A. Holder's 12 h.p. Daimler	2	34	2	0⅖	2	17⅕	26.23	29.90	
5	A11	Hon. John Scott Montagu's 12 h.p. Daimler	2	38⅕	1	57⅘	2	18	26.08	30.56	
6	39	† Century tandem tricycle	2	34⅗	2	24⅗	2	29⅖	24.09	24.93	† Two riders
7	16	3¼ h.p. Gladiator voiturette	2	48⅝	2	22⅛	2	35⅗	23.16	25.31	
8	A31	Mr. Johnson's 6 h.p. Parisian Daimler	3	1⅖	2	10⅘	2	36	23.07	27.52	
9	40	3 h.p. Wolseley voiturette	3	1⅕	2	14⅗	2	37⅘	22.81	26.74	
10	14	3 h.p. De Dion voiturette	2	54⅕	2	33⅘	2	44	21.70	26.00	
11	A3	Mr. T. B. Browne's 6 h.p. Panhard	3	26	2	12⅖	2	49⅕	21.27	27.19	
	A2	Mr. Butler's 6 h.p. Panhard	3	10⅕	‡2	28⅕	2	49⅕	21.27	24.13	‡ With brake slightly on
12	15	3 h.p. De Dion voiturette	3	22⅘	2	47⅕	3	5	19.45	21.53	
		§ Mr. Lord's 7 h.p. Peugeot	2	45	1	58⅕	2	21⅗	26.97	30.45	§ Not officially competing

All the above trials, with the exception of those noted, were made with the driver on board 

The Autocar, Saturday, May 19th, 1900

Preparing cars for the start of Speed Trial at Welbeck Park, Mr. Herbert Austin's Wolseley No. 40: rear view of Gladiator No. 16 driven by Roland le Bars (Photo: Argent Archer)

"Sheffield to Nottingham On the Long Pilgrimage

By Observer from Motor-Car Journal

Nottingham, Friday night

Yesterday was spent at Sheffield, and whatever may be thought of the town, or its hotels, there can be no two opinions as to the hospitality of the Master Cutler and the inhabitants generally. The Automobile Club was right royally entertained, and pleasant are our memories of the great cutlery town.

The committee of gentlemen who became guarantors for the expenses of the visit of the vehicles to Sheffield showed a praiseworthy spirit; and Mr. J. T. Thompson, who filled the arduous post of hon. secretary so efficiently, worked very hard indeed for the success of the venture, sparing neither time nor money in the effort. Many other gentlemen also devoted much of their time to the affair, and it is only right to mention the names of Messrs. W. E. Cope, T. Lonsdale, Cooper Pearson, and F. B. Cauwood amongst those who volunteered for the tedious work in connection with the visit.

So far as the town itself was concerned, it was conceded by all that the tram lines must be the best laid in the whole kingdom – certainly far better laid than those of any other town through which we have passed. And seeing that we have travelled and slipped over many miles of lines we are well qualified to express an opinion. In many places the lines have been abominable – in fact, someone hazarded the opinion that they had been laid in the road and there left until the traffic had ground portions of them in just sufficiently to hold them in.

This morning the wind was cold and the 'control' was long – six miles over tramlines. All the party were punctual, and those who had entered for the racing at Welbeck Abbey had to leave at 6.30a.m. Even those least inclined to be early risers regretted the provision that kept them half-an-hour after the speedy ones had gone. A great deal of interest was taken in the departure of the vehicles, and all along the route to Westhouse Mill Station a sympathetic crowd was seen. Near the control Mr. Frank Butler on his Panhard and Mrs. Kennard driving her De Dion voiturette went by. The succeeding portions of the road were of a switchback description, one steady incline culminating in a sharp rise that caused us to engage the assistance of a few onlookers in reaching the top. In the grey morning, and standing on the top of the hill, it was a weird sight to see the town of Sheffield down in the hollow, with its tall chimney stacks belching forth volumes of smoke. During this part of the journey few cars were seen – in fact the only one that attracted attention was that of Mr. Holder, who was attending to the burners, and trying to remedy bad water circulation by the roadside.

We duly reached Worksop with the first of the Richard cars, and Mr. Mayhew's Peugeot, with Mr. A. Russell aboard and Haxton driving behind. The streets of Worksop were well lined with spectators, an ambulance attracting considerable attention. At the outward we were informed that three horses attached to a cart had run away at sight of a motor-car, and had thrown the driver, who was reported dead. That was ill news – the first of the kind heard during the Trial – and it was with something like relief that the true facts of the accident were ascertained at Lincoln. There we saw a member of the Automobile Club who had been to the hospital, whither the injured man had been taken. It appeared then that he had jumped from the cart and had received a nasty flesh wound. Fortunately it was not regarded as a serious one. As a rule there has been no difficulty in finding the breakfasting places in the towns – these being usually indicated by the police or by a break in the line of spectators – thus leading to the stable yard and hotel. But at Worksop there were no such indications, and we passed through the town to the outward control, thereby missing breakfast. Welbeck Abbey was immediately to the right, and strong was the temptation to go and see the speed trials, but we refrained. Following the instructions in the official programme, we turned to the left and made for Clumber Park. The weather had become bitterly cold, and all the sunshine had long disappeared. But the ride through Clumber Park was, perhaps, the most lovely part of the Trial; here the grass seemed more emerald than ever, and the newly-foliaged trees were simply delightful, elms full of leafage, lovely silver birches, chestnuts and maples thickly leaved and giving broad shadows, oaks and ash all growing to a beauty and height hardly to be rivalled anywhere. How Robin Hood and his merry men would have deplored the presence of so many motor-vehicles in the forest fastnesses. The motorists, however, were delighted with the country associated with so many of his famous exploits. The historic avenue of limes was traversed, and then through a broad belt of oaks we went on at our own pace. Through the well-paved water splash some of the cars dashed with impetuous rush – and their riders had a shower bath. Others who had had experience – such as is given by the Kenilworth water splash – were wiser, and by driving slowly were able to do through drily. The roads through the park were in splendid condition, and towards the Normanton Lodge gates we met one of the stiffest hills of the whole tour. The arrangements for guiding drivers were excellent, and the permission of the Duke of Newcastle to put on full speed was taken advantage of by every car.

From the water splash at Clumber to Saxilby is a distance of fourteen miles – and very different is the scenery to that through the park. Instead of forest monarchs we saw nothing but a well-cultivated stretch of farm land, dotted with cottages and farm buildings, with here and there old square towers of churches and windmills saluting us lazily as we whizzed along. The Great North Road was crossed at Markham Moor Inn, and at East Markham we crossed the railway line before getting to the river Trent. There at Dunham toll bridge arrangements had been made that vehicles engaged in the Trial should pay no toll, the club having paid a certain sum to cover all tolls. Having convinced the somewhat sceptical gatekeeper that we were of the party, we went through – the Richard car, which had been travelling in fine style, coming up and going through with us. Dunham presented a cheerful aspect with its groups of school children and labouring men waiting for the cars. ”

The Motor-Car Journal Saturday, May 19th, 1900

A bird's eye view of the fliers in Welbeck (Photo: *The Autocar*)

Despatching cars on flying start for Speed Trial at Welbeck Park. (Photo: Argent Archer)

AUTO-CAR TRIALS.

SPEED TEST ON A MEASURED MILE.

FROM OUR AUTO-CAR EXPERT.

NOTTINGHAM, Friday Night.

At last it has been made possible to show the full capacities of an auto-car without interference from the police. The Duke of Portland, good sportsman that he is, not only permitted us to drive through his magnificent park at Welbeck to-day without restriction of speed, but even to hold a time test over a measured mile.

A SPEED TEST.

This competition was an optional event. The competing thirteen had a glorious drive through the splendid park. We found the measured mile to be a very gentle gradient with two turns close together and a long straight stretch.

Time keepers were stationed at either end and each car was sent off on the up-grade at intervals of half a minute. They waited at the opposite end until all the competitors had finished the first mile, then each was started at half-minute intervals on the down-grade, and when the times of each competitor for the double journey had been obtained they were halved.

The results were as follows:—

	MIN.	SEC.
Hon. C. S. Rolls' Panhard	1	35 3-5
Mr. Kennard's Napier, and Mr. Mayhew's Panhard	2	1 3-5
Ariel Tricycle and Trailer	2	[illegible]
Mr. [illegible] Daimler	2	17 1-5
Hon. J. S. Montagu's Daimler	2	18
[illegible] Tandem	2	23 2-5
Gladiator Voiturette	2	[illegible]
[illegible] Daimler	2	36
[illegible] Voiturette	2	37 4-5
De Dion Voiturette	2	44
Mr. [illegible] Panhard	2	[illegible] 1-5
Mr. Browne's Panhard	2	40 1-5
Another de Dion Voiturette	3	[illegible]

Mr. Rolls' time on the up-grade was 1min. 46 4-5sec., and on the down 1min. [illegible] 3-5sec., the latter being equal to a rate of 42½ miles an hour.

THE FIRST ACCIDENT.

To-day's run was marred by the only accident to a human being which has yet occurred throughout the tour, and even in this case the fault was not that of the automobilists. Not far from Worksop the Ariel tricycle and trailer was overtaking a big waggon, which, though empty, had a team of three horses.

About fifty yards away Mr. Cheel, who drove the tricycle, sounded his horn, and immediately the horses ran away with the waggon, and pulled the waggoner down. He fell under the wheels, and Mr. Cheel immediately rode off for a doctor, and fetched him to the spot on the trailer, the passenger having meanwhile administered brandy to the waggoner.

The doctor found on examination that no bones were broken, but ordered the injured man's removal to a hospital.

The journey, as a whole, to-day was even more than usually successful, the roads being excellent, and intense enthusiasm being displayed along the line of route from Sheffield to Nottingham, 82½ miles long.

At Lincoln the local committee entertained the visitors to lunch, and the Mayor presided. Several hours were devoted to an exhibition in St. Swithin's-square. Being market day, the town was packed with sightseers.

From Lincoln to Nottingham, a distance of twenty miles, Mr. Graham White's car was driven in excellent style by a lady, and at top speed.

Above:
Photo by kind permission of N.M.M. Beaulieu (Photo: Elizabeth Bennett)

The Hon. C. S. Rolls, needless to say, was one of those who opted to run at Welbeck, and he won by a good margin. Mark Mayhew's 8 h.p. Panhard and S. F. Edge driving the 8 h.p. Napier tied for second place while Edwin Cheel's Ariel tricycle, with pedal-assistance from both riders, and the fourteen-year-old St. John Nixon (lent by the Kennard-Edge team for the occasion) in the trailer, came in third! The local constabulary was in attendance (to ensure fair play?).

What the Newspapers said ...

Pasted into Montague Grahame-White's personal scrapbook is a newspaper report (we are not told from which paper) (see right)

'From our Auto-Car Expert'
Nottingham, Friday night. *(May 11th 1900)*

This describes the Speed Trial at Welbeck Park over the measured mile. It was a first of it's kind for England, and generated much excitement amongst the drivers, after so many days of keeping to the speed limits (maximum 12 mph, with 8 mph in towns). Now they could really see whose car would go fastest!

Perhaps, as was becoming predictable, The Hon. C. S. Rolls would take the honours. The true battle that day and throughout the Trial was for second place!

The Autocar correspondent continues his story after the Welbeck Park Speed Trial.

"Upon retracing our steps for the return journey we again came across Captain Langrishe – whose mishap had put him out of the trials – and stopped to make enquiries. The pump had been disabled by the coming out of a screw which had ground a channel in the side of the pump case and let all the water out, and they were just finishing one of the smartest makeshift jobs we have seen, the pump being patched up and made watertight by means of canvas and red lead, backed up by small pieces of wood wired into position, and with this improvised arrangements they eventually completed the day's run after two hours' delay. Turning from this point we took a short cut towards the main road, having on one steep drop to pull up rather sharply to prevent running over Mrs. Kennard's voiturette, the noise of which prevented her hearing our horns sounded behind. At one part of the run the road took us across a wide ford with probably 6in. of water running over it. We eased up and crawled through slowly. Not so Mr. Mayhew's car which preceded us, and which carried Mr. Bidlake on the footboard, which went through at full speed, the while the mudguardless front wheel threw a beautiful cascade into Bidlake's shoes. The Wolseley car, which was following us, also came through at full speed, and the water splashing up on the exhaust box enveloped her in a cloud of steam. A little later on Mr. Mayhew was passed in difficulties with a punctured tyre, and Messrs. Holder and Edge went by us, the former giving us his dust for some miles, and we had scarcely joined the main road ere a whiff of steam in front denoted the proximity of one of the steam cars, and we shortly found it to be the Brown-Whitney, steaming steadily along at a moderate pace. The Marshall car No. 49 was overhauled shortly after, and then began a chase after the other cars, which were overhauled steadily one by one until our accelerator cord broke, which necessitated a couple of minutes' stoppage, in spite of which we entered the Lincoln control one minute only behind Mr. Holder, our

The cars will, by kind permission of the Mayor and Corporation, be exhibited in St. Swithin's Square, and leave the Exhibition Area at 3.45 p.m. punctually, in the order in which they arrived at Lincoln.

187

1,000-Mile Trial.

LINCOLN,

FRIDAY, 11th MAY, 1900.

AN

EXHIBITION

OF THE

MOTOR VEHICLES

TAKING PART IN THE

1,000-Mile Trial organized by the Automobile Club of Great Britain,

WILL BE HELD IN

ST. SWITHIN'S SQUARE,

By kind permission of THE MAYOR AND CORPORATION,

FROM 1 P.M. TO 3.45 P.M.

A PUBLIC LUNCHEON will be given to the Members of the Automobile Club and the Owners of the Cars taking part in the Run.

The following Gentlemen act as an Honorary Local Committee, to deal with the arrangements in Lincoln and district:—

President:—The Mayor, Ald. J. G. Williams.

Vice-President:—The Ex-City Sheriff, Mr. J. H. Foster.

Messrs. J. H. Foster, T. E. Foster, W. S. White, H. D. B. Ayliffe, Vesey Brown, C.E. F. Brown, J. D. Goy, C. Nelson, C. H. Gilbert, W. Gilbert, G. Lowe, W. Pask, C. E. Wilso W. Cottam, W. Rasdall, W. C. Sneath, W. C. White, J. W. Enderby, F. S. Chambe F. Morris (Lynn), F. Jecock-Heinle, J. Bamber (Gainsborough), Dr. Cragg (Billingborough Dr. A. P. Russel, Dr. Reville (Heighington), C. Holland (Boston), H. Hudson (Newto Williamson Bros. (Retford), R. M. Wright, J. McKerchar, Nainby (Thorganby), W. C. Marty W. F. Bett, F. White, W. B. Surfleet, W. Hall, C. E. Wilson, and

Mr. R. B. Wrenford, National Provincial Bank of England, Lincoln, *Hon. Treasurer.*

"Gazette" and "Echo" Office, Lincoln, *Hon. Secretary.*

Leaving Lincoln
Sidney Straker's Char-à-banc and two International Victoria's Nos. 41 and 44
(Photo: Argent Archer)

car having been running very much better during the latter part of the journey than at the commencement.

Automotor Journal – Tolls

Dunham – (Lincoln) – The Toll-keepers was in the habit of charging 4/- per vehicle; but at the request of the Club, and in consequence of the energetic action of the Hon. Sec. at Lincoln (who presented the toll-keeper with a letter stating that unless a more reasonable charge were made the club would abandon that road) it is believed that the toll-keeper will accept a sum equivalent to 4d per wheel.

During the mid-day halt at Lincoln, the clubmen and others taking part in the tour were entertained to luncheon at the Saracen's Head Hotel, the Mayor of Lincoln occupying the chair. His Worship was supported by Councillor J. H. Foster, Mr. Edmund Turner, Lord Kingsburgh, the Hon. Jno. Scott-Montagu, the Hon. C. S. Rolls, C. Johnson, Henry Sturmey, Colonel McGrath, and others. After the Queen had been duly honoured, the Mayor, in brief but kindly terms, proposed success to the A.C.G.B., and referred in terms of admiration to the great tour which they had so successfully planned and carried out. He was sure that what had been done would go far to educate the people of England and Scotland in the new method of locomotion.

The Hon. Jno. Scott-Montagu, M.P., referred to the pleasure it gave them all to visit the ancient city of Lincoln, and to the gratitude they felt for the warm welcome they had received. Mr. Johnson, who was most warmly received, then gave the health of the 'Local Committee,' and referred specifically to the earnest work performed by the hon sec., Mr. Wilkinson. The Mayor and Mr. Councillor Foster briefly replied, and then the company parted to take the road to Nottingham.

Getting under weigh again, we found that our detour for the speed trial had placed a considerable number of the cars in front of us, so that when we eventually started in our turn, as the motor was going at her best and we were rolling off something very close on thirty over the fine straightaway roads which we now traversed, we overhauled rapidly car after car, Mr. Rolls, however, who had started behind us, giving us the go-by a couple of miles out. Mr. Straker, with the Daimler char-a-banc, was passed adjusting a little later, and shortly afterwards the New Orleans No. 28 was likewise encountered stopped. Next at the bottom of a steep slope, car No. 31 stopped immediately in front of us, and a little later on a farm waggon was seen upon the grass at the roadside with two horses tandem, the front one down, apparently the result of a scare from one of the earlier cars. The horse scrambled to his feet as we passed, and we ran into Newark in twenty-six and a half minutes for the fourteen miles between the controls. At Newark there was a stop for tea, and at the outward control Mr. Siddeley was struggling with a tyre, whilst Mr. Grahame-White was seen getting under weigh with a lady at the helm, and handling the car, too, in a masterly fashion. The majority of the cars were now behind us, and the Richard car No. 46 was passed in difficulties a few miles out, whilst the M.M.C. car No. 8 was seen hung up with a punctured tyre. No. 32 was passed stopped on a hill, and large numbers of cyclists who had come out from Nottingham were met at every corner, whilst the good people of the lace town assembled in considerable crowds to greet the arriving autocars, which were finally stored for the night and placed on exhibition in the carriage repository, which proved the most cramped quarters we were located in during the tour. Here the cars were arranged on one side with their backs to the wall, and 18in. space between each car. When one side

of the space had been filled. Others as they came in were placed head to tail close to the opposite wall, leaving a space of about four feet for the perambulation of the public, and when the cars filled up the entire yard about a dozen of the later comers were placed on a lift and carried upstairs to an upper floor. Most of the cars, with the exception of what has already been recorded, appear to have covered the day's run without incident, save that Mr. Coles's Benz car No. 2 reported the breaking of a front axle, the broken part, however, being promptly replaced by a spare one carried on

Leaving the Control Lincoln (*right to left:*) No. A23 Charles Cordingley MMC. No. 2 A. J. Coles Benz. Today this car suffered a broken front axle, which was promptly replaced by a spare one carried on board.
(Photo: Argent Archer)

board, so that the delay experienced was not great. Happily no other damage accrued, though the shock considerably strained the vehicle and affected its running on the following day. Mrs. Kennard, however, had perhaps the most exciting experience of any to record, for in endeavouring to avoid a cart on the tram rails of Lincoln her De Dion voiturette had completely turned turtle. Although neither car nor occupants appeared much the worse for the mishap, we fear both suffered somewhat from the shock.”

The Autocar, Saturday, May 19th, 1900

"*The Motor-Car Journal* notes that on arrival in Lincoln many motor-vehicles had come out to meet us, and one funny little affair resembling a varnished box on wheels, and driven by an air-cooled motor, made us curious as to its capacity to travel. We had been going strong when suddenly, without a word of warning, our motor stopped dead. The Richard car, which had fallen slightly behind, passed and had got about a dozen yards ahead when it, too, stopped without notice. Nothing wrong could be found with our motor, and we started again after ascertaining that a plug on the Richard car had broken. Then we went straight into the ancient cathedral city, where a large number of motor-vehicles were to be seen – principally of the Benz, Star, and Marshall types, the Daimler not being so well represented.

We were first into Lincoln and in good time, Mr. Siddeley's Parisian being second, followed by an Iveagh phaeton, the other cars following in quick succession. The first of the cars that had been engaged in the speed tests came in in a cold, drizzling rain.

At Lincoln the cars were on exhibition in St Swithin's Square, the automobilists being entertained to luncheon by the mayor and the local committee at the Saracen's Head Hotel – an incident of the run that was greatly appreciated after the morning's trip. Then we started for Nottingham, the run being only broken by a halt at Newark for tea. Shortly after leaving Lincoln we noticed marks on the road which showed that some car, in taking the corner sharply, had slipped straight across the road and had managed to pull up at the edge of a ditch. The roads were rather dusty, but in good condition, and we were welcomed by long lines of people into Nottingham, a steep ascent from the Market Place leading to Starey's Repository in Parliament Street, where the cars were on exhibition in the evening. All seemed glad that the Trial was so nearly at an end, and we were pleased to see that Mr. Pedley, who had been left behind ill at Birmingham, had turned up at Nottingham feeling much better."

The Motor-Car Journal, Saturday, May 19th, 1900

1,000-Mile Trial. 193

NOTTINGHAM,

FRIDAY, 11th MAY, 1900.

AN EVENING

EXHIBITION

OF THE

MOTOR VEHICLES

TAKING PART IN THE

1,000-Mile Trial of the Automobile Club,

WILL BE HELD IN THE

REPOSITORY, NOTTINGHAM,

Open 5 p.m. to 10 p.m.

ADMISSION - - SIXPENCE.

THE PROFITS WILL BE GIVEN TO THE TRANSVAAL WAR FUND.

Local Committee.

Mr. H. Belcher.
„ H. Kirk.
„ J. B. Snook.
„ G. Cowen (*Hon. Treasurer*).
„ M. Ross Brown.

Mr. F. B. Whitty.
„ G. Rimington.
„ G. G. Hardy.
„ G. Kay.
„ B. Winter.

Mr. Dunford.
„ T. Sharpe.
„ F. Stanhope.
„ H. Rimington.

Hon. Secretary—Mr. H. Rimington.

N

"Mr. Grierson had a lively experience with one of the De Dion voiturettes when running to Nottingham on Friday last. With the idea of 'going for' some boys who were throwing caps, he applied the brakes somewhat quickly, getting up at the same time, with the result that he was thrown out in front of the car, which passed right over him, fortunately without any serious result.

Mrs. Malaprop is still alive in the land. on Friday evening, when he arrived at Nottingham, Mr. Searle found the boiler of his Locomobile priming badly, and mentioning the matter to another member of the party, and opining also that the cause thereby was oil in the boiler, he was advised to seek a chemist and procure from him half a pound of caustic soda, to put this in the boiler, and then blow it out. Accordingly, next morning he sought the caustic soda, but as the tour started at seven, it was somewhat early to expect to find shops open, so approaching the landlady he blandly said in his most dulcet tones, 'Could you direct me to a chemist where I would be likely to get some caustic soda?' but he was not prepared for the reply which he received, which was in equally dulcet tones somewhat to this effect, 'It is hardly likely you will get anything from a chemist at this early hour of the morning, but if it will be of any use to you, I could let you have a *Seidlitz powder*.' Tableau!"

The Autocar, Saturday, May 19th, 1900

NOTTINGHAM TO LONDON

SATURDAY 12TH MAY

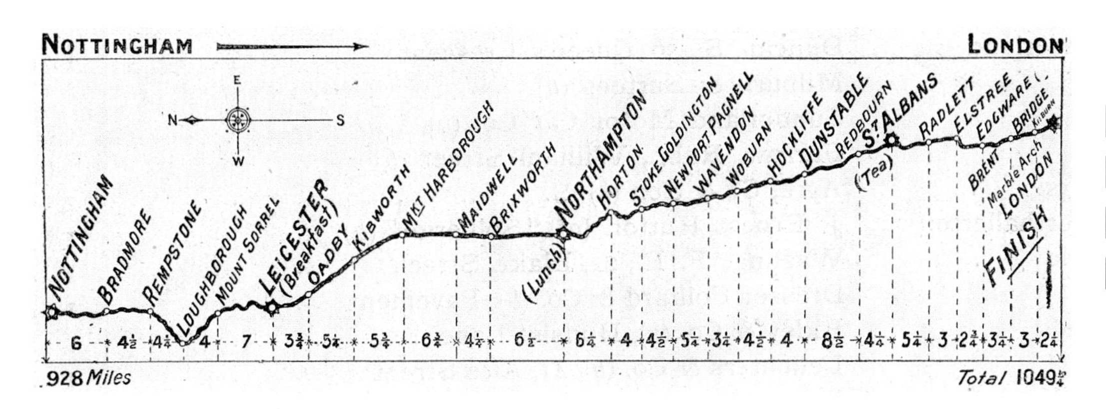

123½ miles via Loughborough, Leicester, Northampton, to London

The Last Driving Day

Nottingham to London and Home

With characteristic thoroughness the Automobile Club had arranged that the last day's run should be the longest, the distance from Nottingham to the Club in London being 123½ miles. Naturally the members of the touring party hoped for a bright day to finish with, but they were disappointed, and in point of weather the 12th of May was the most unpleasant of the whole trip, for it was bitterly cold throughout, with an east wind blowing and light rain falling the greater part of the morning, and although dry roads were experienced towards the close of the run, the driving in the earlier part of the day was exceedingly heavy, and the autocarists required all the leather clothing and wraps they could muster to keep decently comfortable. For our own part, our seat for the day was on car No. 9, one of the Motor Manufacturing Co.'s Iveagh phaetons, with six horse-power Daimler engine, built on the lines of our old 'John-o'-Groater,' and save that the springs had 'gone down' a bit during the run, and occasionally let us down on the frame when passing over crossings or extra large road obstacles, provided most comfortable travelling and enabled us to keep ourselves snug and dry without any trouble or worry about wraps getting into chains, etc. We were four on board all of us more or less heavyweights, our passengers including, besides ourselves, Mr. Schofield, of the Motor Manufacturing Co., and Mr. Freeston, the latter, with us, occupying the snuggery at the back. On arrival at the depot, we found the cars being got out of their cramped positions as rapidly as possible, and promptly at seven, retracing our steps over the Trent Bridge and taking the Loughborough Road, we found ourselves at the outward control. Whilst waiting there Mr. Cordingley shot the control, but we had him passed in the first mile, whilst Mr. Holder on his twelve horse-power Daimler sent us to the rear on the first long hill, and Mr. Stocks and his tandem flew by us on the long down grade on the other side, the Richard No. 46 also passing us at the foot of Bunny Hill. This proved a bit of a teaser, and we saw some fun, as also did the numerous cyclists who had assembled for the purpose at the top. There were several cars in front of us, and Stocks and his passenger quickly dismounted and assisted their mount by shoving. Mr. Friswell's seven horse-power Peugeot likewise required the unloading of the passengers; No. 46 also lightened its load, though not to the same extent; and, somewhat to our surprise, Mr. Montagu's twelve horse-power Daimler, just in front of us, was seen with all passengers out and their shoulders to the wheels, or, rather, to the car. Then came our own turn. We went at the hill, slowed to the bottom speed, the motor hesitated, and the car, in lieu of spragging, was quickly placed across the road, the while we three passengers speedily dismounted, and then she went on her way without trouble with the driver up. ”

The Autocar, Saturday, May 19th, 1900

No. 9, one of the Motor Manufacturing Co.'s Iveagh Phaetons

“ The 1,000 Miles Trial

Bunny Hill Climb

Mr. C. H. Guest and Mr. H. Belcher have favoured us with reports of the manner in which the cars which took part in the 1,000 miles trial climbed 'Bunny Hill,' outside Nottingham. As this was an unexpected hill for all but a few of the drivers, it was, from a spectator's point of view, more interesting than most of the others. The performances of the cars on this particular ascent,which was as steep as anything encountered on the tour, are classified as follow, the observations being taken at the steepest hill as the cars passed:

Very good —

5 The Locomobile Co.'s steam carriage, 2 passengers

Nicely —

A3 Mr. T. B. Browne's 6 h.p. Panhard, 3 passengers

Steady —

The Marshall 5 h.p. carriage, 2 passengers

Well —

A17 Hon. C.S. Rolls's 12 h.p. Panhard, 3 passengers
A10 Mr. Edward Kennard's 8 h.p. Napier, 4 passengers
A25 Mrs. Bazalgette's 3 h.p. Benz Ideal, 2 passengers
A2 Mr. Frank Butler's 6 h.p. Panhard, 3 passengers
A22 Mr. J. A. Holder's 12 h.p. Daimler, 4 passengers
46 Automobile Mfg. Co.'s 7 h.p. Richard car, 4 passengers
36 6 h.p. Daimler, 4 passengers
A23 Mr. C. Cordingley's 6¼ h.p. M.M.C. phaeton, 2 passengers
15 3 h.p. De Dion voiturette, 2 passengers
A21 Mr. E. Pitman's 6 h.p. Daimler, 2 passengers
8 Motor Mfg. Co.'s 6 h.p. phaeton, 3 passengers
A20 Mr. Herbert Ashby's 2¾ h.p. Express motor tricycle, 1 passenger
40 Wolseley voiturette, 3 h.p., 2 passengers
44 3 h.p. International Victoria, 2 passengers
A4 Mr. M. Mayhew's 8 h.p. Panhard, 3 passengers
35 6 h.p. Daimler, 3 passengers
A30 Mr. J. D. Siddeley's 6 h.p. Parisian Daimler, 2 passengers
31 M.M.C. 3½ h.p. Triumph, 1 passenger
38 Daimler 9½ h.p. public service vehicle, 8 passengers
A26 Mr. C. H. Gregson's 6 h.p. Daimler, 3 passengers
37 6 h.p. Daimler Parisian, 3 passengers

Easy —

22 8 h.p. Lanchester carriage, 1 passenger

Tacked up —

47 Automobile Mfg. Co.'s 7 h.p. Richard car, 1 passenger
A24 Mr. R. E. Phillip's 4 h.p. Mors Petit Duc, 2 passengers

Shed passengers to ease or help push —

A11 Hon. J. S. Montagu's 12 h.p. Daimler, 4 passengers
9 Motor Mfg. Co.'s 6 h.p. Iveagh phaeton, 2 passengers
12 Motor Mfg. Co.'s 2¼h.p. tricycle, 1 passenger
27 Burford, Van Toll, and Co.'s 3 h.p. New Orleans, 2 passengers
28 Burford, Van Toll, and Co.'s 3 h.p. New Orleans, 2 passengers
1 Benz 3 h.p. Ideal, 2 passengers
34 Motor Car Co.'s 3½h.p. Decauville, 2 passengers
16 Motor Power Co.'s 3¼ h.p. Gladiator voiturette, 2 passengers
24 5 h.p. Marshall carriage, 2 passengers
41 3 h.p. International Victoria, 2 passengers
14 3 h.p. De Dion voiturette, 2 passengers
11 Motor Mfg. Co.'s 4½ h.p. Princess car, 2 passengers
Also an unnumbered tandem quad, with 2 passengers

Stuck —

4 2¼ Ariel tricycle, with Whippet trailer, 2 passengers
26 8 h.p. Peugeot, 2 passengers
3 3⅛ h.p.Ariel quadicycle, 2 passengers
A29 Mr. M. Mayhew's 7 h.p. Peugeot, 2 passengers
51 Star voiturette, 3½ h.p., 2 passengers
A12 Mr. Henry Edmund's 6 h.p. Daimler, 3 passengers
2 3 h.p. Benz Ideal, 1900 pattern, 2 passengers
Also two unnumbered tricycles with one passenger each.

Shed and stuck —

33 Motor Car Co.'s 3½h.p. Decauville, 1 passenger 

The Autocar, Saturday, May 19th, 1900

Correspondence

The Bunny Hill Climb

We note in this week's issue of *The Autocar* a report made by Messrs. C. H. Guest and H. Belcher on the Bunny Hill climb outside Nottingham, giving the performances of the cars on this particular ascent. In the observations stated to have been the steepest part of the hill as the cars passed, we are classified under the head 'stuck.'

I most emphatically state the Star car did not stick on the hill, or any other hill throughout the run.

Trusting you will find room in your paper to publish this letter in contradiction of the report above referred to.

The Star Cycle Co., Ltd, E. Lisle May 25th

After Bunny Hill (*continued from page 281*)

"A long run down on the other side, with a sharp rise at the finish, brought us into the village of Rempstone, turning into which the strong smell of hot metal told of pump trouble, and, pulling up just round the corner, we found that all our water had vanished. Investigation showed that one of the screws at the back of the pump had come out, thus providing an aperture through which the whole of our water had quietly leaked. The operation of taking off and replacing the pump and filling up again with water occupied us something over an hour, during the greater portion of which it poured steadily, and all the other cars in the run went by us in procession, the Eureka car at 8.45, closely followed by the Brown-Whitney, whilst Mr. Iliffe's tandem made its appearance at nine o'clock, having started late owing to the necessity of completing repairs in the matter of the broken cone before alluded to. We were now right at the tail of the crowd, and many were the speculations as to whether we should reach St. Albans in time to run in with the first detachment – which were timed to leave that place at five. However, the pump difficulty settled, the motor pulled right merrily, and the car ran steadily without a hitch throughout the rest of the day. Mr. Iliffe was passed in Loughborough, and car No. 29 about a mile beyond, whilst we overhauled the Whitney steamer going through Mount Sorrel, and began to feel as if we were on a flier once more. Just inside the Leicester control the New Orleans car (No. 28) was standing, and we had not travelled far within the control, taking the usual pace of eight to ten miles per hour, when a policeman and a flag-holding official suddenly darted at us and called for a four miles an hour pace. We tried to keep to it, but it was crawling. At Leicester an hour and a half were allowed for breakfast and a one hour's exhibition in the yard of the Bell Hotel. Although all the leaders had, by the time of our arrival here, taken their departure, there were still quite a number of cars in the yard, amongst them Captain Langrishe, who reported having lost his way in Nottingham and having been further delayed by pump trouble, the new pump which had been fitted during the night in place of the patched-up one which carried him through the day before having developed a bent spindle. The Motor Manufacturing car No. 8 reported a punctured tyre, and Mr. Coles had been travelling slowly on account of stiff steering, as the result of his breakdown on the previous day, whilst Mr. Johnson, who had not passed us with the others when we were stranded, was reported 'hung up' with some clutch or gear shaft trouble just out of Nottingham. For our part, mindful of the lost hour and a quarter, we stayed at the exhibition but half an hour, and, the rain having obliterated our record card, had no difficulty in getting through the outward control, to which we travelled in the company of two or three other cars, Mr. Gregson leading. Whenever a policeman was encountered, the cars were slowed to an exact four miles an hour. The police in most cases said 'go on,' but Mr. Gregson was inexorable, and the police were shown what four miles an hour meant, and informed the reason why.

We had scarcely got through the control when car No. 8, which had been in front of us, stopped, the while one of its tyres exploded with a loud report, and Mr. Butler was also passed within the control wrestling with the same difficulty. On getting under weigh once more, our car was running well, and No. 12 tricycle was overtaken four miles out. Mr. Edmunds and Mr. Gregson, on their six horse-power Daimlers, were likewise overhauled up the next hill, and a little later on the De Dion No. 14 was in difficulties, and Mr. Phillips, with his 'Pretty Duck' – as some of the irreverent ones christened his 'Petit Duc' – was likewise seen temporarily stranded. Then we overhauled the Parisian Daimler No. 37 with Mr. Pedley once more driving, and reporting the car going very poorly, and at the top of the same hill Mr. Butler, who had repaired his damaged tyre, and whose Panhard was going grandly, went by us at a most respectable speed. Mr. Egerton, on his De Dion, was the next to pass us, whilst we, in our turn, once again overhauled the Brown-Whitney, which had not stopped at all at Leicester, and Mr. Cordingley was once more passed by the road-side shortly before reaching Market Harborough, just out of which place Buck, on the Motor Mfg. Co.'s tricycle No. 12, went by us up a steep hill pedalling very strongly, but stopped at the top, arrived at which point we found Mr. Lord (Peugeot) waiting for a chat with Messrs. Staner, W. C. Iliffe, and Leechman, who had bicycled over through wind and wet from Coventry, and had selected this point of vantage for observing the performances of the cars. We also stopped a few minutes to compare notes, and then headed once more for Northampton. A few miles further on, at the top of a hill, Mr. Johnson, who had evidently put matters right, went by

The gentleman stands as the lady prepares to sit upon the car.
May 12th 1900 – Last day.
(Photo: Friswell Private collection by kind permission of P.H.H.)

us steadily, and at a railway crossing No. 44 International, in charge of Mr. Billing, who had taken her in hand after Mr. Capellan's mishap, was overtaken. Mr. Lord with his Peugeot showed us his back wheels up a strong gradient, car No. 28 was passed, 'adjusting,' a mile and a half beyond Brixworth, and we ran into Northampton in good time for lunch. The cars here were for the dinner hour placed in the carriage repository of Mr. A. F. Mulliner, the overflowing vehicles being accommodated in the yard of the Lamb, the while Mr. Mulliner hospitably carried off many of the party, including ourselves, to his house for luncheon. Here we learned that Mr. Johnson's trouble had been due to a change of quality in the spirit, requiring readjustment of the firing tubes. From Northampton on we experienced much better roads. The rain had ceased, the roads were drier, and as there was no dust, the travelling was excellent, and, but for the cold, cheerless aspect of the skies and the keen air, would have been exceedingly enjoyable. From here to Newport Pagnell the running was excellent. Mr. Mayhew, with his eight horse-power Panhard, went by us seven miles out, but a few miles further on was seen stranded with a punctured tyre, and we ran into Newport in good time, having averaged the run from Northampton at seventeen and a half miles an hour, not at all bad travelling for a solid-tyred touring car with four heavy-weights on board. In Hockliffe we slowed down and waited whilst a funeral procession passed, during which Mr. Johnson, who had left Northampton late, came up, and several local Benz cars were encountered: Mr. Mann, with his Marshall car, was overhauled on the long steady rise into Redbourne, whilst Messrs. Harvey Ducros and C. Sangster, on an Ariel tricycle and trailer, flew by us at a great pace just as we entered St. Alban's control, which we did at 4.7 p.m., Mr. Rolls having arrived at 1.34 p.m. Some twenty or thirty cars were already there, for the most part reporting uneventful runs, save Mr. Holder, who had experienced a couple of punctures, and had gone five miles out of his way. The order at St. Alban's was that the leaders should wait until five o'clock, at which time all cars which had then arrived should proceed at a moderate pace to town, and so finish in close procession, and this was done, the route taking us through the somewhat narrow lanes to

No. A22 J. A. Holder's 12 h.p. Daimler and No. A3 T. B. Browne's 6 h.p. Panhard parked outside Public Benefit Boot Co. and W. Price Wines and Spirits near the Pea Hen Hotel and Pea Hen Stables – London Road St. Albans. (Photo: Friswell Private collection by kind permission of P.H.H.)

Radlett and Elstree. Unfortunately, however, for the comfort of the party and their subsequent appearance on entering London, they apparently had had no rain for some time over this district, and the roads were, as a consequence, very dusty, while the passage of so many pneumatic tyres within the narrow confines of the lanes raised such a cloud of dust that we could scarcely see one another. One or two stoppages for restive horses helped to divide us up, many by mutual consent, after a mile or two of dusty travelling, we rode in a somewhat more open order to avoid at least a little of it until Elstree was reached, where Dr. Acworth was seen with his steamer. Shortly after this Mr. Holder fell out of line with another punctured tyre, but he was up again with the crowd ere we filed into London, which we did in close order, reaching the club at 6.50 p.m., the first batch of cars finishing, as stated above, being the following:

Mr. Rolls, Mr. Kennard, Mr. Cheel's tricycle and trailer, the Richard No. 46, Mr. Mayhew's Peugeot, Mr. Siddeley, the Century tandem, M.C.C. Triumph No. 31, Mr. Stocks on the Ariel quad., Mr Montagu, the Wolseley car, Mr. Ashby's tricycle, Mr. Critchley's Daimler, Dubois and the Decauville No. 34, Mr. Richardson's Daimler, Mr. Friswell, the Richard No. 47, Mr. T. B. Browne, Mr. Butler, Mr. Egerton's De Dion, Mr. Pitman, Mr. Johnson, No. 11 Princess (last day's run only), New Orleans No. 27, M.M.C. Iveagh phaeton No. 9, Mr. Mann's Marshall No. 49, Mr. Mayhew's Panhard, Mr. Pedley's Daimler, Mr. Holder, and the Star.

All these reported good runs for the day, with the exception of the incidents already recorded, and Mr. Coles was said to be stranded with a motor bracket broken between Leicester and Northampton. Most of the cars reaching town by eight o'clock would have qualified for their twelve miles an hour average, and during the evening the following cars registered in the order named: 37, A25, A24, 41, 1, A7, 8, A28, A12, and 32, all these getting in to their twelve miles an hour average, the following additional cars also registering in during the evening: 14, 5, 2, 28, 33, 24, 38, A23, and A26.

On Monday all the cars which ran through the trials were run down to the Crystal Palace, where they have been on view during the week, and will remain there until this (Saturday) evening. ”

The Autocar, Saturday, May 19th, 1900

“How the Last Car Came to Town

By the Deserter

We live in an age of ever-hastening activity and unceasing rush. The motor-car is generally regarded as the embodiment in metal of this characteristic of the century, a monster that goes throbbing through quiet villages and snorting through busy streets with the impartiality of the plague, disturbing sylvan quietness and adding to urban noise. It has been known to go at a pace that no word of police authority could retard, and even in connection with the Great Trial, which was to test the vehicle and not record its speed, chronicles of a mile in four minutes have been told in private conversation. These things distress the easy-going man with a respect for law – and a wife and family. And when commissioned to go to Nottingham and faithfully describe the journey from that busy town, I felt ill at ease, for had I not been used to the familiar cabs and other creeping and crawling things? Mustering courage, and taking a railway ticket, I journeyed to the town from whence come lace curtains, determining to get there before the cars, and select a nice, quiet, steady, sober, and respectable motor-carriage on which to enter London in dignity and in a state of completeness. For those fast machines are monsters. Did not one shed a passenger, and another cause a sheep to flutter into muttonness? And are they not demoralising in making men believe that ‘things (i.e. speeds) are not what they seem’?

Presently the cars arrived – in a style that would have been useful had they been going to a fire. But I was not concerned just then with futurity, and, as I have said, was on the look-out for a machine that was quiet on the road, easy in its internals, safe on its extremities, and not likely to exceed a jog-trot speed. I didn't object to jibbing – provided such antics did not take place in market places and amidst assemblies of people. For there are ribald multitudes who seek to find amusement in the automobile that won't go at all, and wily policeman on the look-out for those that have learned the secret of accelerated motion. Three or four steady cars were pointed out – some had lost nuts, bolts, and minor accessories, and, although thus deformed, were useful. It is not always the spick and span that serves mankind. The old family cat, with eyes

Crowds gather at London Road St. Albans.to welcome the heros – Sir David Salomons (*centre car*) amongst them (Photo: Friswell Private collection by kind permission of P.H.H.)

dim of sight and without a tooth, may yet scare the mice – though it cannot play the offensive among their ranks. And so with a motor-car. Parts may be out of truth and squint with irritating deviations from the straight, but the vehicle can get along with careful tending and gentle shoving uphill.

It was decided that I should go on a car that had done very well thus far. It had never been first; it had never been last. But it had been safe. Its number had never been taken by the police: its driver had never been warned within controls: it had never been taken up a lonely lane to be overhauled out of the sight of men. And yet it was sober and slow – just the car for one who is adverse to rapidly moving scenery, preferring to enjoy the beauty of Nature at a contemplative pace.

And yet don't imagine that there was no lack of enterprise either in the driver or the writer, for we got early to the control and started in the first dozen, going along Parliament Street and down the hill leading across the market in good style. One or two cars behind seemed rather close to our rear works, but none overtook us until we got near the Trent bridge, when the Hon. J. Scott Montagu's Daimler went ahead with Professor Vernon Boys and Mr. C. Cordingley aboard. A few minutes later the Richard car, No. 46, followed, and then we got to the outward control – leaving there eighteen minutes from the start.

The morning was not very bright, and as we got among the fields a nasty drizzling rain was making its influence felt in the greasy state of the road. That, however, did not interfere with the steady running of my car, and it certainly gave promise of what is known to automobilists as a good run. Meanwhile other vehicles were passing by. Mr. Egerton, on a De Dion voiturette, whizzed along in fine style; a few score yards along and International Victoria went ahead, and then a New Orleans car was succeeded by Mrs. Bazalgette on her Benz. There was a pleasing variety in the landscape and also in the cars that passed us. They certainly disturbed the continuity of the view, and were frequent enough to keep one's eyes to the road. Still, the ride was not without interest so far as the next few miles to Loughborough were concerned. No cars had lingered on the roadside, and all seemed anxious to go to the front – probably a reflection of the national idea just now. But why there should be such a rivalry I could not imagine, especially as I understood we were to show the authorities how much below the legal limit a motor-car can be safely driven. Even a huge Noah's-ark sort of car that was advertising the pen with which I write, after keeping doggedly by our side for some time, went ahead – it could stand it no longer. For, horrible to relate, the tire of our off front wheel had punctured, and we were hobbling along on three decent tires and one that was as flabby as an empty sandbag. After that all the small boys and other persons frequenting the road called attention to that punctured tire with a wearying reiteration that tried the patience of passenger and driver alike. They thought they were doing a kindly action in pointing to our misfortune, evidencing a sympathy that would win our appreciation; but their kindness became so monotonous and their sympathy became so tedious that one would have been glad of a peashooter for purposes of revenge. It is no joke to go along with so many sympathisers. They heeded not the quiet and sober dignity of our pace; the superior character of our car was unobserved. All they saw and all they seemed capable of understanding was our misfortune.

Still, we made headway – not so much up the hills as on the descent. But with the help of the Crypto gear we took the hills grandly. I got out to see how well the car advanced towards the heights, and coaxed it from the rear with both hands. The driver thought it would go without help, and I walked by its side with the contemplative attitude of the mute once a feature of every funeral. Then from behind came the familiar 'teuf, teuf,' and I mounted the car again just as we got to the top, and the New Orleans and Wolseley cars came along. Then we had quite a number of pacemakers – the Daimler public-service car, Mr. Mark Mayhew, Mr. R. E. Phillips on his 'Petit Duc' and half a score of others. Somewhere in that district Mr. Swindley was seen on Mr. Lord's Peugeot, and he very considerately pointed to the wayward tire. In fact, scarcely a motorist did not express sympathy. We thank them all for their kind expressions; and can do so all the more heartily now that the trip is over. Nearer Loughborough M. Farman was descried on the roadside admiring a tire, and near Loughborough a 6 h.p. Iveagh phaeton was resting. I thought it was for the convenience of the journalists aboard but afterwards discovered a pump had gone wrong. Happy No. 9 – that was the end of its troubles; ours had scarcely begun. Just before getting to Leicester, M. Farman went along again, and with the baggage van, driven by Mr. Van Toll before us, we went into Leicester in very satisfactory style – for us.

At Leicester I had a few minutes to inspect some of the cars that had recently passed us; but none of the earlier ones were to be seen, and a

St. Albans – Local automobilists come out to encourage the returning heros. (*right:*) No. 27 3 h.p. New Orleans car entered by Burford van Toll & Co. driven by Mr. Astell. (Photo: Friswell Private collection by kind permission of P.H.H.)

good time was spent in replacing the battered tire with a new one. It was merely a tack that had caused our difficulty.

Leaving Leicester we went capitally, passing over the tram lines with a nonchalance that had been impossible before. Right on through Oadby and Kibworth, we took the gradients with ease, and drew well away on the level. While we got ahead of none, none got ahead of us for a while, and then an International Victoria went by. A few miles further on Mr. R. E. Phillips was investigating his car, but caught up and passed us seven miles from Market Harborough.

In Market Harborough a new form of annoyance was commenced by the public, who would persist in asking if we were last. Once the query was varied, and 'Are there any more?' was the form adopted, but the invariable question was, 'Are you the last?' Captain Langrishe was the only motorist we saw in the next few miles, until just after Maidwell Mr. Coles came to greet us, his car standing demurely enough in a blacksmith's shed. He seemed rejoiced – much in the manner of the sailors in 'The Tempest,' who thought each other drowned, and himself the only survivor. Mr. Coles had evidently fancied himself last, and was glad to give us a message for a friend at St. Albans – should we arrive first. A spindle had broken, but was quickly repaired, and his car was into Northampton a few minutes after our steady vehicle.

After the excellent run from Leicester to Market Harborough our car had been going rather slowly, but that did not distress me. Soon after leaving Mr. Coles we slowed down to a stationary position. A trail of water had led to the driver determining on an investigation of the car, when it was found a water joint had gone. Being at the rear of the straggling procession of vehicles, Mr. Rolls was in St Albans by that time – the repair was made without observation. I became water carrier, surprising the good lady at the nearest farmhouse at the quantity of water required. She said the motor-car required more liquid than a horse. Only two motorists passed by – Mr. E. M. Iliffe on his motor-quadricycle, and a Decauville that gave notice of its coming and was speedy in its going. The water-joint skilfully repaired, we restarted. Evidently the rest had done us all good, and the engine seemed refreshed. We took the next hill in fine fashion on the top speed, and then, with encouraging smiles from the police and cheers from the children, we entered Northampton, nearly running over a bullock that crossed our path and alarming a dog that came too near.

When we got to Northampton few vestiges of a motor-car meet remained; and the Plough Inn was deserted. Mr. Banks was just about to depart on his Brown-Whitney steam car; the driver of the New Orleans was ruefully regarding a broken petrol pipe, a Decauville was being got ready for the start, and Mr. Moffatt Ford was preparing to take the M.C.C. Triumph on the last stage of this eventful journey. Thus we had the yard of the Plough Inn to ourselves – and determined to overhaul the car. On opening the back-door, a crack in the bar on which the engine was supported revealed itself. 'Good heavens!' said the driver in a tone that seemed serious indeed. Mr. Coles came along at that moment, and we saw how his repair had been effected. With the help of a local engineer the driver was able to make the necessary repair to our car; but when we got to the outward control no timekeepers could be seen. It was 5.30 p.m.

On through Horton, Stoke Goldington, and Newport Pagnell we went, a few cyclists hinting that the cars had gone by some hours before, and one or two of the facetious ones sadly wanting to know if there were any stray ones about. The evening grew cold, and our prospects of getting to St. Albans before the rest had got to the Crystal Palace were less. We maintained an even pace, such a steady-going rate as I had desired but had never before endured.

> 'O for a seat on a speedier car.
> And a ride on one that would go!'

I don't mean that ours stopped – but it did not go like some are reported to have done. The twilight cast a dullness o'er the landscape, and at Woburn Sands – 81 miles from Nottingham – I could stand it no longer. We were 40 miles from London, and I calculated the car would arrive there at midnight. There was, however, the risk of the delay, and, committing myself to the mercy of the railway company, I took train for Euston.

And thus I came to town. I have since learned the car reached London half an hour past midnight. Next time I go a-motoring give me a car that is speedy as well as sure. ”

The Motor-Car Journal, Saturday, May 19th, 1900

Crowds gather in St. Albans to welcome the last 'procession' to start for London after tea. (photo: Friswell Private collection by kind permission of P.H.H.)

Homeward Bound

BY 'PHANOMEN'

ALTHOUGH considerably interested in the progress of the 1,000-mile Trial, it is one thing to read of the same and another to actually take part in the tour, and when, during the course of last week, an invitation was extended to me to join the cars on the last day's run, there was no hesitation in my acceptance of the offer. Consequently, with great expectations, I journeyed down to the city of lace by the afternoon express on the Great Northern Railway on Friday last, and reached Nottingham just in time to see a number of cars finishing up their day's journey. So far, I was in anxious ignorance of the particular car which was to convey me back to town, so, after attending to the wants of the inner man, I quickly repaired to the Repository, where the evening exhibition of the competing vehicles was being held, to learn my fate. Many times on the way down by train I had cogitated whether I should be dropped on one of the fast cars, or a reliable steady-going car, guaranteed to do its average of twelve miles and hour and no more, or one of those lazier vehicles, whose daily records had been, of somewhat varied character.

Hardly had I entered the Repository when I was greeted by Mr. Percy Richardson, of the Daimler Motor Company Limited, and duly informed by him that he had reserved a seat for me in his wagonette, No. 36. 'Phanomen,' said I to myself, 'your luck's in,' for I have had many previous rides with Mr. Richardson, and know from experience that he always brings his passengers home safely and in good time. My anxiety thus relieved, I spent a pleasant hour in chatting with many of those who had gone through the Trial, and whom I had not seen since the start from Hyde Park Corner, nearly three weeks before. Having had strict instructions not to be late, and acting on a revised version of an old saw, 'Early to bed, early to control,' I retired to rest and dream of the events of the morrow.

Reaching the Repository at 6.15 a.m. on Saturday morning I found a very lively state of affairs already prevailing, several filling up with petrol, others with water, others lighting up their burners, and others vainly endeavouring to work their way out from the rear to get to the control early. By 6.30 nearly all the motors were in operation, and the noise of so many engines at work under one roof made the Repository more like a

Saturday, May 12th 1900 – Cars prepare to leave St. Albans for London. (*centre:*) Mr. & Mrs. Friswell on 8 h.p. Peugeot. (***Right:***) 6 h.p. Daimler driven by Percy Richardson who had carried Lord Justice Clerk of Scotland and Colonel Magrath and on the last day also carried the reporter 'Phanomen' who wrote this account of his experiences. (Photo: Friswell Private collection by kind permission of P.H.H.)

large engineering establishment rather than a stable for horses and vehicles. Our party, which consisted of Lord Kingsburgh, Colonel Magrath, and self, with Mr. Richardson at the wheel, were quickly on board, and running up to the control found already six or seven vehicles in front of us. Although seven o'clock was the official time of starting, in view of the long day's journey – over 120 miles – the signal was given as soon as the bulk of the cars were ready to start, we on No. 36 being timed out at 6.57 a.m. Notwithstanding the early hour a fair number of people turned out to see us depart. The Trent bridge crossed, we quickly arrived at the outward control, and then the open country was reached. There was rather a sharp nip in the air, and the gathering of the clouds overhead did not promise a very enjoyable trip as far as the elements were concerned. Expectations in this direction were not disappointed, for ere long the rain began to come down heavily, and made us glad that we had brought with us a mackintosh in addition to a heavy overcoat. Pointing to a road over the hill-tops some miles distant, we were duly informed that we would shortly have to climb that. It proved to be Bunny Hill one of the steepest in the district. Expecting, no doubt, to see a little fun, quite a number of local automobilists had journeyed to this point – there being five or six cars on the roadside – to see the way the competing vehicles mounted or were pushed up the stiff gradient. So far as we were concerned no pushing was necessary, although the three passengers were politely requested to dismount. The top of Bunny Hill reached, we all quickly made ourselves comfortable again, and were soon travelling at a fair pace. Near Costock, No. 9 was seen at the roadside, the driver devoting his attention to the motor. In due course Loughborough was reached, and by this time the rain had temporarily ceased. The cars as they passed through the town met with a hearty reception, it being the hour when a good many workmen were wending their way to the several large engineering works in the neighbourhood. Mount Sorrel, which, from what we saw of it, is principally noted for the strange colour of the corduroy trousers worn by the men employed in the quarries close by, was next passed, and the miles to Leicester shown by the mile-stones steadily diminished. About five miles from the latter town Messrs. Egerton and Grierson were seen busy at work on the motor of their De Dion voiturette, No. 15, the trouble being, as we afterwards learned, with the exhaust box. A few miles from Leicester we were passed by several cars, including the Wolseley voiturette, Mr. Siddeley's Parisian Daimler, and Mr. Mayhew's Peugeot, and for the first time for many miles we had a sight of the running of a number of vehicles in front of us. In due time the inward control at Leicester was reached, where we gathered that a dozen cars had arrived before us. Probably owing to the inclement weather there were relatively few people out to greet us. The order to travel through the town at a speed of four miles per hour was given at the Great Northern Railway Station, and at this speed we ran into the yard of the Bell Hotel, in Humberstone Gate, where the vehicles had to stay one hour for exhibition purposes.

Breakfast partaken of, a restart for Northampton was made in due course, the cars being held up at the outward control until the appointed time. Several of the Leicester Motor-car Company's Daimler covered wagonettes were observed at work in the public service as we passed out of the town into the suburbs. A mile or so further on we came across Mr. F. H. Butler's car with a punctured tire, which caused him an hour's delay, while not far away Mr. Mark Mayhew was devoting attention to his Panhard car on the roadside. Nothing very exciting occurred to us for some miles until we came upon a herd of cows, which the man in charge left to themselves. However, with but little difficulty we got through, and once more had a clear road, a policeman at a village about nine miles from Market Harborough urging us to go quicker! A few miles further on we came upon Mr. Friswell, enjoying himself on his back under his 8-h.p. Peugeot, trouble with the pump being the cause of his stoppage. Near Kibworth, Mr. Critchley, on his khaki-coloured Parisian Daimler, gave us the go-by, as also did the Gladiator voiturette; both cars were going at a good pace, and the way the last-named vehicle tackled the hills was much commented on. On the outskirts of Market Harborough the male inmates of the workhouse had lined up to witness the passage of the cars, and as we went by there was a good deal of head-nodding at one another, the poor old fellows no doubt talking of the changes that have come over locomotion since they were boys.

This section of the route proved one of the most trying of the whole journey, for it was made up of a series of steep rises and falls, and, as the rain had now begun to be heavy, the roads were too greasy to permit full advantage being taken of the down grades. For some time now we had been speeding on our way alone, not another car being in sight, either in the front or at the rear; but near Maidwell Mr. S. Farman, on the M.C.C.

Mrs. Friswell looks on while her husband discusses the patch on the back tyre (or was it the leaking pump?) of his 8 h.p. Peugeot, will it last to the Finish. (Photo: Friswell Private collection by kind permission of P.H.H.)

Triumph No. 32, came along at a good pace and passed us, as also did Mr. Stocks on the Ariel quad No.3, and Mr. Jackson on the Century tandem tricycle No. 39. By the way, I noticed that this machine was fitted with a 3 h.p. water-cooled De Dion motor and radiator, not a 2¼ h.p. motor as specified in the red book. Near Lamport a very steep descent was met; this we negotiated at a speed which brought the tears to one's eyes. Once more on the level and turning a bend in the road we found the gates at the level crossing at Lamport Station closed against us. This brought us to a stop – the first since leaving Leicester – while a slow coal train went by. At all the cross-roads were encountered groups of interested spectators, and from the number of smart turn-outs of dog-carts, etc., it was evident that the local gentry were taking advantage of the opportunity of seeing for themselves the progress that has been made in motor-cars. We were also pleased to see a couple of ladies on horseback ride behind us for a little distance, thus giving their horses a useful lesson in running quietly in company with automobiles. The red book, which was a most complete encyclopaedia, warned us to beware of the village of Brixworth with its sharp turns. What with these turns and the narrowness of the road at this point many a driver on Saturday was put on his mettle in the handling of his car. We got through safely, however, and were soon running along at a good bat indeed, the nearer our car got to London the better did the motor seem to pull. In fact, as Lord Kingsburgh remarked, it must have known it was going home for a well-earned rest. A few miles further on we overtook the Gladiator voiturette, stopped on the road side, and then M. Jules Dubois on the Decauville No. 34 gave us a taste of his exhaust, and also a demonstration of his agility in jumping off and running along with his little car up the hills. Enjoying a delightful down-hill run we were soon at the Northampton control and on our way to the halting place for lunch. Right in the town we witnessed the nearest approach to a nasty accident on the whole journey. A number of little boys, not content with viewing the cars from the pavement, had placed themselves on the road. A horse attached to a brougham suddenly became restive, and to all the onlookers it appeared that there was no escape for two of the boys whose attention was all for the motor-cars in front of them. Fortunately the driver of the brougham managed to pull his horse a little to the side, but it was a miraculous escape. Running almost to the other end of the town, we found that most of the cars had turned into Messrs. Mulliner's carriage building establishment, so, following suit, we were quickly enjoying a well-earned lunch.

An hour later we started on our last stage of the journey, so far as time records were concerned, viz., to St. Albans, a distance of 44½ miles. We had not gone very far when we came across the Century tandem-tricycle hung up with a punctured tire. At Horton Mr. Friswell came along and left us, while at Stoke Goldington the Century once more passed at a good pace, the riders having effected a quick change of tires. Newport Pagnell was the next town to be passed, and here the sharp turn was safely negotiated, the police rendering assistance in directing the way and keeping the road clear. A mile or so further on the Hon. J. Scott Montagu's car, with Professor Vernon Boys and Mr. C. Cordingley aboard, came along and passed us, while near Waverden we left Mr. Friswell behind us, his pump again giving him trouble. Just before reaching Hockliffe we had to slow down for a flock of sheep which blocked our way. The animals did not apparently like the 'teuf teuf' of the motor, for they stampeded along in front of us at a tremendous pace, one making a somersault on the way. Dunstable had made itself quite gay with bunting to welcome the motor-cars, and the populace were loud in their cheering as we passed along the High Street. A similar reception was accorded us as we ran through Markyate Street and Redbourn, and we quickly found ourselves at the inward control at St. Albans, the timekeepers informing us that we were the seventeenth in order of arrival. Quite a large crowd gathered at the ancient city, who had a good opportunity of inspecting the cars, the order having gone forth in the morning that the vehicles that had arrived up to that time would line up and start in procession at 5 p.m. for London, no passing to take place on the way. Finding the Pea Hen Hotel yard full up, we wended our way to the Queen's Hotel, and, following the example set by earlier arrivals, filled up the time at our disposal by having tea.”

The Motor-Car Journal, Saturday, May 19th, 1900

Assembling in St. Albans for procession into London (photo: Friswell Private collection by kind permission of P.H.H.)

Getting the cars into correct order for procession from St. Albans. No. A11 – John Scott-Montagu arrives with 12 h.p. Daimler.
(Photo: Friswell Private collection by kind permission of P.H.H.)

Postcard of High Street, Dunstable
(Photo: courtesy J. Riddell)

Policemen control the mellée as cars squeeze by to take their place in the procession at St. Albans. (Photo: Friswell Private collection by kind permission of P.H.H.)

"At the outward control at St. Albans a lively scene presented itself. The road being somewhat narrow a little difficulty was experienced in lining up the cars in the same order as that in which they arrived at the inward control. This over, however, a good deal of posing took place for the photographs, and punctually at 5 p.m. the procession, consisting of about thirty vehicles, and headed by the Hon. C. S. Rolls' Panhard, set out for London. Apparently the rain had not been so heavy as further north, the roads being dusty, and those unprovided with goggles had a very trying time. The procession had hardly started when it was brought to a stand, by a restive hay-motor, which did not like passing so many petrol motors at such close quarters as was necessitated by the narrowness of the road at that point. However, the horse was persuaded to behave itself, and we moved along once more. All along the route a large crowd of spectators was met, the number increasing the nearer we got to London, while from St. Albans onwards quite a number of automobilists came out on their cars to welcome us home. Near Elstree Mr. Holder's twin-Daimler was passed, apparently having tire troubles, while at the Welsh Harp the Gladiator voiturette dropped out of the procession. Cricklewood, Kilburn, Maida Vale – it is time the wood paving was repaired here – were soon all behind us, and looking something between a miller and a collier, owing to the dusty twenty miles run from St. Albans, we turned into Oxford Street at the Marble Arch. Along Regent Street, Pall Mall, Charing Cross, Northumberland Avenue we went, and in a few minutes found ourselves outside the Automobile Club's headquarters at 6.43 p.m., fourteen cars being lined up in front of us.

As I said at the beginning, I knew my luck was in when I learned I was to be in the care of Mr. Richardson. His Daimler car, No. 36, ran beautifully the whole distance of 124 miles, with not a single stop except at the appointed places, and the run, but for the heavy rain in the earlier part of the day and the dust at the finish, was most enjoyable, and will long be remembered by the writer."

The Motor-Car Journal, Saturday, May 19th, 1900

Lining up for the procession to London after the last Time Control at St. Albans May 12th 1900. The Hon. C. S. Rolls on his 12 h.p. Panhard prepares to lead the way. (photo: Friswell Private collection by kind permission of P.H.H.)

Detail from the top photograph. Victory in sight – A rare picture of Hon. C. S. Rolls laughing with S. F. Edge and E. Kennard. (Poole, Rolls' mechanician has been defaced in original photo). (Photo: Friswell Private collection by kind permission of P.H.H.)

At last, Mr. & Mrs Friswell move off en route to London after 20 days on the Trial on their 7 h.p. Peugeot. (Photo: Friswell Private collection by kind permission of P.H.H.)

Setting off for London from St. Albans – the last drive. No. A21 Ernest Pitman on 6 h.p. Daimler with T. Weekes his mechanician, followed by No. 11 M.M.C. Princess which joined the Trial on the last day. (Photo: Friswell Private collection by kind permission of P.H.H.)

Tour Jottings

Mr. Shrapnell-Smith, the hon. sec. of the Liverpool Self-propelled Traffic Association, proved himself an expert pump repairer on Friday last. Short of a washer, one was improvised out of a halfpenny piece!

— o§o —

The seven horse-power Peugeot with which Mr. Lord followed the thousand miles tour did the measured mile in Welbeck Park as follows: Uphill, 2m. 45s.; downhill 1m. 58 1-5s; mean time, 2m. 21 3-5s.

— o§o —

The Autocar, Saturday, May 19th, 1900

Loughborough

Much interest was shown in the passage through Loughborough. The first car to arrive was the 12 h.p. Panhard, driven by its owner, the Hon. C. S. Rolls. Two minutes later came Mr. Edward Kennard's 8 h.p. Napier, followed in another minute by a 12 h.p. Daimler, driven by Mr. J. S. Holder. From then the cars came through the town at intervals of one a minute or two till about 8.20, when forty-four had passed. Seven more came along after that time, the last being timed at about 9.30. The 'inward control' for Loughborough was at the Great Central Railway Bridge on the Nottingham Road, from which point a speed limit of eight miles an hour was imposed through the town by way of Nottingham Road, Sparrow Hill, Pinfold Gate, and Leicester Road to the 'outward control' at the Grammar School gates. There the signal was 'right away' for Leicester. At the inward control Mr. A. H. Walker, and at the outward Mr. R. S. Clifford, junior, recorded the times of the passing of each car. A large number of people turned out along the route to watch the procession. For nearly half an hour we had experienced a heavy fall of rain and sleet, which had made the roads somewhat sticky, and the way the cars were handled came in for much commendation, regret being evinced that a stop was not made here to allow of a closer acquaintance being made with the vehicles. The police gave much assistance in regulating the traffic and directing the voyagers on their way.

Northampton

The arrangements for the reception of the vehicles at Northampton were made by Mr. A. F. Mulliner, of Bridge Street, who is a member of the Automobile Club, and is also largely interested in the building of motor-car bodies. The inward control to Northampton Mr. Mulliner arranged to take place at the open space at Kingsthorpe, where the mile-stone to the town stands, and at this control the inward time of each car was taken by Mr. H. W. Dover and Mr. W. B. Shepard. This being done, the cars proceeded at a comparatively slow speed along the Barrack Road, Sheep Street, the Drapery, and down Bridge Street. Several of the cars were cleverly turned into the capacious premises of Mr. A. F. Mulliner, and others were arranged to be placed in the Plough Inn yard. Mr. Mulliner gave a luncheon to a number of members and friends of the Automobile Club. Only a short time was allowed for lunch, as the cars were supposed to leave within an hour after being timed at Kingsthorpe. During the interval several in charge of the cars took advantage to make a thorough overhauling before proceeding on the remainder of their journey. Mr. J. Porteous and Mr. Spencer Downing, both of whom are well known in connection with sport and racing, lent valuable assistance in carrying out the necessary arrangements for the reception of the tourists. The first car to arrive was that of the Hon. C. S. Rolls, Mr. Edge being second. Then came Messrs. Cheel and Newton and Mr. T. A. Holder. Among the later arrivals was the Brown-Whitney steam car and a Marshall car, which required assistance from a local engineer before proceeding on its journey, leaving Northampton about 5.30 p.m. The cars left in the same order that they had entered the town, Messrs. G. H. Bennett and L. Sharman being at the outward control.

Dunstable

What with a brass band contest and the passage through the town of the motor-cars, Dunstable was quite gay on Saturday. The first passed through early in the afternoon, and for over two hours afterwards vehicles came along at irregular intervals, while a few stragglers were seen even later. There was a great crowd, and the railway had brought many from neighbouring places to see the motor-vehicles.

St. Albans

When it became known that the finish of the Trial, so far as time records were concerned, would take place in our town, and that the vehicles which had arrived up to 5 p.m. would then start in procession for London, a large crowd quickly gathered. The first car arrived early in the afternoon, followed quickly by over thirty others. The yard of the Pea Hen Hotel was rapidly filled up, some of the vehicles finding a temporary resting place at the Queen's and others at the Bell Hotel. The procession was formed up near St. Stephen's Church in a somewhat narrow part of the road, and here about thirty vehicles set off in a group for London

The Motor-Car Journal, Saturday, May 19th, 1900

NOTTINGHAM TO LONDON *(continued)*.

4 (later 8) m. p. h. out of Leicester, — Then PROCEED by the Clock Tower, bear a little **L**, along Gallowtree Gate, Granby and London Roads, to the Midland Railway Station, where second control ends. Proceed at 8 m. p. h. for another 2 miles to near the Race Course at Oatby, where control for Leicester ends.

STOP. — Here STOP.

RECORD SHEETS must be filled in here, and be prepared to start away one hour-and-a-half after the time at which you first entered the first inward control of Leicester.

R. A. for 13 m. — Then R. A. 9 miles on at Kibworth, keep **L** at fork by Church.

8 m. p. h. through Market Harborough. — At top of hill, slow to 8 m. p. h., to pass through Market Harborough, keeping church on **L**, and at the end [illegible] crossing the stream.

R. A. for 8 m. — At White Flag, the end [illegible] 8 miles to Lamport Stati[illegible] usually shut. Then go strai[illegible]

Level Crossing. — Be careful at sharp cor[illegible]

STOP. — STOP at the Red Flag [illegible]

RECORD SHEETS [illegible]

8 m. p. h. into Northampton. — Then PROCEED at [illegible]

STOP for Luncheon — Compulsory STOP of [illegible] available for the storage of [illegible]

Level Crossing. — Then PROCEED at [illegible]

8 m. p. h. through Northampton. — over level crossing at Statio[illegible]

STOP. — STOP at the White Fl[illegible]

RECORD SHEET[illegible] to start one h[illegible] the inward co[illegible]

NOTTINGHAM TO LONDON *(continued)*.

Level Crossing. **R. A. for 55 m.** — Then PROCEED R. A. by Route 328, over level crossing at the Station, bearing **L** at fork $1\frac{3}{4}$-miles on.

At the fork, 2 miles beyond Horton, bear slightly **L**.

In Newport Pagnell, $14\frac{3}{4}$ miles, after passing "Swan Inn," turn **L** at Cannon Corner, along St. John's Street and Tickford Street, and at fork at next milestone keep **R** — **L**

In Broughton, 3 miles on, take **L** road at the fork for $\frac{1}{2}$-mile, then bear **R**. At 1 mile keep **L**, and soon after to **R**, leaving Wavendon on **R**-hand. — **L**

Level Crossing. — After passing over a level crossing at Woborn Sands Station, $3\frac{3}{4}$ miles further on, bear **R**.

In Woborn, keep along George Street, leaving Town Hall on **R**; at Hockliffe, $4\frac{1}{2}$ miles on, turn **L** into London Road. Here proceed, by Route 188, direct to St. Albans. — **L**

8 m. p. h. through Dunstable. — On passing under railway bridge, about 4 miles after joining London Road, slow down to 8 m. p. h. to pass through Dunstable.

R. A. — At White Flag, at end of Dunstable, PROCEED R. A., taking care to slow to 8 m. p. h. in the following unflagged villages:—
29th milestone, Markyate Street, 4 miles from Dunstable.
A little beyond 25th milestone, Redbourn, 7 miles from Dunstable.

STOP. — STOP at the 21st milestone on entering the City of St. Albans.

RECORD SHEETS must be filled in here.

8 p. h. ·ough Albans. — Then PROCEED at 8 m. p. h. into St. Albans.

·P for ·ea. — STOP of $\frac{1}{4}$-hour, for Tea.

8 p. h. ıt of Albans. — Then PROCEED at 8 m. p. h. through St. Albans, descending Holywell Hill; at St. Stephen's Church, turn **L**. — **L**

·P. — STOP at White Flag, the end of the control for St. Albans.

RECORD SHEETS must be filled in here.

Tour Jottings

"Our Lincoln correspondent informs us that the perfect control over the cars was a complete revelation to the general public. The short distance in which they could pull up, their silent running, the way they could thread through traffic, and their ease of manipulation, cleared away a lot of prejudice."

— o§o —

London

Report had it that the first car would not reach the Club before 7 p.m., but an hour in advance of that time several well-known members of the automobile world put in an appearance to welcome the 1,000-milers home after their long and trying journey. The cry 'Here they come!' went up when, shortly after 6.30 p.m., the 'toot, toot' of a horn was heard, and the procession, headed by the Hon. C. S. Rolls, on his 12 h.p. Panhard, came in sight. The shaking of hands, the passing of congratulations, and the presentation of handsome bouquets of flowers by Mr. F. R. Simms to the ladies of the party who had completed the 1,000 miles, occupied the next few minutes, after which some little time was spent in posing for the various photographers anxious to get a snapshot of the finish. This

'Arriving Home' Whitehall London 6.45pm 12th May 1900.
(***Left to right:***) No. A17 12 h.p. 4 cylinder Panhard (hot tube and electric ignition) Hon. C. S. Rolls. No. A10 Napier car Mr. Kennard seated, St. John Nixon aged 14 on floor, M. Napier to left of steering wheel with beard. Montague Grahame-White wearing a cap, Harvey du Cros (jun) behind Napier car.
(Photo: Argent Archer)

operation over, the vehicles and their occupants began quietly to disperse – some going to the Crystal Palace and some home, the latter preferring to leave the final journey until the morrow. The thirty-three cars which were lined up at the finish at the Horse Guards Avenue at 7 p.m. on Saturday are shown below in the order of arrival.

The Motor-Car Journal, Saturday, May 19th, 1900

Tour Jottings

“An automobile fête is contemplated at the Crystal Palace on Saturday afternoon, when visitors will be taken for spins round the grounds at a certain charge in the trial cars, and the proceeds handed to Lady Georgina Curzon to swell the total of her admirable Mafeking fund.”

— o§o —

“During the evening a number of other cars came in, the total number which reached the Club on Saturday night according to the official record, being forty-seven.

A17 Hon. C. S. Rolls's 12 h.p. Panhard
A10 Mr. Kennard's 8 h.p. Napier (Mr. S. F. Edge)
4 Ariel tricycle and Whippet trailer
46 Richard car
A20 Mr. Iliffe's Enfield quadricycle
A30 Mr. Siddeley's Parisian Daimler
39 Century tandem tricycle (Mr. Jackson)
31 M.C.C. Triumph (Mr. S. Farman)
3 Ariel quadricycle (Mr. Stocks)
A11 Hon. J. Scott's 12 h.p. Daimler
49 Wolseley voiturette (Mr. Austin)
A20 Mr. Ashby's Empress motor tricycle
35 Daimler Parisian (Mr. Critchley)
34 Decauville voiturette (M. Dubois)
36 Daimler wagonette (Mr. Richardson)
26 8 h.p. Peugeot (Mr. Friswell)
47 Richard car
A3 Mr. T. B. Browne's 6 h.p. Panhard
A2 Mr. F. H. Butler's 6 h.p. Panhard
15 De Dion Voiturette
A21 Mr. E. Pitman's 6 h.p. Daimler
11 Motor Manufacturing Company's Princess car
27 New Orleans car
A31 Mr. Exe's Parisian Daimler
9 Motor Manufacturing Company's Iveagh phaeton
49 Marshall car (Mr. Mann)
A4 Mr. M. Mayhew's 8 h.p. Panhard
37 Daimler Parisian (Mr. Pedley)
A22 Mr. J. A. Holder's 12 h.p. Daimler
51 Star voiturette (Mr. Lisle)
1 Benz Ideal (Mr. Hewetson)
A25 Mrs. Bazalgette's Benz
8 Motor Manufacturing Company's 6 h.p. phaeton (Mr. Burgess)”

St Nixon has a copy – & I
have both a Photo and a
lantern slide

The first car is the 12 HP
4 cyl – Panhard (TUBE AND
electric ignition) – owned &
driven by Charlie Rolls –
The next car is the 1st complete
Napier Car ever made (Napier had made
a very successful ENGINE
& had tried it out in a Panhard
car) The car belonged to Mr
Kennard who is seen seated in it
St John Nixon (aged 14) is sitting on
the floor (as he had done all through
the trial) – Napier himself
is seen a little to the left of the steering
wheel – wearing a beard – & just
beyond him is "Montie" Grahame
White – (brother of Claude G. White
competed (unsuccessfully) against
the French aviator Paulhan in
the London–Manchester flight
for which Harmsworth offered
the second of his series of huge
prizes – Hervey du Cros
junior is seen just behind SJ's
Napier –
The reason my de Dion (No 15
is not in this photo is that
it was very important to the
de Dion Bouton Syndicate
to have a photo of my car at
once (& by itself) for
adv. purposes – hence the
photo of which I sent you a
copy – I could tell you tons
more about the 1000 miles
Trial!

Hubert Egerton's own hand a description of these two photographs on pages 300-302 'Arriving Home'

Tour Jottings

“Owing to an error in the transcription of numbers and subsequent elaboration of our report, we included the Déchamps car as figuring at the bottom of the list of cars which ascended Shap Fell. Needless to say, this is incorrect, for, as already reported, the Déchamps car was smashed up on the Continent on its way to London, and did not take part in the trials at all.”

— o§o —

The Autocar, Saturday, May 19th, 1900

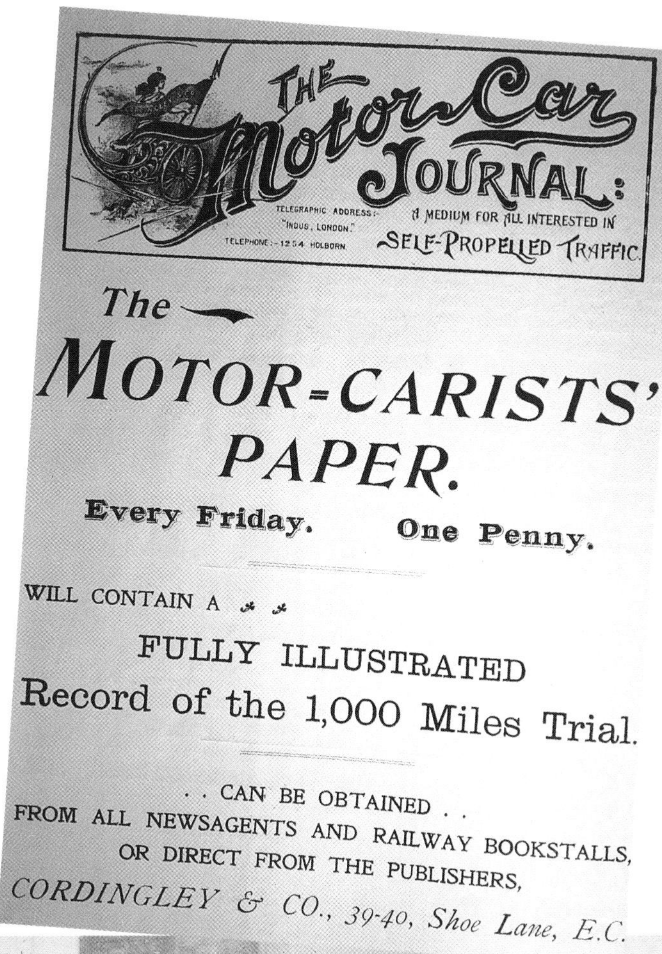

Below:
Arriving at Whitehall May 12th 1900, Hubert Egerton driving De Dion Voiturette – Grierson is his passenger (see reference opposite). – The Motor Manufacturing Co.'s 'Princess' car 4½ h.p. that only ran on the last day of the Trial is shown here in the background.
(Photo: Argent Archer)

34

Arrival in Whitehall – 7 p.m. Saturday, 12th May 1900.
No. 34 Decauville driven by Debois and Hales
No. 36 Daimler driven by Richardson
No. 26 Peugeot driven by Friswell
Right-hand side – pulled out of line No. A2 Frank Hedges Butler's 6 h.p. Panhard. Both Vera Butler and Mrs. Friswell are holding their flowers.
(Photo: Argent Archer)

“ Tour Jottings

Lincoln has taken a keen interest in the autocar movement all along. Quite a dozen local cars met the Automobile Club at Lincoln.

— o§o —

Quite a number of automobilists went out from town on Saturday afternoon to meet the cars on the return journey, several travelling as far as Dunstable.

Mr. F. H. Butler had the misfortune to puncture a tyre immediately on leaving Leicester on Saturday, causing him an hour's delay.

— o§o —

The Lincolnshire and Nottingham roads were about the best traversed on the whole tour. The legal limit of speed was easily maintained on the Lincoln-Newark road, which runs perfectly straight for fourteen miles without a bend.

Whitehall London – 7.15 p.m. Saturday, 12th May 1900. 'Home at last' led by No. 49 5 h.p. Marshall driven by Mr. Mann,
No. 1 Mr. Henry Hewetson's Benz Ideal is visible at the end with more coming around the corner.
(Photo: Argent Archer)

Mr. Mann's bad luck with his Marshall car seemed to take a turn for the better on Saturday. he discovered that in the collision which the car suffered as she was running down to the start of the hundred miles trial which preceded the big round, the backbone which carries the engine was badly cracked right across, and this was really the source of the major portion of his woes. With the other car, the pump of special construction, and which could not be replaced en route, went wrong early in the trip, but by sheer pluck and perseverance these cars were got through, No. 49, on Saturday, coming in well ahead of the cars of her class.

— o§o —

That delightful romanticist Robert Barr (Luke Sharp) was to be observed closely scrutinising the travelled cars at the Crystal Palace last Tuesday. He admitted to being sorely bitten by automobilism. As he lives on the heights of Woldingham, however, he wants a regular cragsman of a car. ”

The Autocar, Saturday, May 19th, 1900

Having brought our travellers home, let us look at a diary of the last four days as seen from a non-competing car Mr. Lord's 7 h.p. Peugeot.

"The A.C.G.B. 1,000 Miles Test

As seen from Mr. Lord's Peugeot

Wednesday, May 9th

Rain fell so heavily on Tuesday night and early on the morning of our run that it had washed clean the streets of Leeds. It had coated the country roads with a mixture of extra slipperiness. Our star was, however, so much in the ascendant that all that was to come down before the clock struck the hour for departing. The cars turned northwards for the breakfast run to Harrogate into the teeth of the coldest wind we can remember. The clouds, too, hung low on the hills, and mist rolled about the valleys so that the beauty of the country through which we passed was quite obscured. On the whole, perhaps, this was for the best, for we would not for worlds have had our driver's attention diverted from the road for even a moment. The grease was awful in places, and put the fear of most things into the heart of an old cyclist, perhaps the most capable person on earth to accurately estimate the possibilities and probabilities of side-slip. That no car travelled broadside on is a testimony to the skill of all our drivers. At the top of a long steep hill a couple of miles out from the Leeds outward control we stopped awhile to see how the leading cars tackled it. Rolls's Panhard seemed to make nothing of it; she must have taken it on her third, heavy as it was, but the Ariel was shortly afterwards with her two riders pedalling furiously. Never have we seen much finer pedalling. Then came the Kennard Napier, the Ariel tricycle with the Whippet combination ascended swathed to the nose in wraps against the bitter, bitter wind. Edge imperturbable as ever, and the little boy (St. John Nixon) sitting as *mécanicien* with that useful accelerator cord in his hand. Holder's Daimler followed quickly, and then Ashby on the Empress motor tricycle, which had done so well up to date. Then Siddeley and Critchley with their respective Parisians, followed by the Gladiator voiturette which Farman drove so well and so fast. They zigzagged almost from the bottom, and the passenger was shed half way up, but they came up bravely enough and held on their way. Then we too proceeded, for standing still was colder work than driving, breakfast awaited at Harrogate, and that nipping blast was stronger than many *apéritifs*. Leeds had not speeded its parting guests to any great extent, but at Harewood the usual crowd was out, and the knots of sightseers grew more numerous as we neared the watering-place. The condition of the descent of Crimple Vale was enough to give a hero qualms, and we are bound to admit that we were thankful to observe that the road surface at the bottom and over the bridge was dry. Even then the corner was sharp enough. Nothing but a morbid craving to see other people in difficulties could have persuaded so many people to rise so early and come so far out from the town as Humphrey Bank. They were there in hundreds, cycles, local autocars, and the common trap by scores had been pressed into their service. As our good friend Lord remarked, Humphrey Bank is a climb, and by a little error of judgement in the important matter of mixture the good Peugeot gave the onlookers some occasion for sniggering. Through no fault of her own, this was the first and last hill on the whole trip at which she really jibbed. There were the two occasions upon which she ran backwards, certainly, but they were due primarily to the fact that the click (*sprag*) was up, and secondly to a constitutional reluctance on the part of her owner to throw in her first speed until the last moment. With a keen recollection of Ness Brow, we mildly suggested click directly Humphrey Bank rose before us, so that unless the car took to tobogganing there could be no backward scurry on this occasion. It was just as well, for on the steepest part where the Harrogatians gathered thickest she jibbed. Mixture, said Lord, and fiddled with the air inlet. In went the clutch, she heaved convulsively forward and jibbed again. Permission to

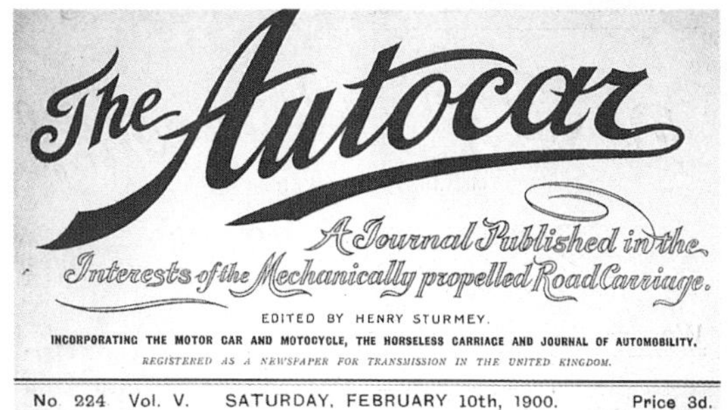

THE British Motor Company, Limited, conjointly with the Dion-Dunlop Company, Limited, control all the De Dion patents, including those upon the new De Dion Voiturette, in England.

Dealers and intending purchasers are warned against buying, selling, or using motors or machines not bearing the proper British License plate.

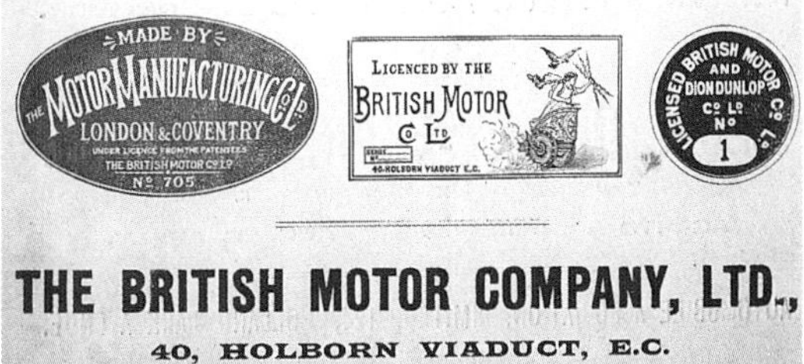

THE BRITISH MOTOR COMPANY, LTD.,
40, HOLBORN VIADUCT, E.C.

descend and walk up was sharply denied us. Better cylinder heads should go, piston rods double up, and gears shear than the cream Peugeot should be shamed by shedding a single ounce of her freight before a sneering crowd. Another wild effort and another jib; and even as the sniggers were becoming guffaws, even as the fool people suggested getting out and shoving even on the very steepest part of that steep hill, she got what she was asking for, and from a standing start flung that grade behind her and sailed up like a bird. Let us do justice to the sniggers and scoffers and put it on record that they cheered. Harrogate was at its windows and in its streets to watch the arrival of the cars, and it, moreover, in all its stateliness, was good to look upon after the depression of Newcastle and the dinginess of Leeds. It carried one's mind back to the majesty of Scotland's capital.

The streets were more thronged than before when we retraced our wheel tracks after breakfast and simply dropped *down* Humphrey's Bank to take the road westward for Otley, Shipley, Bradford, and lunch. Always excepting that first terrible thirty miles out of Manchester, we fancy this section of the route took us over quite the worst roads encountered on the whole trip. The surfaces were greasy and holey, and the hills were raspers. It was cruel work for the low-powered cars, but they got through, which spoke volumes for them. The climb up to Shipley was something to be remembered. The factory hands were out in crowds, and the goggled drivers threw the shawled women into paroxysms of hysterical merriment. In Bradford itself the hugest interest was taken in the vehicles as they stood ranged in order of arrival in the open space before the Town Hall. But for the excellent arrangements the autocars and their occupants might have been mobbed. We do not fancy many orders were booked during the hour's show, but in no place visited were the vehicles more closely or more interestedly examined.

There was a heavy climb out of Bradford, and the paved road was none of the best, but it was lined four deep with operatives, and once the hill was won and the sets left behind, the roads changed for the better, and good surfaces marked the afternoon's running. The Peugeot seemed to be in an excellent humour that afternoon, for notwithstanding the heavy grades she kept touch with Mr. Holder's twelve horse-power Daimler, and Mr. Mark Mayhew's eight horse-power Panhard for a considerable part of the run. The roads deteriorated, but the roadside sightseers increased in numbers for the last few miles into Sheffield, although the scenic reputation of the surroundings of the steel town was well sustained by the scenery passed through. The inconsequent timetable published in the official programme had led the Sheffielders to expect the majority of the cars much later than they really ran in, so that many were disappointed. We think it would have added to the effect of the tour all round if more or less processional entries to such places could have been arranged.

Friday, May 11th

Although our day in Sheffield had been a pleasant one, thanks to the exceeding courtesies of the Master Cutler and the local committee, the tour was now so near its end that no one was sorry to make a start upon the penultimate run. It was an order that the writer and the editor of this paper should be early on the scene of the speed trial in Clumber Park (*Welbeck Park*), so that getting under weigh in good time, and making the best of our way to Worksop, little but the increasing beauty of the countryside as Sheffield with its belching shafts was left behind and Worksop approached was to be noted. After passing through the latter place, Mr. Johnson's, and Mr. Rolls's, and Mr. Kennard's and a few other cars that were up turned into Clumber Park to reach the mile of private road which had been so carefully selected by the Duke of Portland's agent for the flying mile speed trial. Although the landscape lacked the touch of sunlight, the run through the park was delightful. Sheffield wheelfolk are indeed fortunate to have so fine a demesne within holiday reach. The secret of the trial had been excellently kept, for hardly two score people watched the wild scurries of the cars on the upward and downward miles. The pace attained by the high-powered vehicles competing was something of an eye-opener for those fortunate enough to be on the spot, and a keen enjoyment even for the officials concerned. It will be long ere we forget the rush of the Rolls car as she swept by us at the finish of her fastest mile. The trials over, the route was pursued through Clumber Park by Markham Moor Inn to Saxilby and Lincoln, where a right royal greeting awaited us all. The mayor and the committee entertained the club to luncheon, and acted in a most hospitable manner. The cars were the objects of immense interest to the crowds that had come in to Lincoln Market and upon the outgoing progress was at first slow by reason of the immense concourse of people. From Lincoln to Newark (where tea) and on towards Nottingham, as far as Saxondale, we found ourselves once more upon an ancient Roman road, none other than the Fosse Way which in the time of the great old people connected Lincoln to Leicester. It is nearly straight, very nearly level, and of excellent surface, and though for a space within the dreaded confines of Lincolnshire, we fear we speeded the Peugeot. Certainly a certain string not altogether unconnected with the governors was much in demand, and miles were at times covered well inside 2m 30 s. Curiously enough this Fosse Way was almost lined with spectators, and the faster the cars ran the huger their delight. They were much delighted. The speeding on the Fosse Way had so separated the vehicles that Nottingham, too, although keenly expectant, lacked anything processional, and the cars came in by twos and threes. The building selected for the evening show was far from commodious, there being hardly room for two people to pass abreast between the lines of cars. Moreover, a round dozen were hoisted by a carriage lift to a first floor, and there the public had to follow them.

Visitors cars and horse drawn traffic in London Road, St. Albans. (Courtesy P.H.H.)

Saturday, May 12th

It was a scurvy trick on the part of the clerk of the weather to select our last day upon which to visit us with the displeasure of Aquarius. Rain fell fairly heavily after Loughborough was passed, and the roads were once again uncomfortably slippery by the time we gained Mount Sorrel. Bunny Hill tried the hill-climbing powers of some of the weaklings, and the stiff up and down character of the country told upon the pace of the cars. In Leicester we found the police in a terribly stupid condition. These deadly motor cars were not to exceed four miles per hour, and very tenacious were they of their orders. We certainly never touched four miles per hour in the town, but nevertheless were frequently cautioned by very young fresh-coloured policemen of particularly bucolic appearance. Our exit from their town, at least so far as six or eight cars were concerned, is not likely to be forgotten by these blue-coated gentlemen. The automobiles, to the astonishment of all the onlookers, including the force, crawled through the streets at about one mile per hour to the sound of horn and the belch of burnt lubricating oil. From time to time the car drivers complained bitterly to such officers as they saw of the dangerous speed at which tramcars and tradesmen's carts passed them. It was a thing the police did not understand. probably they have not fathomed it yet.

After luncheon at Northampton, where at the George we paid 1s for standing the car for three-quarters of an hour in the open yard, we started on the non-stop run of forty-four and a half miles to St. Albans over glorious roads. The route was by Horton, where the full thousand miles practically finished, Newport Pagnell, Woburn, and Hockliffe, where the Holyhead Road joined, and Dunstable, the full flood of Saturday afternoon cyclists being encountered after the main road was reached. The going was magnificent, the quiet towns and villages along the route being stirred to their depths by the passage of the cars. All the cars arriving at St. Albans by five o'clock formed for procession to London, and if the individuals responsible for this arrangement wished the tourists to wear a travel-stained appearance upon entering town, of a verity they had their desire. The dust raised by the 120 odd wheels in the lanes by Radlett and Elstree caused the occupants of the cars to present the appearance of grimy millers before they reached the Hyde, and this did not pass unnoticed by the spectators 'a long way down the Edgware Road.' The entry into London was a triumphal one, albeit much earlier than was expected by many that went out later to see the much-travelled cars. The trial practically came to an end at St. Albans, but competitors called at the Automobile Club to register on their way to the Crystal Palace, where they may be seen to this day. And so ended an undertaking great and unprecedented in this country, which by its success from start to finish has accomplished marvels in forwarding the interests of automobilism in this realm. ”

The Autocar, Saturday, May 19th, 1900

1,000-Mile Trial. 203

NOTTINGHAM TO LONDON *(continued)*.

R. A. for 11 m.

Then PROCEED R. A. for 11 miles; slowing at first Railway Arch to 8 m. p. h. through Park Street Village, 2 miles from St. Albans (unflagged), and for a total of 1½ miles slow speed should be employed until Colney Street is passed. Use caution in descending short, but steep hill, on leaving Elstree; again 1 mile on, use great caution in descending Brockley Hill, which is very steep at the top.

8 m. p. h. through Edgware.

At the spot where the road from Stanmore joins the main road, at the bottom of the hill, slow to 8 m. p. h. to pass through Edgware.

R. A. for 3 m.

At a Bridge at the end of the village, over a small stream, R. A. for about 3 miles.

8 m. p. h. through Hendon.

At the Hendon Brewery, on **L**, with a tall chimney, slow to 8 m. p. h. to pass through Hendon.

R. A. for 1½ m.

At the Upper Welsh Harp Inn, on **R**, R. A. for about 1½ miles.

STOP.

STOP at the point where the Midland Railway Branch Bridge crosses the road at the foot of a hill, control for London begins.

RECORD SHEETS must be filled in here.

8 m. p. h. through London.

Then PROCEED at 8 m. p. h. along the Edgware Road to Marble Arch, and by Oxford Street, Regent Street, Pall Mall, Northumberland Avenue to the Avenue, Horse Guards.

STOP.

Here STOP.

RECORD SHEETS must be filled in here;

The Vehicles must then be driven immediately to the Crystal Palace and must be left there, under the entire control of the Club, for the Examination of the Judges.

“Tour Jottings

Between Hockliffe and St. Albans it was noticed that several hotels and refreshment caterers had had their signboards repainted lately, and the legend ‘Good accommodation for cycles’ altered to ‘cycles and motor cars.’

— o§o —

When running through Leicester we noticed several of the Leicester Motor Car Co.'s vehicles at work in the public service. They are Daimler ten-seated waggonettes with omnibus top.”

The Autocar, Saturday, May 19th, 1900

“The Small Fry of the Trial

MARY E. KENNARD

The great 1,000-mile Automobile Trial is a thing of the past, but it will live until death in the memory of those who took part in it. From first to last, the tour was a triumphant success, in which the fleet of motors, with but few exceptions, covered themselves with glory. The run over 1,000 miles, however, means motoring is deadly earnest, and hand in hand with great enjoyment went much strenuous endeavour and arduous strain. For it was not all play. The motorcarists had to take the rough with the smooth, and derive consolation often from the fact that they had surmounted difficulties. But is not this the highest kind of enjoyment? Who would give a thank you for success, where all is fair-sailing and monotonous? The variety of motoring constitutes its principal charm. We were only small fry, shrouded in the generous dust of flying Panhard, swift Napier and stately Daimler. They, we knew, looked down upon us; but we did not look down upon ourselves. And as day after day passed, and still we held together in close communion, we felt we were entitled to our self-respect. For did not we scale the rugged heights of dreaded Shap Fell, climb like so many flies over the yet steeper gradients of Dunmail Raise, and struggle through the mountain passes of Birk Hill, in spite of rain overhead and execrable surface under wheel? We came to be a band of brothers, we of the De Dion voiturettes, the Gladiator, the Wolseley, Triumphs, etc., etc. We sympathised with one another's misfortunes; we admired each others feats of valour. The same spirit animated us all. We were determined, with a grim and steadfast determination, to reach the final goal in spite of every obstacle. And when the evening came and we go into port, and recognised our

Mrs. Mary E. Kennard in the back seat of Montague Grahame-White's 12 h.p. Daimler. (Photo:Grahame-White's album courtesy N.M.M. Beaulieu)

brave comrades, how pleased we were! How hearty the greetings and warm the hand-shakings. With almost passionate admiration we hailed that pair of heroes – the Eureka man and he of the Simm's motor-wheel. They worked throughout like Trojans and deserve the Victoria Cross for valour in the field. Brave Jules Dubois, too, conductor of the Décauville, how nimbly he ran when his motor slowed down at some steep eminence; how ably he assisted it on all occasions; what wondrous agility he displayed! Ah! ye proud, high-powered cars, laugh at the poor little struggling small-fry as you will – the honours of the expedition lie with them. You were consistently reliable, we had our troubles – not a few. Punctures, pumps, sparking plugs, ignition, carburettor, all contributed to swell the list, and at some period or other we were afflicted. And yet with all your speed and power you could not shake us off. We clung tenaciously to your vanishing forms, and informed you of our presence at the various controls. We fairly astonished the Benz division and some of the older Daimlers. We were an army of midgets if you like, but an army not to be despised even by the Leviathans who smiled whilst they marvelled at our performance. It was predicted at the start that we should succumb. Not we. We had no idea of giving in. We toiled, we struggled, we laboured, we strove, and success spelt in large capitals crowned our efforts. We proved that the voiturette of to-day is not a mere plaything, but a vehicle capable of surmounting steep gradients, of carrying its passengers in safety over good roads and bad, and of doing 120 miles in the day. A De Dion can be bought for £195, a Gladiator costs £165 or thereabouts, a New Orleans, £140, a Wolseley, £225, and Triumph, £230. Intending purchasers may safely invest in any of these. There is no need to dally for improvements. Improvements, of course there will be in process of time, but Father Time has a soft, slow way of stealing the years, which deprives laggards of untold enjoyment. Be bold, gentle public! Throw aside your caution and procrastination and take what the present offers. Buy a small car, learn to drive it, then exchange for one of higher power, you will never regret your temerity. Troubles you may have, especially at first, until you understand your motor, but given a certain amount of will and intelligence, and you will defy them all. They will melt away as a mirage in the desert. A new world will be opened out to you: an amusement for your youth, an occupation for your middle age, a refuge for your declining years; so, dear public, hurry up, take the plunge, be happy, be courageous, join the band of small fry, who have gained an honourable place in the recent contest, and open inviting arms to you to enter their ranks. ”

The Motor-Car Journal, Saturday, May 19th, 1900

SUMMARY 20

The records of the cars

" *The Autocar* here records, so far as it is possible to ascertain them, the principal causes of stoppage which occurred to the various cars en route, the relation of which will generally account for the comparatively poor performances of the different vehicles upon individual days. Those marked with an asterisk are based upon our own personal observation, the others being obtained officially from the Secretary, as supplied by the drivers themselves. With a few exceptions the mishaps recorded were of a trifling character, and the manufacturers are taking immediate steps to remedy them.

SECTION 1

No. 1 (Benz Ideal, driven by Mr. Hewetson.) No repairs throughout. Attributes bad record between Bristol and Cheltenham to bad petrol. Stud in cap of bearing broke near St. Albans.

No. 2 (Benz Ideal, driven by Mr. Coles.) New spindle to front wheel said to have been broken against kerb. Last day's record bad owing to above mishap, breaking and twisting frame of car, continual stops for heated bearings, main bearings of engine.

No. *3 (Mr. Stocks's Ariel quadricycle.) Had several tyre punctures.

No. *4 (Mr. Cheel's Ariel tricycle with trailer.) In addition to punctures, carried away the petrol and oil connecting tubes, and buckled a wheel near Edinburgh by collision.

No. 5 (Locomobile.) Had trouble with boiler through engine priming. Cone on rear axle replaced, and nipple in water tap. Frequent tyre troubles, four or five new tyres being used, but the near side driving tyre stood throughout. Lost dustcaps on both wrist pins, hence looseness of bearings.

No. 8 (Motor Mfg. Co.'s phaeton, driven by Mr. Burgess.) No part replaced; no causes of delay, except punctures to tyres.

No. 9 (Motor Mfg. Co.'s Iveagh, driven by Mr. Schofield.) Bolt in pump replaced only. No causes of delay.

No. 12 (Motor Mfg. Co.'s tricycle.) Broke axle; has entirely new frame; broke piston.

No. 14 (De Dion voiturette, driven by Mr. Grierson.) Front near spindle broke before Kendal owing to sideslip. Pump failed for lack of water before Newcastle. Sleeve holding universal joint slipped off.

No. 15 (De Dion voiturette, driven by Mr. Egerton.) Two delays by breakages of inlet valve spindle, first outside Haddington, second after Leicester. One puncture only, otherwise tyres not touched.

No. 16 (Gladiator voiturette, driven by M. Farman.) Two new pump rings fitted; one chain changed owing to stretch; compression stay fitted to front axle.

No. *18 (5 h.p. Endurance car.) Retired from the run after leaving Bristol; cause unrecorded.

No. *19 (Orient Express.) Broke her piston; also carried away the end of the countershaft, and retired from the competition between Carlisle and Edinburgh, after running into a ditch through collision with a cow.

No. *20 (Simms's Motor Wheel.) Bent both front axles; broke the supply pipes, and suffered other derangement through upset on greasy tramlines, and finally, from the strain suffered in the upset, broke the backbone in passing over a level crossing near Carlisle.

No. *21 (The four-passenger Lanchester carriage.) broke a valve gear bracket near Savernake Forest; joined the run again at Birmingham. broke the spring of the ignition gear, and the body split in two on the run to Manchester, after which she was withdrawn.

No. 22 (Lanchester, driven by Mr. Millership.) At Bradford cam bush broke; another made. Cam wobbled and broke sliding blocks in Leicester. Stopped there, made good, and put whole car together, to find cam put on wrong, with result – exhausting when should have been firing. Put right, and then did non-stop run Northampton to London. Arrived London 12.10 a.m.

No. 23 (Brown-Whitney.) new chain; new cylinder cover at Edinburgh; trouble with defective water tank, material too thin; trouble from nuts falling off; nuts out of crosshead slide.

No. 24 (Marshall.) Car badly damaged in a collision with railway van a few days before start. Real damage done only discovered last day of trial, when it was found that the stay holding engine was badly cracked, and only held together by two bolts. This was cause of bearings heating, etc.

No. *26 (Mr. Friswell's 8 h.p. Peugeot.) Punctured a tyre, and burst an ignition tube.

No. 27 (New Orleans, driven by Mr. Astell.) Only cause of one day delay a broken carriage spring, and of another lack of current in accumulators caused by some people not charging same in Manchester, although they asserted that this had been done. Belt slipped on Shap.

No. *28 (New Orleans car.) Broke a spring at Derby.

No. *29 (M.C.C. Eureka.) In difficulties several times, and disappeared after Kendal, turning up again at Newcastle.

No. *30 (M.C.C. Eureka.) Was withdrawn after Manchester.

No. 31 (M.C.C. Triumph.) No parts changed. No delays to explain.

No. 32 (M.C.C. Triumph.) Between Edinburgh and Newcastle compensation gear spindle in jack box broke. Lost one day. Carburation spoilt record between Carlisle and Edinburgh, and again between Leeds and Sheffield.

No. 33 (Decauville.) No parts replaced. Only delays punctures, and accident between Reading and Bristol, buckled front wheel. Reached Bristol next morning. Stopped for want of petrol between Birmingham and Manchester. Stopped in Edinburgh one day for driver to go to see after Eureka car.

No. *34 (Decauville, driven by M. J. Dubois.) Broke the end of the sparking plug, which got into the cylinder.

No. 35 (Daimler, driven by Mr. Critchley.) No parts replaced; no failures to report.

No. 36 (Daimler, driven by Mr. Richardson.) One delay first day, caused by breakage of pump pinion.

No. 37 (Daimler Parisian, driven by Mr. Grahame-White.) Delay caused between Edinburgh and Newcastle by breakage, through collision, of steering-gear worm bracket. On Shap burners went out owing to clogging of pressure valve. Stop also between Edinburgh and Newcastle for water in petrol.

No. *38 (Daimler Motor Co.'s public service vehicle.) Broke an induction valve the first day. Broke a supply pipe to one of the burners between Bristol and Cheltenham. A new vaporiser here fitted. Between Carlisle and Edinburgh broke cross head, and jammed the piston into the cylinder. Suffered from a leaky cylinder head, which was replaced at Edinburgh as well as vaporiser.

No. *39 (Century tandem.) Suffered damage in the way of buckled wheel, bent frame, and twisted axle from collision; experienced some trouble with the circulating pump.

No. 40 (Wolseley, driven by Mr. Austin.) Between London and Bristol belt fastening came undone. Bristol and Birmingham, wire cord to choking valve broke, but no stoppage caused. Belt broke. Tyre (old one) burst. Seven miles run on rim. Birmingham and Manchester, tyre puncture; twenty minutes delay. Carlisle and Edinburgh, several punctures; delay about one hour. Edinburgh and Newcastle, tyre punctures; threequarters of an hour delay. Nottingham and London, tyre burst; ten minutes stoppage. Parts replaced, new wire cord to choking valve, new belt, new outer cover to back tyre, new top spring plate to back spring. Breakage caused by running fast over level crossing. new outer cover to back tyre at Edinburgh; ditto at Northampton. Pierced belt at St. Albans. Two passengers, never dismounted for yard of the way, including test hills.

No. 41 (International, driven by Mr. Seyd.) No parts replaced, except two grease boxes on the road. Slow running on last two days due to running out of two batteries.

No. 42 (Hurlingham.) Broke crankshaft between London and Bristol. Car withdrawn.

No. 44 (International, driven by Mr. Capellan.) No parts replaced. Delay between Newcastle and Leeds caused by the driver, Mr. Capellan, breaking a blood vessel.

No. *45 (S.S. carriage.) Broke the front axles by running into a wall in the run down from the Cat and Fiddle into Macclesfield. Broke a chain beyond Kendal, and retired from the competition.

No. 46 (Richard.) New belt on first day. One new inlet valve. Exhaust choked with mud at end of second week and beginning of third. Cause of trouble not suspected.

No. 47 (Richard.) No delays, except for puncture repair and inlet valve sticking outside Carlisle.

No. 49 (Marshall, driven by Mr. Mann.) Pump went wrong first day out, and it being found impossible to replace it in the time given, the car was run through entirely without pump, which was the cause of the delays.

No. 51 (Star, driven by Mr. Lisle.) Broke

swivel before Lancaster; replaced same and two lower frame tubes, two spokes in each wheel, and ball bearing on end of crank-shaft replaced owing to accident.

No. *52 (Roots and Venables.) Broke an axle, and retired at Manchester.

No. *53 (8 h.p. Wolseley carriage.) Joined the run at Birmingham in an untried condition. Fired her bearings, and retired after Manchester.

SECTION II

No. *A1 (Mr. J. E. Hutton's 12 h.p. Panhard.) This car failed the first day through the gear giving way, and went no further. It was a converted vehicle made up from a 6 h.p. Panhard, with another 6 h.p. engine taken out of Mr. Edge's car coupled to it, and was not really calculated to stand the strain of the greater power.

No. *A2 (Mr. Butler's 6 h.p. Panhard.) Experienced several punctures. Ran poorly during the early part of the trial through the piston rings having worked round, thus causing compression to be lost, and a lift pin of one of the valves being worn, putting one cylinder partly out of action.

No. *A3 (Mr. T. B. Browne's 6 h.p. Panhard.) Experienced delay upon one occasion through a stoppage of the pump.

No. *A4 (Mr. Mayhew's 8 h.p. Panhard.) Ran poorly during the early part of the tour through the use of unsuitable spirit on the first day's run. Experienced several punctures.

No. *A7 (Mr. Harmsworth's 6 h.p. Parisian Daimler, driven by Captain Langrishe.) Broke the back pressure pipe. Through sideslip collided with a rock at Matlock, and broke a spring. A loose screw in the pump wore a hole in the pump casing in Welbeck Park. A new pump fitted had a bent spindle. Induction valves required grinding in, and several punctures were experienced.

No. *A9 (Mr. Harvey Ducros' 8 h.p. Napier.) This was a converted 6 h.p. Panhard, and the two top gears gave out on the run to Bristol. The car stopped here.

No. A10 (Mr. Kennard's Napier.) After leaving Hounslow small hole blew in bottom of inlet valve. On second day just before Gloucester pump gland came undone and wait for twenty minutes for engine to cool only. minute's work to tighten nut. At Matlock found cylinder blown a little, remedied by tightening nuts. Two punctures to back wheels, one at Peebles, repaired in eight minutes; second few miles from Northallerton, causing one hour's delay. No other troubles of any kind, save after first day, little trip hammer lost off governor, and run continued without governor.

No. *A11 (Hon. J. Scott-Montagu's 12 h.p. Daimler.) Several punctures caused delay; also some delay from weak lamps.

No. *A12 (Mr. Edmunds's 6 h.p. Daimler) Broke front spring by collision. Skipped the Edinburgh journey, rejoining at Newcastle.

No. *A16 (Mr. A. J. Wilson's Ariel tricycle.) The cross head pin broke and wore channels in the cylinder. The batteries ran out, and the run was relinquished before Edinburgh was reached.

No. *A17 (Hon. C. S. Rolls's 12 h.p. Panhard.) Experienced one puncture, and a slight flare-up through a leakage of the supply pipe to burners.

No. *A19 (Mr. J. R. Hargreaves's 12 h.p. Daimler.) Experienced trouble with new experimental system of cooling tubes, and retired at Calcot Park, rejoining at Birmingham. Carried away a mudguard, and broke a swivel pin of the brake gear by backing into a wall through failure of brakes to grip instantly backwards.

No. *A20 (Mr. Herbert Ashby's Empress tricycle.) Broke a gear pinion near Carlisle.

No. *A21 (Mr. Pitman's 6 h.p. Daimler.) No recorded mishaps.

No. *A22 (Mr. J. A. Holder's 12 h.p. Daimler.) No recorded mishaps, save one or two tyre punctures.

No. *A23 (Mr. Cordingley's 6¼ h.p. M.M.C. phaeton.) Commenced by losing a vulcanised tyre on the first day, and experiencing several minor difficulties through the tour.

No. *A24 (Mr. R. E. Phillip's Mors Petit Duc.) Experienced some difficulties with ignition gear, and during the run from Newcastle the chains came off several times.

No. *A25 (Mrs. Bazalgette's Benz Ideal.) Experienced some ignition troubles on the run to Leeds. No other mishaps recorded.

No. *A26 (Mr. Gregson's 6 h.p. Daimler.) No mishaps recorded.

No. *A27 (Mr. J. R. Hargreaves's 12 h.p. Daimler.) Both the solid front tyres tore away from their retaining wires, and the wires of one of the new ones broke.

No. *A28 (Mr. E. M. Iliffe's Enfield quadricycle.) Wore out gear pinion. broke bearing cone, and experienced several punctures.

No. *A29 (Mr. Mayhew's 7 h.p. Peugeot.) Burst an ignition tube, and broke exhaust pipe.

No. *A30 (Mr. J. D. Siddeley's 6 h.p. Daimler.) Broke a front spring by collision. Experienced a few punctures.

No. *A31 (Mr. Johnson's 6 h.p. Daimler.) Delayed by a punctured tyre one day and by a change of petrol, requiring readjustment of the firing tubes, another. ”

*Information based on *The Autocar* observations

THOUSAND MILE TRIAL, 1900 Results & Prizes

No	Make	H.p.	Entered by	Driver
SECTION I TRADE ENTRIES				
1	Benz	3	Hewetson	Henry Hewetson / W. Randall
2	Benz	3	Hewetsons	E. J. Coles
3	Ariel quad	3¹/₂	Ariel Motor Co Birmingham	Mr. John W. Stocks
4	Ariel trike with Whippet trailer	2¹/₄	Ariel Motor Co Birmingham	Mr. Edwin S. Cheel
5	Locomobile Steam Carriage	2	The Locomobile Co of America	Searles
● 6	MMC Balmoral Charbanc	12	Motor Manuf Co London & Coventry	
● 7	MMC Phaeton	12	Motor Manuf Co London & Coventry	
8	MMC Panhard	6	Motor Manuf Co London & Coventry	Mr. Alfred Burgess
9	MMC Iveagh Phaeton (Daimler)	6	Motor Manuf Co London & Coventry	William White / Mr. Schofield
● 10	MMC "Princess"	4¹/₂	Motor Manuf Co London & Coventry	
11	MMC "Princess"	4¹/₂	Motor Manuf Co London & Coventry	
12	MMC Tricycle	2¹/₄	Motor Manuf Co London & Coventry	E. Buck
● 13	Ariel Panhard Voiturette	3¹/₂	Ariel Motor Co Birmingham	
14	De Dion Voiturette	3	De Dion Syndicate, Ltd	Mr. Grierson
15	De Dion	3	De Dion Syndicate (Egerton)	Mr. Hubert Egerton
16	Gladiator	3¹/₄	Motor Power Co London	Roland le Bars
17	Napier	16	Motor Power Co London	
18	Endurance Car	5	Endurance Motor Co Ltd.	
19	Orient Express	6	Automobile Association Ltd.	
20	Simms Motor Wheel	2³/₄	Motor Carriage Supply Ltd.	Samuel Rowbottom
21	Lanchester carriage	8	Lanchester Engine Co.	
22	Lanchester carriage	8	Lanchester Engine Co.	Archie Millership
23	Brown-Whitney Steam Car		Brown Bros., Ltd.	E. R. Banks
24	Marshall Carriage	5	Marshall & Co.	
● 25	Deschamps	9	J. Burns Oxford St. London	
26	Peugeot	8	Friswell Ltd 18 Holborn Viaduct	Mr. Charles Hain Friswell
27	New Orleans	3	Burford van Toll & Co Twickenham	Mr. Astell
28	New Orleans	3	Burford van Toll & Co Twickenham	I. C. Forrow
29	Eureka car	2¹/₄	Motor Car Co., Ltd	
30	Eureka car	2¹/₄	Motor Car Co., Ltd	
31	M.C.C. Triumph	3¹/₂	Motor Car Co., Ltd	Henry Farman
32	M.C.C. Triumph	3¹/₂	Motor Car Co., Ltd	R. Moffat Ford
33	Decauville	3¹/₂	Motor Car Co 168 Shaftesbury Ave	Frank Strange
34	Decauville	3¹/₂	Motor Car Co 168 Shaftesbury Ave	Jules Dubois and H. K. Hales
35	Daimler	6	Daimler Motor Co Ltd	Mr. J. S. Critchley
36	Daimler	6	Daimler Motor Co Ltd	Mr. Richardson
37	Daimler Parisian	6	Daimler Motor Co Ltd	Mr. M. Grahame-White
38	Daimler Public Service Vehicle	9¹/₂	Daimler Motor Co Ltd	
39	Century Tandem Tricycle	2¹/₄	Century Engineering Manchester	Ralph Jackson
40	Wolseley	3	Wolseley Sheep Shearing Machine Co Birmingham	Mr. Herbert C. Austin
41	International Victoria	3	International Motor Car Co L'don	Mr. Seyd
42	3.5 hp Hurlingham Voiturette	3¹/₂	London Motor Van & Wagon Co Ltd.	
43	5.5 hp Phaeton	5¹/₂	London Motor Van & Wagon Co Ltd.	
44	International Victoria	3	International Motor Car Co London	Mr. Cappellan
45	S.S. Carriage	5¹/₂	S.S. Motor Co.	
46	Richard	7	Automobile Manufacturing Co London	French
47	Richard	7	Automobile Manufacturing Co London	W. C. Bersey + M. Berduil
● 48	Humber voiturette	6	Humber & Co Holborn Viaduct London	

s	Miles driven	No.	Class	Prize	Prize fund	*Daily Mail* Prize	Trophy
v ave speed sectors 2, 6 & 8	523/533	1				£10	
v ave speed sectors 10 & 13	throughout	2	A	1st	£31-3s-8d	£10	
ve speed throughout	throughout	3	E(b)	1st	£31-3s-8d	£10	
ve speed throughout	throughout	4	E(b)	2nd	£15-11s-10d	£10	
v ave speed sectors 1, 2, 3 & 8, 10 missing	throughout	5	A	2nd	£15-11s-10d	£10	
v ave speed sectors 2, 3, 4, 8 & 10	throughout	8	C	2nd	£15-11s-10d	£10	
ve speeds throughout	896 W. White	9	C	2nd		£10	
d for last stage only							
ied with new frame,wheels and engine	throughout						
v eve speed sector 13; 4 & 8 missing							
ve speeds throughout	throughout	15	B	3rd	£9-7s-2d	£10	
ve speeds throughout	throughout	16	£10				
d before Bristol							
d after Bristol							
d after colision with cow Carlisle to Edinburgh							
cords after sector 5	395						
d Manchester with split body							
v ave speed sector 10.13th finished after midnight	951	22				£10	
ds for 6 stages only	throughout						
ges no records 9 stages below 12mph							
starter							
ve except 9mph on sector 2	throughout	26				£10	
v ave speed sectors 4, 8, 9 & 10		27	A	2nd	£15-11s-10d	£10	French Club bronze medal
leted trial but withdrawn due to poor record	621						
peared after Kendall reappeared at Newcastle							
drawn Manchester							
ector records missing: below ave sector 10	throughout	31	B	2nd	£15-11s-10d	£10	
age no records. 6 stages below 12mph		32				£10	
cords 5 stages. 3stages below 12mph	throughout						
ve except 11 mph sector 4		34				£10	
ve speed throughout		35	C	1st		£10	
ave speed sectors 4 & 8		36	C	1st	£31-3s-8d	£10	
ave sector 8		37	C	1st		£10	
cords 7th, 8th stages. 8 stages below 12mph							
v ave stages 10 & 11 no record sector 1	933	39	E(b)	2nd	£15-11s-10d	£10	
ve except sector 11	896	40	B	1st	£31-3s-8d	£10	French Club Silver medal
ave sectors 4, 8, 9 & 10		41				£10	
drawn first day							
ell 1st stage but withdrawn at Bristol with 42							
ave speed sectors 11 & 12		44				£10	
d Kendal							
ave sectors 4, 9 & 10		46				£10	
ave sector 4		47				£10	

No	Make	H.p.	Entered by	Driver
49	Marshall	5	Marshall & Co Belsize Works Manchester	Mr. J. J. Mann
50	Renaux Tricycle		Marshall & Co Belsize Works Manchester	
51	Star Voiturette	3 1/2	Star Motor Co	George Prew
52	Roots & Venables Oil Carriage	2 7/8	Roots & Venables	
53	Wolseley Carriage	15	Wolseley Sheep Shearing Machine Co Birmingham	
SECTION II PRIVATE ENTRIES				
● A1	Panhard	12	J. Ernest Hutton Esq., J.P.	
A2	Panhard	6	Frank H.Butler Esq.	Frank Butler
A3	Panhard	6	T. B. Browne, Esq.	T. B. Browne
A4	Panhard	8	Mark Mayhew L.C.C.	
● A5	Steam Car	12	Cyril Gooch, Esq.	
A6	Panhard	12	Alfred Harmsworth, Esq.	
A7	Daimler	6	Alfred Harmsworth, Esq.	Capt. Hercules Langrishe
A8	not allocated			
● A9	Napier	8	Harvey du Cros Junior, Esq.	
A10	Napier	8	Ed. Kennard, Esq., D.L., J.P.	S. F. Edge (St. John Nixon mech
A11	Daimler	12	Hon. John Scott Montagu J.P.	Hon. J. S. Montagu
A12	Daimler	6	Henry Edmunds Esq.	John Goody/H. Edmunds
● A13	Daimler	6	Ernest Estcourt, Esq.	non starter
● A14	Napier	8	W. D. G. Goff, Esq.	non starter
● A15	petrol Phaeton	5	Robert Mackay Wilson Esq.	non starter
A16	Ariel Tricycle	2 1/4	A. J. Wilson Esq.	A. J. Wilson
A17	Panhard	12	Hon. C. S. Rolls	Hon. C. S. Rolls
● A18	Light Daimler	6	Nevill Copland Esq.	
A19	Daimler	12	John R. Hargreaves J.P.	
A20	Empress Trike	2 3/4	Herbert Ashby Esq.	
A21	Daimler	6	Ernest Pitman Esq.	
A22	Daimler	12	J. A. Holder Esq.	
A23	M.M.C. Phaeton	6 1/4	Chas. Cordingley Esq.	Robert Bunkall
A24	Mors Petit Duc	4	Robert E. Phillips Esq.	
A25	Benz Ideal	3	Mrs. L. Bazalgette	Mrs. L. Bazalgette / Clarkson
A26	Daimler	6	Clarence H. Gregson Esq.	C. G. / Percy Brennan
A27	Daimler Mail Phaeton	12	John R. Hargreaves J.P.	
A28	Enfield Quad	2 1/4	E. M. Iliffe, Esq.	
A29	Peugeot	7	Mark Mayhew L.C.C.	D. Haxton
A30	Daimler	6	J. D. Siddeley, Esq.	J. D. S. /P. Brown
A31	Daimler	6	William Exe, Esq.	Claude Johnson

● (light shading) non-starter

(dark shading) non-finisher

All results were published subject to amendment. Some finishers had incomplete records, and were not eligible for prizes.

s	Miles driven	No.	Class	Prize	Prize fund	*Daily Mail* Prize	Trophy
ave sector 1, 2, 3, 4, 8, 9 & 10		49				£10	
tarter							
age records missing, below ave sector 6	throughout	51				£10	
d Manchester							
d B'ham, retired Manchester							
ave speed 4,8 & 10	throughout	A2					Silver medal & silver vase
ve speed throughout	throughout	A3	C	2nd			Silver medal & silver ACGBI cup
cords for 6th, 7th 8th stages	651						
Times Engineering, Brighton non starter							
arts non-competitively							
ve except 5mph sector 11		A7					Bronze medal & clock
ve speed throughout		A10	C	1st			Bronze Club medal & French silver gilt medal & Club silver cup
ve speed throughout		A11			£5		Bronze medal & silver cup
ave sectors 2, 3, 6, 7, 8, 9 & 10	776/321	A12					Bronze medal & silver cup
d before Edinburgh,full ave sectors 1-6	456						
ve speed throughout	throughout	A17	D	1st	£5		Gold medal Most meritorious irrespective of class & Owers Cup for best in Section II
tarter							
roughout but does not wish to claim records							
cords 4th stage; 6mph on sector 6	throughout	A20	E(a)	2nd			Silver medal
ve speed except 9.5 mph sector 11		A21					Silver medal & silver rose bowl
ve speed except no record sector 5	throughout	A22	D	2nd			Silver medal & silver ACGBI clock
cords 6 stages, 2nd stage 6.5 mph	442						
ave speed sector 10	throughout	A24	B	1st			Silver medal & silver ACGBI cup
ave speed sectors 1, 2, 3, 4, 6, 8, 9 & 10	562/509	A25	A				Silver medal & bracelet
ave speed sectors 8 & 10	641/466	A26					Silver medal & cup
roughout but does not wish to claim records							
avc sectors 4, 8, 9 & 10: 11 no record		A28	E(b)	1st			Silver medal & silver ACGBI cup
cords sectors 3, 11 & 12	976						
ve except 8.5 mph sector 6	831/220	A30	C	2nd			Silver medal & silver ACGBI clock
ve except 9.5 mph sector 9	throughout	A31					Silver medal & silver ACGBI clock

Above:
Trophy presented to Mr. E. Pitman who personally drove the whole distance.

Results

The 1,000 Miles Trial

The records which the different cars made on each day's running, and on the various hill-climbing tests, have now been collated and tabulated by the Automobile Club, though they state that these records are subject to amendment on further examination of the records. The speed rates of the different cars on each period of running are as follows, the periods dealt with being: 1, London to Bristol, 118½ miles; 2, Bristol to Cheltenham, 43 miles; 3, Cheltenham to Birmingham, 49½ miles, 4, Birmingham to Manchester, 101¾ miles; 5, Manchester to Kendal, 73¾ miles; 6, Kendal to Carlisle, 61½ miles; 7, Carlisle to Edinburgh, 100 miles; 8, Edinburgh to Newcastle, 121½ miles; 9, Newcastle to Leeds, 103 miles; 10, Leeds to Sheffield, 74 miles; 11, Sheffield to Lincoln, 46½ miles; 12, Lincoln to Nottingham, 35¾ miles; and 13, Nottingham to London, 122¾ miles. The averages recognised are twelve miles per hour in England, and ten in Scotland.

SECTION I
MAKERS AND AGENTS

CLASS A

(CARS SELLING AT £200 OR LESS.)

No. 1 (Benz Ideal.) Attain its avs. on all but 2nd (9½), 6th (11½), and 8th (11) periods.

No. 2 (Benz Ideal.) Attain its avs. on all but periods 10 and 13, in each of which it scored 11½ m.p.h.

No. 5 (Locomobile steam carriage.) Full avs. on 4th, 5th, 6th, 7th, 9th, 11th, and 12th periods, 11½ m.p.h. on 1st and 13th, 9 on 2nd and 3rd, 9½ on 8th, and no record on 10th.

No. 16 (Gladiator voiturette.) Full avs. all through.

No. 19 (Orient Express.) Full avs. first three days; then retired.

No. 27 (New Orleans.) 11½ miles av. on 4th, 11 on 8th and 9th, and 10 m.p.h. on 10th periods. Full avs. otherwise.

No. 28 (New Orleans.) No records 3rd, 6th, 7th, 8th, and 9th periods, 6 m.p.h. on 5th, 7½ on 4th and 10th, 11½ on 13th, and full av. on remainder.

No. 29 (Eureka car.) Avs. 8 m.p.h. on 2nd, 9½ on 11th, on 6th, and 12 on 5th and 12th periods. No other records.

No. 30 (Eureka car.) No records, save for 2nd day (7 m.p.h.)

No. 33 (Decauville.) Full avs. on periods 5, 6, 7, 11, and 12, 11 m.p.h. on 2nd, 10 on 4th, 9½ on 10th, and no records for others.

No. 34 (Decauville.) Full avs. on all but 4th period (11 m.p.h.)

No. 41 (International Victoria.) 10 m.p.h. on 4th period, 11 on 8th and 9th, 9½ on 10th. Full avs. otherwise.

No. 44 (International Victoria.) Full avs. on all periods but 11th and 12th, when 11 and 10½ m.p.h. respectively are recorded.

No. 51 (Star voiturette.) No record on 5th period, 11 m.p.h. on 6th, and full avs. on all others.

No. 52 (Roots and Venables.) Full avs. first two days, 10½ m.p.h. on 4th. No other records.

CLASS B

(CARS SELLING AT OVER £200, BUT NOT MORE THAN £300)

No. 14 (De Dion voiturette.) Full avs. for first three periods. No record on 4th period. Full avs. for 5th and 6th and 7th periods. No record 8th. Full av. for rest, except last day of 11½ m.p.h.

No. 15 (De Dion voiturette.) Full avs. throughout.

No. 24 (Marshall carriage.) For 1st period 7½ m.p.h., 2nd 9 m.p.h. No records 3rd and 4th days, 11½ m.p.h. 5th period, 10½ on 6th, 9½ on 7th, 9 on 8th and 9th, 5½ on 10th, 8½on 11th, 12 on 12th, and no record for last period.

No. 31 (M.C.C. Triumph.) Full avs. first four periods. No record 5th day. Full avs. 6th, 7th, 8th, and 9th periods, 11 m.p.h. on 10th. Full avs. to finish.

No. 32 (M.C.C. Triumph.) Full avs. first three days, 10 m.p.h. 4th period, 9½ on 5th, full av. on 6th, 9 m.p.h. on 7th, no record 8th, 11 m.p.h. on 9th, 8½ on 10th, 11½ on 11th. Full avs. last two days.

No. 40 (Wolseley voiturette.) Full avs. first ten periods, 10½ m.p.h. on 11th, full avs. on two last days.

No. 45 (S.S. carriage.) Full on first two periods, 8½ on 3rd period. No further records.

No. 49 (Marshall carriage.) 7½ m.p.h. first period, 9½ on 2nd, 11 on 3rd and 4th, full avs. on 5th, 6th, and 7th, 11 on 8th, 11½ on 9th, 5½ on 10th. Full avs. on last three periods.

CLASS C

(CARS SELLING AT MORE THAN £300, BUT NOT MORE THAN £500)

No. 8 (M.M. Co.'s 6 h.p. phaeton.) Full av. first period, 11 m.p.h. on 2nd, 10 m.p.h. on 3rd and 4th, full avs. on 5th, 6th, and 7th, 11 on 8th, full av. on 9th, 10 m.p.h. on 10th. Full avs. to finish.

No. 9 (M.M. Co.'s Iveagh phaeton.) Full avs. from start to finish.

No. 23 (Brown-Whitney steamer.) 11 m.p.h. 1st period, 6½ on second, no record on 3rd, 10 m.p.h. on 4th, no record on 5th, full avs. on 6th and 7th periods, no records 8th, 9th and 10th, 8 m.p.h. on 11th, and no records 12th and 13th.

No. 26 (Peugeot 8 h.p.) Full average 1st period, 9 m.p.h. on 2nd, full avs. to finish.

No. 35 (Daimler 6 h.p.) Full avs. throughout all periods.

No. 36 (Daimler 6 h.p.) Full avs. first three periods, 10 m.p.h. on 4th, full avs. on 5th, 6th, and 7th, 11½ on 8th. Full avs. to finish.

No. 37 (Daimler Parisian.) Full avs. on first seven periods, 10 m.p.h. on 8th. Full avs. to finish.

No. 43 (L.M.V. and Waggon Co.'s phaeton.) Full av. on 1st period; no further records.

No. 46 (Richard car.) Full avs. first three periods, 6½ m.p.h. on 4th. full avs. 5th, 6th, 7th, and 8th, 10 m.p.h. on 9th, 9½ on 10th. Full avs. to finish.

No. 47 (Richard car.) Full avs. first three periods, 11½ m.p.h. on 4th. Full avs. to end.

CLASS D

(Cars selling at more than £500)

No. 22 (Lanchester.) Full avs. first nine periods, 9 m.p.h. on 10th, full avs. 11th and 12th. No record for last day.

CLASS E (a)

(Motor tricycles carrying one person)

No. 12 (Motor Mfg. Co.'s tricycle.) Full av. 1st period, 9 m.p.h. on 2nd, no record 3rd and 4th, full avs. on 5th, 6th, 7th, and 8th, 10½ m.p.h. on 9th, 11 m.p.h. on 10th, full avs. on 11th and 12th. No record on last day.

No. 20 (Simms's Motor Wheel.) Full avs. on first three runs, no record on 4th, full av. on 5th. No further records.

(Motor tricycle carrying two persons)

No. 39 (Century tandem.) No record 1st period, full avs. on 2nd, 3rd, 4th, 5th, 6th, 7th, 8th, and 9th, 11 m.p.h. on 10th, 7 m.p.h. on 11th, and full avs. on 12th and 13th.

CLASS E (b)

(Motor Quads. carrying two persons)

No. 3 (Ariel quad.) Full avs. throughout.

No. 4 (Ariel tricycle with Whippet attachment.) Full avs. from start to finish.

CLASS F

(Public service vehicles)

No. 38 (Daimler.) 9 m.p.h. 1st period, 5½ m.p.h. on 2nd, 7 on 3rd, 6½ on 4th, full av. on 5th, 8½ on 6th, no records on 7th and 8th, 11 m.p.h. on 9th, 8 on 10th, full avs. on 11th and 12th, and 8 m.p.h. on 13th.

SECTION II
PRIVATELY-OWNED VEHICLES

CLASS A

A25 Benz Ideal (Mrs. Bazalgette.) 11½ m.p.h. first period, 7½ on 2nd, 10½ on 3rd and 4th, full av. on 5th, 8 m.p.h. on 6th, full av. on 7th, 8½ on 8th, 8¼ on 9th, 9 on 10th. Full avs. last three days.

CLASS B

A24 Mors voiturette (Mr. R. E. Phillips.) Full avs. first nine periods, 11½ m.p.h. on 10th. Full avs. to end.

CLASS C

A2 Panhard 6 h.p. (Mr. Butler.) Full avs. first three periods, 11 m.p.h. on 4th, full avs. on 5th, 6th, and 7th, 11 on 8th, full av. on 9th, 11 on 10th. Full avs. to finish.

A3 Panhard 6 h.p. (Mr. T. B. Browne.) Full avs. all through.

A7 Daimler 6 h.p. (Mr. A. Harmsworth.) Full avs. on all except 11th period, when record was 5 m.p.h.

A10 Napier 8 h.p. (Mr. E. Kennard.) Full avs. for all periods.

A12 Daimler 6 h.p. (Mr. H. Edmunds.) Full av. 1st period, 11½ m.p.h. on 2nd and 3rd, full avs. 4th and 5th, 5 m.p.h. on 6th, 9½ m.p.h. on 7th, 10 m.p.h. on 8th, 11½ on 9th, 9½ on 10th. Full avs. to end.

A21 Daimler 6 h.p. (Mr. E. Pitman.) Full avs. on twelve periods out of thirteen. On 11th av. was 9½ m.p.h.

A23 M.M. Co.'s 6¼ h.p. (Mr. C. Cordingley.) No record 1st period, 6½ m.p.h. 2nd period, full avs. on 3rd and 4th, no record on 5th and 6th, full av. on 7th, no record on 8th, full av. on 9th, no record on 10th, full avs. on 11th and 12th. No record on last day.

A26 Daimler 6 h.p. (Mr. C. K. Gregson.) Full avs. on first seven periods, 11 m.p.h. on 8th, full av. on 9th, 10 m.p.h. on 10th. Full avs. to the end.

A30 Daimler 6 h.p. (Mr. J. D. Siddeley.) Full avs. on twelve runs; on 6th period av. 8½ m.p.h.

A31 Daimler 6 h.p. (Mr. W. Exe.) Full avs. on twelve runs, and 9½ m.p.h. on 9th period.

CLASS D

A4 Panhard 8 h.p. (Mr. Mark Mayhew.) Full avs. first three periods, 11 m.p.h. on 4th, full av. on 5th, no returns 6th, 7th, and 8th. Full avs. to end.

A11 Daimler 12 h.p. (Hon. J. S. Montagu, M.P.) Full avs. throughout.

A17 Panhard 12 h.p. (Hon. C. S. Rolls.) Full avs. all through.

A22 Daimler 12 h.p. (Mr. J. A. Holder.)

Full avs. first four periods, no return on 5th. Full avs. to finish.

A29 Peugeot 7 h.p. (Mr. Mark Mayhew.) Full avs. first two periods, no return for 3rd, full avs. for 4th, 5th, 6th, 7th, 8th, 9th, and 10th, no returns 11th and 12th. Full av. on last day.

CLASS E (a)

(Motor Tricycles)

A16 Ariel tricycle (Mr. A. J. Wilson.) Full avs. for first six runs; no further returns.

A20 Empress tricycle (Mr. H. Ashby.) Full avs. first three runs, no record 4th period, full av. on 5th period, 7 m.p.h. on 6th. Full avs. to end.

CLASS E (b)

(Motor Quadricycles)

A28 Enfield quad. (Mr. E. M. Iliffe.) Full avs. first three days, 11½ m.p.h. 4th period, full av. on 5th, 6th, and 7th, 11 m.p.h. on 8th and 9th, 11½ on 10th, no record on 11th. Full av. last two days. ”

The Autocar, Saturday, May 19th, 1900

Observations upon the Results

Every endeavour was indeed made by Claude Johnson and his team to collect accurate records. Some Participants, particularly the trade entries were very much aware that this was their greatest advertising opportunity to date for their motorcars. The fact that all the machines were subjected to the same difficulties at the same time was the best comparative exercise that a potential purchaser could wish for. So it was very important not to be spotted particularly by the press – (who, then as now, were always on the lookout for a disaster – good news is no news), if something needed repair. All efforts were made to do this in a quiet corner out of the public eye; and references are found to such furtive repairs going on. For example: in Sheffield a reporter found Mr. Butler dissembling and repairing his Panhard in a 'quiet corner'.

Other moments when the Participant hoped not to be observed were when it was necessary for passengers to dismount, or even, as in the case of Jules Dubois to be seen running alongside the Decauville No. 34 – just after Brixworth on the last day.

Also modifications were made in some instances, so that the car that finished was not the car that started. While this was good for 'Research & Development', it was outside the sporting spirit of the event. The Judges were aware of this possibility, hence their lengthy and painstaking stamping of component parts at the closing of the Exhibition at the Agricultural Hall, London April 14th to 21st, (they worked feverishly to complete this task prior to the start on April 23rd). One feels that the reporter who rode in Mr. Richardson's Daimler No. 36 on the last day, in the company of Lord Kingsburgh and Colonel. Magrath (who had ridden all of the Trial), was perhaps 'fed' a little information. Otherwise how would he have known, when they were passed by the Century tandem tricycle No 39 to make the following casual observation – Quote, 'By the way, I noticed that this machine was fitted with a 3 h.p. water-cooled De Dion motor and radiator, not a 2¼ h.p. motor as specified in the red book.'

Sometimes the press reports exaggerated breakdowns. We read that on the second to last day Mr. A. J. Coles in his Benz suffered a broken front axle on May 10th (*The Autocar*). This was repaired with another he **just happened** to be carrying. The next day *The Motor-Car Journal* reporter says he saw Mr. Coles pulled into a blacksmiths at the side of the road having a broken spindle repaired. When it came to reporting how the car No. 2 Benz had run we are told 'New spindle to front wheel said to be broken against kerb. Last day's record bad owing to above mishap, breaking and twisting frame of car.'

So, when reporting problems, the Participants were in most cases circumspect. Apart from delays from punctures, which seemed 'de rigeur', failures of machinery were played down for obvious reasons. Some breakdowns could not be ignored; but if the car finished (fairly) 1,000 miles in 20 days, what more could a potential purchaser ask?

The other area for confusion to arise is where cars had problems, went for repair, and then rejoined at a later stage. There is even an instance of a car appearing on the last day that had not been seen at all previously (the S. S. Princess car No. 11). So this car was hailed by the public alongside the heroes. Careful inspection of the daily timesheet records is most important! It was common knowledge that the Final Timed Stage ended at St. Albans, and the Participants gathered here to form a procession (in the order in which they arrived in St. Albans) leaving for London at 5 pm. The fact that cars re-joined or even joined for this part must have infuriated the Participants who had driven over 1,000 miles; and further confused reporting!

Unsung Heroes

The Mechanicians (who touched their caps and perhaps worked through the night to rebuild the car while the Driver or Owner was sleeping off his 'Official Welcome' dinner) are very much the unsung heroes of this tale.

Due to the social structure of late Victorian England it is quite difficult to trace these people. Even when photographs were taken their faces seemed to be averted (whether by accident or design we shall never know).

On A17 overall prize winning entry, Poole is recorded as something of a saint, as the Hon. C. S. Rolls was not satisfied with less than perfection.

Clarkson accompanied Mrs Louise Bazalgette on the Benz Ideal A25. He was in fact nominated for a Drivers Certificate at the end of the Trial, and it is recorded that she drove 621 miles, and he drove 562 miles.

T. Weeks accompanied Ernest Pitman on his Daimler A21. They achieved a very near perfect record and should have perhaps gained a second prize. Ernest Pitman was grateful for all the honours he was later awarded, and presented T. Weeks with a silver watch engraved '1,000 Miles Trial 1900' on the back of the case. Inside was a private message 'Presented to T. Weeks By E. Pitman Esqre On the occasion of their winning 2nd prize'

Perhaps the first place was a foregone conclusion saving unforeseen accidents; and one could suggest the real competition was for second place, and Ernest Pitman was grateful to T. Weeks.

Engraved watch case exterior

Far left:
The face of the pocket watch presented to T. Weeks by E. Pitman Esq. It is similar to the ACGBI presentation clocks.

Left:
(*Background:*) No. A21 righthand car with E. Pitman with T. Weeks (*Foreground:*) the watch presented to T. Weeks by E. Pitman.
(Photos: Elizabeth Bennett)

Robert Bunkall drove A23 Mr Cordingley's 6¼ h.p. Phaeton 442 miles. John Goody drove A12 Mr. H. Edmunds' 6 h.p. Daimler 776, while Henry Edmunds drove it 321 miles. P. Brown drove A30 Mr. J. D. Siddeley's 6 h.p. Daimler 220 miles, and accompanied the same throughout entire trial as mechanician. D. Haxton drove A29 Mr. Mark Mayhew's Peugeot 976 miles.

There were also others who were employees of the Companies that made Trade entries. W. Randall shared the driving with his boss Mr. Henry Hewetson on car No. 1, driving the Benz Ideal 533 miles, while Henry Hewetson drove 523 miles.

Searles drove the Locomobile Steam Carriage (No. 5) throughout; and Alfred Burgess (No. 8) the MMC Panhard. W. White drove (No. 9) the MMC Iveagh Phaeton (attributed to Mr Schofield) 896 miles; and E. Buck soldiered on throughout with (No. 12) the much repaired MMC Tricycle. The Brown Whitney steam car (No. 23) was driven throughout by E. R. Banks; and Mr. Astell (No. 27) and Mr. I. C. Forrow. (No. 28) bought the two New Orleans' (built in Twickenham) through the Trial. Henry Farman drove the MCC Triumph (No. 31) throughout; as did Frank Strange on the Decauville (No. 33); Ralph Jackson on the Century Tandem Tricycle (No. 39); and George Prew on (No. 51) the Star voiturette.

The ACGBI recognised that these people, although employed, had made an enormous contributions to the Trial, and Drivers Certificates were issued to them. These must have made a unique contribution to a chauffeur's references.

Automobile Club of Great Britain and Ireland.

1,000 MILES MOTOR VEHICLE TRIAL,
LONDON TO EDINBURGH AND BACK,
23rd APRIL to 12th MAY, 1900.

DRIVING CERTIFICATE.

This is to certify that Mr. Herbert Ashby
is entitled to a Driving Certificate, having driven Motor Vehicle No. A 20 – His Empress Tricycle
throughout the entire trial

Issued by Order of the Committee,
C. Johnson.
Secretary.
4, WHITEHALL COURT, LONDON, S.W.
July, 1900.

NOTE.—This Certificate is awarded without reference to the performance of the above-named Vehicle.

Another observation upon the results was made much later by Lord Montagu of Beaulieu:

'The Trial itself is history. The first of 65-odd vehicles to essay the course left Hyde Park Corner at 7 am, on 23 April 1900, and 35 of these returned to London having travelled the whole way under their own power. A dozen only maintained the legal average speed of 12 mph throughout, though no one made the obvious comment that in order to do so they must all have broken the law.'

Extract from *A Biography of the Hon. C. S. Rolls* by Lord Montagu of Beaulieu

General Conclusions concerning the Tour

"Now that the tour is over, we who have followed it from day to day can look back calmly upon the incidents thereof and form our own conclusions upon the performances of the cars, it must be admitted that the event has been a decided success. In the first place, seeing the apathy which apparently existed throughout the country upon motor matters, we were distinctly surprised at the enthusiastic welcome accorded the autocarists at every point of the thousand miles, not only in the towns but even in the country villages. That the cars favourably impressed every onlooker can scarcely be hoped for, seeing that, following in each other's dust on dusty days, the occupants presented a decidedly dirty appearance, whilst their leather garments and varied headgear and goggles certainly did not add to their beauty. Should another such tour be undertaken, it would be well, if it were possible, either to arrange that the run should be made at greater intervals between the cars or that compulsory halts for a brush down should be made, at any rate, before entering the red flag controls – that is to say, of course, if the object of the tour is to impress the public. Apart from appearance, however, there is ample evidence that the public were impressed, and impressed favourably, with the wonderful ease of management and the general reliability of the cars. Some, we believe, were impressed unfavourably with their speed, but that is a matter upon which opinions largely differ, and speed to the average British mind undoubtedly is an attractive feature. Another point, too, in which, we believe, the tourists distinctly scored was the immunity from serious accident throughout. When it is remembered that the cars passed through many districts where autocars are rarely, if ever, seen, and where, naturally, horses and other animals have not been educated to encounter them without fear, the very little trouble experienced by the automobilists from this cause is remarkable. We were not stopped half-a-dozen times in the whole tour on the cars on which we drove on account of any restive horses, and it is curious to note that the majority of instances of horse-frightening occurred in the case of motor cycles and not with the larger cars. When it is remembered that the aggregate mileage covered by the cars taking part in the tour must have been considerably over 60,000 miles, during which not a single accident of any kind happened to anyone engaged upon them, it is s striking testimony to the safety of autocaring as a pastime and sport. The accidents to others that occurred were caused through the unmanageability of animals, and when all the circumstances are considered, the fact that only one man and one horse were injured in the entire run is ample proof of the safety of the autocar when considered from the point of view of other users of the road as well as of the considerate manner in which the cars were used throughout the tour. In the matter of 'smaller game' as one sportive member put it, 'the bag' was somewhat larger, and may be summed up as seven or eight dogs, a sheep, a cat, and a sparrow. Of the cars themselves, there can be no two opinions about their general behaviour *en route*. Of course most encountered some cause for minor stoppage at one time or another. Circulating pumps, pneumatic tyres, and ignition gear were most generally the cause of delay, but the actual breakdowns were few and far between, and a feature of the tour was, perhaps, the lightning repairs which were in some cases executed, and which enabled cars to continue in the run with but a few hours' delay, which would in ordinary hands and in ordinary times have possibly been stranded for a day or two. The driving generally, although some fast work was put in by the speed cars, was characterised by caution and consideration for the public, and we saw very little in the way of reckless driving, although the French drivers of several of the foreign-built cars apparently could not disabuse themselves of the idea that the whole affair was a race, and they, with one or two others who had personal interests in the cars they drove, were somewhat given to ignoring the green flag controls, and thus picking up time on the faster cars in front, which loyally adhered to the regulations. The hill-climbing contests showed that all the vehicles in the trial were able to be got up the severe gradients they were put at, although several of them could only do so by putting out one or more of their passengers, and some by stoppage and making repeated starts and short runs, and we regret that circumstances prevent our publishing a full record of these incidents, which would, we feel sure, have been of considerable interest and value to our readers. Coming to the performances of the cars themselves, the broad conclusions we arrived at may be stated as follows:

THE BENZ IDEALS got through quite satisfactorily. They did not distinguish themselves greatly as speed vehicles, neither were they remarkable for untoward incidents and stoppages for repairs. They went through at a regular average pace, and well fulfilled the claims of their makers.

THE ARIEL QUADRICYCLE proved itself to be a very speedy vehicle, although, despite its 3⅛ h.p. motor, it had to shed both its passengers at several of the steepest gradients. This could only be obviated by a two-speed gear.

THE ARIEL TRICYCLE, WITH WHIPPET TRAILER, proved itself one of the speediest machines on the road. Whatever may be the comfort or otherwise of riding upon a machine of this kind, there can be no doubt that with two skilled pedallers to assist the motor at critical times it is a combination possessed of very great speed. With the exception of tyre troubles, both these machines stood the severe work of the trials well.

THE LOCOMOBILE (STANLEY) STEAM CAR – Needless to say, a great deal of interest centred in this vehicle, and it must be admitted that she went through the trials a great deal better than many people expected. The prognosticated failure of the boiler before half-way, which more than one had anticipated, did not come off, and she appeared to experience no inconvenience from the various qualities of water picked up en route. Whilst she did not distinguish herself as a speed vehicle, she came through steadily, and, in spite of her light construction, experienced but one mishap – omitting tyre troubles, which were numerous, and which show that the single tube tyre, as used, is too light for the work to which the car was subjected. The light chains and other parts, where breakages were expected by many, stood up throughout the journey. The fitting of the condensers enabled her to avoid visible steam in ordinary running, but not when negotiating steep gradients, or endeavouring to force the pace. The greatest difficulties of working her appeared to exist during a rear gale, when the boiler fires could be, but with difficulty, kept alight.

THE MOTOR MANUFACTURING CO.'S PANHARD TYPE CARRIAGES – with the exception of some tyre troubles, and the failure of a pump on the last day's run, these cars proved themselves to be thoroughly reliable, steady going touring vehicles, able to maintain a good average without difficulties in the way of management. On the company's Princess car, an opinion can scarcely be formed, as she only joined in on the last day. The tricycle of the same company met with bad luck, and the frame was eventually changed for another en route, although by dint of perseverance the whole of the course was covered.

THE DE DION VOITURETTES showed themselves to be possessed of very considerable speed on light gradients, and were apparently very easy of management, though trouble appeared to be experienced by all of them with their pump gear, which, in several instances, underwent replacement. They were somewhat noisy on their gearing, but not more so than the average tricycle

THE GLADIATOR VOITURETTE proved itself one of the speediest vehicles of the party, and a good hill-climber. It met with no serious breakdown, though we saw it stopped at the roadside for adjustments – chiefly with the sparking gear, we believe – a great many times. It is rather low-built, and consequently dusty, but appears likely to prove a fairly satisfactory vehicle of its type, especially where speed is a requisite.

THE 8 H.P. NAPIER CAR was driven for all it was worth, and decidedly made a good showing. Those who rode on her reported more vibration than upon some other cars of the type, but she stood the very hard work she was put to well, and, judging by speed trials, which, after all, are the only really accurate data we have to guide us, in point of speed she equalled the Panhard car of the same power, and considerably distanced two out of the three twelve horse-power cars she competed against. She decidedly proved her position as a car to be reckoned with, and, as a purely English production, she is the equal, power for power, in point of speed, to the best production on the French market.

THE LANCHESTER CARRIAGES scarcely added to the reputation they previously possessed. It was a mistake on the part of the makers to put the second car in the trials, seeing that she was only finished the previous day, and had had no preparatory runs. It was also doubtless a mistake, though done with good intention, to gear the other car down, as, although she proved excellent at hill work, in point of speed, owing to the low gear, she did not show to advantage, and speed in the course of the trials undoubtedly attracted attention. In point of freedom from vibration and comfortable travelling, she distinctly scored, but with eight horse-power engines she would have made a still better showing, if geared somewhat higher.

THE BROWN-WHITNEY STEAM CAR scarcely had a fair test, seeing that she was quite new, and had never been run before, whilst she was also in the hands of an entirely new crew, and virtually an amateur crew at that. Although she was driven right through the trials, she certainly was not seen at her best.

THE MARSHALL CARRIAGES, as recorded elsewhere, had the worst of luck, though they both got through the trials and completed the journey, and Mr. Mann in particular must be complimented on the way he stuck to his car (damaged in the Hatton Garden collision) under all difficulties, and got her through the run. Here again the makers were somewhat unwise in placing an untried system in the trials, their chief troubles arising through difficulties with their pump and water circulation, owing to the fact that whereas hitherto they had depended on natural circulation, for the trials they fitted their cars with water pumps, both of which failed the first day. The cars are possessed of plenty of power and a good speed, and more effective silencers are now being fitted.

THE PEUGEOT CARRIAGES, which went through the trials, proved themselves to be good cars, but, like many another, pump troubles appeared to be the principal difficulties attending their use. They were decidedly speedy, both up hill and on the level, and, power for power, showed themselves well able to rank with the best.

THE NEW ORLEANS CARS distinctly made a good impression, being possessed of a very good turn of speed for small cars, and very fair hill-climbing capacity. Although one of them had plenty of minor troubles, we believe it was more owing to the driver than the car, for the only time we saw Mr. Astell stopped with No. 27 was when his batteries had run out. The very long and trying gradients experienced in many places did not appear to interfere with the effectiveness of their air-cooled motors. The system of cooling worked satisfactorily.

THE EUREKA CARS should never have been entered for such a trial, as they are not intended for heavy touring work. The Eureka is in its place as a little vehicle for running about parks and boulevards, but it could not be expected to show to advantage in the 1,000 miles trial.

THE M.C.C. TRIUMPH CARS – These handsome little vehicles showed themselves possessed of a good turn of speed, and, although inclined to be rather noisy in the gear, got through without any serious troubles, so that they would appear to be established as reliable, handy little cars.

THE DECAUVILLES were probably the least quiet of any of the voiturettes. A very good pace could be got out of them, and they could be got up most hills by shedding their passengers on the steepest parts.

THE DAIMLER VEHICLES naturally attracted much attention, as, especially in the private class, there were more of them running than of any other make. The twelve horse-power cars were considerably slower in the speed trial than the nominally equally horse-powered Panhard with its electric as well as tube ignition, but when it came to the consideration of the company's latest design, the new Parisian six horse-power car, it distinctly scored all along the line. The speed test showed it to be possessed of a very high speed rate when power and weight are considered, and both in the speed trial and throughout the running of the tour it showed itself fully equal – indeed, in many cases superior – to the equivalent cars of the Panhard Company. The new public service vehicle, however, suffered from the same drawback as some of the other cars we have previously mentioned, namely, lack of prior trial.

THE CENTURY TANDEM appears to be a little machine possessed of a very considerable turn of speed, is simple in construction, and easily handled, while the front seat strikes us as being more comfortable than on most tandems. Pump, ignition, and tyre troubles were the cause of delay, many of them due to the Newcastle collision.

THE WOLSELEY CARS – The withdrawal of the larger Wolseley was due mainly to the mistake of taking a new and untried car on the trial. The other one showed a good advantage, and distinctly made a favourable impression, and with longer wheelbase will be a very steady and comfortable car to travel in. She is possessed of good speed and hill-climbing power, is easily handled, and not easily subject to derangement.

THE INTERNATIONAL CARS came through the trials steadily and without mishap. They showed themselves to be fully equal to other vehicles of their class, and may be taken to be steady going, reliable touring cars.

THE RICHARD CARS were very 'in-and-out' in their running, though No. 47 in particular ran much better at the end than at the beginning, when she showed a very fair turn of speed and good hill-climbing capacity. Both these cars were forced to the utmost extent, and proved themselves good all-round vehicles, though, by horse-power comparison, somewhat behind the others of about the same rating.

THE STAR, but for the unfortunate breakage of its axle, and the shaking up it got as the result thereof, scored in its class, being possessed of good speed both on the level and up hill, and

"Several of our readers have expressed curiosity as to why the Endurance car retired from the 1,000 miles trial, and where. For our own part, we lost sight of it at Bristol, and the manufacturers inform us now that they abandoned the run at Cheltenham, largely for two reasons – first because the car was practically an untried one, and only finished two days before, consequently developing minor derangements, which took time to rectify; and also because at Knightsbridge, owing to the car in front pulling up suddenly without warning, they ran into the back of it, seriously damaging their water tank, straining the frame of the car, and causing thereby the heating of the countershaft bearings. This will doubtless be a full and sufficient explanation to those of our readers who take an interest in the Endurance car."

The Autocar, Saturday, May 26th, 1900

making a particularly good showing on the Birkhill climb.

THE PANHARD CARS, all of which, it may be noted, were entered by amateurs, proved themselves the fliers of the tour, especially in the higher-powered vehicles. Judging by the speed test, Mr. Rolls's nominal twelve horse-power car is at least ten miles an hour faster than any other car of similar power. Mr Mayhew's eight horse-power vehicle, owing to unsuitable spirit and troubles attendant thereupon, was not running at her best, but showed conspicuously notwithstanding. With the six horse-power vehicles, however, the showing was not quite so good, for both in the speed test and general running they were not so good as the Daimler Co.'s latest designs of similar power.

THE EMPRESS TRICYCLE made good showing, and possessed a high turn of speed and went through with little in the way of trouble, a worn-out gear pinion being the principal substitution requisite.

THE MORS PETIT DUC struck us, so far as general design and size of car went, as being more nearly what the British public wants than any other car in the run. Without being large, it was roomy enough to be comfortable, and, taken generally, the car behaved well, climbed hills well, was easy to handle, and possessed a good turn of speed. Her causes of delay were in no case serious.

THE ENFIELD QUADRICYCLE, with its two and threequarter horse-power motor, proved also a good and speedy article, and quite equal to anything else in the motor cycle line in the trials in the matter of reliability - possessed of good speed and excellent hill-climbing capacity, although on the very steepest pitches she had to shed her passenger.

In the above notes we have not referred at all to those types of car which did not complete the journey. Their withdrawals are explained in 'the records of the Cars. ”

The Motor-Car Journal

A lighthearted look at fragments from the Trial

Contacts with Officials

Notwithstanding the arrangements made by those who control that out-of-date tollgate on the Dulwich College Road with the Automobile Club, and the letter under the hand of W. G. King addressed to them in which it was promised that a sum of three pence only should be charged to the competing cars en route to the Crystal Palace, the gate-keeper insisted upon regarding the autocars as locomotives, and mulcted all who passed his barrier in the sum of one shilling. As the autocar is a carriage in the eyes of the law, and the toll board is innocent of any mention of carriages, we very much question whether any charge whatever can be made upon autocars passing through the gate. As cyclists had to fight for their freedom from toll at this barrier, so apparently will autocarists.

Police Arrangements

In the large towns the police arrangements have been admirable – contrasting very conspicuously with the peculiar ideas of the Berkshire constabulary. At Manchester it was interesting to see the police urge the automobilists forward, and the action of the Bradford police was even more friendly. The head constable and mounted police kept the way clear, while constables lined the streets, and others held the flags. On leaving the town the vehicles were marshalled in capital style in a long line, and we would congratulate Bradford on the excellent tone adopted by its police authorities.

The Hon. J. Scott Montagu, M.P., interviewed at Gloucester, spoke in high terms of the condition of the roads on the Gloucestershire side of Bristol, and also contrasted the courteous conduct of the police of the county with the brusqueness shown by the authorities in some other districts.

It is gratifying to hear that when the Lancashire County Council first learnt that a hill trial would take place up Shap Fell, the council instructed their surveyor to have the road surface made as good as possible.

It should not be forgotten that the Lord Mayor of Manchester thinks no harm can result from autocars travelling twenty miles per hour on unfrequented country roads. Will the Chief Constable of Berkshire kindly note?

The police of all the counties passed through up to the moment of writing, Berkshire always excepted, have done their utmost to aid in the progress of the cars through their districts. They mount guard at all cross roads and in every village.

It has been suggested by a reader of a legally argumentative inclination that the Automobile Club should take steps against the police authorities of Berkshire for allowing their men to temporarily obstruct the view of persons who wished to read the inscriptions on the milestones. This idea appears to have struck our correspondent as he drove down the Bath Road on the first day of the trial, and found a huge policeman calmly sitting on each milestone, evidently with hostile intentions.

A Point to Remember

Those who follow the order in which the cars have arrived at the leading towns – as given by 'Observer,' and also by our correspondent en route – should remember that in nearly every instance someone has been an hour behind the first starter, owing to the system of controls. Hence it does not follow that the car arriving last has lost so much time as might be supposed.

Marshals were sometimes upset

Mr. William Ward Whittard, of Cheltenham, writes: 'On page 409 of *The Autocar* for April 20th, I notice a reflection on the Cheltenham control, for which there is no excuse. The cars started from the Winter Gardens less than a minute late at my signal. The time in the control was twelve o'clock, and allowing half and hour intervals at the outward control for fifty-eight cars, the time of the last car would be 3h. + 12m. + 29m., or 3.41 about. I believe a short delay occurred at the outward control owing to the obstinacy of one driver, who refused to obey official instructions. It is rather hard that men who give up a whole day (and many days preparation) to assist a thing of this kind should be rated by your correspondent for carefully carrying out their instructions.'

Some of the control officials at the different controls have afforded the occupants of the cars considerable amusement. One particularly energetic member of a certain local committee tried to restrain a six horse-power Parisian Daimler back with his hand, but found he was hardly equal to the effort.

Baggage Wagon

'The trials and tribulations of the baggage waggon' would make good reading. The Daimler waggonette used for this purpose by the company was one of the best cars in the run, and her driver and his car were the 'handy man' of the party. In connection with Mr. Straker's breakdown with the char-a-banc she did good service, standing by the big car all the way from Moffat to Edinburgh, and practically towing the char-a-banc forty-six miles through the night. The larger car required constant fresh supplies of water, and the drivers tell weird tales of tramping over the moors with lamps and canvas buckets in search of the necessary fluid, the while they floundered knee deep in bog holes, and otherwise enjoyed themselves at two o'clock in the morning. They got to Edinburgh at 6.30 a.m. on Saturday, and then worked practically day and night on repairs, doing another night journey to Newcastle, during which their water-hunting adventures were repeated, and reaching the Tyneside capital at four on Monday morning, in time for a clean up for the start at seven. History records that the driver of the baggage car slumbered on his seat during the run to Leeds, and narrowly escaped an upset, and who can wonder at it? Needless to say, the day's rest arranged for at Leeds came as a welcome break in the monotony of work to at least one of those engaged in the tour.

Confused reporting on the number of participants

The First Three Days

On the first day of the Trial sixty cars arrived at Bristol out of the sixty-four that started from London, and forty-four averaged 12 miles an hour; on the second day – from Bristol to Birmingham – fifty-nine cars arrived at the latter place, thirty-four of which averaged 12 miles, and on the run from Birmingham to Manchester thirty-one out of fifty-two which reached the Lancashire city were up to the legal limit. There seems a little confusion as to the actual number that started from Grosvenor Place. Our own observers – stationed at two different points – gave the number of starters at sixty-four, but a report received from Bristol gives the number at sixty-seven. Anyhow, all such little variations may be expected to be cleared up by Mr. Johnson – when he gets a few minutes to spare.

There seems to be a general impression that the full number of entrants for the 1,000 miles trial actually started. As a matter of fact, eighty-five cars did not start, but only sixty-five, and fifty-one of those reached Edinburgh. The others which were put out of the hunt with mishaps which have been detailed in our columns, but practically none of them have been of such a character as to disgrace the carriage. The crankshaft of a railway locomotive breaks occasionally, owing to some hidden flaw in the metal, or through molecular fatigue, and, with one or two exceptions, it has been accidents of this kind which have occurred to the machines which have been left behind. Of course, in a trial of this sort, a few machines were sure to be entered which never had a ghost of a chance of running through, but the Automobile Club could not pick and choose the entries and the failures which have taken place have in one or two instances at least not surprised the keener followers of automobilism.

St John Nixon and Argent Archer.

Argent Archer, the well known photographer at the time of the One Thousand Miles Trial, was commissioned by the organisers to take group photographs around the country – hence the records which we treasure today. Whilst many of the photographs were taken at the various exhibition halls, others were taken at random where the photographer saw a sufficient number of cars gathered

St. John Nixon (*centre*) at Sheffield Drill Hall holding something he wants us to see!

Mr Kennard's Napier. Mr. Edge explaining the functions of the governor (human governor operator 14 year old St. John Nixon to right-hand side) (Photo: *The Autocar*)

together at halting places to record them collectively. In addition he took pictures of individual entries, when requested to do so. It must have been hard work lugging the equipment all over the place. It must be remembered the cameras and tripods were made of wood, thus weighty; and the films were of course heavy glass plates. What, you may well ask has this got to do with St. John Nixon, a young lad of 14?

The beauty of the Argent Archer records is that in some instances the scenes they chose to record were only semi-posed. As a result, many little unrehearsed 'cameos' were captured. This was not, however, the case with young Nixon. The posed photograph taken in the Drill Hall, Sheffield, clearly depicts Nixon sitting in the middle of the Ariel tricycle with Whippet trailer holding a cylindrical object in his right hand for all to see. Now this was obviously quite deliberate; Nixon wanted the photographer to record this. Why? So as to thoroughly emphasize this object he is again seen holding it, this time in his left hand at the close of the Trial in the photographs taken in Whitehall, this time seated in the Napier.

Both Nixon and Edge tell of the arrival of the Napier at Manchester where it was found that the aluminium carburettor had broken in two. It was fixed by Napier himself using plaster of Paris and copper wire. The first carburettor fitted to a Napier was made by Longuemare, according to *The Autocar*, but the cylinder does not look like one of these. So, why is Nixon showing this object astride the Ariel; and then at the end of the Trial in Whitehall London, on the Napier?

Detail of St. John Nixon from Argent Archer photo on opposite page (Photo: Argent Archer)

S. F. Edge possibly tells us in 'My Motoring Reminiscences'.

'On the journey between Birmingham and Manchester the governor-hammer broke, and our method of effecting a repair was one of the jokes of the trial. I must explain that like almost all cars in those days, there was no throttle by means of which the speed of the engine could be controlled. On the timing-shaft, was a centrifugal governor which caused the exhaust valve tappets to move away from the stems of the valves, and thus prevent their opening. When the hammer broke, we had no means of reducing the speed of the engine. As we had no spare governor-hammer in our kit, I procured a long piece of copper wire and one end of this I fastened to the end of the lever which caused the tappets to move, and the other end I threaded round the front cylinder and brought it out through the dashboard. A small piece of wood was attached to this which Nixon, who sat on the footboards, held in his hand. Every time the engine began to race, Nixon pulled the wire, which caused the tappets to move away from the valves; it acted excellently and was quite as efficient as an ordinary governor. When I wished to take out the clutch out or change gear, I shouted 'govern!' and Nixon pulled the wire! The human governor on the Napier was a standing joke, and it worked so well that I did not trouble to get another one from the factory. Throughout the whole trial this was the means of controlling the engine.'

No wonder St. John Nixon thought it worth recording for us all to see one hundred years later!

Horses

In defence of the Low-Bred

The horse is a confirmed conservative; like the cart he drags, his slow mind settles in ruts. In his view man was created to be drawn in a cart, and he asks nothing better than to bear man's mild yoke for ever. Fancy then his perturbation at meeting a procession of vehicles unmistakably horseless moved 'like the wind,' by some mysterious hidden agency! Well may the patient journeying horse be the terror of the watchful motor driver. Poor beast, his powers of expression are limited, but as the car passes, his wild eye and beating hoofs sufficiently attest his alarm. Once, as we descended a hill, we met a splendid black-maned cart horse, lumbering along in dignified leisure. The car whizzes under his nose: he rears on his great haunches pulling his diminutive guardian off his feet, and breaks away in sheer panic. It is interesting to contrast the unfeigned alarm of the simple cart horse with the gentlemanly reserve of the well-bred carriage horse. He is quite as much frightened, but far too refined to show a vulgar lack of self-control. Accordingly, he steps past with a shade of added hauteur. The alarm in his bright eye alone betrays him.

A Narrow 'Squeak'

While on the road from Newcastle to Durham, Mr. Holder had an exciting experience, a horse backing suddenly across the road in front of his car. One of the passengers, relating the incident, says:– 'If we had had tiller steering or solid tires we could not have avoided the onslaught of the cart, but the elasticity of pneumatics and the steadiness of wheel steering enabled us to charge the footpath boldly, although it was about nine inches higher than the road. The car shaved the hedgerow by a bare half-inch and the backing cart just caught the corner of the rear off mudguard, but did no other damage. It was a narrow squeak, however.'

'In Tow'

Just outside the Newcastle control an interesting incident occurred. The cap of the axle of the De Dion voiturette driven by Mr. Egerton fell off broken. Mr. Moffatt Ford came along a few minutes later, and offered to take the De Dion in tow, an offer which Mr. Egerton accepted. With the help of a rope this was done successfully for some time, until the latter found the arrangement unsatisfactory, and throwing the rope away leant over, and with one hand grasped the back of Mr. Ford's car. The journey was thus pursued. Shortly after, as they were turning a corner, a horse drawing a railway lorry was startled, and turning sharply away, broke a lamp post, and nearly struck the adventurous automobilists. There was a great bother, the vanman declaring he did not like 'snakes in the forest,' and exhibiting a contempt for all who drove without horses. Names and addresses were taken, and the crowd that quickly assembled were very much amused.

At the Start

Horse-jobbers took the opportunity of giving their animals a taste of autocars by turning up in numbers at Grosvenor Place, and moving up and down amongst the cars before they left. A wise proceeding indeed.

A Narrow Escape

Among the few occasions on which horses and ponies proved objectionable was one which occurred on the way from York to Leeds. A pony in a trap, in which were two ladies, suddenly swerved across the roadway, but Mr. C. Johnson stopped the motor-car in almost the twinkling of an eye by throwing the machinery out of gear and applying the foot brake. The ladies leaped from the car, the driver was quickly at the pony's head, and all danger at an end.

Southern Horses

The horses met between London and Bristol on Monday last showed remarkably little fear of the cars as they whirled by. On our own account we noticed but one animal that showed any real signs of fear.

Northern Horses

It is very clear that the horses in some of the northern parts of England through which the cars have journeyed are not so well accustomed to the automobile as those in the south. Some have shown a coyness, a shyness, and, sometimes, a restlessness which was never noticed during the earlier stages of the journey, and one collided with Mr. Siddeley's car breaking its leg and disabling the vehicle until the local smith at Keswick put things right.

Horses Undisturbed

The horses on the road from London to Bristol were evidently desirous of sustaining their reputation for good behaviour, and the motorists had nothing to say as to any equine want of manners. At the start we noticed several grooms accustoming their horses to the motors as they stood at ease in Grosvenor Place, and correspondents on the route testify to similar training having been observed near Newbury, Beckington, Box, and other places.

Again the uneducated horse has caused a fatal accident. A pair of them drawing a brewer's dray bolted at New Brompton, having been frightened by a 'road locomotive,' the unfortunate driver being killed. Perchance, when some high and mighty personage has lost his life through this inexcusable equine ignorance, their automobile education may be made compulsory.

A postcard of the day

Accident at Thirsk

On Monday morning the motor-cars passed through Thirsk from Northallerton en route to York and Leeds. Excellent police arrangements had been made by Inspector Cook, who succeeded in keeping the road clear through the market square, it being no easy task, seeing that it was market day, and in addition the principal day of the May Day statutes. .... An accident occurred to the Rev. Mr. Proud, vicar of Kilburn, there were no casualties. In the case referred to Mr. Proud was driving slowly along Inghramgate, when Mr. and Mrs. Chapman, from Hambleton, attempted to drive between Mr. Proud and one of the motor-cars, which was passing at the time, with the result that a collision ensued, and both traps were overturned. The accident was no fault of the motor-cars; and we merely refer to it here as the idea has got abroad that a motor-vehicle was the cause of the mishap.

Contact with dogs and other animals

As already recorded in this column, several dogs met with untimely ends during the course of the tour, and others experienced 'nasty bumps.' On Saturday, running through St. Albans, the Wolseley car ran over no less than three, though that was about the record. We think in all probability a dozen canines met disaster, but in the way of running over things, perhaps the most extraordinary experience was that of Mr. Kennard who, on his Napier, when running fast, actually ran over a sparrow, which was busily engaged with a choice tit-bit in the road. Another curious fatality to an animal occurred on the last day, when Lord Kingsburgh reported that several sheep started away from the side of the road in alarm as his car passed, one of them suddenly falling head over heels and breaking its neck.

The casualties of the week have been, so far as we can learn, few and small. The deaths of one hen and a little chicken are the only fatalities that can be attributed to the motor-cars.

The attitude of dogs towards the autocar varies as much as that of men. Some are plainly scared, and with tails between their legs run away in alarm; others are not so bad, but it is plain they 'don't quite like it,' for they sneak quietly behind their masters or back against the wall. These dogs do not worry the autocarists. It is the other kind. Of this latter class we have the bold animal who rushes at the car headlong with mouthing menace, and either

A cartoon postcard of the day

runs into it or turns tail, and just whisks that appendage from under the wheels in time. This dog is a nuisance, but perhaps the most annoying brute of all is the calmly indifferent dog who plainly fails utterly to comprehend the fact that the car is bearing down upon him, and either stays stolidly where he is or stalks calmly across its path. One or two unfortunate animals have, we believe, been run over and killed in the course of the tour, and we can personally vouch for any number of narrow escapes where these indifferent or aggressive dogs have only been saved from destruction by the smart handling of the drivers, who we find with scarcely an exception are dog lovers, and would no more think of running over one if they could possibly avoid it than slaying their own kith and kin.

Casualties

'The total casualties of the motor-car long-distance Trial were a dead dog and a broken-legged horse. It was distinctly the fault of the animal in each case. The horse injudiciously whipped round at right angles in front of a car, and the dog foolishly believed that a bite out of a tire would do it good.' Later returns include a hen and a sheep, the death of the latter occurring on the last day of the Trial, an illustration of the 'action at a distance' to which Mr. Worby Beaumont referred at Monday's dinner.

Up to Monday night the 1,000 miles tourists had by no means regained the country of educated horses. In the North they still show much fear of cars. Between Boroughbridge and Wetherby a startled pig paced Mr. Lord's Peugeot some two miles in the twilight.

Appearance of the Automobilists

Leather bound
(Photo: *The Autocar*)

The impressions of an outsider who was courteously given a seat on one of the 1,000 miles trial cars, as to the average autocarist's mental equipment, will read with interest by those whom it may concern: 'The outward appearance of the motor car folk is not prepossessing. As to their mental equipment, that seems hardly more attractive to the average person. Already has the motor car industry developed a type. That type has an eager face, as if life was lived at thirty miles per hour, and there was not much time to see what was coming down the road. A scion of the family of Vere de Vere would be sadly out of place on the driver's seat. Furthermore, the face is, at least after the start, a grimy one, in whose wrinkles the dust finds lodging, and the general appearance is akin to that of an employee at the Corporation ash-destructor. The conversational range is strictly confined; it begins and ends with the motor car. A few attempts to engage in talk proved that, only if you could discuss the relative merits of the various makes of motors, or give information as to the surface and profile of the road, were your remarks worth listening to. Any excursion into the scenery to be found on the journey through the Vale of Severn was met with inattention.'

Protection Against the Weather

The great variations in the temperature experienced during the Trial proved to be another sort of trial to many of the participants, and the necessity of special provision in the way of clothing was made clear. Quite a number of those who made the long journey, including ourselves, had in use Burberry's 'Automo Slip-on' Gabardine Combination, and from practical experience we can strongly recommend this as being a most desirable adjunct to the outfit necessary for a motor-car tour. Even when worn over an overcoat we found it exceedingly comfortable and free fitting, and as a protection against sharp winds it was simply invulnerable. Fortunately we had no extended opportunity of testing the water-proof qualities of the Combination, but in this connection those who have adopted it have nothing but praise to offer.

Messrs. Hoare and Sons' autocoats are quite a feature of the 1,000 miles tour. Messrs. Kennard, Swindley, Lord, and Friswell, and Mrs. Kennard and others are sporting them, and right well have their sound protective qualities been appreciated through the cold and wet met with.

Left:
Appearance of the Automobilists (Photo: Argent Archer)

Drivers

Patience, Perseverance, and Philosophy

The man who goes motoring must possess an equable temperament, and be prepared to accept the inevitable without flinching. Such a tour as that upon which the leading automobilists are now engaged calls forth many qualities, and to the exercise of; patience and perseverance the motorist must add the spirit of the philosopher. He must learn not to be exacting in trifles, and to look at general results rather than particular instances. Having got clear of Bristol – the city of spires and charitable institutions – many of the travellers encountered a troublous season owing to the mediocre character of the spirit that had been supplied. Some were annoyed and sought to exercise the feeling of irritation by remarks of denunciatory force and fervour. We will not report their utterances verbatim. In view of the temporary distress they lost their equanimity; but, strangely enough, all reached their destination in good time. Those who had suppressed their indignation showed the philosophic spirit which motorists should seek to cultivate. On such tours the rough paths cannot be wholly avoided, and must be regarded as equally a part of the experience and trial as the smooth and pleasant places.

Concentration

Not only does automobilism induce to the philosophic attitude, but it encourages concentration of thought. As one correspondent wrote of the drivers as they rode into Darlington: 'They looked as if they meant business. Life was real and earnest to them. Manipulating a car looks to an outsider the next serious thing to taking an ironclad into action. You don't speak to the man at the wheel. There is a far-away look in the eyes of the driver, or the owner who is his own driver – on the principle of "every man his own lawyer" – that speaks volumes for the ability of concentration possessed by the human mind.'

Autocar drivers who have passed a cycling novitiate are much more choice in the selection of the road surface over which they steer their cars. The cyclist driver has a keen eye for the best travelling portion of the road, and will be found to get two of his wheels on to it if he cannot get the four.

Three Little Incidents

As the Trial has gone forward the incidents which gave a zest to the performances of the first two or three days have not been repeated, and the contest is settling down into an uneventful parade of reliable and steady cars. On the day of the hill climbing at Taddington Hill there were only three little mishaps to chronicle, and they were of quite minor importance. In one case a governor was broken in the neighbourhood of Lichfield, the victim being the Richard car. In the other a De Dion voiturette broke its front spindle outside Matlock Bridge, but nobody was hurt. A passenger fell out of the car of the Hon. C. S. Rolls while it was descending from the Cat and Fiddle to Macclesfield; altogether a trio of really unimportant matters – unless the descending passenger has a different opinion to offer. Unlikely as this was Poole, his mechanician.

Hon. C. S. Rolls and his 12 h.p. Panhard from Montague Grahame-White's album. (Courtesy N.M.M. Beaulieu)

The Pluck of the Drivers

At Monday's dinner the Hon. C. S. Rolls paid a well-deserved tribute to the pluck and determination shown by the drivers, whose careful attention contributed much to the success of the Trial. To drive a successful car was comparatively an easy matter: but to endure the annoyance of breakages, the inconveniences of punctures, and the comments of the crowd on the belated ones was a trial to many. On the way to Sheffield the driver of one of the Eurekas was on the road from 3 a.m. to half-past one on the following day – a trial of physical strength, no less than a strain on the system as a whole. Nothing, too, could exceed the pluck and determination displayed by the driver of Simms' motor-wheel. All who had an opportunity of seeing how perseveringly he kept on despite the most discouraging circumstances expressed their admiration of his endeavours, which, at times, were almost heroic, displaying a high courage and steady nerve. Mr. Buck, who rode the Motor Manufacturing Company's tricycle, also deserves mention in this connection.

Ladies on the Trial

At various times during the course of the tour ladies occupied seats upon the cars. Four members of the fair sex, however, made the entire journey from start to finish, Mrs. Friswell accompanying her husband, and Miss Butler her father, whilst Mrs. Bazalgette and Mrs. Kennard drove their own vehicles, although the latter was not entered as a contestant. These ladies deserve to be congratulated on the way in which they stuck to the cars, in spite of the, at times, unpleasant weather experienced.

Misses Collis and Fairfax supported the Trial from a distance.
(Photo: P.H.H.)

According to the *Leeds Mercury* one of the cars arriving at Sheffield on Wednesday was the 'Die Don Vatinvette,' bearing a lady who had 'ridden the whole of the 1,000 miles.' Adapted as a draper's delivery vehicle that car might be further disguised as 'The Don Satinette.' Certainly we object to anything of the 'vette' or 'vet' in connection with automobiles.

The Motor-Car Journal, Saturday, May 12th, 1900

Ladies on Tour

While Mr. Edge has been driving Mr. Kennard's Napier, Mrs Kennard has been driving her De Dion voiturette, and, apparently, enjoying the trip. She went up Shap Fell on the quad driven by Mr. J. W. Stocks, and descended at a great pace in front of Mr. Holder's twin Daimler. The three ladies mentioned – Mrs. Bazalgette, Mrs. Friswell, and Miss Butler – are apparently enjoying the experience.

Mrs. Kennard

Mrs. Kennard, the eminent novelist, from whose pen we publish an appreciation of the smaller cars engaged in the recent contest, was, we regret to learn, the victim of her De Dion voiturette having a bad slide slip in Lincoln. It threw both the lady and her man into the road. Her home being at Market Harborough, Mrs. Kennard did not proceed further than Northampton on the 1,000-mile Trial.

Right:
Vera Butler who accompanied her father on entry No. A2 – was also a handy Automobilist

British v. Foreign Cars

That British manufacturers are assuming a good position in the automobile industry is being splendidly demonstrated, and a correspondent describing the exhibition at Leeds says:- 'Roughly, about half the machines whose travel-stained appearance excited such curiosity in the Artillery Drill Hall are of English manufacture. Their present condition and performances en route conclusively prove that the English manufacturer is rapidly making up the somewhat considerable gap which last year existed between the best products of English and French firms. This fact is further emphasised by an analysis of the fifteen cars which have dropped out of the competition, 75 per cent of these being of foreign manufacture.'

The Motor-Car Journal, Friday, May 4th, 1900

Some Experiences — French v. English Cars

One pleasing feature of the Trial, and one upon which British manufacturers are to be congratulated, is the conclusion forced upon all who have followed the trip as to the excellence of the 6 h.p. English cars. these have evidenced a running ability equal to the much-vaunted 6 h.p. Panhards, and have demonstrated that English firms will ultimately hold a very high position in the automobile world.

Many amusing incidents occurred en route, and 'petrol talk' often lasted far into the night. On one occasion, on the day prior to the departure from Edinburgh, some discussion between the owners of two English and French built cars of equal power resulted in a bet by the Englishman – who was Irish

– that his car would reach the first control after Edinburgh first. The bet was accepted, and the owner of the French car finished an easy first, for the simple reason that the genial happy-go-lucky offerer of the wager forgot to fill his petrol tanks, and stopped for lack of fuel a couple of miles from the start. And this at the commencement of a 120 miles run.

Foreign Press Coverage

There was a great deal of British Press coverage, as we have seen. Britain was considered 'backward' in the field of automobilism, so perhaps it is not surprising that there was little interest from foreign correspondants. As the thrust of the exercise was to educate the British public, it is not surprising if this transpires to be a neglected area on the part of the Organisers.

Notwithstanding a representative of 'France Automobile' was present – Maurice Chériére – and his report indicates that he followed the Trial at least until Sheffield.

France Automobile

Maurice Chériére's report concerning the Start (translated into English by Peter Heilbron).

Le Tour d'Angleterre – Londres 23 Avril 1900

'The file of vehicles stretches for nearly a kilometre; there are all the possible models of Phaetons, ducs, petit omnibus, char-a-bancs carrying eight people. Jules Dubois is there on a Decauville, further away I perceive a compatriot who does not know a word of English ...

I recognise again some members of the *Motor-Car Journal* and some great dailies, *Daily Mail*, *The Times* etc., I am the only representative of the French press: it is a loss because this demonstration is worth some trouble.

Amongst the competitors, an intrepid Miss Bacon embarques upon a Werner motorcycle for this long event; others, placed at the side of the driver, seemingly setting off for a pleasure party. If a four seater, they had valises, cases and even hat boxes heaped up on the back seats.

... very obligingly Mr Montague Grahame-White put his vehicle at my disposal and we left for Hounslow at some twenty kilometres from Hyde Park.'

A curious photograph (*see below*) which appeared in a later issue portrays a very unlikely banner and unrecognisable cars. What the French readers made of this we shall never know!

Decauvilles – Depart – 1000 miles non-stop Absolute Trial. (France Automobile 1900). Note the quaint English. (Photo: courtesy P.H.H.)

W. Worby Beaumont author of Comparative Efficiency Table

Comparative Efficiency

Ten-pint can, 5/-

AS SOON AS TABLES of figures were published giving performance of the cars on the hill-climbs, letters started flying to *The Autocar* from readers with a mathematical bent.

The *Daily Mail* published the times for the Taddington Hill Climb on April 28th; and by May 2nd W. G. Little had calculated an efficiency rating from 1 (De Dion voiturette No. 15 and Wolseley No. 40); to 27 for the MMC Iveagh Phaeton No. 9; using the relationship of manufacturer's given horse power to speed. By May 18th L. Ropner had responded that this did not go far enough, and a third factor should be taken into account, namely the weight moved. These gentlemen all generated tables to illustrate their findings, but the most thorough examination of the figures was made by W. Worby Beaumont, in his book *Motor Vehicles and Motors.* The table he generated is given here in full because it gives us an early serious evaluation of the comparative performance of different motorcars all under the same conditions. As was observed at the beginning of this book, this was the first time in the history of the British Motor Industry that this had been made possible; and the figures must have made very serious reading for a potential motorcar purchaser.

Two-pint 1/6.

Worby Beaumont goes on to develop his ideas further by observing that air resistance has not been taken in to consideration in his calculations, surely a first faltering step into the field of motorcar aerodynamics. This is how he sums up the state of play after the Thousand Mile Trial of 1900:

'Air resistance has not been taken into consideration in the calculations in Table XXVI., firstly, because the speeds in most cases were not sufficient to make it important; and, secondly, because on some of the smaller vehicles the riders left the vehicles part of the time. With two of the vehicles, however, the air resistance was important, namely, with the 8 h.p. Napier Daimler on Shap Fell, and the 12 h.p. Panhard of Mr. Rolls on the same hill. In these cases the total power given out at the road wheels was, respectively, 6.6 h.p. and 11.78 h.p. Taking a speed of 950 revolutions of the motor of each vehicle, the power given off by the motors would be, with the Napier Daimler car 9.06 h.p., and with the Panhard car 15.2 h.p. The mechanical efficiency in the two cases would then be, respectively, 73 per cent and 77.5 per cent.

On the whole, although a number of the cars which went through the tour and trials had to be repaired or receive a good deal of careful attention either on the road or at the stopping-places, they have shown that there are now to be had vehicles of several types capable of enduring a great deal of very heavy work under abnormal conditions. The trials on the whole may be taken as gratifying to the Automobile Club and to the motor vehicle industry, and as of great public value. They taught many lessons which will be fully utilised by those manufacturers who are susceptible of instruction and capable of putting it into practice'.

Four-pint can, 2/6.

TABLE XXVI.

Results of the Automobile Club 1,000 Mile Tour, April–May, 1900; Hill-Climbing Trials. Deduced Mechanical Efficiency.

Class.	Number.	Name.	Total weight, including passengers.	Horse-power of Engine stated by maker.	Transmission Gear.	Taddington Hill. Average speed in miles per hour on rise of 651 ft. in 13,320 ft.	Taddington Hill. Average actual HP. at driving road wheels.	Shap Fell (1). Average speed in miles per hour on rise of 840 ft. in 38,300 ft.	Shap Fell (1). Average actual HP. at driving road wheels.	Shap Fell (2). Average speed in miles per hour on rise of 500 ft. in 7,338 ft.	Shap Fell (2). Average actual HP. at driving road wheels.	Dunmail Raise. Average speed in miles per hour on rise of 450 ft. in 9,040 ft.	Dunmail Raise. Average actual HP. at driving road wheels.	Birkhill. Average speed in miles per hour on rise of 460 ft. in 10,560 ft.	Birkhill. Average actual HP. at driving road wheels.	Approximate Mechanical Efficiency of Vehicle.
			cwt. qrs.													per cent.
A.	1	Benz Ideal. Messrs. Hewetson's	13 1	3	Belt, chain	5·39	1·56	—	—	—	—	5·01	1·47	6·0 *d*	1·57	51
"	2	Benz Ideal. Messrs. Hewetson's	13 0	3	Belt, tooth, chain	7·18	2·06	11·5	2·07	4·8	1·76	6·64	1·92	6·6 *d*	1·65	61·5
"	5	Locomobile Steam Carriage	9 1	2 *k*	Chain	9·76	1·86	6·0	—	6·64	1·61	9·79	1·89	10·9	1·98	61 *k*
"	16	Gladiator Voiturette	8 0	3·25	Chain, tooth	8·17	1·24	—	—	—	—	7·67 *e*	1·185	7·5 *d*	0·995	32·6
"	27	New Orleans Car. Messrs. Burford & Van Toll.	8 2	3	Belt, tooth	6·3	1·125	—	—	4·42	0·88	6·22 *d*	0·985	7·7	1·28	35·7
"	28	New Orleans Car. Messrs. Burford & Van Toll.	8 2	3	" "	6·05	1·10	—	—	—	—	4·74	0·80	—	—	31·6
"	33	Decauville Car. The Motor Car Co.	8 3	3·5	Tooth	6·7	1·20	—	—	—	—	5·13	0·84	—	—	34·0
"	34	Decauville Car. The Motor Car Co.	8 2	3·5	"	6·3	1·10	—	—	—	—	6·84	1·21	8·6 *e*	1·23	39·4
"	41	International Victoria	11 0 *a*	3	Belt, chain	5·29	1·26	—	—	—	—	5·55	1·35	—	—	43·5
"	44	International Victoria	10 2 *a*	3	" "	6·17	1·43	—	—	—	—	6·04 *e*	1·33	4·1	—	46
"	51	Star Voiturette	11 2 *a*	3·5	" "	9·15	2·30	—	—	—	—	—	—	8·0	1·76	54·4
"	52	Roots & Venables Car (Kerosene oil)	11 2 *a*	2·87	Chain	5·8	1·205	—	—	—	—	—	—	—	—	50
B.	14	De Dion Voiturette. Mr. R. Fuller	9 2	3	Tooth	—	—	13·5	1·612	7·24	1·79	9·79	1·94	10·9	2·04	61·5
"	15	De Dion Voiturette. The Motor Power Co.	9 2	3	"	10·08	1·975	14·5	1·735	7·58	1·885	—	—	8·0 *e*	1·41	58·3
"	24	Marshall Carriage	15 1	5·0	Belt, chain	—	—	11·5	2·20	4·42	1·81	—	—	—	—	41
"	31	Renault Car. The Motor Car Co.	9 0	3·5 *c*	Tooth	9·45	1·76	—	—	—	—	9·33	1·75	9·6	1·70	58
"	32	Renault Car. The Motor Car Co.	9 0	3·5 *c*	"	7·56	1·41	—	—	—	—	7·33	1·37	—	—	46·3
"	40	Wolseley Voiturette	15 2	3 *l*	Belt, tooth, chain	10·08	3·21	13·0	2·52	6·37	2·59	7·9	2·55	8·6	2·62	89·5 *l*
"	49	Marshall Carriage	14 3	5	Belt, chain	4·94	1·49	10·5	1·94	4·54	1·75	6·04	1·85	6·3	1·83	35·5
C.	8	Daimler Phaeton. Motor Manufacturing Co.	25 2	6	Tooth, chain	5·29	2·785	10·5	3·37	5·14	3·47	5·86	3·13	6·5	3·26	53·5
"	9	Daimler Phaeton. Motor Manufacturing Co.	25 3	6	" "	5·49	3·09	10·5	3·75	4·42	2·84	5·13	2·93	6·3 *e*	3·20	52·8
"	23	Whitney Steam Car. Messrs. Brown Bros.	12 2 *a*	3·8 *b*	Chain	4·56	—	—	—	—	—	7·67	—	8·9	2·36	62
"	26	Peugeot Carriage. Mr. Friswell	19 3	8	Tooth, chain	9·45	3·83	—	—	—	—	9·79	4·03	10·9	4·23	50·5
"	35	Daimler Car. The Daimler Co.	21 2	6	" "	6·3	2·94	13·5	3·98	6·37	3·72	7·9	3·70	6·8	3·03	55·7
"	36	Daimler Car. The Daimler Co.	26 1	6	" "	6·55	3·58	13·5	4·70	4·42	3·05	6·64 *e*	3·72	6·6	3·43	61·6
"	37	Daimler Parisian. The Daimler Co.	22 0	6	" "	9·15	4·12	16	4·27	—	—	8·92	4·06	8·0	3·45	66·2
"	46	Georges Richard Car	21 0	7	Belt, tooth, chain	—	—	—	—	—	—	7·67	3·41	7·5	3·09 *e*	46·5
"	47	Georges Richard Car	21 0	7	" " "	6·43	2·78	—	—	—	—	5·86 *f*	1·86	5·0 *g*	1·98	31·6
D.	22	Lanchester Car. Mr. Millership	16 0 *a*	8	Worm	8·62	3·01	11·5	2·54	4·98	2·22	6·84	2·41	7·7	2·57	31·9
E (*a*).	12	De Dion Tricycle. Motor Manufacturing Co.	3 0 *a*	2·25	Tooth	—	—	—	—	—	—	7·9	0·495	12·6	0·747	27·6
"	20	Simms' Motor Wheel	4 2 *a*	2·75	"	9·45	0·87	—	—	—	—	—	—	—	—	31·6
"	39	Century Tandem Tricycle	5 2 *a*	3	Chain	—	—	—	—	—	—	2·1 *d*	—	10·9 *d*	1·08	36·2
E (*b*).	3	Ariel Quadricycle. Mr. J. Stocks	6 2	3·15	Tooth	15·13 *h*	2·03	20·5	1·67	6·64 *e h*	0·98	11·41 *d*	1·42	13·3 *e*	1·51	48·3
"	4	Ariel Tricycle with Whippet Trailer	5 2	2·25	"	14·4	1·62	20·5	1·41	6·64 *d j*	—	8·22 *d j*	—	12·6 *d j*	—	67·5
A.	A 25	Benz Ideal. Mrs. Bazalgette	12 2	3	Belt, chain	6·7	1·81	—	—	—	—	4·66	1·25	—	—	51
B.	A 24	Mors Voiturette. Mr. Phillips	13 2	4	Tooth, chain	8·39	2·33	—	—	—	—	7·67	2·15	7·5	1·98	53·7
C.	A 2	6 HP. Panhard. Mr. Butler	21 3	6	Tooth, chain	5·69	2·54	10·5	2·86	4·8	2·74	6·22	2·81	5·7	2·43	44·6
"	A 3	6 HP. Panhard. Mr. Browne	20 3	6	" "	8·17	3·49	13·0	3·20	5·68	2·90	7·9	3·06	8·6	3·49	54
"	A 7	6 HP. Daimler. Mr. Harmsworth	18 2 *a*	6	" "	—	—	—	—	—	—	4·66	—	6·6 *e*	2·62	43·6
"	A 10	8 HP. Napier. Mr. Kennard	26 0	8	" "	13·74	7·39	19·0	5·71	—	—	13·69	7·24	11·5	5·86	82
"	A 12	6 HP. Daimler. Mr. Edmunds	20 2	6	" "	6·43	2·89	—	—	—	—	7·08	3·1	—	—	49·8
"	A 21	6 HP. Daimler. Mr. Pitman	24 2 *a*	6	" "	—	—	11·0	3·67	4·42	3·81	6·22	3·33	4·8	—	60·3
"	A 23	6 HP. Daimler. Mr. Cordingly	23 3 *a*	6·25	" "	6·3	—	—	—	—	—	—	—	—	—	—
"	A 26	6 HP. Daimler. Mr. Gregson	25 3	6	" "	5·8	3·26	—	—	—	—	6·84	3·9	4·1 *e*	—	59·7
"	A 30	6 HP. Daimler. Mr. Siddeley	20 2	6	" "	8·39	2·54	13·0	3·37	4·82	2·61	6·92	2·95	7·0	2·84	47·6
"	A 31	6 HP. Daimler. Mr. Johnson	24 2	6	" "	8·17	3·9	11·5	3·35	5·68	3·43	7·9	3·32	8·2	3·93	59·7
D.	A 4	8 HP. Panhard. Mr. Mark Mayhew	20 1 *a*	8	" "	10·08	4·28	12·0	—	5·48	—	—	—	—	—	53·5
"	A 11	12 HP. Daimler. Hon. J. Scott Montagu	23 3 *a*	12	Tooth, chain	11·19	5·46	—	—	—	—	5·26 *f*	—	10·4	4·64	42
"	A 17	12 HP. Panhard. Hon. C. S. Rolls	26 1	12	" "	17·77	9·55	27·5	8·78	17·71	10·9	20·54	11·81	16·0	8·21	82
"	A 22	12 HP. Daimler. Mr. J. A. Holder	30 1	12	" "	14·4	8·94	—	—	7·24	6·4	10·27	6·44	10·9	6·46	57·6
"	A 29	7 HP. Peugeot. Mr. Mark Mayhew	19 2 *a*	7	" "	7·74	3·13	15·5	3·8	7·97	4·1	9·79	3·99	10·0	3·82	53·7
E (*a*).	A 16	Ariel Tricycle. Mr. A. J. Wilson	3 2 *a*	2·25	Tooth	18·91	1·35	18·5	0·815	—	—	5·13	—	6·8 *j*	—	48·3
"	A 20	Empress Tricycle. Mr. H. Ashby	3 2 *b*	2·75	"	—	—	20·0	0·88	15·94	1·46	17·06	1·25	7·5	—	43·2
E (*b*).	A 28	Enfield Quadricycle. Mr. E. M. Iliffe	6 2 *b*	2·25	"	9·15 *e*	1·11	—	—	—	—	9·33 *e*	1·13	12·0 *e h*	1·83	60·5

a Weight based on maker's statement.
b Estimated.
c The de Dion water-cooled engine used in this car is generally stated to give 3 HP., and this figure has been taken in calculating the efficiency.
d Both passengers off temporarily.
e One passenger off temporarily.
f Two passengers off temporarily.
g All off temporarily.
h Pedalling.
j Had to push.
k Brake HP. of engine taken as 3·1.
l Brake HP. of engine here understated. See remarks, p. 618.

Air resistance is not included in these calculations. See p. 622.

21 AFTER THE 1,000 MILES TRAIL

The Minutes of ACGBI reveal all was not over

Extracts from A.C.G.B.I. Minutes

A Mr Ranger Johnson of *Morning Post* put in a claim for compensation from the Club in connection with an accident on the first day of the Thousand Mile Trial. *The Club could not accept any liability.*

Also there was a letter from Messrs Bexcoby & Williamson, concerning an accident which occurred to a farmer (Mr Bingley) near Worksop in connection with the Thousand Miles Trial. *Again it was directed that the Club cannot accept any responsibility in connection with the accident.*

A letter from Mr Fulbrook of Slough was read concerning the Maidenhead Bridge Toll problems.

There were Minutes of votes of thanks for generous hospitality to Mr. & Mrs. Alfred Harmsworth: the Master Cutler of Sheffield: the Reception Committee at Lincoln. Thanks also to the Lord Chief Justice Clerk of Scotland for his personal attendance throughout the Thousand Mile Trial.

Mr. Edmunds had offered prizes for the best photographs of the Thousand Miles Trial, and his offer was accepted.

The ACGBI accorded to the Proprietors of the *Daily Mail* best thanks for the support afforded to them in the organisation of the 1,000 Miles Trial, and to Mr Harmsworth in particular. A letter from Mr Harmsworth was read out; (*insert*) and he was asked to favour the Club with his suggestions as to what might be further done by the Club in respect of the prevention of restrictive legislation.

Original letter to A.C.G.B.I. from Mr. A. C. Harmsworth

The following letter from Mr A. C. Harmsworth having been read:-

Dear Sir, *July* 7, 1900.

Will you very kindly tell the Committee that I gladly accede to their suggestion with regard to the prizes, and I beg to enclose cheque for £410 (four hundred and ten pounds), at the same time congratulating the Club on the great success of the enterprise.

I would like to take this opportunity of urging that we, as a Club, do take every possible step to counteract further restrictive legislation. The present laws seem to me to work excellently, but on all sides one hears of Parliamentary and other pressure that will serve to make the life of the automobilist a burden.

If I may make another suggestion, it is that some person be sent from the Club to all the hotels on the main road, pointing out to hotel-keepers the value of keeping a supply of petrol and lubricating oils, and also a hose-pipe for water supply. In three cases I have brought about the desired effect by merely mentioning the matter.

Yours faithfully,

(Signed) ALFRED HARMSWORTH.

Goliath watch/clock in desk display box closed and opened.
The front of the case hinges open to reveal a giant pocket watch called a 'Goliath' (see trophies on page 342).
(Photos: Elizabeth Bennett)

Presentation of Prizes at the Dinner at The Trocadero Restaurant October 31st 1900

Cups and Prizes were distributed. Drivers Certificates were given to nominated Drivers on the 1,000 Mile Trial.

The Chairman said that these drivers were to be most heartily congratulated in that, owing to their skill, the Trial had demonstrated to a nervous and somewhat inamicable public that 60,000 miles of motor travel over all sorts of roads, over hill and dale, through fair weather and storm, could be accomplished without danger or damage from the cars to other users of the road. On their judgement and skill the success of the Trial had depended, and personally the drivers certificate, had he qualified for one, would have been to him a very valuable possession.

£100 was presented to Claude Johnson contributed by participants and others, together with a Testimonial which read:

> 'Through your able organisation and direction, the Club carried to a successful issue a 1,000 Mile Trial of Motor Vehicles, the result of which not only exceeded all expectations, but marked a distinct era in the History of Locomotion.
>
> We offer you this testimonial as a lasting memento of this important event, with which your name will ever be associated, and in appreciation of the indefatigable energy displayed by you in its conception and promotion.'

Thousand Mile Trial Medal

Far left:
Front view of Herbert Ashby's medal in original box.

Left:
Reverse side of Herbert Ashby's medal with bar detail
(Photos: Elizabeth Bennett)

Mr. Wallace said 'He believed Mr. Johnson had organised the Trial better than any other man in the country could have done it.'

Mr. C. Johnson said he was overwhelmed with the kindness of those who had given him that testimonial. When he first heard of it he wrote to Mr. Rolls (who had the idea to make the testimonial to Johnson) pointing out that what he had done in connection with the Trial, he had done as Secretary of the Club, and he felt the pleasure it had given him was sufficient recompense.

The Trophies
The cups and rose bowl were solid silver. The clocks were made for travelling or for use as a desk timepiece as described on page 341. (Photo: Argent Archer)

A Social Reunion

Under the genial chairmanship of Lord Kingsburgh, the Chief Justice Clerk of Scotland, a goodly number of those who had endured the 1,000-mile Trial met at dinner at the Trocadero Restaurant, London, on Monday evening. Most of those who had come through the ordeal with success were present, and the recounting of experiences gave a lively turn to the conversation.

The tables having been cleared the chairman announced that he had consented to occupy the chair on condition that no speeches were made. With characteristic humour he then proceeded to give the most delightful little address of the evening recalling a visit to America in 1875 and retailing anecdotes in the style of a practised *raconteur*. To set down in print the choice stories of the landing at New York, the hotel-keeper in the far West who had only met one private in the United States army, and of the Jew on board ship on the return voyage, would be to rob the quaint stories of their exquisite setting. Humour, in fact, marked most of the speeches, the brevity of which was generally commendable.

The Hon. C. S. Rolls introduced by the chairman as one who could make some observations on how to 'go up hill slow' had a good reception on rising to give his impressions. Modestly disclaiming the credit of his foremost position, for which the possession of a good machine was, he said, greatly responsible. Mr. Rolls thought that the behaviour of the vehicles which had gone out for the first time was an important matter worth consideration. On the evening before the sealing of the vehicles he discovered that the fourth speed gearwheel of his machine had never been hardened. Mr. T. B. Browne placed at his disposal one of his Panhard cars which was pulled to pieces and the gear replaced between 11.30 p.m. and 6.30 a.m. on the morning of the Trial. They ascertained during the process that the gearing originally designed to transmit 4 h.p. was the identical gear designed for his 12 h.p. machine. In his opinion the most striking vehicle on the tour was the Napier. It was the first vehicle turned out by that firm who had had no experience in that direction before. Without being ashamed to copy the good features of the French vehicles, most important improvements had been made by Mr. Napier which had resulted in it being possible to obtain for £500 a car of the kind they had seen in the Trial. Upon that they should congratulate themselves. If credit was given to the drivers of successful vehicles, even more credit should be given to those whose misfortune it had been to drive vehicles which were hardly ready for a test of that sort, and to the energy and determination to get through amounting to heroism on the part of those drivers was due the credit of having had so many vehicles in at the finish. That was one of the most satisfactory features of the Trial. The fact that out of some sixty starters about fifty got through was bound to deeply impress the public mind. But the credit of that magnificent proportion was due mostly to the way in which the drivers had stuck to their vehicles – sometimes being two or three days behind the rest of the party, yet sticking to their machines, having at heart the determination to contribute their portion to the success of the Trial.

Professor Boys said he had had every advantage in having enjoyed the hospitality of those driving cars, having been 400 miles on the road. As one of the judges he had watched all that had been going on with the greatest interest. Some arithmetical fallacies had been discovered during the course of the trip, and an acquaintance shown with the doctrine of limits. If they divided the distance travelled by the time it took some imagined the rate was thirty miles an hour. But it was only twelve. (Laughter). They thus arrived at a practical exemplification of the mathematical doctrine of limits. It was something new to mathematicians that the doctrine of limits was dependent on the need of the case. In addition to this new experience there was another factor – the geographical one – and the limit, which was found to be twelve in this country, was ten on the other side of the Tweed. (Laughter). An enormous amount of pleasure had been obtained from the Trial, and there had also been an enormous increase in the wealth of the country. He joined the run at Manchester, from whence they passed through thirty solid miles of people. It would be fair to reckon about two to one yard and eight or ten deep on each side of the road. But taking a lower estimate of one person to the yard on each side of the road all the way, or lower still, 1,500 people to the mile on each side they would find the Trial had been witnessed by 3,000,000 people. Some of them travelled some distance and paid 15s. or £1 for the pleasure of the sight of the automobiles. Supposing each person considered the sight of a car worth a penny, 3,300,000 people and fifty cars resulted in 165,000,000 sights of a car or a sum of £687,500. Everyone who ran a car must have spent £100. Fifty cars at £100 a car amounted to £5,000 on the debit side as compared with £687,500 on the credit side. There remained therefore a balance in the possession of the country of £682,500. (Laughter). That was the value of the pleasure

Mr F. K. Butler on his 8 hp Panhard
(Photo: Argent Archer)

which the country had received and not paid for. It might possibly be advantageous to the country that something in the nature of road races should be considered. If for the pleasure of witnessing such miserable speeds as twelve miles an hour such crowds assembled what a revenue could be raised if the top speeds were used? The country might be persuaded that once in a way something in the nature of a road race might be worth having.

The Hon. J. Scott Montagu, M.P. asked to speak on the question of dress, said his own coat had proved very comfortable although it did not perhaps look very smart. As regards special features they remembered the boots of a certain editor and the approved fashion with which some of the drivers were got up. The great question was that of headgear. He had tried the ordinary cap and also the yachting cap and was inclined to believe that the headgear of the automobilist would have to be a sort of mask to go over the head like a fencing mask. The Trial had been a great success and he had found the railwaymen on the line he travelled and the members of the House of Commons equally interested in the results. With regard to future legislation he thought they should license the man and not the vehicle. This would be better than numbering the vehicles. Although automobilists were superior to all the disfigurement that arose from mud, etc., they should recollect that the public had not yet been fully educated in the matter.

Colonel Magrath related some experiences with his motor-car in Ireland, these being chiefly the association of the vehicle, by the natives of the West, with the nether world. He suggested that a party should be got up to go round Ireland.

Mr. S. F. Edge said one of the little engines engaged on the Trial had made 6,312,000 revolutions. Many people had an idea that when they came to a stop motor-cars were in their normal condition. The Trial had done something to dispel that idea. Some of the travellers had seen parts of cars on the road and they turned up as complete cars, seemingly little different to when they started.

Mr. Staplee Firth said the only pleasure he had was to see the cars start. He did not propose to go into the Neolithic age or into matters pre-Adamite. They had authentic records as to the antiquity of the horse for drawing purposes, travel by oxen, ass, elephant, zebra, camel, and other four-legged animals. These had been the only mode of transit supported by the genus shown and he did not think the pace had altered much during the Christian era. He could not understand why men should want to go quicker along the roads than did their forefathers and he put it down to the fact that they were bad bold men. There had been eleven travelling days in the Trial, averaging 96 miles a day, and a coach changing horses every fifteen miles and going nine hours a day would have had to have had 288 horses to cover the distance. It was a great shame

Mr. Chas Jarrott and
Mr. S. F. Edge
(Photo: Argent Archer)

Hon. C. S. Rolls on his racing 12 h.p. Panhard (Photo: Argent Archer)

that 288 horses were thus to be put out of employment. At the same time there was the fact, and it would prove a great awakening in the country.

Mr. E. Kennard thanked Mr. Edge for the splendid way he had controlled his Napier car during the Trial. They might have had some close shaves, but they had gone through safely. The order for the car had been in the hands of Mr. Napier for nine months, at the end of which period he produced a car of which he had every reason to be proud. His 8 h.p. had been a success and even greater things could be anticipated from the 16 h.p.

Mr. Egerton referred to the attitude adopted by various automobilists, varying from complete curves and the upright position to the horizontal attitude sometimes necessitated.

Mr. Mark Mayhew, L.C.C., said he was asked during the Trial to take a gentleman back to his country seat near Sheffield. It was soon evident that that gentleman wanted to try the machine to its utmost. First they ascended a little hill between one in six and one in eight. Then they left the high road to go up a lane in which were two cart ruts seven inches deep. This led to a colliery yard, further on they got to a factory yard, and that opened on to the river. His friend pointed out a ford. Down the steep bank they went and on to the river bed, and the water put out the burners. They got a few men from the colliery to pull the car on to the pavé, and having re-started the engine, climbed the bank backwards successfully.

Mr. C. Cordingley, invited by the chairman to deal with side-slips, said his few experiences had not been very happy ones. He got to Calcot Park very well, but soon after that his trouble began. He lost his tire and had to return part of the way in a style of dot and carry one. It took two hours to do seven miles, and he had had trouble ever since all the way. He had discovered that the exhaust pipe was too small. His burners had been blown out all the way round. He started in bad health and ended in bad health; having indulged in a form of physical exercise to which he was not accustomed. He should not care to again have to do what he had had to do.

Lord Kingsburgh said all engaged on the Trial owed a debt of gratitude to the Secretary, Mr. Johnson. All the arrangements made for carrying out the run had been admirable. There had been no delays, and no chafing, and there had been perfect good humour and kindness all along. A

Mr F. K. Gregson on his 12 h.p. Daimler (Photo: Argent Archer)

great deal of that was to be attributed to the splendid organisation. It was very often in public affairs and in sport of any kind that people took revenge on one another for discomforts to which they were subjected by their officials. Nothing of that kind had occurred in connection with the Automobile Club's Trial. He was quite sure Mr. Johnson would be the last man in the world to desire that all those who had assisted him should not have their full meed of praise, but without a strong hub on the wheel, such as he had been, it would probably have gone to pieces. While they should congratulate him upon the success of the tour they should also congratulate him not only as an official but as a friend – extremely courteous. There never was the right man in the right place more than in the case of Mr. Johnson.

Mr. C. Johnson (Secretary), who was greeted with musical honours, said he was extremely glad to have that opportunity of speaking because there were present some of the gentlemen who had assisted him in connection with the Trial. They had had to do the drudgery whilst he had had to tell them what to do and get all the credit. There were present four of the officials of the club on whom had fallen a vast amount of weary labour which none of them knew anything about. In a case of that sort it was several months' work. He had been able to speak of the provincial committees elsewhere, and would then speak of work done at the Club. There was the permanent official, Mr. Chant, who had had to do work under adverse circumstances; Mr. Joy, who had done invaluable work in connection with the June show, without whose assistance the official programme would not have been what it was; Mr. Tousey also went in, and would sit down at night and begin work, and keep on till four o'clock in the afternoon. The club steward, Mr. Burrows, had been all through the tour, and his constant amiability and willingness to help everywhere in every possible way was also recognised. So far as he (Mr. Johnson) was concerned he was a paid official of the Club, and he simply did his duty. What he had appreciated most was the leniency with which people connected with the tour had taken very abrupt answers. He found that driving a vehicle all day and settling down to work at night was somewhat of a strain. The cordiality that had existed throughout the Trial was remarkable. There had been no friction between any one person and another, and that had been one of the secrets of the success of the Trial. It was very pleasurable to see the owners of competing vehicles helping each other. The attitude of the Press also called for remark. If they took the Press principally concerned with automobilism they might congratulate themselves that they had dealt with the thing fully and fairly. In the general Press certain papers had devoted a very considerable amount of space to the Trial. The papers which had hitherto confined themselves to accidents associated with automobilism were now recognising that motor vehicles were worthy of better notice. In conclusion he thanked them most heartily for the toast, and asked them particularly to remember the assistants who had been associated with him.

Mr. Worby Beaumont referred to the theories of Professor Boys and others with regard to action at a distance, and instanced the case of the sheep that stumbled and pitched its head on the other side of the kerb, converting it forthwith into mutton, as an example of action at a distance. In the days when horses were used to carry people to Birmingham, each horse required 140lbs. of oats per passenger. By train only 2½lbs. of coal per passenger were required, and the saving of time by the train carrying 500 people from London to Birmingham was 1.4 years of the life of a man. He referred to the valley near Dunstable which had been filled up with material taken out of the adjacent hill, and advised automobilists and others to advocate similar improvements of the roads elsewhere.

Mr. Roger Wallace, President of the club, in proposing the health of the Chairman, said the Lord Justice Clerk had done much by his presence and by his addresses to help automobilism.

The Lord Justice Clerk, in responding, said he hoped the judges would give a careful report on certain cars which had not succeeded in completing the run, for he was confident that in most of these the causes of apparent failure were not causes connected with the motor parts of the vehicles, and often with axles and springs, etc., which might happen with any carriage. None could really be attributed to the principle on which the automobile was worked, but to minor details. During the Trial it had been shown that there had been plenty of gentlemen of resource engaged. He had seen a pump which was a curiosity, and might form the beginning of a museum, to be kept at the club, of works performed under difficulties. He suggested that automobiles might usefully be used in connection with railway services. Energy combined with reasonable care as regards capitalisation was required in the production of automobiles, or more harm than good would be done. ”

The Motor-car Journal, Saturday, May 19th, 1900

Mr. Critchley on new Parisian Daimler (Photo: Argent Archer)

During the weeks following the Trial Argent Archer took photographs of several of the Participants both individually and in groups at occasions like Garden Parties, and these are shown in the following pages.

Baron de Sterne's garden Party Strawberry Hill (Photo: Argent Archer)

Mr Frank Butler's Garden Party at Shiplake (Photo: Argent Archer)

Meet of cars at Sheen Club (Photo: Argent Archer)

“

Recognition of Mr. C. Johnson

Monday's pleasant function at the Trocadero was fitly brought to a conclusion with a speech by Mr. Claude Johnson, whose rising caused the company to break the orderliness enjoined by the chairman, and to burst forth into song, 'For he's a jolly good fellow.' That has been recognised all along the route. Never has there been a hitch: the flags have never sent the travellers in the wrong direction: the programme was exact in every detail: the minor arrangements omitted nothing, and altogether the achievement was something notable in the way of organisation. And to this capacity for work Mr. Johnson adds a considerateness for those who have been associated with him that showed itself in his modest reply to the toast of his health. He gratefully recognised the devotion of assistants, and the enthusiasm of local committees, and made graceful tribute to the valuable help he had received from them.

Proposed Testimonial

Quite spontaneously the appreciation of Mr. Johnson by those engaged on the Trial is to be shown in another way, and we are glad to be able to announce that this is to take the form of a present. The subscriptions are limited to £1, and should be sent to the Hon. C. S. Rolls, South Lodge, Rutland Gate, S.W., who is acting as hon. secretary. Services so genially and admirably rendered deserve recognition, and the promptness with which the idea of a testimonial has been taken up is in itself, a tribute which should give enhanced value to the intended gift.”

The Motor-Car Journal, Saturday, May 26th, 1900

Claude Johnson

“

The Roads and the Weather

Automobilists will be glad to read that the *Field* recognises the very satisfactory results obtained by the Automobile Club's Trial. Reviewing the roads encountered and the climatic conditions met with, our contemporary adds: 'During the first fortnight the weather was uniformly favourable, no rain to speak of being encountered; but in the second week a change occurred, and the Monday brought some unpleasant experiences for the travellers, when heavy rains and wet roads were encountered; nor did the interval of Tuesday, which was devoted to exhibition purposes, bring any improvement in the weather, for on Wednesday, the conditions were distinctly worse. Although this experience has been most unpleasant for all concerned, it is satisfactory that the competing vehicles should have been subjected to the severe test which rain, strong winds, heavy mud, and slippery roads impose. These conditions have prevailed, too, over some very hilly parts of the course, which have further added to the severity of the trial. ”

The Motor-Car Journal, Saturday, May 26th, 1900

Overall Reaction from *The Motor-Car Journal*

"
The Automobile Club's 1,000-Mile Trial

The great 1,000-mile Trial is now an event of the past. The Trial, which represents some 50,000 miles of motor travel through crowded cities and dangerously hilly districts, was accomplished without accident to other users of the road being caused through want of control over, or bad driving of, an automobile. All the cars which went through the Trial travelled a minimum of 1,059¼ miles, while some of them totalled 1,107¼ miles. There were eleven actual running days

The beneficial effects of the Trial are beyond measure. To the public it has revealed the fact that motor-cars are by no means toys, but are vehicles which can be relied upon to do their work efficiently

since the competing vehicles left London on April 23, the balance being made up of Sundays and one-day exhibitions in the following towns: Bristol, Birmingham, Manchester, Edinburgh, Newcastle, Leeds, and Sheffield. There were also temporary exhibitions on running days at Kendal, Carlisle, Lincoln, Nottingham, and Leicester. It should be added that on the off days a brief allowance only was made for cleaning and repairs, and that if a car required still more attention the time occupied was deducted from the next running day's journey. There were seven days out of the eleven on which a hundred miles or more was the distance travelled; the longest was the final journey of Saturday, and the shortest was the 61½ miles run from Kendal to Carlisle, which included a hill-climbing competition up Birkhill. The beneficial effects of the Trial are beyond measure. To the public it has revealed the fact that motor-cars are by no means toys, but are vehicles which can be relied upon to do their work efficiently; to the manufacturer it has revealed weak points which needed improvement and modification in a way that no isolated trips of 100 miles or so could possibly do. It has been said that many would-be purchasers of motor-cars have deferred making the plunge until the Trial was completed. Now that such a complete and trying test has been successfully negotiated by so large a number of motor-cars the step need no longer be delayed. It was at first thought that the test was unnecessarily severe, but since it has been successfully carried through the Automobile Club and the motor industry generally can congratulate themselves on having given what should prove an enormous impulse to the automobile movement. "

The Motor-Car Journal, Saturday, May 26th, 1900

A roundup of Newspaper snippets

1,000-Mile Trial Incidents

The Trial should draw attention of British spring and axle makers to the future that lies before them in the automobile industry.

In the list of cars arriving at Newcastle we inadvertently omitted that of Mr. T. B. Browne, No. 3, which was fifth into the city on the Tyne.

Those of the Lincoln local committee who went on the cars as far as Newark returned to the city on two cars lent by Lincoln Motor Bus Company.

As the vehicles passed through Thirsk a hiring fair was in progress, and similar festivities were being indulged in at Leicester when the cars drew up at the Bell Inn.

A large number of people waiting at Barnet to see the arrival of the cars engaged in the 1,000-mile Trial were disappointed – as the route lay through Elstree, a rather doubtful advantage.

Among the many cars seen at Lincoln was a neat-looking Billings voiturette which had been driven over from Gainsborough by Mr. H. W. Bamber of Messrs. Baines and Sons, Limited, Gainsborough.

According to a Woburn journal, the tyre of one of the motor-vehicles burst as it passed through that village on the last day of the Trial, and 'the explosion was heard a long distance, and many thought it was the report of a cannon.'

It is satisfactory to find a number of newspapers remarking that if the 1,000-mile Trial has done nothing more than demonstrate the wonderful control and facile conduct of self-propelled vehicles, a great result may be said to have been achieved.

As Mr. F. H. Butler, the hon. treasurer of the Automobile Club, was pulling up at his door in Pall Mall, after his successful Trial, a horse attached to a carriage took fright at the motor-vehicle and damaged itself so badly that it had to be shot.

Captain Langrishe and Mr. Shrapnell Smith effected quite a smart repair to the pump on Mr. Harmsworth's Parisian Daimler during the course of the journey from Sheffield to Nottinham. Short of a washer, one was improvised out of a halfpenny piece.

As the result of the local exhibitions in connection with the 1,000-mile Trial the following sums have already been handed to the War Fund:- Bristol, £25; Cheltenham, £32 18s.; Carlisle £33 19s. 5d.; Kendal, £12 12s. Total to date, £105 9s. 5d.

As an instance of the scrupulous care that was taken from the first by the promoters of the Trial to provide against accident, it may be mentioned incidentally that a note from the Chief Constable of Newark, drawing attention to the possibility of vehicles and caravans being on the road owing to the nearness of Newark Fair, was given special prominence in the programme.

One of the most stylish-looking vehicles at the Sheffield exhibition was the private carriage of Mr. E. P. Reynolds. the car is of the Daimler type, the body having been built in Sheffield under Mr. Reynolds personal supervision and in appearance it approximates as nearly to the really sightly automobile as anything that the genius of the manufacturer, English or Continental, has yet attained.

The voiturette referred to in our report as having been towed by Mr. Moffat Ford was No. 14. It had had pump troubles, and Mr. Egerton happened to be with it at the time, rendering assistance. Hence the reference to the vehicle as that driven by him. As a matter of fact, the De Dion voiturette No. 15, driven by him, never required extraneous assistance and never fell below the twelve miles average speed.

To be run over by one's own car is rather an unusual incident, but this is what happened to Mr. Grierson, who drove a de Dion voiturette on the journey from Sheffield to Nottingham. Applying the brakes somewhat suddenly, and getting up at the same time, with the intention of giving chase to some boys who had made themselves a nuisance, Mr. Grierson was thrown out in front of the car, the wheels of which went over his leg, fortunately without any serious result.

The rose bowl presented by the Club to Mr. Ernest Pitman

THE END . . . WHICH WAS JUST THE BEGINNING

POSTSCRIPT

A social revolution starts to get a hold

"Lately I had a conversation with an old enemy of motors, bicycles, and every kind of modern method of mechanical locomotion. He has been in not a few law cases in this connection, and was neither always in the right nor succeeded in convincing the court that he was. Imagine my amazement when I met him on Haldon driving an elegant little French motor. 'Oh, yes,' he said. 'I've come round. It was my infernal coachman converted me. You know the kind of fellow I mean – seems to think that the stables and horses are kept for him, and not he for the horses. Talked about 'my horses.' Couldn't do this; couldn't do that; wouldn't do the other. Egad! I sacked him at last and got another. Second ruffian worse than the first. Sacked him too – sick of it – sold horses, carriages, everything – bought four motors of different kinds, and found myself once more master of my own property. Can go anywhere or do anything at any hour – no fear of injuring horses or enraging coachman. Keep an engineer, of course, but we are all amateurs, even to the butler and the boy, and can drive or lend a hand at a pinch. I have been twenty-seven miles to-day, mostly uphill, and I have ten or twelve to go. What price that in comparison with horses. Take my advice – the advice of a man who started in active opposition–buy a motor, and you will be glad of it.'"

An extract from *The Autocar* October 6th 1900

What happened to some of the Participants

Herbert Austin, Lord Austin of Longbridge. – (Drove Entry No. 40 – 3.5 h.p. Wolseley). All Wolseleys' were designed with horizontal engines which continued through 1905 as Austin was totally opposed to the, now popular, vertical ones. The Wolseley amalgamation with J. D. Siddeley resulted in vertical cylinders and Austin's resignation. Aged 40, Austin started his own Company at Longbridge in 1906 and was soon producing cars with conventional engine layout. Knighted KBE in 1917, he stood as an MP from 1919-24, was President of the Institute of Automobile Engineers in 1930 and President of the SMMT in 1934. That same year he was also Master of the Coachmakers and created a Baron in 1936. He died in May 1941 aged 75.

Jules Dubois and **Harold Keates Hales**, M.P. – (Entry No. 34 – 3.5 h.p. Decauville) Jules Dubois was a runner and early racing cyclist. He had many successes often riding with H. O. Duncan, Charron and others. Jules broke the world cycling record in 1894 achieving 38.22 kms in one hour. He rode 500 kms in 17 hours in 1902. He founded Rouxel et Dubois for cycles then abandoned cycle sales for automobiles in 1899 and became commercial agent for La Société Herald. His companion on the Trial, Harold Hales was born in Manchester, April 1868. He claims in his autobiography of 'The Card' to have bought a Beeston motor tricycle in 1898, but, seemingly, prior to that a 2 h.p. Benz in 1897 followed by a De Dion. He also built the first motor garage in the potteries. He had a chequered career, was conservative M.P. for Hanley 1931-35 and donated the Hales Trophy for the Atlantic blue ribband crossings. He died aged 74 in 1942.

Henry Edmunds, M.Inst.C.E, M.I.E.E.E – (Drove Entry No. A12 – 6 h.p. Daimler) was born in 1853 in Halifax, joined the ACGBI in 1898 and was Chairman in 1901. An electrical engineer by training he became a Director of Royce Ltd and owned the third Royce car. He was the man history claims introduced Rolls to Royce.

Sir Charles Hain Friswell 1871–1926 – (Entry No. 26 – 8 h.p. Peugeot) became Chairman of the Standard Motor Co. Ltd. He was knighted in 1909 when he was still only 37. Standard Motors supplied 57 6-cyl. vehicles for George V's Indian Durbar in 1912. Charles travelled widely and was a keen big-game hunter. He also rode and enjoyed sports generally. He died just short of his 55th birthday.

Edward Mauger Iliffe – (Entry No. A28 – 2.25 h.p. Enfield Quadricycle) was M.P. for Tamworth 1923-29, President of the Birmingham Post & Mail, Chairman of Guildhall Insurance and received a Barony in 1933. He was Master of the Coachmakers Livery Co, 1936. Died 1980 at 83.

George H. Lanchester – (Entry No. 21 – 8 h.p. Lanchester Carriage) George married Rose Thomas sister of Fred's wife Minnie in 1907. He became chief designer for his Company, brother Fred resigning in 1914. The Lanchester brothers were at loggerheads with their board of directors over many years. At the end of 1930 Lanchester was sold to BSA/Daimler. George continued with them but did not always see eye to eye with L. H. Pomeroy and resigned in 1936.He was President of the SAE I942-43 and a keen member of the VCC. He was disqualified more than once for arriving too early on the Brighon Run on a 1901 twin-cylinder 12 h.p. Lanchester. He retired from consultancy at the age of 83, and married Mary Stevenson. He died Feb 13th 1970 aged 95. He had, at that time, been making plans to participate in the VCC 70th anniversary of the Thousand Mile Trial.

Sir Hercules Robert Langrishe, Bt. – (Entry No. A7 – 6 h.p. Daimler) Langrishe was the 5th Baronet, a friend and yachting companion of Edward VII, and Master of Kilkenny Fox Hounds. He was 84 when he died in 1943.

Archibald James Walter Millership – (Entry No. 22 – 8 h.p. Lanchester carriage), left Lanchester to join Herbert Austin in his new venture in 1908. He returned to Lanchester to take charge of sales in the North of England a few years later. After BSA bought out Lanchester in 1931, Archie became an agent for Opel and later, Buick cars in Birmingham. His business ended as war loomed. He died around 1951 and was buried in Clent churchyard near Stourbridge.

John Edward Douglas Scott-Montagu KCIE, CSI, FRGS, AICE, AIME, M.P. 2nd Baron, Montagu of Beaulieu, – (Entry No. A11 12 h.p. Daimler). At the time of the 1,000 Mile Trial Montagu was 34. He said of that time 'A curious feature was the number of motorists who knew each other, for those who actually owned their own cars in this country were very few, and in fact, so small was the number that one knew almost everyone who owned a car of any importance at all. I well remember driving from the New Forest to London in those days on several occasions and not meeting one motor car in the whole of 90 miles.' Montagu was elevated to the peerage in 1905. He lived a very full life, enjoyed shooting and fishing on the 10,000 acre Beaulieu estate, sailing and golf. He travelled widely and died aged 62 in 1929.

St. John Cousins Nixon – (Mechanician for S. F. Edge on Entry No. A10 – 8 h.p. Napier) Although mechanically inclined, Nixon earned his living in motor insurance and also as an author. In that respect he was again involved with Edge in the publication of Edge's book *My Motoring Reminiscences* and a number of others, including a history of the ACGBI/RAC, and *Romance Amongst Cars*. Nixon was an early and much involved member of the VCC and was first editor of the Gazette. On the 50th anniversary of the 1000 Mile Trial Nixon drove the first 1899 Wolseley over the original course and again at the 60th anniversary. To cap it all, he took the Wolseley once more for a remarkable third time on the 70th anniversary. He died a few weeks later aged 84.

John Davenport Siddeley CBE, FRAES, 1st Baron Kenilworth – (Entry No. A30 – 6 h.p. Daimler), became an agent for Peugeot but then decided he wanted to engage in manufacture. With Lionel Rothschild an approach was made to Vickers who owned the Wolseley Tool & Motor Car Co. Wolseleys' still had horizontal engines but Siddeley favoured verticality and Vickers went along with this. The Siddeley Motor Car Co, was formed in 1903. He was High Sheriff for Warwickshire 1932, and knighted that year. He became Chairman and Managing Director of Vickers Armstrong-Siddeley Motors and was Master of the Coachmakers, 1934. He was created Baron in 1937 and was President of the SMMT in the same year. He died in 1953 aged 87.

John W. Stocks – (Entry No. 3 – 3.5 h.p. Ariel Quadricyle) drove in the Gordon Bennett Irish race in 1903 together with Edge and Jarrott. Edge considered him to be a great racing driver. He was General Manager for De Dion-Bouton Ltd. London at the time war broke out in 1914, when he joined the Navy. After the war he had a motor agency and garage in Birmingham.

researched PHH: edited EB

1960
Diamond Jubilee Re-enactment Run – St. John Cousins Nixon driving Herbert Austin's 1899 Wolseley – being received in Main Street Kendal by the Mayor. He drove over the original course for the 50th Anniversary, 60th Anniversary, and the 70th Anniversary.

BIBLIOGRAPHY

Books

BIRD, A. & HUTTON-STOTT, F. *Lanchester Motor Cars.* London:Cassell, 1965

CLARK, C. S. *The Lanchester Legacy.* Coventry: Coventry University, 1995

DUNCAN, H. O. *The World on Wheels, Vol II.* Paris: Duncan,1926

EDGE, S. F. *My Motoring Reminiscences.* London: Foulis, n.d.

GRAHAME-WHITE, M. *At the Wheel Ashore and Afloat.* London: Foulis, 1934

HARMSWORTH, A. *The Badminton Library: Motors.* London: Longmans Green, 1902

HOOPER, W. EDEN. *The Motor Car.* London: Butterworth & Co 1908

JARROTT, C. *Ten Years of Motors and Motor Racing.* London: Grant Richards, 1906

JOHNSON, C. *1,000 Miles Motor Vehicle Trial.* Official programme. London: A.C.G.B.I., 1900.

– *An Early History of Motoring.* Cheltenham: Burrows, c1927

JOHNSON, E. *The Dawn of Motoring.* Milton Keynes: Mercedes-Benz, 1986

MONTAGU OF BEAULIEU, LORD. *A Biography of the Hon.C.S.Rolls.* (*pub & date)

– *The First Ten Years of Automobilism, 1896-1906.* London: Car Illustrated, 1906

NAGLE, E. & SEDGEWICK, M. *V.C.C. – 50 years Pictorial History.* London: Veteran Car Club, 1981

NICHOLSON, T. R. *The Motor Book: an anthology 1895-1914.* London: Methuen, 1962

NIXON, ST. J. C. *Daimler 1896-1946.* London: Foulis, 1946

– *Romance Amonst Cars.* London: Foulis, 1937

– *The Simms Story, from 1891.* London: Simms, 1955

– *The Story of the S.M.M.T. 1902-1952.* London: S.M.M.T.,1952

– *Wolseley.* London: Foulis, 1949

NOBLE, D. (ed). *R.A.C. Jubilee Book, 1897-1947.* London: R.A.C., 1946

NOBLE, D & JUNNER, G.M. *Vital to the Life of the Nation.* London: S.M.M.T., 1946

OLDHAM, W. J. *The Hyphen in Rolls-Royce.* London: Foulis, 1967

SAUNIER, B. *de. Annual.* Paris: B de Saunier 1906

SAUNIER, DOLLUS et GEOFFROY. *Histoire de la Locomotion Terrestre.* Paris: L'illustration, 1935

TROUBRIDGE, LADY & MARSHALL, A. *John, Lord Montagu of Beaulieu.* London: Macmillan, 1930

WORBY BEAUMONT, W. *Motor Vehicles and Motors.* London: Constable, 1900 & 1902

Journals, etc.

A.C.G.B.I. Minutes

The Autocar, 1899-1900

Automotor Journal, 1899-1900

Car Illustrated, 1902

La France Automobile, 1900

The Motor-Car Journal, 1900

Motoring Annual (Motorist's Year Book), A.C.G.B.I., 1903-1904

Newspapers

Berwick Advertiser

Carlisle Express

Cheltenham Examiner

Darlington and Stockton Times

Evening Press, York

The Patriot, Carlisle

Peebles News and County Advertiser

The Scotsman

Yorkshire Post

INDEX

Page numbers in *italics* refer to illustrations, those in ***heavy type*** refer to illustrations dating from the time of the Trial. Numbers in parentheses are those used in the Trial; a star indicates a non-starter. Incidental mentions of cars and people have not been indexed.

D

E